GRE WORDLIST

VOCABULARY WITH MEMORY TRIGGERS

T0381179

PARTRIDGE
A Penguin Random House Company

Copyright © 2014 by Dr. Prasad Raju.

ISBN: Hardcover   978-1-4828-3701-8
               Softcover   978-1-4828-3703-2
               eBook   978-1-4828-3702-5

All rights reserved. No part of this book may be used or reproduced by any means, graphic, electronic, or mechanical, including photocopying, recording, taping or by any information storage retrieval system without the written permission of the publisher except in the case of brief quotations embodied in critical articles and reviews.

Because of the dynamic nature of the Internet, any web addresses or links contained in this book may have changed since publication and may no longer be valid. The views expressed in this work are solely those of the author and do not necessarily reflect the views of the publisher, and the publisher hereby disclaims any responsibility for them.

To order additional copies of this book, contact
Partridge India
000 800 10062 62
orders.india@partridgepublishing.com

www.partridgepublishing.com/india

GRE WORDLIST

VOCABULARY WITH MEMORY TRIGGERS

Prasad Raju V.V.N.R. Pathapati, Ph.D

Preface

Dr. Raju's Memory Triggers for vocabulary wisdom

It is a matter of memory and more... what we mean is a "trigger". Learning thousands of words in thirty days or even less is indeed a task; so we need a capsule called the "memory trigger", before venturing out for a successful score in the most sort after competitive tests such as GRE, SAT, CAT, GMAT, TOEFL and the like.

Here's a trigger- when you come across a word, it must stimulate your mind with related thoughts, and at once- in a flash- the given word must be revealed! And how?! Enter into the world of Dr. Raju's Memory Triggers that introduces you to hitherto never explored techniques of vocabulary learning. It is not complicated or taxing, rather it is a fun learning experience based on over a decade of practical research on vocabulary acquisition, retention and usage. Well, good vocabulary is a must and not just that, having a good knowledge of the advanced words that appear in varied tests is equally advantageous.

If you are one of those students seeking vocabulary wisdom, you've found the right book. "Dr Raju's Memory Trigger Based Vocabulary," will teach you the words you need to know- swiftly and efficiently. Here you are not just acquainting with the words (which is what most vocabulary books do), but the words are rather ingrained into your memory disk! This is because it uses an absolutely unique tactic called the "memory trigger"---that is guaranteed to etch each word and it's meaning, pronunciation and also its usage eternally in your mind. For sure, the learner here will be equipped with a substantial foundation of advanced, university level glossary that is needed for a high score and more!

Memory experts' agree that mnemonics (or memory aids) are the surest, fastest and easiest way to remember names, places, events, words and anything else one needs to remember. The presentation of this information, centered on a memory trigger, creates a memorable connection to the meaning of the word. Well, in simple words, a memory trigger is a device that helps by associating what you are trying to remember with something you already know. So, without a glitch or a hitch, won't you get rich with the wealth of words?! Why not...

Contents

Introduction

How to use this book

Each word consists of four elements.

1. **The main word:** The word you wish to learn. It is followed by phonetic pronunciation and a definition.

    Example: AESTHETIC (es THET ik), Concerned with beauty; artistic

2. **The Trigger:** The trigger is a simple word or words which rhyme or sound like the main word.

    Example: ATHLETIC

3. **The link:** The link connects the main word and the trigger in a sentence.

    Example: ATHLETIC body appears **AESTHETIC.**

4. **Sample Sentence:** Geetha molded the lump of clay into an aesthetically pleasing masterpiece.

AESTHETIC (es THET ik): a. Concerned with beauty; artistic

    Trigger: AESTHETIC-ATHLETIC

    Trigger Sentence: ATHLETIC body appears AESTHETIC.

The Memory Trick Method:

The first step in using this method is to find a key word for the word you are trying to learn. For example, let's say you're trying to learn the word ASSUAGE. A good key word for the word ASSUAGE is MASSAGE because it follows two rules-

1. The word either sounds acoustically similar or looks similar to the target word.

2. The word is common or familiar to the learner, which makes it easier to draw or visualize.

Note : Triggers & Trigger Sentences are only meant to stimulate your imagination and recollect a particular word. They need not / necessarily be grammatically or logically correct, but definitely will make sense in memorizing the given word.

ASSUAGE (uh SWAYJ): v. Sooth, make less severe

   Trigger: ASSUAGE-MASSAGE

   Trigger Sentence: The MASSAGE ASSUAGE and relieved my pain.

   Sample Sentence: Refreshing winds assuage the summer's heat.

The second step is to connect the key word to the target definition. More simply, we need to link the word massage to "make less severe or sooth."

When tested against other methods, the memory trick word strategy repeatedly proved to be superior technique for acquiring vocabulary for subjects of nearly all ages, and with periodic review, one of the best methods for long term retention.

How to review

To review the word ASSUAGE:

1.   Recall the key word MASSAGE.

2.   Visualize some picture of a girl massaging a man's tired body.

3.   Connect the visualization to the meaning of the target word (referring to the soothing effect).

4.   Think about how the word was used in a sentence or try to make up a sentence of your own.

Types of memory tricks used in this book

1.   **Synonym Triggers:** The meaning of the memory trick that is familiar to the reader is similar to the target word.

Example: A

DAWDLE (DAW dul): v. Delay, waste time

   Trigger: DAWDLE-IDLE

   Trigger Sentence: DAWDLE is to IDLE; dawdle and idle are synonyms.

Hard work pays later...
Laziness pays now !

Example: B
IRASCIBLE (i RAS uh bul):
 a. Hot-tempered; irritable
Trigger: IRASCIBLE-IRRITABLE
 Trigger Sentence: IRASCIBLE
 person is usually IRRITABLE.

2. **Antonyms Triggers:** The meaning of the trigger that is familiar to the reader is opposite to the target word.

Example :
CRAVEN (KRAY vuhn): a. fearful,
 cowardly ;dastard
 Trigger: CRAVEN- BRAVE +N
 Trigger Sentence: CRAVEN and
 BRAVE are antonyms.

3. **Manipulation of Some Letters:** The meaning of the memory trick that is familiar to the reader is obtained by addition, subtraction or rearrangement of few letters in the target word.

Example :
ROTUND (roh TUND): n. Round in Shape; Fat
 Trigger: ROTUND-ROUND
 Trigger Sentence: A ROTUND
 person is ROUND in shape.

4. **The words with similar sound:** The trigger sounds acoustically similar to the target word and forms an indelible connection.

Example : A
RIFE (ryfe): a. abundant ; current
   Trigger: RIFE-LIFE
   Trigger Sentence: The ocean is RIFE with LIFE.

Example : B
RAPACIOUS (ruh PEY shuhs): a. Greedy, Selfish; Predatory
   Trigger: RAPACIOUS-"RAPES"
   Trigger Sentence: He might be a RAPIST as he looks at women so RAPACIOUSLY!

Example : C
EXIGENCY (EK si juhn see):
               n. Urgent situation
   Trigger: 1. EXIGENCY -URGENCY;
2. EXIGENT-URGENT
   Trigger Sentence: 1. URGENCY, EMERGENCY and EXIGENCY are synonyms.
2. EXIGENT is equal to URGENT.

5 . **Part of the word:** The meaning of the memory trick that is familiar to the reader is obtained by extracting few letters from the target word.

Cry Cry Cry...

Example :

LACHRYMOSE (lak-ruh-mohs): a. Tearfu

   Trigger: CHRY-CRY

   Trigger Sentence: 1. LACHRYMOSE "la +CHRY + mose".

   2. LACHRYMOSE things arouse CRY

6. **The Memory Trick Word That requires Imagination:** The word is common or familiar to the learner, which makes it easier to draw or visualize.

Me a word wizard!

Example : A

ACUMEN (AK yoo mun): n. Shrewdness, keenness and depth of perception

   Trigger: 1.ACU (IQ)+MEN, 2. ACUMEN -A CUTE MAN

   Trigger Sentence: A CUTE MAN of strong "IQ" possesses ACUMEN.

   Sample sentence: Financial acumen is an asset in the share market.

COOL! I CAN PLUG IN MY ELECTRIC SHAVER OUT DOORS !

Example : B

SEVER (SEV ur): v. Cut, separate

   Trigger: SEVER-SHAVER

   Trigger Sentence: A SHAVER SEVERS; cuts or SEPARATES.

   Sample sentence: The guillotine was an execution device invented to sever the head.

7. **Using Suffixes and Prefixes and Root Words:** Using roots, prefixes and suffixes to determine a word's meaning can help you greatly. This method in combination with trigger method forms a powerful tool to remember the words for a long time.

Example : A

INFALLIBLE (in FAL ah bul): a. Unfailing

   Trigger: NO FALL-NO FAIL

   Trigger Sentence: UNFAILING-
   INFALLIBLE people NEVER FALL or FAIL.

Example : B

DISABUSE (dih suh BYUZE): v. Correct
   a false impression; undeceive

   Trigger: DIS + ABUSE-" DON'T ABUSE"

   Trigger Sentence: Remove ABUSE;
   DON'T ABUSE him; he is free from error.

Example : C

CREED (kreed): n. Any system of religious beliefs

   Trigger: CREED-BREED

   Trigger Sentence: Every BREED (Hindu breed;
   Islam breed, Christian BREED etc.,) has
   some CREED; Hindu BREED has Hindu CREED

NOTE: *All CRED-; CREED-; prefixes are associated
with belief, trust and faith

1. **CREDO** (n) : system of religious or ethical belief
2. **CREDULITY** (n): tendency to believe too readily ; gullibility
3. **INCREDULITY** (n) : disbelief
4. **CREDULOUS:** willing to believe too readily
5. **CREDENCE** (n): belief, credit
6. **INCREDULOUS** (a): Disbelieving, skeptical

Who would most benefit from this book?

Vocabulary triggers are designed for anyone wishing to build a stronger vocabulary. However, they are particularly recommended for students studying for Pre-Scholastic Aptitude Test (PSAT), Scholastic Aptitude Test (SAT) and Graduate Record Examination (GRE) and CAT (IIM). Remember that approximately 90% of university courses require reading comprehension. And to be good reader you must have an extensive vocabulary.

A Typical Exercise for Memory Check

Match each word and its memory trick to the corresponding definition

SL No.	WORD	MEMORY TRIGGER	SL No.	DEFINITIONS
1	AESTHETIC	How ATHLETIC body looks??	A	A system of religious beliefs
2	CREED	Hindu BREED Hindu Creed	B	Abundant ; current
3	LACHRYMOSE	CHRY	C	Concerned with beauty ; artistic
4	RIFE	LIFE	D	Correct a false impression; Undeceive
5	EXIGENCY	URGENCY	E	Cut, separate
6	DISABUSE	DON'T ABUSE	F	Delay, waste time
7	INFALLIBLE	NO FALL-NO FAIL	G	Fearful, cowardly
8	SEVER	SHAVER does what??	H	Greedy, Selfish; Predatory
9	ACUMEN	A CUTE MEN-IQ MEN	I	Hot-tempered; irritable
10	RAPACIOUS	RAPES	J	Round in Shape; Fat
11	ROTUND	ROUND	K	Shrewdness, keenness and depth of perception
12	ASSUAGE	MASSAGE	L	Sooth, make less severe
13	IRASCIBLE	IRRITABLE	M	Tearful
14	DAWDLE	DAWDLE -IDLE	N	Unfailing
15	CRAVEN	BRAVE is antonym.	O	Urgent situation

Memory Check Answers:

1	2	3	4	5	6	7	8	9	10	11	12	13	14	15
C	A	M	B	O	D	N	E	K	H	J	L	I	F	G

Introduction to the Word Groups:

Effective speakers and writers rule the roost in the kingdom of language. Impressive speaking and writing skills help you get a good job and move up the ladder of success. NASSCOM says that employees who negotiate better command 30% more salaries than their peers. When you confidently communicate your feelings, ideas, hopes, and fears; people think you're hot stuff. And you are!

One relatively easy way to consolidate your vocabulary (word power) is to master tomes of synonyms and antonyms in the form of **word groups**. Armed with an awesome range of words, you can express yourself more confidently and more stylishly and become an influential speaker and impactful writer.

Understanding connotations of words in groups, categories, or clusters is a brilliant way of rapidly increasing your vocabulary. For example, instead of addressing someone as *stubborn*; why don't you call him/her *recalcitrant*, *obdurate* or *hidebound*?

By grouping words, you can become skilled at replacing a monotonous word with two or three or even a dozen substitute words. These fillers or add-ons give you the lowdown on synonyms and antonyms, explain how this vocabulary strengthens your communication, and offers you plethora of examples to give you an idea of how many new and exhilarating words you can encounter and incorporate into your everyday language.

Group of words aren't always exact synonyms. For example, calling someone **rotund**, meaning plump, is not the same as referring to him or her as **obese**, meaning excessively overweight.

A synonym never means exactly the same thing as the word it replaces. No word is ever an exact synonym for another word because there is always a slight difference in meaning between the two words. Consider some synonyms for those famous opposites, love and hate:

Love: adore, cherish, treasure, adulate, worship, revere, esteem

Cherish and **treasure** imply that the loved object is highly esteemed; **revere** and **worship** show that the admired person is **venerated** as a god.

Hate: abhor, scorn, dislike, shun, abominate, despise, detest

Even though all these words are synonyms, their meanings differ contextually. For example, **scorn** implies not only hatred but also mockery and even avoidance. When you **scorn** someone, you ridicule him/her and try to shun his/her company. The words **detest** and **abominate** suggest that the hatred is so strong that the speaker can't even bear to be in the person's presence. Thus, we can clearly see the difference in the intensity of dislike.

However, if you group the words together by their general meanings, you can understand them well enough, which is all that's demanded in the competitive exams. No question in CAT, SAT, GRE, or any other standardized test asks for a precise definition.

You're never given a blank piece of paper and asked to write the meaning of a word. Instead, you use the context to come up with basic idea of what you want. If you need a word that means slim, you are not given both **svelte** (pleasantly, fashionably slim) and **emaciated** (over thin and malnutritioned) in the same set of answers. You get either one or the other. As long as you know that both of them fall in the category of "thin", you're okay.

When you cluster the words, you can also remember them in an **antithetical** (opposite) manner. That is, review all the words that mean thin, and then all the words that mean overweight. Study all the words that mean lucky, then all the words that mean unlucky. You can become a walking thesaurus before you realize it!!

Important NOTE: A word in one group may also appear in other groups since it can have several shades of connotations.

Word List Day-1

ABANDON (uh BAN dun): v. Give up (an action or practice) completely.

> **Trigger:** "ABANDON" -"A-BANNED"
>
> **Trigger Sentence:** He was ABANDONED from the country for possessing BANNED narcotics.
>
> **Sample Sentence:** Animal activists are campaigning against *abandonment* of old and sick animals on the streets.

ABASE (uh BAYS): v. Humiliate, degrade

> **Trigger:** ABASE- A BASE
>
> **Trigger Sentence:** Such BASE ideas will ABASE your reputation.
>
> **Sample Sentence:** Teacher *abased* the student by criticizing him in front of the girls!
>
> Related Words: DEBASE- n. degrade, humiliate

ABASH (ah BASH): v. Embarrass

> **Trigger:** 1. ABASH-ABASE. 2. A BASH
>
> **Trigger Sentence:** 1. When the teacher ABASED him, he felt ABASHED. 2. When the teacher BASHED him in front of the girls, he felt ABASHED.
>
> **Sample Sentence:** He was *abashed* by her open admiration.
>
> Related Words: UNABASHED- a. not embarrassed, not ashamed

ABATE (ah BEYT): v. Reduce; become less

> **Trigger:** 1. ABATE-"A BITE". 2. ABATE-REBATE
>
> **Trigger Sentence:** 1. My hunger ABATED after I took A BITE of an apple. 2. The store is REBATING refrigerators this week, so it ABATED some financial burden on me.
>
> **Sample Sentence:** The tornado *abated* soon, but with it, it took lot of lives!

ABDICATE (AB di keyt): v.Give up; renounce

> **Trigger:** ABDICATE- "AB (ABSENT) + DICTATE"
>
> **Trigger Sentence:** The emperor has now NO power to DICTATE the terms, as he has ABDICATED his throne.
>
> **Sample Sentence:** The king *abdicated* his throne in order to marry an ordinary woman.

ABERRANT (uh BER unt): a. Deviant; abnormal

> **Trigger:** 1. ABERRANT-ERR-ERROR. 2. ABERRANT-OFF CURRENT
>
> **Trigger Sentence:** 1. If you continue to repeat the same ERRORS, your life will become ABBERRANT. 2. ABERRANT & CURRENT are antonyms. 3. Wearing bell-bottom pants is ABERRANT now-a-days as this trend is OFF CURRENT.

Sample Sentence: Raju's method of teaching English words with Triggers is totally *aberrant*. But it works like magic!

Related Words: ABERRATION- n. deviation, abnormality

ABET (uh BET): v. Help or encourage, usually in some wrongdoing

Trigger: 1.ABET- "A-BET". 2. ABET-SET

Trigger Sentence: 1. In IPL league some cricket players ABET the bookies and help them illegally during A BETTING game. 2. ABET is to SET UP an action.

Sample Sentence: The bank's security guard himself *abetted* the thief in robbing the bank.

ABEYANCE (uh BEY uns): n. Suspended Action; temporary inactivity

Trigger: ABEYANCE-"AB+YAWNS"

Trigger Sentence: Stop YAWNING and start working. You can't keep your work in ABEYANCE any more.

Sample Sentence: The research scholars held their projects in *abeyance* for lack of funds from the university.

ABHOR (ab HOR): v.Hate, dislike

Trigger: 1. ABHOR-A BORE 2. ABHOR-ADORE (** antonyms)

Trigger Sentence: 1. 'The Satanic Verses' is a BORING book. I ABHOR reading it.

2. People ABHOR Hitler, but I ADORE him. 3. ABHOR (dislike) and ADORE (love) are antonyms.

Sample Sentence: John *abhorred* his boring new job at the Super market.

Related Words: ABHORRENCE -n. disgust, hate

ABIDING (uh BAHY ding): a. Continuous; permanent

Trigger: 1.ABIDING -A BINDING. 2. ABIDING - A BONDING

Trigger Sentence: 1. I will ABIDE by the faith, since I have a BINDING trust on you.

2. BONDING in marriage reflects that both the couple ABIDE to each other forever.

Sample Sentence: 1. Soldiers in the battle need to have an *abiding* faith in themselves. 2. If you make a promise you must *abide* by it.

Related Words: ABIDE- v. accept or act in accordance with

ABJECT (AB jekt): a. Utterly hopeless; shameful

Trigger: ABJECT-REJECT-DEJECT

Trigger Sentence: My girl friend REJECTED me, since I am in ABJECT condition.

Sample Sentence: *Abject* poverty still prevails in India.

ABJURE (ab JOOR): v. Renounce upon oath; deny

Trigger: ABJURE-ASSURE

Trigger Sentence: 1. ABJURE (give up on oath) and ASSURE (promise) are antonym variants. 2. In front of the JURY (group of judges), Bill Clinton ABJURED Monica instead of giving her the ASSURANCE.

Sample Sentence: He *abjured* his relations with his girl friend.

ABOLISH (uh BOL ish): v. Cancel, put an end to

Trigger: 1.ABOLISH-ESTABLISH (** antonyms). 2. ABOLISH-DEMOLISH

Trigger Sentence: 1. ABOLISH (cancel or put an end) and ESTABLISH (set up or create) are antonyms. 2. Talibans DEMOLISHED the Bamiyan Buddha and ABOLISHED the construction of monuments of other religions.

Sample Sentence: Slavery was *abolished* in the mid 19th century in America and in Russia.

ABOMINATE (uh BOM ih nate): v. Hate; to dislike

Trigger: ABOMINATE-"A BOMB I HATE"

Trigger Sentence: 1. I ABOMINATE BOMBS. 2. If someone DOMINATES me, I usually ABOMINATE them.

Sample Sentence: Peace lovers *abominate* nuclear weapons.

Related Words: ABOMINABLE - a. very bad; terrible

ABORTIVE (uh BOR tiv): a. Unsuccessful, fruitless

Trigger: ABORTIVE-"ABORTION"

Trigger Sentence: Both ABORTIVE and ABORTION words imply the meaning for unsuccessful efforts.

Sample Sentence: They made *abortive* efforts by struggling for a separate State.

ABOUND (uh BOUND): v. be plentiful; overflow with

Trigger: ABOUND-ABUNDANT

Trigger Sentence: Be ABUNDANT or plentiful is known as ABOUND.

Sample Sentence: They live in a region where mango grooves *abound.*

Related Words: ABUNDANCE - n. plentifulness; richness

ABRASIVE (uh BREY siv): a. Harsh in manner; a substance that abrades

Trigger: 1.ABRASIVE-ABUSIVE-AGGRESSIVE. 2. ABRASIVE-RAZOR

Trigger Sentence: 1. My ABRASIVE boss is an ABUSIVE and an AGGRESSIVE character. 2. The RAZOR causes ABRASION and EROSION.

Sample Sentence: My lady boss is an *abrasive* and an aggressive character.

Related Words: ABUSIVE - a. using foul language; mistreating

ABREAST (uh BREST): a. Up-to-date; side by side; well-informed

Trigger: 1.ABREAST-"AB"+BREAST. 2. A&B

Trigger Sentence: 1. Angelina Jolie kept herself ABREAST with the information about BREAST cancer before she went ahead with mastectomy. 2. "A & B" are side by side alphabets. "A" knows about "B".

Sample Sentence: It's amazing how young Arjun keeps himself *abreast* of all the latest software in the IT industry.

ABRIDGE (uh BRIJ): v. Shorten

Trigger: 1.ABRIDGE- "A BRIDGE". 2. "ABRI"- A BRIEF

Trigger Sentence: 1.A BRIDGE between the two places has drastically ABRIDGED the distance between them. 2. A BRIEF way of putting things is known as ABRIDGEMENT.

Sample Sentence: The teacher *abridged* over 5000 years of Indian history into a lucid and succinct documentary film.

Related words: UNABRIDGED- a. complete, not shortened

ABROGATE (AB ruh geyt): v. Abolish; cancel officially

Trigger: ABROGATE-"AB+NEGATE"

Trigger Sentence: ABROGATE is to NEGATE (by being negative) the effect of the efforts.

Sample Sentence: Congress government *abrogated* the old law for a renewed and altered bylaws.

ABRUPT (uh BRUPT): a.Unexpectedly sudden; curt; rude

Trigger: 1.RUPT-RUPTURE. 2. INTERRUPT

Trigger Sentence: 1. After a RUPTURE to the tire, the car came to an ABRUPT stop. 2. He ABRUPTLY INTERRUPTED me.

Sample Sentence: He interrupted me in an *abrupt* way while I was delivering my speech.

ABSCISSION (ab SIZH un): n. The act of cutting off

Trigger: AB+SCISSION-"SCISSOR"

Trigger Sentence: With SCISSORS, The doctors made an ABSCISSION.

Sample Sentence: *Abscission* from the core group of managers did dishearten Jack.

ABSCOND (ab SKOND): v. Depart secretly and hide

Trigger: 1. ABSCOND-JAMES BOND. 2. AB (ABSENT)-SECOND

Trigger Sentence: 1. JAMES BOND ABSCONDS from the trap set by his villains. 2. The spy ABSCONDED with in SECONDS from the den of a villain.

Sample Sentence: He has abandoned his wife and children, and has *absconded*.

ABSOLUTE (AB suh loot): a. Complete, totally unlimited, certain

Trigger: 1. ABSOLUTE ZERO. 2. GOD IS ABSOLUTE

Trigger Sentence: 1. At ABSOLUTE ZERO as per thermodynamics, there is no disorder, COMPLETE CERTAINTY. 2. GOD IS ABSOLUTE. He is omnipotent, omnipresent, and omniscient.

Sample Sentence: GOD is *absolute*, he is there every where.

ABSOLVE (ab ZOLV): v. Pardon; forgive an offense

Trigger: ABSLOVE-SOLVE

Trigger Sentence: Court case is SOLVED and I am ABSOLVED of accusation.

Sample Sentence: After viewing the evidence the jury agreed to *absolve* John of any criminal intent in the car accident.

ABSTAIN (ab STEYN): v. Avoid, refrain from

Trigger: ABS-ABSENT

Trigger Sentence: 1. "ABS" implies ABSENCE; he is ABSENT from taking any drug for two months.

Sample Sentence: The doctors often advise the liver patients to *abstain* from alcohol.

ABSTEMIOUS (ab STEE mee us): a. Self- control, especially in the consumption of food and drink

Trigger: 1. "ABS"-"SIX PACK-ABS". 2. ABSTEMIOUS-ABSENTIOUS-ABSENT

Trigger Sentence: 1. If you want to develop 6 -pack ABS you got to be ABSTEMIOUS. 2. ABSENT from food and drink, is known as ABSTEMIOUS.

Sample Sentence: The absentminded scientist is very *abstemious* as he takes his food sparingly. Related Words: ABSTINENCE - n. Avoidance, restrain from eating and drinking.

ABSTRACT (AB strakt): a.Theoretical; difficult to understand, n. summary

Trigger: 1.ABSTRACT-ABS+TRACK. 2. ABSTARCT-CONTRACT

Trigger Sentence: 1. a. The train with ABSENCE OF TRACKS is an ABSTRACT (theoretical concept). 2. Secretary, take an extract of this ABSTRACT and present me in a CONTRACT version.

Sample Sentence: 1. I don't expect you to give me a minute to minute detail of the whole conference, just an *abstract* will do for the file records. 2. Epigenetics is an *abstract* subject as it is highly intractable.

ABSTRUSE (ab STROOS): a. Ambiguous, difficult to understand; obscure

Trigger: 1. ABSTRUSE-CONFUSE. 2. ABSTRUSE –"ABS (absent) + TRUTH"

Trigger Sentence: 1. Theory of Special Relativity CONFUSES people because it is a very

ABSTRUSE concept. 2. Modern psychologists argue that Freud's psychological theories are mostly ABSTRUSE as there is ABSENCE OF TRUTH in his claims.

Sample Sentence: Quantum mechanics is an *abstruse* subject for many students.

ABUT (uh BUT): v. To border upon; adjoin

Trigger: ABUT-("AB"-"UT")

Trigger Sentence: Alphabets A and B are ADJOINING letters. Similarly "U&T" alphabets ABUT each other.

Sample Sentence: 1. England *abuts* Scotland. 2. The temple *abutting* the river made a picturesque view.

ABYSMAL (uh BIZ mul): a. Immeasurably deep or wretched; bottomless

Trigger: 1. "ABYSMAL-"A-DISMAL". 2. ABYSMAL-"A- BE-SMALL"

Trigger Sentence: 1. Imagine a DISMAL or ABYSMAL performance in an exam. 2. I am A VERY SMALL person in the society and I am leading an ABYSMAL life.

Sample Sentence: It the secrets of the sea fascinate some, others are terrified by its mysterious deep *abysmal.*

Related Words: ABYSS – n. a bottomless pit; chasm

ACCEDE (ak SEED): v. Agree, assent

Trigger: 1. ACCEDE-ACCEPT- AGREED. 2. ACCEDE-CEDE (SEED)

Trigger Sentence: 1. ACCEDE and ACCEPT are synonyms. 2. Low SEEDED player ACCEDES defeat to the top SEEDED player in any sport.

Sample Sentence: The government *acceded* (bowed) to the military pressure.

ACCENTUATE (ak SEN choo yet): v. Stress or emphasize; intensify

Trigger: 1.ACCENTUATE "POWERFUL ACCENT".2. ACCENTUATE (ACCENT--tone)

Trigger Sentence: Dr. Rao ACCENTUATED (with powerful ACCENT) physical exercises in addition to a change in diet to overcome diabetes and high blood pressure.

Sample Sentence: Certain syllables in English are *accentuated* with sharp accent.

ACCESSORY (ak SES uh ree): n. Additional object; useful but not essential thing

Trigger: ACCESSORY-other than NECESSARY (**antonym).

Trigger Sentence: An ACCESSORY is a secondary object which complements anything that is NECESSARY.

Sample Sentence: She bought an attractive handbag as an *accessory* for her dress.

Related Words: 1. ANCILLARY – n. secondary; subordinate. 2. AUXILIARY –n. additional; supporting

ACCLAIM (uh KLAYM): v. Praise publicly

Trigger: 1. ACCLAIM-A CLAIM. 2. ACLAim-ACLA-A CLAP

Trigger Sentence: 1. Indian cricket team CLAIMED the trophy and everyone ACCLAIMED the team. 2. A CLAP of the hands is a sign of PRAISING.

Sample Sentence: Critics have *acclaimed* the Indian musician A.R. Rehman as the best Indian music composer of recent times.

ACCOLADE (AK uh layd): n. An expression of praise; award

Trigger: 1.ACCOLADE-APPLAUD (** synonyms). 2. ACCOLADE-ACT OF LAUD

Trigger Sentence: 1. An ACT OF LAUD (APPLAUD-praise) is an ACCOLADE. 2. He received APPLAUDS and ACCOLADES for his performance.

Sample Sentence: The emotive and realistic play received *accolades* from the media.

ACCOMPLICE (ah KAM plis): n. Partner in crime

Trigger: ACCOMPlice-ACCOMPANY-COMPANY

Trigger Sentence: The ACCOMPLICE ACCOMPANIED the criminals in a bank robbery

Sample Sentence: The police caught the thief and his *accomplice* driver.

Related Words: COMPLICITY - n. partnership (in wrongdoing or crime)

ACCORD (uh KORD): n. Agreement, v. to grant, give

Trigger: 1. ACCORD-AGREED. 2. ACCORD- ACCEPT. 3. ACCORD-AWARD

Trigger Sentence: 1. n. we AGGREED to peace ACCORD. 2. v. ACCORD is to ACCEPT. 3. The Academy ACCORDED me an AWARD.

Sample Sentence: 1. We are in *accord* with your proposal. 2. The national assembly *accorded* (granted) him more power.

ACCOUNT (uh KOUNT): v. Give a view; n. Explanation, report

Trigger: ACCOUNT-AMOUNT

Trigger Sentence: Bank sent me an ACCOUNT of AMOUNT what I owe.

Sample Sentence: He gave an inaccurate *account* of the plot to kill the president.

Related Words: RECOUNT - v. tell, narrate; count again

ACCRETION (uh kREE shun): n. An increase in amount; addition

Trigger: 1.ACCERETION-ACCUMULATION. 2. ACCRETION-ATTRITION

Trigger Sentence: 1. ACCRETION, ADDITION and ACCUMULATION are synonyms.

2. ACCRETION and ATTRITION are antonyms.

Sample Sentence: The NGOs' strong fund - raising activities have *accreted* the old-age-homes' resources.

Related Words: ATTRITION- n. wearing away

ACCUSE (uh KYOOZ): v.place blame, charge with a crime

Trigger: 1. ACCUSE-ABUSE. 2. ACCUSE- A CURSE

Trigger Sentence: 1. They ACCUSED the parents for ABUSING their children. 2. The witch was ACCUSED for CURSING

Sample Sentence: He has been *accused* of lying and swindling of office funds.

Related Words: ABUSE- v. insult; injure

ACERBIC (uh SUR bik): a. Bitter; sharp-tempered

Trigger: ACERBIC-ACIDIC

Trigger Sentence: Lemon taste is ACERBIC and ACIDIC; my boss's nature and his tongue is ACERBIC!

Sample Sentence: She lost all her good friends due to her *acerbic* attitude.

Related Words: ACERBITY -n. sourness; bitterness (of temper)

ACKNOWLEDGE (ak NOL ij): v. Recognize; admit

Trigger: ACKNOWLEDGE-A KNOWLEDGE

Trigger Sentence: I've KNOWLEDGE about it; and I KNOW how to ACKNOWLEDGE your greetings.

Sample Sentence: It is important to *acknowledge* the work of others in one's own writing.

ACME (AK mee): n.Top; peak

Trigger: 1. ACME-ACE. 2. ACME-ACNE

Trigger Sentence: 1. ACE has got highest points in a card game. 2. ACE (like Ussian Bolt)

is an expert; he reached ACME of his career in running. 3. ACNE-high point on skin (pimple); ACME-highest point in one's life.

Sample Sentence: The *ace* batsman at the *acme* of his career sadly met with an accident.

ACOLYTE (AK uh lahyt): n. An assistant or follower

Trigger: ACOLYTE-"A CO PILOT"

Trigger Sentence: He is such a popular pilot...many CO-PILOTS want to be his ACOLYTES.

Sample Sentence: The spiritual guru was chanting at the temple with few of his *acolytes.*

ACQUIESCENCE (ak wee ES uns) : n. Passive acceptance; yielding

Trigger: 1. ACQUIESCENCE-ACCEPTANCE. 2. ACQUIESCENCE- A QUIET SENSE

Trigger Sentence: 1. ACQUIESCENCE and ACCEPTANCE are synonyms. 2. A QUIET SENSE exists when there is an ACQUIESCENCE.

Sample Sentence: Thankfully the bank has given *acquiescence* to my appeal for extension of loan repayment.

Related Words: ACQUIESCE -v. accept; agree passively

ACQUISITIVE (uh KWIZ i tiv): a. Strongly desirous of acquiring and possessing

Trigger: ACQUIRE-REQUIRE

Trigger Sentence: When you are ACQUISITIVE, you are going to ACQUIRE more than REQUIREMENT.

Sample Sentence: The *acquisitive* developers are trying to tear down the historic home and build a shopping mall.

Related Words: 1.ACQUIRE - v. obtain, attain. 2. ACQUISITION - n. The action of possessing

ACQUIT (uh KWIT): v.Discharge, set free; exonerate

Trigger: 1.ACQUIT-A QUIT. 2. ACQUIT-CONVICT (** antonyms)

Trigger Sentence: 1. After "THE QUIT" India movement led by Mahatma Gandhi, India was ACQUITTED (released) from the British rule. 2. ACQUIT and CONVICT are antonyms.

Sample Sentence: Shockingly the *convict* was acquitted of the murder charges against him.

Related Words: ACQUITTAL – n. act of freeing from a debt or blame

ACRID (AK rid): a. Sharp; bitterly pungent

Trigger: ACRID-ACID

Trigger Sentence: Her ACRID remarks and ACID comments make her many more enemies for her; ACID taste and smell are ACRID in nature.

Sample Sentence: The *acrid* odor of burnt gunpowder pervaded the room after the pistol had been fired.

ACRIMONY (ak ri MOW nee) : n. Bitterness or ill feeling

Trigger: 1.ACRImony-ACRID-ACID. 2. ACRIMONY-A CRIME ON ME

Trigger Sentence: 1. ACRID-ACID taste is bitter and relationships between couples can also get bitter. 2. A CRIME ON ME charged by my colleague brings ACRIMONY between us.

Sample Sentence: An *acrimonious* dispute between wife and husband brought bitter separation.

Related Words: ACRIMONIOUS - a. bitter in words or manner

ACTUATE (AAK choo ayt): v. Activate, motivate

Trigger: 1. ACTUATE-ACTIVATE. 2. ACTUATE- MOTIVATE

Trigger Sentence: ACTUATE is to ACTIVATE and MOTIVATE.

Sample Sentence: The union leader *actuated* the workers to protest against the management for a salary hike.

ACUMEN (AK yoo mun): n.Shrewdness, keenness and depth of perception.

Trigger: 1.ACU (IQ) +MEN. 2. ACUMEN -A CUTE MAN

Trigger Sentence: 1. A CUTE MEN of high "IQ" possess ACUMEN. 2. He was A CUTE MAN with high business ACUMEN.

Sample Sentence: The business *acumen* of Dhirubhai Ambani was very sharp.

ACUTE (uh KYOOT): a. Shrewd, mentally sharp, critical

Trigger: ACUTE-A CUTE

Trigger Sentence: 1. A CUTE guy is smart (ACUTE) and CLEVER. 2. ACUTE angle is SHARP-POINTED.

Sample Sentence: Vishwanathan Anand's *acute* sense of gambits has made him one of the greatest chess players in the world.

Related Words: OBTUSE -a. slow, stupid

ADAMANT (AD uh munt): a.Hard; stubborn, rigid

Trigger: ADAMANT-A DIAMOND

Trigger Sentence: A DIAMOND (like person) is a very ADAMANT and RIGID substance.

Sample Sentence: He was *adamant* in his determination to punish the corrupt officials.

ADDLE (AD l): v. Confuse; mix up

Trigger: ADDLE-RIDDLE

Trigger Sentence: My ADDLED brain could not make any sense of a RIDDLE.

Sample Sentence: My son is *addled* up in his head, and how can he solve these riddles!

ADDRESS (uh DRES): v. Speak to, deal with; discuss

Trigger: ADDRESS - EXPRESS

Trigger Sentence: ADDRESS is to EXPRESS; where is your ADDRESS, SPEAK to me?!

Sample Sentence: He needs to *address* his complicated medical issues with the experts.

ADDUCE (uh DYOOS): v. To cite as evidence; offer as an example

Trigger: ADDUCE-PRODUCE

Trigger Sentence: ADDUCE is to PRODUCE some proof as EVIDENCE.

Sample Sentence: The murder victims' blood stained cloths were collected as *adduce* to further the investigations.

ADEPT (uh DEPT): a.Skilled, expert

Trigger: 1. ADEPT-"A+DEPTH". 2. ADD APT-"ADD APTITUDE"

Trigger Sentence: 1. ADEPT person possess lot of "A DEPTH" in his field of study. 2. ADEPT and INEPT are antonyms.

Sample Sentence: She is *adept* at computing any given maths problem.

Related Words: INEPT - a. incompetent; awkward or clumsy

ADHERE (ad HEER) : v. Stick fast to; be devoted to.

Trigger: 1.ADHERE-ADHESIVE 2. ADHERE- ADD HER

Trigger Sentence: 1. Just like an ADHESIVE (glue-sticky) she ADHERES to our party. 2. ADD HER in to our group, since she is an ADHERENT follower.

Sample Sentence: 1.She *adheres* scrupulously to the Judaic laws. 2. Rahul Gandhi praised congress *adherents* for their support and hard work.

Related Words: ADHERENT - n. Supporter

ADJUNCT (AJ unkt): n. Something added on or attached; supplement

Trigger: ADJUNCT- "ADD + JUNK".

Trigger Sentence: ADJUNCT- ADD JUNK to the main thing.

Sample Sentence: The bar room was an *adjunct* to the minister's original dining hall.

ADMONISH (ad MAWN ish): v.Warn, scold

Trigger: 1.ADMONISH-"ADD + PUNISH". 2. adMONIsh-MONITOR

Trigger Sentence: 1. I will ADD PUNISHMENT if you don't do the work- I ADMONISHED him. 2. The MONITOR (supervisor) ADMONISHED the lazy workers.

Sample Sentence: The principal *admonished* the back benchers for creating a racket in the class.

Related Words: PREMONITION - n. forewarning

ADORE (uh DOHR): v. Admire, venerate

Trigger: ADORE-ADMIRE

Trigger Sentence: ADORE and ADMIRE are synonyms.

Sample Sentence: He is such an *adorable* talented young man...!

Related Words: ADORATION - n. admiration, veneration

ADORN (uh DAWRN): v.Decorate, enhance

Trigger: ADD +ORN (ORNAMENT)

Trigger Sentence: People ADD ORNAMENTS to ADORN their body.

Sample Sentence: The crown princess was *adorned* with jewelry studded with precious gems.

Related Words: UNADORNED - a. undecorated, simple

ADROIT (uh DROIT): a. Clever, skillful

Trigger: 1. ADROIT-A DRAW IT. 2. ADROIT-- ANDROID

Trigger Sentence: 1. M.F.HUSSIAN is an ADROIT artist; he can DRAW IT perfectly; MALADROIT can't DRAW it. 2. ANDROID mobile phones are so ADROIT that they can perform dozens of functions.

Sample Sentence: The finesse and *adroitness* of the surgeon impressed the medical students in the operation theatre.

Related Words: MALADROIT - a. clumsy

ADULATION (ad you LAY shun): n. Excessive admiration, flattery

Trigger: 1. ADULATION-ADORATION. 2. ADULATION-ADMIRATION

Trigger Sentence: ADMIRATION, ADORATION and ADULATION are synonyms.

Sample sentience: Film stars enjoy a lot of *adulation* because their admirers express their adoration for them.

ADULTERATE (uh DUHL ter it): v. Make impure, spoil

Trigger: 1. ADULTERATE-ADD + ALTER. 2. ADULT MOVIES

Trigger Sentence: 1. ADULTERATE is to make (something) poorer in quality by ADDING an ALTER substance. 2. ADULT MOVIES ADULTERATE the minds of children.

Sample Sentence: It is a crime to sell *adulterated* foods.

Related Words: UNADUTERATED - a. pure

ADUMBRATE (a DUM brayt): v.To suggest or disclose partially; foreshadow

Trigger: ADUMBRATE-"AD-UMBRA-(UMBRELLA)".

Trigger Sentence: UMBRELLA gives PARTIAL SHADOW; under an UMBRELLA the lovers ADUMBRATE their love making.

Sample Sentence: Her constant nagging over the job *adumbrated* her intent of quitting sooner than later!

ADVERSARY (AD ver see ree): n.Enemy; rival

Trigger: 1. ADVERSE-adVERSE-WORSE. 2. ADVERSE-REVERSE

Trigger Sentence: 1. An ADVERSARY brings ADVERSE and WORSE situation. 2. An ADVERSARY REVERSES your progress.

Sample Sentence: Saina defeated her *adversary* in the race for Badminton title by a sure victory.

ADVERSE (ad VURS): a.Bad; miserable

Trigger: ADVERSE-"ADD+WORSE"

Trigger Sentence: The weather ADDed WORSE conditions; we were in an ADVERSE situation.

Sample Sentence: The worse thing is that even in *adverse* conditions he doesn't shun his laziness.

ADVOCACY (AD vuh kuh see): n. Support

Trigger: 1.ADVOCACY-ADVOCATE. 2. ADVOCATE-ADD +VOICE

Trigger Sentence: 1. My ADVOCATE always SUPPORTS me. 2. He ADDS VOICE in favor of me; and also ADVISES me.

Sample Sentence: He *advocates* equal rights for boys and girls.

Related Words: ADVOCATE – v. support; n. supporter, champion

AESTHETIC (es THET ik): a.Concerned with beauty; artistic

Trigger: 1.AESTHETIC-ARTISTIC. 2. AESTHETIC- ATHLETIC

Trigger Sentence: 1. ARTISTIC people are AESTHETIC in nature. 2. ATHLETIC body appears AESTHETIC

Sample Sentence: Geetha molded the lump of clay into an *aesthetically* pleasing work of art.

AFFABLE (AF uh bul): a. Good-natured and sociable; friendly

Trigger: "AFFABLE-"AFFECTION-ABLE"

Trigger Sentence: 1. AFFECTIONATE people are AFFABLE. 2. Affable, likable, lovable, sociable, amiable, amicable, amenable are synonyms.

Sample Sentence: Unlike our earlier boss, the present boss is so *affable* that we can approach him without any inhibitions.

AFFECT (uh FEKT): n.Influence, attack (of a disease)

Trigger: AFFECT-EFFECT

Trigger Sentence: AFFECT is to "make a difference to" and EFFECT is to "bring to result".

Sample Sentence: The grammer teacher said that, "Affect and Effect are commonly confused. Affect is primarily a verb meaning 'make a difference to'. EFFECT is used both as a noun and a verb, meaning 'a result' or 'bring about a result'."

AFFECTED (uh FEK tid): a. Artificial; faked to impress

> **Trigger:** 1. AFFECTED- "A FAKED". 2. AFFECT-EFFECT
>
> **Trigger Sentence:** 1. A FAKED behavior is AFFECTED in nature. 2. Cinema "EFFECTS" or "tricks" are AFFECTED and UNNATURAL.
>
> **Sample Sentence:** The *affected* student talked excitedly about US universities, though he had never been to US.
>
> Related Words: 1.UNAFFECTED -a. natural, genuine 2. AFFECTATION - n. artificial manner

AFFINITY (uh FIN uh tee): n. Attraction; closeness

> **Trigger:** 1. AFFINITY-AFFECTION+UNITY. 2. AFFINITY-AFFAIR
>
> **Trigger Sentence:** 1. As we have UNITY there is an AFFINITY among us.
>
> 2. We have a love AFFAIR, since there is an AFFINITY between us.
>
> **Sample Sentence:** Bob has an *affinity* for good food and loves to cook.
>
> Related Words: AFFILIATION - n. association

AFFIRM (uh FURM): n. State to be true; confirm

> **Trigger:** 1.AFFIRM-CONFIRM. 2. AFFIRM-FIRM
>
> **Trigger Sentence:** His AFFIRMATIVE approach CONFIRMED the theory.
>
> **Sample Sentence:** "I need an *affirmation* from you that you will not abandon my work half way through".
>
> Related Words: AFFIRMATION- n. declaration that something is true

AFFLICTION (uh FLIK shun): n. Suffering, pain; torment

> **Trigger:** AFFLICTION-INFECTION
>
> **Trigger Sentence:** Any viral INFECTION causes AFFLICTION.
>
> **Sample Sentence:** Malnutrition is one of the common *afflictions* in the Third World countries.
>
> Related Words: AFFLICT - v. cause suffering

AFFLUENT (AF loo unt): a. Wealthy, plentiful

> **Trigger:** AFFLUENT -FLUENT
>
> **Trigger Sentence:** Many AFFLUENT persons are FLUENT communicators; if you are AFFLUENT you can easily INFLUENCE.
>
> **Sample Sentence:** In our city, all the *affluent* families live on the river side homes.
>
> Related Words: AFFLUENCE -n. wealthy

AFFRONT (uh FRUNT): v. Insult, offend

> **Trigger:** 1.AFFRONT-FRONT-CONFRONT. 2. AFFRONT-OFFEND
>
> **Trigger Sentence:** 1. Don't AFFRONT me IN FRONT OF others. 2. He CONFRONTED and AFFRONTED me in the public.
>
> **Sample Sentence:** Such aggressive behavior by these boys is an *affront* to our school's reputation.

AGGRANDIZE (uh GRAN diez): v. Increase, Enhance, Exaggerate

> **Trigger:** 1. AGGRANDIZE -A GRAND SIZE. 2. AGGRANDIZE-ADD GRAND- SIZE
>
> **Trigger Sentence:** He AGGRANDIZED his position by erecting his GRAND SIZED statues.
>
> **Sample Sentence:** One cannot *aggrandize* his position simply by erecting one's grand sized statues.

Memory Test-1 : Match each word and its memory trick to the corresponding definition.

S.N	WORD	MEMORY TRIGGER	S.N	DEFINITIONS	KEY
1	ABANDON	He BANNED smoking----	A	Cancel officially; abolish	
2	ABASE	Show your BASE to ABASE him	B	Be plentiful; overflow with	
3	ABASH	teacher BASHED me –I feel ABASHED	C	Cancel, put an end to	
4	ABATE	REBATE—a bite of an apple ABATES	D	Continuous; permanent	
5	ABDICATE	I don't want DICTATOR power	E	Deviant; abnormal	
6	ABERRANT	You are an ERROR in the society	F	Embarrass	
7	ABET	A BET- time- ABET your friends	G	Give up (an action) completely	
8	ABEYANCE	AB+YAWNS..no action	H	Give up; renounce	
9	ABHOR	I ABHOR a bore guy..I never ADORE	I	Harsh in manner; a substance that abrades	
10	ABIDING	A BINDING-or A bonding	J	Hate, dislike	
11	ABJECT	She REJECTED -- I'm in ABJECT state	K	Dislike, Hate	
12	ABJURE	In front of JURY, I ABJURED her	L	Help (usually in some wrongdoing)	
13	ABOLISH	ESTABLISH is an antonym-demolish	M	Humiliate, degrade	
14	ABOMINATE	a BOMB I hate	N	Reduce; become less	
15	ABORTIVE	Just like "ABORTION"	O	Renounce upon oath; deny	
16	ABOUND	abundance	P	Shorten	
17	ABRASIVE	RAZOR-abusive-abrasion	Q	Suspended Action; temporary inactivity	
18	ABREAST	Two BREASTS abreast	R	Unsuccessful, fruitless	
19	ABRIDGE	A BRIEF; A BRIDGE is constructed	S	Up-to-date; side by side	
20	ABROGATE	AB+NEGATE- negative to an action	T	Utterly hopeless; shameful	

Memory Test-2 : Match each word and its memory trick to the corresponding definition.

S.N	WORD	MEMORY TRIGGER	S.N	DEFINITIONS	KEY
1	ABRUPT	Ruptured ; interrupted	A	Additional object	
2	ABSCISSION	SCISSORS are used for	B	Agree, assent	
3	ABSCOND	Absent in a second –James Bond	C	Agreement ; to grant, give	
4	ABSOLUTE	God is ABSOLUTE	D	An expression of praise; award	
5	ABSOLVE	Court case is SOLVED	E	An increase in amount; addition	
6	ABSTAIN	Abs-ABSENT from doing	F	Avoid, refrain from	
7	ABSTEMIOUS	ABS-6 pack ABS ..so no food & drink	G	Complete, certain	
8	ABSTRACT	Imagine a train WITHOUT TRACKS	H	Difficult to understand; obscure	
9	ABSTRUSE	CONFUSE	I	Give a view; Explanation	
10	ABUT	A&B are joining letters	J	Immeasurably deep; bottomless	
11	ABYSMAL	ABYSMAL-DISMAL; ABYSS-no base	K	Leave secretly and hide	
12	ACCEDE	ACCEPT or AGREED	L	Pardon; forgive an offense	
13	ACCENTUATE	With powerful ACCENT he ACCENTUATED	M	Partner in crime	
14	ACCESSORY	Other than NECESSARY	N	Praise publicly	
15	ACCLAIM	A CLAP to ACCLAIM	O	Self- control (esp. in the eating and drinking)	
16	ACCOLADE	Act of laud- APPLAUD	P	Stress or emphasize; intensify	
17	ACCOMPLICE	Accompany - illegal	Q	The act of cutting off	
18	ACCORD	AGREED - also awarded	R	Theoretical; difficult to understand	
19	ACCOUNT	TELL ME about your bank ACCOUNT	S	To border upon; adjoin	
20	ACCRETION	Acceleration-accumulation	T	Unexpectedly sudden; curt; rude	

Answers	Ex.No	1	2	3	4	5	6	7	8	9	10	11	12	13	14	15	16	17	18	19	20
	1	G	M	F	N	H	E	L	Q	J	D	T	O	C	K	R	B	I	S	P	A
	2	T	Q	K	G	L	F	O	R	H	S	J	B	P	A	N	D	M	C	I	E

Memory Test-3 : Match each word and its memory trick to the corresponding definition.

S.N	WORD	MEMORY TRIGGER	S.N	DEFINITIONS	KEY
1	ACCUSE	ABUSE-A CURSE	A	Activate, motivate	
2	ACERBIC	ACIDIC nature	B	An assistant or follower	
3	ACKNOWLEDGE	I've a A KNOWLEDGE	C	Bitter; sharp-tempered	
4	ACME	1.ACE. 2.ACNE	D	Bitterness or ill feeling	
5	ACOLYTE	A CO PILOT	E	Blame, charge with a crime	
6	ACQUIESCENCE	Acceptance	F	Confuse; mix up	
7	ACQUISITIVE	Acquiring more than required	G	Hard; stubborn, rigid	
8	ACQUIT	Quit him from your hands	H	mentally sharp, shrewd, critical	
9	ACRID	Acid taste	I	Passive acceptance; yielding	
10	ACRIMONY	A crime on me ?? acrid-acid	J	Recognize; admit	
11	ACTUATE	activate	K	Set free; exonerate	
12	ACUMEN	1.IQ –MEN and 2. A CUTE MEN	L	Sharp; bitterly pungent	
13	ACUTE	a CUTE GUY possesses ???	M	Shrewdness, keenness	
14	ADAMANT	A DIAMOND–what type of material ?	N	Skilled, expert	
15	ADDLE	Riddle ??	O	Something added on or attached	
16	ADDRESS	I EXPRESS- when I ADDRESS	P	Speak to, deal with; discuss	
17	ADDUCE	PRODUCE evidence	Q	Stick fast to; be devoted to	
18	ADEPT	He's A DEPTH of knowledge	R	Strongly desirous of acquiring	
19	ADHERE	ADHESIVE	S	To cite as evidence; offer as an example	
20	ADJUNCT	Add +Junk	T	Top; peak	

Memory Test-4 : Match each word and its memory trick to the corresponding definition.

S.N	WORD	MEMORY TRIGGER	S.N	DEFINITIONS	KEY
1	ADMONISH	I will PUNISH- I ADMONISHED	A	Admire, venerate	
2	ADORE	ADORE-ADMIRE	B	Artificial; faked to impress	
3	ADORN	add ORNAMENT	C	Attraction; closeness	
4	ADROIT	ANDROID- he can DRAW IT	D	Bad; miserable	
5	ADULATION	ADMIRATION-ADORATION	E	Clever, skillful	
6	ADULTERATE	ADULT movies ADULTERATE kids	F	Concerned with beauty; artistic	
7	ADUMBRATE	UMBRELLA gives shadow	G	Decorate, enhance	
8	ADVERSARY	A REVERSE Person	H	Enemy; rival	
9	ADVERSE	WORSE condition	I	Excessive admiration, flattery	
10	ADVOCACY	my ADVOCATE-ADDS VOICE to me	J	Increase, Exaggerate	
11	AESTHETIC	How an ATHLETIC body looks???	K	Influence, attack (of a disease)	
12	AFFABLE	AFFECTION + BLE	L	Insult, offend	
13	AFFECT	AFFECT-EFFECT; INPUT-OUTPUT	M	Make impure, spoil	
14	AFFECTED	A FAKED	N	Sociable; friendly	
15	AFFINITY	AFFECTION-AFFAIR-UNITY	O	State to be true; confirm	
16	AFFIRM	Firm-CONFIRM	P	Suffering, pain; torment	
17	AFFLICTION	INFECTION causes ???	Q	Support	
18	AFFLUENT	Money is FLUENT and flowing	R	To disclose partially; foreshadow	
19	AFFRONT	Firing in the FRONT	S	Warn, scold	
20	AGGRANDIZE	A GRAND SIZE	T	Wealthy, plentiful	

Answers	Ex.No	1	2	3	4	5	6	7	8	9	10	11	12	13	14	15	16	17	18	19	20
	3	E	C	J	T	B	I	R	K	L	D	A	M	H	G	F	P	S	N	Q	O
	4	S	A	G	E	I	M	R	H	D	Q	F	N	K	B	C	O	P	T	L	J

WORD GROUPS DAY-1

★ **CRITICIZE / CRITICISM**

NOUNS: animadversion, anathema, aspersion, calumny, defamation, disapprobation, fulmination, libel, malediction, opprobrium, obloquy, slander; diatribe, harangue, invective, philippic, tirade

VERB: admonish, belittle, berate, castigate, censure, chastise, condemn, declaim, deprecate, denigrate, denounce, decry, deride, disparage, discredit, excoriate, expostulate, gainsay, impugn, lambaste, malign, objurgate, pillory, revile, rebuke, remonstrate, reprimand, reprove, rail, upbraid, vilify, vituperate

ADJECTIVE: abusive, defamatory, derogatory, insulting, pejorative, scurrilous, scandalous

ANTONYMS: v. praise, commend, applaud, extol

★ **PRAISE/PRAISING**

VERB: acclaim, aggrandize, applaud, commend, compliment, eulogize, extol, exalt, esteem, hail, venerate, rave about, revere, laud, lionize, honor

NOUNS: accolade, encomium, kudos, laurels, paean, panegyric, eulogy

ADJECTIVE: laudatory, flattering; commendable, laudable

ANTONYMS: censure, calumny, slander

★ **SAD/SADNESS**

ADJECTIVES: bleak, crestfallen, dejected, despondent, disconsolate, dispirited, doleful, dolorous, elegiac, forlorn, funeral, glum, gloomy, lachrymose, lugubrious, melancholy, mournful, morose, rueful, saturnine, sullen, woeful, woebegone

NOUNS: anguish, despair, depression, misery

VERB: bewail, grieve, lament, mourn, regret

ANTONYMS: adj. ebullient, exuberant, festive, merry, high-spirited, vivacious

★ **HAPPY/HAPPINESS**

ADJECTIVES: content, blissful, cheerful, jocular, merry, gleeful, gratified, jubilant, buoyant, radiant, sunny, beatific, thrilled, elated, exhilarated, ecstatic, euphoric, exultant, exuberant, overjoyed, rapturous

NOUNS: jubilation, rapture

VERB: rejoice, exult

ANTONYMS: v. depress, mourn; n. elegy

★ **PLENTY/ABUNDANCE**

ADJECTIVES: ample, bountiful, copious, plethora, profuse, extensive, generous, inexhaustible, lavish, fulsome, lush, overflowing, numerous, prolific, rife, replete

NOUN: abundance, glut, profusion, cornucopia, plenty, plenitude, multitude, surfeit, surplus

VERB: burgeon, flourish, inundate, proliferate, teem.

ANTONYMS: adj. dearth, paucity, scarcity, sparse, scanty

★ **LACK/SCARCITY**

NOUN: dearth, deficiency, insufficiency, lack, paucity, poverty, scarcity, want

ADJECTIVES: exiguous, inadequate, meager, paltry, slender, scanty, sparse

VERB: want, be devoid of.

ANTONYMS: abundance, plenitude, surfeit.

Emotional blackmail ?! ABRUPT end to my bachelorhood !!

If you don't get hooked to me... I will put ABRUPT end to my life by hooking myself !

ABRUPT : un expectedly sudden, curt, rude

Word List Day-2

AGGREGATE (AG ruh gut): v. Gather; n. Accumulate

  Trigger: AGGREGATE-SEGREGATE (SEPARATE)

  Trigger Sentence: 1. Aggregate and segregate are antonyms. 2. AGGREGATE is to gather and SEGREGATE is to separate.

  Sample Sentence: 1.They purchased an *aggregate* (n) of 3000 shares in the company. 2. They *aggregated (v)* lot of wealth during share market boom.

  Related Words: SEGREGATE – v. separate; divide

AGGRIEVE (uh GREEV): v. Cause sorrow; offend

  Trigger: AGGRIEVE-A GRIEF

  Trigger Sentence: A GRIEF (sorrow) stricken Sugreev (Vali's brother in Ramayana) AGGRIEVED in front of Rama.

  Sample Sentence: She *aggrieved* over lays of her jewelry.

  Related Words: AGGRAVATE – v. make worse; annoy

ALACRITY (uh LAK ri tee): n. Promptness; cheerful readiness

  Trigger: ALACRITY-"ALARM+CITY"

  Trigger Sentence: When the celebration ALARM buzzed in the CITY, everyone moved with ALACRITY.

  Sample Sentence: He accepted the invitation from a beautiful girl with *alacrity*.

ALARMING (uh LAHR ming): a. Worrisome, a warning of danger

  Trigger: 1.ALARMING-HARMING. 2. ALARMING-A WARNING

  Trigger Sentence: ALARMING signal sent A WARNING notice about A HARMING danger.

  Sample Sentence: We *alarmed* the new neighbors about the burglaries in our colony.

ALBEIT (awl BEE it): conj. Although, even though

  Trigger: ALBEIT-ALL BUT

  Trigger Sentence: The conjunctions... ALBEIT, although and BUT are synonyms.

  Sample Sentence: It was a wonderful trip *albeit* expenses and long hours of train travel.

ALCHEMY (AL kuh mee): n. A medieval chemistry

  Trigger: alCHEMY-CHEMISTRY

  Trigger Sentence: ALCHEMY is a PSEUDO (fake) CHEMISTRY in medieval period, which focused on the transmutation of base metals into gold.

  Sample Sentence: The *alchemy* of cosmetics transforms ugly girls into beautiful damsels.

ALIENATE (EY lee uh neyt): v.To make unfriendly, separate

  Trigger: ALIEN-ALLY (*antonyms)

  Trigger Sentence: 1. He is an ALIEN and stranger; let us get ALIENATED from him. 2. ALIEN is an ENEMY & ALLY is a FRIEND.

  Sample Sentence: If you insist on marrying that *alien*, we have no other option but to *alienate* you.

  Related Words: INALIENABLE - a. non-transferable

ALLAY (au LAY): v. Calm; pacify

    Trigger: alLAY-LAY

    Trigger Sentence: After 6 hours of arduous play, LAY BACK for a while; it ALLAYS all your pain and fatigue.

    Sample Sentence: The Father sat by her consoling and helped *allay* her agony.

ALLEGE (uh LEJ): v. State without proof

    Trigger: 1.ALLEGE-ALL LEGAL.2.ALLEGE-ALL LEAGUE

    Trigger Sentence: 1. When you ALLEGE, an ALLEGATION is thrown on someone WITHOUT a LEGAL PROOF. 2. ALL IPL LEAGUES are corrupted; it is an ALLEGATION and not yet proven.

    Sample Sentence: Because Modi was not proven guilty in the court, the newspapers can only refer to him as the "*alleged* corrupt official".

    Related Words: ALLEGED - a. declared but not proved; suspect

ALLEGORY (AL uh gawr ee): n. Fable; symbolic story, metaphor

    Trigger: 1. ALLEGORY- A LEGEND STORY. 2. ALLEGORY-ALLIGATOR STORY

    Trigger Sentence: 1. AN ALLEGORY is A SYMBOLIC STORY. 2. AN ALLIGATOR STORY is a type of an ALLEGORY

    Sample Sentence: "Alice in Wonderland", can be interpreted as an *allegory*.

    Related Words: ALLEGORICAL - a. metaphorical

ALLEVIATE (uh LEE vee ayt): v. Relieve; lessen the severity of...

    Trigger: 1. ALLEVIATE-A LEAVE HE ATE. 2. ALLEVE-RELIEVE

    Trigger Sentence: 1. Herbs RELIEVE the pain or disease. A LEAVE HE ATE to ALLEVIATE the pains. 2. "ALLEVE" sounds like "RELIEVE".

    Sample Sentence: She got completely relieved once she had been *alleviated* from a rare form of cancer.

ALLOY (AL oy): v.Mix metals; corrupt by adding other substances

    Trigger: ALLOY-ALL TOYS

    Trigger Sentence: ALL TOYS are ALLOYED; they are a fake of a model.

    Sample Sentence: Bronze is an *alloy* consisting of copper and tin.

    Related Words: UNALLOYED - a. pure, complete

ALLUDE (uh LOOD): v. To refer indirectly; hint

    Trigger: 1. ALLUDE- "A LOUD"- (not a loud). 2. ALLUDE-NOT RUDE

    Trigger Sentence: 1. When we ALLUDE, we won't tell in A LOUD manner, we just HINT. 2. Don't tell him RUDELY; ALLUDE him that his behavior is RUDE.

    Sample Sentence: Don't *allude* from here. He can't understand your hints. Instead speak loud.

    Related Words: ALLUSION - n. Indirect reference

ALLURE (uh LUHR): v. Tempt, attract

    Trigger: ALLURE-"ALL LOVE"

    Trigger Sentence: ALL LOVE happens because of ALLURE and ATTRACTION. I got ALLURED by ALL his LOVE letters.

    Sample Sentence: We were *allured* by the delicious-looking food.

    Related Words: LURE – v. Tempt; entice

ALOOF (uh LOOF): a. Reserved or reticent; Indifferent; detached

    Trigger: ALOOF-ALONE

    Trigger Sentence: ALOOF wants to be ALONE and reserved.

    Sample Sentence: David Thoreau mostly remained *aloof* because he loved to be alone.

ALTERCATION (awl tur KAY shun): n. Noisy quarrel

    Trigger: "ALTER-ACTION-REACTION"

    Trigger Sentence: There is an ALTER ACTION and REACTION when an ALTERCATION broke out among the people.

    Sample Sentence: An *altercation* broke between the southern and northern students due to regional sentiments.

ALTRUISM (AL troo iz um): n.Unselfish; philanthropy

    Trigger: ALTRUISM-ALL TRUE ISM

    Trigger Sentence: ALL TRUE people follow ALTRUISM. ALTRUISTS have TRUE love towards all his/her fellow human beings.

    Sample Sentence: That rich woman is *altruistic*; she pays the expenses for poor students to go to college.

    Related Words: ALTRUISTIC -n. unselfish, generous

AMALGAM (uh MAL gum): n. A mixture or blend

    Trigger: 1.AmalGAM-A GUM. 2. amalgaMATE-MATE

    Trigger Sentence: 1. A GUM is used for BLENDING two or more things. 2. MATE means join two things together.

    Sample Sentence: The dentist filled the large cavity with an *amalgam* of gold and silver.

    Related Words: AMALGAMATE - v. to unite into a single body.

AMATEUR (AM uh choor): a.Not professional, novice

    Trigger: AMATEUR-"A+ MATURE"- NO MATURE

    Trigger Sentence: AMATEURS are NOT yet MATURE. They are not professional. They do things for pleasure.

    Sample Sentence: He is an *amateur* sports person; he is not yet professional.

AMBIGUOUS (am BIG yoo us): a. Doubtful or uncertain in meaning

    Trigger: AMBIGUOUS-OBVIOUS

    Trigger Sentence: AMBIGUOUS and OBVIOUS are antonyms.

    Sample Sentence: Confused by *ambiguous* (not obvious to the mind) instructions, the parents were unable to assemble the toy.

    Related Words: 1. AMBIGUITY - n. lack of clarity 2.UNAMBIGUOUS - a. clear

AMBIVALENCE (am BIV uh luns): n.A state of having both positive and negative feelings towards a subject

    Trigger: AMBIVALENCE-"A NO BALANCE"

    Trigger Sentence: 1. A person with NO BALANCE of mind tends to be AMBIVALENT; sometimes positive and sometimes negative. 2. Ambivalent, ambiguous and ambivalence are synonym variants.

    Sample Sentence: Initially Dr. Raju was *ambivalent* whether to take up a job or to attend graduate studies abroad. Well, he landed up doing both!

AMELIORATE (uh MEEL yuh rayt): v. Improve; get better

    Trigger: 1. A MEAL RATE. 2. AMELIORATE-DETERIORATE

Trigger Sentence: 1. If A MEAL RATE is decreased poor people's condition will be AMELIORATED. 2. AMELIORATE (improve) and DETERIORATE (decline) are antonyms.

Sample Sentence: Many social workers have attempted to *ameliorate* the conditions of people living in the slums.

AMENABLE (uh MEEN uh bul): a.Easily managed; willing

    Trigger: 1.AMENable-AMEN (OK). 2. AMENABLE-AMENDABLE

    Trigger Sentence: 1. AMENABLE person says AMEN (ok) 2. AMENABLE people are AMENDABLE

    Sample Sentence: Many a women can turn ruffian men into *amenable* persons.

AMEND (uh MEND): v. Change; correct

    Trigger: AMEND-"A MIND + BEND"

    Trigger Sentence: When you AMEND your MIND, you can BEND it in any direction.

    Sample Sentence: The club *amended* the membership rules to allow the younger generation.

    Related Words: EMEND –v. correct; amend

AMITY (AM uh tee): n. Friendship, friendly ties

    Trigger: AMITY-ENMITY

    Trigger Sentence: AMITY and ENMITY are antonyms.

    Sample Sentence: If you show *amity* to others, they don't show any enmity against you.

    Related Words: 1. AMIABLE - a. friendly 2. AMICABLE - a. friendly

AMOROUS (AM ur us): n.Full of love; loving

    Trigger: AMOROUS-AFFAIRS (of LOVE)

    Trigger Sentence: My AFFAIRS with that girl were full of AMOROUS moonlight rides.

    Sample Sentence: Romeo and Juliet is a *amorous* love story, which however ends in tragedy.

    Related Words: ENAMORED - a. in love, charmed

AMORPHOUS (ay MOHR fus): a.Formless; lacking shape or definition

    Trigger: AMORPHOUS-FORMLESS

    Trigger Sentence: AMORPHOUS LACKS any FORM; AMOEBAS are AMORPHOUS.

    Sample Sentence: 1. Nebulas in the space are *amorphously* dreamlike and formless! 2. John created an *amorphous* creature in his stories that changed its form or escaped into thin air!!!

AMPLE (AM puhl): a. Plenty, full

    Trigger: 1.AMPLE-I'M FULL. 2. AMPLITUDE- MAGNITUDE- PLENITUDE

    Trigger Sentence: 1. AMPLE sounds like I'M FULL. 2. I have just had AMPLE food. I AM FILLED.

    Sample Sentence: The government sent an *ample* supply of food and medicines to the train accident victims.

    Related Words: AMPLIFY - v. to make larger

AMPLIFY (AM pluh fi): v. Intensify; make stronger; clarify by expanding

    Trigger: AMPLIFY-AMPLIFIER

    Trigger Sentence: AMPLIFIER AMPLIFIES or increase the power or current.

    Sample Sentence: The stadium's sound system with an excellent *amplifier* could reach out to thousands of audiences.

ANACHRONISM (uh NUK ruh niz um): n.Something or someone misplaced in time.

Trigger: ANACHRONISM (OUT OF TIME); SYNCHRONISM (SAME TIME)

Trigger Sentence: CHRONOLOGICAL means according to the ORDER OF TIME; ANACHRONISM is something is OUT OF ORDER OF TIME.

Sample Sentence: Space and time are not an *anachronism* in Special Relativity. They are synchronised into what is called space-time continuum.

Related Words: SYNCHRONISM -n. simultaneous; coincidence

ANALOGOUS (uh NAL uh gus): a.Similar, comparable

Trigger: 1. ANALOGOUS-HOMOLOGOUS. 2. ANALOGOUS- ANOMALOUS

Trigger Sentence: 1. In GRE/SAT (old pattern) ANALOGY- we were seeking SIMILAR pairs (Homo-same). 2. ANALOGOUS means SAME; ANOMALOUS (abnormal) means DIVERGENT

Sample Sentence: Brains and computers are often considered *analogous*.

Related Words: ANALOGY -n. similarity

ANARCHY (AN ur kee): n. Lawlessness, absence of government

Trigger: ANARCHY- MONARCHY

Trigger Sentence: 1. People are prepared even for ANARCHY rather than living in a MONARCHY. 2. MONARCH -single ruler; PATRIARCH-male head; MATRIARCH-female head; ANARCH —no head; rebel

Sample Sentence: The day the substitute teacher arrived, *anarchy* broke out in class.

Related Words: 1. MONARCHY – n. rule by a single person. 2. OLIGARCHY –n. rule by a few elite people. 3. MATRIARCHY –n. rule by a female head. 4. PATRIARCHY – n. rule by a male head

ANATHEMA (uh NATH uh muh): n. Curse; solemn curse

Trigger: ANATHEMA- AN ASTHMA

Trigger Sentence: For many patients ASTHMA is an ANATHEMA.

Sample Sentence: It is indeed an *anathema* for people living and working in such poor and unhygienic environment.

ANECDOTE (AN ik doht): n. A short entertaining story describing an amusing incident

Trigger: 1. ANECDOTE –AN EX DATE. 2. ANECDOTE -A NARRATE

Trigger Sentence: AN AMUSING NOTE of AN EX-DATED incident is called an ANECDOTE

Sample Sentence: My teacher made his lectures quite interesting my interspersing and connecting funny *anecdotes*.

ANIMADVERSION (an uh mad VUR zhun): n.Criticism; aspersion

Trigger: 1. ANIMADVERSION. 2. ANY MAD VERSION

Trigger Sentence: 1. ANTI + MAD + VERSION; MAD PEOPLE VERSION is full of ANIMADVERSION. 2. ANY MAD VERSION represents ANTI TALK against someone.

Sample Sentence: *Animadversions* you may cast against my failures, I shall soon emerge a winner like a phoenix!

ANIMATED (AN uh mey tid): a.Lively, energetic

Trigger: ANIMATED- ANIMAL+ACTIVATED

Trigger Sentence: The ACTIVATED ANIMALS are quite ANIMATED in Tom and Jerry cartoon movies.

Sample Sentence: By watching those cute *animation* films, kids get *animated* with joy.

Related Words: INANIMATE - a. weak, lifeless

ANIMOSITY (an ih MAHS uh tee): n.Strong hostility or enmity

    Trigger: 1.ANIMosITY-ENMITY. 2. ANIMOSITY-"ENEMY + CITY"

    Trigger Sentence: 1. In an ENEMY CITY you will find ANIMOSITY. 2. ANIMITY (in the word ANIMOSITY) sounds like ENMITY when we remove "OS".

    Sample Sentence: After fighting over the same girl friend, the two brothers developed a strong *animosity* against each other.

    Related Words: ANIMUS -n. ill feeling

ANNEX (uh NEKS): v. Extension, add

    Trigger: ANNEX-"ADD + NEXT"

    Trigger Sentence: Alexander ANNEXED lot of kingdoms by ADDING NEXT to his empire.

    Sample Sentence: Our neighbors *annexed* the common road and used it as their private parking area!

ANNIHILATE (uh NY uh layt): v. To destroy completely

    Trigger: 1. ANNIHILATE-ELIMINATE. 2. ANNIHIL (ANNUL-a NIL)

    Trigger Sentence: 1. AN ANT HILL is ANNIHILATED by a snake. 2. ANNIHILATE, ANNUL (NULL is to make NIL) and ELIMINATE are synonyms.

    Sample Sentence: The plague *annihilated* an entire civilization.

ANNOTATE (AN uh teyt): v.Make explanatory notes; comment

    Trigger: ANNOTATE-"ADD NOTES"

    Trigger Sentence: When we ANNOTATE, we ADD FOOT- NOTES for additional explanation.

    Sample Sentence: He gave a quick look at the *annotations* in his notebook before the exam.

ANNUL (uh NUHL): v. Cancel; make invalid

    Trigger: ANNUL-"AN+NUL (NIL)"

    Trigger Sentence: ANNUL is to make everything NIL (VOID).

    Sample Sentence: The parents of the eloped couple tried to *annul* their marriage.

ANODYNE (AAN uh dyen): a. Reducing pain; soothing

    Trigger: ANODYNE-"A NO PAIN"

    Trigger Sentence: When we use ANODYNE- there is NO PAIN.

    Sample Sentence: No *anodyne* could relieve him of his pain.

ANOINT (uh NOINT): v.Consecrate; rub oil on a person's head.

    Trigger: 1.ANOINT-AN OINT. 2. ANOINT-APPOINT

    Trigger Sentence: In a religious APPOINTMENT an OINTMENT is rubbed on a person's head to ANOINT him as the chief.

    Sample Sentence: 1. Neil Starr was *anointed* as the crown prince. 2. My granny *anointed* my hair with oils blended with a paste of herbs and other aromatic seeds.

ANOMALY (uh NAH muh lee): n.Irregularity, Abnormality

    Trigger: ANOMALY-ABNORMALLY

    Trigger Sentence: Something which represents ABNORMAL (out of NORMAL) condition is termed as an ANOMALY.

    Sample Sentence: A cold day in May at Mumbai is an *anomaly*.

    Related Words: ANOMALOUS -a. abnormal

ANONYMOUS (uh NON uh mus): a.Not named, unknown

    Trigger: ANONYM-"A NO NAME"

Trigger Sentence: Having NO NAME is known as ANONYMOUS.

Sample Sentence: An *anonymous* writer does not reveal his name.

ANTAGONIST (an TAG uh nist): n. Adversary; opponent

Trigger: ANTAGONIST-"ANTI & AGAINST"

Trigger Sentence: An ANTAGONIST is ANTI and AGAINST; an ANTAGONIST ANTAGONIZES (cause agony).

Sample Sentence: Don't *antagonize* your boss, just obey his orders; the boss is always right!

Related Words: ANTAGONISM - n. hostility

ANTECEDENT (an tuh SEED unt): n. something going before...

Trigger: ANTECEDE-PRECEDE

Trigger Sentence: 1. ANTECEDE-PRECEDE; ANTERIOR-PRIOR; ANTECEDENT-PRECEDENT; ANTEDATE-PREDATE; ANTE-PRE (BEFORE). 2. ANTECEDE and PRECEDE are synonyms.

Sample Sentence: The Buddha was *antecedent* of Jesus whereas Jesus was precedent of Prophet Mohammad.

ANTEDATE (AN ti dayt): v. To be of older date than; precede in time

Trigger: 1. ANTEDATE-OLD DATE. 2. ANTEDATED-ANTEQUATED

Trigger Sentence: OLD DATE or PREDATE is referred as ANTEDATE.

Sample Sentence: These Cholla period temples *antedate* the Vijayanagara temples by over 500 years and yet both depict the same themes.

Related Words: PREDATE - v. occur prior to.

ANTEDILUVIAN (an tee di LOO vee uhn): a. Ancient; antiquated

Trigger: ANTEDILUVIAN-ANTIQUATED- ANTIQUE

Trigger Sentence: 1. ANTIQUATED, ANTIQUE, and ANTEDILUVIAN represents the things which are VERY OLD. 2. ANTIQUES are ANTEDILUVIAN are displayed in museums.

Sample Sentence: The *antediluvian* customs have not changed for thousands of years when it comes to suppression of women.

Related Words: ANTEDILUVIAL - a. period before the Biblical flood.

ANTICIPATE (an TIS uh peyt): v. Look forward to; expect

Trigger: 1.ANTICIPATE-ANTE SEE FATE. 2. UNANTICIPATED-UNEXPECTED

Trigger Sentence: The financial wizards ANTE-SEE (FORESEE) the FATE of share prices of the many stock market listed companies.

Sample Sentence: The meteorologists *anticipated* thunder storms and heavy rains in the next few days.

Related Words: UNANTICIPATED - a. not expected; not foreseen

ANTIDOTE (an ti DOTE): n. A remedy to counteract a poison or disease

Trigger: ANTIDOTE-"ANTI-DOSE"

Trigger Sentence: An ANTIDOTE acts like A DOSE of medicine ANTI to the effects of poison.

Sample Sentence: We carried a medical kit with an *antidote* for snake bite in the jungle.

ANTINOMIAN (an ti NOH mee uhn): n. One who rejects a socially established morality.

Trigger: ANTINOMIAN-"ANTI "

Trigger Sentence: An ANTINOMIAN is simply ANTI towards orthodox rules of morality.

Sample Sentence: Mao was an *antinomian* because he was anti-cultural or anti-traditional and wanted to obliterate the old influence through Cultural Revolution in

China during 1960s.

ANTIPATHY (an TIP uh thee): n. Aversion, hatred

Trigger: ANTIPATHY-"ANTI + PITY"

Trigger Sentence: Hitler had ANTIPATHY against mercy. He was AGAINST the act of PITY.

Sample Sentence: Politicians created an *antipathy* among people so they could divide and rule!

ANTIQUATED (AN ti kwey tid): a. Out-of-date, obsolete

Trigger: 1. ANTIQUATED-ANTIQUE. 2. ANTIQUATED-OUTDATED

Trigger Sentence: An OUTDATED thing like an ANTIQUE is termed as ANTIQUATED.

Sample Sentence: You got such *antiquated* objects in your house that it appears like a museum!

ANTITHETIC (an tuh THET ik): a. Opposing; negating

Trigger: ANTIthetical-ANTI

Trigger Sentence: 1. ANTI and ANTITHETIC are synonyms. 2. Antagonistic, anti, anti-establishment, antipathetic, antipodal, antinomian, antithesis, antithetical, antonymous; all are belong to same family.

Sample Sentence: It's foolish to deliver *antithetical* speeches among staunch believers.

Related Words: ANTITHESIS – n. opposite

APATHY (AP uh thee): n. No feeling, indifferent

Trigger: 1.APATHY- NO PITY. 2. APATHY-SYMPATHY-ANTIPATHY

Trigger Sentence: APATHY means NO PITY; I've neither SYMPATHY nor ANTIPATHY. "Apathy-no feelings"; "antipathy-opposite feeling"; "sympathy, empathy-same feelings"; "pathos-feelings"

Sample Sentence: Shylock shows no pity for Antanio. He was *apathetic* to his pitiful condition. In fact, he shows antipathy against him.

Related Words: APATHETIC - a. indifferent

APEX (AY peks): n. The highest or culminating point; climax

Trigger: APEX-A PEAK

Trigger Sentence: 1. A PEAK point is an APEX. 2. VERTEX (most VERTICAL POINT) and APEX are synonyms.

Sample Sentence: He was at the *apex* of his career when he decided to quit!

APHORISM (AF uh riz um): n. Concise saying; pithy

Trigger: 1.APHORISM-A PHRASE ISM. 2. APHOR (A FOR) +ISM

Trigger Sentence: A PHRASE like "an apple ("A FOR"-"apple") a day keeps the doctor away," is an APHORISM.

Sample Sentence: He often uses *aphorisms* like "penny saved is a penny earned", "friend in need is a friend indeed", etc.

APLOMB (uh PLOM): n. Self-confidence

Trigger: APLOMB-A BOMB

Trigger Sentence: I feel like, I am A BOMB. I have APLOMB. I never worry about A BOMB.

Sample Sentence: USA can attack its enemies with *aplomb* because its forces can bomb on enemy territories using their invisible B2 stealth bomber aeroplanes.

APOCRYPHAL (uh POK ruh fuhl): a. Not genuine; untrue

Trigger: APOCRYPHAL-HYPOCRITICAL

Trigger Sentence: HYPOCRITICAL praise is NOT GENUINE; similarly APOCRYPHAL things are NOT GENUINE.

Sample Sentence: His comments are considered hypocritical because his criticism is *apocryphal*.

APOLITICAL (ey puh LIT i kul): a. Not political; not interested in politics.

Trigger: APOLITICAL-POLITICAL

Trigger Sentence: I am NOT interested in POLITICAL affairs; I'm APOLITICAL

Sample Sentence: His *apolitical* statement is politically neutral.

APOLOGIST (uh POL uh jist): n. One who speaks in defense of something; advocate.

Trigger: 1. APOLOGIST-ANTAGONIST. 2. APOLOGIST-"A PROTAGONIST"

Trigger Sentence: 1. ANTAGONIST is always AGAINST; PROTAGONIST (protector) is a SUPPORTER. 2. Apologist and antagonist are antonyms. 3. Apologist and protagonist are synonyms.

Sample Sentence: USA was an *apologist* of capitalism whereas USSR was its antagonist during 1917-91.

APOSTATE (uh POS tit): n. Traitor; one who abandons his religious or political beliefs.

Trigger: APOSTATE-"OPP. STATE"

Trigger Sentence: APOSTATE goes to OPP. (OPPOSITE) STATE; leaves his former faith and belief.

Sample Sentence: Kim Philby, a former British Secret Agent, turned into an *apostate* because he worked against his own state and passed on information to an opposite state.

Related Words: APOSTASY - n. disloyalty

APPALLING (uh PAWL ing): a. Shocking, horrifying

Trigger: APPALLING-FALLING (FALLING is SHOCKING)

Trigger Sentence: 1. Sudden FALLING brings APPALLING experience. 2. APPALL- is to make you FALL and to shock you too.

Sample Sentence: The scandalous behavior of this actress *appalled* her fans.

Related Words: APPALL – v. horrify, dismay

APPARENT (uh PAR unt): a. Readily perceived or understood; obvious.

Trigger: APPARENT- APPEARING

Trigger Sentence: APPARENT things APPEAR; so they are OBVIOUS

Sample Sentence: He *apparently* appears to be against our marriage.

APPARITION (ap uh RISH un): n. A ghost; phantom

Trigger: APPARITION-APPEARANCE

Trigger Sentence: Any supernatural APPEARANCE can be termed as an APPARITION-it is a GHOSTLY appearance.

Sample Sentence: Films on *apparitions* and imaginative creatures do entertain all age groups.

APPEASE (uh PEEZ): v. Soothe, relieve

Trigger: 1. APPEASE-TO EASE. 2. APPEASE-A-PLEASE

Trigger Sentence: TO EASE is TO APPEASE.

Sample Sentence: If we ease public hunger, we can *appease* their anger.

APPELLATION (ap uh LAY shun): n. Name, title

    Trigger: 1.APPEL-APPLE. 2. APPELLATION-APPLICATION

    Trigger Sentence: 1. APPLE is an APPELLATION of a fruit. 2. Whenever we write an APPLICATION for a post (e.g. Apple Company), we have to mention our APPELLATION.

    Sample Sentence: 1. The kindergarten teachers created *appellations* like "red bear" and "devil frog" for their stuffed animals to entertain the kids. 2. I was officially given the *appellation* of the editor-in-chief.

APPOSITE (uh POZ it): a. Appropriate

    Trigger: APPOSITE-A POSITIVE

    Trigger Sentence: He always gives A POSITIVE remark which is APPOSITE to the occasion.

    Sample Sentence: His *apposite* remarks create an appropriate and a positive impact.

APPRAISE (uh PRAYZ): v. Estimate value

    Trigger: APPRAISE-A PRICE (VALUE)

    Trigger Sentence: A PRICE for your work is APPRAISED by your boss.

    Sample Sentence: The accounts department of a company *appraises* the cost price of its goods.

APPRECIATE (uh PREE shee yet): v. 1. Be thankful for. 2. Rise in value or price. 3. Be fully aware

    Trigger: APPRECIATE-DEPRECIATE

    Trigger Sentence: 1. Whenever we APPRECIATE we either PRIZE or RISE THE PRICE of someone or something. 2. APPRECIATE and DEPRECIATE are antonyms.

    Sample Sentence: 1. "Thank you; I *appreciate* your concerns for me and my family". 2. Her land value got *appreciated* during the real-estate boom.

APPREHEND (ap ri HEND): v. Arrest (someone) for a crime.

    Trigger: 1. APPREHEND-A FREE HAND. 2. UP HAND

    Trigger Sentence: 1. When I ARREST (APPREHEND) a person, I won't give him A FREE HAND (antonym memory trick). 2. UP HAND (HANDS-UP) is a gesture made to ARREST.

    Sample Sentence: The police *apprehended* the suspected criminals.

APPREHENSION (ap ri HEN shun): a. Anxious or fearful especially of future evil: foreboding

    Trigger: APPREHENSION- UPPER TENSION

    Trigger Sentence: When people are in a state of APPREHENSION, they develop HYPER (UPPER) TENSION.

    Sample Sentence: They were *apprehensive* about letting their 17-year-old daughter drive alone.

    Related Words: 1.APPREHENSIVE - a. worried; 2.APPREHEND - v: arrest, understand

APPRISE (v. uh PRYZE): Inform

    Trigger: 1. APPRISE-ADVERTISE. 2. APPRISE-A PRIZE

    Trigger Sentence: 1. When you win A PRIZE you are going to ADVERTIZE and APPRISE it to everybody. 2. I won't be SURPRISED, since I was already APPRISED.

    Sample Sentence: I *apprised* him that his house rent was due.

APPROBATION (ap ruh BAY shun): n. Approval; praise

    Trigger: APPROBATION —APPROVES

    Trigger Sentence: APPROBATION is to APPROVE

    Sample Sentence: The Government paid rich *approbation* to the young entrepreneur and approved a million dollar loan.

Related Words: DISAPPROBATION - n. disapproval, condemnation

APPROPRIATE (uh PROH pree it): v. Take without permission, a. Suitable

Trigger: APPROPRIATE- "A-PRO-PIRATE"

Trigger Sentence: 1. v. A PIRATE APPROPRIATES money without permission.
2. a. Appropriate, apropos, apposite and apt are synonym variants.

Sample Sentence: 1. This adult film is not *appropriate (adj)* for children. 2. The invaders *appropriated* (v) the land and property of the inhabitants.

Related Words: EXPROPRIATE - v. confiscate. 2. MISAPPROPRIATE –v. take dishonestly

APROPOS (ap ruh POH): a. Appropriate; relevant, suitable

Trigger: APROPOS-A PROPER

Trigger Sentence: A PROPER statement delivered by the speaker APROPOS.

Sample Sentence: It's absolutely *apropos* that the principal gave the credit to the coach for creating a victorious football team out of a bunch of (otherwise) bully boys!

APT (APT): a. Appropriate; intelligent

Trigger: APT-APTITUDE

Trigger Sentence: When you have an APTITUDE, you can talk APT.

Sample Sentence: Beena being kind hearted and compassionate, is an *apt* choice to work as the manager of the orphanage.

Related Words: APTITUDE - a. skill; talent

ARABLE (AR uh buhl): a. Fit for growing crops

Trigger: ARABLE-FARMABLE

Trigger Sentence: ARABLE lands are FARMABLE and tillable.

Sample Sentence: It's like an oasis to find a piece of *arable* terrain in this concrete jungle city!

ARBITRARY (AHR buh trer ee): a. 1. Based on random choice; capricious 2. Autocratic

Trigger: "ARBIT+RARY"-"ORBIT+VARY"

Trigger Sentence: Imagine something VARY from one ORBIT to another ORBIT RANDOMLY.

Sample Sentence: 1.The dictator takes an *arbitrary* decision. 2. When you lack the information to judge what to do next, you will be forced to make an *arbitrary* decision.

when you grow up i do not want you to work like this ass !

i feel like an ass already !

ASSIDUOUS - tirelessly working

Memory Test-5 : Match each word and its memory trick to the corresponding definition.

S.N	WORD	MEMORY TRIGGER	S.N	DEFINITIONS	KEY
1	AGGREGATE	Aggregate –segregate (antonyms)	A	A medieval chemistry	
2	AGGRIEVE	A GRIEF	B	A blend or a mixture	
3	ALACRITY	ALARM buzzed in the CITY	C	Although, even though	
4	ALARMING	Some sign is HARMING	D	Calm; pacify	
5	ALBEIT	All BUT	E	Cause sorrow; offend	
6	ALCHEMY	some CHEMISTRY	F	Doubtful or uncertain in meaning	
7	ALIENATE	He is an ALIEN—not ALLY	G	Gather; accumulate	
8	ALLAY	LAY for a while –take REST	H	Mix metals; corrupt by mixing	
9	ALLEGE	Without LEGAL proof	I	Noisy quarrel	
10	ALLEGORY	An alligator STORY	J	Not professional, novice	
11	ALLEVIATE	A LEAVE HE ATE; herbs -why???	K	Promptness	
12	ALLOY	ALL TOYS are made of alloys	L	Relieve; lessen the severity of…	
13	ALLUDE	When I ALLUDE, I'll never talk LOUD	M	Reserved or reticent; detached	
14	ALLURE	He ALLURES me with ALL his LOVE !!!	N	State without proof	
15	ALOOF	Want to be ALONE	O	symbolic story; metaphor	
16	ALTERCATION	Alter action & reaction	P	Tempt, attract	
17	ALTRUISM	ALL TRUE people follow ALTRUISM	Q	To make unfriendly, separate	
18	AMALGAM	A mal GUM	R	To refer indirectly; hint	
19	AMATEUR	NO MATURE in sport	S	Unselfish; philanthropy	
20	AMBIGUOUS	not OBVIOUS - it is AMBIGUOUS	T	Worrisome, a warning of danger	

Memory Test-6 : Match each word and its memory trick to the corresponding definition.

S.N	WORD	MEMORY TRIGGER	S.N	DEFINITIONS	KEY
1	AMBIVALENCE	NO BALANCE of mind	A	A short entertaining story	
2	AMELIORATE	A MEAL RATE is decreased.. so ??	B	Change; correct	
3	AMENABLE	He says AMEN (ok)- AMENDABLE	C	Criticism; aspersion	
4	AMEND	bend your MIND	D	Curse; solemn curse	
5	AMITY	no ENMITY-no enemy	E	Easily managed; willing	
6	AMOROUS	AFFAIRS (of love)	F	Extension, add	
7	AMORPHOUS	No morphs	G	Formless; lacking shape or definition	
8	AMPLE	I am FULL	H	Friendship, friendly ties	
9	AMPLIFY	MAGNIFY	I	Full of love; loving	
10	ANACHRONISM	ANTI- to CHRONOMETER	J	Improve; get better	
11	ANALOGOUS	Homologous	K	Intensify; make stronger	
12	ANARCHY	No monarchy-no patriarchy	L	Lawlessness, absence of government	
13	ANATHEMA	My ASTHMA is an ANATHEMA	M	Lively, energetic	
14	ANECDOTE	A NARRATE-an ex date	N	Make explanatory notes; comment	
15	ANIMADVERSION	any mad VERSION	O	Mixed feelings (both negative & positive)	
16	ANIMATED	ANIMATED movies are full of life	P	Plenty, full	
17	ANIMOSITY	ENMITY—NO AMITY	Q	Similar, comparable	
18	ANNEX	No monarchy-no patriarchy	R	Something or someone misplaced in time	
19	ANNIHILATE	ant hill ate -ELIMINATE	S	Strong hostility or enmity	
20	ANNOTATE	ADD NOTES to explain	T	To destroy completely	

Answers	EX.NO	1	2	3	4	5	6	7	8	9	10	11	12	13	14	15	16	17	18	19	20
	5	G	E	K	T	C	A	Q	D	N	O	L	H	R	P	M	I	S	B	J	F
	6	O	J	E	B	H	I	G	P	K	R	Q	L	D	A	C	M	S	F	T	N

Memory Test-7 : Match each word and its memory trick to the corresponding definition.

S.N	WORD	MEMORY TRIGGER	S.N	DEFINITIONS	KEY
1	ANNUL	make NIL	A	A remedy to counteract a poison	
2	ANODYNE	A NO PAIN	B	Adversary; opponent	
3	ANOINT	Apply OINT to a king	C	Ancient; antiquated	
4	ANOMALY	abnormally	D	Aversion, hatred	
5	ANONYMOUS	A no NAME	E	Cancel; make invalid	
6	ANTAGONIST	He is ANTI and AGAINST	F	Concise saying; pithy	
7	ANTECEDENT	ANTECEDE-PRECEDE	G	Consecrate; rub oil on HEAD	
8	ANTEDATE	PREDATE-previous date	H	Irregularity, Abnormality	
9	ANTEDILUVIAN	antiquated-antique	I	Look forward to; expect	
10	ANTICIPATE	Anti-see-fate; I'll see fate of future	J	No feeling, indifferent	
11	ANTIDOTE	Anti-DOSE	K	Not genuine; untrue	
12	ANTINOMIAN	ANTI—to NORMAL rules	L	Not named, unknown	
13	ANTIPATHY	ANTI+PITY	M	One who rejects orthodoxy	
14	ANTIQUATED	ANTIQUE +DATED	N	Opposing; negating	
15	ANTITHETIC	it is ANTI to my thesis	O	Out-of-date, obsolete	
16	APATHY	NO PITY	P	Reducing pain; soothing	
17	APEX	A PEAK-vertex	Q	Self-confidence	
18	APHORISM	A PHRASE+ ISM	R	Something going before	
19	APLOMB	I feel like I am A BOMB	S	The highest point; climax	
20	APOCRYPHAL	HYPOCRITICAL-hypocrisy	T	To be of older date than; predate	

Memory Test-8 : Match each word and its memory trick to the corresponding definition.

S.N	WORD	MEMORY TRIGGER	S.N	DEFINITIONS	KEY
1	APOLITICAL	NO POLITICAL	A	A ghost; phantom	
2	APOLOGIST	A PROTAGONIST	B	Anxious or fearful; foreboding	
3	APOSTATE	he goes to OPP. STATE	C	Appropriate	
4	APPALLING	FALLING is SHOCKING	D	intelligent ; appropriate	
5	APPARENT	APPARENT things APPEAR	E	Appropriate; relevant, suitable	
6	APPARITION	supernatural APPEARANCE	F	Approval; praise	
7	APPEASE	TO EASE is to APPEASE	G	Arrest (someone) for a crime	
8	APPELLATION	APPLE is an APPELLATION of a fruit	H	Capricious ; autocratic	
9	APPOSITE	A POSITIVE remark	I	Estimate value	
10	APPRAISE	A PRICE for your work is APPRAISED	J	Fit for growing crops	
11	APPRECIATE	Appreciate –depreciate (antonyms)	K	Inform	
12	APPREHEND	UP HAND (HANDS-UP)	L	Name, title	
13	APPREHENSION	HYPER (UPPER) TENSION	M	not interested in politics	
14	APPRISE	ADVERTISE; I've won a PRIZE	N	Obvious; readily perceived	
15	APPROBATION	APPROBATION is to APPROVE	O	One who speaks in defense; advocate	
16	APPROPRIATE	A-PRO-PIRATE appropriates money	P	Rise in value ; be thankful for	
17	APROPOS	A PROPER statement	Q	Shocking, horrifying	
18	APT	you have an APTITUDE	R	Soothe, relieve	
19	ARABLE	FARMABLE	S	Take without permission; suitable	
20	ARBITRARY	ORBIT+VARY-varying decisions	T	Traitor	

EX.NO	1	2	3	4	5	6	7	8	9	10	11	12	13	14	15	16	17	18	19	20
7	E	P	G	H	L	B	R	T	C	I	A	M	D	O	N	J	S	F	Q	K
8	M	O	T	Q	N	A	R	L	C	I	P	G	B	K	F	S	E	D	J	H

WORD GROUPS DAY-2

★ **FAT/PLUMP BODY**

ADJECTIVES: buxom, corpulent, flabby, obese, paunchy, portly, rotund, squat

NOUNS: rotundity

VERB: fatten

ANTONYMS: adj. lean, skinny, thin

★ **SLIM-LEAN BODY**

ADJECTIVES: angular, anorexic, emaciated, gaunt, haggard, inadequate; lanky, slender, slim, svelte

NOUNS: lankiness

VERB: slim, diet

ANTONYMS: adj.fat, plump

★ **HUGE/GIGANTIC**

ADJECTIVES: huge, enormous, elephantine, gargantuan, gigantic, giant, humongous, leviathan, massive, colossal, behemoth, mammoth, monumental, prodigious, titanic, towering

NOUN: enormity, immensity, massiveness

VERB: aggrandize, enlarge, magnify

ANTONYMS: little, miniscule, small, tiny

★ **VERY SMALL/TINY**

ADJECTIVES: diminutive, minute, minuscule, puny, tiny

NOUN: miniature

VERB: diminish

ANTONYMS: huge, enormous, giant

★ **OBEDIENT/ SUBMISSIVE NATURE**

ADJECTIVES: amenable, acquiescent, complaisant, compliant, docile, deferential, dutiful, malleable, obedient, obeisant, pliant, pliable, submissive, slavish, subservient, tame, tractable, unassertive, yielding

NOUN: compliance, passivity, resignation, servility

VERB: abide, comply, confirm, defer, heed, obey

ANTONYMS: adj. intransigent, intractable; v. repudiate.

★ **STUBBORN/UNYIELDING NATURE**

ADJECTIVES: dogged, froward, contrary, headstrong, implacable, inflexible, inexorable, intractable, intransigent, mulish, obstinate, obdurate, contrary, perverse, pig-headed, recalcitrant, refractory, resolute, uncompromising, unrelenting, willful

NOUN: contumacy, tenacity, pertinacity.

ANTONYMS: amenable, pliant, tractable, submissive, relenting.

★ **TALKATIVE /WORDY**

ADJECTIVES: loquacious, long-winded, fluent, garrulous, grandiloquent, prolix, verbose, voluble, conversational, communicative, babbling, blathering, effusive, redundant, wordy

NOUN: circumlocution, verbiage, verbosity, prolixity

VERB: expatiate, elaborate, prate, palaver

ANTONYMS: reticent, taciturn, laconic; brief, concise, curt, sententious, pithy

hey friends, you know what happened ?.....!

he is indeed

VOCIFEROUS !

VOCIFEROUS : voluble voice, loud

Word List Day-3

ARCANE (ar KAYN): a. Secret, mysterious; understood by few

Trigger: 1. ARCANE -DARK LANE .2. ARCANE- ARC-DARK

Trigger Sentence: 1. In DARK LANES many ARCANE things do happen. 2. ARC sounds like DARK; when you keep something in DARK, it will be SECRET and MYSTERIOUS; and difficult to understand too.

Sample sentence: Many of the symbols inside the pyramids are *arcane* for the visitors to understand and decode.

ARCHAIC (ahr KAY ik): a. Ancient; no longer used

Trigger: 1. ARCHAIC-ARCHEOLOGY. 2. ARCHAIC- ARCH LIKE

Trigger Sentence: 1. ARCHEOLOGY is the study of ARCHAIC or old things. 2. ARCH LIKE structures are ARCHAIC and rarely seen in the modern world.

Sample sentence: With the arrival of personal computers, typewriters have become *archaic*.

ARCHETYPE (AHR kuh type): n. Original model, prototype

Trigger: 1. ARCHETYPE-PROTOTYPE. 2. ARCHETYPE-FIRST TYPE

Trigger Sentence: Both ARCHETYPE and PROTOTYPES usually precede something else; Swastika was the ARCHETYPE of Hitler. He made it the PROTOTYPE of Nazis.

Sample sentence: The Wright Brother's first airplane was an *archetype* that led to the advanced airplanes in the future.

ARDOR (AHR dur): n. Enthusiasm; fervor

Trigger: ARDOR-ADORE

Trigger Sentence: When we ADORE/ADMIRE something we do that with ARDOR.

Sample sentence: With all her *ardor* and devotion, Gayatri worshiped the Shirdi Saibaba.

Related Words: ARDENT- a. intense, passionate, zealous

ARDUOUS (AR joo us): a. Hard, laborious

Trigger: ARDUOUS-"HARD + PLUS"

Trigger Sentence: ARDUOUS jobs are HARD and TOUGH to complete; "ARD" sounds like"HARD".

Sample sentence: GRE students spend many *arduous* hours on learning the wordlists, well I have an easy solution for them called `memory trigger'!!

ARID (AR id): a. Dry, barren

Trigger: 1. ARID-ARD-HARD. 2. ARAB-ARID

Trigger Sentence: 1. ARAB LANDS are ARID because of desert. 2. HARD LANDS are ARID.

Sample sentence: It is very hard for Arabs to survive on *arid* lands.

ARISTOCRATIC (uh ris tuh KRAT ik): a. Of the noble class; refined

Trigger: ARISTOCRATIC-"ARISTOTLE LIKE"

Trigger Sentence: ARISTOTLE was Greek philosopher and NOBLE man.

Sample sentence: During the times of yore, tiger hunting was an *aristocratic* activity.

Related Words: PLUTOCRATIC - a. of wealthy and ruling class

ARRAIGN (uh REYN): v. Accuse; indict

> **Trigger:** 1.ARRAIGN-ARREST. 2. ARRAIGN-ERR AGAIN
>
> **Trigger Sentence:** When you ERR AGAIN people are going to ARRAIGN and ARREST.
>
> **Sample sentence:** He was *arraigned* on charges of aiding and abetting terrorists.

ARTICULATE (ar TIK yuh lit): v. Clearly express; effective

> **Trigger:** 1.ARTICULATE-"ART + ARTICLE". 2. ARTICULATE-ARTICLE
>
> **Trigger Sentence:** 1. He has an ART of writing and SPEAKING ARTICLES. 2. He expresses his ARTICLES in an ARTICULATE manner. 3. A, E, I, O, U- "ARTICLES" are spoken with clarity when we pronounce them. But some of the vowels such as "P" in Psychology are not pronounced.
>
> **Sample sentence:** Hitler was *articulate* not just in his speech, but also in the art of writing.
>
> Related Words: INARTICULATE - v.Unclear; not understandable

ARTIFICE (AHRT uh fus): n. Trickery; deception

> **Trigger:** 1. ARTIFICE-ARTFUL. 2. ARTIFICE-"ART + FICTION"
>
> **Trigger Sentence:** ARTFUL (cunning art) guy uses ARTIFICE (FICTITIOUS ART) to deceive people.
>
> **Sample sentence:** Many swindlers *artifice* art lovers by selling them artificial paintings.
>
> Related Words: ARTFUL - a. clever

ARTLESS (ART lis): a. Without guile; open and honest

> **Trigger:** ART-LESS
>
> **Trigger Sentence:** ARTFUL people are CUNNING and ARTLESS people are INNOCENT.
>
> **Sample sentence:** Surprisingly her simple and *artless* charm won us over instantly.

ASCENT (uh SENT): n. Climbing; rising up; upward slope

> **Trigger:** ASCEND-DESCEND
>
> **Trigger Sentence:** ASCEND is to go up; DESCEND is to go down.
>
> **Sample sentence:** The Himalayan mountain rage has many *ascents* and descents.
>
> Related Words: 1. ASCENDENCY - n. domination. 2. DESCENT – n. come down

ASCERTAIN (as ur TAYN): v. Find out for certain; clarify

> **Trigger:** ASCERTAIN-CERTAIN
>
> **Trigger Sentence:** ASCERTAIN is to MAKE something CERTAIN.
>
> **Sample sentence:** I want to *ascertain* whether the diamond is fake or genuine.

ASCETIC (uh SET ik): a. A person who practices self-denial; austere

> **Trigger:** ASCETIC-MONASTIC
>
> **Trigger Sentence:** 1. MONK-MONASTIC-ASCETIC. 2. ASCETICS live MONASTIC life.
>
> **Sample sentence:** The wealthy man could not understand the *ascetic* life of the monks.

ASCRIBE (uh SKRYBE): v. Attribute to, charge to

> **Trigger:** ASCRIBE-DESCRIBE
>
> **Trigger Sentence:** Whenever scribes DESCRIBE someone, they ASCRIBE some quality to them.
>
> **Sample sentence:** Newton *ascribed* his success to patient observation.

ASPERITY (ah SPER ah tee): n. Sharpness, bad temper

> **Trigger:** 1. ACERBITY-ACIDITY-ASPERITY. 2. ASPERITY-SEVERITY
>
> **Trigger Sentence:** These remarks, spoken with ASPERITY, stung the boys with ACERBITY to whom they had been directed.

Sample sentence: Being offended by the paparazzi, she responded with *asperity* in her tone.

Related Words: ASPERSION - n.slander, damaging remark

ASPERSION (uh SPUR zhun): n. Slander; false rumor

Trigger: 1. ASPERSION-"ANTI-PERSON". 2. ASPERSION -AS POISON

Trigger Sentence: With an ASPERSION she spreads POISON on people's mind.

Sample sentence: Shahi spread *aspersions* against me as she aspired to take my position.

Related Words: ASPERITY - n. harshness of tone or manner.

ASPIRE (uh SPYRE): v. Seek to attain a goal, dream for...

Trigger: 1. ASPIRE-INSPIRE-DESIRE. 2. ASPIRE-aspHIGHER

Trigger Sentence: 1. My sir INSPIRED me to ASPIRE for HIGHER GRE scores. 2. You got to PERSPIRE (sweat) to achieve your DESIRED goals.

Sample sentence: Preetham studied hard because he *aspired* to be the class first.

Related Words: ASPIRATION - n. a will to succeed

ASSAIL (ah SAIL): v. Assault, attack

Trigger: 1. ASSAIL-MISSILE. 2. ASSAIL-ASSAULT

Trigger Sentence: With MISSILES a ship sail was ASSAILED.

Sample sentence: Indian army *assailed* the terrorists with missiles.

Related Words: UNASSAILABLE - a.not able to be attacked.

ASSENT (uh SENT): v. Agree, n. accept

Trigger: 1. ASSENT-SAME SENTI. 2. ASSENT-CONSENT

Trigger Sentence: 1. ASSENT means SAME SENTIMENTS; therefore we agree. 2. Dissent-different sentiments; therefore we disagree. 3. CONSENT and ASSENT are synonyms.

Sample sentence: There was an at once *assent* between the two parties with same sentiments.

Related Words: 1. CONSENT –v.agree. 2. DISSENT –v.disagree

ASSERT (uh SURT): v. State strongly

Trigger: 1. ASSERT-ASSET. 2. ASSERTIVE- AGGRESSIVE

Trigger Sentence: 1. This is my ASSET; I ASSERT with certainty. 2. AN ASSERTIVE talk is an AGGRESSIVE talk.

Sample sentence: Why don't you *assert* your rights and do something about getting your rightful share of the property?

Related Words: ASSERTION - n. a confident statement of fact.

ASSIDUOUS (uh SIJ oo us): a. Hardworking, diligent

Trigger: ASSIDUOUS-"ASS + DOES"

Trigger Sentence: He is very ASSIDUOUS. He works like an ASS DOES.

Sample sentence: Only the *assiduous* students were invited to attend the conference.

ASSIMILATE (uh SIM uh layt): v. Fully understand; absorb

Trigger: ASSIMILATE-"AS SIMILAR"

Trigger Sentence: When you ASSIMILATE information, you keep it AS SIMILAR impression as possible in the brain.

Sample sentence: The monk *assimilated* the teachings of Buddha.

ASSUAGE (uh SWAYJ): v. Sooth, make less severe

    Trigger: ASSUAGE-MASSAGE

    Trigger Sentence: The MASSAGE ASSUAGED and relieved my pain.

    Sample Sentence: Refreshing winds *assuage* the summer's heat.

ASTONISHING (uh STON i shing): a. Surprising, shocking

    Trigger: ASTON-STUN

    Trigger Sentence: I was STUNNED at her ASTONISHING performance.

    Sample sentence: He *astonishingly* expanded his business in over six countries in a short span.

ASTOUNDING (uh STOUN ding): a. Amazing, Shocking

    Trigger: ASTOUNDING-STUNNING

    Trigger Sentence: I was STUNNED at the race horse's ASTOUNDING triumph.

    Sample sentence: People were stunned by the *astounding* performance of the gymnast.

ASTRAY (uh STREY): v. Away from the correct direction

    Trigger: 1. ASTRAY-AWAY. 2. A STRAY

    Trigger Sentence: A STRAY dog is AWAY from right path.

    Sample sentence: A bullet went *astray* and killed a bystander.

ASTUTE (uh STOOT): a. Clever; keen, shrewd

    Trigger: 1.ASTUTE-ACUTE-CUTE. 2. ASTUTE-TUTOR

    Trigger Sentence: 1. ASTUTE and ACUTE are synonyms; 2. A CUTE guy is SMART and BRILLIANT.

    Sample sentence: You will become *astute* only when your observation becomes acute.

ASUNDER (uh SUN dur): a. Into separate parts

    Trigger: ASUNDER-A THUNDER

    Trigger Sentence: A THUNDER torn ASUNDER the intimate lovers who were hugging tightly.

    Sample sentence: The thunderstorm uprooted and tore *asunder* the trees in our estate.

ASYLUM (uh SYE lum): n. Shelter, refuge

    Trigger: ASYLUM-ASHRAM

    Trigger Sentence: Tibetan refugees take ASYLUM in India in the ASHRAM place of Dharmashala.

    Sample sentence: My alcoholic brother was sent to the `asylum` for de-addiction.'

ATAVISTIC (at uh VIS tic): a. Characteristic of a former era

    Trigger: ATAVISTIC- A TAIL V STICK

    Trigger Sentence: A TAIL STICKING at the end was common in ATAVISTIC characters of early human being.

    Sample sentence: The *atavistic* behavior of this street gang is a throwback to the days of caveman.

ATONE (ah TONE): v. Make amends for; pay for

    Trigger: 1. ATONE-AT ONE. 2. ATONE-OWN.

    Trigger Sentence: 1. To ATONE is to "OWN" a mistake and amend the sins. 2. To be AT ONE with god the Indian sadhus ATONE in Himalayas.

    Sample sentence: Bob tried to *atone,* by accepting his disobedience.

ATROCITY (uh TROH city): n. Cruel act of violence

Trigger: 1. ATROCITY-"METRO-CITY". 2. ATROCITY-A TROY CITY

Trigger Sentence: 1. In Mumbai METRO-CITY there was an ATROCITY of terrorists on hotel Taj. 2. In A TROY CITY there was an ATROCITY.

Sample sentence: The book details the *atrocities* committed by Hitler.

Related Words: ATROCIOUS - a.horrifyingly wicked.

ATROPHY (A truh fee): n. Wasting away

Trigger: ATROPHY-"ASTRO+PHYSICIST"

Trigger Sentence: ASTROPHYSICIST Stephen Hawking suffers with ATROPHY.

Sample sentence: Laziness will lead you to *atrophy* of your talents; when will you start making good use of yourself?!

ATTAIN (uh TAYN): v. To accomplish, gain

Trigger: ATTAIN-A+GAIN

Trigger Sentence: ATTAIN is TO GAIN

Sample sentence: This Ferrari car can *attain* a speed of 300 miles per hour.

Related Words: ATTAINMENT - n. achievement

ATTENUATE (uh TEN u wayt): v. Make thin; weaken

Trigger: 1.atTENUate-TENU-THIN. 2. TENUOUS-THINNISH

Trigger Sentence: 1. ATTENUATE-TENUOUS-EXTENUATE belong to same family. 2."TENUOUS" means THINNISH.

Sample sentence: The patient has *attenuated* so much that he is becoming thin by the day.

Related Words: 1.TENUOUS – a. thin. 2. EXTENUATE - v.make smaller; reduce

ATTEST (uh TEST): v. Testify; bear witness

Trigger: ATTEST-TEST-TESTIFY

Trigger Sentence: The certificate given after TESTING and verification of original documents ATTESTS the authenticity of the painting.

Sample sentence: The banker asked John to *attest* his pictures along with the signatures of the witnesses in his loan application.

ATTRITION (ah TRISH un): n. Gradual decrease in numbers; wearing down by friction

Trigger: 1. ATTRITION-"A- FRICTION". 2. AT-RECESSION. 3. EROSION-ABRASION

Trigger Sentence: 1. Due to A FRICTION there is an ATTRITION of the surface. 2. AT RECESSION period there is an ATTRITION of people from a company.

Sample sentence: *Attrition* of houses is common in these sea facing constructions; the high tides do erode the outer walls of the houses by the sea.

ATTUNED (uh TYOON ed): a. in harmony; in sympathetic relation

Trigger: ATTUNED-TUNED (** synonyms)

Trigger Sentence: The industry is ATTUNED/TUNED with the demands of the market.

Sample sentence: After years spent in India, he's finding it difficult to *attune* himself to the American culture.

ATYPICAL (ay TIP uh kul): a. Unusual, not normal

Trigger: NOT TYPICAL

Trigger Sentence: ATYPICAL behavior of present day kids...NOT the accepted TYPE of response that we expect from children.

Sample sentence: 1. It's *atypical* to find a dog without a curve in its tail! 2. It's *atypical* of my husband not to loose his car keys!

AUDACIOUS (aw DAY shis): a. Bold; daring

Trigger: 1. AUDACIOUS-AUDIENCE. 2. AU-DASH-IOUS- "A DASHING NATURE"

Trigger Sentence: 1. The leader (like HITLER) was an AUDACIOUS man, when he stood before millions of AUDIENCE. 2. When you face AUDIENCE you require AUDACIOUS nature.

Sample sentence: Gayatri made an *audacious* decision to climb over Mount Everest all alone.

AUGMENT (awg MENT): v. Increase; add to

Trigger: 1.AUGMENT-SEGMENT. 2. AUGMENT -ADD+ MOUNT

Trigger Sentence: Whenever we SEGMENT, we cut something into different units. However when we AUGMENT, we do it by add-ons.

Sample sentence: Deduction in fee structure actually *augmented* admissions in the college.

AUGURY (AW guh ree): n. Omen; prediction

Trigger: 1. AUGURY-AA + GURU. 2. AUGURY-INAUGURATE (IN +AUGUR+ATE)

Trigger Sentence: 1. An Indian GURU in the Himalayas tells AUGURY. 2. If the AUGURY is good, you are going to INAUGURATE a new venture.

Sample sentence: The staunch Hindus believe in the *augury* of astrologers and soothsayers.

Related Words: AUGUR - v.predict; foretell

AUSPICIOUS (aw SPISH us): a. Favorable, beneficent

Trigger: AUSPICIOUS- WISH US

Trigger Sentence: The best WISHES for our new business are AUSPICIOUS to us.

Sample sentence: With favorable weather, it was an *auspicious* moment to set on sail.

AUSTERE (aw STEER): a. Severely simple; unadorned; strict

Trigger: 1. AUSTERE-EASTER. 2. AUSTERE-"AWE+SEVERE"

Trigger Sentence: 1. During EASTER FASTING time, people are usually AUSTERE. 2. AUSTERE people are SEVERE.

Sample sentence: During the severe Economic Depression of 1929 people lived *austere* lives.

Related Words: AUSTERITY - n.modesty, ascetic simplicity

AUTHENTICATE (aw THEN ti keyt): v. Prove genuine

Trigger: AUTHENTICATE-AUTHENTIC

Trigger Sentence: AUTHENTIC documents are AUTHENTICATED.

Sample sentence: The tests at the forensic lab *authenticated* the murderer.

AUTHORITARIAN (uh THAWR uh tayr ee un): a. Demanding absolute obedience to authority; dictatorial

Trigger: AUTHORITARIAN -AUTHORITY

Trigger Sentence: An AUTHORITARIAN boss exhibits AUTHORITY over his subordinates.

Sample sentence: Mr. Tedd as a boss was an *authoritarian* and a disciplinarian; his subordinates were nervy in his presence.

AUTHORITATIVE (uh THOR tey tiv): a. Commanding; reliable

    Trigger: AUTHORITATIVE- "AUTHORITY+ GIVE"

    Trigger Sentence: If one has an AUTHORITY in a field of one's skill gives a statement, it is going to be AUTHORITATIVE or reliable.

    Sample sentence: 1. A book written by an expert on a certain subject is an example of an *authoritative* book. 2. The lecturer spoke to the students in an *authoritative* manner.

AUTONOMY (aw TON uh mee): n. Independence; self-government

    Trigger: AUTONOMY-AUTOCRACY-DEMOCRACY

    Trigger Sentence: In an AUTOCRACY there is NO DEMOCRACY; in an "AUTONOMY" there will be FREEDOM and INDEPENDENCE.

    Sample sentence: The partitioning of India created two separate and *autonomous* jute economies.

    Related Words: AUTONOMOUS - a. self-governing.

AVANT-GARDE (uh vant GARD): a. Radically new or original; unusually new

    Trigger: "AVANT-GARDE"-"A-ONE-GRADE"

    Trigger Sentence: A-ONE-GRADE people are usually AVANT-GARDE (ORIGINAL) thinkers.

    Sample sentence: The National Institute of Fashion Technology produces *avant-garde* designers.

AVARICE (AV er is): n. Greed; lust for power or wealth

    Trigger: AVARICE-A+VERY+RICH

    Trigger Sentence: A VERY RICH person possesses AVARICE

    Sample sentence: Men of *avarice* would like to become very rich in no time.

AVER (uh VER): v. To declare true; affirm

    Trigger: 1.AVER-AVOW. 2. AVER- SWEAR

    Trigger Sentence: 1. To AVER (avow, vow) is to SWEAR. 2. AVER is to give A VERY confident statement to declare truth.

    Sample sentence: A witness usually avows on a holy book and *avers* his/her evidence.

    Related Words: AVOW –v. declare; acknowledge

AVERSE (uh VURS): a. Strongly disliking or opposed

    Trigger: AVERSE-A WORSE FEELING

    Trigger Sentence: AVERSE is to have WORSE FEELINGS about an opponent.

    Sample sentence: I do not want to be a house wife as I have an *aversion* to spend time at home.

    Related Words: AVERSION - n.firm dislike

AVERT (uh VERT): v. Prevent, turn away

    Trigger: 1. AVERT-DIVERT. 2. AVERT-AVOID

    Trigger Sentence: 1. He AVERTED an accident by DIVERTING and turning sharply to a corner. 2. AVERT is to AVOID.

    Sample sentence: In order to *avert* danger, the mountaineers avoided avalanche slopes.

AVID (AV id): a. Keen interest; greedy

    Trigger: 1. AVID-CUPID (god of desire). 2. AVID- A VID (A-VIDEO)

    Trigger Sentence: 1. People have AVIDITY and CUPIDITY for NUDITY. 2. He is an AVID VIDEO game player.

Sample sentence: Sohila is an *avid* horse rider.

Related Words: AVIDITY - n. desirousness

AVOCATION (av uh KEY shun): n. Hobby or minor occupation

Trigger: AVOCATION-VOCATION (JOB)

Trigger Sentence: During summer VACATION, I've an AVOCATION; VOCATION is a MAIN OCCUPATION.

Sample sentence: She did keep herself occupied by choosing an *avocation* of tailoring.

Related Words: VOCATIONAL - a. of or relation to a vocation or occupation.

AVOW (uh VOW): v. Declare; confess

Trigger: 1.AVOW-A OATH. 2. AVOWAL- A IS A VOWEL

Trigger Sentence: 1. A VOW is AN OATH. 2. AVOWAL- "A IS VOWEL"; I accept and DECLARE it as TRUE

Sample sentence: Vamsi *avowed* his love for Madhu even after she ditched him.

Related Words: AVOWAL - n.declaration

AVUNCULAR (uh VUNG kyuh lur): a. Like an uncle

Trigger: AVUNCULAR-AN UNCLE

Trigger Sentence: AN UNCLE of mine is AVUNCULAR; he gives me money whenever I'm in need.

Sample sentence: The teacher's *avuncular* attitude made him nearer and dearer to his students.

AWE (AW): n. Solemn wonder

Trigger: AWE-JAW

Trigger Sentence: In a JAW-DROPPING surprise, I watched the episode in AWE

Sample sentence: 1. Chandrahasa was *awe* struck to see her favorite star Hrithik Roshan! 2. The scenic beauty of the hills was *awe* inspiring!

AWRY (uh RYE): a. Distorted; crooked

Trigger: AWRY-AWAY

Trigger Sentence: My plan for the trip went into AWRY; AWAY from what I had expected.

Sample sentence: Our plans of a vacation went *awry* due to heavy rains.

AXIOMATIC (ak see uh MAT ik): a. Self-evident truth requiring no proof, certain

Trigger: AXIOMATIC-MATHEMATIC

Trigger Sentence: AXIOMATIC things require no MATHEMATIC proof; such as "earth is spinning on an AXIS".

Sample sentence: The sun is round is an *axiomatic* statement. It needs no mathematical proof.

lungi DANCE
lungi DANCE
lungi DANCE

all the rajini fans DANCED in FRENZY

FRENZY: funny, whirl, passion, emotion

BADINAGE (BAD n ij): n. Witty conversation

Trigger: BADINAGE-"BAD –LANGUAGE"

Trigger Sentence: BADINAGE need not be BAD; but you got to use some BAD LANGUAGE to evoke laughter.

Sample sentence: The friends congratulated the newlyweds with jolly good *badinages*.

BAFFLE (BAF ul): v. Confuse; frustrate

Trigger: 1. BAFFLE-BE + FOOL. 2. BAFFLE-PUZZLE

Trigger Sentence: I got myself - "BE FOOLED" and BAFFLED after I had seen that PUZZLE.

Sample sentence: The new code *baffled* the enemy agents.

BALEFUL (BAYL ful): a. Harmful, Threatening, Malevolent

Trigger: 1.BALEFUL-BALL FALL. 2. BALEFUL-BALE FALL

Trigger Sentence: 1. When a BALL FALLS on a batsman it will be BALEFUL and HARMFUL. 2. If a BALE of cotton FALLS on someone, it is going to be HARMFUL.

Sample sentence: When the ball fell on the head of the fielder, he suffered a *baleful* injury.

BALK (BAWK): v. Refuse to proceed, foil; block

Trigger: 1.BALK-BACK. 2. BALK-BLOCK

Trigger Sentence: 1. He is going BACK because a tiger BLOCKS his movement. 2. BALK is to go BACK; never proceed.

Sample sentence: When our soldiers *balked* in the battlefield, we had to turn back.

BALM (BALM): n. Something that relieves pain

Trigger: BALM-CALM

Trigger Sentence: If something irritates, the BALM is going to make you CALM.

Sample sentence: He is a gentle *balm* of a friend who supported me during my failures.

Related Words: BALMY - a.calm, soothing

BANAL (buh NAL): a. Lacking originality; ordinary

Trigger: BANAL-BANANA

Trigger Sentence: 1. A BANANA is an everyday fruit; nothing new. 2. BANANA fruit is abundantly grown here. Its usage in various dishes is quite BANAL here.

Sample sentence: The teacher's story was so *banal* that the students fell asleep.

Related Words: BANALITY - n.commonplace, lacking originality.

BANEFUL (BAYN ful): a. Destructive, harmful

Trigger: 1.BANE-PAIN. 2. BANEFUL-PAINFUL

Trigger Sentence: 1. PAIN is a BANE (curse); BOON is a BLESSING and BANE is HARMFULL. 2. It is quite BANEFUL when someone makes PAINFUL comments at you.

Sample sentence: It is a *bane* to suffer from pain of failure.

Related Words: 1.BANE - n.poison, misfortune .2.BOON –n. gift; blessing

BANISH (BAN ish): v. Expel; dismiss

Trigger: BANISH-BAN

Trigger Sentence: The treacherous were BANISHED from the land.

Sample sentence: Lenin was *banished* to Siberia because he took part in a banned organization.

Related Words: BANISHMENT - n.expulsion

BARD (BAHRD): n. A poet

Trigger: BARD-BIRD (LOVE BIRD)

Trigger Sentence: The LOVE BIRDS are in the garden attempting poetry as if they were BARDS.

Sample sentence: Shakespeare was a famous *bard*.

BAROQUE (buh ROHK): a. Highly ornate

Trigger: 1. BAROQUE-BAR. 2. BAROQUE-BARACK

Trigger Sentence: 1. BARACK Obama's BAR looks BAROQUE. 2. BARS are gaudily DECORATED to attract customers.

Sample sentence: Michael Jackson is identified with *baroque* exuberance in printed silk shirts.

BARREN (BAR uhn): a. Infertile, unproductive

Trigger: BARREN-BARE

Trigger Sentence: BARE LANDS (naked lands-without trees) are BARREN.

Sample sentence: The Thar desert in India is *barren* except for an occasional oasis of palm trees.

Related Words: BARE – a. hardly; naked

BARRICADE (BAR ih keyd): n. Blockade, barrier; obstruction

Trigger: BARRICADE-BARRIER

Trigger Sentence: BARRICADE the way by erecting BARRIERS with BARS and DEBAR the people from entering.

Sample sentence: The Street where the President lives is always *barricaded* for security reasons.

Related Words: 1. BAR - v. block, barricade. 2. DEBAR - v. exclude or prohibit. 3. BARRIER- n. obstacle

BASK (BASK): v. Luxuriate; derive pleasure in warmth

Trigger: 1.BASK-BASKET. 2. BASK-BATHE-SUN BATHE

Trigger Sentence: 1. BASKET ball – I BASK in playing in the sun. 2. Taking sun BATHE...I am BASKING in sun BATHE.

Sample sentence: She *basked* in glory after being awarded as the best dancing diva!

BAWDY (BAW dee): a. Vulgar, obscene

Trigger: 1.BAWDY-BODY. 2. BAWDY-BADDY (BAD GUY)

Trigger Sentence: A BADDY is showing his BODY and is singing a BAWDY song.

Sample sentence: They published a collection of Elizabethan *bawdy* jokes, *bawdy* pictures.

BEACON (BEE kun): v. Warning light; lighthouse; guide

Trigger: BEACON- (BEAM-ON)

Trigger Sentence: 1. On a hill a BEAM is ON and it acts like BEACON to warn of danger. 2. A steady BEAM BEACONS from the shore guiding the ships.

Sample sentence: 1. *Beacon* is a light or fire on the top of a hill that acts as a warning or signal. 2. She was a *beacon* of hope in troubled times.

BEDIZEN (bih DIZ un): v. To dress in a vulgar manner

Trigger: BEDIZEN-"BAD DESIGN"

Trigger Sentence: The BEDI girl wears a BAD DESIGN- BEDIZEN dress to a function.

Sample sentence: Sex workers are often seen *bedizening* themselves to attract customers!

BEDLAM (BED lum): n. A scene of uproar and confusion

Trigger: BEDLAM- BAD JAM

Trigger Sentence: When there was BAD JAM (traffic jam), there was a BEDLAM.

Sample sentence: Following the world cup cricket match, the stadium was in a state of *bedlam.*

BEFUDDLE (bih FUHD l): v. Confuse thoroughly

Trigger: 1.beFUDDLE-RIDDLE. 2. Be FUDDLE-ADDLE

Trigger Sentence: 1. ADDLE, MUDDLE and BEFUDDLE are synonyms; whereas FUDDLED is ADDLED after alcohol. 2. This RIDDLE BEFUDDLED even the teacher.

Sample sentence: John was completely *befuddled* when he was introduced to my identical twin.

BEGUILE (bih GYLE): v. Mislead, deceive; charm

Trigger: 1.BEGUILE-BE + GUILE (refer). 2. GUILE-GUY ILL

Trigger Sentence: An ILL minded GUY- BEGUILED a gullible GAL.

Sample sentence: He always remains agile. You can't *beguile* him.

Related Words: GUILE - n. fraud; cunning

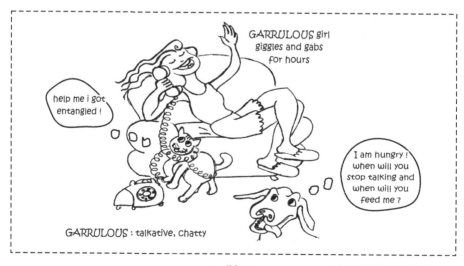

Memory Test-9 : Match each word and its memory trick to the corresponding definition.

S.N	WORD	MEMORY TRIGGER	S.N	DEFINITIONS	KEY
1	ARCANE	DARK LANE- things are arcane	A	A person who practices self-denial	
2	ARCHAIC	ARCHEOLOGY is the study of ARCHAIC	B	Accuse; indict	
3	ARCHETYPE	PROTOTYPE	C	Agree, accept	
4	ARDOR	we ADORE/ADMIRE with ARDOR	D	Ancient; no longer used	
5	ARDUOUS	HARD + PLUS	E	Assault, attack	
6	ARID	HARD LANDS are ARID	F	Clearly express; effective	
7	ARISTOCRATIC	ARISTOTLE LIKE	G	Climbing; upward slope	
8	ARRAIGN	ERR AGAIN-arrest	H	Dry, barren	
9	ARTICULATE	ARTICLES are expressed	I	Enthusiasm; fervor	
10	ARTIFICE	fictitious ART they use ..	J	Find out for certain; clarify	
11	ARTLESS	no art of trapping people	K	Hard, laborious	
12	ASCENT	ASCEND is to go up	L	Of the noble class; refined	
13	ASCERTAIN	Make CERTAIN	M	Open and honest; without guile	
14	ASCETIC	ASCETICS live MONASTIC life.	N	Original model, prototype	
15	ASCRIBE	scribes DESCRIBE & ascribe	O	Refer to; attribute to	
16	ASPERITY	ACERBITY-ACIDITY-ASPERITY	P	Secret, understood by few	
17	ASPERSION	she spreads POISON on me	Q	Seek to attain a goal	
18	ASPIRE	ASPIRE-I'll aspHIGHER	R	Sharpness, bad temper	
19	ASSAIL	With MISSILES	S	Slander; false rumor	
20	ASSENT	We have same sentiments	T	Trickery; deception	

Memory Test-10 : Match each word and its memory trick to the corresponding definition.

S.N	WORD	MEMORY TRIGGER	S.N	DEFINITIONS	KEY
1	ASSERT	ASSERTIVE- AGGRESSIVE talk	A	Amazing, Shocking	
2	ASSIDUOUS	ASS + DOES assiduous work	B	Away from the correct direction	
3	ASSIMILATE	SIMILAR impression in brain	C	Characteristic of a former era	
4	ASSUAGE	The MASSAGE ASSUAGED	D	Clever; keen, shrewd	
5	ASTONISHING	I was STUNNED	E	Cruel act of violence	
6	ASTOUNDING	astounding-stunning	F	Fully understand; absorb	
7	ASTRAY	A STRAY dog is AWAY	G	Hardworking, diligent	
8	ASTUTE	ASTUTE - ACUTE – a cute guy	H	In harmony	
9	ASUNDER	THUNDER torn ASUNDER	I	Into separate parts	
10	ASYLUM	ASYLUM-ASHRAM	J	Make amends for; pay for	
1	ATAVISTIC	A TAIL V STICK at the end	K	Make thin; weaken	
12	ATONE	To ATONE is to "OWN" a mistake	L	Shelter, refuge	
13	ATROCITY	A TROY CITY	M	Sooth, make less severe	
14	ATROPHY	ASTROPHYSICIST Stephen Hawking	N	State strongly	
15	ATTAIN	attain-A+GAIN	O	Surprising, shocking	
16	ATTENUATE	TENUOUS" means THINNISH	P	Testify; bear witness	
17	ATTEST	TESTIFY	Q	To accomplish, gain	
18	ATTRITION	A FRICTION there is an ATTRITION	R	Unusual, not normal	
19	ATTUNED	Same TUNED	S	Wasting away	
20	ATYPICAL	He not of our type	T	Wearing down; gradual decrease	

Answers	EX.NO	1	2	3	4	5	6	7	8	9	10	11	12	13	14	15	16	17	18	19	20
	9	P	D	N	I	K	H	L	B	F	T	M	G	J	A	O	R	S	Q	E	C
	10	N	G	F	M	O	A	B	D	I	L	C	J	E	S	Q	K	P	T	H	R

Memory Test-11 : Match each word and its memory trick to the corresponding definition.

S.N	WORD	MEMORY TRIGGER	S.N	DEFINITIONS	KEY
1	AUDACIOUS	au-dash-ious- DASHING	A	Commanding; reliable	
2	AUGMENT	AUGMENT -add+ mount	B	Bold; daring	
3	AUGURY	GURU predicts	C	Declare; confess	
4	AUSPICIOUS	AUSPICIOUS- WISH US for good	D	Demanding obedience to authority	
5	AUSTERE	EASTER fasting -maintain AUSTERE	E	Distorted; crooked	
6	AUTHENTICATE	AUTHENTIC	F	Favorable, beneficent	
7	AUTHORITARIAN	Authority	G	Greed; lust for power or wealth	
8	AUTHORITATIVE	AUTHORITY+ GIVES	H	Hobby or minor occupation	
9	AUTONOMY	AUTO -RULE ; no autocracy	I	Increase; add to	
10	AVANT-GARDE	How A+ONE+GRADE think ???	J	Independence; self-government	
11	AVARICE	AVARICE want to be A VERY RICH	K	Keen interest; greedy	
12	AVER	to SWEAR	L	Like an uncle	
13	AVERSE	A WORSE feeling	M	Prediction; omen	
14	AVERT	AVOID and DIVERT	N	Prevent, turn away	
15	AVID	CUPID-AVID of A VIDEO game	O	Prove genuine	
16	AVOCATION	second VOCATION	P	Radically new or original	
17	AVOW	Avow-A OATH	Q	Severely simple; strict	
18	AVUNCULAR	Uncle	R	Solemn wonder	
19	AWE	AWESOME- open your JAW	S	Strongly disliking or opposed	
20	AWRY	AWAY from straight line	T	Declare true; affirm	

Memory Test-12 : Match each word and its memory trick to the corresponding definition.

S.N	WORD	MEMORY TRIGGER	S.N	DEFINITIONS	KEY
1	AXIOMATIC	MATHEMATIC wise 100% correct	A	A poet	
2	BADINAGE	Bad language	B	A scene of uproar and confusion	
3	BAFFLE	BE + FOOL- PUZZLE	C	Barrier; obstruction	
4	BALEFUL	BALE or BALL FALLING on me	D	Confuse thoroughly	
5	BALK	BACK - BLOCK	E	Confuse; frustrate	
6	BALM	Makes you CALM	F	Derive pleasure in warmth	
7	BANAL	BANANA–every day we get	G	Destructive, harmful	
8	BANEFUL	something PAINFUL	H	Dress in a vulgar manner	
9	BANISH	BAN that man	I	Highly ornate	
10	BARD	Love birds turn bards	J	Harmful, Threatening	
11	BAROQUE	Barak Obama BAR- how it looks ??	K	Expel; dismiss	
12	BARREN	BARE Lands	L	Infertile, unproductive	
13	BARRICADE	barrier	M	Lacking originality; ordinary	
14	BASK	BASKET ball game at beach	N	Mislead, deceive; charm	
15	BAWDY	Baddy scenes	O	Refuse to proceed; block	
16	BEACON	BEAM-ON	P	Self-evident truth, certain	
17	BEDIZEN	BAD-DESIGN dress	Q	Something that relieves pain	
18	BEDLAM	BAD JAM creates traffic jam	R	Vulgar, obscene	
19	BEFUDDLE	This RIDDLE BEFUDDLED me	S	Warning light; guide	
20	BEGUILE	BE GUILE - guys are guile	T	Witty conversation	

Answers

EX.NO	1	2	3	4	5	6	7	8	9	10	11	12	13	14	15	16	17	18	19	20
11		B	I	M	F	Q	O	D	A	J	P	G	T	S	N	K	H	C	L	R	E
12		P	T	E	J	O	Q	M	G	K	A	I	L	C	F	R	S	H	B	D	N

WORD GROUPS DAY-3

★ UNCOMMUNICATIVE/ LESS WORDY

NOUN: taciturnity, reticence, reserve

ADJECTIVES: brusque, concise, curt, laconic, pithy, reticent, reserved, succinct, terse

ANTONYMS: adj. garrulous, loquacious, prolix, voluble

★ STRENGTH/STRONG/STRENGTHEN

ADJECTIVES: potent, puissant, robust, virile, vigorous; sturdy, hardy, burly, sinewy

NOUNS: energy, vim, vitality

VERB: corroborate, bolster, fortify, buttress, invigorate, reinforce

ANTONYMS: adj. impuissant, impotent; v. undermine, enervate

★ WEAK/WEAKEN

ADJECTIVES: frail, feeble, flaccid, fragile; infirm, debilitated, enervated, effete, emaciated, exhausted, incapacitated, indisposed, decrepit; tired, fatigued, jaded

NOUNS: impotence, decrepitude

VERB: adulterate, debilitate, flag, effete, exhaust, enervate, enfeeble, incapacitate, invalidate, sap, vitiate, wither; exacerbate, stultify; undermine, undercut

ANTONYMS: adj.strong, powerful; v.reinforce, invigorate

★ QUARRELSOME NATURE

ADJECTIVES: antagonistic, bellicose, belligerent, confrontational, contentious, disputatious, combative, cantankerous, choleric, irascible, hostile, polemical, peevish, pugnacious, querulous, truculent

NOUNS: altercation, clash, contention, feud, dispute, discord, dissension, skirmish, spat, strife

VERB: bicker, contend, squabble, wrangle

ANTONYMS: adj. affable, amiable, complaisant, genial, neutral

★ FRIENDLY NATURE

ADJECTIVES: amiable, amicable, cordial, congenial, genial, harmonious

NOUNS: amity, affinity, benevolence, comity, consanguinity, camaraderie, propinquity, rapport, harmony; intimacy, empathy, sympathy, accord, concord, kinship

VERB: associate, consort, fraternize

ANTONYMS: n. animosity, enmity, inimical, hatred, hostility

★ BEGINNER/YOUNG/IMMATURE

ADJECTIVES: callow, dabbler, dilettante, juvenile, infantile, naïve, puerile, uninitiated, untrained, unworldly; inchoate, embryonic, nascent

NOUNS: apprentice, fledgling, initiate, neophyte, novice, novitiate, recruit, tyro

VERB: initiate, inaugurate

ANTONYMS: n. connoisseur, virtuoso, veteran, sophisticated

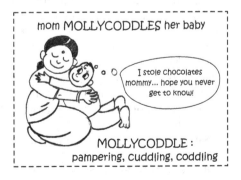

mom MOLLYCODDLES her baby

I stole chocolates mommy... hope you never get to know!

MOLLYCODDLE :
pampering, cuddling, coddling

Word List Day-4

BEHEMOTH (buh HEE muth): a. A huge creature

    Trigger: BHEEM -GOLIATH

    Trigger Sentence: The GOLIATH BHEEM in Mahabarath looked like a BEHEMOTH.

    Sample sentence: The luxury resort with no customers has become a *behemoth* to maintain.

BEHOLDEN (bih HOHL dun): a. Obligated; indebted; in debt

    Trigger: BEHOLDEN -BE+HOLD; "BE UNDER SOMEONE'S HOLD"

    Trigger Sentence: I will BE UNDER YOUR HOLD, if you give me your golden ring.

    Sample sentence: I am *beholden* for your hospitality during my stay in your country. Thank you.

BELEAGUER (be LEE gur): v. Harass; besiege; attack

    Trigger: 1. BIG LEAGUER -SMALL LEAGUER. 2. BELEAGUE-PLAGUE

    Trigger Sentence: 1. BIG LEAGUE players always BELEAGUER the small LEAGUERS. 2. In olden days people were often BELEAGUERED or attacked by PLAGUE.

    Sample sentence: Those bossy and boisterous boys *beleaguered* this young stammering kid.

BELIE (bi LYE): v. Show to be false; contradict; fake

    Trigger: BELIE-"BE+LIE"

    Trigger Sentence: TO LIE is to CONTRADICT.

    Sample sentence: His tenderness towards children *belies* his outwardly rude appearance.

    Related Words: BELIED - a.negated

BELITTLE (bi LIT ul): v. Disparage; decry

    Trigger: BELITTLE-"BE+LITTLE"

    Trigger Sentence: BELITTLE is to make someone LITTLE in front of others.

    Sample sentence: Donot *belittle,* but encourage your weak students.

BELLICOSE (BEH lih cohs): a. Warlike; combative

    Trigger: 1. BELLI + COSE-REBELLIOUS. 2. BELLI-BULLY

    Trigger Sentence: 1. People with BELLICOSE nature are REBELLIOUS; bellicose and belligerent are synonyms. 2. BELLICOSE people usually BULLY others.

    Sample sentence: They took their *bellicosely* behaving son to the angry management consoler.

BELLIGERENT (buh LIJ er unt): a. Quarrelsome; aggressive

    Trigger: 1. "BELLI + GERENT"-"REBEL+GENT". 2. BELLI-BULLY

    Trigger Sentence: 1. BELLIGERENT people are REBELLIOUS in nature. 2. BELLIGERENT people BULLY others.

    Sample sentence: Sheela's *belligerent* sister-in-law is indeed an embarrassment to the family.

    Related Words: BELLICOSE- a. belligerent; quarrelsome

BEMUSE (bi MYOOZ): v. Confuse

    Trigger: BEMUSE-CONFUSE

    Trigger Sentence: The persistent fever BEMUSED the CONFUSED doctor.

    Sample sentence: The electric wiring is a *bemusing* me; call an electrician to look into the circuit.

BENEDICTION (ben uh DIK shun): n. Blessing

    Trigger: 1.BEN (good) + DICTATION. 2. BENEDICT (POPE)

    Trigger Sentence: 1. GOOD DICTION or GOOD DICTATION of words on someone can be called BENEDICTION. 2. The Pope BENEDICT gave me a BENEDICTION.

    Sample sentence: Every Sunday Pope leads a *benediction* service in the church at Vatican City.

BENEFACTOR (BEN uh fak tur): n. Sponsor, donor

    Trigger: BENEFACTOR-"BENEFIT+ACTOR"

    Trigger Sentence: A BENEFACTOR gives BENEFITS to other people.

    Sample sentence: The actor was a *benefactor* of PFA with his financial contributions.

BENEFICENT (buh NEF uh sent): a. Kind; good

    Trigger: 1.BENEFIcent-BENEFIT. 2. BENEFICENT-EFFICIENT

    Trigger Sentence: BENEFICENT man gives BENEFITS to others.

    Sample sentence: Rockefeller was a *beneficent* philanthropist. He benefited the US society with his liberal contributions.

BENEFICIARY (ben uh FISH uh ree): n. One who benefits from something; heir

    Trigger: BENEFICIARY-BENEFITS

    Trigger Sentence: A BENEFICIARY receives BENEFITS from BENEFACTORS.

    Sample sentence: *Beneficiary* is a person who gains benefit from something, especially a Will.

BENEVOLENT (buh NEV uh lunt): n. Generous, kind

    Trigger: 1. BENEVOLENT-(BE+ NO+ VIOLENT) .2. BENEVOLENT-BENEFACTOR

    Trigger Sentence: 1. BENEFACTOR and BENEVOLENT persons always provide BENEFITS to other people. 2. A BENEVOLENT person tends to BE A NON-VIOLENT person.

    Sample sentence: I always wanted the qualities of *benevolence* and chivalry in my man.

BENIGN (bi NYNE): a. Favorable and not harmful; not malignant

    Trigger: 1.BE + NINE-BENEFIT. 2. BENIGN-MALIGN (** antonyms)

    Trigger Sentence: 1. NINE (9!!!) symbol gives lot of BENEFITS. 2. Gandhi had BENIGN thoughts whereas Hitler MALIGNED the German minds.

    Sample sentence: Martin is a young politician known for his *benign* behavior and brotherhood.

    Related Words: MALIGN - a. evil; harmful

BENISON (BEN uh zun): n. Blessing, benediction

    Trigger: 1.BENISON-BENEDICTION. 2. BENISON-BEND-SON

    Trigger Sentence: 1. BENEDICTION and BENISON are synonyms. 2. BEND down my SON, I'll give my BENISON.

    Sample sentence: The pilgrims took *benisons* from the priest before their arduous journey.

BENT (BENT): n. A strong inclination or interest; natural talent

Trigger: BENT-"BEND-MIND"

Trigger Sentence: I BENT upon playing cricket, since my MIND BENDS towards my liking.

Sample sentence: She developed a gradual *bent* towards fine arts, though she studied Math.

BEQUEATH (bih KWEETH): v. Leave property to someone in a will; hand down

Trigger: BEQUEATH- BEFORE DEATH

Trigger Sentence: Elders usually BEQUEATH their property to their children through a Will BEFORE DEATH.

Sample sentence: My aunt *bequeathed* me all her jewelry.

Related Words: BEQUEST - n. inheritance, legacy

BERATE (bih REYT): v. Scold strongly

Trigger: BERATE- "BAD-RATE"

Trigger Sentence: The critics BERATED the movie by giving very BAD RATING.

Sample sentence: The officer *berated* the butler for not polishing his shoes.

BEREFT (bih REFT): a. Deprived of; lacking

Trigger: 1. beREFT-LEFT. 2. BEREFT-BURY+LEFT

Trigger Sentence: After I LEFT you at the BURIAL ground, I am BEREFT of you.

Sample sentence: It is a sad thing that my maid's children are kept *bereft* from basic education.

Related Words: BEREAVED - a. bereft, suffering from loss

BESEECH (bih SEECH): v. Beg; to request earnestly.

Trigger: BESEECH-"BEG + SEEK"

Trigger Sentence: BESEECH is to BEG and SEEK. BEGGARS BESEECH for alms when they SEEK some favour from others.

Sample sentence: I *beseech* you to be seated patiently; the speaker will join us soon...

BESIEGE (bih SEEJ): v. Surround a place, esp. with an army, harass

Trigger: BESIEGE-"TROY SIEGE"

Trigger Sentence: 1. Troy was under SIEGE. 2. BESIEGE-BESET-BELEAGUER are synonyms.

Sample sentence: When the pop star tried to leave the hotel she was *besieged* by journalists.

Related Words: SIEGE - v.attack

BETRAY (bih TREY): v. Be disloyal, reveal a secret.

Trigger: 1.BETRAY-BE TRICK. 2. BETray-BET

Trigger Sentence: 1. BETRAYED-BE TRICKED. 2. BETting and match fixing during the game season, saw some cricketers & football players BETRAY their own teams.

Sample sentence: The insurance company *betrayed* me by not granting the entire money.

BEWILDERING (bih WIL der ing): a. Extremely confusing

Trigger: 1.BEWILDERING-WILD. 2. BEWILDERING-BAFFLING (** synonyms)

Trigger Sentence: WILD life at the Amazon rain forests BEWILDERED (v) the adventurers.

Sample Sentence: We were *bewildered* when a golfer was found dead in the maple woods.

BIASED (BAHY ust): a. Bias, n. a partiality, a. biased, favoring one person over other

Trigger: BIAS-BOSS

Trigger Sentence: MY BOSS is BIASed towards girls.

Sample sentence: There is no gender *bias* between male and female officers in the military.

Related Words: UNBIASED – a. impartial; unprejudiced

BIFURCATE (BAHY fer keyt): v. split into two, divide into two

Trigger: BIFURCATE-BI+FORK

Trigger Sentence: The FORK BIFURCATED the beef.

Sample sentence: The road *bifurcated*.

BIGOT (BIG aht): n. A person who is one-sided and prejudiced in his views; intolerant

Trigger: 1.BIGOT (BHAGATH). 2. BI GOT- BY GOD-MY GOD

Trigger Sentence: 1. BHAGATH Singh was a BIGOT as he never tolerated British. A BIGOT possesses BIGOTRY. 2. BIGOT says that MY GOD is only great; other gods are waste; he never tolerates others beliefs.

Sample sentence: Broad minded Harsha was taken aback by his *bigotry* and biased classmates.

Related Words: BIGOTRY - n. intolerance of differing ideas or beliefs

BILIOUS (BIL yus): a. Irritable; cranky

Trigger: BILIOUS-BILES-PILES

Trigger Sentence: 1. When BILE (in liver) is abnormal, a person feels BILIOUS. 2. PILES disease brought BILIOUS mood.

Sample sentence: He is *bilious* old man who keeps cribbing for attention and help.

BILK (BILK): v. Cheat; defraud

Trigger: BILK- BILL (Clinton)

Trigger Sentence: BILL (Clinton) BILKED (cheated) his wife.

Sample sentence: Jack was *bilked* out of his inheritance by a lawyer who handled his estate.

BIZARRE (bih ZAR): a. Very strange or unusual; odd

Trigger: BIZARRE-BAZAAR

Trigger Sentence: Indian BAZAARS look BIZARRE for foreigners.

Sample sentence: Singer Lady Gaga is famous for her *bizarre* dressing sense.

BLAND (BLAND): a. Tasteless; mild; boring

Trigger: 1.BLAND-LAND.2. BLAND- BLAH TASTE

Trigger Sentence: LAND taste is BLAH & BLAND.

Sample sentence: My elderly in-laws need *bland* and softly cooked food.

BLANDISH (BLAND ish): v. Coax with flattery; persuade

Trigger: 1. BLANDISH-"BRAINWASH". 2. BLANDISH-"BLONDE +ISH"

Trigger Sentence: Guys BLANDISH (flattery) a BLONDE by BRAINWASH.

Sample sentence: Manufacturers *blandish* people by brainwashing them through ads.

Related Words: BLANDISHMENT - n. flattery

BLASÉ (blah ZEY): a. Bored with pleasure or dissipation

Trigger: 1.BLASÉ-(party) BLAST .2. BLASÉ-"BLAH+ LIFE"

Trigger Sentence: 1. Daily party BLAST makes someone BLASÉ; excessive parties are too boring. 2. BLAH LIFE is known as BLASÉ.

Sample sentence: My uncle has a *blasé* nonchalant attitude, he simple says- "let go... let god... this moment will pass too"!

BLASPHEMOUS (BLAAS fuh mus): a. Irreverent; sacrilegious; profane

Trigger: BLASPHEMOUS-"BLAST +FAMOUS"

Trigger Sentence: If you BLAST FAMOUS people such as Gandhi, Pope, Imam etc., it is known as BLASPHEMOUS.

Sample sentence: It was nothing short of *blasphemy* for Gadsy to say that Gandhi told lies.

Related Words: 1. BLASPHEMY - n. irreverence. 2. INFAMY - n. public shame

BLATANT (BLAYT unt): a. Loudly offensive; extremely obvious

Trigger: BLATANT-"BLAST + AUNT"

Trigger Sentence: BLAST (BLAST is loud and offensive). Our BLATANT neighbouring AUNT BLASTED at the boys when the cricket ball broke her window pane.

Sample sentence: Surya *blatantly* turned up his stereo to disrupt his parent's dinner party.

BLEAK (BLEEK): a. Depressing, unhappy, sad

Trigger: BLEAK-BLACK

Trigger Sentence: BLACK color signifies that life is BLEAK.

Sample sentence: In this symbolic art, white represents bright future and *black* for *bleak* days.

BLEMISH (BLEM ish): n. Flaw, fault, defect

Trigger: 1.BLEMISH-"BLAME +ISH". 2. BLEM-PROBLEM

Trigger Sentence: 1. People BLAME others, because of BLEMISHES. 2. You face many PROBLEMS if you live a BLEMISHED life.

Sample sentence: This poor report on the officer will certainly leave a *blemish* on his record.

BLIGHT (BLYTE): n. Disease, decay

Trigger: BLIGHT- "BAD-LIGHT"

Trigger Sentence: When you get exposed to sun LIGHT you may get BLIGHT; UV -LIGHT might cause BLIGHT.

Sample sentence: Having spent over a decade in the dark dingy cells of Andaman Islands, the prisoner was completely *blighted* both physically and mentally.

Related Words: BLIGHTED - a.destroyed

BLITHE (BLYTH): a. Happy; carefree

Trigger: BLIthe-BLISS

Trigger Sentence: 1. The BLISSFUL Buddha BLITHELY forgot his surrounding while he meditated. 2. MENTALLY LIGHT hearted people are usually BLITHE.

Sample sentence: The beach babies with their boy friends *blithely* partied on the seashore.

Related Words: BLITHELY –adv. carelessly

BLUDGEON (BLUD jun): v. To hit forcefully; n. club

Trigger: 1.BLUDGEON-"BLOOD + GUN". 2. BLUDGEON-"BLOOD + GEN"

Trigger Sentence: The BLOOD was GENERATED from the criminal when the spy had used his GUN as a BLUDGEON.

Sample sentence: After *bludgeoning* her to death, the murderer tried to escape.

BLUNT (BLUNT): a. 1. Characterized by truthfulness in speech, curt. 2. Not sharp

   Trigger: BLUNT-BLANK-"POINT-BLANK"

   Trigger Sentence: I was BLUNT in asking him POINT-BLANK whether he wanted the job.

   Sample sentence: He was *blunt* and gruff with most people; but was always gentle with kid.

BOGUS (BOE guss): a. Not genuine; artificial, sham

   Trigger: 1. BOGUS–"BOYS+GUYS". 2. "BOGUS-BABAS"

   Trigger Sentence: 1. Some BABAS (saints) are BOGUS. They preach one thing, but practice another thing. 2. GALS say that GUYS/BOYS are GUILE and BOGUS.

   Sample sentence: Many people get away by submitting bogus certificates to beget a job!

BOHEMIAN (boh HEE mee un): a. Unconventional (in an artistic way)

   Trigger: BOHEMIAN-"BOY-HE+MAN"

   Trigger Sentence: For BOYS, HE-MAN looks BOHEMIAN. For young BOYS - Superman, Spiderman, HE-MAN, Batman etc - signify BOHEMIAN symbols of adventure.

   Sample sentence: He is an artist and a real *bohemian*.

BOISTEROUS (BOI ster us): a. Noisy; violent, rough

   Trigger: 1.BOIS (BOYS) + TEROUS (TERRORS). 2. BOIS-NOISE

   Trigger Sentence: BOYS are BOISTEROUS in nature.

   Sample sentence: The vociferous boys have turned this peaceful neighbourhood into a *boisterous* location.

BOLSTER (BOHL ster): v. Support, reinforce

   Trigger: BOLSTER-BOOSTER

   Trigger Sentence: BOOSTER vaccinations BOLSTER immunity of infants.

   Sample sentence: The Indian team had a pep rally in order to *bolster* their team before the big game.

BOMBAST (BOM bast): n. Pompous; using inflated language

   Trigger: 1. BOMBAST-BOAST. 2. BOMBAST-BOMB + BLAST

   Trigger Sentence: 1. BOASTERS BOMBAST about their achievements. 2. When a BOMB BLASTS there's a loud noise; similarly, when BOMBASTIC words are said, they SOUND HIGH but have no meaning.

   Sample sentence: Such a *bombastic* fellow he is, he made us listen to his so called success stories.

   Related Words: BOMBASTIC - a.inflated

BONHOMIE (bohn uh MEE): n. Good-natured friendliness

   Trigger: BONHOMIE-"BORN+HOMELY"

   Trigger Sentence: He is BORN HOMELY (simple); that BONHOMIE which won the hearts of all who knew him.

   Sample sentence: I met some strangers who were quite *bonhomie* towards me in Boston.

BOON (BOON): n. Benefit; blessing

Trigger: BOONS-BONUS

Trigger Sentence: To be BORN into a wealthy family is a BOON (BONUS) from god.

Sample sentence: Your employer confers a *boon* on you when he/she declares a bonus.

Related Words: BANE - n. harm; poison

BOOR (BOO r): n. A rude or insensitive person

Trigger: 1.BOOR-BOO. 2. BOOR-BEAR

Trigger Sentence: 1. BOOR person usually BOOS. 2. The BOORS behave like BEARS

Sample sentence: The *boorish* boys booed the captain when he returned to the pavilion after scoring a duck.

Related Words: BOORISH - a.uncivilized

BOWDLERIZE (BOWD lur ize): v. Expurgate; purify

Trigger: BOWDLERISE-"BOWLES+RINSE (RISE sounds like RINSE)

Trigger Sentence: In order to purify the intestines, BOWDLERIZE your BOWLS by RINSING with an enema.

Sample sentence: Sensitive parts of the film were *bowdlerized* to pass through sensor.

BRAGGART (BRAAG urt): n. Boaster, show off

Trigger: BRAGGER-BOASTER

Trigger Sentence: BRAGGART is a DRAGGER & BOASTER

Sample sentence: A *braggart* keeps boasting about his accomplishments.

Related Words: 1. BRAGGER - n. boaster. 2. BRAGGADOCIO - n. boastful behavior

BRANDISH (BRAN dish): v. Wave around; exhibit aggressively

Trigger: 1.BRANDish-BRAND. 2.BRANDIsh-BANDIT

Trigger Sentence: 1. Any new BRAND they buy, people exhibit or BRANDISH to everyone. 2. A BANDIT BRANDISHED a knife in a drunken state.

Sample sentence: Riding on a horse back the warrior princess *brandished* her sword and led the soldiers into the battle field.

BRAZEN (BRAY shun): a. Shameless or arrogant

Trigger: 1.BRAzen-BRA. 2. BRAZEN-BRASH-RASH

Trigger Sentence: 1. When the girl wears only BRA, then people usually calls her BRAZEN. 2. RASH minded people are BRASH and BRAZEN (reckless).

Sample sentence: The models *brazenly* exhibited the new bra.

Related Words: BRASH- a.rash; reckless

BREACH (BREECH): n. Violation; crack, gap

Trigger: BREACH-BREAK (of rules)

Trigger Sentence: When you BREAK something unlawfully, it is called BREACH or violation of rules. When you BREAK the law, there is going to be a BREACH.

Sample sentence: They found a *breach* in the enemy's fortifications to penetrate.

BREVITY (BREV i tee): n. Briefness, shortness

Trigger: BREvity-BREIF

Trigger Sentence: 1. BREVITY is a BRIEF statement. Its hallmark is its precision. 2. ABBREVIATE, BREVILOQUENT, BREVITY, and BRIEFNESS, belong to same family.

Sample sentence: *Brevity* is what we need in your editorial, not a lengthy piece of script.

BRIDLE (BRAHYD I): v. Bring under control

Trigger: BRIDLE-BREAK PEDDLE

Trigger Sentence: BREAK PEDDLE BRIDLES the speeding vehicle.

Sample sentence: Hold your horses! I mean *bridle* yourself and wait for your turn to come, we will surely listen to your concepts and choose you if you are the best among the presenters.

BRISTLING (BRIS uling): a. Showing irritation; raising like bristles

Trigger: 1.BRISTLE-WRESTLE 2. BRISTLE-BRUSH

Trigger Sentence: 1. In a WRESTLE the fighters BRISTLE at the sight of each other. 2. Imagine a tooth BRUSH BRISTLE.

Sample sentence: The dog *bristled* at the sight of the cat.

BRITTLE (BRIT I): a. Likely to break; fragile; frail

Trigger: BRITTLE-BOTTLE

Trigger Sentence: A glass BOTTLE is made of BRITTLE material; it can be broken pretty easily.

Sample sentence: It was a *brittle* apology from him that was anything but heartfelt.

BROACH (BROHCH): v. Introduce; open up

Trigger: 1.BROACH-BROCHURE. 2. BROACH-APPROACH

Trigger Sentence: 1. A BROCHURE is given by the counselor to BROACH about the institute. 2. When a boy APPROACHES a girl for the first time, he needs to BROACH.

Sample sentence: At the lunch meeting, Tiwari waited for the right time to *broach* on pay hike.

BROOK (BROOK): v. Tolerate; bear

Trigger: BROOK-BROKEN (** near antonyms)

Trigger Sentence: The guy could not BROOK his life with a BROKEN HEART and so committed suicide.

Sample sentence: The new secretary had to *brook* unprofessional remarks from her colleagues.

BRUSQUE (BRUSK): a. Curt, abrupt; rude

Trigger: BRUSQUE-ABRUPT

Trigger Sentence: 1. I asked for a cup of coffee and received an ABRUPT reply from my BRUSQUE wife: "I don't have time." 2. A BRUTE behaves in a BRUSQUE manner.

Sample sentence: *Brusque* behavior is not welcome in old age homes- be compassionate.

BRUTALITY (broo TAL ih tee): n. Cruelty, ruthless

Trigger: BRUTAL-BEAT ALL

Trigger Sentence: A BRUTAL man BEATS ALL people

Sample sentence: There was lot of *brutality* against Jews during the Hitler regime.

Related Words: BRUTAL - a.cruel, harsh

BUCOLIC (byoo KAHL ik): a. Rural, pastoral

Trigger: BUCOLIC-BULLOCK cart

Trigger Sentence: BULLOCK-cart is a symbol of BUCOLIC life.

Sample sentence: I often have dreams of *bucolic* fields and butterflies... may be subconsciously I want to escape away from this cacophonous city life into the beautiful serene countryside.

BUNGLE (BUHNG gul): v. Mismanage, blunder

Trigger: BUNGLE-BLUNDER

Trigger Sentence: He committed BLUNDERS and BUNGLED the job.

Sample sentence: I was afraid you would *bungle* up your assignment.

BUOYANT (BOI uhnt): n. Able to float; cheerful; optimistic

Trigger: BUOYANT-BOUNCY ANT

Trigger Sentence: The BOUNCY ANT is quite BUOYANT after seeing the sweet in my house.

Sample sentence: The dancers *buoyantly* prepared themselves for the evening's show.

BUREAUCRACY (byoo RAHK ruh see): n. Any large administrative system with numerous rules and regulations

Trigger: 1.AUTOCRACY. 2. DEMOCRACY.3. BUREAUCRACY

Trigger Sentence: DEMOCRACY-where people rule; BUREAUCRACY-where OFFICERS RULE with numerous rules and regulations

Sample sentence: He is an honest *bureaucrat* who strictly follows *bureaucratic* rules and cannot be bullied by gangsters.

Related Words: 1. PLUTOCRACY – n. government by wealthy people. 2. ARISTOCRACY – n. noble class

BURGEON (BUR jun): v. To grow rapidly; blossom

Trigger: 1.BURGEON-BURGER ON. 2. BURGEON- BULGE ON

Trigger Sentence: 1. BURGERS ON and ON -your stomach is going to BURGEON. 2. BULGE ON- growing rapidly

Sample sentence: The *burgeoning* population in India will put a lot of burden on resources.

BURLESQUE (bur LESK): n. Comic imitation

Trigger: BURLESQUE-BURRA MASQUE

Trigger Sentence: By wearing a MASQUE, the BURRA (great) people like Gandhi are always target of BURLESQUE

Sample sentence: Bob is good at *burlesquing* and mocking the behavior patterns of his teachers.

BURNISH (BER nish): v. Make shiny by rubbing, polish

Trigger: BURNISH-VARNISH -POLISH

Trigger Sentence: 1. When we apply VARNISH, the objects are going to BURNISH. 2. The shoemaker BURNISHED the shoes with a POLISH.

Sample sentence: The maid *burnished* the brass lamps until they reflected light.

BUTTRESS (BUT rus): v. Support, reinforce

Trigger: 1.BUTTRESS-"BUTT+REST". 2. BUTTRESS-MISTRESS

Trigger Sentence: 1. My big BUTT supports the REST of the body. 2. My MISTRESS BUTTRESSES me all the time.

Sample sentence: The mediaeval century temple pillars were *buttressed* with sculptures of flying seraphs.

BYZANTINE (BIZ un teen): a. Excessively complicated

Trigger: 1. BYZANTINE-BUSY LINE. 2. BYZANTINE-LABYRINTHINE (refer)

Trigger Sentence: The BUSY LANES of Hyderabad roads are so outrageously BYZANTINE that it is impossible to maneuver my car during BUSY morning hours.

Sample sentence: The monks practice a *byzantine* form of Zen meditation.

CABAL (kuh BAL): n. A Small group of secret plotters, group of conspirators

    Trigger: CABAL-KABUL

    Trigger Sentence: In KABUL (Afghan capital-Taliban) there was a CABAL; culprits behind terrorist attacks on many countries

    Sample sentence: The Kabul Taliban *cabal* failed, as its scheme was exposed by the Intelligence.

CACOPHONY (kuh KAFH uh nee): n. Discord, harshness in sound

    Trigger: CACOPHONY-CELL PHONE

    Trigger Sentence: In the middle of an important meeting if a CELL-PHONE rings, it causes a lot of CACOPHONY.

    Sample sentence: Crows created a *cacophony* while we silently stood at the funeral ground.

    Related Words: CACOPHONOUS - a. harsh-sounding, jarring.

CADGE (KAJ): v. Beg for money

    Trigger: CADGER-BEGGAR

    Trigger Sentence: CADGER and BEGGAR are synonyms; a BEGGAR wears a BADGE and CADGES in the street.

    Sample sentence: He has a habit of *cadging* cigarettes from his friends.

CAJOLE (kuh JOHL): v. Tempt, persuade with flattery

    Trigger: 1. CAJOLE- JOLIE- Angelina JOLIE. 2. CAJOLE-KAJAL

    Trigger Sentence: 1. Bradd Pitt CAJOLED Angelina JOLIE. 2. Heroine KAJAL CAJOLED the hero Ajay Devgon.

    Sample sentence: I *cajoled* my husband to take me out on a cruise holiday.

CALAMITY (kuh LAM uh tee): n. Disaster; catastrophe

    Trigger: CALAMITY-CALL ALMIGHTY

    Trigger Sentence: CALL ALMIGHTY (god) to stop the CALAMITY and disaster in the world.

    Sample sentence: A hurricane would cause a *calamity* at these low-lying coastal regions.

    Related Words: CALAMITOUS - a.disastrous, miserable

CALLOUS (KAL uss): a. Hard; heartless; unsympathetic

    Trigger: CALLOUS-CARELESS

    Trigger Sentence: My husband has become CALLOUS and CARELESS

    Sample sentence: The *callousness* of the doctor resulted in the patient's death.

    Related Words: CALLOUSED – a. emotionally hardened

CALLOW (KAL oh): a. Inexperienced; very young

    Trigger: 1.CALLOW-HOLLOW. 2. CALLOW-CAL (CALIBER) + LOW

    Trigger Sentence: 1. My brain is HOLLOW, since I'm a CALLOW. 2. CALLOW youth tend to have LOW CALIBER.

    Sample sentence: Rohan was just a *callow* boy of sixteen when he arrived in Paris.

CALUMNY (KAL um nee): n. A false statement to injure the reputation; slander

    Trigger: 1.CALUMNIOUS- "CALL +U+ MINUS". 2. CALL BAD

    Trigger Sentence: 1. In a CALUMNIOUS phone call, the opposition CALLED YOU with MINUS words. 2. CALL with BAD words is known as CALUMNY

    Sample sentence: Political parties are *calumnious* towards their opposing parties.

    Related Words: CALUMNIOUS - a.tending to discredit or malign.

CAMOUFLAGE (KAM uh flahzh): n./v. Disguise; conceal; hide

    Trigger: 1. CAM- POSE. 2. "CAMOUFLAGE-"CAME UNDER FLAG"

    Trigger Sentence: 1. Web CAM (camera) was used to disclose his CAMOUFLAGE. 2. He CAME UNDER FLAG to cover his face to HIDE and DECEIVE

    Sample sentence: Soldiers *camouflaged* themselves in the jungle in brown patchy uniforms.

CANDID (KAAN did): a. Honest, open

    Trigger: 1. CANDID-"CON DID". 2. CANDID-CANDLE

    Trigger Sentence: 1. A CON man never DID in a CANDID manner. 2. CANDLE light gives OPENNESS; the leader's speech was as CANDID and fiery as a CANDLE flame.

    Sample sentence: The photographer took *candid* and natural shots of the village market.

WRATH :
anger, rage, fury

Memory Test-13 : Match each word and its memory trick to the corresponding definition.

S.N	WORD	MEMORY TRIGGER	S	DEFINITIONS	KEY
1	BEHEMOTH	BHEEM +GOLIATH	A	Beg; to request earnestly	
2	BEHOLDEN	I will BE under your HOLD	B	Blessing	
3	BELEAGUER	PLAGUE disease –BELEAGUERS	C	Blessing, benediction	
4	BELIE	Show it to BE a LIE	D	Confuse	
5	BELITTLE	She makes me LITTLE	E	Deprived of; lacking	
6	BELLICOSE	REBEL-POSE	F	Disparage; decry	
7	BELLIGERENT	REBEL-BELLI-BULLY mentality	G	Favorable and not harmful	
8	BEMUSE	Bemuse-amuse-confuse	H	Generous, kind	
9	BENEDICTION	He dictates good	I	Harass; besiege; attack	
10	BENEFACTOR	He provides Benefits	J	Huge creature	
11	BENEFICENT	It gives benefits	K	Kind; good	
12	BENEFICIARY	He receives benefits	L	Leave property to someone in a will	
13	BENEVOLENT	He also provides Benefits	M	Obligated; indebted; in debt	
14	BENIGN	NOT MALIGN- only BENEFITS	N	One who benefits from something	
15	BENISON	Bend my son--benediction	O	Quarrelsome; aggressive	
16	BENT	My mind BENDS towards	P	Scold strongly	
17	BEQUEATH	BEFORE DEATH my parents gave ???	Q	Show to be false; contradict	
18	BERATE	Critics RATE the movie	R	Sponsor, donor	
19	BEREFT	After you LEFT, I'm BEREFT	S	Strong inclination or interest	
20	BESEECH	Beg and seek	T	Warlike; combative	

Memory Test-14 : Match each word and its memory trick to the corresponding definition.

S.N	WORD	MEMORY TRIGGER	S.N	DEFINITIONS	KEY
1	BESIEGE	Troy was under SIEGE	A	Partiality; favoring one person	
2	BETRAY	BE TRICK them & betray	B	A person who is one-sided & prejudiced	
3	BEWILDERING	WILD forest. I 'm BEWILDERED	C	Be disloyal, reveal a secret	
4	BIASED	My BOSS is BIASED towards girls	D	Bored with pleasure or dissipation	
5	BIFURCATE	BI+ FORK	E	Cheat; defraud	
6	BIGOT	BIGOT says - MY GOD is only great	F	Coax with flattery; persuade	
7	BILIOUS	PILES disease - BILIOUS mood.	G	Curt;rude; not sharp	
8	BILK	BILLClinton BILKED his wife	H	Depressing, unhappy, sad	
9	BIZARRE	Indian BAZAARS look BIZARRE	I	Disease, decay	
10	BLAND	LAND taste is BLAH & BLAND	J	Extremely confusing	
11	BLANDISH	a BLONDE is brainwashed	K	Flaw, fault, defect	
12	BLASÉ	BLASÉ-"BLAH+ LIFE"	L	Happy; carefree	
13	BLASPHEMOUS	blast +famous people	M	Hit forcefully; club	
14	BLATANT	blast of the aunt	N	Disrespectful; sacrilegious	
15	BLEAK	BLACK color- life is BLEAK	O	Irritable; cranky	
16	BLEMISH	BLEM-PROBLEM	P	Loudly offensive; extremely obvious	
17	BLIGHT	BAD-LIGHT gives blight	Q	Split into two	
18	BLITHE	BLITHE-BLISS	R	Surround a place and harass	
19	BLUDGEON	BLOOD + GUN	S	Tasteless; mild; boring	
20	BLUNT	POINT-BLANK talk	T	Very strange or unusual; odd	

Answers	EX.NO	1	2	3	4	5	6	7	8	9	10	11	12	13	14	15	16	17	18	19	20
	13	J	M	I	Q	F	T	O	D	B	R	K	N	H	G	C	S	L	P	E	A
	14	R	C	J	A	Q	B	O	E	T	S	F	D	N	P	H	K	I	L	M	G

Memory Test-15 : Match each word and its memory trick to the corresponding definition.

S.N	WORD	MEMORY TRIGGER	S.N	DEFINITIONS	KEY
1	BOGUS	BOYS are GUILE and BOGUS	A	Benefit; blessing	
2	BOHEMIAN	HE-MAN looks BOHEMIAN	B	Boaster, show off	
3	BOISTEROUS	BOIS-NOISE	C	Briefness, shortness	
4	BOLSTER	booster -bolster	D	Bring under control	
5	BOMBAST	boasters bombast	E	Curt, abrupt; rude	
6	BONHOMIE	BORN+HOMELY	F	Exhibit aggressively; wave around	
7	BOON	BONUS	G	Expurgate; purify	
8	BOOR	BOOR-BOO	H	Good-natured friendliness	
9	BOWDLERIZE	BOWLES+RINSE	I	Introduce; open up	
10	BRAGGART	bragger-boaster	J	Likely to break; fragile; frail	
11	BRANDISH	Any new BRAND I brandish	K	Noisy; violent, rough	
12	BRAZEN	Brazen girl wears only a BRA	L	Not genuine; artificial, sham	
13	BREACH	BREAK (of rules)	M	Pompous; using inflated language	
14	BREVITY	BREvity-BREIF	N	Rude or insensitive person	
15	BRIDLE	break peddle BRIDLES	O	Shameless or arrogant	
16	BRISTLING	In WRESTLE the fighters BRISTLE	P	Showing irritation	
17	BRITTLE	glass BOTTLE is BRITTLE	Q	Support, reinforce	
18	BROACH	brochure-approach	R	Tolerate; bear	
19	BROOK	BROKEN HEART- I can't brook	S	Unconventional	
20	BRUSQUE	A BRUTE talk in a brusque manner	T	Violation; crack, gap	

Memory Test-16 : Match each word and its memory trick to the corresponding definition.

S.N	WORD	MEMORY TRIGGER	S.N	DEFINITIONS	KEY
1	BRUTALITY	Brutal-beat all people	A	A small group of secret plotters	
2	BUCOLIC	I find BULLOCK cart in	B	Able to float; cheerful; optimistic	
3	BUNGLE	BLUNDER	C	Administrative system with many rules	
4	BUOYANT	BOUNCY ANT	D	Beg for money	
5	BUREAUCRACY	Bureaucrats RULE	E	Comic imitation	
6	BURGEON	BURGERS ON and ON	F	Cruelty, ruthless	
7	BURLESQUE	wearing a MASQUE	G	Disaster; catastrophe	
8	BURNISH	VARNISH -POLISH	H	Harshness in sound , discord	
9	BUTTRESS	BUTT+REST	I	Disguise; conceal; hide	
10	BYZANTINE	BUSY LINE is byzantine	J	Excessively complicated	
11	CABAL	KABUL-Taliban	K	False statement to injure; slander	
12	CACOPHONY	CELL PHONE sound	L	Grow rapidly; blossom	
13	CADGE	cadger-beggar	M	Heartless; unsympathetic	
14	CAJOLE	Brad Pitt cajoled JOLIE	N	Inexperienced; very young	
15	CALAMITY	CALL ALMIGHTY to save	O	Make shiny, polish	
16	CALLOUS	callous -careless	P	Mismanage, blunder	
17	CALLOW	low caliber guy	Q	Open ; honest	
18	CALUMNY	calumnious- call +u+ minus	R	Rural, pastoral	
19	CAMOUFLAGE	He CAME UNDER FLAG	S	Support, reinforce	
20	CANDID	I talk candid- I can do	T	Tempt, persuade with flattery	

Answers	EX.NO	1	2	3	4	5	6	7	8	9	10	11	12	13	14	15	16	17	18	19	20
	15	L	S	K	Q	M	H	A	N	G	B	F	O	T	C	D	P	J	I	R	E
	16	F	R	P	B	C	L	E	O	S	J	A	H	D	T	G	M	N	K	I	Q

WORD GROUPS DAY-4

★ EXPERT/SKILL

ADJECTIVES: adept, adroit, consummate, deft, dexterous, ambidextrous, accomplished; proficient, sophisticated, virtuoso

NOUNS: aesthete, connoisseur, guru, pundit, sage, savant, veteran

VERB: expertise, master

ANTONYMS: n.novice, neophyte; adj. callow, maladroit

★ FICKLE/CHANGEABLE NATURE

ADJECTIVES: arbitrary, changeable, erratic, fickle, flighty, impulsive, inconstant, irresolute, mercurial, mutable, labile, quirky, random, temperamental, unpredictable, unstable, vagarious, volatile, wayward, whimsical

NOUNS: caprice, crotchet, whim, whimsy, vagary, quirk

VERBS: waver, hesitate, dither, equivocate, oscillate, vacillate, fluctuate

ANTONYMS: adj. consistent, stable, steadfast, unwavering, dependable

★ STEADY NATURE

ADJECTIVES: abiding, certain, constant, consistent, enduring, equable, steadfast, unfaltering, unwavering; composure, self-possession; serenity, tranquility, equilibrium; poise, sangfroid

NOUNS: equability, equanimity, equilibrium

VERBS: stabilize

ANTONYMS: adj. unstable, wobbly; unfaithful

★ RESPECT /RESPECTED/RESPECTFUL

VERB: admire, defer, esteem, honor, idolize, revere, venerate

ADJECTIVES: august, distinguished, estimable, revered, venerable

NOUNS: courtesy, deference, reverence, veneration

ANTONYMS: v. disregard, disrespect, insult, ridicule; n. contempt

★ RIDICULE-MOCKERY

VERB: banter, deride, lampoon, mock, jeer at, scorn, satirize, scoff, tease, taunt, chaff

ADJECTIVES: derisive, jeering, scoffing, taunting

NOUNS: badinage, banter, burlesque, caricature, contempt, derision, disdain, disparagement, farce, gibe, irony, jeer, mockery, parody, persiflage, sarcasm, satire, taunt, travesty

ANTONYMS: v. respect , praise

★ SHY/SHYNESS

ADJECTIVES: bashful, coy, demure, diffident, timid, timorous, reserved, reticent, introverted, retiring, self-effacing, withdrawn, nervous, inhibited, repressed, embarrassed

NOUNS: timidity

VERB: shy, recoil

ANTONYMS: adj. brazen, bold, unashamed

this PUG dog is PUGNACIOUS

aggressive, confrontational, argumentative

Word List Day-5

CANDOR (CAN dur): n. Openness, sincerity

Trigger: CANDOR-CAN DO

Trigger Sentence: I may do means- I may do it or I may not do it; it lacks openness; but if you say, I CAN DO- it signifies FRANKNESS; I CAN DO sentence itself implies the "CANDOR"

Sample Sentence: Speaking with *candor*, the minister called for political reforms.

CANONICAL (kuh NON i kuhl): a. Conforming to orthodox rules

Trigger: CANON-COMMON

Trigger Sentence: COMMON people usually follow their religious CANON

Sample Sentence: The world is moving forward but for my father who is *canonically* struck to traditional values!

Related Words: CANON - n. accepted principle; church law

CANT (KANT): n. 1. Hypocrisy, false religiousness. 2. Jargon

Trigger: 1. CANT-SAINT. 2. CANT-CHANT

Trigger Sentence: 1. Some of the CHANTING SAINTS are involved in CANT (false religiousness). 2. Sanskrit CHANT can be understood only by Hindu SAINT. It is their religious CANT or JARGON.

Sample Sentence: 1. The *saint's* complicated *cants* are misleading to his disciples. 2. They don't speak our *cant* (slang or lingo) but manage to understand!

CANTANKEROUS (kan TANK er us): a. Bad-tempered, irritable

Trigger: CANTANKEROUS-"CANT + ANKER (ANGER) + OUS"

Trigger Sentence: "ANKER" in the word sounds like "ANGER". CANTANKEROUS person exhibits lot of ANGER like a Military TANKER

Sample Sentence: The psycho was *cantankerous* in public only as an act of self protection.

CANYON (KAN yun): n. A deep narrow valley with steep sides

Trigger: CANYON-Y ("Y" shaped or "V" shaped)

Trigger Sentence: CANYON De Chelly is actually a "Y" shaped CANYON which is fairly shallow near its mouth.

Sample Sentence: The famous Grand *Canyon* will be my next holiday destination.

CAPACIOUS (kuh PAY shush): a. Spacious, comfortable

Trigger: CAPACIOUS-SPACIOUS

Trigger Sentence: SPACIOUS and CAPACIOUS are synonyms.

Sample Sentence: The location was *capacious* enough to accommodate a spacious stadium.

CAPITULATE (kah PICH uh layt): v. Surrender

Trigger: CAPITULATE-"CAPITAL + ATE"

Trigger Sentence: After the "CAPITAL WAS ATE" by enemy forces, the king eventually CAPITULATED.

Sample Sentence: Only after a tough resistance, the enemy *capitulated*.

CAPRICIOUS (kuh PRISH us): a. Fickle, changeable; impulsive

Trigger: caPRICIOUS-PRICES

Trigger Sentence: Share PRICES are CAPRICIOUS- UNPREDICTABLE; likewise human behavior too is UNPREDICTABLE

Sample Sentence: He is a *capricious* traveler for he never sticks to his scheduled tour.

Related Words: CAPRICE - n. a sudden change of mood or behavior.

CAPTIOUS (KAP shus): a. Fault-finding, picky

Trigger: 1. CAPTIOUS-CAPTAINS. 2. CAPTIOUS-CAPTURE US

Trigger Sentence: 1. A CAPTIOUS CAPTAIN CAPTURED US when we committed mistakes. 2. The CAPTAIN was so CAPTIOUS that no player was willing to work under him.

Sample Sentence: I was hurt when my boss passed those *captious* remarks at me.

CARDINAL (KAHRD nul): n. Main, chief

Trigger: 1. CARDINAL-CAPITAL. 2. CARDINAL-CARDIAC

Trigger Sentence: 1. Delhi CAPITAL is CARDINAL for India. 2. CARDIAC (related to heart) condition is CARDINAL for human survival.

Sample Sentence: Computers have become *cardinal* in our everyday life!

CARICATURE (KAR uh kuh chur): n. Comical distortion

Trigger: 1. CARICATURE-CARTOON FEATURE. 2. CARICATURE-CARRY-JIM CARRY

Trigger Sentence: 1. He could draw a CARTOON or a CARICATURE with masterly hand. 2. Jim CARRY facial FEATURE is famous for CARICATURES.

Sample Sentence: The cartoonist captured the characteristics of politicians in his *caricatures.*

CARNAGE (KAR nij): n. Destruction of life

Trigger: CARNAGE-"CAR DAMAGE"

Trigger Sentence: In the CARNAGE that followed the politician's demise, my CAR was completely DAMAGED.

Sample Sentence: Will this *carnage* of cattle be banned in these inhuman slaughter houses?!

CARNAL (KAHR nl): a. Fleshly; Sensual

Trigger: 1.CARNAL-CARNIVOROUS. 2. CARNAL-CARS

Trigger Sentence: 1. CARNIVOROUS people have a CARNAL delight in FLESH eating. 2. These days the lovers in CARS derive CARNAL pleasures.

Sample Sentence: Nityananda, the spiritual guru was tarnished for having *carnal* desires.

CARP (KAWRP): v. Find fault

Trigger: CARP-COP (police cop)

Trigger Sentence: A CARPING COP always FINED FAULTS in others.

Sample Sentence: My editor keeps *carping* about our reports for not being challenging enough!

CASTIGATE (KASS tuh gate): v. Criticize; scold; punish

Trigger: 1.CASTigate-CASTE. 2. CASTIGATE-CURSE THE GATE

Trigger Sentence: 1. In Indian CASTE system, it is usual that one CASTE people CASTIGATE other CASTE people. 2. In a CASTIGATION (n) a drunken man CURSED THE closed GATE of his home.

Sample Sentence: It's unlawful to *castigate* someone in the name of caste or religion.

CATACLYSM (KAT ah kliz um): n. A violent upheaval or disaster; earthquake, flood

Trigger: 1.CATACLYSM-CAT KILLED. 2.cataCLYSMIC-SEISMIC or CYCLONIC

Trigger Sentence: 1. Many CATS were KILLED in a CATACLYSM. 2. Intense SEISMIC/ CYCLONIC activity caused CATACLYSMIC tsunami on earth.

Sample Sentence: The day is not far when earth will show her *cataclysmic* avatar unless we stop being arrogant on our environment and start conserving nature.

CATALYST (KAT l ist): n. Cause of change; stimulus

Trigger: CATALYST-CYCLIST

Trigger Sentence: The CYCLIST Lance Armstrong acted as a CATALYST in the drug scam

Sample Sentence: The cyclist Lance Armstrong was proud to be a *catalyst* for cancer survivors.

CATASTROPHE (kuh TAS truh fee): n. Disaster, calamity, cataclysm

Trigger: CATASTR--DISASTER

Trigger Sentence: CATASTAR" sound like "DISASTER"

Sample Sentence: The Spanish Influenza *catastrophe* of 1918 was a disaster killing millions.

CATEGORICAL (kat uh GOR uh kul): a. Absolute, certain; without reservations

Trigger: CATEGORICAL-CATEGORY

Trigger Sentence: I can CATEGORICALLY say that Brazilian forests come under the CATEGORY of rain forests.

Sample Sentence: O.J. Simpson's *categorical* denial of the murder of his wife did make news.

Related Words: CATEGORICALLY – adv. definitely, decisively

CATER TO (KEY ter to): v. Supply something desired; pamper

Trigger: CATER-EATER

Trigger Sentence: The waiter CATERED dinner for all the EATERS at the restaurant.

Sample Sentence: I can't go through the toil of cooking and *catering* to guests everyday.

CATHARSIS (kuh THAR sis): n. Emotional cleansing through drama; purging

Trigger: CATHARSIS--OASIS

Trigger Sentence: In OASIS there was a CATHARSIS. When the thirsty travellers saw an OASIS in the desert, they experienced an intense CATHARSIS.

Sample Sentence: Dancing is a means of *catharsis* for her.

Related Words: CATHARTIC – a. Purifying, cleansing

CATHOLIC (KATH lik): a. Universal; embracing everything; liberal

Trigger: 1.CatHOLic-HOLISTIC-WHOLE .2. CATHOLIC-COSMIC (** synonyms)

Trigger Sentence: 1. CATHOLIC approach is a HOLISTIC approach. 2. CATHOLICS believe that Mother Mary is HOLISTIC.

Sample Sentence: He was oriental and *catholic,* and read everything in the library.

Related Words: HOLISTIC – a. dealing with wholeness rather than focusing on its parts

CAUSAL (KAW zuhl): a. Related cause and effect

Trigger: CAUSE

Trigger Sentence: There is a CAUSAL link between poverty and crime; CAUSE is poverty and effect is CRIME.

Sample Sentence: There is a *causal* correlation between scarcity and higher prices.

CAUSTIC (KAW stik): a. Corrosive, sarcastic; biting comments

   Trigger: CAUSTIC-SARCASTIC

   Trigger Sentence: SARCASTIC statements raise CAUSTIC feelings.

   Sample Sentence: This ladies club has women making *caustic* remarks at each other!

   Related Words: SARCASTIC – a. satirical, derisive

CAVIL (KAV ul): v. Make petty or unnecessary objections

   Trigger: 1.CAVIL-EVIL. 2. CAVIL-CRITICAL

   Trigger Sentence: EVIL minded aunty CAVIL endlessly with the neighbors.

   Sample Sentence: My father *cavils* with merchants; he loves to bicker and bargain over prices.

CEASE (SEES): v. End; stop

   Trigger: 1. CEASE-CLOSE (*synonyms). 2. CEASE-PAUSE (*synonyms)

   Trigger Sentence: The fighting along the border has temporarily CEASED/PAUSED.

   Sample Sentence: The ordnance factory was forced to *cease* its illegal production.

CEDE (SEED): v. Yield; surrender

   Trigger: 1.CEDE-SEED. 2. ACCEDE-CONCEDE-CEDE

   Trigger Sentence: 1. Low SEEDED tennis player CEDED to the top SEEDED player. 2. ACCEDE (or accept) and CONCEDE is to ACCEPT the defeat.

   Sample Sentence: The illegal settlers did *cede* to the police and moved out of encroachments.

CELERITY (sah LER i tee): n. Alacrity, rapidity, speed

   Trigger: CELERITY-ACCELERATE

   Trigger Sentence: The Swift car is ACCELERATED and now it is moving with ALACRITY

   Sample Sentence: Though not in best of physical forms, Ussain Bolt did move with *celerity*.

CELIBATE (SEL uh bit): n. Away from sensual (sexual) desires; unmarried

   Trigger: 1.CELIBATE-CELEBRATE. 2. CELEBRITY-CELIBATE

   Trigger Sentence: 1. CELIBATE never CELEBRATES Valentine's Day. 2. CELEBRITIES usually don't practise CELIBACY.

   Sample Sentence: Sheela swore that she would remain a *celibate* until her marriage.

   Related Words: CELEBRATED – a. famous; well known

CENSORIOUS (sen SOHR ee us): a. Fault finding; critical

   Trigger: CENSORIOUS-CENSOR

   Trigger Sentence: CENSOR people are usually CENSORIOUS; they are FAULT-FINDING committee of the movies

   Sample Sentence: "In a *censorious* world, good work gets criticized", nagged the social worker.

   Related Words: CENSOR - v. to examine to suppress anything considered objectionable.

CENSURE (SEN shur): v. Blame; criticize

   Trigger: CENSURE--CENSOR

   Trigger Sentence: CENSOR board CENSURED the film director for vulgar scenes.

   Sample Sentence: The defense minister was *censured* for his role in the guns' scam.

CEREBRAL (suh REE brul): a. 1. n. An Intellectual Person, 2.a. Relating To the Brain

Trigger: CEREBRAL-CERELAC

Trigger Sentence: Mom feeds me with CERELAC (cereal powder), assuming that I will become CEREBRAL like my dad.

Sample Sentence: Geetha likes the *cerebral* type of men who make arm- chair-intellectuals!

Related Words: CEREBRATION - thought

CEREMONIOUS (ser uh MOH nee us): a. Formal; polite

Trigger: CEREMONIOUS-CEREMONY

Trigger Sentence: In a CEREMONY (example -marriage ceremony) people are very polite and behave well; Sanskrit pundits speak CEREMONIOUS or FORMAL language.

Sample Sentence: The president's dinner is an annual *ceremonious* event.

CERTITUDE (SUHR tih tood): n. Certainty, sureness

Trigger: CERTITUDE-CERTAIN-CERTAINTY

Trigger Sentence: Job CERTAINTY provides CERTITUDE to life.

Sample Sentence: Every year, it is mandatory for my mother to give her *certitude* as "living" to her bank to beget her monthly pension.

CESSATION (se SAY shun): n. Stopping, ceasing

Trigger: 1. CEASE-CLOSE. 2. CESSATION-CONCLUSION

Trigger Sentence: 1. CEASE means CLOSE or PAUSE. 2. CESSATION & CONCLUSION are synonyms; the process of CEASING is known as CESSATION.

Sample Sentence: The factory workers threatened a *cessation* if their demands were not met.

Related Words: CEASE - v. stop, close

CHAGRIN (shuh GRIN): n. Displeasure, strong feelings of embarrassment

Trigger: CHAGRIN- GRIN

Trigger Sentence: 1. Her wicked GRIN CHAGRINNED (v) him deeply. 2. GRIN means smile; CHAGRIN means DISPLEASURE.

Sample Sentence: Sally was completely *chagrined* with her boss's misbehavior, so she quit.

CHAMPION (CHAM pee un): v. Defend, support

Trigger: CHAMPION

Trigger Sentence: Sachin is a CHAMPION cricketer who CHAMPIONED (supported) and defended India with his extraordinary batting skills.

Sample Sentence: Mahatma Gandhi *championed* the Indian freedom struggle against British.

CHANT (CHANT): n. Sing, recite

Trigger: CHANT-CHIRP; * NOTE: Learn chant based words here.

Trigger Sentence: CHANTEY (a sailor's song); CHIRP (a small singing sound made by birds), CHOIR (singing group), CHORALE (hymn tune), CHORUS (singing group); DESCANT (another *chant*, second melody).

Sample Sentence: The Guru *chanted* a prayer and we recited in chorus.

Related Words: CHANTEUSE - n. A female singer especially in pubs and cabarets.

CHAOS (KAY ahs): n. Complete disorder and confusion

    Trigger: 1. COSMOS –ORDER. 2. CHAOS-DISORDER

    Trigger Sentence: 1. CHAOTIC-COSMETIC; COSMETIC surgery we do it for ORDER OF features; CHAOTIC means DISORDER. 2. Cosmos - order; chaos-disorder.

    Sample Sentence: It's an absolute *chaotic* situation in the university, due to the students' strike.

    Related Words: CHAOTIC - a. totally lacking order, confused.

CHARISMA (kuh RIZ muh): n. A personal attractiveness

    Trigger: CHARISMA-CHARisMa-CHARM

    Trigger Sentence: A CHARMING girl possesses CHARISMA

    Sample Sentence: The *charismatic* actress mesmerizes her spectators with her charm.

CHARLATAN (SHAR luh tun): n. Fraud, one who claims more skill or knowledge than he has.

    Trigger: 1.CHARLATAN-CHARLES Sobhraj. 2. CHARLATAN-CHEAT ON

    Trigger Sentence: 1. The notorious international criminal CHARLES Sobhraj is a CHARLATAN. 2. CHARLATANS wait for an opportunity to CHEAT simpletons.

    Sample Sentence: Oh' you charlatan, please don't dupe people with your half cooked ideas.

CHARY (CHAR ee): a. Careful, cautious, wary

    Trigger: CHARY-WARY-(BEWARE)

    Trigger Sentence: 1. CHARY and WARY are synonyms. 2. BEWARE of the dog; he is WARY of dogs.

    Sample Sentence: Ajay is very *chary* while investing in real estate companies.

CHASTE (CHAYST): n. Pure, Virginal, Modest

    Trigger: 1.CHASTE-TASTE. 2. CHASTE-(skirt) CHASER (** near antonyms)

    Trigger Sentence: 1. Person who never TASTES sex is called a CHASTE. 2. SKIRT CHASERS are NOT CHASTE.

    Sample Sentence: Marry is an innocent girl who became a nun to lead a *chaste* life.

CHASTEN (CHEY suhn): v. To punish; discipline

    Trigger: 1. CHASTEN-CHASE+SIN. 2. CHASTEN-SOFTEN (** near antonyms)

    Trigger Sentence: 1. Police CHASE SIN people to CHASTEN them. 2. CHASTEN (someone) and SOFTEN (someone) are antonyms.

    Sample Sentence: The pastor *chastened* him to stop chasing sins.

CHASTISE (chas TYZE V): Punish; criticize harshly

    Trigger: 1.CHASTISE-CRITICIZE. 2. CHASTISE-CHASTEN (**synonyms)

    Trigger Sentence: 1. CHASTISE is to CRITICIZE. 2. Priests CHASTISE common folk and CRITICIZE their way of living.

    Sample Sentence: The exam invigilator *chastised* the students for talking during the test.

CHAUVINIST (SHOH vuh nist): n. Person who is extremely patriotic; person who is excessively devoted to his own sex, race etc.

    Trigger: CHAUVINISM-HINDUISM-ISLAMISM-NATIONALISM

    Trigger Sentence: Various ISMS incites people towards CHAUVINISM

    Sample Sentence: `MCP' is commonly used as a slang to refer to `Male *Chauvinistic* Pigs'- pointing at men who think they are of superior sex!

CHECK (CHEK): v. To block; stop motion

Trigger: CHECK-BREAK-BLOCK (** synonyms)

Trigger Sentence: 1. At the CHECK post the police CHECKED my belongings. 2. CHECK whether the BREAKS of your vehicle are working or not.

Sample Sentence: Inflation must be held under *check* if the US dollar is to have any value.

Related Words: BREAK - v. prevent

CHECKERED (CHEK erd): a. Marked by various changes in fortune

Trigger: CHINESE CHECKER-CHESS BOARD

Trigger Sentence: CHINESE CHECKER or CHESS BOARD is marked with many variations (of colors); similarly his business career is also CHECKERED.

Sample Sentence: His success story depicts his journey through a *checkered* life, and how he ducked through his checkmates to ultimately be the king!

CHERISH (CHER ish): v. Relish; love

Trigger: 1.CHERISH-CHERRY. 2. CHERISH-RELISH-DELISH

Trigger Sentence: 1. I CHERISH CHERRY. 2. I CHERISH and RELISH the DELICIOUS food.

Sample Sentence: I shall *cherish* those wonderful moments we spent together in the train trip.

CHIC (SHEEK): a. Elegantly and stylishly fashionable

Trigger: CHIC-she LOOK

Trigger Sentence: She LOOKS CHIC.

Sample Sentence: She has got a *chic* sense of dressing.

CHICANERY (shi KAY nuh ree): n. Trickery; deception

Trigger: 1.CHICANERY-TRICKERY. 2. CHIC-TRICK

Trigger Sentence: 1. To trap a CHIC, you got to use CHICANERY and TRICKERY. 2. "CHIC" in the word sounds like "TRICK".

Sample Sentence: The foreign tourists fall victims to the local priests' *chicanery* at Banaras.

CHIDE (CHIDE): v. Scold, yell at

Trigger: 1. CHILD. 2. CHIDING-SCOLDING

Trigger Sentence: 1. Don't CHIDE the CHILD in front of others. 2. CHIDING and SCOLDING are synonyms.

Sample Sentence: Mom *chided* my brother for bunking his school.

CHIMERICAL (ki MAYR uh kul): a. Illusory; imaginary

Trigger: 1.chiMERICAL-MIRACLE .2.CHIMERA-CAMERA

Trigger Sentence: 1. The MIRACLE of the Greek ORACLE is only CHIMERICAL.
2. CAMERA captures CHIMERA (images).

Sample Sentence: Bobby has some *chimerical* schemes to make diamonds by crushing bottles.

Related Words: CHIMERA - n. imaginary monster, illusion, delusion.

CHIVALROUS (SHIV uh l rus): a. Courteous, Courageous

Trigger: CHIVALROUS-SHIVA + VALOROUS

Trigger Sentence: Lord SHIVA is CHIVALROUS and VALOROUS; he is COURAGEOUS and COURTEOUS.

Sample Sentence: The *chivalrous* soldiers valorously fought in the battlefield.

CHOLERIC (kahl UR ik): a. Quick to Anger

    Trigger: 1.CHOLERIC-CHOLERA .2. CHOLERIC-COLLAR

    Trigger Sentence: 1. After she was smitten by CHOLERA, she became CHOLERIC. 2. The CHOLERIC man gets hot under the COLLAR.

    Sample Sentence: Mohan is *choleric*, especially when disturbed while he is reading.

CHRONIC (KRAHN ik): a. Lasting (as of an illness); constant

    Trigger: CHRONIC-CLINIC

    Trigger Sentence: People who suffer with CHRONIC disease always visit CLINIC.

    Sample Sentence: Tom had to see an orthopedic for his *chronic* back pain.

CHRONOLOGY (krah NOL uh gee): a. An order of events from the earliest to the latest

    Trigger: CHRONOLOGY-CHRON (time)-LOGY (study)

    Trigger Sentence: CHRON- (root word) means TIME. Logy- (root word means study); "study according to time;" CHRONICLE is record of time in the form of history. CHRONIC disease remain with time; CHRONOLOGY-study according to time; CHRONOMETER —instrument for measuring time.

    Sample Sentence: The chronicle recorded all the events in its log book in a *chronological* order.

    Related Words: CHRONOLOGICAL - a. in order of time; sequential

CHURLISH (CHUR lish): a. Boorish; rude

    Trigger: 1. CHURLISH-not POLISHED. 2. CHURLISH-GIRLISH.

    Trigger Sentence: 1. The UNPOLISHED behavior is known as CHURLISH. 2. GIRLISH girls are DELICATE; CHURLISH people are RUDE

    Sample Sentence: Girls don't tolerate *churlish* behaviour.

CIPHER (SYE fer): v./n. Code, a secret method of writing

    Trigger: CIPHER-C FOR "CODE"

    Trigger Sentence: A for an apple; B for a boy; C FOR CODE. It is not easy to CIPHER a code and then to DECIPHER it.

    Sample Sentence: The cave temple walls had *ciphers* that seemed like an ancient inscription.

    Related Words: 1.ENCIPHER - v. encode. 2. DECIPHER - v. Decode

CIRCUITOUS (sur KYOO uh tus): a. Roundabout, not direct

    Trigger: CIRCUITOUS-CIRCUITS

    Trigger Sentence: 1. Like a CIRCUIT (circle) the path is CIRCUITOUS.2. The neural CIRCUITS in the brain are CIRCUITOUS.

    Sample Sentence: The road to the fort is *circuitous* and steep with many twisty turns.

CIRCUMLOCUTION (sur kum loh KYOO shun): n. Indirect or roundabout expression; verbosity

    Trigger: 1. CIRCUMLOCUTION- CIRCLE+ TALK is under CIRCULATION

    Trigger Sentence: 1. CIRCUMLOCUTION is beating around the bush. It's not a straight talk. It's a CIRCULAR TALK. 2. When a gossip is under CIRCULATION, people talk with CIRCUMLOCUTION.

    Sample Sentence: Politicians are notorious for *circumlocution*, talking much but doing little.

CIRCUMSCRIBE (SUR kum skrybe): a. Limit; confine

    Trigger: 1.CIRCUMSCRIBE-CIRCLE INSCRIBED. 2.CIRCUMSCRIBE-PROSCRIBE (refer)

    Trigger Sentence: 1. Laxman CIRCUMSCRIBED Sita by drawing a CIRCUMFERENCE around her. A CIRCLE is CIRCUMSCRIBED in a triangle. 2. CIRCUMSCRIBE-limit; PROSCRIBE-ban; PRESCRIBE-allow.

Sample Sentence: The goon politician was jailed so as to *circumscribe* his illegal activities.

Related Words: PROSCRIBE - v. prohibit; banish

CIRCUMSPECT (SUR kum spekt): v. Cautious; prudent

Trigger: CIRCUMSPECT-CIRCLE INSPECT

Trigger Sentence: The CIRCUMSPECT CIRCLE INSPECTOR has thoroughly INSPECTED law and order in his CIRCLE.

Sample Sentence: *Circumspection* is a must in the investigation department.

CIRCUMVENT (sur kum VENT): v. Outwit; baffle; surround

Trigger: CIRCUMVENT-"CIRCLE + PREVENT"

Trigger Sentence: The forces formed a CIRCLE AROUND (SURROUND) the enemy camp and SECRETLY PREVENTED them from attacking, thus, CIRCUMVENTING the enemy.

Sample Sentence: The general *circumvented* the enemy by attacking through the rearend.

CITE (SITE): v. Quote, commend

Trigger: CITE-SITE

Trigger Sentence: Wikipedia WEBSITE CITES lot of information on any topic

Sample Sentence: Dr. Prasad's research paper on fuel cells has been *cited* by the scientists.

Related Words: 1.CITED - a. quoted. 2. CITATION - n. quotation; official praise

CIVILITY (si VIL i tee): n. Politeness, courtesy, graciousness

Trigger: CIVILITY-CIVILIZED+ FORMALITY

Trigger Sentence: 1. CIVILITY is reflected in FORMALITY of dressing.2. CIVILIZED people are POLITE. UNCIVILIZED people are CRUDE and rough.

Sample Sentence: They greeted each other with the usual exchange of *civilities*.

Related Words: CIVIL – a. polite, non-military, non-religious

CLAIRVOYANCE (klair VOI uns): n. Extrasensory perception, sixth sense

Trigger: CLAIRVOYANCE-CLEAR + VOICE

Trigger Sentence: In the sixth sense movie the boy possesses CLAIRVOYANCE and he can hear CLEAR VOICE from the death people too.

Sample Sentence: Some mystics claim to be *clairvoyant* and can communicate with the dead!

CLAMOR (KLAM er): n. Loud Noise

Trigger: 1.CLAMOR-HAMMER. 2. CALMER-CLAMOR (*antonym Trigger)

Trigger Sentence: 1. The sudden HAMMER of fists produced CLAMOR. 2. The CALMER person never produces CLAMOR.

Sample Sentence: Varma hated the *clamor* of the city traffic.

CLANDESTINE (klan DES tin): a. Done secretly

Trigger: 1.CLANDESTINE-INTESTINE. 2. CLANDESTINE-PLAN THIS TIME

Trigger Sentence: 1. The trafficker CLANDESTINELY transported marijuana in the INTESTINE of a dog. 2. PLAN THIS TIME in a CLANDESTINE manner.

Sample Sentence: Unless you *clandestinely* plan out, you will not succeed in your plot.

CLANGOR (KLANG er): n. Loud resounding noise

Trigger: CLANGOR-BANGER

Trigger Sentence: The BANGER was making a CLANGOR.

Sample Sentence: The *clangor* of the alarm woke me up.

CLAUSTROPHOBIA (klaw struh FOH bee uh): n. Fear of enclosed places

Trigger: CLAUSTROPHOBIA-CLOSER PHOBIA

Trigger Sentence: CLAUSTROPHOBIA is an irrational fear of being in a CLOSED space.

Sample Sentence: I don't go in elevators because I am *claustrophobic*.

Related Words: 1.ACROPHOBIA: n. abnormal fear of heights. 2. PHOBIA: n. irrational fear

CLEMENCY (KLEM un see): n. Grace, mercy, leniency

Trigger: CLEMENCY-"cle + MENCY "(MERCY)"

Trigger Sentence: "MENCY" in the word sounds like "MERCY"; Ms. MERCY requested the judge to show CLEMENCY.

Sample Sentence: The government should impose absolutely no *clemency* on kidnappers.

Related Words: 1. CLEMENT - a. merciful; mild. 2. INCLEMENT: cruel; unmerciful

CLERGY (KLUR jee): n. People who work in religious ministry

Trigger: CLERGY-CLERK

Trigger Sentence: A religious CLERK is known as CLERGY. He works as a Head CLERK in the CLERGY of Vatican.

Sample Sentence: A local *clergy* was participated in the international - interfaith conference.

Related Words: CLERICAL - a. spiritual

CLICHE (klee SHAY): n. Overused (expression or phrase); trite remark

Trigger: 1.CLICHÉ-CLUTCH. 2. CLICHÉ-CLASS SAY

Trigger Sentence: 1. For majority of American presidents the sentence "God bless America" is a CLICHÉ. They use it as regularly as a motorist uses a CLUTCH. 2. In the CLASS, our boring teachers always SAY CLICHÉS

Sample Sentence: A *cliché* proverd is- "an apple a day keeps a doctor away."

CLOAK (KLOHK): v. Cover, conceal

Trigger: CLOAK-LOCK

Trigger Sentence: In a CLOAK room you have separate LOCKER facility.

Sample Sentence: Their plans were made in a *cloak* of secrecy.

CLOISTER (KLOY stur): v. Shut away; seclude

Trigger: 1.CLOISTER-OYSTER. 2. CLOISTER-CLOSET

Trigger Sentence: 1. She CLOISTERED herself in a CLOSET. 2. An OYSTER usually dwells in a CLOISTER (n).

Sample Sentence: After the death of his beloved wife, Oliver *cloistered* himself in the house.

CLOYING (KLOY ing): a. Distaste because of excessively sweet or sentimental.

Trigger: CLOYING-LOVING (**OVERLY LOVING to the point of distaste)

Trigger Sentence: Overly LOVING sentiments are CLOYING in nature.

Sample Sentence: Beware of her a *cloying* behavior; she is a sugar coated knife!

COAGULATE (ko AG yoo late): v. Thicken; become clotted

    Trigger: COAGULATE-COLGATE

    Trigger Sentence: The COLGATE tooth paste is in COAGULATED form.

    Sample Sentence: The patient was given blood thinners to prevent his blood from *coagulating*.

COALESCE (koh uh LES): v. Combine, fuse

    Trigger: COALESCE-"COLA + WHISKY"

    Trigger Sentence: Many people COALESCE (combine) the COLA and WHISKY before they drink.

    Sample Sentence: The two rivers *coalesced* into one large lake.

    Related Words: COALITION - n. Union

COARSE (KOHRS): a. Rough texture; crude

    Trigger: 1. COARSE-no GRACE. 2. COARSE-CRASS-MASS

    Trigger Sentence: 1. The COARSE man lacks GRACE. 2. COARSE-CRASS-MASS are synonyms. The popular actor's COARSE voice appeals to MASSES.

    Sample Sentence: Kavita always preferred a *coarse* canvas for her paintings than a smooth one.

a demon emerged out of the professors' book and created PANDEMONIUM

PANDEMONIUM : uproar, mayhem, chaos

Memory Test-17 : Match each word and its memory trick to the corresponding definition.

S.N	WORD	MEMORY TRIGGER	S.N	DEFINITIONS	KEY
1	CANDOR	I CAN DO implies candor	A	Certain; without reservations	
2	CANONICAL	COMMON people follow cannon	B	Bad-tempered, irritable	
3	CANT	CHANT of SAINTS is a cant	C	Cause of change; stimulus	
4	CANTANKEROUS	"ANKER" - "ANGER"	D	Comical distortion	
5	CANYON	"Y" shaped	E	Conforming to orthodox rules	
6	CAPACIOUS	SPACIOUS	F	Criticize; scold; punish	
7	CAPITULATE	CAPITAL WAS ATE-	G	Deep narrow valley with steep sides	
8	CAPRICIOUS	Share PRICES are CAPRICIOUS	H	Destruction of life	
9	CAPTIOUS	Captain CAPTURED us	I	Disaster, cataclysm	
10	CARDINAL	CARDIAC condition is CARDINAL	J	Fault-finding, picky	
11	CARICATURE	CARTOON feature	K	Fickle, changeable; impulsive	
12	CARNAGE	CAR gets DAMAGED	L	Find fault	
13	CARNAL	Carnivorous - CARNAL delight	M	Fleshly; Sensual	
14	CARP	A carping COP	N	Jargon; false religiousness	
15	CASTIGATE	CURSE THE GATE	O	Main, chief	
16	CATACLYSM	CAT KILLED	P	Openness, sincerity	
17	CATALYST	Cyclist was a CATALYST	Q	Spacious, comfortable	
18	CATASTROPHE	CATASTAR" - "DISASTER	R	Supply something desired	
19	CATEGORICAL	100% CATEGORY	S	Surrender	
20	CATER TO	Cater to the eaters	T	Violent disaster; flood	

Memory Test-18 : Match each word and its memory trick to the corresponding definition.

S.N	WORD	MEMORY TRIGGER	S.N	DEFINITIONS	KEY
1	CATHARSIS	In OASIS there was a CATHARSIS	A	Alacrity, rapidity, speed	
2	CATHOLIC	catholic-HOLISTIC-WHOLE	B	Away from sensual desires	
3	CAUSAL	CAUSE	C	Blame; criticize	
4	CAUSTIC	sarcastic	D	Certainty, sureness	
5	CAVIL	EVIL minded aunty CAVILS	E	Defend, support	
6	CEASE	CEASE-CLOSE or pause	F	Disorder and confusion	
7	CEDE	Low SEEDED	G	Displeasure	
8	CELERITY	CELERITY-ACCELERATE	H	Emotional cleansing through drama	
9	CELIBATE	CELIBATE never CELEBRATES	I	End; stop	
10	CENSORIOUS	CENSOR people are CENSORIOUS	J	Fault finding; critical	
11	CENSURE	CENSOR board CENSURED	K	Formal; polite	
12	CEREBRAL	Cerebral cortex	L	Make petty objections	
13	CEREMONIOUS	Ceremony language	M	Personal attractiveness	
14	CERTITUDE	CERTAINTY	N	Related cause and effect	
15	CESSATION	CONCLUSION	O	Relating To the Brain	
16	CHAGRIN	sad GRIN	P	Sarcastic; corrosive,	
17	CHAMPION	Sachin was a CHAMPION	Q	Sing, recite	
18	CHANT	CHANT-CHIRP	R	Stopping, ceasing	
19	CHAOS	Cosmos-chaos	S	Universal; embracing everything	
20	CHARISMA	CHARMING girl	T	Yield; surrender	

Answers	EX.NO	1	2	3	4	5	6	7	8	9	10	11	12	13	14	15	16	17	18	19	20
	17	P	E	N	B	G	Q	S	K	J	O	D	H	M	L	F	T	C	I	A	R
	18	H	S	N	P	L	I	T	A	B	J	C	O	K	D	R	G	E	Q	F	M

Memory Test-19 : Match each word and its memory trick to the corresponding definition.

S.N	WORD	MEMORY TRIGGER	S.N	DEFINITIONS	KEY
1	CHARLATAN	CHARLES Sobhraj	A	An order of events in time	
2	CHARY	wary-(beware)	B	Block; stop motion	
3	CHASTE	never TASTES sex	C	Boorish; rude	
4	CHASTEN	Why Police CHASE SIN ??	D	Careful, cautious, wary	
5	CHASTISE	chastise-criticize	E	Code, a secret method of writing	
6	CHAUVINIST	Hinduism-Islamism-nationalism	F	Constant (as of an illness)	
7	CHECK	check-break-block	G	Courageous , Courteous	
8	CHECKERED	checker-chess board	H	Elegantly fashionable	
9	CHERISH	I cherish CHERRY	I	Fraud	
10	CHIC	she LOOKS chic	J	Illusory; imaginary	
11	CHICANERY	CHIC-TRICK	K	Marked by various changes	
12	CHIDE	Don't CHIDE the CHILD	L	Person who is extremely patriotic	
13	CHIMERICAL	MIRACLE appears	M	Criticize harshly; punish	
14	CHIVALROUS	Lord SHIVA is VALOROUS	N	punish; discipline	
15	CHOLERIC	He catches COLLAR	O	Quick to Anger	
16	CHRONIC	Always CLINIC	P	Relish; love	
17	CHRONOLOGY	CHRON (time)-LOGY (study)	Q	Roundabout, not direct	
18	CHURLISH	not POLISHED	R	Scold, yell at	
19	CIPHER	C FOR "CODE"	S	Trickery; deception	
20	CIRCUITOUS	CIRCUITS	T	Virginal, Modest, Pure	

Memory Test-20 : Match each word and its memory trick to the corresponding definition.

S.N	WORD	MEMORY TRIGGER	S.N	DEFINITIONS	KEY
1	CIRCUMLOCUTION	It's a CIRCULAR talk	A	Cautious; prudent	
2	CIRCUMSCRIBE	Circle INSCRIBED	B	Combine, fuse	
3	CIRCUMSPECT	Circle INSPECT	C	Cover, conceal	
4	CIRCUMVENT	CIRCLED and PREVENTED	D	Crude; rough texture	
5	CITE	WEBSITE CITES	E	Distaste with an excess	
6	CIVILITY	civilized+ formality	F	Done secretly	
7	CLAIRVOYANCE	CLEAR + VOICE from death	G	Extrasensory perception	
8	CLAMOR	HAMMER sound	H	Fear of enclosed places	
9	CLANDESTINE	PLAN THIS TIME	I	Limit; confine	
10	CLANGOR	BANGER sound	J	Loud Noise	
11	CLAUSTROPHOBIA	Closer phobia	K	Loud resounding noise	
12	CLEMENCY	MENCY-MERCY	L	Mercy, leniency	
13	CLERGY	A religious CLERK	M	Overused expression	
14	CLICHÉ	In CLASS they SAY cliché	N	People who work in religious ministry	
15	CLOAK	CLOAK-LOCK	O	Politeness, courtesy	
16	CLOISTER	OYSTER in a cloister	P	Quote, commend	
17	CLOYING	Overly LOVING sentiments	Q	Roundabout expression	
18	COAGULATE	COLGATE tooth paste	R	Shut away; seclude	
19	COALESCE	cola + whisky	S	Surround; outwit; baffle	
20	COARSE	CRASS-MASS; no grace	T	Thicken; become clotted	

Answers

EX.NO	1	2	3	4	5	6	7	8	9	10	11	12	13	14	15	16	17	18	19	20
19	I	D	T	N	M	L	B	K	P	H	S	R	J	G	O	F	A	C	E	Q
20	Q	I	A	S	P	O	G	J	F	K	H	L	N	M	C	R	E	T	B	D

WORD GROUPS DAY-5

★ COURAGEOUS

ADJECTIVES: audacious, adventurous, courageous, dauntless, doughty, gallant, intrepid, plucky, valiant, valorous, venturesome, undaunted

NOUNS: bravery, mettle, valor

VERB: venture

ANTONYMS: cowardly, craven, pusillanimous.

★ TIMID/COWARD NATURE

ADJECTIVES: craven, pusillanimous, timid, trepid, timorous; diffident

NOUNS: trepidation, apprehension

VERB: flinch, cringe, recoil, quail, wince, shy

ANTONYMS: adj. bold, brave

★ UNIMPORTANT/INSIGNIFICANT ISSUES

ADJECTIVES: trivial, frivolous, incidental, inconsequential, inconsiderable, insignificant, irrelevant, little, meager, nugatory, paltry, petty, piddling, superficial, trifling; marginal, tangential, peripheral

NOUNS: triviality, inconsequence, non-essential

VERB: trifle with

ANTONYMS: adj. consequential, significant, valuable, weighty, worthwhile

★ IMPORTANT/SIGNIFICANT ISSUES

ADJECTIVES: appreciable, considerable, major, momentous, notable, indispensible, weighty, far-reaching, substantial, significant, serious; crucial, crux, critical, decisive, essential, gist, key, pith, pivotal, salient

NOUNS: consequence, significance, supremacy, preeminence, prominence

VERB: signify

ANTONYMS: adj. insignificant, little, nonessential, trivial, unimportant, unsubstantial

★ NARROW-MINDED/INTOLERANT

ADJECTIVES: conservative, dogmatic, doctrinaire, intolerant, illiberal, insular, hidebound, opinionated, parochial, provincial, prejudiced, bigoted

NOUNS: bigotry, sectarianism, chauvinism, jingoism

VERB:

ANTONYMS: adj. broad-minded, liberal, tolerant

★ BROAD-MINDED

ADJECTIVES: catholic, cosmopolitan, dispassionate, flexible, indulgent, liberal, permissive, progressive, tolerant, unbiased, unprejudiced

NOUNS: liberality

VERB:

ANTONYMS: adj.bigoted, biased

★ SCOLD-SCOLDING

NOUNS: admonishment, castigation, censure, reproach, reproof, remonstration

VERB: admonish, berate, chastise, chide, rebuke, reprimand, reproach, reprove, upbraid

ADJECTIVE: admonitory, reproachful, reproving

ANTONYMS: v. compliment, flatter, praise

Word List Day-6

COAX (KOHKS): v. Persuade (someone) by flattery; tempt

Trigger: 1.COAX-COKES. 2. COAX-COERCE

Trigger Sentence: 1. Guys offer COKES to COAX girls. 2. Don't COERCE children, COAX them.

Sample Sentence: Sheeba managed to *coax* her boss into granting her a months' leave!

CODA (KOH duh): n. Concluding section; finale

Trigger: CODA-COMA

Trigger Sentence: "COMA" —"END of the life"; "CODA"- "END of music".

Sample Sentence: The *coda* of the film fittingly ends as the heroine emerges out of coma.

CODICIL (KOD uh sul): v. A supplement to a will

Trigger: CODICIL-CO ADD WILL

Trigger Sentence: In a CODICIL a clause is ADDED to the WILL.

Sample Sentence: My dad added a *codicil* to the registered will to clarify certain conditions.

COERCE (koh URS): v. Force, compel to do something

Trigger: COERCE-FORCE

Trigger Sentence: COERCE is to FORCE the people to do things.

Sample Sentence: They forced him to obey the orders, but only with great *coercion*.

Related Words: COERCION - n. use of force

COEVAL (koh EE vul): a. Living at the same time as; contemporary

Trigger: 1.COEVAL-RIVAL. 2. COEVAL-"CO-EVOLVE"

Trigger Sentence: 1. All RIVALS are COEVAL; (primeval-primordial; primitive, ancient); (medieval-related to Middle Ages). 2. COEVALS are CO-EVOLVED.

Sample Sentence: Gandhi and Hitler were *coeval,* but they were not rivals.

Related Words: 1. PRIMEVAL - a. ancient; primitive. 2. MEDIEVAL – a. middle ages

COGENT (KOH junt): a. Convincing

Trigger: COGENT- AGENT

Trigger Sentence: Marketing AGENTS have to use COGENT words to sell a product.

Sample Sentence: She presented *cogent* arguments to the jury.

COGITATE (KHAZ uh tayt): v. Contemplate, think over

Trigger: COGITATE-MEDITATE

Trigger Sentence: She reached to a decision only after much COGITATION and MEDITATION.

Sample Sentence: Baba said he was *cogitating* over the meaning of life, while he actually slept!

COGNIZANT (KAWG nu zunt): a. Having knowledge; aware

Trigger: COGNIZANT-RECOGNIZE

Trigger Sentence: I can easily RECOGNIZE; I'm COGNIZANT of it.

Sample Sentence: A child starts to recognize, when *self-cognizance* sets in at 18 to 24 months.

Related Words: INCOGNIZANT - a. lacking knowledge; unaware

COHERENT (koh HEER unt): a. Logically connected; understandable; consistent

    Trigger: 1.coherENT-ENT. 2. COHERENT- CAN HEAR IT

    Trigger Sentence: 1. ENT - "ear, nose and throat are COHERENT"-logically connected. 2. I CAN HEAR IT when you talk COHERENTLY.

    Sample Sentence: Only if mathematical steps are consistent, there will be a *coherent* solution.

    Related Words: INCOHERENT – a. inconsistent; unintelligible

COHESIVE (koh SEE iv): a. Union; well integrated

    Trigger: COHESIVE-ADHESIVE

    Trigger Sentence: When an ADHESIVE is applied the joined parts will be COHESIVE.

    Sample Sentence: The members of the family are *cohesive* and adhere to each other.

    Related Words: COHESION - n. sticking together

COLLABORATE (kuh LAB uh reyt): v. Work together, cooperate

    Trigger: COLLABORATE-COOPERATE

    Trigger Sentence: They COLLABORATED and COOPERATED in the project.

    Sample Sentence: In a *collaborative* effort 28 countries co-operated during the 1990 Gulf-war.

COLLUSION (kuh LOO zhun): n. Conspiracy

    Trigger: 1.COLLUSION-ILLUSION. 2. COLLUDE-DELUDE (refer)

    Trigger Sentence: 1."COLLUSION" is to keep the other people under "FALSE ILLUSION" by scheming and plotting. 2. COLLUSION is a COLLABORATION in doing wrong things.

    Sample Sentence: There was *collusion* among some of the office workers.

    Related Words: COLLUDE - v. cooperate for deceptive purposes.

COLORED (KUHL erd): a. Influence; biased; deceptive

    Trigger: COLORED-preferred COLOR

    Trigger Sentence: The COLORED opinion of the jury favored the white COLORED people.

    Sample Sentence: The lives of most of us are *colored* by politics.

COLOSSUS (kuh LOS uhs): n. Very big statue; something that is huge

    Trigger: 1.COLOSSUS -COLOSSUS OF RHODES. 2.COLOSSUS –COLUMN (HUGE COLUMN)

    Trigger Sentence: A COLOSSUS of Apple at Rhodes is a VERY BIG STATUE and is one of the past Seven Wonders of the World.

    Sample Sentence: We faced *colossus* losses during the recent earth quake.

    Related Words: COLOSSAL – a. enormous; gigantic

COMBATIVE (kom BAT iv): a. Eager to fight

    Trigger: COMBATIVE-"COME+BATTLE"

    Trigger Sentence: Goaliath challenged David to COME for a BATTLE against him in a COMBAT.

    Sample Sentence: With a *combative* courage the activists blocked the roads defying laati charge.

COMELY (KUHM lee): a. Attractive, pretty

    Trigger: 1.COMELY-LOVELY. 2. COMELY-HOMELY

    Trigger Sentence: 1. She is LOVELY & COMELY. 2. COMELY means beautiful where as HOMELY means ugly in Western countries.

    Sample Sentence: The lovely lady was so *comely* that all her suitors were charmed by her.

COMMENDABLE (kuh MEN duh bul): a. Deserving praise

Trigger: 1.COMMEND-RECOMMEND. 2. COMMEND-nice COMMENT

Trigger Sentence: In RECOMMENDATION letters the professor always COMMEND others with NICE COMMENTS.

Sample Sentence: I recommend all employees to follow the *commendable* performance of Tom.

COMMENSURATE (kuh MEN sur it): a. Equal in extent; having a common measure

Trigger: COMMENSURATE-COMMON+MEASURE

Trigger Sentence: 1. When we COMMENSURATE, we have a COMMON-MEASURE. 2. The COMMON MEASURE that COMMENSURATES your salary is your experience.

Sample Sentence: Her new position came with a *commensurate* level of responsibility.

COMMISERATE (kuh MIZ uh reyt): v. Sympathize, empathize, feel sorrow for, pity

Trigger: COMMISERATE-"CO + MISERABLE"

Trigger Sentence: We COMMISERATED with them for their MISERABLE loss.

Sample Sentence: Prasad was drowned in sorrow over his father's death, when his friends came to *commiserate* and pay their condolences.

COMMODIOUS (kuh MOH dee uhs): a.Spacious, comfortable

Trigger: COMMODIOUS-ACCOMMODATE

Trigger Sentence: COMMODIOUS room ACCOMMODATES many people.

Sample Sentence: The limousine is so *commodious* that it accommodates a big family.

COMMONPLACE (KOM un pleys): a. Ordinary, everyday; uninteresting

Trigger: COMMONPLACE-COMMON

Trigger Sentence: COMMONPLACE things are COMMONLY seen

Sample Sentence: Cell phones have become a *commonplace* in the world!

COMMOTION (kuh MOH shun): n. Confusion, turmoil

Trigger: COMMOTION-MOTION (CONFUSED MOTION)

Trigger Sentence: The CONFUSED MOTION of the children created a COMMOTION at the park.

Sample Sentence: I prefer the silence of the fields and forests than the *commotion* of the city.

COMPATIBLE (kum PAT uh bul): a. Harmonious; agreeable

Trigger: COMPATIBLE - COMPANION + ABLE

Trigger Sentence: I have an able COMPANION who is COMPATIBLE with my temperament.

Sample Sentence: Sai and Mai are *compatible*; they both like movies and dogs.

Related Words: INCOMPATIBLE - a. incongruous, unsuitable

COMPELLING (kum PEL ing): a. Powerful; convincing

Trigger: 1. COMPELLING-TELLING. 2. COMPEL-PROPEL-IMPEL

Trigger Sentence: 1. The way she is TELLING is COMPELLING and CONVINCING. 2. COMPEL-IMPEL-PROPEL-----all are forceful.

Sample Sentence: His style of telling stories is so *compelling* that kids do not like to leave him.

Related Words: 1. COMPEL - v. force, influence. 2. IMPEL – v. urge; drive.3. PROPEL- v. push

COMPENDIUM (kum PEN dium): n. A brief summary of a larger work

Trigger: COMPENDIUM-"COMPACT+ END"

Trigger Sentence: COMPACT (contract in size) ENDING reflects the meaning of COMPENDIUM.

Sample Sentence: The author was asked to submit a *compendium* of his book by the publisher.

COMPLACENT (kum PLAY sunt): a. Self-satisfied, overly pleased with oneself

Trigger: COMPLACENT-self PLEASANT

Trigger Sentence: The hare was COMPLACENT and SELF-PLEASANT with his attitude. That is the reason hare lost to the slow moving turtle in the race.

Sample Sentence: The strong financial system has made people *complacent*.

Related Words: COMPLACENCY: n. self-satisfaction; smugness

COMPLAISANT (kum PLAY zunt): a. Willing to please others; obliging

Trigger: 1. comPLAISANT -PLEASANT – PLEASE. 2. COMPLAISANT- COMPLIANT-COMPLY

Trigger Sentence: 1. The host's COMPLAISANT disposition was PLEASANT and PLEASING. 2. COMPLYING attitude is called COMPLAISANT attitude.

Sample Sentence: The host's *complaisant* manner made everyone feel at home.

Related Words: COMPLAISANCE: n. willingness to please.

COMPLEMENT (KAHM pluh munt): v. Complete; be the perfect counterpart

Trigger: 1.COMPLEMENT-COMPLETE. 2. COMPLEMENT-SUPPLEMENT

Trigger Sentence: To get the COMPLETE taste I need some pepper to COMPLEMENT the soup.

Sample Sentence: Perfect couples *complement* each other on looks and in demeanor.

COMPLIANT (kum PLY unt): a. Yielding, ready to comply

Trigger: 1. COMPLiant-COMPLY. 2. COMPLIANT-no COMPLAINT

Trigger Sentence: COMPLIANT people arouse NO COMPLAINTS; they are OBEDIENT

Sample Sentence: It is necessary to be *compliant* with the state traffic laws for your own safety.

Related Words: 1. PLIANT – a. flexible; easily influenced. 2. COMPLY – v. obey

COMPLICITY (kum PLIS uh tee): n. Partnership (in wrongdoing or crime)

Trigger: COMPLICITY-COMPANY

Trigger Sentence: 1. COMPLICITY implies giving COMPANY to a friend in doing wrong things. 2. An ACCOMPLICE ACCOMPANIED with me in a robbery.

Sample Sentence: The *complicity* of the couple in cheating naïve people baffled the police.

Related Words: ACCOMPLICE : n. partner in crime

COMPORT (kum POHRT): v. Behave; bear oneself

Trigger: 1. COMPORT-REPORT. 2. COMPORT-COMPOSE

Trigger Sentence: 1. There is a GOOD REPORT that you COMPORT well with dignity all the time. 2. He COMPORTS himself with COMPOSURE.

Sample Sentence: They *comported* (conducted) themselves well during those difficult times.

COMPOSED (kum POHZD): a. Self-controlled, calm

Trigger: COMPOSED-CALM POSE

Trigger Sentence: The CALM POSE of Buddhist monks reminds me to remain COMPOSED.

Sample Sentence: She finally stopped crying on the death of her dog and *composed* herself.

Related Words: COMPOSE - v. create; calm one-self

COMPOSURE (kum POH zhur): n. Calmness

Trigger: COMPOSURE -CALM + POSE

Trigger Sentence: When I look at the CALM POSTURE of the Buddha, I experience a sense of COMPOSURE.

Sample Sentence: You may feel nervous, but don't lose your *composure* in front of the camera.

Related Words: DISCOMPOSURE: n. confusion, lack of order.

COMPREHEND (kom pri HEND): v. Understand; apprehend

Trigger: COMPREHEND-completely UNDERSTAND

Trigger Sentence: When I COMPREHEND, I completely UNDERSTAND everything.

Sample Sentence: I can *comprehend* from this letter that she has a soft corner for you.

Related Words: 1.MISAPPREHENSION: n. improper understanding.
2.INCOMPREHENSION:n. lack of understanding

COMPREHENSIVE (kom pruh HEN siv): a.Thorough; inclusive, complete

Trigger: COMPREHENSIVE-INTENSIVE & EXTENSIVE

Trigger Sentence: A COMPREHENSIVE education consists of INTENSIVE as well as EXTENSIVE knowledge of a subject.

Sample Sentence: This intensive course with extensive information is meant for a *comprehensive* knowledge.

COMPROMISE (KOM pruh myze): n. 1. To come to agreement by mutual concession (positive sense) 2. Bring into disrepute or danger by reckless behavior (negative sense)

Trigger: 1.COMPROMISE-"COME+PROMISE" (positive sense) 2. Break PROMISE (negative sense)

Trigger Sentence: 1. The two rivals CAME forward and PROMISED to COMPROMISE. 2. The PROMISCUOUS man BROKE the marriage PROMISE and hence COMPROMISED his integrity.

Sample Sentence: 1. They were caught red handed in a *compromising* position! 2. My vote on this issue was a sure *compromise* against my principles.

CONCATENATE (kon KAT n eyt): v. Link together, connect one to another

Trigger: CONCATENATED-CONNECTED

Trigger Sentence: In a pet CONNECTION of a circus show, one cat was CONCATENATED to another cat.

Sample Sentence: Seems like our fates are *concatenated* as we keep bumping into each other.

CONCAVE (kahn KAYV): a.Curving inward; hollow

Trigger: CONCAVE-CAVE

Trigger Sentence: The underground CAVES are in CONCAVE shape.

Sample Sentence: You have lost so much weight that your stomach is almost *concave*!

Related Words: CONVEX (adj): curved outward; arched

CONCEDE (kun SEED): v. Admit; yield

Trigger: 1.CONCEDE-ACCEDE. 2. CONCEDE-SUPERCEDE-SUCCEED

Trigger Sentence: 1. CONCEDE-ACCEDE-ACCEPT are synonyms. 2. SUPERSEDE never CONCEDES and never admits his SURRENDER to lower SEEDED player.

Sample Sentence: Federer superseded Rafael Nadal when he *conceded* defeat due to his injury.

CONCEIT (kon SEET): n. Self love; arrogance; a fanciful notion

Trigger: 1.CONCEIT–SEAT. 2. CONCEIT-CONCEPT

Trigger Sentence: The people who are on SEAT (or in power) exhibit CONCEIT.

Sample Sentence: She is under the *conceit* that she is the most beautiful woman in the world!

CONCEPTION (kun SEP shun): n. Creation; beginning of an idea

Trigger: 1. CONCEPTION-CONTRACEPTION. 2. CONCEPTION-CONCEPT

Trigger Sentence: 1. CONTRACEPTION prevents CONCEPTION of pregnancy .
2. The theoretical CONCEPT of making INCEPTION movie from its CONCEPTION stage it was destined to become huge success.

Sample Sentence: From its *conception* the plan was doomed to failure.

Related Words: CONCEPTUAL: a. relating to mental concepts

CONCILIATE (kun SIL ee eyt): v. Reunite, make friendly; appease; calm; pacify

Trigger: CONCILIATE-"CONCILiate"-"COUNSEL MATE"

Trigger Sentence: The COUNSELOR tried to CONCILIATE the estranged couple (MATES).

Sample Sentence: She managed to *conciliate* the angry customer.

Related Words: RECONCILE - v. settle (a quarrel); reunite.

CONCISE (Kun SYSE): a.Brief; succinct; terse

Trigger: CONCISE-Short SIZE

Trigger Sentence: We were asked to CONCISE the original draft into a SMALL SIZE.

Sample Sentence: I prefer e mails in *concise* format.

CONCOCT (kun KAHKT): v. Invent

Trigger: 1. conCOCT-COCKTAIL. 2. CONCOCT-CONCEPT-CONSTRUCT

Trigger Sentence: 1. A COCKTAIL is CONCOCTED by mixing various alcohols and juices.
2. The CONCEPT for the movie story is CONCOCTED.

Sample Sentence: He *concocted* a plan to get rich the easy way!

CONCOMITANT (kun KAHM uh tunt): a. Occurring together; accompanying

Trigger: CONCOMITANT-CONCURRENT-(CO-OCCURRING)

Trigger Sentence: CONCURRENT things are CONCOMITANT; they CAN COME together and provide COMPANY to each other.

Sample Sentence: Naturally, old age comes with a *concomitant* loss of memory.

CONCORD (KAHN cord): n. Harmony, agreement

Trigger: CONCORD-ACCORD-AGREED

Trigger Sentence: CONCORD and ACCORD (ACCORD means AGREED) are synonyms. The ACCORD brought CONCORDANCE between the warring nations.

Sample Sentence: The sisters are now in *concord* about the toys they will have to share.

Related Words: CONCORDANCE: n. agreement; harmony

CONCUR (kun KER): v. Agree, work together

Trigger: CONCUR-CONCORD (refer)

Trigger Sentence: CONCORD and CONCUR are synonyms

Sample Sentence: Did you *concur* with the decision of the court or did you find it unfair?

CONDENSED (kun DENST): a. Made shorter; reduced to dense form

Trigger: CONDENSED-DENSE

Trigger Sentence: By making it DENSER they released the book in a CONDENSED format.

Sample Sentence: 1.Congress *condensed* the three-year plan into a six-month plan. 2. Gayatri makes tasty- yummy- hot *condensed* soups.

Related Words: DENSE : a. compact; thick; slow

CONDESCEND (KAHN duh send): v. 1. To descend to the level of one considered inferior; humiliate 2. Act in a proud manner

Trigger: 1. conDESCEND-DESCEND. 2. ASCEND-CONDESCEND--DESCEND

Trigger Sentence: When you CONDESCEND, you treat others in a DESCENDING manner.

Sample Sentence: The senior students behave in a *condescending* manner to control the juniors.

CONDIGN (kun DAHYN): a. Well-deserved; merited

Trigger: 1.CONDIGN-CON+DIE+N. 2.CONDIGN-CON +DIGN (dignity)

Trigger Sentence: 1. A death penalty for a CON MAN (convict) is a CONDIGN (well deserved) punishment (CON-DIE-signifies a death penalty for a CON). 2. DIGNITY (the state of being worthy).

Sample Sentence: The captain's bravery awards were conqueringly *condign*.

CONDONE (kun DOHN): v. Forgive, pardon

Trigger: CONDONE-PARDON

Trigger Sentence: 1. When the culprit CONDONED over his actions, the victim felt PARDONING him. 2. AIDS disease PARDONS the people who wear CONDOM.

Sample Sentence: She *condoned* her husband's occasional infidelities.

CONDUCIVE (kun DYOO siv): v. Encouraging, helpful

Trigger: 1.CONDUCE-PRODUCE. 2. CONDUCIVE-CONTRIBUTIVE (** SYNONYMS)

Trigger Sentence: PRODUCE organic food that is CONDUCIVE to better health.

Sample Sentence: The school is creating a *conducive* atmosphere for the adult learners.

CONFER (kun FER): v. Give, grant, or bestow

Trigger: CONFER-OFFER

Trigger Sentence: When we CONFER we OFFER something

Sample Sentence: She *conferred* a knighthood on him.

Related Words: PROFFER: v. offer; propose

CONFINE (kun FAHYN): v. Limit, restrict

Trigger: CONFINE-FINITE

Trigger Sentence: FINITE is LIMITED: INFINITE is UNLIMITED: CONFINE is to keep something within FINITE.

Sample Sentence: I will *confine* my remarks to the subject we came here to discuss.

CONFORMIST (kun FORM ist): n. One who conforms to the established norms.

    Trigger: CONFORM-UNIFORM

    Trigger Sentence: We must CONFORM to the school norms by wearing its UNIFORM.

    Sample Sentence: Wearing uniforms to school is *confirming* to the system's policy.

    Related Words: NONCONFORMIST: n. one who does not conform to conventional values.

CONFOUND (kun FOUND): v. Confuse; puzzle

    Trigger: 1. CONFOUND-CONFUSE. 2. CONFOUND-DUMBFOUND

    Trigger Sentence: 1. I got CONFOUNDED and CONFUSED when identical twins appeared. 2. A solution CAN'T BE FOUND!!! I got CONFOUNDED and DUMFOUNDED.

    Sample Sentence: I got *confounded* between fiction and fact; good and bad; virtue and vice.

    Related Words: CONFOUNDED: a. confused, puzzled, perplexed

CONFRONT (kun FRONT): v. Stand face to face; challenge

    Trigger: CONFRONT-COME FRONT

    Trigger Sentence: The commandant CAME to the FRONT and CONFRONTED the enemy.

    Sample Sentence: It was our plan to *confront* the other team with a show of strength.

    Related Words: CONFRONTATIONAL : a. aggressive, conflicting

CONGENIAL (kun JEAN ee ul): a. Pleasant; friendly

    Trigger: 1. CONGENIAL-GENIAL-JOVIAL. 2. CONGENIAL-CONVIVIAL

    Trigger Sentence: CONGENIAL, CONVIVIAL, JOVIAL, GENIAL are synonyms; He is not only GENIAL and JOVIAL with his family but also CONGENIAL with others.

    Sample Sentence: This atmosphere is so *congenial* and inspiring to work.

CONGRUITY (kun GROO ih tee): n. The quality of agreeing; being suitable

    Trigger: 1.CONGRUENT. 2. CONGRUITY-CONFORMITY (** synonyms)

    Trigger Sentence: CONGRUENT triangles are identical in form; so they AGREE TO EACH OTHER

    Sample Sentence: There is an obvious *congruity* between congruent triangles.

    Related Words: 1.CONGRUENT: a. agreeing. 2. INCONGRUITY: n. inconsistency; lack of harmony.

CONGRUOUS (KONG groo us): a. In agreement or harmony

    Trigger: 1.CONGRUENT. 2. conGRUOUS- GROUPS

    Trigger Sentence: 1. CONGRUOUS, CONGRUENT and CONGRUITY belong to same family. 2. Remember CONGRUENT triangles. They agree each other in all aspects.

    Sample Sentence: The architecture should be in *congruous* with the surrounding environment.

    Related Words: INCONGRUOUS: n. unsuitable; inharmonious

CONNIVE (kuh NYVE): v. Plot, scheme, conspire

    Trigger: CONNIVING-CUNNING

    Trigger Sentence: The CUNNING government CONNIVED in the rebel's military buildup.

    Sample Sentence: They *connived* behind my back to use unethical ways to fight.

CONNOISSEUR (kon uh SUR): n. Expert, aesthete; judge of art

    Trigger: 1.CAN KNOW SIR. 2. CAN KNOW SURE

Trigger Sentence: 1. A CONNOISSEUR CAN know FOR SURE whether this portrait is an original one or a fake. 2. I CAN KNOW from your appearance, SIR that you are a CONNOISSEUR of art.

Sample Sentence: She is not an artist but is an avid *connoisseur* of classical sculpture.

CONNOTATION (kon uh TEY shun): Suggested or implied meaning of an expression

Trigger: CONNOTATION-DENOTATION-NOTATION

Trigger Sentence: 1. DENOTATION represents DIRECT or DICTIONARY meaning; CONNOTATION represents IMPLIED meaning. 2. CONNOTATION is inference of something with indirect NOTATION or DENOTATION.

Sample Sentence: The title "Doctor" doesn't always *connote* a medical degree.

Related Words: DENOTATION: n. indication; definition

CONSANGUINITY (kon sang GWIN i tee): n. Kinship, connection

Trigger: 1.con + sang +UNITY .2. CONSANGUINITY-COMMUNITY

Trigger Sentence: There is UNITY in CONSANGUINITY.

Sample Sentence: *Consanguinity* is important among people for a harmonious community.

CONSCIENTIOUS (kon see EN shus): a. Thorough and assiduous; careful

Trigger: 1. CONSCIENTIOUS-SCIENTISTS. 2. CONSCIENTIOUS-CONSCIENCE

Trigger Sentence: 1. SCIENTISTS are CONSCIENTIOUS before they make their hypotheses public. They are very CAUTIOUS and CAREFUL. 2. CONSCIENTIOUS individuals follow their CONSCIENCE.

Sample Sentence: Every inch of the space ship was *conscientiously* examined by the NASA.

CONSENSUS (kun SEN sus): n. General agreement

Trigger: 1.conSENSUS-SENSE. 2. CONSENSUS-CONSONANCE (** near synonyms)

Trigger Sentence: CONSENSUS arises when there is a SENSE of unity among all members.

Sample Sentence: The committee members came to a *consensus* and closed the issue.

CONSENT (kun SENT): v. Agree; approve

Trigger: CONSENT-CONSENSUS-SAME SENSE-SAME SENTI

Trigger Sentence: When we CONSENT (combined sentiments) there will be CONSENSUS.

Sample Sentence: The CEO has given his *consent* for the new project launch.

CONSEQUENTIAL (kon si KWEN shul): a. Resultant, subsequent, important

Trigger: SEQUENCE

Trigger Sentence: 1. In a SEQUENCE one thing FOLLOWS other. 2. SEQUENCE is MOST IMPORTANT in a playing card game.

Sample Sentence: *Consequential* to the weakening of the economy of USSR, many East European communist governments collapsed in a sequence.

Related Words: INCONSEQUENTIAL: a. unimportant, insignificant

CONSERVATISM (kon SUR va tizm n): Desire to preserve traditions, resistance to change

Trigger: CONSERVE-PRESERVE

Trigger Sentence: CONSERVATISM tries to CONSERVE and PRESERVE the existing culture of the society; like Hinduism-Islamism-Conservatism.

Sample Sentence: Surya knew, his English girl friend will clash with his parent's *conservatism*.

Related Words: CONSERVATIVE: a. resisting changing; cautious

CONSIDERABLE (kun SID er uh bul): a. Substantial, Notably large

Trigger: CONSIDERABLE-CAN SIZABLE

Trigger Sentence: CONSIDERABLE and SIZABLE are synonyms

Sample Sentence: We received *considerable* number of complaints, to act on the problem.

Related Words: 1.INCONSIDERATE: v. unkind; heedless. 2. CONSIDER : v. regard

CONSIDERATE (kun SID er it): a. Thoughtful; respectful; kind

Trigger: CONSIDERATE-CAN SIDE

Trigger Sentence: He is on my SIDE always!!! He is quite CONSIDERATE towards me.

Sample Sentence: To me, he was always quiet and calm, soft spoken and always *considerate*.

Related Words: 1.INCONSIDERATE: a. unkind; heedless .2. CONSIDER: v. think over; believe.

CONSOLE (kun SOHL): v. Lessen the suffering of; encourage

Trigger: CONSOLE- CALM SOUL

Trigger Sentence: Her SOUL was CALMED down when he CONSOLED her

Sample Sentence: He *consoled* the widow.

Related Words: 1.SOLACE: v. comfort; console. 2. CONDOLE: v. express sympathy

CONSOLIDATE (kun SAHL uh dayt): v. Make stronger or more solid, merge

Trigger: 1.conSOLIDate-SOLID .2.CONSOLIDATE-"COMBINE SOLIDS"

Trigger Sentence: 1. CONSOLIDATE is to make more SOLID and STRONG. 2. COMBINE two SOLIDS for a MERGER.

Sample Sentence: Israel *consolidated* its position amidst Arab countries with support from USA.

Related Words: CONSOLIDATION: n. strengthening; unification

CONSPICUOUS (kun SPIK yoo us): a. Noticeable, easy to see

Trigger: CONSPICUOUS-CAN SEE PICS

Trigger Sentence: I CAN SEE PICS (pictures) of a heroine; they are CONSPICUOUS to my eye.

Sample Sentence: Can you see these pics? Aren't they *conspicuous*?

Related Words: INCONSPICUOUS: v. unnoticeable, unobtrusive

CONSPIRACY (kun SPEER uh see): n. Plot; secret plan

Trigger: CONSPIRACY- CON +SPY+ PRIVACY

Trigger Sentence: The intelligence team uncovered the SPY CONSPIRACY.

Sample Sentence: The French revolution was a *conspiracy* to overthrow the ruling royalty.

CONSTERNATION (kahn stur NAY shun): n. Fear or dismay

Trigger: CONSTERNATION- MONSTER+ NATION

Trigger Sentence: The MONSTER has created the CONSTERNATION in the NATION.

Sample Sentence: Much to her parents' *consternation*, she has decided to become an actress.

CONSTRAINT (kun STREYNT): n. Compulsion; repression of feelings

Trigger: 1.CONSTRAIN-RESTRAIN-RESTRICT. 2. STRAIN

Trigger Sentence: 1. CONSTRAIN is to RESTRAIN and RESTRAIN is to RESTRICT or LIMIT. 2. Don't RESTRICT him. Talent cannot be CONSTRAINED for long.

Sample Sentence: After two pegs of whisky, they were able to talk without *constraint*.

Related Words: CONSTRICT : v. make smaller, tighten

CONSTRICT (kun STRIKT): v. squeeze; compress; restrict the freedom of

Trigger: 1.CONSTRICT- CONTRACT (** synonyms).2. CONSTRICT-RESTRICT-STRICT

Trigger Sentence: 1. Her throat CONSTRICTED/CONTRACTED. 2. The declining economy has CONSTRICTED job opportunities and RESTRICTED the financial resources.

Sample Sentence: The students were *constricted* from going out of the college campus.

Related Words: RESTRICT: v. limit; constrict; curb

CONSTRUE (kun STROO): v. Interpret; explain

Trigger: CONSTRUE-CONSTRUCT-INSTRUCT

Trigger Sentence: How to CONSTRUCT my house?? Then the architect INSTRUCTOR CONSTRUES.

Sample Sentence: What message do you *construe* in this letter?

Related Words: MISCONSTRUE: v. misinterpret; misunderstand

CONSUMMATE (KON sum it): v. Perfect, fulfill, complete

Trigger: CONSUMMATE-CAN+SUMMIT

Trigger Sentence: 1.Their happiness CONSUMMATED by reaching SUMMIT of Mount Everest. 2. He reached the SUMMIT of the Mount Everest with CONSUMMATE mountaineering skill.

Sample Sentence: I make stupid errors; you are a *consummate* idiot.

Memory Test-21 : Match each word and its memory trick to the corresponding definition.

S.N	WORD	MEMORY TRIGGER	S.N	DEFINITIONS	KEY
1	COAX	COKES to COAX girls	A	Attractive, pretty	
2	CODA	Coma —END of the life	B	Biased; influence	
3	CODICIL	co add will	C	Concluding section; finale	
4	COERCE	Coerce is to FORCE	D	Conspiracy ; secret agreement	
5	COEVAL	CO-EVOLVE	E	Contemplate, think over	
6	COGENT	Marketing AGENTS are	F	Convincing	
7	COGITATE	Meditate	G	Deserving praise	
8	COGNIZANT	RECOGNIZE	H	Eager to fight	
9	COHERENT	CAN HEAR IT	I	Force, compel to do something	
10	COHESIVE	Adhesive	J	Having a common measure; equal	
11	COLLABORATE	COOPERATE	K	Having knowledge; aware	
12	COLLUSION	CO- ILLUSION to deceive	L	Living at the same time	
13	COLORED	preferred COLOR	M	Persuade by flattery; tempt	
14	COLOSSUS	Colossus of Rhodes	N	Spacious, comfortable	
15	COMBATIVE	COME+BATTLE	O	Supplement to a will	
16	COMELY	LOVELY looking	P	Sympathize, feel sorrow for	
17	COMMENDABLE	Recommend	Q	Understandable; consistent	
18	COMMENSURATE	COMMON+MEASURE	R	Union; well integrated	
19	COMMISERATE	Co + miserable	S	Very big statue; huge	
20	COMMODIOUS	Accommodate	T	Work together, cooperate	

Memory Test-22 : Match each word and its memory trick to the corresponding definition.

S.N	WORD	MEMORY TRIGGER	S.N	DEFINITIONS	KEY
1	COMMONPLACE	COMMONLY seen	A	1. agree. 2. bring into disrepute	
2	COMMOTION	The Confused MOTION	B	Admit; yield	
3	COMPATIBLE	COMPANION + ABLE	C	Arrogance; self love; a fanciful notion	
4	COMPELLING	TELLING with force	D	Behave; bear oneself	
5	COMPENDIUM	COMPACT+ END	E	Brief summary of a larger work	
6	COMPLACENT	self PLEASANT	F	Calm, Self-controlled	
7	COMPLAISANT	PLEASANT; complying	G	Calmness	
8	COMPLEMENT	COMPLETE-supplement	H	Complete; make perfect	
9	COMPLIANT	NO COMPLAINTS-comply	I	Confusion, turmoil	
10	COMPLICITY	Provide COMPANY	J	Connect one to another	
11	COMPORT	At Airport comport well	K	Curving inward; hollow	
12	COMPOSED	CALM POSE	L	Harmonious; agreeable	
13	COMPOSURE	CALM + POSE	M	Ordinary, everyday; uninteresting	
14	COMPREHEND	Understand	N	Partnership (wrongdoing)	
15	COMPREHENSIVE	Intensive & extensive	O	Powerful; convincing	
16	COMPROMISE	We compromised	P	Self-satisfied	
17	CONCATENATE	CONNECT	Q	Thorough; inclusive, complete	
18	CONCAVE	CAVE shape	R	Understand; apprehend	
19	CONCEDE	Concede-accede-cede	S	Willing to please others; obliging	
20	CONCEIT	people who are on SEAT	T	Yielding, ready to comply	

Answers

EX.NO	1	2	3	4	5	6	7	8	9	10	11	12	13	14	15	16	17	18	19	20
21	M	C	O	I	L	F	E	K	Q	R	T	D	B	S	H	A	G	J	P	N
22	M	I	L	O	E	P	S	H	T	N	D	F	G	R	Q	A	J	K	B	C

Memory Test-23 : Match each word and its memory trick to the corresponding definition.

S.N	WORD	MEMORY TRIGGER	S.N	DEFINITIONS	KEY
1	CONCEPTION	CONCEPTUAL stage	A	Agree, work together	
2	CONCILIATE	COUNSEL- MATE	B	Brief; succinct; terse	
3	CONCISE	Small size	C	Conforms to the established norms	
4	CONCOCT	New COCKTAIL	D	Confuse; puzzle	
5	CONCOMITANT	Concurrent	E	Creation; beginning of an idea	
6	CONCORD	Concord-accord-agreed	F	Encouraging, helpful	
7	CONCUR	CONCORD - CONCUR	G	Forgive, pardon	
8	CONDENSED	making it DENSER	H	Give, grant, or bestow	
9	CONDESCEND	DESCENDING manner	I	Harmony, agreement	
10	CONDIGN	DIGNITY is good	J	In agreement or harmony	
11	CONDONE	Please PARDON	K	Invent	
12	CONDUCIVE	CONTRIBUTIVE	L	Limit, restrict	
13	CONFER	OFFER	M	Lower oneself ; act proudly	
14	CONFINE	Within FINITE	N	Occurring together; accompanying	
15	CONFORMIST	We must CONFORM	O	Pleasant; friendly	
16	CONFOUND	Confuse	P	Reduced to dense form; made shorter	
17	CONFRONT	COME FRONT	Q	Reunite; appease	
18	CONGENIAL	Genial-jovial	R	Stand face to face; challenge	
19	CONGRUITY	CONGRUENT triangles	S	The quality of agreeing; being suitable	
20	CONGRUOUS	Congruous- GROUPS	I	Well-deserved; merited	

Memory Test-24 : Match each word and its memory trick to the corresponding definition.

S.N	WORD	MEMORY TRIGGER	S.N	DEFINITIONS	KEY
1	CONNIVE	Conniving- Cunning	A	Agree; approve	
2	CONNOISSEUR	CAN KNOW SIR	B	Complete; perfect; fulfill	
3	CONNOTATION	Implied NOTATION	C	Desire to preserve traditions	
4	CONSANGUINITY	COMMUNITY	D	Easy to see , noticeable	
5	CONSCIENTIOUS	Scientists are CONSCIENTIOUS	E	Expert ; judge of art	
6	CONSENSUS	SENSE of unity	F	Fear or dismay	
7	CONSENT	Same sense-same senti	G	General agreement	
8	CONSEQUENTIAL	SEQUENCE	H	implied meaning of an expression	
9	CONSERVATISM	PRESERVE the existing	I	Interpret; explain	
10	CONSIDERABLE	SIZABLE	J	Kinship, connection	
11	CONSIDERATE	He considers	K	Lessen the suffering of ; encourage	
12	CONSOLE	CALM SOUL	L	Make stronger or more solid	
13	CONSOLIDATE	make more SOLID	M	Plot, scheme, conspire	
14	CONSPICUOUS	CAN SEE PICS	N	Plot; secret plan	
15	CONSPIRACY	SPY plan	O	Respectful; kind ; thoughtful	
16	CONSTERNATION	MONSTER threatens	P	Restriction; repression	
17	CONSTRAINT	Restrain-restrict	Q	Squeeze; restrict the freedom of	
18	CONSTRICT	CONTRACT in size	R	Subsequent, important	
19	CONSTRUE	He INSTRUCTS	S	Substantial, Notably large	
20	CONSUMMATE	CAN+SUMMIT- sum it	T	Thorough and assiduous; careful	

Answers

EX.NO	1	2	3	4	5	6	7	8	9	10	11	12	13	14	15	16	17	18	19	20
23	E	Q	B	K	N	I	A	P	M	T	G	F	H	L	C	D	R	O	S	J
24	M	E	H	J	T	G	A	R	C	S	O	K	L	D	N	F	P	Q	I	B

WORD GROUPS DAY-6

★ FLATTERY

ADJECTIVES: obsequious, groveling, ingratiating, sycophancy, servile, unctuous

NOUNS: adulation, blandishments, fawning, blarney, cajolery

VERB: cajole, coax, inveigle, wheedle, persuade, serenade

ANTONYMS: v. criticize, condemn, insult, offend, reject

★ LIVELY NATURE

ADJECTIVES: agile, alert, animated, blithe, blithesome, buoyant, bustling, effervescent, enterprising, frolicsome, jocund, keen, merry, nimble, snappy, spirited, sprightly, spry, vibrant, vigorous, vivacious, vivid.

NOUNS: liveliness, vim, vigor, vitality.

VERB: bask, enjoy, relish savor

ANTONYMS: apathetic, dispirited, inactive, lethargic

★ SLOW-LAZY NATURE

ADJECTIVES: apathetic, listless, slothful, sluggish, languid, torpid

NOUNS: hesitation, indolence, inertia, languor, lassitude, lethargy, reluctance, tardiness, torpor

VERB: dawdle, dally, laze, linger, loiter, saunter, plod, trudge

ANTONYMS: v. hurry, haste, expedite, precipitate

★ EVERYDAY-ROUTINE THINGS

ADJECTIVES: banal, mundane, hackneyed, clichéd, pedestrian, prosaic, vapid, commonplace, ordinary, conventional, orthodox, stereotyped, stale, stock, trite, tired, unoriginal, uninteresting, unremarkable, bland, insipid, humdrum, dull

NOUNS: platitude, cliché, banality, bromide

VERB: typecast, conventionalize

ANTONYMS: adj. original, imaginative, extraordinary

★ ORIGINALITY-NOVELTY

ADJECTIVES: innovative, creative, imaginative, novel, refreshing; avant-garde, unusual, unconventional, unorthodox, pioneering, unique, distinctive

NOUNS: ingenuity, novelty

VERB: pioneer, originate

ANTONYMS: adj. banal, time-worn

★ RUDE BEHAVIOR

ADJECTIVES: impolite, coarse, discourteous, disrespectful, impertinent, insolent, impudent, sassy; churlish, curt, brusque, brash, derogatory, uncivil.

NOUNS: boor, churl, lout

VERB: insult, humiliate, affront

ANTONYMS: adj. courteous, polite, urbane, genteel.

★ POLITENESS

ADJECTIVES: courteous, mannerly, deferential, well bred, genteel, gracious, urbane; tactful, diplomatic, sophisticated, refined

NOUNS: nicety, chivalry, courtesy, urbanity

VERB: court

ANTONYMS: adj. rude, uncivilized

Word List Day-7

CONTEMPLATE (KON tem playt): v. To consider carefully; look at thoughtfully

Trigger: 1. CONTEMPLATE-TEMPLE. 2. CONCENTRATE

Trigger Sentence: 1. In a TEMPLE a Sadhu was CONTEMPLATING/MEDITATING on the inner god. 2. When we CONTEMPLATE, we usually CONCENTRATE on an issue.

Sample Sentence: Concentrate, to *contemplate* on difficult scientific ideas like 'time travel'.

CONTEMPT (kum TEMPT): v. Disdain; disrespect

Trigger: CONTEMPT-CONTEMN- CONDEMN

Trigger Sentence: One should CONDEMN racial segregation. It is showing CONTEMPT toward your fellow human being.

Sample Sentence: I have developed *contempt* against my lazy workers.

Related Words: 1.CONTEMPTIBLE - a. despicable; nasty. 2. CONTEMPTUOUS- a. insulting

CONTEND (kun TEND): v. Compete; struggle

Trigger: CONTEND-CONTEST

Trigger Sentence: In an election CONTEST, he CONTENDS for the president post.

Sample Sentence: He *contends* against a mighty opponent.

CONTENTION (kun TEN shun): n. Contest; Conflict

Trigger: conTENTION-TENSION

Trigger Sentence: An Election CONTEST gives lot of TENSION and leads to CONFLICT between the people.

Sample Sentence: The *contention* between USA and USSR athletes used to create tension in the Olympics.

CONTENTIOUS (kun TEN shus): a.Quarrelsome

Trigger: CONTENTIOUS-CONTEST-CONTROVERSIAL

Trigger Sentence: Election CONTESTS are CONTENTIOUS in nature

Sample Sentence: Made for each other, husband is quarrelsome and wife equally *contentious*.

CONTEST (KON test): n.Dispute, competition, match

Trigger: CONTEST-(election) CONTEST

Trigger Sentence: Imagine a boxing CONTEST or an election CONTEST... where there is a dispute.

Sample Sentence: The two contestants are eagerly awaiting the results of the *contest*.

CONTIGUOUS (kun TIG yoo us): a.Touching; Adjacent

Trigger: CONTIGUOUS-CONTINUOUS

Trigger Sentence: CONTIGUOUS things are CONTINUOUS in nature

Sample Sentence: The *contiguous* border of China and Mongolia continuous for thousands of kilometres.

CONTINGENT (kun tin JUNT): a.Dependent upon, happening by chance; n. representative group

Trigger: 1. CONTINGENT-"CO+TANGENT". 2. CONTINGENT-CONTINENT+GENTS

Trigger Sentence: 1. It is CONTINGENT upon the placement of two circles whether the line is a COMMON TANGENT. 2. The CONTINGENT of Indian SUB-CONTINENT GENTS (Indian CONTINGENT) is gathering in USA.

Sample Sentence: 1. a. The merger of the two companies is *contingent* upon Government's approval. 2. n. A *contingent* of firemen was swiftly dispatched to the fire accident location.

CONTRADICTION (kon truh DIK shun): n.Statement opposite to what was already said

Trigger: CONTRAdiction-CONTRA-CONTRAST

Trigger Sentence: The statement like "he is brave and he is not brave" is a CONTRADICTION.

Sample Sentence: A *contradiction* arises when there is a contrast of opinions among people.

Related Words: 1.CONTRADICT - v.deny, refute, oppose. 2. CONTRARY – a. opposed; contradictory

CONTRAVENE (kon truh VEEN): a.Oppose; contradict

Trigger: 1. CONTROVERSY. 2. CONTRA-; COUNTER-; CONTRO

Trigger Sentence: 1. If you CONTRAVENE with our proposal, it will spark a CONTROVERSY. 2. Prefixes which start with "CONTRA-;" "COUNTER-;" "CONTRO-:" provide OPPOSE sense

Sample Sentence: The advocate's counter argument *contravenes* the public prosecutor.

CONTRITE (kun TRITE): a.Penitent; sorry

Trigger: CONTRITE-"CAN'T-RIGHT"

Trigger Sentence: I CAN'T make it RIGHT; I'm WRONG and now I feel CONTRITE and SORRY about it.

Sample Sentence: Asha's *contrite* tears had no affect on the judge while imposing penalty.

Related Words: CONTRITION - n.regret

CONTRIVED (kun TRYVED): a.Forced; artificial; not spontaneous

Trigger: 1.CONTRIVING-CUNNING. 2. CONTRIVE-CONCEIVE

Trigger Sentence: 1. CONTRIVING, CONNIVING and CUNNING are synonyms. 2. CONTRIVE is to CONCEIVE an idea to DECEIVE the people.

Sample Sentence: His behavior is *contrived*. I doubt that he is a cunning person.

CONTROVERT (KON truh vurt): v.Refute; oppose, challenge

Trigger: 1.CONTROVERT-CONTRADICT. 2. "CONTRA-;"- "CONTRO-;"- "COUNTER"

Trigger Sentence: In a COUNTER ACT they CONTRADICTED/CONTROVERTED my statement.

Sample Sentence: The lawyer's counter argument *controverts* all evidence.

Related Words: INCONTROVERTIBLE - a.impossible to debate

CONTUMACIOUS (kon tyoo MAY shus): a.Rebellious; head strong

Trigger: CONTUMACIOUS-"CANT + MAKE + US"

Trigger Sentence: 1. You CAN'T MAKE US to do anything; we are CONTUMACIOUS and REBELLIOUS people. 2. INTIMACY (close friendship) doesn't lead to CONTUMACY (disobedience)

Sample Sentence: The *contumacious* mob shouted defiantly at the police.

Related Words: 1.CONTUMACY - n.obstinacy, disobedience. 2.CONTUMELY- a. rudeness

CONTUMELY (kun TOO muh lee): n. Rudeness; contemptuous behavior

Trigger: CONTUMELY- CONTEMPTIBLY

Trigger Sentence: They yelled CONTEMPTIBLE language in retaliation when the rival heaped CONTUMELY on them.

Sample Sentence: The senior scientists *contumely* snubbed the junior scientist at the seminar.

CONUNDRUM (kuh NUN drum): n.Difficult problem; dilemma
Trigger: CONUNDRUM-"CO-NONE-DRUM"
Trigger Sentence: NO OTHER DRUM is available in the company; so for a DRUMMER, to beat on a SINGLE DRUM is going to be a CONUNDRUM.
Sample Sentence: Dancer Pradeesh was in a *conundrum* when the judges asked him to choreograph an abstract dance depicting the nebulas in the space!

CONVALESCE (kahn vul EHS): v. Recover, get well after sickness
Trigger: CONVALESCE-CAN WELL SICK
Trigger Sentence: He is CONVALESCING from his leg injuries. He CAN soon become WELL after this SICKNESS by physiotherapy treatment.
Sample Sentence: After his heart attack, he went through a period of *convalescence* at home.

CONVENTIONAL (kun VEN shu nl): a.Ordinary; routine; formal
Trigger: 1. CONVENTIONAL-CONVENT+TRADITIONAL. 2. UNCONVENTIONAL-UNUSUAL
Trigger Sentence: 1. CONVENTIONAL people follow TRADITIONAL (old & routine) methods. 2. In a CONVENT, nuns follow CONVENTIONAL rules.
Sample Sentence: Our *conventional* behavior stems from our traditional beliefs.
Related Words: UNCONVENTIONAL - a.unusual

CONVERGE (kun VERJ): v.Meet, come together
Trigger: CONVFRGE-"COME + MERGE"
Trigger Sentence: Come let us MERGE, we CONVERGE
Sample Sentence: The two roads merge gradually, and *converge* into one at the Y junction.
Related Words: DIVERGE - v.to move in different direction.

CONVERSE (KAHN vurs): n.Opposite
Trigger: CONVERSE-REVERSE
Trigger Sentence: CONVERSE is to give a REVERSE statement
Sample Sentence: The couple is completly *converse*. Their relationship has turned worse.

CONVICTION (kun VIK shin): n.A determined belief, declaration of guilt (*second sense)
Trigger: conVICTion-VICTORY
Trigger Sentence: If you have CONVICTION in yourself, VICTORY is yours.
Sample Sentence: With *conviction* and confidence the orator took to the mike and enthralled all.
Related Words: CONVICT - v.declare guilty

CONVIVIAL (kun VIV ee ul): a.Friendly; cheerful, jolly
Trigger: 1.CONVIVIAL-JOVIAL .2.CONVIVIAL-CARNIVAL
Trigger Sentence: 1. CONVIVIAL people are JOVIAL and FRIENDLY. 2. The CONVIVIAL people created a CARNIVAL atmosphere.
Sample Sentence: The *convivial* atmosphere in the carnival was electrifying.

CONVOKE (kun VOHK): v.Call together, call to meeting, summon
Trigger: 1.CONVOKE-CONVENE. 2. CONVOKE-CONVOCATION
Trigger Sentence: The students were CONVOKED in the auditorium for CONVOCATION
Sample Sentence: An emergency *convoke* was held by the management to handle the crisis.

CONVOLUTED (KAHN vuh loo tid): a.Twisted; involved, intricate

Trigger: 1.CONVOLUTED-REVOLVED. 2. CONVOLUTED-COMPLICATED

Trigger Sentence: 1. A problem has been REVOLVED/TWISTED ... and it has now become CONVOLUTED and COMPLICATED. 2. CONVOLUTION problem INVOLVES lot of complexity

Sample Sentence: The theory is *convoluted*. Readers find it very complicated to comprehend.

Related Words: INVOLVED - a.complicated

COPIOUS (KOH pee us): a.Bountiful; abundant, plentiful

Trigger: 1.COPIOUS-COPIES. 2. COPIOUS-COUNTLESS

Trigger Sentence: I've COPIOUS and COUNTLESS amounts of COPIES

Sample Sentence: She has a *copious* number of copies of this text material.

CORDIAL (KOR jul): a.Friendly; warm; heartfelt

Trigger: 1.CORDIAL-CARD. 2. CORDIAL-CONVIVIAL- CONGENIAL

Trigger Sentence: 1. The CORDIAL couple sent me an invitation CARD for their marriage anniversary. 2. CONGENIAL, CONVIVIAL, and CORDIAL are synonyms.

Sample Sentence: The management at the hotel reception is quite *cordial* and helpful.

CORNUCOPIA (kor nyoo KOH pee uh): n. Abundance, plenty; a symbol of plenty

Trigger: CORNUCOPIA-"CORN + COPIOUS" (refer)

Trigger Sentence: Farmers are growing CORNUCOPIA of CORN for COPIOUS amount of people.

Sample Sentence: There is a *cornucopia* of creative energy among the young and restless.

COROLLARY (kuh ROL uh ree): a.Something that naturally follows; result

Trigger: COROLLARY- CO ROLL

Trigger Sentence: Blind jealousy is a frequent COROLLARY of passionate love. Jealousy ROLLS just behind love.

Sample Sentence: During winter nights, fog is a sort of *corollary* to darkness.

CORPOREAL (kawr PAWR ee ul): a.Bodily; material

Trigger: 1.CORPOREAL-MATERIAL. 2. CORPOREAL-CORPORATION (BODY)

Trigger Sentence: 1. All MATERIAL things are CORPOREAL; corp-, corporation, corpse (dead body) all are related to body. 2. A registered corporation has a *corporeal* existence in the eye of the Companies Law of 1956.

Sample Sentence: He was not a churchgoer; he was interested only in *corporeal* matters.

CORPULENT (KOR pew lent): a.Fat, obese

Trigger: 1.CORPulent. 2. CORPULENT-CORPORAL

Trigger Sentence: 1. CORPULENT people can eat entire CROP of a year. 2. Corporal-material; bodily; corporation-business body; corpulent person possess lot of physical body.

Sample Sentence: I dread being *corpulent* because it's in my genes. So I am a cautious eater!

CORROBORATE (kuh ROB uh rayt): v.Confirm; support with evidence

Trigger: CORROBORATE-"CO+ ROBBERS" -COOPERATE.

Trigger Sentence: 1. The ROBBERS & CO, CORROBORATE each other in the movies like "ocean- 11", "ocean- 12" etc. 2. CORROBORATION and CONFIRMATION are synonyms.

Sample Sentence: If you cooperate, I can easily *corroborate* evidence to support this hypothesis.

COSMOPOLITAN (kahz muh PAHL uh tun): a.Sophisticated; related to the whole world.
  Trigger: COSMOPOLITAN-COSMOPOLITE-POLITE
  Trigger Sentence: You should learn how to be POLITE if want to be a part of a COSMOPOLITAN culture.
  Sample Sentence: Hong Kong is a *cosmopolitan* city with people from all over the world.

COUNTENANCE (KOWNT uh nanz): n./ v.(n) Appearance; face, (v) Tolerate; support
  Trigger: 1. COUNTENANCE-"COUNT+NUNS". 2. COUNTENANCE-COUNTER STANCE
  Trigger Sentence: 1. (n) COUNT how many NUNS are there; When someone ENCOUNTERS remember their COUNTENANCE. 2. (v) COUNTER (COUNTER-ATTACKED) and COUNTENANCE are antonym variants. The COUNTENANCE of Russia is usually a COUNTER STANCE to USA.
  Sample Sentence: The *countenance* of the innocent nun made every patient chrish her help.

COUNTERFEIT (KOUN ter fit): a.Forged, fake, false
  Trigger: COUNTERFEIT-COUNTER FAKE
  Trigger Sentence: In a bank COUNTER many COUNTERFEIT (FAKE) dollar bills were detected
  Sample Sentence: *Counterfeit* currency was detected by the bank officials.

COUNTERMAND (koun ter MAND). v.Cancel an order
  Trigger: COUNTERMAND-"COUNTER + COMMAND"
  Trigger Sentence: COMMAND is an ORDER; COUNTER means AGAINST; i.e. "cancel a previous order".
  Sample Sentence: The judge *countermanded* the counter argument.

COUNTERPOINT (KOUN ter point): n.Emphasize by contrast
  Trigger: COUNTERPOINT-COUNTER
  Trigger Sentence: The violence of the movie is COUNTERPOINTED by ironic humor
  Sample Sentence: She *countered* the discrimination of caste politics in the society.
  Related Words: 1. COUNTERBALANCE - v.adjust or make up for; oppose and mitigate the effects of by contrary actions. 2. COUNTEREXAMPLE - n.example that refutes a theory or claim. 3. COUNTERINTUITIVE - a. contrary to what common sense would suggest. 4.COUNTERPART - n. things very much alike; a thing that completes another. 5. COUNTERPRODUCTIVE - a. nonadvantageous, hindering the attainment of a goal. 6.COUNTERWEIGHT - n. an equivalent counterbalancing weight. 7. ENCOUNTER - v. face; clash

COUP (KOO): n. A victorious accomplishment; sudden attack
  Trigger: 1.COUP-TRAP. 2. COUP-TROUP
  Trigger Sentence: A TROUPE (military) applies a TRAP in a COUP to overthrow the established government.
  Sample Sentence: The killing of Osama Bin Laden was a *Coup* employed by US.

COURT (KOHRT): v. Seek to gain; seek love
  Trigger: COURT-HEART-SWEET HEART
  Trigger Sentence: I COURT my date; I COURT my sweet HEART.
  Sample Sentence: He was courting his college sweetheart.
  Related Words: COURTESY - n. politeness

COVERT (KOH vert): a. Secret, hidden
    Trigger: COVERT-COVERED
    Trigger Sentence: Spies usually operate COVERTLY by COVERING their faces
    Sample Sentence: The *covert* covered his activities under the guise of religion.
    Related Words: OVERT – a. visible; undisguised

COVETOUS (KOW it us): a. Having a great desire; greedy, envious
    Trigger: COVET+OUS- LOVE AT US
    Trigger Sentence: I COVET her means, I LOVE TO have her.
    Sample Sentence: He has a *covetous* eye on the dancer as he loves her graceful movements.

COWER (KOW ur): v. Shrink with fear
    Trigger:1.COWER-FEAR. 2. COWER- COWARD FEAR
    Trigger Sentence: 1. To shrink with FEAR is known as COWER. 2. The COWARD COWERED to pressure.
    Sample Sentence: Oh! Stop *cowering* dear doggie, I am only applying medicine on your wound.

COZEN (KUHZ un): v. Cheat; deceive
    Trigger: COzeN-CON GENT
    Trigger Sentence: The CON GENT or con man COZENED several elderly ladies into believing that he was intending marriage.
    Sample Sentence: How could he *cozen* the poor old man for money!

CRAFTY (KRAF tee): a. Cunning, deceptive
    Trigger: CRAFT-ART-ARTFUL
    Trigger Sentence: CRAFTY and ARTFUL guys are skillful, but in a derogatory sense; they possess CUNNING SKILL.
    Sample Sentence: Pick-pocketing is so *crafty*, that a pick-picketer should be a master of this art.

CRASS (KRAS): a. Rude, ill-mannered
    Trigger: 1.CRASS-MASS. 2. CRASS-NO CLASS
    Trigger Sentence: 1. MASS people are CRASS minded. 2. CRASS minded people have NO CLASS; they are identified with GROSS mentality.
    Sample Sentence: If the film should appeal to mass, the character of the hero should be *crass*.

CRAVEN (KRA ven): a. Fearful, cowardly; dastard
    Trigger: CRAVEN- BRAVE +N
    Trigger Sentence: CRAVEN and BRAVE are antonyms.
    Sample Sentence: How can a *craven* stranger keep a brave countenance?!

CREDENCE (KREED ns): n. Belief, credit
    Trigger: 1.CREDENCE-CREED (ref). 2. CREDENCE-CONFIDENCE (** synonyms)
    Trigger Sentence: A CREED (Hindu BREED-Hindu BELIEF) has CREDENCE/CONFIDENCE to its religion.
    Sample Sentence: The confident contestant gave *credence* to the people for supporting him.
    Related Words: 1.CREED – n. faith; religion. 2. CREDO - n. any system of beliefs

CREDIBLE (KRED uh bul): n. Reliable; dependable
    Trigger: CREDIBLE-RELIABLE
    Trigger Sentence: CREDIBLE and RELIABLE are synonyms.
    All CRED-; CREED-; prefixes are associated with *belief, trust and faith.*
    Sample Sentence: We buy ornaments from this *credible* and skillful goldsmith.
    Related Words: INCREDIBLE - a. unbelievable; fabulous

CREDULITY (kruh DYOO li tee): n. Tendency to believe too readily; gullibility
    Trigger: CREDULITY-CREDIT
    Trigger Sentence: 1. The CREDIT offered to the defaulters reflects the CREDULITY of the bank personnel. 2.*All CRED-; CREED-; prefixes are associated with belief, trust and faith.
    Sample Sentence: The quack sells the fake medicine to the *credulous* (a) people.
    Related Words: 1.INCREDULITY - n. disbelief. 2. CREDULOUS - a. willing to believe too readily

CREED (KREED): n. Any system of religious beliefs
    Trigger: CREED-BREED
    Trigger Sentence: Every BREED (Hindu breed; Islam breed, Christian BREED etc.,) has some CREED; Indian BREED has Hindu CREED. *All CRED-; CREED-; prefixes are associated with belief, trust and faith.
    Sample Sentence: People of many *creeds* and cultures coexist in India.
    Related Words: CREDO - n. system of religious or ethical belief.

CRESCENDO (kruh SHEN doh): n. Gradual increase in loudness of the music, swelling, climax
    Trigger: ASCEND-DESCEND-TRANSCEND-CRESCENDO
    Trigger Sentence: 1. ASCEND-go up. 2. DESCEND-go down. 3. TRANSCEND-rise above (go beyond in success). 4. CRESCENDO-ascend of music; CRESCENDO means gradual ASCEND of music.
    Sample Sentence: The *crescendo* of the music transcended the mood of the audience.

CRESTFALLEN (KREST fawl un): a. Sad and disappointed
    Trigger: crestFALLEN-FALLEN (from EVEREST)
    Trigger Sentence: When he had FALLEN ill, he appeared CRESTFALLEN.
    Sample Sentence: Instead of being *crestfallen* at his failure, he got engaged in a fresh project.

CRINGE (KRINJ): v. Shrink back, flinch; recoil (in surprise or fear)
    Trigger: CRINGE-SYRINGE
    Trigger Sentence: Kids CRINGE when they see SYRINGE.
    Sample Sentence: I *cringed* with pain when I got to know of the inhumanity of slaughter houses.
    Related Words: CRINGING a./ n. bending in fear or servility.

CRONYISM (KROH nee iz um): n. Favoritism shown to friends
    Trigger: CRONY-ENEMY
    Trigger Sentence: CRONY means close friend which is opposite to ENEMY.
    Sample Sentence: The mayor was accused of *cronyism* for deploying relatives in key positions.
    Related Words: CRONY - n. buddy, friend

CROTCHETY (KROCH i tee): a. 1. Bad-tempered. 2. Having unusual ideas
    Trigger: 1. CROTCH - C (COCK) + ROACH. 2. CROTCHETY-CROW + CHUTNEY

Trigger Sentence: 1. I get *crotchety* after I see the cockroach face. 2. Dipping the condiment into a COCK ROACH CHUTNEY or CROW CHUTNEY is something an ECCENTRIC idea.

Sample Sentence: I could not have a healthy logical conversation with this *crotchety* man.

CRUDE (KROOD): a. Unrefined; natural; rudimentary

Trigger: CRUDE-RUDE

Trigger Sentence: His RUDE behavior reveals his CRUDE brought up.

Sample Sentence: "You are so *crude* and uncouth" cried out Cathe at Scott's sexual advances.

CRUX (KRUKS): n. Essential or main point

Trigger: CRUX-CRUCIAL-CRUC (CRUC + IAL)

Trigger Sentence: This is the CRUX of the issue. We need to understand this CRUCIAL (CRITICAL) point.

Sample Sentence: The *crux* of the matter is that you must work hard to become a word wizard.

Related Words: CRUCIAL- a. critical; very important

CRYPTIC (KRIP tik): a. Secret; furtive; mysterious

Trigger: 1.CRYPT-SCRIPT. 2. CRYPTIC-MYSTIC

Trigger Sentence: 1. The SCRIPT was so CRYPTIC, we could not decode it. 2. MYSTIC things are MYSTERIOUS. The MYSTIC spoke in a CRYPTIC language.

Sample Sentence: His *cryptic* remarks could not be interpreted.

CULMINATE (KUL muh nayt): v. Climax; end, conclude

Trigger: CULMINATE-TERMINATE

Trigger Sentence: CULMINATE and TERMINATE are synonyms. We CULMINATED the school year by a trip to New York and it TERMINATED at empire state building.

Sample Sentence: The love story *culminated* with a teary separation of the lovers.

CULPABLE (KUL puh bul): n. Deserving blame

Trigger: CULPRIT-CONVICT

Trigger Sentence: A CULPRIT is CULPABLE. CULPRIT and CONVICT are synonyms

Sample Sentence: The act of the convict was *culpable;* he had to be given punishment.

Related Words: 1. EXCULPATE – v. free from blame. 2. INCULPABLE – a. not guilty; innocent

CUMBERSOME (KUM bur sum): a. Burdensome, heavy

Trigger: CUMBERSOME-TIMBER SOME

Trigger Sentence: TIMBER is HEAVY; lifting the TIMBER is CUMBERSOME.

Sample Sentence: The application process is *cumbersome* and time-consuming.

Related Words: ENCUMBER – v. burden; hamper

CUPIDITY (kyoo PID ih tee): n. Greed

Trigger: CUPIDITY-NUDITY

Trigger Sentence: 1. CUPIDITY strikes when you look at NUDITY. 2. CUPID is the god of LUST.

Sample Sentence: The evidence revealed the *cupidity* of the company's directors.

Related Words: CUPID - n. god of love

CURMUDGEON (kur MUJ un): n. Ill-tempered, stingy person, spoilsport

Trigger: 1. CURMUDGEON-"CRUDE +GENT". 2. CURMUDGEON-"CURSE"

Trigger Sentence: 1. He is not a GENTLEMAN. He is CRUDE. He is a CURMUDGEON. 2. The CURMUDGEON CURSES others all the time.

Sample Sentence: His staff curses and considers him a *curmudgeon* for not giving salaries.

CURSORY (KUR suh ree): a. Casual, hastily done

Trigger: 1. CURSOR. 2. CURSORY-CASUALLY

Trigger Sentence: 1. We move the CURSOR on a computer in a HASTY manner. 2. Even CURSORY (CASUAL) love (on Orkut, Face book etc.,) happens with the computer CURSOR.

Sample Sentence: A *cursory* examination of the ruins indicates the possibility of arson.

CURT (KURT): a. Rudely brief; abrupt

Trigger: 1. CURT-CUT SHORT. 2. CURT-lack of COURTESY

Trigger Sentence: 1. He CURTLY CUT SHORT my explanation. 2. CURT manners LACK COURTESY

Sample Sentence: My husband's *curt* criticism on of my paintings cuts down my spirits!

CURTAIL (ker TALE): v. Reduce, cut short

Trigger: CURTAIL-"CUT +TAIL"

Trigger Sentence: To CURTAIL their ambition, we should CUT their TAILS in the bud.

Sample Sentence: New policies were introduced to *curtail* the powers of select departments.

CYNIC (SIN ik): n. A person who disbelieves

Trigger: 1. CYNIC-SIN +ic. 2. CYNIC-CRITIC

Trigger Sentence: 1. A CYNIC finds SIN even in the virtuous. 2. The CRITIC was criticized for his CYNIC comments.

Sample Sentence: These *cynics* have not understood the concept; they think it is not realistic.

Related Words: CYNICAL - a. Sarcastic

CYNOSURE (SIN uh shoor): n. Center of attraction

Trigger: 1.CYNOSURE-CINE STAR. 2. CYNOSURE- DINOSAUR

Trigger Sentence: 1. CINE-STARS are the CYNOSURES of the common public. 2. In Jurassic Park movie DINOSAUR was the CYNOSURE.

Sample Sentence: Dinosaurs make *cynosures* characters in the story books for children.

DABBLE (DAB ul): v. To work superficially
    Trigger: DABBLE-SCRIBBLE
    Trigger Sentence: SCRIBBLE (scribe) is to write carelessly; DABBLE is to do carelessly and superficially.
    Sample Sentence: He was a *dabbler*, trying out the basics of many arts but mastering none.

DAMPEN (DAM pun): n. Make moist; discourage
    Trigger: 1.DAMPEN-DAMP-DEADEN. 2. DAMPEN-DEADEN
    Trigger Sentence: The DAMP atmosphere at tropical beach DEADENS our spirits.
    Sample Sentence: The rains have *dampened* our picnic plans.
    Related Words: DAMPER - n. depression; restraint

DAUNT (DAWNT): v. To scare; intimidate
    Trigger: DAUNT-HAUNT
    Trigger Sentence: He was timid; always backing up at DAUNTING conditions like going into HAUNTED houses.
    Sample Sentence: It is a *daunting* task to live in this haunted house.
    Related Words: 1.DAUNTLESS - a. bold, fearless. 2. UNDAUNTED - a. fearless

DAWDLE (DAW dull): v. Delay, waste time
    Trigger: DAWDLE-IDLE
    Trigger Sentence: If you DAWDLE, you will be identified as an IDLE person.
    Sample Sentence: Don't *dawdle* when you take your nightly strolls, come back soon.

DAZZLE (DAZ ul): v. Amaze, fascinate; blind with bright light
    Trigger: DAZZLE-PUZZLE
    Trigger Sentence: The archeologist was DAZZLED with the amazing PUZZLING skills of Mayan people.
    Sample Sentence: Sheela was a *dazzling* bar dancer who always wore shimmering cloths.
    Related Words: DAZE - v. to confuse with intense light; shock

DEARTH (DURTH): n. A scarcity; lack of something
    Trigger: DEARTH-DEATH
    Trigger Sentence: Severe DEARTH of food results in DEATH of thousands of persons every year.
    Sample Sentence: There is no *dearth* of talent in the extremely smart young generation.

DEBACLE (di BAHK ul): n. Downfall; defeat; disaster
    Trigger: 1.DEBACLE-THE BUCKLE. 2. DEBACLE-DEFEAT
    Trigger Sentence: 1. If you BUCKLE, the match will end in a DEBACLE for us. 2. DEBACLE and DEFEAT are synonyms.
    Sample Sentence: If we get defeated again, the tournament will end in a *debacle* for us.

DEBASE (di BAYS): v. Lower the value or character of; degrade

Trigger: DEBASE -THE BASE

Trigger Sentence: If you DEBASE your teachers, it reflects your BASE (low) character.

Sample Sentence: My integrity, self respect and conviction can never get *debased* due to gossip.

Related Words: ABASE - v. Humiliate, degrade

DEBAUCHERY (di BAW shuh ree): n. Excessive indulgence in sex, alcohol, or drugs

Trigger: DEBAUCHERY-THE BACHELOR PARTY

Trigger Sentence: THE BACCHANALIAN BACHELOR'S party is usually full of DEBAUCHERY and drunken revelry.

Sample Sentence: Thy lived a horrific life full of violence, wild sex, and general *debauchery*.

DEBILITATE (di BIL uh tayt): v. Make very weak; incapacitate

Trigger: DEBILITY-NO ABILITY

Trigger Sentence: Physical INABILITY has not DEBILITATED the spirit of Stephen Hawking.

Sample Sentence: The virus *debilitates* the body's immune system.

DEBRIS (DEB ree): n. Scattered rubbish or remains; fragments

Trigger: 1. DEBRIS-THE BRICKS. 2. DEBRIS-DE + BREAKS

Trigger Sentence: When THE BRICKS, BREAK there will be DEBRIS (fragments).

Sample Sentence: Construction *debris* dumped into the lakes are the reason for them to vanish.

DEBUNK (di BUNK): v. Ridicule, expose as false; disprove

Trigger: DEBUNK- DE+ BUNK

Trigger Sentence: When I was in college, my lecturers used to DEBUNK me for I BUNKED my classes quite regularly.

Sample Sentence: The physicist *debunked* the psychic for hallucinating of a flying horse.

DECADENCE (DEK uh dens): n. Decline, decay

Trigger: DECAY-DECLINE

Trigger Sentence: As you age, your energy DECLINES. Hence, you should be more active to arrest body DECADENCE.

Sample Sentence: The *decadence* of Mughal Empire gave rise to the British rule in India.

Memory Test-25 : Match each word and its memory trick to the corresponding definition.

S.N	WORD	MEMORY TRIGGER	S.N	DEFINITIONS	KEY
1	CONTEMPLATE	In temple-concentrate	A	Compete; struggle	
2	CONTEMPT	contemn- condemn someone	B	Conflict; contest	
3	CONTEND	election CONTEST they contend	C	Contemptuous behavior; rudely	
4	CONTENTION	TENSION between us	D	Contradict; Oppose	
5	CONTENTIOUS	contentious-contest	E	Dependent upon, happening by chance	
6	CONTEST	boxing CONTEST	F	Difficult problem; dilemma	
7	CONTIGUOUS	continuous	G	Disdain; disrespect	
8	CONTINGENT	common + tangent	H	Dispute, competition, match	
9	CONTRADICTION	CONTRAST statement	I	Artificial; forced; not spontaneous	
10	CONTRAVENE	contradict	J	look at thoughtfully	
11	CONTRITE	CAN'T RIGHT-I am wrong	K	Meet, come together	
12	CONTRIVED	contriving-cunning	L	Oppose, challenge ; refute	
13	CONTROVERT	CONTRADICT	M	Opposite	
14	CONTUMACIOUS	You cant + make + us	N	Opposition (opp. statement)	
15	CONTUMELY	contumely- contemptibly	O	Ordinary; routine; formal	
16	CONUNDRUM	I am beating my head drum	P	Quarrelsome	
17	CONVALESCE	CAN WELL SICK	Q	Rebellious; head strong	
18	CONVENTIONAL	convent+traditional	R	Recover, get well after sickness	
19	CONVERGE	come + merge	S	Sorry; penitent	
20	CONVERSE	REVERSE	T	Touching; Adjacent	

Memory Test-26 : Match each word and its memory trick to the corresponding definition.

S.N	WORD	MEMORY TRIGGER	S.N	DEFINITIONS	KEY
1	CONVICTION	VICTORY will be there	A	Abundance, plenty; a symbol of plenty	
2	CONVIVIAL	JOVIAL	B	Bodily; material	
3	CONVOKE	Convene a meeting	C	Bountiful; abundant, plentiful	
4	CONVOLUTED	revolved/twisted	D	Call together, call to meeting	
5	COPIOUS	countless amounts of copies	E	Cancel an order	
6	CORDIAL	convivial- congenial	F	Confirm; support with evidence	
7	CORNUCOPIA	corn + copious	G	Determined belief, declaration of guilt	
8	COROLLARY	They CO ROLL	H	Emphasize by contrast	
9	CORPOREAL	MATERIAL	I	Face, Appearance; Tolerate	
10	CORPULENT	eat entire CROP of an year	J	Fat, obese	
11	CORROBORATE	co+ robbers -cooperate	K	Forged, fake, false	
12	COSMOPOLITAN	POLITE	L	Friendly; cheerful, jolly	
13	COUNTENANCE	COUNT+NUNS	M	Friendly; warm; heartfelt	
14	COUNTERFEIT	counter fake	N	Having a great desire; greedy, envious	
15	COUNTERMAND	counter + command	O	Secret, hidden	
16	COUNTERPOINT	COUNTER point	P	Seek to gain; seek love	
17	COUP	coup-trap; coup- troupe	Q	Something that naturally follows; result	
18	COURT	heart-sweet heart	R	Sophisticated; related to the whole world	
19	COVERT	covered	S	Twisted; involved, intricate	
20	COVETOUS	love at us with lust	T	Victorious accomplishment; sudden attack	

Answers

EX.NO	1	2	3	4	5	6	7	8	9	10	11	12	13	14	15	16	17	18	19	20
25	J	G	A	B	P	H	T	E	N	D	S	I	L	Q	C	F	R	O	K	M
26	G	L	D	S	C	M	A	Q	B	J	F	R	I	K	E	H	T	P	O	N

Memory Test-27 : Match each word and its memory trick to the corresponding definition.

S.N	WORD	MEMORY TRIGGER	S.N	DEFINITIONS	KEY
1	COWER	Coward fear	A	Bad-tempered; unusual ideas	
2	COZEN	con gent	B	Belief, credit	
3	CRAFTY	craft-art-artful	C	Burdensome, heavy	
4	CRASS	mass- crass-no class	D	Cheat; deceive	
5	CRAVEN	Not BRAVE	E	Climax; end, conclude	
6	CREDENCE	creed -credit	F	Cunning, deceptive	
7	CREDIBLE	credible-reliable	G	Deserving blame	
8	CREDULITY	They give credit everyone	H	Essential or main point	
9	CREED	Hindu breed-Hindu creed	I	Favoritism shown to friends	
10	CRESCENDO	Slowly ASCEND	J	Fearful, cowardly; dastard	
11	CRESTFALLEN	Fallen from Everest	K	Gradual increase in loudness	
12	CRINGE	Kids CRINGE - SYRINGE	L	Reliable; dependable	
13	CRONYISM	CRONY-not ENEMY	M	Rude, ill-mannered	
14	CROTCHETY	crotchety - seeing cockroach	N	Sad and disappointed	
15	CRUDE	RUDE behavior	O	Secret; furtive; mysterious	
16	CRUX	crux-crucial issue	P	Shrink back(in fear)	
17	CRYPTIC	cryptic-mystic script	Q	Shrink with fear	
18	CULMINATE	culminate-terminate	R	System of religious beliefs	
19	CULPABLE	culprit-convict	S	Tendency to believe; gullibility	
20	CUMBERSOME	TIMBER is heavy	T	Unrefined: natural: rudimentary	

Memory Test-28 : Match each word and its memory trick to the corresponding definition.

S.N	WORD	MEMORY TRIGGER	S.N	DEFINITIONS	KEY
1	CUPIDITY	cupidity strikes- nudity	A	Amaze; blind with bright light	
2	CURMUDGEON	crude +gent or curses	B	Casual, hastily done	
3	CURSORY	cursory-casually	C	Center of attraction	
4	CURT	CUT SHORT	D	Cut short, reduce	
5	CURTAIL	CUT +TAIL	E	Decline, decay	
6	CYNIC	they always find sin	F	Delay, waste time	
7	CYNOSURE	Cine star	G	Downfall; defeat; disaster	
8	DABBLE	Just SCRIBBLE	H	Excessive indulgence in sex etc.,	
9	DAMPEN	dampen-damp-deaden	I	Greed	
10	DAUNT	daunt-haunt	J	Ill-tempered	
11	DAWDLE	IDLE	K	Lower the value; degrade	
12	DAZZLE	DAZZLE-puzzle	L	Make moist; discourage	
13	DEARTH	results in DEATH	M	Make very weak; incapacitate	
14	DEBACLE	debacle-defeat	N	Person who disbelieves	
15	DEBASE	the base	O	Ridicule, expose as false	
16	DEBAUCHERY	The bachelor party	P	Rudely brief; abrupt	
17	DEBILITATE	debility-no ability	Q	Scarcity; lack of something	
18	DEBRIS	debris-the bricks	R	Scare; intimidate	
19	DEBUNK	BUNKED –they debunked	S	Scattered rubbish; fragments	
20	DECADENCE	Decay-decline	T	Work superficially	

Answers	EX.NO	1	2	3	4	5	6	7	8	9	10	11	12	13	14	15	16	17	18	19	20
	27	Q	D	F	M	J	B	L	S	R	K	N	P	I	A	T	H	O	E	G	C
	28	I	J	B	P	D	N	C	T	L	R	F	A	Q	G	K	H	M	S	O	E

WORD GROUPS DAY-7

★ GREED-DESIRE

ADJECTIVES: avid, gluttonous, grasping, insatiable, ravenous, rapacious, voracious

NOUNS: avarice, cupidity, rapacity

VERB: covet, crave, hanker, yearn

ANTONYMS: n. content; adj. generous

★ GENEROUS-GENEROSITY

ADJECTIVES: liberal, magnanimous, benevolent, altruistic, charitable, noble; unselfish, self-sacrificing

NOUNS: largesse, munificence, philanthropy; patron, benefactor

VERB: donate, grant , bestow

ANTONYMS: adj. selfish, parsimonious, penurious

★ INCREASE

ADJECTIVES: enlarged, aggrandized, exaggerated

NOUNS: accretion, inflation, dilation, distention, proliferation

VERB: amplify, aggrandize, augment, escalate, enhance, intensify, magnify, wax

ANTONYMS: v.subside, diminish; n.deflation, attenuation, attrition.

★ DECREASE

ADJECTIVES: flagging, diminished

NOUNS: deflation, descent, depression, recession, slump

VERB: abate, abbreviate, bate, depreciate, deteriorate, dwindle, diminish, ebb, flag, recede, subside, taper, wane; shrink, shrivel

ANTONYMS: v. aggrandize, amplify, magnify, increase ; enhance, flourish

★ LITERAL: word for word; exact, real

ADJECTIVES: accurate, actual, authentic, genuine, methodical, not figurative, plain, true, unexaggerated, verbal, verbatim, veritable, written

NOUNS: exactness

VERB: literalize

ANTONYMS: adj. exaggerated, figurative, imaginative

★ FIGURATIVE: not literal, but symbolic

ADJECTIVES: allegorical, denotative, emblematic, florid, flowery, illustrative, metaphorical, pictorial, poetical, representative

NOUNS: figurativeness

VERB: figure , depict

ANTONYMS: adj. literal, real, straightforward

★ RELIGIOUS

ADJECTIVES: canonical, clerical, devout, divine, ecclesiastical, holy, hollowed, moral, orthodox, pious, pontifical, reverent, righteous, sacred, sacrosanct, sectarian, spiritual, supernatural, theological

NOUNS: creed, cult, faith; piety, devotion; sermon, homily, discourse

VERB: consecrate, hollow; proselytize; preach

ANTONYMS: adj. agnostic, atheistic, irreligious, ungodly; secular

they can wag their tails
with same energy
and SYNERGY !

SYNERGY : cooperation, combined action

Word List Day-8

DECEITFUL (dih SEET ful): a. Deceptive, dishonest

    Trigger: DECEITFUL-DECEIVE FULL

    Trigger Sentence: It was a DECEITFUL/DECEPTIVE plot to escape paying taxes

    Sample Sentence: Aren't most of the advertisements outrageous, *deceitful* and misleading?!

    Related Words: DECEPTIVE - a. misleading, deceitful

DECIDUOUS (dih SIH joo us): a. Falling off as leaves; short-lived

    Trigger: 1.DECIDUOUS-DESCENDS. 2. DECIDUOUS- RESIDUOUS

    Trigger Sentence: 1. DECIDUOUS leaves DESCEND from trees. 2. Under the DECIDUOUS trees one can find RESIDUOUS leaves.

    Sample Sentence: He chose not to fret about the *deciduous* discomforts of his existence.

DECIMATE (DES uh mayt): v. Kill a large part of...

    Trigger: 1. DECIMATE-CHECK MATE. 2. DECIMATE-DECIMAL

    Trigger Sentence: 1. In the game of chess when we CHECK-MATE, we DECIMATE the opposite king. 2. If you keep showing this kind of DISMAL performance, it will DECIMATE your career.

    Sample Sentence: Budget cuts have *decimated* public services in small towns.

DECIPHER (dih CIE fur): v. Decode; interpret

    Trigger: DECIPHER-DE + CIPHER; (CIPHER-"C-FOR" MEANS "CODE")

    Trigger Sentence: CIPHER is to CODE; DECIPHER is to DECODE; ENCIPHER is to ENCODE; (a for an apple; b for boy and c FOR- CODE).

    Sample Sentence: I could not *decipher* the doctor's handwriting.

    Related Words: INDECIPHERABLE - a. cannot be decoded.

DECLAIM (dee KLEYM): v. To speak loudly and pompously

    Trigger: DECLAIM-DECLARE

    Trigger Sentence: DECLAIM is to DECLARE a speech loudly; I DECLARE that it is mine.

    Sample Sentence: He *declaimed* against the wasteful ways of modern society.

    Related Words: DECLAMATORY - a. ostentatiously lofty in style

DECLIVITY (dih KLIH vih tee): n. Descent, slope, decline

    Trigger: DECLIVITY-DECLINE

    Trigger Sentence: DECLINE and DECLIVITY are synonyms.

    Sample Sentence: They hiked until they came to a gentle *declivity* leading down to the stream.

    Related Words: 1.DECLENSION - n. decline; deterioration. 2. ACCLIVITY – n. upward slope

DECOROUS (DEK ur us): a. Polite; socially correct

    Trigger: DECOROUS-DECENTNESS

    Trigger Sentence: DECOROUS means DECENT and INDECOROUS means INDECENT

    Sample Sentence: If you maintain *decorous* appearance, people will admire your decency.

    Related Words: INDECOROUS - a. improper, unseemly

DECORUM (di KOH rum): n. Good manners; politeness

Trigger: 1. DECORUM-DECORATE-DECENT. 2. DECORUM-NO RUM

Trigger Sentence: 1. People who maintain DECORUM look DECENT and proper. 2. The celebration was held in DECORUM. There was NO serving of RUM.

Sample Sentence: He acts with *decorum* in public, while at home his wife knows his true colors.

Related Words: DÉCOR - n. decoration

DECREPIT (dee KREP it): a. Weak, frail; worn out by age

Trigger: DECREPIT-DECREASE + FIT

Trigger Sentence: The DECREPIT old man looked frail with DECREASED FITNESS.

Sample Sentence: Once a dandy dude zipping on a bike; now *decrepit* at 70 uses a walking stick.

Related Words: DECREPITUDE - n. State of collapse caused by illness or old age.

DECRY (di KRY): v. Condemn; denounce; criticize

Trigger: DECRY-CRY

Trigger Sentence: People CRY on other people's success and DECRY on them.

Sample Sentence: Critics *decry* his dramas for being unabashedly sensational.

DEDUCE (dee DOOS): v. Derive by reasoning

Trigger: 1.DEDUCE-DE+DICE-THE DICE. 2. DEDUCTIVE - DETECTIVE

Trigger Sentence: 1. I can DEDUCE the digits when you roll THE DICE in a game of dice. 2. Using the DEDUCTIVE reasoning the DETECTIVE came to a conclusion.

Sample Sentence: I can *deduce* where each of these numbers must go in the puzzle.

Related Words: DEDUCIBLE – a. derived by reasoning

DEEM (DEEM): v. Regard in a specified way: suppose

Trigger: DEEM-ASSUME

Trigger Sentence: When you DEEM something, you ASSUME something.

Sample Sentence: I *deem* it fitting that at this solemn occasion we pray for peace.

DEFACE (dih FAYS): v. Destroy; disfigure

Trigger: de + FACE -DEFORM

Trigger Sentence: Hitler tried to DEFACE Jews. He made attempts to DEFORM their community.

Sample Sentence: We will not *deface* the rock by chopping or adding holes.

DEFAME (di FAYME): v. Damage the good reputation of; malign

Trigger: de (DECREASE) + FAME

Trigger Sentence: DEFAME is to DECREASE the FAME of a famous person

Sample Sentence: The hospital was *defamed* with the new managements' carelessness.

DEFAULT (dih FAWLT): n. Failure to act; Failure to pay loan on time.

Trigger: DEFAULT-THE FAULT

Trigger Sentence: Since it is a FAULT, if the borrower DEFAULTS, the bank can take the house

Sample Sentence: As her husband failed to appear in the court, she got divorce by *default*.

DEFER (dih FUR): v.1.Postpone, delay; 2.respect (second sense)

> **Trigger:** 1. DEFER-"DO-LATER." 2. DEFER-OFFER (OFFER respect)
>
> **Trigger Sentence:** 1. DEFER is to DO LATER. 2. When in want of a job OFFER we got to DEFER (respect) the boss.
>
> **Sample Sentence:** If you demand for *defer* in the course, you will end up paying extra fee.

DEFERENCE (DEF ur uns): n. Respect, reverence

> **Trigger:** 1.DEFERENCE-REVERENCE (**synonyms). 2. DEFERENCE —NO+ DIFFERENCE
>
> **Trigger Sentence:** 1. If we show REVERENCE to our parents, our children will show us DEFERENCE. 2. The host showed NO DIFFERENCE in treatment of his guests. He paid the same DEFERENCE to every participant.
>
> **Sample Sentence:** Her relatives treat one another with *deference*.
>
> Related Words: DEFERENTIAL -a. respectful

DEFIANT (dih FAHY unt): a. Resisting, opposing

> **Trigger:** DEFIANT –DEFY-DENY
>
> **Trigger Sentence:** DEFIANT people DEFY (or DENY). The DEFIANT Porus DENIED surrendering to Alexander.
>
> **Sample Sentence:** King Charles remained *defiant* in the face of imminent defeat.
>
> Related Words: DEFY - v. oppose, challenge

DEFICIT (DEF uh cit): n. Lack; shortage

> **Trigger:** 1. DEFICIT–NOT SUFFICIENT. 2. DEFICIENCY-LACK OF SUFFICIENCY
>
> **Trigger Sentence:** DEFICIENCY (DEFICIT) is opposite to SUFFICIENCY (SUFFICIENT).
>
> **Sample Sentence:** *Deficit* with electric supply issues, we could not finish the work.
>
> Related Words: DEFICIENCY - n. lack, shortage

DEFILE (di FYLE): v. To make dirty or filthy; to pollute

> **Trigger:** 1.DEFILE-DO ILL. 2. DEFILE-DESPOIL (SPOIL)
>
> **Trigger Sentence:** "DEFILE" is to "DO ILL" &"SPOIL" the place.
>
> **Sample Sentence:** The hoodlums *defiled* the church with their scurrilous writing.

DEFINITIVE (di FIN uh tiv): a. Decisive; most reliable

> **Trigger:** 1.DEFINITE-THE FINAL. 2. DEFINITIVE-DECISIVE (** synonyms)
>
> **Trigger Sentence:** After THE FINAL round of meeting, a DEFINITIVE/DECISIVE policy will be declared.
>
> **Sample Sentence:** Online trading is aiming at a *definitive* source of futuristic shopping.
>
> Related Words: DECISIVE –a. conclusive; final

DEFLECT (dih FLEKT): v. Divert; deviate

> **Trigger:** DEFLECT-DIVERT
>
> **Trigger Sentence:** He DEFLECTED his competitors by DIVERTING the confrontation.
>
> **Sample Sentence:** Let us *deflect* our personal animosity and concentrate on the cause.

DEFT (DEFT): a. Adept, skillful

> **Trigger:** 1.DEFT-DEAF. 2. LEFT-HAND
>
> **Trigger Sentence:** 1. Many DEAF people (Helen Keller, Beethoven, and Mozart) are DEFT in art. 2. Ivan Lendl was a DEFT LEFT- HAND tennis player.
>
> **Sample Sentence:** Though he is deaf, he is *deft* in handling difficult tasks.

DEFUNCT (dee FUNGKT): v. Dead; no longer in use

    Trigger: DEFUNCT-NO FUNCT

    Trigger Sentence: NO more FUNCTIONING; it is already DEAD.

    Sample Sentence: Doctors believe that appendix has no function. It's a *defunct* organ.

DEGENERATE (di JEN uh rayt): v. Deteriorate; become worse

    Trigger: DEGENERATE-de +GENERATE

    Trigger Sentence: GENERATE is to create; whereas DEGENERATE is to destroy

    Sample Sentence: The conditions in the Indian slums are *degenerating* by the day.

    Related Words: DEGENERACY - n. decline, state of having low moral values.

DEGRADE (di GRAYD): v. To reduce in status, rank etc., demote

    Trigger: A-GRADE; D-GRADE

    Trigger Sentence: If you secure a D- GRADE, it will DEGRADE your rank.

    Sample Sentence: She tends to *degrade* her younger women colleagues.

    Related Words: DEGRADATION - n. humiliation

DEIFY (DEE uh fahy): v. Turn into god; Idolize

    Trigger: DEIFY-DEITY

    Trigger Sentence: The people DEIFIED the emperor by treating him like a DEITY

    Sample Sentence: Admire the rock star all you want; but just don't *deify* him, he is no a deity!

    Related Words: DEIFICATION - n. act of making divine

DEJECTED (di JEK tid): v. Depressed, sad

    Trigger: DEJECTED-REJECTED

    Trigger Sentence: 1. As he was REJECTED by is sweet-heart, he became DEJECTED. 2. DEJECTION is known as a DEPRESSION.

    Sample Sentence: Mohan is *dejected* with the deteriorating health condition of his father.

DELECTABLE (di LEK tuh bul): a. Delicious; delightful

    Trigger: 1. DELECTABLE-THEY LICK THE BOWL. 2. DELECTABLE-DELIGHTFUL-DELICIOUS

    Trigger Sentence: 1. As the pudding was DELECTABLE, we LICKED THE BOWL. 2. DELECTABLE and DELIGHTFUL are synonyms.

    Sample Sentence: The *delectable* and aromatic spread on the table was tempting.

DELETERIOUS (del uh TIR ee us): a. Harmful

    Trigger: DELETERIOUS-DELETES

    Trigger Sentence: 1. Natural Selection naturally DELETES DELETERIOUS genes. 2. DELETE the spam mails in mail box; since they are DELETERIOUS to the computer.

    Sample Sentence: The chemical is *deleterious* to the environment.

DELIBERATE (di LIB ur hut): a. To think carefully, intentional, methodical

    Trigger: DELIBERATE-"de +LIBERATE"

    Trigger Sentence: LIBERATE your kids SLOWLY AND CAREFULLY.

    Sample Sentence: USA liberated Kuwait in 1991 with a *deliberate* plan.

DELINEATE (di LIN ee ayt): v. Describe or portray

    Trigger: 1.DELINEATE-THE LINE. 2. DELINEATE –DEFINE (** synonyms)

Trigger Sentence: With an OUTLINE diagram the machine was DELINEATED.

Sample Sentence: Bright floral pattern of the mural was *delineated* against the dark wall.

Related Words: DEPICT –v. portray; describe

DELUDE (di LOOD): v. Deceive, to mislead

Trigger: DELUDE-MISLEAD

Trigger Sentence: DELUDE is to MISLEAD.

Sample Sentence: They *deluded* us with their misleading moral values.

Related Words: DELUSION - n. illusion

DEMAGOGUE (DEM uh gog): n. False leader of people

Trigger: DEMAGOGUE-DEMO + ROGUE

Trigger Sentence: ROUGE LEADERS of DEMOCRACY can be represented as DEMAGOGUES.

Sample Sentence: Hitler and Mussolini were *demagogues* and responsible for World War II.

DEMARCATE (DEE mahr keyt): v. Set apart; Mark off the boundaries

Trigger: DEMARCATE-THE MARK IT

Trigger Sentence: DEMARCATE between INDIA and PAK by MARKING a line.

Sample Sentence: Make the *demarcation* marks conspicuous.

DEMEAN (di MEEN): v. Humiliate, degrade

Trigger: DEMEAN-"DE + MEAN".2.DEMEAN-DEMON

Trigger Sentence: 1. The DEMON was DEMEANED with bad MEANINGS. 2. DEMEAN, DEBASE, DEGRADE, DECRY, DEROGATE belong to same family.

Sample Sentence: He acted like a demon to *demean* such a wonderful person.

DEMEANOR (di MEE nur): n. Behavior, conduct; bearing

Trigger: DEMEANOR- "THE MANNER"

Trigger Sentence: DEMEANOR is to maintain the MANNERS

Sample Sentence: Judging from her *demeanor*, I would say she is uncomfortable being here.

Related Words: MISDEMEANOR - n. wrong doing; error

DEMISE (di MIZE): n. Death

Trigger: 1. DEMISE-DIM EYES. 2. DEMISE-DECEASE

Trigger Sentence: 1. EYES get DIM before the DEATH or DEMISE. 2. DEMISE and DECEASE are synonyms.

Sample Sentence: He suffered from dim eye-sight before his *demise*.

DEMOTIC (dih MOT ik): a. Of the common people, popular

Trigger: DEMOTIC-DEMOCRATIC

Trigger Sentence: In a DEMOCRATIC society more DEMOTIC ideas will flourish.

Sample Sentence: Passing of an aristocratic society to a *demotic* lowered the standards.

DEMUR (dih MUR): v. Object; hesitate

Trigger: 1.DEMUR-DIFFER. 2. DEMUR-MURMUR

Trigger Sentence: 1. I DIFFER (means disagree-DIFFERENCE of opinion-objection) and DEMUR to the controversial statement. 2. Hey students DON'T MURMUR; teacher DEMURS.

Sample Sentence: I *demurred* to comment, so they thought I differed from their conclusion.

DEMURE (di MYOOR): a. Calm and polite; modest; coy

Trigger: 1.DEMURE-THE MATURE. 2. DEMURE-THE PURE

Trigger Sentence: 1. The MATURE girl exhibits DEMURE manners. 2. THE PURE girl is DEMURE.

Sample Sentence: Mary Louise was so gentle and *demure;* she never raised her tone of voice.

DEMYSTIFY (dee MIS tuh fahy): a. Clarify; free from mystery or obscurity

Trigger: DEMYSTIFY-NO MYSTERY

Trigger Sentence: DEMYSTIFY is to REMOVE the MYSTERY from the obscure story.

Sample Sentence: The history class is intended to *demystify* the myths.

Related Words: MYSTERIOUS – a. puzzling; unexplainable

DENIGRATE (DEN ih grate): v. Criticize; blacken

Trigger: 1. DENIGRATE-DEGRADE. 2. DENIGRATE-"DENY +GREAT"

Trigger Sentence: 1. DEGRADE and DENIGRATE are synonyms. 2. You can't DENY the historical importance of THE GREAT by simply DENIGRATING them.

Sample Sentence: Jack's father would *denigrate* him for minor things when angry.

DENOTATIVE (DEE noh tey tiv): n. Indicating; representing, naming

Trigger: DENOTATIVE-DENOTE

Trigger Sentence: 1. DENOTATION DENOTES a NAME or MEANING. 2. DENOTATIVE is dictionary meaning; CONNOTATIVE is implied meaning.

Sample Sentence: "Free market" does not *denote* "doesn't cost anything" for that "free" part.

DENOUEMENT (dey noo MAHN): n. Outcome; final result; conclusion (in a novel, play, film etc.)

Trigger: DEN U END

Trigger Sentence: In the action oriented movies the DENOUEMENT usually takes place in the villain's DEN.

Sample Sentence: The film had a different *denouement* with the prodigal daughters' escape.

DENOUNCE (di NOWNS): v. Condemn; criticize

Trigger: DENOUNCE-DE + NOUNS-BAD NOUNS

Trigger Sentence: DENOUNCE is to talk about someone by using BAD NOUNS openly.

Sample Sentence: The captured soldiers were *denounce* and abused by the terrorists.

Related Words: DENUNCIATION - n. condemnation

DEPICT (di PIKT): v. Portray; describe

Trigger: DEPICT-THE + PICT-THE PICTURE

Trigger Sentence: I like the way she DEPICTS the characters in THE PICTURES of her novels.

Sample Sentence: The documentary film *depicts* the life and culture of the tribes.

DEPLETE (di PLEET): v. Empty, reduce

Trigger: DEPLETE-"Opp. REPLETE or COMPLETE"

Trigger Sentence: The Country has been DEPLETED off its natural resources COMPLETELY

Sample Sentence: The Government Exchequer has *depleted*. We should find ways to replete it.

Related Words: DEPLETION - n. emptying

DEPLORE (di PLOHR): v. Disapprove of; regret

Trigger: DEPLORE- THE POOR

Trigger Sentence: I DEPLORE for THE POOR condition of the students in the public schools who are studying on THE FLOOR.

Sample Sentence: We *deplore* the recent outbreak of violence in our city.

Related Words: DEPLORABLE – a. regrettable; miserable

DEPOSE (dih POHS): v. Dismiss; remove from the office

Trigger: DEPOSE-DEMOTE

Trigger Sentence: A military junta DEPOSED the dictator after he had DEMOTED the noble man of the country.

Sample Sentence: Margaret Thatcher was *deposed* as leader of the British Conservative Party.

DEPRAVITY (di PRAV ih tee): n. Corruption; moral perversion

Trigger: DEPRAVITY-"THE PRIVATE" + "RAVE PARTY"

Trigger Sentence: 1. The private RAVE PARTY is full of DEPRAVITY. 2. DEPRAVITY means LACK of PURITY.

Sample Sentence: *Depravity* and dissolution of morals in a society is the main cause of unrest.

DEPRECATE (DEP ri kayt): v. Disapprove; belittle

Trigger: 1. DEPRECATE-APPRECIATE. 2. DEPRICATE-DEPRECIATE (** near synonyms)

Trigger Sentence: Stop DEPRECATING others' importance and start APPRECIATING others' virtues.

Sample Sentence: That comedian is best known for *deprecating* himself in a funny way.

Related Words: DEPRECIATE – v. reduce the value of

DEPRIVE (dih PRAHYV): v. Prevent from having; take away; deny

Trigger: DEPRIVE-DE+ PREVENT

Trigger Sentence: To DEPRIVE is to DENY and PREVENT; the communist government DEPRIVED the public by DENYING possessing any private property.

Sample Sentence: 1. The dictators *deprived* the basic rights of the people. 2. While my friends go out parting all night, my parents *deprive* me of the fun by not allowing me to go.

DERELICTION (der uh LIK shun): n. Neglecting of one's duty, negligence

Trigger: 1. DERELICTION-NEGLECTION. 2. DERELICT-NEGLECT

Trigger Sentence: 1. NEGLECTION of duties is called DERELICTION. 2. DERELICT person is NEGLECTED by the society.

Sample Sentence: Captain John got suspended from his services on charges of *dereliction*.

Related Words: DERELICT - a. neglected; abandoned

DERIDE (di RYDE): v. Mock, ridicule, sneer

Trigger: 1.DERIDE-RIDE-RIDICULE. 2. DERIDE-DEGRADE

Trigger Sentence: 1. He DERIDED his opponent with RIDICULOUS comments. 2. I am being DEGRADED by other people.

Sample Sentence: Opposing coaches *derided* our team because we haven't won a single game.

Related Words: DERISION - n. ridicule; scorn

DERIVATIVE (di RIV uh tiv): a. Copied or adopted; lacking originality

Trigger: DERIVATIVE-"NOT-CREATIVE"

Trigger Sentence: His ideas are DERIVATIVE. They are NOT CREATIVE.

Sample Sentence: Her music concert was disappointingly mechanical and *derivative*.

DEROGATIVE (dih ROG uh tiv): a. Belittling, disparaging

Trigger: DEROGATIVE-THE NEGATIVE

Trigger Sentence: He made a DEROGATIVE remark which has a NEGATIVE effect on my status.

Sample Sentence: Nazis developed a *negative* opinion about Jews due to Hitler's *derogative* comments.

Related Words: DEROGATORY - a. expressing a low opinion.

DESCRY (dih SKRIE): v. See from far away

Trigger: DESCRY-DISCOVER

Trigger Sentence: DESCRY is to DISCOVER

Sample Sentence: Telescope can *descry* objects from far to discover the universe.

DESECRATE (DES ih krayt): v. Damage the sacred places; insult

Trigger: 1.DESTROY SACRED. 2. DESECRATE-CONSECRATE

Trigger Sentence: 1. DESECRATE is to DESTROY the SACRED things. 2. Though it is very easy to DESECRATE something, it is very difficult to CONSECRATE it.

Sample Sentence: Vandals *desecrated* the temple, removing statues and breaking pillars.

Related Words: CONSECRATE - v. make sacred; dedicate

DESICCATE (DESS ih kayt): v. To dry out completely

Trigger: DESICCATE-DESERT CAKE

Trigger Sentence: DESERT CAKE is usually DESICCATED or DRIED up

Sample Sentence: It didn't rain for two months, and Emma's garden got *desiccated*.

DESIST (di ZIST): v. Stop; cease

Trigger: DESIST-RESIST

Trigger Sentence: I DESIST from alcohol by RESISTING the temptations.

Sample Sentence: The cease fire orders from the government, did *desist* the fight.

DESOLATE (DES uh lit): a. Abandoned, neglected

Trigger: DESOLATE-ISOLATE

Trigger Sentence: The ISOLATED house was DESOLATED many years ago.

Sample Sentence: How can a mother *desolate* her own children?!

Related Words: DESOLATE - v. rob of joy; abandon

DESPAIR (dih SPAIR): n. To lose all hope

Trigger: DESPAIR-DESPERATE

Trigger Sentence: The DESPERATE girl is in DESPAIR

Sample Sentence: His *despair* for a job is obvious in his desperate attempts to find one.

Related Words: DESPERATE -a: hopeless; bad

DESPICABLE (DES pi kuh bul): a. Deserving hatred and contempt; abominable

Trigger: DESPICABLE- NOT SPEAKABLE

Trigger Sentence: Her DESPICABLE behavior is UNSPEAKABLE

Sample Sentence: He is a *despicable* offender who has a list of crimes in his kitty.

DESPISE (dih SPAHYZ): v. To regard with hate; scorn

Trigger: 1.DESPISE- DE+SPICE. 2. DESPISE-DE+SPOUSE

Trigger Sentence: 1. I DESPISE the food that is without SPICE. 2. I DESPISE my SPOUSE since she is NOT SPICY anymore

Sample Sentence: She *despises* use of spices in Indian recipes.

Related Words: DESPICABLE - a. deserving hatred and contempt

DESTITUTE (DES tuh toot): a. Poor, Penniless

Trigger: 1. DESTITUTE-DUSTY+TOOTH. 2. DESTITUTE-NO INSTITUTE

Trigger Sentence: 1. A DESTITUTE person possesses DUSTY TOOTH and DUSTY LOOK. 2. A DESTITUTE has NO INSTITUTE to pursue his academics

Sample Sentence: There exists no institute in this big city to take care of the *destitute*.

DESUETUDE (DES wi tood): n. A state of non use

Trigger: DISUSED

Trigger Sentence: DESUE - sounds like DISUSE

Sample Sentence: This ship was disused and is in the state of *desuetude* for over a decade.

DESULTORY (DES ul tor ee): a. Aimless, random; digressing

Trigger: 1. DESULTORY—DEVIATORY. 2. DESULTORY-DULL STORY

Trigger Sentence: 1. The DULL STORY of the DESULTORY film provoked wrath of many film critics. 2. The DESULTORY teenager is in a DEVIATORY path.

Sample Sentence: Because of Peter's *desultory* attitude, his sergeant refused to write a recommendation for him.

DETACHED (dih TACHT): a. Not attached; aloof; impartial

Trigger: DETACHED-ATTACHED (** near antonyms)

Trigger Sentence: One cannot simultaneously remain both DETACHED and ATTACHED with the same person.

Sample Sentence: He is a *detached* observer in all the company's affair.

Related Words: DETACHMENT - n. separation; disinterest, aloofness

DETAIN (di TANE): v. Delay; arrest

Trigger: DETAIN-RETAIN-RESTRAIN

Trigger Sentence: She RETAINED him by DETAINING in her hugs.

Sample Sentence: The travelers at the airport were *detained* due to a bomb scare.

DETERIORATE (dih TEER ee uh reyt): v. Get worse; weaken

Trigger: 1.DETERIORATE-DECELERATE-DECLINE. 2. AMELIORATE-ACCELERATE

Trigger Sentence: DETERIORATING means DECLINING; If rainfall continues to DECLINE, forests will DETERIORATE fast.

Sample Sentence: These medicines *deteriorate* if not stored in a cool dark place.

DETER (dee TUR): v. Discourage, prevent

    Trigger: DETER-DEBAR

    Trigger Sentence: The principal DETERRED the student that he would DEBAR him.

    Sample Sentence: A woman *deterred* her attacker by yelling for police help.

    Related Words: DETERRENT - a. serving to stop

DETERMINISTIC (dih tur muh niz um): a. Pertaining to determinism (doctrine which states that there is a reason for everything and all is predestined)

    Trigger: DETERMINISTIC -DETERMINED

    Trigger Sentence: Ancestors understood that our fate is DETERMINED by a DETERMINISTIC power.

    Sample Sentence: My mother believes that all marriages are *deterministic*, made in heaven!

    Related Words: DETERMINATE - a. fixed; definite.

DETRACTOR (di TRAK tur): n. Critic; one who belittles

    Trigger: 1. DETRACTOR-THE ACTOR. 2. DETRACTOR-DEROGATOR

    Trigger Sentence: THE ACTOR had many DETRACTORS; the DEROGATOR DETRACTS the actor in the movie.

    Sample Sentence: *Detractor* is the one who disparages or belittles the worth of something.

    Related Words: DETRACTION - n. slandering; aspersion

DETRIMENTAL (deh trih MEN tul): a. Injurious, harmful

    Trigger: detriMENTAL-MENTAL

    Trigger Sentence: MENTAL pressure is DETRIMENTAL to one's health.

    Sample Sentence: Pirated software has a *detrimental* effect on the economy as well.

DEVASTATE (DEV uh steyt): v. Destroy; ruin

    Trigger: 1.DEVASTATE-BAD STATE. 2. DEVASTATE- WASTE (** synonyms)

    Trigger Sentence: The flood DEVASTATED the STATE.

    Sample Sentence: Coastal Sri Lanka was totally *devastated* by the Indian Ocean tsunami.

DEVIATE (DEE vee ate): v. Turn away from a norm; depart, diverge

    Trigger: DEVIATE-"DE + VIA (WAY)"

    Trigger Sentence: VIA means WAY; DEVIATE-NOT following or doing in the USUAL WAY.

    Sample Sentence: Oh, please don't try to *deviate* from the topic and jeopardize our plans.

DEVIOUS (DEE vee us): a. Not straightforward; erratic; dishonest

    Trigger: 1. DEVIOUS-BOGUS. 2. DEVIOUS-NOT OBVIOUS

    Trigger Sentence: 1. DEVIOUS people DEVIATE from straight honest path. 2. This is a DEVIOUS scheme. Don't become a victim to this BOGUS temptation. 3. DEVIOUS things are NOT OBVIOUS.

    Sample Sentence: Vinod *deviously* faked in the office of headache, to go to his girlfriend.

DEVISE (dih VAHYZ): v. Plan, invent; think up

    Trigger: 1.DEVISE-THE WISE. 2. DEVISE-DEVICE

    Trigger Sentence: 1. THE WISE people DEVISE and PLAN things properly.

2. He has DEVISED new DEVICE with his ingenious thinking.

Sample Sentence: They *devised* a plan to take over the director's office and pull him down.

DEVOID (di VOID): a. Lacking; empty

Trigger: DEVOID-THE VOID

Trigger Sentence: VOID means EMPTY; If you are DEVOID of spirit, your life will turn to a VOID.

Sample Sentence: The Island was *devoid* of drinking water, so the shipwrecked sailors suffered.

Related Words: VOID - a. empty; null

Memory Test-29 : Match each word and its memory trick to the corresponding definition.

S.N	WORD	MEMORY TRIGGER	S.N	DEFINITIONS	KEY
1	DECEITFUL	Deceive full	A	Condemn; denounce; criticize	
2	DECIDUOUS	Residues- DESCENDS	B	Damage the good reputation of	
3	DECIMATE	Check mate king is gone	C	Deceptive, dishonest	
4	DECIPHER	DECIPHER is to DECODE	D	Decode; interpret	
5	DECLAIM	DECLARE loudly	E	Derive by reasoning	
6	DECLIVITY	DECLINE	F	Descent, decline	
7	DECOROUS	Decentness	G	Destroy; disfigure	
8	DECORUM	DECENT and no rum	H	Failure to act; Failure to pay loan	
9	DECREPIT	Decrease + fit	I	Falling off as leaves; short-lived	
10	DECRY	People CRY on other	J	Good manners; politeness	
11	DEDUCE	DETECTIVE analysis	K	Kill a large part of	
12	DEEM	Assume	L	Lack; shortage	
13	DEFACE	DEFORM face	M	Make dirty; to pollute	
14	DEFAME	Decrease + fame	N	Polite; socially correct	
15	DEFAULT	The fault	O	Postpone, delay; respect	
16	DEFER	DO-LATER	P	Resisting, opposing	
17	DEFERENCE	Reverence- no difference	Q	Respect, reverence	
18	DEFIANT	DEFY-DENY	R	Speak loudly and pompously	
19	DEFICIT	Not sufficient	S	Suppose; regard in a specified way	
20	DEFILE	Do ill- despoil -spoil	T	Weak, frail; worn out by age	

Memory Test-30 : Match each word and its memory trick to the corresponding definition.

S.N	WORD	MEMORY TRIGGER	S.N	DEFINITIONS	KEY
1	DEFINITIVE	decisive	A	Adept, skillful	
2	DEFLECT	divert	B	Behavior, conduct; bearing	
3	DEFT	left- hand is deft	C	Dead; no longer in use	
4	DEFUNCT	No functioning	D	Death	
5	DEGENERATE	Opposite to generate	E	Deceive, to mislead	
6	DEGRADE	A-GRADE to D-GRADE	F	Decisive; most reliable	
7	DEIFY	Treat someone like deity	G	Delicious; delightful	
8	DEJECTED	My love was REJECTED	H	Depressed, sad	
9	DELECTABLE	delightful-delicious	I	Describe or portray	
10	DELETERIOUS	virus deletes	J	Deteriorate; become worse	
11	DELIBERATE	LIBERATE your kids SLOWLY	K	Divert; deviate	
12	DELINEATE	DEFINE with lines	L	False leader of people	
13	DELUDE	MISLEAD	M	Harmful	
14	DEMAGOGUE	DEMO + ROGUE	N	Humiliate, degrade	
15	DEMARCATE	Mark them	O	Object; hesitate	
16	DEMEAN	You are a demon	P	Of the common people, popular	
17	DEMEANOR	The manner	Q	Reduce in status, rank etc., demote	
18	DEMISE	DIM EYES-decease	R	Set apart; Mark off the boundaries	
19	DEMOTIC	democratic	S	Think carefully, intentional	
20	DEMUR	DIFFER- I differ	T	Turn into god; Idolize	

Answers	EX.NO	1	2	3	4	5	6	7	8	9	10	11	12	13	14	15	16	17	18	19	20
	29	C	I	K	D	R	F	N	J	T	A	E	S	G	B	H	O	Q	P	L	M
	30	F	K	A	C	J	Q	T	H	G	M	S	I	E	L	R	N	B	D	P	O

Memory Test-31 : Match each word and its memory trick to the corresponding definition.

S.N	WORD	MEMORY TRIGGER	S.N	DEFINITIONS	KEY
1	DEMURE	Mature girl is pure	A	Belittling, disparaging	
2	DEMYSTIFY	NO MYSTERY at all !!	B	Calm and polite; modest; coy	
3	DENIGRATE	Deny +great- degrade	C	Clarify; free from mystery	
4	DENOTATIVE	It DENOTEs	D	Condemn; criticize	
5	DENOUEMENT	DEN U END	E	Copied; lacking originality	
6	DENOUNCE	BAD NOUNS are used	F	Criticize; blacken	
7	DEPICT	Picturize	G	Damage the sacred places; insult	
8	DEPLETE	No complete	H	Disapprove; belittle	
9	DEPLORE	THE POOR state	I	Dismiss; remove from the office	
10	DEPOSE	DEMOTE-de +POSE	J	Empty, reduce	
11	DEPRAVITY	RAVE PARTY	K	Final result; outcome	
12	DEPRECATE	Depreciate	L	Indicating; representing, naming	
13	DEPRIVE	DE+ PREVENT	M	Mock, ridicule, sneer	
14	DERELICTION	Neglect ion	N	moral perversion; corruption	
15	DERIDE	Ride-ridicule	O	Neglecting of one's duty	
16	DERIVATIVE	Not-creative	P	Portray; describe	
17	DEROGATIVE	The negative	Q	Prevent from having; take away	
18	DESCRY	Descry-discover	R	Regret; disapprove of	
19	DESECRATE	Destroy SACRED	S	See from far away	
20	DESICCATE	Desert CAKE	T	Dry out completely	

Memory Test-32 : Match each word and its memory trick to the corresponding definition.

S.N	WORD	MEMORY TRIGGER	S.N	DEFINITIONS	KEY
1	DESIST	Resist from moving	A	Abandoned, neglected	
2	DESOLATE	ISOLATE someone	B	Aimless, random; digressing	
3	DESPAIR	Desperate	C	Critic; one who belittles	
4	DESPICABLE	UNSPEAKABLE acts	D	Delay; arrest	
5	DESPISE	You are not spicy	E	Deserving hatred; abominable	
6	DESTITUTE	DUSTY + tooth	F	Destroy; ruin	
7	DESUETUDE	Disused	G	Discourage, prevent	
8	DESULTORY	Deviatory	H	Get worse; weaken	
9	DETACHED	No attachment	I	Injurious, harmful	
10	DETAIN	Retain-restrain	J	Lacking; empty	
11	DETERIORATE	Decelerate-decline	K	Lose all hope	
12	DETER	DEBAR	L	Not attached; aloof; impartial	
13	DETERMINISTIC	Already DETERMINED	M	Not straightforward; dishonest	
14	DETRACTOR	The bad actor	N	Pertaining to determinism	
15	DETRIMENTAL	MENTAL fellow acts	O	Plan, invent; think up	
16	DEVASTATE	Keep Bad state	P	Poor, Penniless	
17	DEVIATE	De +via	Q	Regard with hate; scorn	
18	DEVIOUS	Not obvious	R	State of nonuse	
19	DEVISE	How to DEVICE	S	Stop; cease	
20	DEVOID	The void	T	Turn away from a norm; diverge	

Answers

EX.NO	1	2	3	4	5	6	7	8	9	10	11	12	13	14	15	16	17	18	19	20
31		B	C	F	L	K	D	P	J	R	I	N	H	Q	O	M	E	A	S	G	T
32		S	A	K	E	Q	P	R	B	L	D	H	G	N	C	I	F	T	M	O	J

WORD GROUPS DAY-8

★ IRRELIGIOUS

ADJECTIVES: agnostic, atheistic, blasphemous, heathen, iconoclastic, impious, irreverent, pagan, sacrilegious, unholy

NOUNS: blasphemy, sacrilege

VERB: desecrate, defile, profane

ANTONYMS: adj. agnostic, atheistic, irreligious, ungodly; secular

★ SERIOUS NATURE

ADJECTIVES: austere, dour, deadpan, earnest, grave, grim, pensive, resolute, sedate, severe, sober, somber, solemn, staid, steady, stern, weighty

NOUNS: gravity, solemnity

VERB:

ANTONYMS: adj. flippant, funny, happy, light

★ DROLL: amusing, farcical

ADJECTIVES: comical, diverting, facetious, funny, hilarious, humorous, jocose, jocund, jocular, quaint, risible, waggish, whimsical, wry

NOUNS: antic, buffoon, clown, droll, harlequin, jester, zany

VERB: joke

ANTONYMS: adj. somber, grave

★ EQUAL-SIMILAR

ADJECTIVES: commensurate, comparable, corresponding, duplicate, egalitarian, equivalent, homogenous, identical, indistinguishable, invariable, matching, parallel, proportionate, synonymous, tantamount, uniform, unvarying

NOUNS: alter-ego, peer, rival

VERB: match, resemble

ANTONYMS: adj.different, discriminatory

★ DISSIMILAR- UNEQUAL

ADJECTIVES: antithetical, antonymous, contradictory, contrary, different, disparate,

distant, divergent, diverse, heterogeneous, opposite, unique, various

NOUNS: divergence, variance, dissimilitude

VERB: diverge

ANTONYMS: adj.alike, compatible, equal, similar

★ BETRAYAL: disloyalty

ADJECTIVES: fickle, treacherous, traitorous, subversive, renegade

NOUNS: disloyalty, duplicity, deception, perfidy, treachery, treason.

VERB: betray

ANTONYMS: faithfulness, loyalty, support

★ LOYAL/LOYALTY

ADJECTIVES: steadfast, staunch, dependable, reliable, trustworthy, unchanging, unwavering, unswerving; patriotic

NOUNS: allegiance, adherence, fealty, fidelity

VERB: abide by

ANTONYMS: adj. disloyal, undependable, unfaithful

MONASTIC monks in meditation

MONASTIC
simple, basic, ascetic

Word List Day-9

DEXTEROUS (DEK ster us): a. Skillful

Trigger: DEXTEROUS-TEXT WRITES

Trigger Sentence: 1. DEXTEROUS people WRITE TEXT books; they are very CLEVER.
2. DEFT people are DEXTEROUS.

Sample Sentence: She is so *dexterous* in text writing that she trains teachers on calligraphy.

Related Words: AMBIDEXTERITY - n. ability to use both right and left hands with equal ease

DIABOLIC (dahy uh BOL ik): a. Devilish, wicked

Trigger: DIABOLIC-"DIE +PUBLIC"

Trigger Sentence: 1. Many persons in the PUBLIC DIED in the hands of the DIABOLIC tyrant. 2. DIABOLIC, DEMONIC and SATANIC; all are related to devils and demons family.

Sample Sentence: The police quickly mobilized to track down the *diabolical* serial killer.

DIAPHANOUS (dahy AF uh nus): a. Filmy, transparent; sheer

Trigger: 1. DIAPHANOUS-CELL PHONES. 2. DIAPHANOUS-DIAPERS

Trigger Sentence: 1. DIAPERS (absorbent cloths worn by babies (as underpants)) are usually DIAPHANOUS in nature. 2. Many of the CELL PHONES outer coverings appear DIAPHANOUS.

Sample Sentence: The hall had *diaphanous* curtains to separate the seating for women.

DIATRIBE (DYE uh tryb): n. An angry speech; criticism

Trigger: DIATRIBE-TRIBE -"DIALOGUES ON TRIBE"

Trigger Sentence: DIALOGUES ON TRIBES are said in a CRITICIZING MANNER.

Sample Sentence: The author's 'Dialogues on Tribe' has received a *diatribe* from literary critics.

DICEY (DAHY see): a. Dangerous, risky; uncertain

Trigger: 1.DICEY-DICE. 2. DICEY-DIES

Trigger Sentence: 1. If you play DICE, you will face a DICEY situation in your life one day. 2. A man DIES in DICEY situation.

Sample Sentence: Unable to face the *dicey* situation, the main character dies in the story.

DICHOTOMY (dye KAHT uh mee): n. Split, branching into two parts (especially contradictory)

Trigger: DICHOT-"DI + CUT"

Trigger Sentence: DICHOTOMY means DIVISION or CUT into two parts.

Sample Sentence: There is a *dichotomy* in my mind; I can't think of a conclusion to this crisis.

DIDACTIC (dahy DAK tik): a. Instructive, teaching

Trigger: DIDACTIC-THE TACTIC

Trigger Sentence: The teaching TACTICS are DIDACTIC in nature.

Sample Sentence: Some colleges are already being *didactic* about safe computing.

DIFFER (DIF er): v. Be dissimilar, distinct

Trigger: DIFFER-DIFFERENT

Trigger Sentence: I am afraid I DIFFER from you because I hold a DIFFERENT perspective.

Sample Sentence: The two schools of thought, Jainism and Buddhism, *differ* in their approach.

DIFFERENTIATE (dif uh REN shee eyt): v. Distinguish, make different

Trigger: DIFFERENTIATE-DIFFERENCE

Trigger Sentence: To make out or mark the DIFFERENCE is known as DIFFERENTIATION.

Sample Sentence: I could not *differentiate* the difference between real and the fake!

DIFFIDENCE (DIH fih duns): n. Shyness

Trigger: DIFFIDENCE-Opp. CONFIDENCE

Trigger Sentence: Lack of CONFIDENCE is known as DIFFIDENCE; if you LACK CONFIDENCE you'd be SHY.

Sample Sentence: If you have excessive *diffidence*, you will never improve your confidence.

DIFFUSE (di FYOOZ): v. Scatter; a. Wordy, rambling

Trigger: 1. DIFFUSE-FUSE. 2. DIFFUSIVE-EXCESSIVE wordy

Trigger Sentence: 1. FUSE (fusion) means join or COMBINE; DIFFUSE (diffusion) means spread out or SCATTER. 2. DIFFUSIVE also means EXCESSIVE talk.

Sample Sentence: In the *diffused* lighting effects on stage, the dancers moved like shadows.

Related Words: DIFFUSIVE- a. tending to spread out.

DIGRESSION (di GRESH un): n. Deviation from the main point

Trigger: 1. DIGRESSION-DIVERSION. 2. DIGRESSION-DEVIATION

Trigger Sentence: DIGRESSION is a DEVIATION from the main topic.

Sample Sentence: Speakers are requested to avoid *digression* and not *deviation* from the topic.

DILAPIDATED (di LAP uh day tid): v. Spoiled because of neglect

Trigger: DILAPIDATED-OUTDATED (expiry DATED)

Trigger Sentence: The building is so OUTDATED that it is almost in a DILAPIDATED state.

Sample Sentence: Many *dilapidated* heritage buildings are being neglected by the government.

DILATE (dye LAYT): v. Expand, enlarge

Trigger: 1. DILATE-INFLATE. (** synonyms). 2. DILATE-DEFLATE (** antonyms)

Trigger Sentence: 1. DILATE & INFLATE (expand) are synonyms. 2. DILATE (expand) & DEFLATE (shrink) are antonyms.

Sample Sentence: The doctor put eye drops in my eyes to *dilate* my eyeballs for examination.

DILATORY (DIL uh tohr ee): a. Delaying

Trigger: DILATORY-DELAYER-DELAY

Trigger Sentence: DELAYER exhibits DILATORY attitude.

Sample Sentence: I don't tolerate your *dilatory* tactics. Finish the work without further *delay*.

DILETTANTE (DIL i tahnt): a. Superficial, amateur; dabbler

Trigger: 1.DILETTANTE- DILUTES ART. 2. DILET-DELIGHT

Trigger Sentence: By being a DILETTANTE he has DILUTED his passion for the ART. Now he paints art only for the DELIGHT.

Sample Sentence: Hasa wants to be an artist. But she's only a *dilettante* with an ability to paint.

DILIGENT (DIL uh gent): a. Industrious, hard-working

Trigger: DILIGENT-NEGLIGENT

Trigger Sentence: DILIGENT and NEGLIGENT (neglecting duties, careless) are antonyms.

Sample Sentence: If you are negligent, you'll not understand the value of a *diligent* person.

Related Words: DILIGENCE - n. perseverance, industriousness

DIMINUTION (di muh NYOO shun): n. Reduction, decrease

Trigger: DIMINUTION-"DI + MINUTE"

Trigger Sentence: MINUTE means MINI or SMALL in size.

Sample Sentence: His physical appearance is *diminutive*. But his success is not *minute*.

Related Words: DIMINISH - v. make smaller

DIN (DIN): n. A loud continued noise

Trigger: DIN-TIN

Trigger Sentence: Drop a TIN, it will make a DIN.

Sample Sentence: As Jim caught the ball, a *din* from the crowd did not let him hear the anchor.

DIRE (DYE ur): a. Terrible, Disastrous

Trigger: 1.DIRE-FIRE. 2. DIRE-DIED

Trigger Sentence: 1. Don't play with FIRE; you will have to face DIRE consequences. 2. Lot of people DIED in DIRE situations.

Sample Sentence: The struggle for power between the brothers lead to a *dire* fallout.

DISABUSE (dih suh BYUZE): v. Correct a false impression; undeceive

Trigger: DIS + ABUSE-"DON'T ABUSE"

Trigger Sentence: REMOVE ABUSE; DON'T ABUSE him; he is free from error.

Sample Sentence: No point trying to *disabuse* your abusive acts as the matter is in the court.

DISAFFECTED (dis uh FEK tid): a. 1. Not satisfied. 2. Disloyal

Trigger: DISAFFECTED-NO AFFECTIONS

Trigger Sentence: My hubby is NOT showing any AFFECTION towards me; he has become DISAFFECTED; he has become REBEL and DISLOYAL.

Sample Sentence: Why do you stay in a meaningless and *disaffected* marriage?!

DISAPPROBATION (dis ap ruh BEY shun): n. Disapproval, condemnation

Trigger: DISAPPROBATION-DISAPPROVE

Trigger Sentence: DISAPPROBATION is to DISAPPROVE.

Sample Sentence: The *disapprobation* was universal. Every member *disapproved* the proposal.

Related Words: APPROBATION- n. approval; praise

DISARRAY (dis uh RAY): n. Lack of order, mess

  Trigger: DISARRAY-DISARRANGE

  Trigger Sentence: With the DISARRANGED furniture the room was in DISARRAY.

  Sample Sentence: My room is in such *disarray* that I can neither find my car keys nor my office dossier.

DISAVOWAL (DIS uh vowl): n. Denial, rejection

  Trigger: DISAVOWAL-"D IS A VOWEL"

  Trigger Sentence: If you say 'D IS A VOWEL', it is a DISAVOWAL because D is a consonant.

  Sample Sentence: She *disavowed* her own stories fearing she might get caught for her lies.

DISCERN (di SURN): a. To see things clearly; recognize

  Trigger:1. DISCERN-DISCOVER. 2.DISCERN-LEARN. 2. DISCERNING-LEARNING

  Trigger Sentence: 1. I can DISCERN/DISCOVER right from wrong. 2. LEARNING gives DISCERNING mind. 3. When you LEARN you can easily PERCEIVE.

  Sample Sentence: A scientist should be *discerning*. Then only can he keep *discovering* new things.

  Related Words: INDISCERNIBLE - a. impossible to see or clearly distinguish

DISCLOSE (dis CLOZ): v. Reveal

  Trigger: DIS (not) + CLOSE

  Trigger Sentence: DISCLOSE is opposite to CLOSE; OPEN the SECRET and REVEAL it to the others

  Sample Sentence: When she *disclosed* the secrets of the president, it virtually closed his chance of being re-elected.

DISCOMFIT (dis KUM fit): v. Make uneasy, discomfort

  Trigger: DISCOMFIT -DISCOMFORT

  Trigger Sentence: 1. DISCOMFIT is to cause DISCOMFORT. 2. DISCOMFIT is to make someone UNFIT

  Sample Sentence: We could perceive the *discomfort* of our guest. His *discomfit* stemmed from unfamiliarity with the subject.

DISCONCERT (dis cun SURT): v. Upset; disorder; confuse

  Trigger:1.DISCONCERT-BAD CONCERT. 2. DISCOMFORT

  Trigger Sentence: People were DISCONCERTED and felt DISCOMFORT during a BADLY organized musical CONCERT.

  Sample Sentence: The constant attention from a young man however *disconcerted* the nun.

  Related Words: DISCONCERTING - a. upsetting; disturbing

DISCORD (DIS kord): n. Disagreement, Disharmony

  Trigger: DISCORD-DISACCORD- DISAGREED

  Trigger Sentence: ACCORD means AGREED; DISCORD means DISAGREED

  Sample Sentence: The *discord* between the two nations occurred when they *disagreed* over a number of things.

  Related Words: DISCORDANT - a. Disagreeing; conflicting

DISCOUNT (dis KOUNT): v. Disregard, ignore

  Trigger: DISCOUNT-DON'T COUNT

  Trigger Sentence: DISCOUNT is to REDUCE the value of a person in front of others---

like a price is DISCOUNTED

Sample Sentence: Why are you giving *discount* to his misbehavior towards women in the office??!!

DISCREDIT (diss KRED it): n. Defame; destroy confidence in; disbelieve

Trigger: DISCREDIT -NO CREDIT

Trigger Sentence: DON'T give CREDIT to those who have brought DISCREDIT

Sample Sentence: When you *discredit* my contribution to the organization, then it means you are not willing to give me any credit.

DISCREET (di SKREET): v. Careful; diplomatic; subtle

Trigger:1. DISCREET-THIS SECRET. 2. DISCRETION-"THIS CAUTION"

Trigger Sentence: 1. You must be DISCREET about THIS SECRET code. 2. I CAUTION you to use your DISCRETION about THIS issue.

Sample Sentence: You should be *discreet* enough whether to reveal this secret or not.

Related Words: DISCRETION - n. caution, careful judgment

DISCREPANCY (dis KREP un see): n. Lack of consistency; difference

Trigger:1. DISCREPANT-DIFFERENT. 2.DISCRE (DISAGREE)+ PANCY

Trigger Sentence: 1. DISCREPANT and DIFFERENT are synonyms variants. 2. "DISCRE" in the word sounds like DISAGREE

Sample Sentence: We disagree over the reason behind the *discrepancy*.

Related Words: DISCREPANT - a. differing, disagreeing

DISCRETE (dih SKREET): a. Separate and distinct

Trigger:1.DISCRETE-DISSECT. 2. DISCRETE-DISPARATE (** synonyms)

Trigger Sentence: 1. There are DISCRETE methods to DISSECT a corpse. 2. DISCRETE-DISTINCT-DIFFERENT are synonym variants

Sample Sentence: Two *discrete* people united in a marriage is indeed amazing!

DISCRETION (dis KRESH in): n. Caution, careful judgment

Trigger: THIS CAUTION-DIS (THIS) +CRETION (CAUTION)

Trigger Sentence: If you've DISCRETION, you'd usually do the things with CAUTION

Sample Sentence: The employees were expected to maintain *discretion* while on duty.

DISCRIMINATE (di SKRIM uh nayt): v. Recognize a difference, treat differently (*negative sense*)

Trigger: DISCRIMinate-THIS CRIME

Trigger Sentence: 1. Who is GOOD and who is CRIMINAL; the judge can DISCRIMINATE. 2. Sometimes judges are PARTIAL too; it is called prejudiced attitude. 3. DISCRIMINATE and DIFFERENTIATE are synonyms

Sample Sentence: The art critic could easily *discriminate* between the original and the fake copy.

DISDAIN (dis DAYN): v. To view with disrespect or scorn

Trigger: DISDAIN-THIS STAIN

Trigger Sentence: I DISDAIN the people with STAIN marks.

Sample Sentence: The millionaire lottery winner treated her former friends with *disdain*.

DISENCHANT (dis en CHAHNT): v. Let down; disappoint

Trigger: DISENCHANT -DISAPPOINT

Trigger Sentence: FREE from ENCHANTMENT or DISAPPOINTMENT is known as DISENCHANTMENT.

Sample Sentence: He gradually became bored and *disenchanted* due to lack of patronization for his music.

DISENFRANCHISE (dis en FRAN chyze): v. Deprive of civil rights

Trigger: DIS+ EN + FRANCHISE

Trigger Sentence: NO FRANCHISE- NO FREEDOM TO VOTE

Sample Sentence: Hitler *disenfranchised* all civil rights from German citizens. People lost even their basic franchises.

Related Words: 1.ENFRANCHISE (v) : give a person some rights; liberate. 2.FRANCHISE (n) : grant the right to vote

DISENTANGLE (dis en TANG guhl): v. Free from complex position, extricate

Trigger: TANGLE- "BERMUDA TRIANGLE"

Trigger Sentence: Bermuda TRIANGLE is a TANGLE (or ENTANGLEMENT); Scientists DISENTANGLED the enigma of BERMUDA TRIANGLE.

Sample Sentence: The bookkeeper *disentangled* the records and cleared up mistakes.

Related Words: ENTANGLE - a. involve in complicated circumstances.

DISGRUNTLED (dis GRUN tld): a. Angry or dissatisfied

Trigger: DISGRUNTLED-"THIS GUN TOLD"

Trigger Sentence: THIS GUN TOLD that you are DISGRUNTLED

Sample Sentence: The man was so *disgruntled* with his old gun that he threw it into a lake.

Related Words: DISGRUNTLE - v. displease

DISHEARTEN (dis HAHR tun): a. Discourage; dispirit

Trigger: DISHEARTEN- HEART ATTACK

Trigger Sentence: We were DISHEARTENED by the news that our grandfather had a HEART ATTACK.

Sample Sentence: We were absolutely *disheartened* to learn that our luxury cruise trip got cancelled!

Related Words: 1. HEARTEN (v) : encourage.2. WHOLEHEARTED (adj); sincere; devoted

DISHEVELED (di SHEV uld): a. Untidy, disordered

Trigger: DISHEVEL-"DIS (NOT) + SHAVE + WELL"

Trigger Sentence: He DOESN'T SHAVE WELL; he looks untidy and DISHEVELED

Sample Sentence: People at the pub party looked tired and *disheveled*, but generally excited.

DISINCLINATION (dis in kluh NEY shun): v. Dislike; unwillingness

Trigger: DISINCLINATION-NO INCLINATION

Trigger Sentence: He has NO INCLINATION to read; so he has DISINCLINATION to books.

Sample Sentence: Though hailing from a family of classical musicians, Devansh was always *disinclined* towards music.

Related Words: INCLINATION (n): tendency; liking

DISINGENUOUS (dis in JEN yoo us): a. Insincere, not naïve, hypocritical

Trigger: DISINGENUOUS-NOT GENUINE

Trigger Sentence: He is DISINGENUOUS. His actions are NOT GENUINE.

Sample Sentence: The ex-criminal was *disingenuous* about his background when he applied for a job.

Related Words: INGENUOUS - a. innocent; frank

DISINTERESTED (dis IN truh stid): a. Free from selfish motive; unbiased

Trigger: DISINTERESTED OF INTEREST

Trigger Sentence: LACK OF SELF-INTEREST is termed as DISINTERESTED; it represents total IMPARTIALITY

Sample Sentence: Scientists are reputed as devotees of the *disinterested* pursuit of truth.

DISJOINTED (dis JOIN tid): a. Disconnected, disordered

Trigger: DISJOINTED-NO JOINT

Trigger Sentence: The story is DISJOINTED; there is NO JOINT between scenes to scene.

Sample Sentence: His treatise is an incomplete and *disjointed* narrative.

DISJUNCTION (dis JUHNGK shun): n. State of being disconnected

Trigger: DISJUNCTION-NO JUNCTION

Trigger Sentence: There was DISJUNCTION between theory and practice.

Sample Sentence: The first point the critic makes, is the complete *disjunction* of the art world from that of day-to-day life.

Related Words: JUNCTURE - n. place where two things meet and join; connection

DISMAY (dis MAY): v. Dishearten

Trigger: DISMAY-DISMAL

Trigger Sentence: DISMAL performance by the players in the football match DISMAYED the coach

Sample Sentence: His dismal performance in the exam *dismayed* his parents.

DISPARAGE (di SPAR ij): v. Belittle; discourage

Trigger:1. DIS(NOT) + PRAISE. 2. DISPARAGE -DISCOURAGE

Trigger Sentence: DIS (NO) + PRAISE —CRITICIZE

Sample Sentence: His employer's *disparaging* comments discouraged him.

DISPARATE (DIS pur it): v. Dissimilar, different

Trigger: DISPARATE-THIS SEPARATE

Trigger Sentence: DISPARATE and SEPARATE are not disparate

Sample Sentence: Our personalities were *disparate*; Janet liked to socialize, and I liked quiet times alone.

DISPARITY (dih SPAR i tee): n. Inequality; difference

Trigger: DISPARITY-DIS (not) + PARITY

Trigger Sentence: In THIS PARTY there is a DISPARITY; NO EQUALITY- [PAR-PEER-EQUALS]

Sample Sentence: Economic *disparity* is inherent in Capitalism. The slogan of Socialism is equality.

Related Words: 1.PARITY (n) : equality. 2. PAR (n) : standard; equal status

DISPASSIONATE (dis PASH uh nut): a. Impartial; calm

Trigger: DISPASSIONATE -DIS (NO) +PASSION

Trigger Sentence: NO PASSION (NO PERSONAL FEELING) for anyone; DISPASSIONATE people are IMPARTIAL

Sample Sentence: We need a leader who has no personal passion. Only such a person can remain *dispassionate* and solve our problems.

Related Words: IMPASSIONED - a. full of passion; emotional

DISPEL (dis PELL): v. Scatter, expel, drive away

Trigger: 1.DISPEL-EXPEL. 2.DISPEL-DISPERSE.

Trigger Sentence: 1. Instead of DISPELLING workers' fears, the management EXPELLED the workers themselves.2. DISPEL and DISPERSE are synonyms

Sample Sentence: An exorcist was called-in to *dispel* the evil spirits.

Related Words: DISPERSE - v. scatter

DISPIRIT (dis PIR ut): v. Dishearten, discourage

Trigger: DISPIRIT -DIS (NO) + SPIRIT

Trigger Sentence: Lack of SPIRIT in sports shown by her child DISPIRITED her.

Sample Sentence: When dad announced that he could not get tickets for the film, we became a bunch of *dispirited* souls!

Related Words: SPIRITED - a. lively ; energetic

DISPOSITION (dis puh ZISH un): n. Your usual mood; character

Trigger: DISPOSITION-HIS POSITION

Trigger Sentence: Find out HIS POSITION at this moment; is he in a happy DISPOSITION or in a sad DISPOSITION?

Sample Sentence: Rahul Gandhi's *disposition* is still getting shaped. He has no clear position on his foreign policy.

Related Words: 1.PREDISPOSITION - n. previous tendency, susceptibility .
2. INDISPOSED (adj); a. sick; unwilling

DISPUTATIOUS (dis pyoo TEY shus): a. Fond of having arguments

Trigger: DISPUTATIOUS -DISPUTES

Trigger Sentence: DISPUTATIOUS arguments are going to cause DISPUTES

Sample Sentence: A *disputatious* professor could give you an argument on just about anything.

Related Words: INDISPUTABLE - a. unquestionable; certain

DISQUIET (dis KWYE ut): n. Anxiety, uneasiness

Trigger: DIS (NOT) + QUIET

Trigger Sentence: DISQUIET is to remove the QUIETNESS in a person and make him feel ANXIOUS

Sample Sentence: That horror movie *disquieted* my kids so much that they slept with me for a week.

Related Words: DISQUIETUDE - n. anxiety, lack of calm.

DISSEMBLE (di SEM bul): v. Disguise, pretend

Trigger: DISSEMBLE-RESEMBLE

Trigger Sentence: To DISSEMBLE is to RESEMBLE like someone else and deceive them

Sample Sentence: Christina often *dissembles* about her grades. Her actual grades do not have any sort of *resemblance* to the actual ones.

Related Words: DISSIMULATE - v. dissemble; act in a false manner

DISSEMINATE (di SEM uh nayt): v. To scatter or spread widely

Trigger: DISSEMINATE-THIS SEMINAR

Trigger Sentence: The participants have DISSEMINATED a lot of useful information in THIS SEMINAR.

Sample Sentence: Food and water packets were *disseminated* to the flood victims from the helicopter along the river beds of Orissa.

DISSENT (di SENT): v. Disagree

Trigger:1.DIS (NO) + SENTI. 2. DISSENSION-DISSONANCE

Trigger Sentence: 1. When we have DIFFERENT SENTIMENTS there is going to be a DISSENSION; there is no CONSENSUS. 2. DISSONANCE and DISSENSION are synonyms.

Sample Sentence: Inter-personal *dissent* usually results in social dissonance.

Related Words: DISSENSION - n. disagreement, strife

DISSIDENT (DIS uh dunt): a. Opposing, dissenting

Trigger: DISSIDENT-DISSENT

Trigger Sentence: DISSIDENT (n) is a person who DISSENTS from established policy.

Sample Sentence: During his stay in Pakistan, he was considered a *dissident* for being an Indian patriot.

DISSIPATE (DIS uh payt): v. Waste (money, energy, or resources); squander

Trigger: DISSIPATE-"THE SIP+ATE"

Trigger Sentence: He DISSIPATES money on THE SIPS (alcohol) and excessive EATING.

Sample Sentence: He *dissipated* all of his family fortunes in casinos and bars!

DISSOLUTE (DIS uh loot): a. Loose in moral

Trigger: DISSOLUTE-PROSTITUTE

Trigger Sentence: Many SOCIALITES lead a DISSOLUTE life with PROSTITUTES.

Sample Sentence: The rap singer led a wild and *dissolute* life.

DISSOLUTION (dis uh LOO shun): n. Separation, death of morals

Trigger: DISSOLUTION-DISSOLVE

Trigger Sentence: 1. Whenever we SOLVE the problem we DISSOLVE the problem in to SEPARATE steps. 2. INTEGRITY represents HONESTY; DISSOLUTENESS represents DISHONESTY

Sample Sentence: Shahi is a *dissolute* person with no moral integrity, how can I employ her?!

Related Words: DISSOLUTE - a. corrupt

DISSONANCE (DIS uh nuns): n. Discord; difference

Trigger:1.DIS (BAD) + SONO (SOUND). 2. DISSONANCE -DIFFERENCE

Trigger Sentence: The DIFFERENCE in SOUNDS filled the air with barbaric DISSONANCE

Sample Sentence: They ended their marriage because of *dissonances* in their relationship.

Related Words: CONSONANACE - n. harmony; agreement

DISSUADE (dih SWEYD): v. Discourage; persuade not to do.

Trigger: DISSUADE-DISS DO

Trigger Sentence: They tried to DISSUADE a friend from making a mistake; they DISSED him from DOING anything wrong.

Sample Sentence: Negative campaigning *dissuaded* people from voting.

Related Words: PERSUADE -v. convince; sway

DISTEND (di STEND): v. Swell, expand

    Trigger: DISTEND-EXTEND-EXPAND

    Trigger Sentence: 1. DISTENTION can be an EXTENSION. 2. As technology DISTENDS, possibilities EXPAND.

    Sample Sentence: The grains got *distended* after soaking up over night.

    Related Words: DISTENTION - n. expansion

DISTILL (dih STIL): a. Purify; refine; extract an essence

    Trigger: DISTILL-DISTILLATION

    Trigger Sentence: DISTILL is to remove impurities from, increase the concentration of, and separate through the process of DISTILLATION.

    Sample Sentence: I need *distilled* water to cool my car.

DISTINCT (di STINKT): a. Clearly different

    Trigger: DISTINCT-DIFFERENT

    Trigger Sentence: DISTINCT is to identify the DIFFERENT things or species clearly

    Sample Sentence: Leonardo Da Vin Ci showed *distinct* talent in *different* fields.

    Related Words: DISTINCTION - n. difference, uniqueness; excellence

DISTINGUISH (di STING gwish): v. See as different; recognize

    Trigger: DISTINGUISH- DISTINCT

    Trigger Sentence: 1. DISTINCT and DISTINGUISH are synonyms. 2.He is a DISTINCT individual; he can easily DISTINGUISH between what is logical and what is illogical.

    Sample Sentence: The *distinguished* dignitaries present in the International Conference of Young Engineers were impressed with Surya's concepts on storing up solar energy.

    Related Words: INDISTINGUISHABLE - a. same; exactly alike.

DISTORT (dih STAWRT): v. Deform; falsify; twist

    Trigger: DISTORT -THIS TORQUE

    Trigger Sentence: THIS TORQUE is due to the DISTORTION caused by spin of an object.

    Sample Sentence: The odd camera angle *distorted* her figure in the photograph.

    Related Words: TORTUOUS -a. full of twists ; complex

DISTRAUGHT (dis TRAWT): a. Upset; distracted by anxiety

    Trigger: 1. DISTRAUGHT- DISTRACTED. 2. THIS DRAUGHT

    Trigger Sentence: 1. DISTRAUGHT over the health of her child the parents are DISTRACTED with grief. 2. THIS DRAUGHT made the people DISTRAUGHT.

    Sample Sentence: The *distraught* parents frantically searched the ravine for their lost child.

    Related Words: OVERWROUGHT -a. deeply agitated

DIURNAL (dye UR nul): a. Daily; active during the day

    Trigger: 1.DIURNAL-DIARY + JOURNAL. 2. URINAL

    Trigger Sentence: 1. My DIARY (or journal) records DAILY activities of the DAY time. 2. Going to URINALS is a DIURNAL activity rather than NOCTURNAL (night time) activity.

    Sample Sentence: I cannot imagine working in the nights because I am a complete *diurnal* person like the Sun flower!

    Related Words: NOCTURNAL -a. active during the night

DIVERGE (dih VURJ): v. Vary and go in a different direction

Trigger: 1.DIVERGE-CONVERGE. 2. DIVERGE-DIVERT (** near synonyms)

Trigger Sentence: CONVERGE and DIVERGE are antonyms; our ideas do not CONVERGE. In fact, they DIVERGE.

Sample Sentence: He *diverged* from the original text and interpreted it otherwise.

DIVERSE (di VURS): a. Different, varied

Trigger: 1.DI-VARIOUS. 2. DIVERSE-VERSATILE

Trigger Sentence: He is a person of VERSATILE and DIVERSE (various) talents.

Sample Sentence: The "Gangam" song by the Korean pop singer Psy appealed to *diverse* audiences.

Related Words: VARIED -a. diverse; changing

DIVEST (di VEST): v. Strip; deprive

Trigger: DIVEST-INVEST (** near antonyms)

Trigger Sentence: The Nazis DIVESTED the Jews of all their INVESTMENTS.

Sample Sentence: Since Martin grew in a boarding school he was *divested* from his parents love.

Related Words: 1.DIVESTITURE - n. the act of stripping. 2. INVESTITURE - n. the act or ceremony of investing

DIVISIVE (dih VIS iv): a. Creating disunity

Trigger: DIVISIVE-DIVIDE

Trigger Sentence: DIVISIVE plans DIVIDE the group into two parts.

Sample Sentence: The *divisive* forces in the organization will eventually *divide* it into two.

DIVULGE (di VULGE): v. Reveal, disclose

Trigger: DIVULGE-THE BULGE

Trigger Sentence: The BULGE of the stomach DIVULGES the fat body of a person or pregnancy in a woman.

Sample Sentence: Until he *divulges* the secret, his bulged belly does not deflate.

Memory Test-33 : Match each word and its memory trick to the corresponding definition.

S.N	WORD	MEMORY TRIGGER	S.N	DEFINITIONS	KEY
1	DEXTEROUS	Text writes	A	loud continued noise	
2	DIABOLIC	Die +public-- plan	B	Amateur; dabbler, superficial	
3	DIAPHANOUS	Diapers are diaphanous	C	Angry speech; criticism	
4	DIATRIBE	Dialogues on tribe	D	Be dissimilar, distinct	
5	DICEY	DIES in DICEY situation	E	Dangerous, risky; uncertain	
6	DICHOTOMY	Di + cut	F	Delaying	
7	DIDACTIC	The tactic	G	Deviation from the main point	
8	DIFFER	Be Different	H	Devilish, wicked	
9	DIFFERENTIATE	Make Difference	I	Disastrous; terrible	
10	DIFFIDENCE	Opp. CONFIDENCE	J	Expand, enlarge	
11	DIFFUSE	EXCESSIVE wordy	K	Filmy, transparent; sheer	
12	DIGRESSION	Diversion-deviation	L	Industrious, hard-working	
13	DILAPIDATED	Outdated (expiry DATED)	M	Make different; distinguish	
14	DILATE	Dilate-inflate	N	Reduction, decrease	
15	DILATORY	Delayer-delay	O	Scatter; Wordy, rambling	
16	DILETTANTE	Dilute art	P	Shyness	
17	DILIGENT	He is not Negligent	Q	Skillful	
18	DIMINUTION	mini	R	Split, branching into two parts	
19	DIN	Drop a TIN- make a DIN	S	Spoiled because of neglect	
20	DIRE	Play with FIRE ??	T	Teaching , instructive	

Memory Test-34 : Match each word and its memory trick to the corresponding definition.

S.N	WORD	MEMORY TRIGGER	S.N	DEFINITIONS	KEY
1	DISABUSE	Remove abuse	A	Careful; diplomatic; subtle	
2	DISAFFECTED	No affections	B	Caution, careful judgment	
3	DISAPPROBATION	Disapprove	C	Correct a false impression	
4	DISARRAY	Disarrange	D	Defame; disbelieve	
5	DISAVOWAL	D is a vowel ?? no	E	Denial, rejection	
6	DISCERN	Discover	F	Deprive of civil rights	
7	DISCLOSE	(not) + CLOSE	G	Difference; lack of consistency	
8	DISCOMFIT	Discomfort	H	Disagreement, Disharmony	
9	DISCONCERT	Bad concert; Discomfort	I	Disapproval, condemnation	
10	DISCORD	Disaccord- disagreed	J	Discomfort , Make uneasy	
11	DISCOUNT	Don't count	K	Ignore; disregard	
12	DISCREDIT	No credit	L	Lack of order, mess	
13	DISCREET	Discretion-This caution	M	Let down; disappoint	
14	DISCREPANCY	Discre (disagree)	N	Not satisfied; Disloyal	
15	DISCRETE	Dissect	O	recognize ; see things clearly	
16	DISCRETION	This CAUTION	P	Recognize a difference	
17	DISCRIMINATE	What is GOOD & CRIME	Q	Reveal	
18	DISDAIN	This stain	R	Separate and distinct	
19	DISENCHANT	Disenchant -disappoint	S	Upset; disorder; confuse	
20	DISENFRANCHISE	No franchise	T	View with disrespect or scorn	

Answers	EX.NO	1	2	3	4	5	6	7	8	9	10	11	12	13	14	15	16	17	18	19	20
	33	Q	H	K	C	E	R	T	D	M	P	O	G	S	J	F	B	L	N	A	I
	34	C	N	I	L	E	O	Q	J	T	H	K	D	A	G	R	B	P	S	M	F

Memory Test-35 : Match each word and its memory trick to the corresponding definition.

S.N	WORD	MEMORY TRIGGER	S.N	DEFINITIONS	KEY
1	DISENTANGLE	DISENTANGLED a tangle	A	Angry or dissatisfied	
2	DISGRUNTLED	THIS GUN TOLD	B	Anxiety, uneasiness	
3	DISHEARTEN	Heart attack	C	Discourage; belittle	
4	DISHEVELED	Dis- shave well	D	Disconnected, disordered	
5	DISINCLINATION	No inclination	E	Discourage; dispirit	
6	DISINGENUOUS	Not genuine	F	Disguise, pretend	
7	DISINTERESTED	Lack of self-interest	G	Dishearten	
8	DISJOINTED	No joint	H	Dishearten, discourage	
9	DISJUNCTION	No junction	I	Dislike; unwillingness	
10	DISMAY	DISMAL performance	J	Dissimilar, different	
11	DISPARAGE	Dis (no) + praise	K	Fond of having arguments	
12	DISPARATE	separate	L	Free from complex position	
13	DISPARITY	(not) + PARITY	M	Free from selfish motive; unbiased	
14	DISPASSIONATE	(no)-passion for anyone	N	Impartial; calm	
15	DISPEL	Expel	O	Inequality; difference	
16	DISPIRIT	Lack of SPIRIT	P	Insincere, hypocritical	
17	DISPOSITION	His position	Q	Scatter, expel, drive away	
18	DISPUTATIOUS	Disputes	R	State of being disconnected	
19	DISQUIET	(Not) + quiet	S	Untidy, disordered	
20	DISSEMBLE	RESEMBLE like other	T	Usual mood; character	

Memory Test-36 : Match each word and its memory trick to the corresponding definition.

S.N	WORD	MEMORY TRIGGER	S.N	DEFINITIONS	KEY
1	DISSEMINATE	This seminar -disperse	A	Clearly different	
2	DISSENT	Different sentiments	B	Creating disunity	
3	DISSIDENT	Dissident-dissent	C	Daily; active during the day	
4	DISSIPATE	The sip+ate	D	Difference ; discord	
5	DISSOLUTE	Dissolute-prostitute	E	Disagree	
6	DISSOLUTION	Dissolve integrity	F	Discourage; persuade not to do	
7	DISSONANCE	Dissonance -difference	G	Distracted by anxiety	
8	DISSUADE	Diss do	H	Go in a different direction	
9	DISTEND	Distend-extend-expand	I	Loose in moral	
10	DISTILL	Distillation	J	Opposing, dissenting	
11	DISTINCT	Distinct-different	K	Purify; extract an essence	
12	DISTINGUISH	Distinguish- see distinct	L	Reveal, disclose	
13	DISTORT	This torque	M	Scatter or spread widely	
14	DISTRAUGHT	Distracted	N	See as different; recognize	
15	DIURNAL	Dialy+ journal	O	Separation, death of morals	
16	DIVERGE	Diverge-divert	P	Strip; deprive	
17	DIVERSE	Diverse-versatile	Q	Swell, expand	
18	DIVEST	Vest is removed	R	Twist ; deform; falsify	
19	DIVISIVE	Divisive-divide	S	Varied, different	
20	DIVULGE	The bulge tells	T	Waste (money); squander	

Answers

EX.NO	1	2	3	4	5	6	7	8	9	10	11	12	13	14	15	16	17	18	19	20
35	L	A	E	S	I	P	M	D	R	G	C	J	O	N	Q	H	T	K	B	F
36	M	E	J	T	I	O	D	F	Q	K	A	N	R	G	C	H	S	P	B	L

WORD GROUPS DAY-9

★ **FLAW:** defect, imperfection

ADJECTIVES: unsound, faulty, distorted, erroneous, fallacious, flawed, misleading

NOUNS: blemish, failing, flaw, foible, glitch, speck, stain, vice

VERB: mar, deface, mutilate

ANTONYMS: perfection, strength

★ **FLAWLESS:** perfect, impeccable

ADJECTIVES: absolute, consummate, immaculate, impeccable, irreproachable, pristine, perfect, unblemished, unerring ,unmarred; exemplary, model, ideal

NOUNS: perfectness

VERB: refine, perfect

ANTONYMS: flawed, imperfect

★ **PROPER BEHAVIOR**

ADJECTIVES: decorous , seemly, befitting, genteel, demure

NOUNS: propriety, decorum, decency, protocol, courtesy, politeness, rectitude, sobriety, dignity, civility

VERB: behave, comport

ANTONYMS: n. impropriety, indecorum.

★ **IMPROPER BEHAVIOR**

ADJECTIVES: indecorous, impropriety, unseemly, unbecoming, immodest, indelicate, indecent; inappropriate, ill-bred

NOUNS: indecorum, impropriety, unseemliness, indecency, indelicacy

VERB: misbehave, misconduct

ANTONYMS: adj. decorous, seemly

★ **FOOLISH- RIDICULOUS**

ADJECTIVES: asinine , daft, fatuous, inane, obtuse, vacuous; preposterous, nonsensical, irrational, ridiculous, ludicrous, absurd; maladroit, inept, impolitic , tactless, imprudent, injudicious

NOUNS: folly, idiocy, imbecility, inanity, foolhardiness, recklessness; dolt, oaf;

VERB: err, bungle

ANTONYMS: adj. sagacious, judicious, wise, perspicacious, discerning.

★ **WISDOM-WISE**

ADJECTIVES: astute, wise, sage, sagacious; discerning, judicious, canny, clearheaded, perceptive, shrewd, prudent, insightful, perspicacious

NOUNS: acumen, acuity, sagacity, wit, perspicacity, prudence, circumspection, discretion; cerebral, cerebration.

VERB: coruscate

ANTONYMS: asinine, fatuous, inane, insensate, obtuse, stupid

★ **HATRED-HATE**

ADJECTIVES: abominable, despicable, execrable, obnoxious, odious, repugnant

NOUNS: abhorrence, aversion, hostility, ill will, enmity, animosity, animus, antipathy, rancor; revulsion, disgust, contempt, odium

VERB: abominate, abhor , despise, detest, disdain, execrate, loathe, eschew, spurn, scorn, imprecate

ANTONYMS: v.adore, admire, venerate, cherish.

Word List Day-10

DOCILE (DAHS ul): a. Manageable, obedient

    Trigger: DOCILE -"DO-SILENT"

    Trigger Sentence: 1. The DOCILE boy DOES work very SILENTLY. 2. DOCTORS are DOCILE.

    Sample Sentence: The graduate students were *docile* and eager to learn.

DOCTRINAIRE (dok truh NAIR): n. /a. A person who tries to apply some doctrine or theory; inflexible; dogmatic

    Trigger: 1.DOCT-DOCUMENT. 2. NAIRS (OF KERALA)

    Trigger Sentence: 1. A DOCTRINAIRE is strictly according to religious DOCUMENTS (like Bible; Quran, Bagavath Geetha). 2. NAIRS of Kerala are said to be DOCTRINAIRE (extremely orthodox).

    Sample Sentence: A *doctrinaire* documents all the dos and don'ts.

    Related Words: 1. DOCTRINE- n. set of beliefs. 2. INDOCTRINATE- v. teach doctrines to

DOCTRINE (DOK trin): n. Set of guide lines to a particular subject, opinion; dogma

    Trigger: 1.DOCT-DOCUMENT. 2. DOCTR-DOCTOR

    Trigger Sentence: 1. A religious DOCUMENT is called a DOCTRINE. 2. A DOCTOR gives his DOCTRINE (a set of rules; prescription) to his patients.

    Sample Sentence: The *doctrines* of our holy texts are meant to discipline our society.

    Related Words: INDOCTRINATE- a. instruct in a particular doctrine; brainwash

DOGGED (DAW gid): a. Determined, stubborn

    Trigger: DOGGED-"DOG- GOOD"

    Trigger Sentence: Just like a POLICE DOG (which is good at sensing smell) the DOGGED DOG was determined to catch the criminal.

    Sample Sentence: The good dog never lacked *doggedness* in helping his master.

DOGMA (DAWG muh): n. System of religious laws or beliefs

    Trigger: DOGMA-AM GOD (Reverse READING)

    Trigger Sentence: DOG (reverse "GOD" for clue) is famous for loyalty & BELIEF; but DOGMA is a RELIGIOUS BELIEF.

    Sample Sentence: According to Stephen Hawking the belief in God is a *dogma*.

DOGMATIC (dawg MAT ik): a. Opinionated, rigid, authoritative

    Trigger: 1.DOGTAIL. 2. DOGMA-I'AM GOD (reverse)

    Trigger Sentence: 1. DOG TAIL is DOGMATIC; you can never make it straight; it is stubborn. 2. You can't argue with a DOGMATIC person who says that he is GOD.

    Sample Sentence: A *dogmatic* man can't be convinced like you can't make a *dog-tail* straight.

DOLDRUMS (DOHL drums): n. A dull, depressed mood; Lack of energy

    Trigger: 1. D +OLD +DRUMS. 2. DULL DRUMS

    Trigger Sentence: 1. THE OLD DRUMS are in DOLDRUMS. 2. DULL DRUMS are in DULL mood.

    Sample Sentence: The sound of those drums is so dull that listeners experience *doldrums*.

DOLEFUL (DOHL ful): a. Sad, sorrowful

    Trigger: 1. CONDOLE. 2. WOEFUL-DOLEFUL-RUEFUL (** near synonyms)

Trigger Sentence: 1. During CONDOLENCE meeting everyone appeared DOLEFUL. 2. WOEFUL, RUEFUL, SORROWFUL and DOLEFUL are synonym variants.

Sample Sentence: My *condolences* to the *doleful* family for the death of their pet dog.

DOLOROUS (DOL er uhs): a. Sorrowful

Trigger: CONDOLE- DOLEFUL-DOLOROUS-DOLDRUMS

Trigger Sentence: People are DOLOROUS during a CONDOLENCE meeting; CONDOLE-DOLEFUL-DOLOROUS-DOLDRUMS are synonym variants.

Sample Sentence: He could not face doldrums, so he put an end to his *dolorous* life.

DOLT (DOHLT): n. Stupid person

Trigger: DOLT-DULL+T

Trigger Sentence: A DOLT guy is a DULLARD.

Sample Sentence: Only a *dolt* would were his pants inside out!

DOMINANT (DOM uh nent): a. Most prominent, controlling, powerful

Trigger: 1.DOMAIN. 2.DOMINATE. 3.DOMINANT-PROMINENT

Trigger Sentence: He remains completely DOMINANT in his DOMAIN.

Sample Sentence: When the man became prominent, he started to behave *dominantly*.

Related Words: DOMINANCE - n. control, domination

DON (DON): v. To put on

Trigger: "D- ON" —"DRESS ON"

Trigger Sentence: DON means to PUT ON.

Sample Sentence: He *dons* a new avatar with a new dress every day.

Related Words: 1. DOFF – v. remove; put off. 2. DON - n. a person of great importance.

DORMANT (DOR munt): a. Inactive, Sleeping, Lazy

Trigger: 1.DORM-DORMITORY. 2. DOOR-MAT

Trigger Sentence: 1. Your life remains DORMANT as long as you live in a DORMITORY. 2. A DOOR-MAT lies DORMANT because it is lifeless.

Sample Sentence: Bears hibernate in caves and remain *dormant* throughout the winter.

DOSSIER (DAW see ey): n. A file of documents or records; detailed report

Trigger: DOSSIER-CASHIER

Trigger Sentence: CASHIER maintains a financial DOSSIER. Dossier is a file containing details.

Sample Sentence: I dug into the *dossiers* to trace out our ancestral property.

DOUR (DOWR): a. Gloomy; unfriendly; stubborn

Trigger: DOUR-SOUR

Trigger Sentence: His DOUR behaviour made us feel SOUR.

Sample Sentence: We *dourly* stood at the door and resisted the enemies coming inside.

DOWNRIGHT (DOUNrahyt): a. Straightforward; utter, complete

Trigger: DOWNRIGHT-OUTRIGHT (** synonyms)

Trigger Sentence: He is DOWNRIGHT/OUTRIGHT dishonest.

Sample Sentence: The tsunami was *downright* disturbing.

Related Words: 1.DOWNPLAY - v. understate; minimize. 2. DOWNCAST - a. depressed, dejected, disheartened. 3. DOWNSIZE - v. make smaller.

DRAB (DRAB): a. Dull, cheerless, lacking color

Trigger: 1.DRAB-DRAG. 2. FAB-DRAB

Trigger Sentence: 1. The novel becomes DRAB as it is DRAGGED unnecessarily. 2. Remove this DRAB dress and where this FAB (fabulous) dress.

Sample Sentence: Jane feels that life is a *drab* in towns as compared to the thrilling city life.

DRACONIAN (dray KOH nee un): a. Excessively harsh; cruel

Trigger: DRACONIAN-DRAGON-DRACULA

Trigger Sentence: Athenian lawmaker DRACO whose DRACONIAN laws prescribed death for almost every offense.

Sample Sentence: The millitants were *draconian* and chopping fingers of people who opposed.

DREAD (DRED): n. Fear; terror

Trigger: DREAD-DEAD

Trigger Sentence: I DREAD the thought of seeing a DEAD person.

Sample Sentence: He *dreads* dogs, so he dare not enter into my house which has drooling dogs!

DROLL (DROHL): a. Humorous, odd, funny

Trigger: DROLL-ROLL

Trigger Sentence: Comedian's humor was so DROLL that people were ROLLING on the ground.

Sample Sentence: I rolled down to laugh at the *droll* drama of my students.

DROUGHT (DROWT): n. Lack of rain, abnormally dry weather

Trigger: DROUGHT-"DRY OUT"

Trigger Sentence: During DROUGHTS, all the wells in the village DRY OUT.

Sample Sentence: India is struggling to cope with the consequences of a devastating *drought*.

DRUDGERY (DRUJ ur ee): n. Tiring work; menial labor

Trigger: DRUDGERY-no LUXURY

Trigger Sentence: Some people enjoy LUXURY at the cost of others DRUDGERY.

Sample Sentence: The workers were put through a lot of *drudgery* in this factory.

DUBIOUS (DOO bee us): a. Doubtful; questionable

Trigger: 1.DUBIOUS-OBVIOUS. 2. DUBIOUS-BOGUS

Trigger Sentence: 1. DUBIOUS is opposite to OBVIOUS. 2. BOGUS things evoke DUBIOUS feelings

Sample Sentence: I was already *dubious* about the bogus appearance of the saint.

Related Words: INDUBITABLE – a. obvious; unquestionable

DUCTILE (DUHK til): a. Malleable, flexible

Trigger: 1. DUCT. 2. DUCTILE-TRACTILE

Trigger Sentence: 1. The DUCTS which carry water are usually DUCTILE. 2. DUCTILE and TRACTILE (tractable) are synonyms.

Sample Sentence: Clay being *ductile* and tactile, most of the sculptors use it for modeling.

DULCET (DULL set): a. Sweet sounding, melodious

    Trigger: DULCET- DIL SE +T

    Trigger Sentence: "DIL SE" song of A.R. Rahman is a DULCET tone.

    Sample Sentence: The Vedic priest chanted the mantras with a gentle *dulcet* pitch.

DUPE (DOOP): v. Deceive, trick; n. fool

    Trigger: 1. DUPLICATE-DUPED. 2. DUPE-DOPE

    Trigger Sentence: 1. DUPES (n) are easily DUPED with DUPLICATE goods. 2. The DUPE (n) has been DOPED.

    Sample Sentence: 1. (n) It was hard to make out who was a killer and who a mere *dupe*. 2. (v) Clark's attempted to *dupe* the store owner with counterfeit bills resulted in his arrest.

DUPLICITY (doo PLIS uh tee): n. Double dealing; hypocrisy

    Trigger: DUPE-DUPLICATE (MONEY)

    Trigger Sentence: 1. DUPLICATE money creators are involved in DUPLICITY. 2. The DUPLICITY in the DUPLICATE copy is apparent.

    Sample Sentence: *Duplicity* can only lead to dejection as you are draining yourself by scheming.

DURESS (duh RESS): n. Coercion, forcible restraint

    Trigger: 1.DURESS-PRESS. 2. DURESS-ARREST

    Trigger Sentence: During his ARREST, he was kept under DURESS.

    Sample Sentence: The culprit confessed to his murder only after *duress*.

DWINDLE (DWIN dul): v. Reduce; shrink

    Trigger: DWINDLE-WRINKLE

    Trigger Sentence: The WRINKLED old man strength has been DWINDLED.

    Sample Sentence: Her bundles of money got swindled, and her savings *dwindled!*

EARNEST (UR nist): n. Seriousness, industriousness

    Trigger: EARNEST-EARN

    Trigger Sentence: To EARN anything (like to earn 99 percentile in GRE score) one has to make an EARNEST effort.

    Sample Sentence: I *earnestly* request you to consider my ill health and post me to my village.

EBULLIENT (i BUL yunt): a. Full of energy; excitement

    Trigger: EBULLIENT-Red BULL

    Trigger Sentence: You become EBULLIENT after drinking RED BULL energy drink.

    Sample Sentence: Pamella was *ebullient* when she told her friends about her first date.

Related Words: 1.EBULLIENCE - n. excitement.2.EXUBERANCE - n. abundance; high spirits.

ECCENTRIC (ek SEN trik): a. Irregular, Odd; bizarre

Trigger: ECCENTRIC-"EC - CENTRIC"-"OUT OF CENTER"

Trigger Sentence: CENTRIC means CENTRAL; while everybody follows (or goes in) the CENTRAL PATH, the ECCENTRIC deviates from it.

Sample Sentence: The professor was well-known for his *eccentric* antics.

ECCLESIASTIC (ih klee zee AS tik): a. Pertaining to the church or religion

Trigger: 1.ECCLESIASTIC- MONASTIC-MONK. 2. ECCLES (EGG LESS) + ASCETIC

Trigger Sentence: 1. ECCLESIASTIC people live MONASTIC (monk) life. 2. EGG LESS (religious people like Buddhist Monks never eat eggs) ASCETICS usually lead ECCLESIASTIC life.

Sample Sentence: This young man is already like an *ecclesiastic* and he will make a perfect priest.

ECHELON (ESH uh lon): n. level; rank

Trigger: 1.ECHELON-A LINE. 2. ECHELON-ELECTRON

Trigger Sentence: 1.In A LINE of an organization there will be an ECHELON, where people are arranged in an organized way according to their rank. 2. ELECTRONS of an atom or molecule are configured in an ECHELON.

Sample Sentence: The School is ranked within the upper *echelons* of engineering institutes.

ECLECTIC (i KLEK tik): a. Selecting from various sources

Trigger: 1.ECLECTIC-ELECTRIC. 2.ECLECTIC-SELECTION

Trigger Sentence: ELECTRIC power can be ECLECTIC. We can SELECT from Hydel, thermal, nuclear, renewable energy etc.

Sample Sentence: Sally's home décor is *eclectic*; she likes a both modern and antique.

ECLIPSE (i KLIPS): v. Darken, surpass

Trigger: ECLIPSE (lunar or solar)

Trigger Sentence: During lunar or solar ECLIPSE one celestial body DARKENS another celestial body.

Sample Sentence: Shyama believed that her ill fate was like an *eclipse*.

ECSTASY (EK stuh see): n. Joy; rapture

Trigger: 1. ECSTATIC-EXCITE STATE. 2. ECSTASY -EC (out) + STASY (static)

Trigger Sentence: 1. In ECSTASY a person reaches an EXCITED STATE. 2. When STATIC condition is OUT it is called DYNAMIC and ENERGETIC STATE.

Sample Sentence: She danced like a peacock in *ecstasy* under the cascading rainfalls!

Related Words: ECSTATIC - a. blissful

EDIFICATION (ed uh fi KEY shun): n. Education, instruction

Trigger: 1. EDUCATION. 2. EDIFY-EDUCATE

Trigger Sentence: 1. Moral EDUCATION is known as EDIFICATION. 2. EDIFY is to EDUCATE.

Sample Sentence: Educate your children and they will *edify* (v) their character.

Related Words: EDIFY - v. educate

EFFACE (uh FACE): v. Erase, rub-out

Trigger: EFFACED-ERASED (** synonyms)

Trigger Sentence: To EFFACE your bad memories you should ERASE your past memories.

2. Sometimes we SELF-EFFACE from the public by living an anonymous life.

Sample Sentence: To assure that he left no clues, the thief *effaced* his fingerprints on the safe.

Related Words: SELF-EFFACING – a. make inconspicuous; shy

EFFECTUAL (ih FECT choo ul): a. Effective; able to produce the desired effect

Trigger: 1.EFFECTUAL-EFFECTIVE (** synonyms). 2. EFFECTUAL--EFFICIENT

Trigger Sentence: The sermon eFFECTUALly brought an EFFECTIVE change in the listeners.

Sample Sentence: His efficient work *effectually* transformed the company's fortunes.

Related Words: INEFFECTUAL - a. inefficient; futile

EFFERVESCENT (ef er VES unt): a. Full of energy; producing bubbles of gas

Trigger: 1.EFFERVESCENT-A FERVOR SENSE. 2.FERVOR (FEVER OF LOVE-full of passion)

Trigger Sentence: 1. She has a SENSE OF FERVOR and she is EFFERVESCENT. 2. FERVOR-FERVID-FERVENT-EFFERVESCENT-PERFERVID-all belong to same family; full of LOVE and PASSION.

Sample Sentence: The freshers were refreshingly *effervescent*, bubbly and bright!

EFFETE (ih FEET): a. worn-out, exhausted; decadent

Trigger: 1. EFFETE-DEFEAT. 2. NO-EFFECTIVE

Trigger Sentence: His condition is EFFETE after the DEFEAT. He is NO more EFFECTIVE.

Sample Sentence: The *effete* self-proclaimed intellectuals tried to dominate young thinkers.

EFFICACY (EF i kuh see): a. Effective; effectiveness

Trigger: 1. EFFICIENCY–EFFICACY. 2. EFFICACIOUS- EFFICIENT

Trigger Sentence: 1. EFFICACY brings in EFFICIENCY. 2. This training programme is very EFFICACIOUS. It turns your employees into an EFFICIENT lot.

Sample Sentence: A series of tests measured the *efficacy* of the new cancer drug.

Related Words: EFFICACIOUS - a. effective

EFFRONTERY (e FRUNT ur ee): n. Shameless Boldness; impudence

Trigger: EFFRONTERY —"ZIP-FRONT"

Trigger Sentence: 1. If you remove your pant ZIP in FRONT of others, then you are characterized as EFFRONTERY. 2. His EFFRONTERY IN FRONT of such a distinguished crowd was shocking.

Sample Sentence: Only Teja had the *effrontery* to tell the teacher that he was goofing around.

EFFULGENT (ih FUHL juhnt): a. Radiant, shining brightly

Trigger: EFFULGENT-"A BLUE DETERGENT"

Trigger Sentence: The new BLUE DETERGENT can make even a dirty cloth EFFULGENT.

Sample Sentence: The stage was lit by a hundred lamps to create an *effulgent* aura.

EFFUSIVE (ih FYOO sihv): a. Gushing; Overflowing

Trigger: EFFUSIVE-EXCESSIVE (EMOTIONS)

Trigger Sentence: Mother kisses her baby EFFUSIVELY filling with EXCESSIVE EMOTION.

Sample Sentence: A person of excessive emotions offered *effusive* gratitude for our help.

Related Words: EFFUSION - n. pouring forth

EGALITARIAN (e gal uh TARE ee un): n. Advocate of equal rights.

Trigger: 1.EGAL-EQUAL. 2. EGALITY-EQUALITY

Trigger Sentence: An EGALITARIAN believes in the EQUALITY of all people.

Sample Sentence: Osho preached an *egalitarian* philosophy.

Related Words: EGALITY - n. equality

EGREGIOUS (i GREE jus): a. Outrageously bad, clearly wrong

Trigger: 1. EGREGIOUS-EGG RAISES. 2.EGREGIOUS-OUTRAGEOUS

Trigger Sentence: 1. When one gives an EGREGIOUS speech during a gathering, EGG RAISES or EGG REACHES them; people RAISE EGGS and throw at them. 2. OUTRAGEOUS acts of cruelty are known as EGREGIOUS crimes.

Sample Sentence: Kavitha's son was not just mischievous; he was an *egregious* terror.

ELATED (ih LEY tid): a. Happy; overjoyed

Trigger: ELATED-ELEVATED-(PROMOTED)

Trigger Sentence: When he was ELEVATED in his designation, he was ELATED.

Sample Sentence: My mother was *elated* to see my sister after over three years.

Related Words: 1. ELATION - n. high spirits; joy. 2. ELEVATE - v. exalt; lift, raise high.

ELEGY (EL uh jee): n. Sorrowful poem; lament

Trigger: 1. ELEGY-A LEGENDARY. 2. ELEGY-EULOGY (refer)

Trigger Sentence: 1. Whenever A LEGENDARY figure dies people usually sing an ELEGY. 2. ELEGY is a poem of sorrow whereas EULOGY is a poem of praise.

Sample Sentence: The princess sang an emotional *elegy* in the memory of her slain prince.

Related Words: ELEGIAC - a. mournful

ELICIT (i LIS it): v. Extract from; draw out by discussion

Trigger: 1. ELICIT-A LIP SAID. 2. ELICIT-ILLICIT (ILLEGAL)

Trigger Sentence: 1. A girl LIP SAID something. Can you ELICIT what she said? 2. Media ELICIT information from ILLICIT (illegal affair) love affairs of Bill Clinton.

Sample Sentence: It is difficult to *elicit* responses from these set of dumb students.

ELITE (i LEET): n. A group of people considered to be superior in a society or organization.

Trigger: 1.ELITE-ELECT. 2. ELITE-SOCIALITE

Trigger Sentence: 1. We ELECT the ELITE (the best) people. 2. SOCIALITES are treated as ELITE.

Sample Sentence: Usually only individuals of *elite* class get elected to responsible positions.

ELIXIR (e LIX ur): n. Cure-all; panacea

Trigger: ELIXIR-A LIQUOR

Trigger Sentence: LIQUOR is AN ELIXIR for pains; some people take A LIQUOR to forget pains.

Sample Sentence: Economists predicted that liberalization would be an *elixir* for financial woes.

ELOQUENCE (EL uh kwuns): n. Fluent or persuasive speaking

Trigger: ELOQUENT-FLUENT

Trigger Sentence: FLUENCY is needed to be ELOQUENT and expressive.

Sample Sentence: Arjun has a great vocabulary and he spoke with *eloquence*.

Related Words: ELOQUENT - a. expressive

ELUCIDATE (i LOO so dayt): v. Make clear, explain

> **Trigger:** ELUCIDATE-LUCID (refer)
>
> **Trigger Sentence:** 1. LUCID-CLEAR; ELUCIDATE-MAKE CLEAR; PELLUCID-CLEAR; LUC-LOOK; LOOK everything is LUCID (clear). 2. She ELUCIDATED the point LUCIDLY.
>
> **Sample Sentence:** Doctors should always *elucidate* test results to their patients.
>
> Related Words: LUCID - a. clear

ELUDE (ih LOOD): v. Evade, avoid

> **Trigger:** ELUDE-EVADE- AVOID
>
> **Trigger Sentence:** 1. The fox succeeded in ELUDING (EVADING-AVOIDING) the hunters. 2. Elude, evade and avoid are synonyms.
>
> **Sample Sentence:** He evades repaying by *eluding* his lenders.
>
> Related Words: ELUSIVE - n. evasive

ELUSIVE (i LOO siv): a. Difficult to catch; evasive

> **Trigger:** 1.ELLUSIVE-ILLUSIVE. 2. ELUDE-EVADE-AVOID (refer)
>
> **Trigger Sentence:** ILLUSIVE things such as MIRAGES are ELUSIVE (difficult to catch).
>
> **Sample Sentence:** The *elusive* God particle is no more *evasive*. It has been explained.

EMACIATE (i MAY see ayt): v. Make lean, make thin

> **Trigger:** EMACIATE-NO MASS HE ATE
>
> **Trigger Sentence:** As HE ATE NO MASS, he EMACIATED beyond recognition.
>
> **Sample Sentence:** Thousands of children in Ethiopia are *emaciated* due to hunger.

EMANCIPATE (i MAN suh peyt): v. Set free; liberate

> **Trigger:** EMANCIPATE –E (out) + MAN
>
> **Trigger Sentence:** From the manual labor A MAN is EMANCIPATED.
> (Prefix "e": "e-out"; "ex-out";"ef-out".)
>
> **Sample Sentence:** The dishwasher *emancipated* women from the domestic drudgery.

EMBARGO (em BAHR goh): n. A legal prohibition on commerce; ban

> **Trigger:** 1.EMBARGO-"END + CARGO". 2. BAR-BAN
>
> **Trigger Sentence:** 1. USA imposes EMBARGO (END OF CARGO (shipment)) on many dictatorial governments. 2. BAR is to DEBAR and BAN.
>
> **Sample Sentence:** Petrol prices will increase if there is an *embargo* on oil imports from Arab.

EMBELLISH (im BEL ish): v. Adorn, ornament, and decorate

> **Trigger:** BELLE- BELLY
>
> **Trigger Sentence:** A BELLE (beautiful girl) EMBELLISHES her BELLY.
>
> **Sample Sentence:** Chandrahasa's dance ornaments are *embellished* with diamonds and rubies.

EMBEZZLE (im BEZ ul): v. Steal

> **Trigger:** 1. BEZZANT (gold coin in Byzantine Empire period). 2. BUZZ.
>
> **Trigger Sentence:** 1. They EMBEZZLED thousands of BEZZANTS. 2. The alarm BUZZED when there was EMBEZZLEMENT in the bank.
>
> **Sample Sentence:** The accountant was caught *embezzling* money from the bank.

EMBLEMATIC (em bluh MAT ik): v. Symbolic

    Trigger: EMBLEM-SYMBOL

    Trigger Sentence: A crown SYMBOL is EMBLEMATIC of royalty.

    Sample Sentence: The market's free fall is *emblematic* of the declining economy.

EMBROIL (im BROYL): v. In a difficult situation; entangle

    Trigger: 1. I AM BROILED-EMBROILED. 2. BOIL (cook) + BROIL (roast)

    Trigger Sentence: 1. I am in A BROIL, totally in EMBROILED state. 2. The cook is in an EMBROILED state, whether to BOIL or BROIL the mutton.

    Sample Sentence: As the country is *embroiled* in Civil War, people are boiling in dissatisfaction.

    Related Words: IMBROGLIO - n. an extremely confused or complicated situation.

EMEND (ee MEND): v. Correct errors; improve

    Trigger: 1.AMEND-EMEND-MEND. 2. MEND-BEND

    Trigger Sentence: 1. By MENDING his ways he AMENDED the expletive content in his book. 2. AMEND, MEND and EMEND are synonyms.

    Sample Sentence: The author wanted to *emend* his book due to printing errors.

EMINENT (EM ih nent): a. Famous, prominent

    Trigger: 1.EMINENT- EMINEM. 2. PROMINENT-EMINENT

    Trigger Sentence: 1. Rapper EMINEM is an EMINENT person. 2. Usually PROMINENT people become more EMINENT in human society.

    Sample Sentence: Michael Jordan is the most *eminent* basketball player of this century.

    Related Words: EMINENCE - n. high position.

EMPATHY (EM puh thee): n. Understanding, sympathy

    Trigger: EMPATHY-SYMPATHY (SAME-PITY)

    Trigger Sentence: People with EMPATHY express right amount of SYMPATHY.

    Sample Sentence: I *empathize* with Kim and commiserate with her health conditions.

EMPHATIC (em FAT ik): a. Forceful, definite, clear

    Trigger: EMPHATIC -EMPHASIZE

    Trigger Sentence: They EMPHASIZED his idea with EMPHATIC clarity.

    Sample Sentence: The orders are absolute and *emphatic*...no alterations will be entertained.

    Related Words: 1.EMPHASIZE – v. stress the importance of. 2. DE-EMPHASIZE –v. play down

EMPIRICAL (em PIR uh kul): a. Based on experience

    Trigger: 1. EMPIRICALLY-EXPERIMENTALLY. 2. UMPIRE

    Trigger Sentence: 1. EMPIRICAL experiences help us learn things EXPERIMENTALLY. 2. UMPIRES are usually EMPIRICAL in their approach.

    Sample Sentence: *Empirical* evidence is what required in understanding the gene pool.

EMULATE (IM u late): v. Imitate; rival

    Trigger: EMULATE-IMITATE-SIMULATE

    Trigger Sentence: EMULATE is to IMITATE; and SIMULATE also means IMITATE.

    Sample Sentence: My competitor tried his best to *emulate* my style of teaching but failed!

    Related Words: SIMULATE - v. imitate; pretend

ENAMOUR (ih NAM er): a. Be filled with love.

    Trigger: 1. ENAMOUR-I AM YOUR. 2. EN-AMOUR (AFFAIR-LOVE)

    Trigger Sentence: 1. When you are ENAMORED with someone, you will say I AM YOURS. 2. I'm IN AMOUR (AFFAIR) with a girl. Bill Gates had an AFFAIR with Monica who ENAMOURED him.

    Sample Sentence: I am completely *enamored* by the beauty of Taj Mahal.

ENCHANT (en CHANT): v. Delight; charm

    Trigger: EN+ CHANT - (CHARM)

    Trigger Sentence: To CHARM someone; when a girl CHARMS a boy, he CHANTS her name.

    Sample Sentence: The charm of Marilyn Monroe *enchanted* millions of people in the world.

    Related Words: 1.ENCHANTING - a. charming .2.DISENCHANT – v. let down; disappoint

ENCOMIUM (en KOME ee um): n. Praise, eulogy

    Trigger: 1.INCOME (ENCOM). 2. IN-COMELY (EN+COMI+UM)

    Trigger Sentence: 1. If you donate your INCOME, people are going to give you an ENCOMIUM. 2. You look so COMELY....He paid a rich ENCOMIUM on her COMELY and lovely appearance.

    Sample Sentence: Who does not seek *encomiums*?

    Related Words: OPPROBRIUM- n. humiliation; insult

ENCOMPASS (en KUHM puhs): v. Include comprehensively; enclose

    Trigger: 1. ENCOMPASS- IN COMPASS. 2. ENCOMPASS-ENCLOSE-ENCIRCLE

    Trigger Sentence: When we ENCOMPASS, we draw a CIRCLE with a COMPASS and ENCLOSE.

    Sample Sentence: He *encompassed* the globe by encircling it in a jetliner.

ENCROACH (en KROACH): v. Trespass, occupy beyond set limits

    Trigger: 1.ROACH. 2. ENCROACH-EN+CRASH

    Trigger Sentence: 1. The COCKROACHES ENCROACH wherever there is food. 2. He CRASHED the gates and ENCROACHED the building.

    Sample Sentence: The estate had warning signs against *encroaching* trespassers.

ENCUMBER (en KUHM ber): v. Burden

    Trigger: ENCUMBER-LUMBER-TIMBER

    Trigger Sentence: 1. LUMBER, TIMBER, ENCUMBER; all are heavy and represent burden. 2. Imagine a large CUCUMBER and you will be ENCUMBERED by its heaviness.

    Sample Sentence: He said the campaign did not *encumber* the public funds.

ENDEAVOR (in DEV ur): v. Try hard; make an effort to achieve a goal

    Trigger: ENDEAVOR-ENDURE

    Trigger Sentence: He ENDURED lot of pain in an ENDEAVOR to achieve 6-pack body

    Sample Sentence: Hundreds of runners *endeavored* to win the Olympic Marathon.

ENDEMIC (en DEM ik): a. Native, local, limited to an area.

    Trigger: 1.ENDEMIC. 2.ENDEMIC-INDIGENOUS

    Trigger Sentence: 1. Malaria EPIDEMIC is ENDEMIC and especially belongs to tribal region. 2. Something ENDEMIC is also known as INDIGENOUS.

    Sample Sentence: Caste system was an *endemic* culture among the natives.

ENDORSE (en DAWRS): v. Approve; support
>   **Trigger:** 1.ENDORSE-HORSE. 2. ENDORSE-NURSE
>   **Trigger Sentence:** 1. The jockey ENDORSED his HORSE. 2. The NURSE ENDORSED the medicine.
>   **Sample Sentence:** My project got *endorsed* by the government.

ENDOW (en DOW): v. Grant; give especially a large gift; give ability
>   **Trigger:** 1.ENDOW-WIDOW. 2. ENDOW- DOWRY
>   **Trigger Sentence:** 1. The WIDOW was ENDOWED with money. 2. I ENDOWED DOWRY.
>   **Sample Sentence:** My Grandfather John *endowed* his alma-mater with a trust fund.

ALLEVIATED : relieve pain, lessens, makes tolerable

RAMSHACKLED : falling to pieces, rickety

Memory Test-37 : Match each word and its memory trick to the corresponding definition.

S.N	WORD	MEMORY TRIGGER	S.N	DEFINITIONS	KEY
1	DOCILE	They Do-silent	A	controlling, powerful	
2	DOCTRINAIRE	Strictly document	B	Determined, stubborn	
3	DOCTRINE	Religious DOCUMENT	C	Dull, cheerless, lacking color	
4	DOGGED	Dog- good	D	Dull, lack of energy	
5	DOGMA	I Am god -dogma	E	Excessively harsh; cruel	
6	DOGMATIC	dog tail is dogmatic	F	Fear; terror	
7	DOLDRUMS	Dull drums	G	File of documents; detailed report	
8	DOLEFUL	Woeful-doleful-rueful	H	Gloomy; unfriendly; stubborn	
9	DOLOROUS	Condole- doleful-dolorous	I	Humorous, odd, funny	
10	DOLT	DOLT guy -DULLARD	J	Inactive, Sleeping, Lazy	
11	DOMINANT	Dominate	K	inflexible; dogmatic	
12	DON	on	L	Obedient , manageable	
13	DORMANT	Door-mat is DORMANT	M	Put on	
14	DOSSIER	Cashier has a dossier	N	Rigid, opinionated, authoritative	
15	DOUR	DOUR - SOUR	O	Sad, sorrowful	
16	DOWNRIGHT	OUTRIGHT	P	Set of guide lines , opinion	
17	DRAB	Dragging	Q	Sorrowful	
18	DRACONIAN	Dragon-dracula behavior	R	Straightforward; complete	
19	DREAD	If I see Dead-dread	S	Stupid person	
20	DROLL	People are ROLLING	T	System of religious laws or beliefs	

Memory Test-38 : Match each word and its memory trick to the corresponding definition.

S.N	WORD	MEMORY TRIGGER	S.N	DEFINITIONS	KEY
1	DROUGHT	Dry out	A	Coercion, forcible restraint	
2	DRUDGERY	No LUXURY	B	Darken, surpass	
3	DUBIOUS	Opp. to OBVIOUS	C	Deceive, trick ; fool	
4	DUCTILE	Ducts are ductile	D	Double dealing; hypocrisy	
5	DULCET	DIL SE tone is dulcet	E	Doubtful; questionable	
6	DUPE	Duplicate-duped	F	Education, instruction	
7	DUPLICITY	Duplicate man	G	Effective	
8	DURESS	Press- Duress-arrest	H	Erase, rub-out	
9	DWINDLE	Size Wrinkled	I	Full of energy; excitement	
10	EARNEST	To Earn make effort	J	Irregular, Odd; bizarre	
11	EBULLIENT	Red BULL	K	Joy; rapture	
12	ECCENTRIC	Out of center	L	Lack of rain, abnormally dry	
13	ECCLESIASTIC	monastic-monk	M	Level; rank	
14	ECHELON	A LINE of rule	N	Malleable, flexible	
15	ECLECTIC	Eclectic-selection	O	Reduce; shrink	
16	ECLIPSE	ECLIPSE (lunar)	P	Related to the church or religion	
17	ECSTASY	Excite state	Q	Selecting from various sources	
18	EDIFICATION	Education	R	Seriousness, industriousness	
19	EFFACE	Effaced-erased	S	Sweet sounding, melodious	
20	EFFECTUAL	Effectual-effective	T	Tiring work; menial labor	

Answers	EX.NO	1	2	3	4	5	6	7	8	9	10	11	12	13	14	15	16	17	18	19	20
	37	L	K	P	B	T	N	D	O	Q	S	A	M	J	G	H	R	C	E	F	I
	38	L	T	E	N	S	C	D	A	O	R	I	J	P	M	Q	B	K	F	H	G

Memory Test-39 : Match each word and its memory trick to the corresponding definition.

S.N	WORD	MEMORY TRIGGER	S.N	DEFINITIONS	KEY
1	EFFERVESCENT	A fervor sense	A	Advocate of equal rights	
2	EFFETE	No-effective	B	Cure-all; panacea	
3	EFFICACY	Efficiency	C	Difficult to catch; evasive	
4	EFFRONTERY	Zip-front	D	Draw out by discussion;extract	
5	EFFULGENT	A blue detergent	E	Effective; effectiveness	
6	EFFUSIVE	Excessive (emotions)	F	Evade, avoid	
7	EGALITARIAN	Egal-equal	G	Fluent or persuasive speaking	
8	EGREGIOUS	Outrageous	H	Full of energy; bubbly	
9	ELATED	Elevated	I	Gushing; Overflowing	
10	ELEGY	A legendary dies	J	Happy; overjoyed	
11	ELICIT	A lip said	K	legal ban on commerce	
12	ELITE	Elite-socialite	L	Make clear, explain	
13	ELIXIR	A liquor	M	Make lean, make thin	
14	ELOQUENCE	Fluent	N	Outrageously bad, clearly wrong	
15	ELUCIDATE	Lucid	O	Radiant, shining brightly	
16	ELUDE	Elude-evade- avoid	P	Selected as the best	
17	ELUSIVE	Elusive-evasive	Q	Set free; liberate	
18	EMACIATE	He ate no mass	R	Shameless Boldness; impudence	
19	EMANCIPATE	A MAN is free	S	Sorrowful poem; lament	
20	EMBARGO	End + cargo	T	Worn-out, exhausted	

Memory Test-40 : Match each word and its memory trick to the corresponding definition.

S.N	WORD	MEMORY TRIGGER	S.N	DEFINITIONS	KEY
1	EMBELLISH	A belle embellishes	A	Approve; support	
2	EMBEZZLE	Bezzant -buzz	B	Based on experience	
3	EMBLEMATIC	Symbol	C	Be filled with love	
4	EMBROIL	I am broiled	D	Burden	
5	EMEND	Emend-mend	E	Correct errors; improve	
6	EMINENT	Eminem	F	Decorate and adorn	
7	EMPATHY	Sympathy (same-pity)	G	Delight; charm	
8	EMPHATIC	Emphasize	H	Famous, prominent	
9	EMPIRICAL	Experimentally	I	Forceful, definite, clear	
10	EMULATE	Imitate-simulate	J	Grant; give ability	
11	ENAMOUR	I am your	K	Imitate; rival	
12	ENCHANT	En+ chant -charm	L	In a difficult situation; entangle	
13	ENCOMIUM	You are so comely	M	Include comprehensively; enclose	
14	ENCOMPASS	enclose-encircle	N	Native, local, limited to an area	
15	ENCROACH	En+crash	O	Praise, eulogy	
16	ENCUMBER	Lumber-timber	P	Steal	
17	ENDEAVOR	Endeavor-endure	Q	Symbolic	
18	ENDEMIC	Endemic-indigenous	R	Trespass	
19	ENDORSE	Endorse-nurse	S	Try hard; make an effort	
20	ENDOW	Endow- give dowry	T	Understanding, sympathy	

Answers	EX.NO	1	2	3	4	5	6	7	8	9	10	11	12	13	14	15	16	17	18	19	20
	39	H	T	E	R	O	I	A	N	J	S	D	P	B	G	L	F	C	M	Q	K
	40	F	P	Q	L	E	H	T	I	B	K	C	G	O	M	R	D	S	N	A	J

WORD GROUPS DAY-10

★ PASSION-PASSIONATE

ADJECTIVES: ardent, fervid, fervent, frenzied, enthusiastic, passionate, impassioned, intense, vehement, wholehearted, earnest

NOUNS: ardor, fervor, gusto, spirit, verve, zeal, zealot, zest

VERB: arouse, enthuse, excite, rhapsodize, galvanize

ANTONYMS: n. apathy, indifference, lethargy, languor, torpor, impassiveness.

★ LOVE -LIKE

ADJECTIVES: cherished

NOUNS: adulation, allegiance, amour, ardency, ardor, enchantment, fervor, fidelity, hankering, idolatry, infatuation, passion, piety, rapture, worship, yearning, zeal; aptitude, bent, disposition, leaning, penchant, predilection, predisposition, proclivity, proneness, propensity, yen

VERB: cherish, dote, relish

ANTONYMS: n. standard

★ FALSEHOOD

ADJECTIVES: affected, apocryphal, bogus, disingenuous, duplicitous, erroneous, phony, counterfeit, factitious, fallacious, fictitious, fraudulent, feigned, hypocritical, specious, spurious, sham

NOUNS: lying, artifice, deceit, deception, mendacity, untruthfulness, fabrication, perjury, posturing, pretence, treachery; equivocation, prevarication

VERB: conceal, dissemble, equivocate, feign, mislead, prevaricate

ANTONYMS: n.truth, fact, veracity, reality

★ TRUTH –TRUTHFUL

ADJECTIVES: candid, frank, honest, legitimate, ingenuous, open, forthright, straightforward, reliable

NOUNS: candor, credibility, credence, integrity, veracity, verity, verisimilitude, sincerity, honesty; validity, factuality, authenticity

VERB: be honest, tell truth

ANTONYMS: artifice, mendacity, falsify

★ TRICKY/FRAUD NATURE

ADJECTIVES: dissembling, fraudulent

NOUNS: charlatan, hypocrite, mountebank, impostor, quack, swindler; chicanery, duplicity, fraud, guile, skullduggery, sophistry, subterfuge

VERB: bamboozle, camouflage, disguise, dissemble, masquerade, dupe, feign, gull, hoax, hoodwink, sham, simulate

ANTONYMS: adj. naïve, forthright, straightforward, n. candor, truthfulness

★ METICULOUS: very careful and precise

ADJECTIVES: accurate, conscientious, diligent, demanding, exact, fastidious, finicky, meticulous, methodical, pedantic, punctilious, painstaking, scrupulous, thorough

NOUNS: perfectionist, pedant, purist, stickler thoroughness

VERB: heed

ANTONYMS: adj. casual, careless, carefree; lenient

Word List Day-11

ENDURING (en DYOOR ing): v. Lasting; surviving

   Trigger: DURABLE

   Trigger Sentence: Anything that is DURABLE is ENDURING.

   Sample Sentence: Known for its durable goods, the company has *endured* the tough market.

   Related Words: 1.ENDURE - v. tolerate. 2. DURABLE – a. long-lasting

ENERVATE (EN er veyt): v. Weaken, tiring

   Trigger: 1.ENERVATE-NO ENERGY. 2. ENERVATE-HE NEVER ATE

   Trigger Sentence: 1. After ENERVATING work, I LOST all my ENERGY. 2. As HE DID NOT EAT anything last week, he was ENERVATED.

   Sample Sentence: The cancer treatment has *enervated* her, she has no energy.

ENFRANCHISE (en FRAN chyze): v. Give the right to vote to

   Trigger: ENFRANCHISE-FRANCHISE (free)

   Trigger Sentence: Mc Donald's ENFRANCHISES its business to its FRANCHISEES.

   Sample Sentence: Women were not *enfranchised* and could not vote in earlier times.

ENGAGE (en GEYJ): v. Attract; employ; commit; confront

   Trigger: ENGAGE-GAZE

   Trigger Sentence: The young age girl's GAZE ENGAGED the boy.

   Sample Sentence: Video games kept him *engaged* throughout the day.

   Related Words: 1. ENGAGING - a. charming; attractive. 2.DISENGAGE – v. disconnect; etach

ENGENDER (en JEN dur): v. Produce, cause

   Trigger: GENDER-GENERATE

   Trigger Sentence: Male GENDER and female GENDER ENGENDER (GENERATE) another gender.

   Sample Sentence: Gender bias *engenders* conflict in society.

ENHANCE (en HANS): v. Improve; Increase

   Trigger: ENHANCE-ADVANCE

   Trigger Sentence: ENHANCE is to ADVANCE

   Sample Sentence: I *enhanced* my computer's modem. I can work faster now.

ENIGMA (uh NIG muh): n. A mysterious thing

   Trigger: AN EGG or MA!!!- DILEMMA

   Trigger Sentence: Which is born first-An EGG or its MA? I am in a DILEMMA-It is AN ENIGMA.

   Sample Sentence: She remained an *enigma* with many secrets buried in her heart!

   Related Words: ENIGMATIC - a. obscure, puzzling

ENLIGHTENED (en LAHYT nd): a. Knowledgeable, broad-minded

   Trigger: ENLIGHTEN-LIGHT

   Trigger Sentence: Follow god's LIGHT....you will be ENLIGHTENED.

   Sample Sentence: 1. The results of our research *enlightened* our colleagues.2.Goutama Buddha was *enlightened* under the Bodhi Tree.

ENMITY (EN mi tee): n. Hatred; animosity

    Trigger: ENMITY-ENEMY

    Trigger Sentence: The political ENEMIES had experienced the feudal ENMITY for years.

    Sample Sentence: The *enmity* between the feuding landlords is the center of the story.

ENNUI (AHN wee): n. Boredom

    Trigger: ENNUI-(refer)-ANNOY (ANTI-JOY)

    Trigger Sentence: The perennial ENNUI ANNOYS the members of the aesthetic club.

    Sample Sentence: I expected some excitement but ended up in *ennui*.

ENORMITY (i NOR muh tee): n. Hugeness (in a bad sense); immensity

    Trigger: eNORMity-NORM-NORMAL

    Trigger Sentence: More than NORMAL size or intensity can be termed as ENORMITY.

    Sample Sentence: The *enormity* of the universe is an enchanting mystery!

ENRAGE (in RAGE): v. Infuriate, anger

    Trigger: 1. ENRAGE-RAGE-ROUSE. 2. ENRAGE-ANGREZ

    Trigger Sentence: 1. The chief's ENRAGE ROUSED the feelings of the employees. 2. Indians were ENRAGED with the ANGREZ before independence.

    Sample Sentence: The *enraged* crowd pelted stones at the glass building.

ENRICH (en RICH): v. Improve the quality or value of, make better

    Trigger: ENRICH-RICH

    Trigger Sentence: The RICH experience ENRICHED her understanding.

    Sample Sentence: This memory trick book *enriched* my English vocabulary.

ENSCONCE (en SKONS): v. Settle comfortably; install; establish; hide

    Trigger: ENSCONCE-INSCONCE-ISKCONS

    Trigger Sentence: In ISKCONS temple lord Krishna's sculpture is ENSCONCED.

    Sample Sentence: After retirement, he wants to *ensconce* with his wife in a simple village.

ENSHROUD (en SHROUD): v. To shroud; conceal, to cover

    Trigger: ENSHROUD-"IN CLOUD"

    Trigger Sentence: IN CLOUDS sun is ENSHROUDED; sun is covered by CLOUDS.

    Sample Sentence: For thousands of years the cave temple was *enshrouded* in thick jungle.

    Related Words: SHROUD -: v. conceal, obscure

ENTAIL (in TAYL): v. Necessitate; require; involve

    Trigger: 1. ENTAIL-"END-TAIL". 2. ENTAIL-DETAIL

    Trigger Sentence: 1. TAIL is a NECESSARY part for most of the animals; Lord Hanuman role ENTAILS a TAIL at the END. 2. The project ENTAILS considerable DETAILS of related issues.

    Sample Sentence: Any financial investment *entails* some degree of risk.

ENTANGLE (en TANG gul): v. To complicate; to twist together

    Trigger: 1.ENTANGLE-"IN TANGLE". 2. ENTANGLE- IN TRIANGLE

    Trigger Sentence: 1. Bermuda TRIANGLE is a TANGLE; TANGLE and ENTANGLE are synonyms. 2. She is ENTANGLED in a romantic TRIANGLE.

    Sample Sentence: I became *entangled* in a court case.

    Related Words: DISENTANGLE - n. free, release

ENTHRALL (en THRAWL): v. Captivate, enslave

Trigger: ENTHRALL-THRILL

Trigger Sentence: The crime THRILLER film was ENTHRALLING.

Sample Sentence: We were *enthralled* and thrilled at the Disney Park.

ENTICE (in TICE): v. Tempt, attract; lure

Trigger: 1. ENT (ENTRAP) + ICE (EYES). 2. ENTRAP WITH ICE (EYES)

Trigger Sentence: 1. She ENTRAPs with her ENTICING EYES. 2. She ENTICES me with ICY phrases.

Sample Sentence: Food and entertainment contribute to the *enticement* of a cruise vacation.

ENTITLE (en TAHYT l): v. Give the right to; give a title to

Trigger: ENTITLE-TITLE

Trigger Sentence: Vivian Richard's extraordinary batting in his cricket career ENTITLED him to win the knighthood TITLE- "Sir".

Sample Sentence: The card *entitles* me to get a discount in this store.

ENTRENCH (en TRENCH): v. Settle comfortably; encroach

Trigger: 1. ENTRENCH-IN TRENCH. 2. ENTRENCH -ENCROACH

Trigger Sentence: 1. IN a TRENCH he ENTRENCHED. 2. ENTRENCH also means ENCROACHING.

Sample Sentence: After years of hard work, they finally *entrenched* themselves in business.

ENUMERATE (i NOO muh rayt): v. Mention one by one, list

Trigger: ENUMERATE- A+ NUMBER+ RATE

Trigger Sentence: The doctor ENUMERATED the list of NUMBER of advantages of the drug.

Sample Sentence: The salesman *enumerated* all the special features of the car.

ENUNCIATE (ee NUN see ayt): v. Speak clearly

Trigger: 1. ENUNCIATE-PRONOUNCE-ANNOUNCE. 2. ENUNCIATE-COMMUNICATE.

Trigger Sentence: 1. ENUNCIATE is to COMMUNICATE properly. 2. He ENUNCIATED all the syllables with nice PRONUNCIATION.

Sample Sentence: Prasad must learn to *enunciate* before he becomes a public speaker.

ENVISION (in VIZH un): v. To picture or visualize; imagine

Trigger: ENVISION -IN VISION (IMAGE) - VISUALIZE

Trigger Sentence: 1. When you ENVISION, you are under a VISION or IMAGE about your life. 2. What kind of career do you ENVISION for yourself?

Sample Sentence: I *envision* India to be corrupt free, hope my visualization becomes a reality.

Related Words: ENVISAGE - v. visualize, imagine

EPHEMERAL (i FEM ur al): a. Short-lived, fleeting

Trigger: 1. EPHEMERAL -A FUNERAL. 2. EPHEMERAL-ETERNAL(** near antonyms)

Trigger Sentence: 1. In A FUNERAL we're reminded of the fact that human life is EPHEMERAL. 2. Life is EPHEMERAL, it is not ETERNAL.

Sample Sentence: My first love was the sweetest, but was an *ephemeral* experience.

EPIDEMIC (ep i DEM ik): n. /a. Plague, something which spreads quickly (i.e. a disease)

Trigger: ENDEMIC-PANDEMIC-EPIDEMIC

Trigger Sentence: EPIDEMIC (PANDEMIC) like a plague is something that spreads to vast area and ENDEMIC (like congenital diseases) is confined to small area.

Sample Sentence: Corruption is growing like an *epidemic* in our country.

EPIGRAM (EP ih gram): n. Short and witty saying

Trigger: 1.TELEGRAM. 2. EPIGRAM-EPIC (** near antonyms)

Trigger Sentence: 1. On TELEGRAM we generally WRITE CONCISELY. 2. An EPIC is a long narrative poem; whereas EPIGRAM is a shorter one.

Sample Sentence: Sally's favorite epigram is, "A friend in need is a friend indeed."

EPILOGUE (EP uh log): n. Short speech at conclusion

Trigger: EPILOGUE-END DIALOGUE

Trigger Sentence: EPILOGUE is the conclusion or END-DIALOGUE of a book or a speech.

Sample Sentence: The whole book was so boring but for the *epilogue*!

EPISODIC (ep uh ZOD ik): a. Occurring at irregular intervals

Trigger: 1. EPISODE-1; EPISODE-2; EPISODE-3 2. IN EPISODES

Trigger Sentence: 1. Star Wars episode-1; episode-2; episode-3; they occur EPISODICALLY. 2. Harry potter -7th novel was made into TWO SEPARATE EPISODES.

Sample Sentence: The long novel was filmed for television as an *episodic* soap opera.

EPISTLE (ih PIS uhl): n. Long formal letter, missive

Trigger: EPISTLE-"A POSTAL"

Trigger Sentence: In A POSTAL service he sent lengthy EPISTLES to her.

Sample Sentence: An *epistle* is long postal letter carried by an apostle.

Related Words: 1. EPISTOLARY - n. related to a long formal letters. 2. MISSIVE - : letter

EPITOME (i PIT uh mee): n. Perfect example; embodiment

Trigger: EPITOME-"EPIC+ OME"

Trigger Sentence: In Hindu EPIC – OME is a perfect symbol or EPITOME of divinity.

Sample Sentence: Mahatma Gandhi is an *epitome* of peace, harmony and non violence.

Related Words: TOME –n. large book

EQUABLE (EK wuh bull): a. Uniform, steady; calm

Trigger: 1. EQUABLE-STABLE. 2. EQUABLE-EQUAL

Trigger Sentence: EQUABLE climate means STABLE climate.

Sample Sentence: Southern Florida lays claim to a pleasant and *equable* temperature.

EQUANIMITY (ek wuh NIM uh tee): n. Calmness; composure; emotional stability

Trigger: EQUANIMITY-EQUALITY-EQUAL

Trigger Sentence: If you have a mind of EQUANIMITY, you will show EQUAL emotion.

Sample Sentence: The young soldier faced his death with *equanimity*.

EQUILIBRIUM (ek wuh LIB ree um): n. Balance

Trigger: EQUAL +LIBRA (balance)

Trigger Sentence: 1. EQUILIBRIUM; EQUANIMITY; EQUIPOISE; all are synonym variants. 2. The state of economy reaches EQUILIBRIUM with EQUAL BALANCE in demand and supply.

Sample Sentence: A bad cocktail drink can cause dizziness or loss of *equilibrium*.

EQUIPOISE (EK wuh poiz): n. Balance, equilibrium, stability

Trigger: EQUIPOISE- EQUAL POSE

Trigger Sentence: EQUAL POSE on both left & right (sad & happy) represents A BALANCED mind.

Sample Sentence: In this hour of loss and sadness, Vishal stood with *equipoise*.

EQUITABLE (EK wuh tuh bul): a. Fair and impartial

Trigger: EQUITABLE-EQUALITY

Trigger Sentence: Socialist countries follow EQUITABLE policy and provide EQUAL opportunities.

Sample Sentence: The panel of adjudicators is supposed to maintain an *equitable* judgment.

EQUIVOCAL (i KWIV uh kul): a. Ambiguous; intentionally misleading

Trigger: EQUIVOCAL-DOUBLE VOCAL

Trigger Sentence: 1. DOUBLE VOCAL (or VOICE) people are EQUALLY VOCAL to the both sides of any issue. 2.DOUBLE VOCAL (or DOUBLE TONGUE) people MISLEAD others.

Sample Sentence: He gave an *equivocal* directional route map that we ended up nowhere!

Related Words: UNEQUIVOCAL - v. clear, unambiguous

EQUIVOCATE (ee KWIV oh kayt): v. Lie; mislead; use words with double meanings

Trigger: EQUIVOCATE-EQUIVOCAL-DOUBLE VOCAL

Trigger Sentence: 1. DOUBLE VOICE people MISLEAD.2. An EQUIVOCAL talk has DOUBLE interpretation.

Sample Sentence: He *equivocated* in his report on the stolen antiques to the press.

ERADICATE (ee RAD i kayt): v. Destroy

Trigger: 1. ERASE. 2. ERADICATE-A RADIUM ACT

Trigger Sentence: 1. ERASE is to WIPE OUT...ERADICATE an evil. 2. RADIUM (radiation therapy) ERADICATED cancer; RADIATION generally DESTROYS.

Sample Sentence: My father is on a little mission to *eradicate* the weeds in our backyard.

Related Words: 1. ERADICATION - n. destruction. 2. ERODE –v. wear away

ERODE (ih ROHD): n. Wear away; eat away

Trigger: ERODE-ERASE

Trigger Sentence: With gradual EROSION the roads have been ERODED.

Sample Sentence: The rain *eroded* the rocks and created an engraved pattern on them.

ERRATIC (i RAT ik): a. Odd; unpredictable

Trigger: ERRATIC-ERR

Trigger Sentence: 1. ERRATIC people make ERRS. 2. ERRATIC & ECCENTRIC are synonyms.

Sample Sentence: The little boy's *erratic* behavior worried his parents.

ERRONEOUS (ih RONE ee us): a. False; wrong

Trigger: ERROR NEWS-ERROR

Trigger Sentence: ERRORS IN NEWS should be rectified. Remove ERRONEOUS information.

Sample Sentence: She *erroneously* identified the wrong man as the main culprit.

ERSATZ (uhr SAHTZ): a. An artificial or inferior substitute or imitation
   Trigger: ERSATZ- OTHER STAT-PHOTOSTAT
   Trigger Sentence: PHOTOSTAT is an ERSATZ- an artificial substitute.
   Sample Sentence: The complex is designed as an *ersatz* Egyptian pyramid.
ERSTWHILE (URST wahyl): adv. Formerly, previously
   Trigger: ERSTWHILE-EARLIEST WHILE
   Trigger Sentence: My ERSTWHILE friend's EARLIEST work reflects EARLY renaissance period.
   Sample Sentence: Our *erstwhile* partner companions have now become our political enemies.
ERUDITE (ER yoo dyte): a. Learned, educated
   Trigger: "E + RUDE+ITE"-"A RUDE OUT"
   Trigger Sentence: RUDE fellows are ILLITERATES; if RUDENESS is OUT you could be ERUDITE.
   Sample Sentence: Most professional speakers are *erudite* and intelligent.
   Related Words: ERUDITION - n. learning, knowledge
ESCHEW (ES choo): v. Avoid
   Trigger: 1.ESCHEW-CHEW. 2. ESCHEW-ESCAPE (** synonyms)
   Trigger Sentence: 1. People should ESCHEW CHEWING tobacco.2. ESCHEW also means ESCAPE.
   Sample Sentence: We were advised to *eschew* riding at midnight.
ESOTERIC (es uh TER ik): a. Hard to understand; known only to the chosen few
   Trigger: 1.ESOTERIC-HISTORIC. 2. ESO sounds like EASY; but NOT EASY.
   Trigger Sentence: 1. HISTORIC things are ESOTERIC to common people; only knowledgeable people can understand. 2. ESO sounds like EASY...but NOT EASY-very difficult to understand.
   Sample Sentence: Quantum Mechanics is *esoteric* because it is not easy to follow it.
ESPOUSE (eh SPOWZ): v. Adopt; support
   Trigger: ESPOUSE-OPPOSE (** antonyms)
   Trigger Sentence: 1. I ESPOUSE my SPOUSE (wife). 2. ESPOUSE and OPPOSE are antonyms.
   Sample Sentence: These days' artists are not being *espoused* by the government.
ESTIMABLE (ES thu muh bul): a. Admirable; worthy
   Trigger: 1.ESTIMATE HIGH. 2. ESTEEM-BEST TEAM
   Trigger Sentence: 1. When we ESTEEM someone like Tendulkar, we have HIGH ESTIMATION on him. 2. My team is BEST TEAM; I've a GREAT RESPECT for it.
   Sample Sentence: She has an *estimable* reputation for delivering the work on time.
   Related Words: ESTEEM - v. respect, value
ESTRANGE (eh STRANJ): v. Separate from, Make unfriendly
   Trigger: ESTRANGE-STRANGE
   Trigger Sentence: When my ESTRANGED wife sought a divorce, she looked so STRANGE to me.
   Sample Sentence: He is my *estranged* lover.

ETERNAL (ih TUR nl): a. Lasting; without end

Trigger: ETERNAL-A TERMINAL-NO TERMINAL

Trigger Sentence: ETERNAL things have NO TERMINAL point.

Sample Sentence: The terminal truth of existence seems to be *eternally* difficult to understand.

Related Words: EPHEMERAL –a. short-lived

ETHOS (EE thos): n. Beliefs or character of a group

Trigger: ETHOS-ETHICS

Trigger Sentence: Medical ETHICS -medical CHARACTERISTICS; business ETHICS-business CHARACTERISTICS.

Sample Sentence: The tribal communities of Madhya Pradesh have their own ethos and *ethics*.

ETIQUETTE (ET i ket): n. Social behavior; protocol

Trigger: ETIQUETTE-"ETHIC + STICK"

Trigger Sentence: He STICKS to ETHICS; right ETHICAL behavior is known as ETIQUETTE.

Sample Sentence: You cannot teach *etiquette* with the help of a stick of ethics.

Related Words: PROTOCOL –n. rules of behavior

EULOGY (YOO luh jee): n. Praise, commendation

Trigger: 1.EU (GOOD) + LOG (DIALOGUE). 2. EULOGIZE- YOUR LARGE EYES

Trigger Sentence: 1. GOOD DIALOGUE about someone is called an EULOGY. 2. YOU'VE LARGE EYES- a guy EULOGIZES a beautiful girl.

Sample Sentence: When I heard the dialogue of the two scientists, I paid them rich *eulogy*.

Related Words: EULOGIZE – v. speak in praise of someone.

EUPHEMISM (YOO fuh miz um): n. A good word substituted for an offensive word

Trigger: euPHEMISM-FORMALISM

Trigger Sentence: 1. "He DIED" is offensive way of expressing about the death of a person; "HE PASSED AWAY" is termed as EUPHEMISM in such case. 2. In FORMALISM-we use mild dialogues (like WASH ROOM for a TOILET); in slang we use OFFENSIVE dialogues.

Sample Sentence: *Euphemism* is formal, a gentle way of expressing hard things.

EUPHONY (YOO fuh nee): n. Sweet sound

Trigger: EU (good) + PHONE

Trigger Sentence: GOOD PHONE -GOOD SOUND; CACOPHONY and EUPHONY are antonyms.

Sample Sentence: The *euphony* in the tune of the phone was mellifluous, and I kept humming.

EUPHORIA (yoo FOR ee uh): n. A feeling of intense happiness and elation

Trigger: 1. EUPHORIA-EU + FOUR. 2. EUPHORIA - RIO (Rio De Janeiro)

Trigger Sentence: 1. When Sachin hits the ball for a FOUR, the crowd goes into EUPHORIA. 2. People had an EUPHORIA at RIO DE JANEIRO beaches.

Sample Sentence: *Euphoria* of Brazil's Soccer World Cup win echoed on all four sides of stadium.

EVADE (ee VADE) : v. Avoid, shirk

    Trigger: 1.EVADE-AVOID(** synonyms). 2. EVADE-EVA-AWAY FROM

    Trigger Sentence: The borrower EVADED paying the money back and AVOIDED the lender.

    Sample Sentence: I hid behind a wall to *evade* my father's attention after came home drunk!

    Related Words: EVASIVE - a. elusive, avoiding

EVANESCENT (ev uh NES unt): a. Vanishing; temporary

    Trigger: EVANESCENT —"EVAPORATING -SCENT"

    Trigger Sentence: SCENT smell is temporary; it EVAPORATES or DISAPPEARS like VAPOR.

    Sample Sentence: A quality scent is not *evanescent*. It doesn't evaporate quickly.

    Related Words: EVANESCENCE - n. fading away; disappearing

EVENHANDED (EE vuhn HAN did): n. Fair; impartial

    Trigger: EVEN HAND

    Trigger Sentence: For a man of EVENHANDED bearing assumes that both the HANDS are EVEN; he never treats left hand as clumsy hand.

    Sample Sentence: The judges made an *evenhanded* assessment at the dog show.

    Related Words: LOPSIDED –a. unblalanced ; leaning to one side

EVERLASTING (ever LAS ting): a. Continuing forever; eternal

    Trigger: EVERLASTING-LASTING FOREVER

    Trigger Sentence: The EVERLASTING themes of love and revenge will LAST FOREVER.

    Sample Sentence: This material has excellent thermal properties and is virtually *everlasting*.

    Related Words: 1.LONG-LASTING - a. existing for a long time .2.LASTING - a. continuing

EVINCE (i VINS): v. Show clearly

    Trigger: EVINCE-EVIDENCE

    Trigger Sentence: She EVINCED the EVIDENCE.

    Sample Sentence: The lawyer *evinced* clear evidence in support of the innocence of his client.

EVOKE (ee VOKE): v. Wake, recall to the conscious mind

    Trigger: EVOKE-A WAKE- (A WAKE UP CALL)

    Trigger Sentence: I always cherish my sweet childhood memories, they WAKE or EVOKE joy.

    Sample Sentence: The horror film was all about *evoking* evil spirits!

    Related Words: EVOCATIVE - a. serving to bring to mind

EXACERBATE (ig ZAS ur bayt): v. Worsen, aggravate

    Trigger: 1. EXAGGERATE (BAD). 2. EX+ ACERBITY (ACIDITY-BITTER)

    Trigger Sentence: 1. EXAGGERATE (increase in NEGATIVE direction) is called EXACERBATE. 2. Already on existing pain, if you pour EXTRA ACID, the pain INTENSIFIES.

    Sample Sentence: North Korea exaggerates its military might, *exacerbating* its affairs with USA.

EXACTING (ig ZAK ting): a. Extremely demanding; precise

    Trigger: EXACTING-EXACT

Trigger Sentence: An EXACTING boss wants thing to be too EXACT and demands PRECISENESS.

Sample Sentence: My work is *exacting* because my boss is fussy, and hence wants exact results.

Related Words: INEXACT –a. imprecise

EXALT (ig ZAWLT): v. Raise in rank; praise

Trigger: EXALT-EXCESS SALT

Trigger Sentence: EXCESSIVE SALT RAISES- BP. Psychological RAISING is called PRAISING.

Sample Sentence: Elizabeth's teachers *exalted* her bravery in saving the drowning boy.

EXASPERATE (ig ZAS per it): v. Vex

Trigger: 1. VEX (just keep "V" before "EX"). 2. EXASPERATE-"EXAGGERATE BAD"

Trigger Sentence: My EX (wife) EXASPERATED me; I got VEXED with her and gave divorce.

Sample Sentence: The train journey was *exasperating* because of the dely.

EXCERPT (EK surpt): n. Selected portion

Trigger: EXCERPT-"EXTRACT – EXPERT"

Trigger Sentence: The EXPERTS EXTRACT the quotations from many great authors.

Sample Sentence: An *excerpt* from the book on Gandhi was used in the newspaper article.

EXCISE (ek SYZE): v. To remove by cutting

Trigger: 1.EXCISE-EXTRA SIZE. 2. EXCISE-INCISE

Trigger Sentence: Surgeons EXCISE the EXTRA SIZE of their patients with the help of liposuction.

Sample Sentence: You have to incise before you *excise* the tumour from the body.

EXCLUSIVE (ik SKLOO siv): a. Limited to a select few; expensive

Trigger: EXCLUSIVE-EXCLUDE

Trigger Sentence: The EXCLUSIVE restaurants and EXPENSIVE bars EXCLUDE general public.

Sample Sentence: He attended an *exclusive* Ivy-League school.

Related Words: INCLUSIVE – a. comprehensive; all-embracing, extensive

EXCORIATE (ek SKOR ee ayt): v. Criticize strongly

Trigger: 1. EXCORIATED- X-RATED. 2. EX + CORIA (Korea) +ATE

Trigger Sentence: 1. X-RATED MOVIES were EXCORIATED by critics. 2. USA EXCORIATED North KOREA, Iran and Cuba as rogue nations.

Sample Sentence: It is not appropriate to *excoriate* members of one's family in public.

EXECRABLE (ig ZEK ruh bul): a. Extremely bad or unpleasant

Trigger: EXECRABLE-EXTRA TROUBLE

Trigger Sentence: The EXTRA TROUBLES the couple faced in separation ware EXECRABLE.

Sample Sentence: Living conditions in Ethiopia are *execrable*.

EXECRATE (EK si kreyt): v. Extreme hate; to dislike strongly; curse

Trigger: 1. EXECRATE- EXTRA HATE. 2. EXECRATE-BAD RATE

Trigger Sentence: 1. When you EXECRATE someone, it reflects all your EXTRA HATE against the person.2. The critics EXECRATED the film and gave it a BAD RATING. 3. Something that gives EXTRA-TROUBLE is EXECRABLE (very bad and unpleasant).

Sample Sentence: We *execrate* the unscientific methods of animal testing in the labs.

Related Words: EXECRABLE - a. extremely bad or unpleasant.

EXEMPLARY (eg ZEM pluh ree): a. Serving as a model or example, outstanding

Trigger: EXEMPLARY-EXAMPLE

Trigger Sentence: The EXEMPLARY behaviour of Gandhi remains as an EXAMPLE for centuries.

Sample Sentence: George Washington is depicted as the *exemplar* of a true patriot.

Related Words: EXEMPLIFY –v. illustrate; serve as an example

EXCULPATE (EK skuhl peyt): v. Clear from blame

Trigger: EXCULPATE -EX+CULPRIT

Trigger Sentence: He is EX-CULPRIT. NOT a CULPRIT. The judge EXCULPATED the EX-CULPRIT.

Sample Sentence: We got witnesses to his heinous crime; the convict can never be *exculpated*.

Related Words: INCULPATE - v. charge with a crime; blame

EXHORT (ig ZOHRT): v. Urge; encourage strongly

Trigger: 1. EXCITE-HEART. 2. EXHORT -EXERT

Trigger Sentence: 1. He EXCITED my HEART and EXHORTED me to finish my graduate study. 2. When we EXHORT a person we ask them to EXERT (exercise) pressure in a field of their choice.

Sample Sentence: The crowd *exhorted* the Indian Cricketers by flashing flags.

Related Words: HORTATORY – a. encouraging; stimulating

EXIGENCY (ig ZIG un see): n. Urgent situation

Trigger: 1. EXIGENCY -URGENCY. 2. EXIGENT-URGENT

Trigger Sentence: 1. URGENCY, EMERGENCY and EXIGENCY are synonyms. 2. EXIGENT is equal to URGENT.

Sample Sentence: In times of *exigencies* one cannot afford to sit back to contemplate!

Related Words: EXIGENT - a. urgent

EXODUS (EK suh dus): n. Mass departure

Trigger: 1. EXIT + BUS. 2. EXO-ENDO

Trigger Sentence: 1. People are on an EXODUS in a BUS. 2. EXO (outside); ENDO (inside).

Sample Sentence: During the partition *exodus* of the natives was obvious.

EXONERATE (ig ZON uh reyt): v. Free from burden; Acquit

Trigger: 1. EXONERATE -EX + OWNER. 2. EXONERATE-EXCULPATE

Trigger Sentence: 1. I'm an EX-OWNER; so there is NO BURDEN; no ownership- no burden!!! 2. EXONERATE & EXCULPATE are synonyms.

Sample Sentence: I felt *exonerated* when the judge exculpated me from all charges against me.

Related Words: ONEROUS –a. burdensome

EXORBITANT (eg ZORB ih tant): a. Excessive

Trigger: EXORBITANT-Extra ORBIT

Trigger Sentence: 1. ORBIT TRAVEL is EXORBITANT. 2. The prices at INORBIT MALL are EXORBITANT.

Sample Sentence: The airline fare was *exorbitant*, and I had no choice but to buy.

CHIDE : scold, rebuke, to find fault

NURTURE :
care for, rear, cultivate

Memory Test-41 : Match each word and its memory trick to the corresponding definition.

S.N	WORD	MEMORY TRIGGER	S.N	DEFINITIONS	KEY
1	ENDURING	DURABLE	A	Attract; employ; commit	
2	ENERVATE	he never ate-no energy	B	Boredom	
3	ENFRANCHISE	franchise	C	Captivate, enslave	
4	ENGAGE	Girl's gaze ENGAGED	D	Complicate; to twist together	
5	ENGENDER	GENERATE	E	Give a title or the right to	
6	ENHANCE	ADVANCE	F	Give the right to vote to	
7	ENIGMA	an egg or MA- DILEMMA	G	Hatred; animosity	
8	ENLIGHTENED	LIGHT in the brain	H	Hugeness ;immensity	
9	ENMITY	Enemy	I	Improve the quality	
10	ENNUI	Ennui- ANNOYS	J	Improve; Increase	
11	ENORMITY	More than NORMAL	K	Infuriate, anger	
12	ENRAGE	rage-ROUSE	L	Knowledgeable, broad-minded	
13	ENRICH	Make it RICH	M	Lasting; surviving	
14	ENSCONCE	ISKCONS temple	N	Mysterious thing	
15	ENSHROUD	in CLOUD	O	Necessitate; require; involve	
16	ENTAIL	END-TAIL required	P	Produce, cause	
17	ENTANGLE	in love TANGLE	Q	Settle comfortably; hide	
18	ENTHRALL	THRILL	R	Shroud; conceal, to cover	
19	ENTICE	ENTRAP with EYES	S	Tempt, attract; lure	
20	ENTITLE	TITLE	T	Weaken, tiring	

Memory Test-42 : Match each word and its memory trick to the corresponding definition.

S.N	WORD	MEMORY TRIGGER	S.N	DEFINITIONS	KEY
1	ENTRENCH	ENCROACH	A	Ambiguous; intentionally misleading	
2	ENUMERATE	A+ number+ rate	B	Balance	
3	ENUNCIATE	Pronounce-ANNOUNCE	C	Balance, stability	
4	ENVISION	In vision- VISUALIZE	D	Calmness; emotional stability	
5	EPHEMERAL	A FUNERAL	E	Destroy	
6	EPIDEMIC	Pandemic-epidemic	F	Fair and impartial	
7	EPIGRAM	TELEGRAM	G	Lie; use words with double meanings	
8	EPILOGUE	End DIALOGUE	H	Long formal letter, missive	
9	EPISODIC	Come in EPISODES	I	Mention one by one, list	
10	EPISTLE	In a A POSTAL	J	Occurring at irregular intervals	
11	EPITOME	Epic+ OME (ॐ)	K	Perfect example; embodiment	
12	EQUABLE	STABLE mind	L	Picture or visualize; imagine	
13	EQUANIMITY	EQUALITY-equal mind	M	Plague, that spreads quickly	
14	EQUILIBRIUM	EQUAL +LIBRA	N	Settle comfortably; encroach	
15	EQUIPOISE	Equal POSE	O	Short and witty saying	
16	EQUITABLE	Equality to all	P	Short speech at conclusion	
17	EQUIVOCAL	DOUBLE VOCAL attitude	Q	Short-lived, fleeting	
18	EQUIVOCATE	double vocal	R	Speak clearly	
19	ERADICATE	A radium act- ERASED	S	Uniform, steady; calm	
20	ERODE	Erode-corrode-ERASE	T	Wear away; eat away	

Answers	EX.NO	1	2	3	4	5	6	7	8	9	10	11	12	13	14	15	16	17	18	19	20
	41	M	T	F	A	P	J	N	L	G	B	H	K	I	Q	R	O	D	C	S	E
	42	N	I	R	L	Q	M	O	P	J	H	K	S	D	B	C	F	A	G	E	T

Memory Test-43 : Match each word and its memory trick to the corresponding definition.

S.N	WORD	MEMORY TRIGGER	S.N	DEFINITIONS	KEY
1	ERRATIC	ERR from normal	A	Admirable; worthy	
2	ERRONEOUS	Error news-ERROR	B	Artificial substitute or imitation	
3	ERSATZ	PHOTOSTAT is an ERSATZ	C	Avoid	
4	ERSTWHILE	EARLIEST WHILE	D	Avoid, shirk	
5	ERUDITE	A RUDE OUT- no rudeness	E	Beliefs or character of a group	
6	ESCHEW	Eschew-ESCAPE	F	Fair; impartial	
7	ESOTERIC	Not EASY	G	False; wrong	
8	ESPOUSE	My spouse espouses	H	Feeling of intense happiness	
9	ESTIMABLE	Estimate HIGH	I	Formerly, previously	
10	ESTRANGE	Make STRANGE	J	Good word for an offensive word	
11	ETERNAL	A terminal-NO TERMINAL	K	Hard to understand	
12	ETHOS	Ethics of a group	L	Lasting; without end	
13	ETIQUETTE	Ethic + stick	M	Learned, educated	
14	EULOGY	Eu (good) + log (dialogue)	N	Odd; unpredictable	
15	EUPHEMISM	FORMALISM we talk mild	O	Praise, commendation	
16	EUPHONY	EU (good) + PHONE	P	Separate from, Make unfriendly	
17	EUPHORIA	rio de janeiro	Q	Social behavior; protocol	
18	EVADE	EVADE-AVOID	R	Support ; adopt	
19	EVANESCENT	Evaporating -scent	S	Sweet sound	
20	EVENHANDED	EVEN HAND for all	T	Vanishing; temporary	

Memory Test-44 : Match each word and its memory trick to the corresponding definition.

S.N	WORD	MEMORY TRIGGER	S.N	DEFINITIONS	KEY
1	EVERLASTING	Lasting forever	A	Clear from blame	
2	EVINCE	evidence	B	Continuing forever; eternal	
3	EVOKE	A wake- a wakeup call	C	Criticize strongly	
4	EXACERBATE	Exaggerate (bad)	D	Excessive	
5	EXACTING	EXACT-100%	E	Extreme hate; curse	
6	EXALT	Excess salt raises BP	F	Extremely bad or unpleasant	
7	EXASPERATE	Vex-separate	G	Extremely demanding; precise	
8	EXCERPT	EXTRACT – expert	H	Free from burden; Acquit	
9	EXCISE	Extra size- incise	I	Limited to a select few; expensive	
10	EXCLUSIVE	Exclude others	J	Mass departure	
11	EXCORIATE	X-rated	K	Raise in rank; praise	
12	EXECRABLE	EXTRA TROUBLE	L	Remove by cutting	
13	EXECRATE	Extra HATE	M	Selected portion	
14	EXCULPATE	Ex+culprit	N	Serving as a example, outstanding	
15	EXEMPLARY	EXAMPLE	O	Show clearly	
16	EXHORT	Hearten	P	Urgent situation	
17	EXIGENCY	Urgency	Q	Urge; encourage strongly	
18	EXODUS	EXIT + BUS	R	Vex	
19	EXONERATE	EX + OWNER	S	Wake, recall to the conscious mind	
20	EXORBITANT	Extra ORBIT travel	T	Worsen, aggravate	

Answers

EX.NO	1	2	3	4	5	6	7	8	9	10	11	12	13	14	15	16	17	18	19	20
43	N	G	B	I	M	C	K	R	A	P	L	E	Q	O	J	S	H	D	T	F
44	B	O	S	T	G	K	R	M	L	I	C	F	E	A	N	Q	P	J	H	D

WORD GROUPS DAY-11

★ CARELESS ATTITUDE

ADJECTIVES: slapdash, slipshod, slovenly, sloppy, negligent, lax, slack, disorganized, hasty, hurried; negligent, remiss; heedless, feckless, irresponsible, impetuous, reckless; indiscreet, unconcerned; unstudied, nonchalant, insouciant

NOUNS: negligence, dereliction, disregard

VERB: shirk, disregard

ANTONYMS: adj. careful, meticulous

★ POVERTY-POOR

ADJECTIVES: destitute, impecunious, impoverished, lacking, mendicant

NOUNS: indigence, penury, need

VERB: impoverish, pauperize, bankrupt

ANTONYMS: adj.wealthy, affluent, abundant

★ WEALTHY

ADJECTIVES: affluent, luxurious, sumptuous, plutocratic, prosperous

NOUNS: opulence, lucre

VERB: enrich

ANTONYMS: v.poor, impoverished

★ BEG-SEEK

ADJECTIVES: supplicant, suppliant

NOUNS: supplication, petition; mendicant, beggar

VERB: beseech, cadge, entreat, implore, importune, supplicate, solicit

ANTONYMS: v.command, demand; earn

★ MODERATE LIFE

ADJECTIVES: abstemious, austere, ascetic, even-tempered, restrained, temperate, sparing

NOUNS: sobriety, temperance

VERB: adjust, restrain, regulate

ANTONYMS: adj.immoderate, inordinate, intemperate, unrestraint, over-indulgent.

★ IMMODERATE LIFE

ADJECTIVES: extravagant, exorbitant, intemperate, immoderate, inordinate, overindulgent, profligate, unrestrained, uncontrolled, unbridled, wanton, zealous

NOUNS: dissipation, debauchery, intemperance profligacy, fanatic, frenzy

VERB: indulge, luxuriate

ANTONYMS: adj.moderate, temperate, modest

★ AGREEMENT-HARMONY

ADJECTIVES: congruent, congruous, compatible, consonant, harmonious

NOUNS: accord, amity, amicability, assent, compatibility, concord, concurrence, consensus, conciliation, consent, harmony

VERB: concur; compromise, reconcile; integrate, synthesize

ANTONYMS: n. animosity, antagonism, discordant, enmity, inimical, hostility

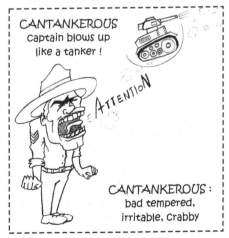

CANTANKEROUS captain blows up like a tanker !

ATTENTION

CANTANKEROUS : bad tempered, irritable, crabby

Word List Day-12

EXORCISE (EK ser sahyz): v. Expel an evil spirit

Trigger: EXORCISE-EXORCIST

Trigger Sentence: In EXORCIST movie, the EXORCIST EXORCISES the devils; when we OSTRACIZE, we drive out the criminals; when we EXORCISE we drive out the devils.

Sample Sentence: An exorcist *exorcised* the evil from the victim's body.

EXOTIC (ig ZOT ik): a. Strange; foreign; not native

Trigger: EXO (outside) - ENDO (inside)

Trigger Sentence: EXOGENOUS- outside factors; ENDOGENOUS- internal factors; ENDOSCOPY-internal examination; EXOTIC- outside of the place; not native.

Sample Sentence: Alice's Wonder Land is an *exotic* place because you see all odd things there.

EXPATIATE (ik SPEY shee eyt): v. Talk at length, amplify, elaborate

Trigger: 1.EXPATIATE-EXPAND TALK. 2. EXPATIATION-EXPLANATION

Trigger Sentence: He EXPANDS an EXPLANATION by EXPATIATING.

Sample Sentence: In an *expatiating* talk he explained how to expand the rule over the country.

Related Words: EXPATIATION - n. tendency to speak at great length

EXPATRIATE (eks PAY tree ayt): n. One who lives in a foreign country; exile

Trigger: EXPATRIATE –"EX (OUT) + PATRIOT"

Trigger Sentence: He lives as an EXPATRIATE in USA, yet he is PATRIOTIC to his former nation.

Sample Sentence: There is an *expatriate* Indian community in USA.

EXPEDIENT (ik SPEE dee unt): a. Convenient and practical; wise

Trigger: 1. EXPEDIENT –EXPERIENCED. 2. EXPEDIENT -EXPERIMENT

Trigger Sentence: 1. EXPERIENCE gets EXPEDIENCY in thinking. 2. EXPEDIENT is CONVENIENT.

Sample Sentence: Tom Hash is an experienced scientist with an *expedient* approach to testing.

Related Words: EXPEDIENCY - n. practicality

EXPEDITE (EK spi dyte): v. Hasten, to speed up

Trigger: EXPEDITE-EX SPEED IT

Trigger Sentence: When you want to EXPEDITE, you got to do with EXTRA SPEED.

Sample Sentence: Our chartered accountant *expedited* the filing of our taxes.

Related Words: EXPEDITIOUS - a. quick, efficient

EXPEND (ik SPEND): v. Spend; use up

Trigger: EXPEND-SPEND

Trigger Sentence: EXPEND is to SPEND and consume.

Sample Sentence: If we *expend* our natural resources, nothing will be left to spend in future.

EXPIATE (EK spee ayt): v. Make amends for a sin

> **Trigger:** EXPIATE-"EX + PIRATE"
>
> **Trigger Sentence:** He is an EX-PIRATE (NOT a PIRATE); the PIRATE EXPIATED god to purify him.
>
> **Sample Sentence:** By clearing up all the vet bills, Tina did *expiate* for hitting my dog with her car.
>
> Related Words: EXPIATION - n. penance

EXPLICIT (ik SPLIS it): a. Clearly expressed; definite; outspoken

> **Trigger:** 1.EXPLICIT-EXPLAINS IT. 2. EXPLICIT-EXPRESS
>
> **Trigger Sentence:** 1. EXPLICIT is to EXPLAIN, EXPRESS. 2. She EXPLICITLY EXPRESSED her love.
>
> **Sample Sentence:** His point of view is so *explicit* that it is self-explanatory.
>
> Related Words: 1. EXPLICITLY –adv. clearly. 2. IMPLICIT –a. implied

EXPONENTIAL (ek spoh NEN shul): a. Characterized by extremely rapid increase

> **Trigger:** math's EXPONENT
>
> **Trigger Sentence:** 10^3 is an EXPONENTIAL expression. It represents EXTREMELY RAPID growth.
>
> **Sample Sentence:** At EXPONENTIAL speeds of 3*10 EXPONENT 8, material acquires vast energy.

EXPOSTULATE (ik SPAHS chu layt): v. Protest

> **Trigger:** EXPOSE+tulate- EXPOSE-OPPOSE
>
> **Trigger Sentence:** EXPOSE in the word sounds like OPPOSE; EXPOSE someone's mistake and ARGUE about that mistake is known as EXPOSTULATION.
>
> **Sample Sentence:** The opposition parties have expressed their *expostulation* to the Martial Law.
>
> Related Words: EXPOSITION - n. public exhibition; clarification

EXPUNGE (ik SPUHNJ): v. Remove, cancel

> **Trigger:** 1.EXPUNGE-A SPONGE. 2. EXPUNGE-A PUNCH
>
> **Trigger Sentence:** 1. A SPONGE mop EXPUNGES dirt better than a cloth mop. 2. He EXPUNGED the opponent with single heavy PUNCH.
>
> **Sample Sentence:** Since a lot of historical records were *expunged*, it is difficult to decode dates.

EXQUISITE (EKS kwi zit): a. Very beautiful and delicate, intense

> **Trigger:** 1. EXQUISITE-EXECUTIVE. 2. EXQUISITE-"EX+SQUEEZE IT"
>
> **Trigger Sentence:** 1. A LADY EXECUTIVE looks EXQUISITE. 2. Don't SQUEEZE her; she is EXQUISITE and EXTREMELY DELICATE.
>
> **Sample Sentence:** The new lady executive has given us an *exquisite* dinner.

EXTANT (EK stunt): a. Still existing; current

> **Trigger:** 1. EXTANT-EXTINCT. 2. EXTANT-EXIST
>
> **Trigger Sentence:** Dinosaurs are EXTINCT and Tigers are still EXTANT; EXTANT means EXIST.
>
> **Sample Sentence:** Existing species are called *extant* species.

EXTEMPORE (ik STEM puh ree): a. Spontaneous, impromptu, without prior preparation

> **Trigger:** EXTEMPORARY-TEMPER

Trigger Sentence: The short TEMPERED man explodes with EXTEMPORE comments.

Sample Sentence: His *extempore* talk was a breath of fresh air, after those boring paper reads.

EXTENUATE (ik STEN yoo yet): v. Lessen; weaken

   Trigger: EXTENT +ATE

   Trigger Sentence: The EXCUSE EXTENUATED the EXTENT of the crime.

   Sample Sentence: The police could *extenuate* the crimes to a certain extent.

EXTINCT (ik STINKT): a. No longer living

   Trigger: EXTANT-EXTINCT

   Trigger Sentence: Dinosaurs are EXTINCT and Tigers are still EXTANT.

   Sample Sentence: Soon many species will become *extinct* due to global warming.

EXTIRPATE (EK stir payt): v. Destroy, uproot

   Trigger: EXTIRPATE-EXTERMINATE

   Trigger Sentence: Some people EXTERMINATE the garden insects by EXTIRPATING with poison.

   Sample Sentence: To conserve any heritage building it is important to *extirpate* termites.

EXTOL (ik STOHL): v. Exalt, praise

   Trigger: 1. EXTOL - EXTRA TOLD. 2. EXTOL -EXALT (refer)

   Trigger Sentence: 1. EXTRA TOLD ---TOLD more than they deserved. Eg. You are extraordinarily beautiful. 2. EXTRA TALL girls are EXTOLLED as beauties. 3. EXALT and EXTOL are synonyms.

   Sample Sentence: We were told to extra praise the late leader by *extolling* his greatness.

EXTRANEOUS (ik STRAY nee us): a. Not essential, Superfluous

   Trigger: 1.EXTRAS. 2. EXTRANEOUS-EXTRA NEWS

   Trigger Sentence: 1. EXTRAS are unnecessary and irrelevant. 2. Lot of TV channels unnecessarily supplying the EXTRA NEWS and there by spreading EXTRANEOUS information.

   Sample Sentence: The speaker did not appreciate the *extraneous* comments from the audience.

EXTRAPOLATE (ik STRAP uh layt): v. Guess; infer

   Trigger: EXTRAPOLATE-"EXTRA + POLE"

   Trigger Sentence: 1st, 2nd, 3rd POLE locations are known. Mathematically, thinking about "where is the 4th POLE?" is called EXTRAPOLATION.

   Sample Sentence: Amundsen's team could not *extrapolate* the exact location of the South Pole.

   Related Words: INTERPOLATE –v. insert something new

EXTRAVAGANT (ik STRAV uh gunt): a. Wasteful, lavish, costly

   Trigger: EXTRAVAGANT –"EXTRA-SPEND"

   Trigger Sentence: An EXTRAVAGANT unnecessarily SPENDS EXTRA money.

   Sample Sentence: The film is notable for its *extravagant* settings and special effects.

EXTRICATE (EK struh kayt): v. Free, disentangle

   Trigger: 1.INTRICATE-COMPLICATE. 2.EXTRICATE-EXTRACT

Trigger Sentence: 1. INTRICATE means COMPLICATED. 2. EXTRACT from INTRICATE or COMPLICATE position is known as EXTRICATION.

Sample Sentence: He *extricated* me from a complicated situation.

Related Words: INEXTRICABLE - a. impossible to disentangle.

EXTRINSIC (iks TRINZ ik): a. External, not essential, extraneous

Trigger: 1. EXTRINSIC-EXTERNAL. 2. EXTRAS

Trigger Sentence: 1. EXTERNAL is EXTRINSIC. 2. EXTRAS are UNNECESSARY and EXTRINSIC.

Sample Sentence: Extra artists are *extrinsic* to a film.

Related Words: INTRINSIC - v. belonging naturally; essential

EXTROVERT (EKS truh vurt): n. An outgoing person

Trigger: EXTROVERT-INTROVERT-AMBIVERT

Trigger Sentence: An EXTROVERT (external) is social; an INTROVERT (internal) is reserved; an AMBIVERT can be both social & reserved.

Sample Sentence: Jim being an *extrovert* is often a comic relief in our otherwise serious office.

Related Words: INTROVERT –n. one who tends to focus on his own thoughts and feelings.

EXUBERANT (ig ZOO buh runt): n. Cheerful; abundant, plentiful

Trigger: 1.EXUBERANT-EBULLIENT (refer). 2. EXUBERANT-ABUNDANT

Trigger Sentence: 1. EBULLIENT (RED BULL drink gives lot of LIVELINESS) and EXUBERANT are synonyms. 2. ABUNDANT money made me EXUBERANT.

Sample Sentence: His *exuberant* performance has made the audience feel ebullient.

Related Words: EXUBERANCE - n. abundance, high spirits

EXULT (igz UHLT): v. Be happy, rejoice

Trigger: EXULT-EXAM RESULT

Trigger Sentence: 1. The EXAM RESULT was good and therefore he EXULTED with joy. 2. EXULTATION and EXHILARATION are synonyms.

Sample Sentence: When he received the news of his *exaltation*, he was exulted.

FABRICATED (fab rih KAY tid): a. Fake, forged; made up

Trigger: FABRICATE-FAKE CREATE

Trigger Sentence: They FABRICATED and CREATED a FAKE story.

Sample Sentence: *Fabricated* news is fake news because it is created intentionally.

Related Words: FABRICATE - v. fake, construct

FACADE (fuh SAHD): n. Front face (of a building); artificial or deceptive front face

Trigger: FAÇadE-FACE

Trigger Sentence: Front FACE of a building is known as FACADE; it is usually a false FACE.

Sample Sentence: Behind their *façade* of happiness was a spell of gloom.

FACETIOUS (fuh SEE shus): a. Humorous, inappropriate joking

Trigger: FACETIOUS-"FACE TEASES US"

Trigger Sentence: Imagine a TEASING or FUNNY FACE which creates FACETIOUS comments.

Sample Sentence: Jim Carrey's *facetious* face amuses us.

FACILE (FAS il): a. Easily done, oversimplified (*negative sense)

Trigger: 1.FACILE-FACE SMILE. 2. FAC-FACTORY JOB

Trigger Sentence: 1. SMILE JOB is FACILE; when the job is FACILE the FACE SMILES. 2. FACTORY JOB is difficult; FACILE JOB is easy.

Sample Sentence: Her smiling face makes us feel even a difficult task appear *facile*.

FACILITATE (fuh SILL uh tate): v. To make easier; promote

Trigger: FACILITATE-FACILITY

Trigger Sentence: FACILITIES are provided to MAKE LIFE EASIER.

Sample Sentence: The Company's bus facility has *facilitated* our journey to and from our office.

FACTIOUS (FAK shus): a. Quarrelsome, dissentious

Trigger: FACTIOUS

Trigger Sentence: The FACTIONS are FIGHTING in a FACTIOUS party.

Sample Sentence: The university admin had difficulty in dealing with the *factious* students.

Related Words: FACTIONAL –a. related to a partisan group

FACTITIOUS (fak TISH us): a. False, artificial

Trigger: 1. FACTITIOUS-FICTITIOUS. 2. FACTORY

Trigger Sentence: 1. All FACTORY products are FACTITIOUS and ARTIFICIAL. 2. FICTITIOUS things are FACTITIOUS most of the time.

Sample Sentence: She was shocked to find out that her dazzling necklace was *factitious*.

FALLACIOUS (fuh LEY shus): a. False; misleading

Trigger: FALLACIOUS-FALSE reason

Trigger Sentence: A FALSE statement is logically FALLACIOUS.

Sample Sentence: The marketing agent promoted *fallacious* schemes on investments.

FALLIBLE (FAL uh buhl): a. Liable to fail

Trigger: 1. FALL-FAIL. 2. FALLIBLE-FALSE

Trigger Sentence: 1. FALLIBLE people FALL DOWN or FAIL by committing FALSE things. 2. INFALLIBLE never FALL DOWN; they are PERFECT. 3. FALLIBLE is LIABLE TO FAIL.

Sample Sentence: Napoleon's failure at Waterloo shows, everybody is *fallible* at sometime.

Related Words: INFALLIBLE - a. never failing.

FALLOW (FAL oh): a. Uncultivated; plowed but not sowed

Trigger: FALLOW-no FOLLOW up

Trigger Sentence: If you don't take the FOLLOW UP action it will be USELESS and FOLLOWED.

Sample Sentence: If there is no follow up through ploughing, this land will become *fallow*.

FALTER (FALL tur): v. Hesitate to act; waver

Trigger: 1. "FALTERED-FAILED". 2. FALTER-HALTER

Trigger Sentence: 1. FALTER is FAILURE. 2. Like HALTER (bus halt, bus stops) FALTER - hesitate.

Sample Sentence: His regular failures *faltered* him many times in his life.

Related Words: UNFALTERING - a. steady or resolute.

FANATIC (fuh NAT ik): a. Extreme, radical, zealous

Trigger: FANATIC -FAN

Trigger Sentence: The FANS are FANATIC about their hero.

Sample Sentence: The *fanatics* were fervently publicizing their religious guru.

FANCY (FAN see): n. Idea; illusion; whim

Trigger: FANCY -FANTASY

Trigger Sentence: As a school girl I was FANCY about reading romantic FANTASIES

Sample Sentence: She *fancied* becoming a super model.

Related Words: 1.FANCIFUL –a. Imaginary; whimsical; strange. 2. FANTASY - n. illusion

FASTIDIOUS (fa STID ee us): a. Over particular, difficult to please

Trigger: FASTIDIOUS-FAST & TIDINESS

Trigger Sentence: 1. FASTIDIOUS people FAST to the TIDINESS. 2. So many FASTINGs I've done, but god is FASTIDIOUS (DIFFICULT TO PLEASE).*note: fasting is usually done to please the god.

Sample Sentence: The *fastidious* nature of our boss compelled us to be fast and tidy.

FATHOM (FA thum): v. Comprehend; investigate

Trigger: 1. FATHOM-GAUTAM. 2. FATHOM-"FATE + ATOM"

Trigger Sentence: 1. GAUTAM Buddha FATHOMED on life. 2. The FATE OF ATOM will be FATHOMED by collider experiments.

Sample Sentence: Radiation was known when scientists *fathomed* about the fate of atom.

Related Words: UNFATHOMABLE - a. incomprehensible

FATUOUS (FACH oo us): a. Stupid; silly

Trigger: FATUOUS-VACUOUS

Trigger Sentence: 1. My brain is VACUOUS (vacuum); that is the reason I'm FATUOUS; silly and foolish. 2. Most of the FAT people appear FATUOUS.

Sample Sentence: The audience made *fatuous* comments during the serious play.

FAWN (FAWN): v. To seek favor by flattering

Trigger: 1.FAWN-FAN. 2. FAWNING-FAN SWINGING

Trigger Sentence: 1. Servants used to FAWN their kings as they SWUNG FANS next to throne. 2. FANS usually FAWN behind heroes and heroines.

Sample Sentence: Andrea's cat *fawns* her by rubbing alongside her leg when she is hungry.

Related Words: FAWNING - a. flattering, acting in a servile manner in order to gain favor.

FAZE (FEYZ): n. Frighten; disturb

Trigger: FAZE-EASE

Trigger Sentence: 1. The meditation will EASE his FAZED state. 2. FAZE and EASE are antonyms

Sample Sentence: Failures have never *fazed* them; they continued to do what they believed in.

FEALTY (FEE uhl tee): n. Loyalty, faithfulness

    Trigger: FEALTY-LOYALTY

    Trigger Sentence: FEALTY and LOYALTY are synonyms.

    Sample Sentence: The loyal employees at a king's court were recognized for their fealty.

FEASIBLE (FEE zub bul): a. Possible, likely

    Trigger: FEASIBLE-POSSIBLE

    Trigger Sentence: If it is POSSIBLE, it is FEASIBLE too.

    Sample Sentence: Wise people don't keep impossible goals before measuring *feasibility* in work.

    Related Words: UNFEASIBLE - n. not practicable

FECKLESS (FEK lis): a. Careless and irresponsible

    Trigger: 1. FECKLESS-RECKLESS. 2. FECKLESS-USELESS

    Trigger Sentence: FECKLESS fellows are RECKLESS and USELESS in nature.

    Sample Sentence: Cuckoo mother is so *feckless* that it recklessly puts its eggs in other bird nests.

FECUNDITY (fi KUHN di tee): n. Fertility; fruitfulness

    Trigger: 1. FECUNDITY-FERTILITY. 2. FECUND-FERTILE

    Trigger Sentence: FECUNDITY and FERTILITY are synonyms.

    Sample Sentence: The *fecundity* of a queen bee is awesome. During its days of fertility it gives birth to thousands of worker bees.

    Related Words: FECUND - a. fertile; fruitful

FEEBLE (FEE bul): a. Weak

    Trigger: FEEBLE-UNABLE

    Trigger Sentence: She is UNABLE to do the chores, since she is FEEBLE from her long illness.

    Sample Sentence: He made *feeble* attempts to find a job and support his family.

    Related Words: FOIBLE - n. weakness; fault

FEIGN (FAYN): v. Pretend

    Trigger: FEIGN-FAKE

    Trigger Sentence: 1. He FAKED (FEIGNED) that he was FAINT. 2. FEIGN and FAKE are synonyms.

    Sample Sentence: Anshula *feigned* of stomachache so as to avoid going to school.

    Related Words: 1.UNFEIGNED –a. genuine. 2. FEINT –n. deception

FEINT (FAINT): v. To trick by cunning

    Trigger: FEINT-FRONT-"FALSE FRONT"

    Trigger Sentence: FALSE FRONT (doing back tactics) is a FAKE attempt.

    Sample Sentence: False saints exhibit tricks with their *feint* hands in front of their followers.

    Related Words: FEIGN - v. fake, pretend

FELICITOUS (fi LIS i tuhs): a. Well chosen or apt, pleasing

   Trigger: FELICITOUS-FEEL EASY TO US

   Trigger Sentence: We FEEL EASY TO US since your remarks are FELICITOUS.

   Sample Sentence: His *felicitous* nature made us feel easy in his company.

FELICITY (fuh LIS uh tee): n. Happiness; ability

   Trigger: 1. FELICITY-FACILITY. 2. FELICITY-FEEL + CITY

   Trigger Sentence: 1. Good FACILITY brings FELICITY. 2. He expressed FEELINGS FOR THE CITY life with his customary FELICITY.

   Sample Sentence: The Indian immigrants waiting for their green cards dreamt of *felicity* in USA.

   Related Words: FELICITATE - v. congratulate, offer good wishes

FEND (FEND): v. Ward off; resist

   Trigger: 1.FEND-DEFEND. 2. FEND-FENCE

   Trigger Sentence: In a FENCING sport he DEFENDED the rival by FENDING off blows.

   Sample Sentence: The batsman had to *fend* against the intimidating fast bowler.

FERAL (FEHR ul): a. Wild, untamed

   Trigger: 1.FEAR ALL. 2. FATAL

   Trigger Sentence: 1. FERAL animals FEAR ALL the people. 2. The FERAL cats are FATAL.

   Sample Sentence: South African jungles are famous for *feral* cats.

   Related Words: FEROCIOUS –a. cruel ; brutal

FERVENT (FUR vunt): a. Ardent; hot

   Trigger: 1.FERVENT-ARDENT. 2. FERVID-FERVOR-FERVENT

   Trigger Sentence: 1. With an ARDENT love they ignited a FERVENT love affair. 2. Fervor, fervid and fervent belongs to same family.

   Sample Sentence: Joshua hails from a family of *fervent* followers of Gandhian principles.

FERVOR (FUR ver): n. Intense and passionate feeling

   Trigger: FERVOR -FEVER (love fever)

   Trigger Sentence: 1. When I'm in LOVE FEVER, I've lot of FERVOR for her FOREVER. 2.FERVOR-FERVENT-FERVID-PERFERVID-EFFERVESCENT; all belong to the same family of PASSION.

   Sample Sentence: The fever of cricket became *fervor* during the finals of the World Cup.

   Related Words: 1. FERVID - a. fervent, passionate. 2. FERVENT - a. Passionate; intense, hot.

FESTER (FES tur): v. To cause irritation; rankle

   Trigger: 1.FEST-INFEST-INFECT. 2. FESTER-BLISTER

   Trigger Sentence: 1. The INFESTED house FESTERED them. 2. BLISTERS FESTERD him in summer.

   Sample Sentence: Srikanth got *festered* by those constant marketing calls.

   Related Words: FESTERING - a. inflamed; rot

FETID (FET id): a. Unpleasant smell

   Trigger: FETID- FEET

   Trigger Sentence: Sweat FEET give off FETID odor.

   Sample Sentence: Municipality left the *fetid* garbage on the streets for days!

FETTER (FET ur): v. Chain; hamper

Trigger: FETTER-"FEET+TIE+R" .2. UNFETTER-RUN BETTER

Trigger Sentence: 1. TIE his FEET, so that they are FETTERED. 2. If you are UNFETTERED, you can RUN BETTER since you have full of freedom.

Sample Sentence: The prisoners were *fettered* with iron chains around their ankles.

Related Words: UNFETTERED - a. free of restraint.

FIASCO (fee AS koh): n. A complete failure

Trigger: FIASCO - PSYCHO -DISCO

Trigger Sentence: 1. The DISCO of a PSYCHO is a FIASCO; a PSYCHO is a failure in the society. 2. My marriage with a PSYCHO was a FIASCO.

Sample Sentence: The disco concert, which we performed last week, was a big *fiasco*.

FICKLE (FIK ul): a. Changeable, faithless

Trigger: FICKLE-FLICKER

Trigger Sentence: 1. Because of his FICKLE nature, thoughts FLICKER through his mind. 2. In a windy room the FLICKER of the candle is UNSTEADY.

Sample Sentence: She's so *fickle* minded that she cannot decide on which subject to opt.

FICTITIOUS (fik TISH uhs): a. Not real; imaginary

Trigger: FICTITIOUS-FICTIONAL (*synonyms)

Trigger Sentence: The FICTIONAL book has many FICTITIOUS stories

Sample Sentence: Science fiction stories are not real; they are *fictitious* scientific stories.

FIDELITY (fuh DEL uh tee): n. Loyalty

Trigger: 1. FIDELITY-FEALTY-LOYALTY. 2. CONFIDENCE

Trigger Sentence: 1. FEALTY, LOYALTY and FIDELITY are synonyms. 2. I've CONFIDENCE in my friend; since he has FIDELITY towards me.

Sample Sentence: *Fidelity* between people depends upon the amount of confidence they keep.

Related Words: INFIDELITY - n. disloyalty

FIGURATIVE (FIG yur uh tiv): a. Using a figure of speech; metaphorical; not literal

Trigger: FIGURE-LITERAL

Trigger Sentence: There are two ways of speech: 1. Explain in FIGURATIVE sense like "he is like a lion"; FIGURE is an imagination. 2. Explain with words-in LITERAL sense; word for word.

Sample Sentence: When Surya told Hasa she was dumb as a brick, he was speaking *figuratively.*

FILIAL (FIL ee uhl): a. Relating to a son or daughter

Trigger: 1.AFFILIATION-FILI. 2. FILIAL-FAMILIAL-FAMILY

Trigger Sentence: 1. AFFILIATION means ATTACHMENT. 2. FAMILIAL relationships are FILIAL.

Sample Sentence: Many *filial* family members of Einstein still live in USA.

FILIBUSTER (FILL ih buss ter): v. Block legislation by making long speeches

Trigger: FILIBUSTER-"BLOCK-BUSTER"

Trigger Sentence: FILIBUSTER sounds like BLOCK BUSTER; if you take only "BLOCK" in the MT (MEMORY TRICK) then you would get the direct meaning.

Sample Sentence: The Minister *filibustered* the proceedings with his long speech.

FINESSE (fi NES): n. Delicate Skill; subtlety

Trigger: FINENESS-FINE TALENT

Trigger Sentence: The FINESSE of the artiste was exhibited through her FINE artistic TALENT.

Sample Sentence: The ice skater skates with *finesse,* twirling with graceful movements.

FINICKY (FIN i kee): a. Excessively particular, fussy

Trigger: 1. FINE +PICKY. 2. FINE-OVER FINE

Trigger Sentence: 1. Boss is FINICKY and PICKY. 2. FINICKY artist strives for OVER FINE quality.

Sample Sentence: It is so difficult to travel with *finicky* partners overtly conscious of hygiene.

FITFUL (FIT ful): a. Intermittent; sporadic

Trigger: FITFUL-"BIT FULL"-BIT by BIT

Trigger Sentence: In a TV serial, the makers are not going to show complete or FULL episode; they do it BIT by BIT; so FITFUL means ...BIT...BIT...BIT

Sample Sentence: Through the bouts of *fitful* grit the sculptor finished his big task bit by bit.

FLABBY (FLAB ee): v. Weak; drooping; loose

Trigger: 1.FLABBY-CHUBBY. 2. FLABBY-FEEBLE

Trigger Sentence: 1. The CHUBBY baby playfully exhibited her FLABBY belly. 2. The FLABBY muscles of the old fat man appeared FEEBLE.

Sample Sentence: The firm, in its fourth generation of family ownership, has grown *flabby.*

FLACCID (FLASS id): a. Flabby; not firm; soft

Trigger: FLACCId-FLABBY-CHUBBY-FATTY

Trigger Sentence: 1. FLACCID body of sea elephant is filled with FLABBY fat. 2. FATTY acids turn a person's body FLACCID.

Sample Sentence: After a long sickness the athlete's muscles became *flaccid* and floppy.

FLAG (FLAG): v. Grow weak, Droop

Trigger: 1.FLAG-LAG. 2. FLAG-FAG

Trigger Sentence: If you take too many FAGS your energy FLAGS; you will be LAGGING behind.

Sample Sentence: With an *unflagging* zeal Mother Teresa worked for the poor and needy.

Related Words: UNFLAGGING - a. tireless, constant

FLAGRANT (FLAY grunt): a. Visibly bad; outrageous; blatant

Trigger: 1.FLAG BURNT. 2. FLAG RENT.

Trigger Sentence: 1. A country's FLAG is BURNT by terrorists; it is a FLAGRANT violation. 2. It is FLAGRANT mistake when a country's FLAG is given for RENT.

Sample Sentence: Daniel's *flagrant* disregard for Victoria's feelings is what upset her the most.

FLAMBOYANT (flam BOY ant): a. Showy, ornate

Trigger: 1.FLASHY BOY-SHOWY. 2. FLAMBOYANT -FLAME + BOY

Trigger Sentence: The FLAMBOYANT BOY was FLASHY as well as SHOWY.

Sample Sentence: She was one of the most *flamboyant* actresses in the theater.

FLAW (FLAW): n. Fault or weakness

    Trigger: FLAWLESS- FAULTLESS

    Trigger Sentence: FLAWLESS work means FAULTLESS work.

    Sample Sentence: The *flaw* was so obvious that you should have noticed the *fault* immediately.

    Related Words: FLAWLESS -a. perfect

FLEDGLING (FLEJ ling): n. Inexperienced

    Trigger: FLEDGLING -FRESH WING

    Trigger Sentence: A FLEDGLING bird is trying to fly with FRESH WINGS

    Sample Sentence: A *fledgling* bird takes a few weeks before it gets its fresh wings.

    Related Words: UNFLEDGED - a. immature

FLEETING (FLEE ting): a. Temporary; transient

    Trigger: 1.FLEETING-"F-LEAVING". 2. FLEETING-FADING

    Trigger Sentence: FLEETING moment means LEAVING or FADING moment; it is TEMPORARY.

    Sample Sentence: Time is so *fleeting* that it turns into a fading memory.

FLIMSY (FLIM zee): a. Delicate; thin; poorly made; weak

    Trigger: FLIMSY-FILMY-FILMS

    Trigger Sentence: The transparent FILM is FLIMSY.

    Sample Sentence: The movie flopped because of its *flimsy* plot.

Memory Test-45 : Match each word and its memory trick to the corresponding definition.

S.N	WORD	MEMORY TRIGGER	S.N	DEFINITIONS	KEY
1	EXORCISE	Exorcist-sizes spirits	A	Clearly expressed; outspoken	
2	EXOTIC	EXO (outside) - ENDO (inside)	B	Destroy, uproot	
3	EXPATIATE	Expand talk	C	Exalt, praise	
4	EXPATRIATE	Ex (out) + patriot	D	Expel an evil spirit	
5	EXPEDIENT	EXPERIENCE brings EXPEDIENCY	E	Extremely rapid increase	
6	EXPEDITE	Ex speed it	F	Foreign; not native; strange	
7	EXPEND	Spend	G	Lessen; weaken	
8	EXPIATE	Ex + pirate-no more pirate	H	Make amends for a sin	
9	EXPLICIT	Explains it	I	No longer living	
10	EXPONENTIAL	Math's EXPONENT	J	Not essential, Superfluous	
11	EXPOSTULATE	Expose-OPPOSE	K	One who lives in a foreign country	
12	EXPUNGE	A SPONGE	L	Protest	
13	EXQUISITE	lady executive- exquisite	M	Remove, cancel	
14	EXTANT	Extant-exist	N	Speed up ; hasten	
15	EXTEMPORE	Sudden temper	O	Spend; use up	
16	EXTENUATE	Extent +ATE	P	Spontaneous, impromptu	
17	EXTINCT	Extant-extinct	Q	Still existing; current	
18	EXTIRPATE	EXTERMINATE	R	Talk at length, elaborate	
19	EXTOL	Extra told-exalt	S	Very beautiful and delicate, intense	
20	EXTRANEOUS	extra news	T	Wise ; convenient and practical	

Memory Test-46 : Match each word and its memory trick to the corresponding definition.

S.N	WORD	MEMORY TRIGGER	S.N	DEFINITIONS	KEY
1	EXTRAPOLATE	Where is Extra + pole ?	A	An outgoing person	
2	EXTRAVAGANT	Extra-spend	B	Be happy, rejoice	
3	EXTRICATE	Extract from intricate	C	Cheerful; abundant, plentiful	
4	EXTRINSIC	External- Extras	D	Easily done; oversimplified	
5	EXTROVERT	Extrovert-introvert	E	External, not essential, extraneous	
6	EXUBERANT	Ebullient- abundant	F	Fake, forged; made up	
7	EXULT	Exam result is good	G	False, artificial	
8	FABRICATED	FAKE CREATE	H	False; misleading	
9	FACADE	Front FACE	I	Free, disentangle	
10	FACETIOUS	Face TEASES US	J	Front face (of a building)	
11	FACILE	Face smile job	K	Guess; infer	
12	FACILITATE	Facility	L	Hesitate to act; waver	
13	FACTIOUS	Factions	M	Humorous, inappropriate joking	
14	FACTITIOUS	FICTITIOUS	N	illusion; whim; idea	
15	FALLACIOUS	FALSE reason	O	Liable to fail	
16	FALLIBLE	fail	P	Make easier; promote	
17	FALLOW	No FOLLOW up	Q	Quarrelsome, dissentious	
18	FALTER	Faltered-failed to act	R	Uncultivated; plowed but not sowed	
20	FANATIC	Fan is fanatic	S	Wasteful, lavish, costly	
19	FANCY	Fantasy	T	Zealous, extreme, radical	

Answers	EX.NO	1	2	3	4	5	6	7	8	9	10	11	12	13	14	15	16	17	18	19	20
	45	D	F	R	K	T	N	O	H	A	E	L	M	S	Q	P	G	I	B	C	J
	46	K	S	I	E	A	C	B	F	J	M	D	P	Q	G	H	O	R	L	T	N

Memory Test-47 : Match each word and its memory trick to the corresponding definition.

S.N	WORD	MEMORY TRIGGER	S.N	DEFINITIONS	KEY
1	FASTIDIOUS	Fast to tidiness	A	Careless and irresponsible	
2	FATHOM	Gautam Fathomed	B	Cause irritation; rankle	
3	FATUOUS	VACUOUS –vacuum brain	C	Disturb; frighten	
4	FAWN	Fan swinging	D	Fertility; fruitfulness	
5	FAZE	Faze-ease; NO EASE	E	Happiness; ability	
6	FEALTY	Fealty-LOYALTY	F	Hot; Ardent	
7	FEASIBLE	POSSIBLE	G	Intense and passionate feeling	
8	FECKLESS	Reckless -useless	H	Investigate; comprehend	
9	FECUNDITY	Fecund-fertile	I	Loyalty, faithfulness	
10	FEEBLE	I'm UNABLE	J	Over particular, difficult to please	
11	FEIGN	Feign-FAKE	K	Pleasing, well chosen or apt	
12	FEINT	Front-"FALSE FRONT"	L	Possible, likely	
13	FELICITOUS	Feel easy to us	M	Pretend	
14	FELICITY	Felicity-FEEL + CITY	N	Resist; ward off	
15	FEND	Defend--fence	O	Seek favor by flattering	
16	FERAL	Fear all- Fatal	P	Stupid; silly	
17	FERVENT	Fervid-fervor-fervent	Q	Trick by cunning	
18	FERVOR	love FEVER	R	Unpleasant smell	
19	FESTER	Fest-infest-INFECT	S	Weak	
20	FETID	Sweat FEET - FETID odor	T	Wild, untamed	

Memory Test-48 : Match each word and its memory trick to the corresponding definition.

S.N	WORD	MEMORY TRIGGER	S.N	DEFINITIONS	KEY
1	FETTER	Feet+tie+r	A	Block by making long speeches	
2	FIASCO	PSYCHO is a failure	B	Chain; hamper	
3	FICKLE	Flicker	C	Changeable, faithless	
4	FICTITIOUS	FICTIONAL	D	Complete failure	
5	FIDELITY	Fidelity-fealty-loyalty	E	Delicate Skill; subtlety	
6	FIGURATIVE	Figure-literal	F	Delicate; thin; weak	
7	FILIAL	Filial-familial-family	G	Excessively particular, fussy	
8	FILIBUSTER	Block-buster	H	Fault or weakness	
9	FINESSE	FINE TALENT	I	Flabby; not firm; soft	
10	FINICKY	Fine-OVER FINE	J	Grow weak, Droop	
11	FITFUL	BIT FULL-BIT by BIT	K	Inexperienced	
12	FLABBY	Chubby;Flabby-feeble	L	Intermittent; sporadic	
13	FLACCID	Flabby-chubby-fatty	M	Loose; Weak; drooping	
14	FLAG	Lagging	N	Loyalty	
15	FLAGRANT	FLAG BURNT	O	Not real; imaginary	
16	FLAMBOYANT	FLASHY boy-showy	P	Relating to a son or daughter	
17	FLAW	Fault	Q	Showy, ornate	
18	FLEDGLING	Fresh wing	R	Temporary; transient	
19	FLEETING	F-LEAVING	S	Using a figure of speech; not literal	
20	FLIMSY	FILMY-films	T	Visibly bad; outrageous; blatant	

Answers	EX.NO	1	2	3	4	5	6	7	8	9	10	11	12	13	14	15	16	17	18	19	20
	47	J	H	P	O	C	I	L	A	D	S	M	Q	K	E	N	T	F	G	B	R
	48	B	D	C	O	N	S	P	A	E	G	L	M	I	J	T	Q	H	K	R	F

WORD GROUPS DAY-12

★ DISAGREEMENT-DISHARMONY

ADJECTIVES: incongruent, inconsonant, discrepant, incompatible, incongruous, inconsistent; divisive, antagonistic, irreconcilable

NOUNS: contention, controversy, dissent, dispute, disaccord, discord, polarity, schism, variance; disharmony, altercation, squabble, wrangle; discrepancy, disparity, divergence, deviation, nonconformity; incompatibility, contradiction, conflict, clash, contrast

VERB: gainsay, take issue , differ .

ANTONYMS: n. acquiescence, harmony, peace

★ UNINTELLIGIBLE: impossible to understand

ADJECTIVES: abstruse, ambiguous, arcane, esoteric, recondite, cryptic, Delphic, inscrutable, incomprehensible, impenetrable, nebulous, obscure, opaque, unintelligible, unfathomable, vague

NOUNS: ambiguity, enigma, conundrum, quandary

VERB: equivocate, obfuscate, perplex, rarefy, mystify

ANTONYMS: adj.intelligible, lucid

★ LUCID: easy to understand, bright

ADJECTIVES: explicit, intelligible, comprehensible, cogent, coherent, fathomable, clear, lucid, limpid, transparent, patent, unambiguous; luminous.

NOUNS: pellucidity, transparency

VERB: elucidate, illuminate, explicate

ANTONYMS: adj.confusing, obscure, murky, vague

★ THEORY-THEORETICAL

ADJECTIVES: abstract, hypothetical, conjectural, conceptual, academic, ideological, quixotic, philosophical, speculative, notional, assumed, presumed, untested, unproven

NOUNS: notion, postulate, assumption, supposition, premise; axiom, maxim, theory

VERB: postulate, posit, presume, suppose, presuppose, assume, premise

ANTONYMS: empirical, practical, heuristic, experimental

★ EXPERIMENTAL-PRACTICAL

ADJECTIVES: empirical, hands-on, hardheaded, applied, heuristic, experiential; feasible, pragmatic, practicable, realistic, viable, workable, possible.

NOUNS: practicability, functionality

VERB: prove, experiment

ANTONYMS: adj. theoretical, impractical

★ TEMPORARY

ADJECTIVES: ephemeral, evanescent, fleeting, momentary, temporal, transitory, transient, vanishing, fugitive; interim, provisional, tentative

NOUNS: impermanence, transitoriness

ANTONYMS: adj.enduring, everlasting, eternal, perpetual, permanent

Word List Day-13

FLINCH (FLINCH): v. Shrink, hesitate
    Trigger: 1. FLINCH-(FT-INCH). 2. FLINCH-PINCH-PUNCH
    Trigger Sentence: 1. The FOOT length becomes INCH when it FLINCHES. 2. She FLINCHED when they PUNCHED her boy friend.
    Sample Sentence: She *flinched* at the very thought of eating raw fish at the sea!

FLIPPANCY (FLIP an see): n. Careless attitude, disrespectfulness
    Trigger: 1. FLIPPANCY–FANCY. 2. FLIPPANT-"SLIP-IN-PANT"
    Trigger Sentence: 1. FANCY or showy guys exhibit FLIPPANCY. 2. FLIPPANT guys keep SLIP IN PANTS during the exams; he is CARELESS and DISRESPECTFUL towards the rules.
    Sample Sentence: If you are *flippant*, you will slip down.
    Related Words: FLIPPANT - a. Lacking in seriousness; superficial.

FLORID (FLOR id): a. Flowery; overly decorated; reddish
    Trigger: FLORID-"FLOWERED"
    Trigger Sentence: The Institute is FLOWERED with FLORID red color FLOWERS.
    Sample Sentence: A wide range of flowers has been arranged very *floridly* in the flower show.

FLOUNDER (FLOWN dur): v. Struggle; move awkwardly
    Trigger: 1.FLOP+UNDER. 2. FLOUNDER-BLUNDER
    Trigger Sentence: 1. She was a FLOP UNDER her interior, FLOUNDERING- not knowing quite what to say. 2. FLOUNDER and BLUNDER are synonyms.
    Sample Sentence: His *floundering* speech made his opponents underestimate his caliber.

FLOURISH (FLOOR ish): v. Prosper; grow well
    Trigger: FLOURISH-"FLOWER +ISH"
    Trigger Sentence: My FLOWER business is FLOURISHING; the FLOWERS are GROWING.
    Sample Sentence: In a botanical park, flowers *flourish* everywhere.

FLOUT (FLOWT): v. Reject; mock
    Trigger: 1.FLOUT-SHOUT. 2. FLOUT-"FOUL+ OUT"
    Trigger Sentence: 1. My boss FLOUTS me with SHOUTS and SLIGHTS me always. 2. When one FLOUTS one tends to use FOUL language.
    Sample Sentence: My rude neighbor *flouted* my new car out of jealousy.

FLUCTUATE (FLUHK choo eyt): v. Waver; change
    Trigger: FLUCTUATE-FLUX
    Trigger Sentence: The FLUX always FLUCTUATES; there is FLUCTUATION in the electrical FLUX.
    Sample Sentence: Since our electric voltage *fluctuated* all day, I could not work on computer.

FOIBLE (FOY bul): n. Weak point; a minor flaw
    Trigger: 1.FAIL+ABLE. 2. FOIBLE-FEEBLE-UNABLE.
    Trigger Sentence: FEEBLE minded people usually possess FOIBLES.
    Sample Sentence: The opposition is on the lookout for a *foible* to make a mountain out of mole.

FOIL (FOYL): v. Defeat, frustrate
    Trigger: FOILED-FAILED

Trigger Sentence: FOIL is to make something FAIL.

Sample Sentence: The prisoners' escape attempt was *foiled*.

FOLLY (FOL ee): n. Foolishness

    Trigger: 1. FOLLY-FOOL. 2. FOLLY-FOOLERY-FOOLISHNESS

    Trigger Sentence: FOLLY is known as FOOLISHNESS.

    Sample Sentence: Human *folly* is not rare. There is a degree of *foolishness* inherent in humans.

FOMENT (foh MENT): v. Stir up, stimulate

    Trigger: FOMENT- FLAME IT

    Trigger Sentence: To FLAME IT, we got to FOMENT (stir up)

    Sample Sentence: Vivek's presence *fomented* Sarita's secret crush for him.

FOOLHARDY (FOOL har dee): a. Rash, fearless

    Trigger: FOOL +HARD

    Trigger Sentence: FOOLISHLY HARD and BRAVE guy exhibits FOOLHARDY nature.

    Sample Sentence: *Foolhardily* they went hiking without warm clothes in winter!

FORAGE (FOR uj): v. Search for food; raid

    Trigger: FORAGE-FOREST

    Trigger Sentence: In FOREST animals FORAGE (search and raid) for the food.

    Sample Sentence: We decided to pick up the rifle and go *foraging* into the jungles.

FORBEARANCE (for BAYR ans): n. Tolerance; Patience

    Trigger: 1. BEAR WITH. 2. FORBEARANCE- FOR TOLERANCE

    Trigger Sentence: 1. She BEARS with FORBEARANCE. 2. FORBEARANCE - FOR TOLERANCE.

    Sample Sentence: Social workers do possess *forbearance* to deal in difficult situations.

FORBID (fer BID): v. Ban; prohibit

    Trigger: 1. FORBIDDEN FRUIT. 2. FORBID-"FOR + BAD". 3. CAN'T BID

    Trigger Sentence: 1. FORBIDDEN fruit is PROHIBITED 2. FOR BAD effects some things are FORBIDDEN. 3. You can't BID when something is FORBIDDEN.

    Sample Sentence: The firm is *forbidden* from issuing shares to public for it has a bad record.

FOREBODE (for BODE): v. To predict or foretell

    Trigger: FOREBODE-FORECAST-FORETELL

    Trigger Sentence: FORECAST-FORETELL-FOREBODE---they just convey BEFOREHAND, what is going to happen in FUTURE???

    Sample Sentence: We did have a *foreboding* that rains were round the corner!

    Related Words: BODE - v. portend, presage

FOREGROUND (FOHR ground): v. Move into the foreground to make more visible or prominent

    Trigger: FOREGROUND-BACKGROUND-UNDERGROUND (** antonym variants)

    Trigger Sentence: The news FOREGROUNDED the politician's infamous UNDERGROUND acts.

    Sample Sentence: Public discussion was meant to *foreground* the issue of women's' safeties.

FORENSIC (fuh REN sik): a. Legal; relating to the public debate

    Trigger: FORUM + SEEK

    Trigger Sentence: The FORENSIC experts seek the public FORUMS to SEEK INFO on legal issues.

    Sample Sentence: *Forensic* medicine is a medical finding that can provide info on crimes.

FORESEE (fohr SEE): v. Be aware of beforehand; predict

Trigger: FORESEE- SEE BEFORE

Trigger Sentence: I have SEEN it BEFORE in my dream! I can FORESEE myself as the president!

Sample Sentence: I can *foresee* future consequences of our actions.

Related Words: 1.UNFORESEEABLE - a. incapable of being predicted. 2. FOREKNOWLEDGE - n. advance knowledge, knowing beforehand. 3. FORETHOUGHT - n. thinking in advance, foresight

FORESIGHT (FAWR sahyt): v. Ability to foresee

Trigger: FORESIGHT-SEE IT BEFORE; FORESIGHT-FORETHOUGHT

Trigger Sentence: If you possess FORESIGHT you can SEE IT BEFORE what happens in future.

Sample Sentence: If you have forethought, it reflects your *foresight*.

Related Words: 1.INSIGHT –n. perception; intuition. 2. FARSIGHTED –a. having foresight

FORESTALL (fawr STAWL): v. Prevent by taking advance action

Trigger: 1. FORE + STALL (STILL). 2. FORESTALL-STANDSTILL-MAKE STILL

Trigger Sentence: STALL is to STILL or STOP; FORESTALL is to STALL someone BEFORE they act.

Sample Sentence: The Republicans *forestalled* the debt ceiling bill forcing a *standstill* in the rule.

Related Words: STALL –v. cause to stop

FORFEIT (FOR fit): v. Lose; surrender

Trigger: FORFEIT-DEFEAT

Trigger Sentence: After the world cup cricket DEFEAT, Australia FORFEITED the trophy.

Sample Sentence: Our team had to *forfeit* the game since we didn't have enough players.

FORGO (for GO): v. Go without; to give up.

Trigger: FORGO-GO--LET'S GO

Trigger Sentence: LET' GO...LET'S NOT DO IT; FORGO is to GO WITHOUT.

Sample Sentence: Let's *forgo* the game and go out in protest of biased umpiring.

FORMIDABLE (FAWR muh dih bul): a. Fearsome; redoubtable

Trigger: FORMIDABLE-"FORM-DEVIL"

Trigger Sentence: DEVIL is in FORM; when someone is in FORM (esp. sports) they are FORMIDABLE and look like DEVIL to the opponents.

Sample Sentence: When you are *formidable* mentally, no devil form will frighten you.

FORSAKE (for SAYK): v. Desert; abandon; renounce

Trigger: FOR SEEK-NEVER SEEK

Trigger Sentence: When you FORSAKE you will NEVER SEEK

Sample Sentence: Hitler tried to *forsake* Jews. He never wanted Jews in Germany.

FORTE (for TAY): n. Strong point, special talent

Trigger: FORTE -FORT

Trigger Sentence: A FORT'S FORTE is its surrounding wall.

Sample Sentence: Athletics was always her *forte*.

Related Words: FORTIFY - v. strengthen; reinforce.

FORTHRIGHT (FOWRTH ryt): a. Frank; direct

Trigger: FORTHRIGHT-RIGHT-STRAIGHT

Trigger Sentence: He is RIGHT always; FRANK and STRAIGHTFORWARD.

Sample Sentence: As long as you behave *forthright*, you are always right.

Related Words: DOWNRIGHT - a. straightforward

FORTITUDE (FOHR tih tood): n. Courage; bravery

Trigger: FORTITUDE -FORT DUDE

Trigger Sentence: This DUDE has got COURAGE; he PROTECTS the FORT from enemies' invasion.

Sample Sentence: Your forte is your charisma, dude. Use this *fortitude* to your advantage.

Related Words: FORTRESS - n. stronghold

FORTUITOUS (for TWO uh tus): a. By chance; accidental

Trigger: FORTUITOUS-FORTUNE

Trigger Sentence: FORTUNE nature is FORTUITOUS; FORTUNE happens by CHANCE.

Sample Sentence: Fortune always favors me. I *fortuitously* escaped the accident.

FOSTER (FAWS tur): v. Encourage, nurture

Trigger: FOSTER-BOOSTER

Trigger Sentence: A BOOSTER always FOSTERS me by giving BOOST.

Sample Sentence: My *foster* parents boosted my confidence with encouragement.

FOUNDER (FOWN dur): v. Sink; fail completely

Trigger: FOUNDER-"GO UNDER"

Trigger Sentence: When you FOUNDER, you will GO UNDER water and then SINK.

Sample Sentence: The Titanic began to *founder* after hitting the iceberg.

FRACAS (FRAK us): n. Noisy quarrel; brawl

Trigger: FRACAS-FRACTURES.

Trigger Sentence: The FRACTURES were the result of FRACAS in a bar.

Sample Sentence: The *fracas* in the parliament ended with some of the members suspended.

FRACTIOUS (FRAK shuhs): a. Rebellious, unruly

Trigger: 1. FRACT (REACT) +ious. 2. FRACTIOUS-REACTIONS

Trigger Sentence: "FRACT" sounds like REACT; FRACTIOUS people show REACTIONS.

Sample Sentence: The reaction of the workers against the management became *fractious*.

Related Words: INFRACTION –n. breach; violation

FRAIL (FRAYL): a. Weak; fragile

Trigger: 1. FRAIL-FAIL. 2. FRAIL-AIL- (AIL-ILL)

Trigger Sentence: 1. FRAIL things always FAIL; for they are weak. 2. The AILING man is FRAIL.

Sample Sentence: Doctors say that the patient's organs are so *frail* that they eventually fail.

Related Words: 1.FRAILTY - n. weakness. 2. FRAGILE –a. easily broken; weak

FRANTIC (FRAN tik): a. Wild; highly excited

Trigger: 1. FRANTIC-FRENETIC-FRENZY (refer). 2. FRANTIC-full of PANIC

Trigger Sentence: 1. FRANTIC-FRENETIC-FRENZY-CRAZY; are synonyms. 2. In a FRENZY, the mob frantically broke everything in their way.

Sample Sentence: Jackson's fans screamed *frantically* on seeing him.

Related Words: FRANTICALLY –adv. madly

FRAUDULENT (FRAW juh lunt): a. Deceitful; dishonest

Trigger: FRAUDULENT-FRAUD

Trigger Sentence: FRAUDULENT schemes are based on FRAUD.

Sample Sentence: Officers involved in this *fraudulent* scam were finally caught by the CBI.

Related Words: DEFRAUD –v. cheat; swindle

FRENETIC (fruh NET ik): a. Wildly excited; frenzied

    Trigger: 1. FRENETIC-FRANTIC- FRENZY (refer). 2. FRENETIC

    Trigger Sentence: 1. FRENZY means CRAZY, MADNESS. 2. EXTREMELY ENERGETIC is FRENETIC.

    Sample Sentence: The energetic hero does all sorts of *frenetic* acts in any average film.

FRENZY (FREN zee): n. Uncontrollable Excitement

    Trigger: FRENZY-CRAZY

    Trigger Sentence: They celebrated New Year in a CRAZY and FRENZY manner.

    Sample Sentence: If you ignite that crazy fellow, he will go *frenzy*.

    Related Words: FRENZIED - a. wildly excited

FRESCO (FRES koh): n. Fresh painting on a plaster

    Trigger: FRESCO-"FRESH-PICASSO"

    Trigger Sentence: A FRESH painting of PICASSO was executed in FRESCO.

    Sample Sentence: The Gothic cathedral is famous for beautiful *frescoes* and stain glass.

FRIVOLOUS (FRIV uh luhs): a. Lacking in seriousness, carefree

    Trigger: 1. FRIVOLOUS-FREE LOVES. 2. FRI-FREE. 3. FRIVOLOUS-FOOLISH (** synonyms)

    Trigger Sentence: 1. This is a FREE LOVING FRIVOLOUS guy. Don't trust his LOVE. 2. How FOOLISH are you to love this FRIVOLOUS guy.

    Sample Sentence: Nancy enjoyed Bill's *frivolous* and funny ways.

    Related Words: FRIVOLITY - n. flippancy, silliness.

FROWARD (FROH werd): a. Contrary, rebellious

    Trigger: FROWARD-FORWARD-BACKWARD

    Trigger Sentence: FROWARD guy moves FORWARD when I say move BACKWARD.

    Sample Sentence: The inspector had to deal with a *froward* prisoner who was difficult to handle.

FRUCTIFY (FROOK tuh fahy): v. To make fruitful

    Trigger: FRUCT-FRUIT

    Trigger Sentence: FRUCTIFY is to make FRUITFUL.

    Sample Sentence: I *fructified* my sabbatical by completing the research in time.

FRUGAL (FROO gul): a. Economical, care in spending

    Trigger: 1. FRUGAL-"FEW+GAL". 2. Opposite to PRODIGAL (refer)

    Trigger Sentence: A FRUGAL spends FEW to the GALS.

    Sample Sentence: If you are *frugal*, few gals will date with you.

    Related Words: 1.FRUGALITY - n. thrift; economy. 2. PRODIGAL –a. wasteful; generous

FULMINATE (FUL muh nayt): v. Explode; strongly attack

    Trigger: 1. MINE-EXPLODES. 2. FULL +MINUS - FULL NEGATIVE WORDS.

    Trigger Sentence: My boss always FULMINATES on employees by using FULL MINUS words.

    Sample Sentence: When he *fulminates*, he reminds me of a mine explosion.

FURTIVE (FUR tiv): a. Stealthy; secret

    Trigger: 1. FURTIVE-SECRETIVE. 2. FURT-FART

    Trigger Sentence: 1. FURTIVE-SECRETIVE are synonyms. 2. People oust FARTS in a FURTIVE way.

    Sample Sentence: She did her religious rituals in a *furtive* manner.

FUSION (FYOO zhun): n. Combination; union
Trigger: FUSION-FISSION
Trigger Sentence: Nuclear FUSION (union) and nuclear FISSION (separation) are contradictory.
Sample Sentence: Modern choreographers often love *fusion* of different dance forms.

FULSOME (FUL sum): a. Disgustingly excessive
Trigger: FULSOME-OVERFULLNESS
Trigger Sentence: FULSOME means EXCESSIVELY FULL to the level of being disgusting.
Sample Sentence: I cannot stand his *fulsome* attitude; he is otherwise a sugar coated knife!

FUTILE (FYOOT ul): n. Useless; worthless
Trigger: 1. FUTILITY-NO UTILITY. 2. FUTILE-NOT FERTILE
Trigger Sentence: 1. UTILITY -USEFULNESS; FUTILITY- USELESSNESS. 2. FUTILE is NOT FERTILE.
Sample Sentence: It is *futile* for an infertile couple to give birth without medical help.
Related Words: UTILITARIAN –a. useful; practicable

GADFLY (GAD fly): n. An irritating person
Trigger: "GAD-FLY"-"BAD FLY"
Trigger Sentence: He is just like a BAD FLY; he IRRITATES us.
Sample Sentence: He is a GADFLY. Bad language effortlessly flows from his tongue.

GAFFE (GAF): n. An embarrassing blunder; mistake
Trigger: 1.GAFFE-GOOFY. 2. GAFFE-LAUGH
Trigger Sentence: 1. In Disney cartoons GOOFY usually commits GAFFE. 2. He committed GAFFE by LAUGHING loudly at the meeting.
Sample Sentence: How can you expect this *goofy* guy doing things without gaffes?

GAINSAY (gayn SAY): v. Deny; contradict
Trigger: GAIN+SAY- "AGAINST SAY"
Trigger Sentence: 1. GAINSAY is to SAY AGAINST. 2. If you SAY AGAINST him, he GAINSAYS it.
Sample Sentence: You are *gainsaying* your own version of the story by giving conflicting info.
Related Words: NAYSAY - v. refuse

GALLANT (GAL unt): a. Brave; courageous
Trigger: 1.GALLANT-MILLITANT. 2. GALLANT-TALENT
Trigger Sentence: 1. MILITARY man is GALLANT. 2. A MILITANT is GALLANT, but irrational.
Sample Sentence: The *talented* soldier put up a *gallant* resistance to the attackers.
Related Words: GALLANTRY - n. courage; courtesy

GALVANIZE (GAL vuh nyze): v. Stimulate; shock or excite.
    Trigger: 1.GAL. 2. GALVANIZE-ENERGIZE
    Trigger Sentence: The hottie GAL GALVANIZED and ENERGIZED the boys.
    Sample Sentence: The new gal has *galvanized* the entire college on the first day itself.

GAMBIT (GAM bit): n. An opening action that is calculated to gain an advantage; tactic
    Trigger: 1.GAMBIT–GAME. 2. GAMBLE A BIT
    Trigger Sentence: In any GAME you got to GAMBLE a BIT (GAMBIT) to win the GAME.
    Sample Sentence: The coach's *gambit* paid off when his players won the football match.

GAMBOL (GAM buhl): v. To jump about playfully; skip
    Trigger: GAMBOL-"GAME BALL"
    Trigger Sentence: In a basket-BALL GAME, the BALL GAMBOLS and players GAMBOL.
    Sample Sentence: When the team won the basket ball game trophy, its players *gamboled*.

GARBLED (GAR buld): v. Confused; mixed up, jumbled
    Trigger: 1. GARBLE-GARBAGE. 2. GARBLE-GARGLE
    Trigger Sentence: 1. GARBAGE we mix-up everything; so GARBAGE TALK is CONFUSED and GARBLED. 2. Don't speak while you GARGLE. Your speech becomes GARBLED.
    Sample Sentence: He was so sleepy that his speech had become *garbled*.

GARGANTUAN (gar GAN shoo in): a. Enormous, huge
    Trigger: GARGANTUAN-GIGANTIC-TITANIC
    Trigger Sentence: 1. a GIGANTIC (GARGANTUAN) man is TITANIC. 2. You need to have a GARGANTUAN appetite to accomplish this GIGANTIC work.
    Sample Sentence: The losses are almost *gargantuan* due to recession in the market.
    Related Words: GIGANTIC –a. huge; tremendous

GARNER (GAHR ner): v. Gather; store up
    Trigger: GARNER-GATHER
    Trigger Sentence: GARNER is to GATHER; in GRAIN BIN we GARNER the GRAINS.
    Sample Sentence: Political parties *garner* support by organizing large gatherings.

GARRULOUS (GAR uh lus): a. Unnecessarily talkative; wordy
    Trigger: GARRULOUS-GIRLS
    Trigger Sentence: GIRLS are usually GARRULOUS in nature.
    Sample Sentence: Our *garrulous* uncle made us spend more time than we planned.
    Related Words: GARRULITY - n. talkativeness

GAUCHE (GOHSH): a. Awkward; clumsy
    Trigger: GAUCHE-GRACE-lack of GRACE
    Trigger Sentence: GAUCHE means LACK OF GRACE.
    Sample Sentence: In spite of looking *gauche*, Lenin didn't lack grace.
    Related Words: GAUCHERIE - n. awkwardness; lack of social grace.

GAUDY (GAW dee): a. Vulgarly showy; flashy
    Trigger: GAUDY-BODY
    Trigger Sentence: The country LADY on her BODY wears GAUDY clothing.
    Sample Sentence: Some people can effortlessly carry *gaudy* clothing and loud makeup!

GAUNT (GAWNT): a. Lean; haggard; angular
    Trigger: GAUNT (lean)-GIANT (huge)
    Trigger Sentence: 1. a GIANT looks HUGE; and a GAUNT looks LEAN and THIN. 2. This former GIANT has turned into a GAUNT individual.
    Sample Sentence: Many of the models today maintain a hanger like *gaunt* bodies.

GAWKY (GAW kee): a. Awkward, clumsy
> **Trigger:** gAWKy-AWKWARD
> **Trigger Sentence:** GAWK sounds like AWKWARD. He is so GAWKY that he does even simple things as AWKWARD as possible.
> **Sample Sentence:** His dressing is *gawkier* than he himself is!
> Related Words: GAWKISH - a. clumsy

GENERIC (je NER ik): a. Referring to a class or group; not specific
> **Trigger:** GENERIC-GENERAL-GENES
> **Trigger Sentence:** A GENERIC is pertaining to same GENRE-GENES; it is GENERAL- "not specific".
> **Sample Sentence:** Christmas has become a *generic* festival, celebrated by people of all religions.

GENRE (ZHAHN ruh): n. Particular type, category (esp of art, literature)
> **Trigger:** 1.GENRE-GENERATION-TYPE. 2. GENDER
> **Trigger Sentence:** 1. Every GENERATION has its GENRE of art and literature. 2. Male GENDER-male GENRE; female GENDER-female GENRE.
> **Sample Sentence:** Of all the *genres* of literature, my favorite is romantic prose poetry.

GERMANE (jur MAYN): a. Relevant, appropriate
> **Trigger:** GERMANE-GERMAN
> **Trigger Sentence:** GERMAN language is GERMANE to GERMANY.
> **Sample Sentence:** It is not *germane* to walk out rudely from the debate program.

GERMINAL (JUR muh nl): a. Creative; Original
> **Trigger:** 1. GERMINAL-TERMINAL. 2. GERMINAL-SEMINAL (SEMEN)
> **Trigger Sentence:** 1. GERMINAL-beginning; TERMINAL-end. 2. SEMINAL and GERMINAL are synonyms. SEMEN means seed. It is ORIGINAL.
> **Sample Sentence:** *Germinal* ideas of one discipline can influence the growth of another.

GIGANTIC (ji GAN tik): a. Huge; tremendous
> **Trigger:** GIGANTIC-TITANIC
> **Trigger Sentence:** TITANIC is a GIGANTIC ship
> **Sample Sentence:** At 67 years of age, Mark André climbed the *gigantic* Himalayan heights!

GLUT (GLUT): n. Excessive supply, overabundance
> **Trigger:** gLUT-LOT
> **Trigger Sentence:** GLUT is to have a LOT.
> **Sample Sentence:** This *glut* of water is the result of lots of rainfall occurred recently.

GLUTTON (GLUT en): n. Overeater
> **Trigger:** 1. GLUTTON-MUTTON. 2. GUT+TON
> **Trigger Sentence:** 1. GLUTTON eats MUTTON. 2. GLUTTON GUT weighs TON as he overeater.
> **Sample Sentence:** My dog is a *glutton* and eats everything that he chances to grab upon!

GINGERLY (JIN jer lee): a. Cautiously, Carefully
> **Trigger:** 1. GINGERLY-GENTLY. 2. GINGERLY- GUARDEDLY
> **Trigger Sentence:** 1. Add GINGER in tea GENTLY and GINGERLY. 2. Night guards survey GUARDEDLY and GINGERLY.
> **Sample Sentence:** The cat *gingerly* walked on the wall before it dived over the dogs.

GIST (JIST): n. Essence; main idea
    Trigger: 1.GIST-LIST OUT. 2. GIST-BEST POINT
    Trigger Sentence: 1. GIST is to LIST OUT the main points of study. 2. Write down the BEST POINTS of your idea in a GIST.
    Sample Sentence: List out the *gist* of the hypothesis in a simple report.

GLIB (GLIB): a. Fluent but insincere; slick
    Trigger: 1. GLIB-LIP. 2. GLIB-GLIDE
    Trigger Sentence: 1. For a GLIB talker the words from LIP flow LIB (liberally).
    2. GLIDE is to WALK SMOOTHLY; GLIB is to TALK SMOOTHLY.
    Sample Sentence: She glides through any situation with her masterly *glib*.

GLOAT (GLOHT): v. Boast greatly; express evil self-satisfaction
    Trigger: 1. GLOAT-GLORY. 2. GLOAT-GLOW
    Trigger Sentence: 1. They GLOAT over SELF-GLORY and GLOAT over the misfortune of enemy. 2. Their faces were in GLOW when they GLOAT over their victory.
    Sample Sentence: My big brother always *gloats* on how he always beats me in chess.

GLUM (GLUM): a. Dejected; gloomy; ill-natured
    Trigger: GLUM-GLOOMY
    Trigger Sentence: They became GLUM when they heard the GLOOMY news.
    Sample Sentence: The dark *dungeon* has a glum atmosphere.
    Related Words: GLOOMY - a. sad; dark

GOAD (GOHD): v. Urge on
    Trigger: 1. GOAD-GO & DO. 2. GOAD-GOAL
    Trigger Sentence: 1. GO GO GO and DO IT. 2. He GOADED us to achieve a GOAL.
    Sample Sentence: You should *goad* yourself continuously towards your goal.

GORGE (GAWRJ): v. Stuff oneself with food; n. Deep ravine
    Trigger: GORGE-LARGE
    Trigger Sentence: George Bush GORGED himself with a LARGE ice-cream.
    Sample Sentence: 1. They *gorged* themselves on meat and liquor. 2. The *gorge* between the valleys was dark and deep.
    Related Words: DISGORGE - v. vomit, eject forcefully

GOSSAMER (GOSS uh mer): a. Very light, delicate
    Trigger: GOSSAMER-"GO in SUMMER"
    Trigger Sentence: We usually "GO in SUMMER" with GOSSAMER (light weight & delicate) cloths.
    Sample Sentence: Hiding behind those *gossamer* curtains, the princess gestured and whispered to her lover, those sweet little secret words.

GOUGE (GOWJ): v. Over charge; swindle
    Trigger: 1.GOUGE- HUGE CHARGE. 2. GOUGE-GUAGE
    Trigger Sentence: 1. They GOUGED money from the football fans by CHARGING HUGE money on black tickets. 2. The Indian petrol GAUGES GOUGE money from public.
    Sample Sentence: The oil companies *gouge* money in the name of unknown charges.

GRADATION (grey DEY shun): n. Gradual change; phase; transition in stages
    Trigger: GRADATION-GRADUAL
    Trigger Sentence: There are subtle GRADATIONS/GRADUAL CHANGES in color.
    Sample Sentence: *Gradation* means a smooth transition between one color to another color.

Memory Test-49 : Match each word and its memory trick to the corresponding definition.

S.N	WORD	MEMORY TRIGGER	S.N	DEFINITIONS	KEY
1	FLINCH	Feet becomes INCH	A	Ability to foresee	
2	FLIPPANCY	FANCY attitude	B	Area closest to the viewer	
3	FLORID	FLOWERED-red	C	Ban; prohibit	
4	FLOUNDER	Flop+under	D	Be aware of beforehand	
5	FLOURISH	Flower +ish	E	Careless attitude, disrespectfulness	
6	FLOUT	Shout	F	Defeat, frustrate	
7	FLUCTUATE	Fluctuate-FLUX	G	Flowery; overly decorated; reddish	
8	FOIBLE	Fail+able	H	Foolishness	
9	FOIL	Make it FAIL	I	Predict or foretell	
10	FOLLY	Folly-FOOLERY	J	Prosper; grow well	
11	FOMENT	Flame it-foam it	K	Rash, fearless	
12	FOOLHARDY	Fool +hard—die hard	L	Reject; mock	
13	FORAGE	FOREST animals FORAGE	M	Relating to the public debate; legal	
14	FORBEARANCE	Bear with	N	Search for food; raid	
15	FORBID	Forbidden fruit	O	Shrink, hesitate	
16	FOREBODE	Forecast-foretell	P	Stir up, stimulate	
17	FOREGROUND	background-underground	Q	Struggle; move awkwardly	
18	FORENSIC	Forum + seek	R	Tolerance; Patience	
19	FORESEE	Foresee- see before	S	Waver; change	
20	FORESIGHT	See it before	T	Weak point; a minor flaw	

Memory Test-50 : Match each word and its memory trick to the corresponding definition.

S.N	WORD	MEMORY TRIGGER	S.N	DEFINITIONS	KEY
1	FORESTALL	Standstill-make still	A	By chance; accidental	
2	FORFEIT	Forfeit-defeat	B	Courage; bravery	
3	FORGO	Let's go	C	Deceitful; dishonest	
4	FORMIDABLE	FORM-devil	D	Renounce; desert; abandon	
5	FORSAKE	NEVER SEEK	E	Encourage, nurture	
6	FORTE	Fort	F	Fearsome; redoubtable	
7	FORTHRIGHT	Right-straight	G	Frank; direct	
8	FORTITUDE	Fort DUDE	H	Fresh painting on a plaster	
9	FORTUITOUS	FORTUNE is FORTUITOUS	I	Go without; to give up	
10	FOSTER	BOOSTER - FOSTERS	J	Highly excited; wild	
11	FOUNDER	Go under	K	Lacking in seriousness, carefree	
12	FRACAS	Fractures after fracas	L	Lose; surrender	
13	FRACTIOUS	reactions	M	Noisy quarrel; brawl	
14	FRAIL	Frail-AIL- ILL	N	Prevent by taking advance action	
15	FRANTIC	Frenetic-FRENZY	O	Rebellious, unruly	
16	FRAUDULENT	Fraud	P	Sink; fail completely	
17	FRENETIC	Frantic- FRENZY	Q	Strong point, special talent	
18	FRENZY	Frenzy-CRAZY	R	Uncontrollable Excitement	
19	FRESCO	Fresh-Picasso	S	Weak; fragile	
20	FRIVOLOUS	FREE loves -foolish	T	Wildly excited; frenzied	

Answers	EX.NO	1	2	3	4	5	6	7	8	9	10	11	12	13	14	15	16	17	18	19	20
	49	O	E	G	Q	J	L	S	T	F	H	P	K	N	R	C	I	B	M	D	A
	50	N	L	I	F	D	Q	G	B	A	E	P	M	O	S	J	C	T	R	H	K

Memory Test-51 : Match each word and its memory trick to the corresponding definition.

S.N	WORD	MEMORY TRIGGER	S.N	DEFINITIONS	KEY
1	FROWARD	Forward-backward	A	Awkward; clumsy	
2	FRUCTIFY	Fruitful	B	Brave; courageous	
3	FRUGAL	FEW+GAL	C	Combination; union	
4	FULMINATE	Mine-EXPLODES	D	Confused; mixed up, jumbled	
5	FURTIVE	Expel FARTS - FURTIVE	E	Contradict; deny	
6	FUSION	Fusion-fission	F	Contrary, rebellious	
7	FULSOME	Overfullness	G	Disgustingly excessive	
8	FUTILE	NOT fertile	H	Economical, care in spending	
9	GADFLY	Bad fly	I	Embarrassing blunder; mistake	
10	GAFFE	Gaffe-laugh	J	Enormous, huge	
11	GAINSAY	Against say	K	Explode; strongly attack	
12	GALLANT	Militant are gallant	L	Gather; store up	
13	GALVANIZE	ENERGIZE	M	irritating person	
14	GAMBIT	GAMBLE a bit	N	jump about playfully; skip	
15	GAMBOL	Game BALL	O	Make fruitful	
16	GARBLED	Garbage talk	P	Stealthy; secret	
17	GARGANTUAN	Gigantic-TITANIC	Q	Stimulate; shock or excite	
18	GARNER	Garner-gather	R	Tactic; trick in a game	
19	GARRULOUS	GIRLS are GARRULOUS	S	Unnecessarily talkative; wordy	
20	GAUCHE	Lack of GRACE	T	Useless; worthless	

Memory Test-52 : Match each word and its memory trick to the corresponding definition.

S.N	WORD	MEMORY TRIGGER	S.N	DEFINITIONS	KEY
1	GAUDY	showing body	A	Awkward, clumsy	
2	GAUNT	GAUNT- opp. GIANT	B	Boast greatly	
3	GAWKY	Gawky-AWKWARD	C	Cautiously, Carefully	
4	GENERIC	Generic-general-genes	D	Dejected; gloomy; ill-natured	
5	GENRE	Particular Generation	E	Essence; main idea	
6	GERMANE	German -GERMANY	F	Excessive supply, overabundance	
7	GERMINAL	Germinal-seminal	G	Fluent but insincere; slick	
8	GIGANTIC	Gigantic-TITANIC	H	Gradual change; phase	
9	GLUT	Glut-LOT	I	Huge; tremendous	
10	GLUTTON	MUTTON eating	J	Lean; haggard; angular	
11	GINGERLY	Handle GENTLY	K	Original; Creative	
12	GIST	list out best	L	Over charge; swindle	
13	GLIB	Lip- -glides	M	Overeater	
14	GLOAT	Self GLORY- glow	N	Particular type, category	
15	GLUM	Glum-GLOOMY	O	Referring to a group; not specific	
16	GOAD	Go & DO	P	Relevant, appropriate	
17	GORGE	LARGE food t once	Q	Stuff oneself with food	
18	GOSSAMER	I GO in SUMMER	R	Urge on	
19	GOUGE	HUGE charge	S	Very light, delicate	
20	GRADATION	GRADUAL change	T	Vulgarly showy; flashy	

Answers	EX.NO	1	2	3	4	5	6	7	8	9	10	11	12	13	14	15	16	17	18	19	20
	51		F	O	H	K	P	C	G	T	M	I	E	B	Q	R	N	D	J	L	S	A
	52		T	J	A	O	N	P	K	I	F	M	C	E	G	B	D	R	Q	S	L	H

WORD GROUPS DAY-13

★ **PERMANENT-PERMANENCE**

ADJECTIVES: abiding, constant, enduring, everlasting, eternal, lasting, perpetual, perennial, unending, imperishable, interminable.

NOUNS: immortality, perpetuity.

VERB: eternalize, immortalize

ANTONYMS: adj. temporary, transitory, ephemeral

★ **FRUGAL-PARSIMONIOUS**

ADJECTIVES: frugal, thrifty, sparing; canny, provident; parsimonious, penurious, mean, miserly, niggardly, ungenerous, tight-fisted, stingy;

NOUNS: frugality, thrift; parsimony

VERB: economize, conserve, husband

ANTONYMS: adj. prodigal, extravagant, wasteful

★ **PRODIGAL**

ADJECTIVES: extravagant, spendthrift, profligate, wasteful; improvident, imprudent; profuse, lavish, rich

NOUNS: prodigality, profligacy, dissipation; wastrel

VERB: squander, waste, exhaust

ANTONYMS: adj.thrifty, mean; frugal

★ **HARMLESS**

ADJECTIVES: innocuous, innocent, naïve, benign, inoffensive

NOUNS: benignancy

VERB:

ANTONYMS: adj. harmful, offensive, noxious, injurious

★ **HARM-HARMFUL**

ADJECTIVES: baleful, detrimental, deleterious, inimical, insidious, invidious, hostile, hazardous, lethal, malign, malignant,

malevolent, minatory, noxious, ominous, pestilential, sinister, subversive, pernicious

NOUNS: malice, malevolence

VERB: injure, mar, impair, impale, ravage, vitiate

ANTONYMS: v. benevolent, salubrious, salutary

★ **IMPARTIAL ATTITUDE**

ADJECTIVES: disinterested, detached, dispassionate, objective, egalitarian, equitable, even-handed, fair, just; unbiased, unprejudiced, neutral, non-partisan

NOUNS: equity, objectivity, neutrality

VERB: neutralize

ANTONYMS: adj.partial, prejudice

★ **PARTIALITY**

ADJECTIVES: biased, discriminatory, inequitable, prejudiced, partisan, one-sided, slanted, coloured,

NOUNS: bias, discrimination, prejudice, inequity

VERB: discriminate, bias, prejudice

ANTONYMS: n. impartiality, disinterestedness

is it a TABOO for women to smoke TOBACCO ?!

TABOO :
forbidden,
unthinkable,
banned

Word List Day-14

GRANDILOQUENT (gran DIL uh kwunt): a. Pompous, loud, excessively eloquent
> **Trigger:** GRAND+ELOQUENT
>
> **Trigger Sentence:** He is GRANDILOQUENT as he speaks ELOQUENTLY with GRAND gestures.
>
> **Sample Sentence:** With grace and *grandiloquence* of the royalty, Martin delivered his dialogues.

GRANDIOSE (GRAN dee ohs): a. Magnificent; exaggerated
> **Trigger:** GRANDIOSE-"GRAND+POSE"
>
> **Trigger Sentence:** 1. GRAND is known as GRANDIOSE. 2. GRANDIOSE is to give GRAND POSE.
>
> **Sample Sentence:** Egyptian emperors built *grandiose* structures to exhibit their grandeur.

GRANDSTAND (GRAN stand): v. perform showily in order to impress the audience
> **Trigger:** GRANDSTAND-STAND GREAT
>
> **Trigger Sentence:** She is a GRANDSTANDER and never misses a chance to GRANDSTAND.
>
> **Sample Sentence:** The politician doesn't hesitate to *grandstand* to makes his point.

GRATIFY (GRAT uh fahy): v. Satisfy, please
> **Trigger:** GRATIFICATION-SATISFACTION
>
> **Trigger Sentence:** To make someone FEEL GREAT you got to GRATIFY and SATISFY them.
>
> **Sample Sentence:** The guest is satisfied with the *gratifying* dinner.

GRATIS (GRA tus): a. Free of charge.
> **Trigger:** GRATIS -GRANT IS
>
> **Trigger Sentence:** I will GRANT you this GRATIS; GRANT is GRATIS; GRANT IS always FREE.
>
> **Sample Sentence:** Banks don't *grant* loans gratis interest.

GRATUITOUS (gruh TOO uh tus): a. Given freely; unjustified
> **Trigger:** 1. GRANTS. 2. GRATUITY
>
> **Trigger Sentence:** 1. GRANT money but don't GRANT ADVICES which are GRATUITOUS (free of cost).2. The Indian Government gives GRATUITY to its employees at retirement GRATUITOUSLY.
>
> **Sample Sentence:** It is unfair for the US Government to sanction grants *gratuitously*.
>
> Related Words: GRATUITY-n. tip; bonus

GRAVITY (GRAV i tee): a. Seriousness or importance
> **Trigger:** 1. GRAVE (YARD). 2. GRAVITY-LEVITY
>
> **Trigger Sentence:** 1. Gravity of sadness in a graveyard. 2. GRAVITY-serious; LEVITY-not serious.
>
> **Sample Sentence:** We didn't realize the *gravity* of Steven's drug addiction until it got worse.
>
> Related Words: LEVITY –n. lack of seriousness

GREGARIOUS (gri GAIR ee us): a. Fond of company

    Trigger: 1. GREGARIOUS – CONGREGATION. 2. GREGARIOUS-"GRE + VARIOUS"

    Trigger Sentence: 1. A GREGARIOUS person loves to be in a CONGREGATION. 2. His GREGARIOUS contacts are as varied as VARIOUS GRE words.

    Sample Sentence: The next compartment in the train had a bunch of *gregarious* singing girls.

GRIEVOUS (GREE vus): a. (Of something bad) very serious

    Trigger: GRIEVOUS-GRIEF to US

    Trigger Sentence: Causing GRIEF or sorrow is known as GRIEVOUS.

    Sample Sentence: Abolition of Child labor is indeed a *grievous* issue to be addressed.

GRISLY (GRIZ lee): a. Ghastly

    Trigger: GHASTLY-GRISLY-GHOSTLY

    Trigger Sentence: The GRIZZLY bear before us appears GRISLY and GHASTLY

    Sample Sentence: Poe is renowned for telling *grisly* tales in many of his works.

GROTESQUE (grow TESK): a. Fantastic, absurdly odd, ugly

    Trigger: GROTESQUE -GROW+TUSK

    Trigger Sentence: When you GROW TUSK on your head, you would look GROTESQUE.

    Sample Sentence: *Grotesque* is the word that stands apt for Chandana Khan's horrible paintings!

GROVEL (GRUV ul): v. Plead; crawl abjectly on ground

    Trigger: 1.GROVEL- BOW WELL. 2. GROVEL--GROW-WELL

    Trigger Sentence: 1. GROVEL is to BOW WELL in front of the superiors. 2. In order to"GROW WELL" in life you got to BEG and GROVEL superiors.

    Sample Sentence: John Jones makes his employees *grovel* if they really needed a favour.

GUFFAW (guh FAW): v. To laugh loudly

    Trigger: GUFFAW-"HEE-HAW-HAW"

    Trigger Sentence: I GUFFAWED hee haw haw very loudly.

    Sample Sentence: How could you *guffaw* at the funeral?! You embarrassed us all!

GUILE (GYLE): n. Cunning; trickery

    Trigger: 1.GUILE-"GUY + ILL". 2. GUY-GAL

    Trigger Sentence: 1. I feel sick to see that GUY'S ILL GUILE. 2. GUYS, and also GALS are GUILE.

    Sample Sentence: 1. Due to his *guile* activities, Bob's had a bad reputation. (Beguile is the action of guile, verb.) 2. Bharath *beguiled* his friends out of their savings and investments.

    Related Words: 1.GUILELESS - a. naive, sincere. 2. BEGUILE - v. deceive; charm

GUISE (GYZE): n. Outward appearance; mask

    Trigger: GUISE-DISGUISE

    Trigger Sentence: The guile GUYS are in GUISE to DISGUISE their true nature.

    Sample Sentence: My neighbor under the *guise* of friendship betrayed me.

    Related Words: DISGUISE –v. hide; conceal

GULLIBLE (GUL ih bul): a. Credulous; easy to deceive

    Trigger: GULL (refer)-GULLIBLE

Trigger Sentence: We can easily GULL (guile; gull-to deceive) the GULLIBLE people.

Sample Sentence: You are mistaken to imagine that Shreya is an innocent *gullible* girl.

Related Words: GULLIBILITY - n. credulity, quality of being easily deceived.

HABITAT (HAB i tat): n. The natural home

   Trigger: 1.HABITAT-"HABIT AT". 2. INHABIT

   Trigger Sentence: 1. It is NATURAL HABIT to reach HABITAT after the day's work. 2. INHABITANTS belong to a HABITAT.

   Sample Sentence: We replicated the turtle's *habitat* in our backyard.

HACKNEYED (HAK need): a. Routine, overused, commonplace

   Trigger: HACKNEY + ED - LACK NEW

   Trigger Sentence: Here is a HACKNEYED script of the movie; there is LACK of anything NEW in it.

   Sample Sentence: The theatre critics criticized her story because of its *hackneyed* plot.

HAGGARD (HAG erd): a. Looking exhausted; worn out

   Trigger: 1.HAGGARD-HAGRID. 2. HAGGARD-BEGGER

   Trigger Sentence: 1. In Harry Potter film HAGRID is gigantic; as opposite to HAGGARD. 2. BEGGARS wear a HAGGARD look.

   Sample Sentence: Her face was drawn and *haggard* due to hunger and sleeplessness.

HALCYON (HAL see un): a. Calm, happy

   Trigger: 1.HALCYON-CYCLONE. 2. HAL + CYON- HALL+DYAN.

   Trigger Sentence: 1. The severe CYCLONE disturbed the HALCYON atmosphere. 2. When you do DYAN (meditation) in a HALL... life will be HALCYON!!!

   Sample Sentence: As the cyclone weakened, the people began to see *halcyon* days again.

HALE (HALE): a. Robust, healthy

   Trigger: 1.INHALE + EXHALE. 2. HALE-PALE (** near antonyms)

   Trigger Sentence: Practice rhythmic INHALING and EXHALING, you will be HALE and healthy.

   Sample Sentence: Your face very PALE. Obviously you are not HALE and healthy.

   Related Words: PALE –a. weak; pallid; blanch

HALLMARK (HAUL mark): n. Specific feature; emblem

   Trigger: 1.MARK-FEATURE. 2. HALLMARK -TRADE MARK

   Trigger Sentence: 1. A MARK or feature is known as HALL MARK.2.Our TRADE MARK stands for HALLMARK of quality.

   Sample Sentence: These days' women prefer buying pure gold with a *hallmark* certificate.

HALLOWED (HAL owed): a. Holy; sacred

    Trigger: 1. HALLOW-HOLY. 2. HALLOWED-HONORED

    Trigger Sentence: 1. The HOLY Jerusalem is HALLOWED. 2. HALLOWED and HOLY are synonyms.

    Sample Sentence: Those *hallowed* hills of Tirupati are being visited by millions of devotees daily.

HAMPER (HAM pur): v. Impede, delay

    Trigger: HAMPER -HALTER (HALT)

    Trigger Sentence: 1. A bus HALTERS at a HALT. 2. HAMPER, HALTER and HINDER are synonyms

    Sample Sentence: This HALTING journey will HAMPER my chances of reaching on time.

    Related Words: 1.UNHAMPERED - a. unhindered, not delayed. 2. HALTER –v. prevent

HAPHAZARD (HAP haz urd): a. Lacking order; random

    Trigger: HAP + HAZARD

    Trigger Sentence: 1. HAPS (or happenings) in life are HAPHAZARD; HAP (luck) and HAZARD (danger) in life occur HAPHAZARDLY. 2. It is HAZARDOUS to work HAPHAZARDLY on machine.

    Sample Sentence: My studio is usually *haphazard* and nothing is in its right place!

HAPLESS (HAP lis): a. Unfortunate

    Trigger: HAPLESS -HAPPY LESS

    Trigger Sentence: He is HAPLESS and HOPELESS after a bad beginning.

    Sample Sentence: The *hapless* accident victim waited for hours to get help.

    Related Words: 1. MISHAP - n. unlucky accident, misfortune. 2. HAP- chance

HAPPENSTANCE (HAP uhn stans): n. Chance; fate

    Trigger: HAPPEN CHANCE

    Trigger Sentence: Something that HAPPENS by CHANCE is represented as HAPPENSTANCE.

    Sample Sentence: In a *happenstance* of fate, a beggar by chance happened to win the lottery.

HARANGUE (huh RAANG): n. / v. Aggressive or scolding speech

    Trigger: 1. HARANGUE-"HARASS-TONGUE". 2. HARANGUE-HER ANGER

    Trigger Sentence: 1. The boss's HARASSING TONGUE is throwing a HARANGUE at some poor creature. 2. When HER ANGER is fitful, she tends to hurl a HARANGUE at the receiver.

    Sample Sentence: Do not drive away your students by *haranguing* them to submit home works.

HARBINGER (HAR bin jur): n. Fore runner; indication

    Trigger: HARBINGER-MESSENGER-BRINGER-BEGINNER

    Trigger Sentence: 1. Clouds are HARBINGERS and MESSENGERS of the rain. 2. HARBINGER-MESSENGER-BRINGER-BEGINNER; all are synonyms.

    Sample Sentence: Mikhail Gorbachev is the *harbinger* and messenger of world peace.

HARDHEADED (HARD HED id): a. Practical; stubborn

    Trigger: 1.HARDHEADED-PRACTICAL HEADED. 2.HEARDHEADED-HEADSTRONG

Trigger Sentence: The PRACTICAL-HEADED capitalist took a HARDHEADED approach in investing.

Sample Sentence: The businessman gave *hardheaded* advice to his subordinates.

Related Words: HARD-NOSED - a. stubborn; uncompromising

HARMONY (HAR mu nee): n. Unity, symmetry

Trigger: HARMONY-HARM NO (** NO HARM)

Trigger Sentence: When there is HARMONY, people never HARM each other.

Sample Sentence: There is no harm living in *harmony*.

Related Words: 1.HARMONIOUS- a. marked by agreement; melodious. 2. DISHARMONY - discord

HARROWING (HARE oh ing): a. Extremely painful; distressing

Trigger: 1.HARROWING-ARROW + IN. 2. HARROWING -HARASSING

Trigger Sentence: 1. Imagine an ARROW INside of your body-- it will be a HARROWING experience. 2. HARROWING, HORRIFYING and HARASSING are synonyms.

Sample Sentence: The *harrowing* incident still harasses me.

Related Words: 1.HARROW - v. trouble, hurt. 2. HARRY - v. harass; destroy

HASTEN (HAY sen): v. Expedite, stepped up

Trigger: HASTEN –FAST run

Trigger Sentence: You have to HASTEN up. You should RUN FAST to catch the train.

Sample Sentence: Bring a computer and replace this typewriter to *hasten* your work.

HAUGHTY (HAUT ee): a. Arrogantly superior

Trigger: HAUGHTY -HOTTIE GAL

Trigger Sentence: HOTTIE GIRLS are ARROGANT and HAUGHTY in nature.

Sample Sentence: When I questioned by boyfriend, he only gave me a *haughty* reply.

HAVEN (HAY vin): n. A place of safety

Trigger: HAVEN-HEAVEN

Trigger Sentence: HEAVEN is the safest place; HELL is the most dangerous place.

Sample Sentence: Christians believe that heaven is God's abode and it is a safe *haven*.

HAVOC (HAV ahk): n. Destruction; disorder

Trigger: HAVOC - VOLCANO

Trigger Sentence: The VOLCANO eruption created HAVOC

Sample Sentence: The students created *havoc* in the lecture hall and ran out hither thither!

HAZARDOUS (HAZ er dus): a. Dangerous

Trigger: HAZARDOUS-HUNDRED DIES

Trigger Sentence: 1. HUNDRED DIED in a HAZARDOUS accident. 2. HAZARDOUS and JEOPARDOUS (refer) are synonyms.

Sample Sentence: My mom thinks, paragliding is a *hazardous* sport, so she wouldn't allow me.

HEARKEN (HAHR kun): v. listen; pay attention to

Trigger: HEARKEN-HEAR

Trigger Sentence: *HEARKEN*! I HEAR the distant beat of the hooves of many horses.

Sample Sentence: He sings the song of the Sirens... he *hearkens* to the barking of the

Sphinx.

HEARTEN (HAHR tn): v. Encourage; comfort

Trigger: BRAVE-HEART

Trigger Sentence: In BRAVE HEART movie, the hero Mel Gibson HEARTENS the Scots in their first war of independence.

Sample Sentence: People received *heartening* words of encouragement by the minister.

Related Words: DISHEARTEN - v. discourage, dispirit

HEDONIST (HI duhn ist): n. Pleasure seeker

Trigger: HEDONIST -HE DON IST

Trigger Sentence: The Underworld DON is a HEDONIST; HE enjoys life to the full extent.

Sample Sentence: He is a *hedonist* habitually holidaying on those luxury cruises.

HEED (HEED): v. Pay attention to; take notice of

Trigger: 1. HEED-NEED. 2. HEEDFUL-MINDFUL. 3. HEEDLESS-RECKLESS-CARELESS

Trigger Sentence: 1. You NEED to HEED my advice. 2. HEEDFUL and MINDFUL are synonyms.

Sample Sentence: *Heed* to the teacher's advice, and you'll surely pass the examination.

Related Words: HEEDLESS - a. not noticing; careless

HEGEMONY (hi JEM uh nee): n. Authority over others

Trigger: HEGEMONY-HE'S MONEY

Trigger Sentence: HE HAS MONEY; so he exhibits HEGEMONY over poor people.

Sample Sentence: Right now as a ruling party Congress has the *hegemony*.

HEINOUS (HAY nus): a. Hatefully bad; or shockingly evil

Trigger: 1. HEINOUS- HYENA. 2. HEINOUS-"HE"-VILLAINOUS

Trigger Sentence: 1. HYENA habits are HEINOUS. 2. HEINOUS and VILLAINOUS are synonyms.

Sample Sentence: The villainous criminal has committed many *heinous* crimes.

HERALD (HER uld): v. To give notice of; announce

Trigger: 1. HERALD-"HEAR + ALL +d". 2. "UNHERALDED"- "UNHEARD"

Trigger Sentence: 1.HEAR ALL, when voice HERALDED. 2. UNHERALDED things are NOT HEARD.

Sample Sentence: The Vijayanagara dynasty *heralded* a new beginning of civilization in Humpi.

Related Words: UNHERALDED –a. not previously announced.

HERESY (HER uh see): n. Opinion contrary to popular belief, unorthodox religious belief

Trigger: HERESY –HETERODOXY (** synonyms)

Trigger Sentence: ORTHODOXY - HETERODOXY are antonyms; HERESY - HETERODOXY are synonyms.

Sample Sentence: The Catholic Church used to consider it *heresy* to eat meat on Friday.

Related Words: HERETICAL - a. unorthodox, deviation from accepted beliefs

HERETICAL (huh RET i kul): a. Unorthodox, radical

Trigger: HERETICAL- (THEORETICAL-PRACTICAL)

Trigger Sentence: HERE PRACTICAL guy, HERETICAL towards the THEORETICAL stuff proposed by orthodox people.

Sample Sentence: You can be *heretical* but don't pass negative comments on orthodox people.

HERMIT (HUR mit): n. One who lives alone; RECLUSE

  Trigger: HERMIT -NO PERMIT

  Trigger Sentence: 1. A HERMIT never PERMITS anyone. 2. HERMETIC means tightly sealed; If it is HERMETIC it doesn't PERMIT anything.

  Sample Sentence: This *hermit* lived in the extreme conditions in the caves of Himalaya.

  Related Words: HERMETIC - a. sealed; mysterious

HETERODOX (HET er uh doks): a. Unorthodox; Unconventional

  Trigger: HETERO-ORTHO (** antonyms)

  Trigger Sentence: HETERO means different; ORTHODOX is an antonym for HETERODOX.

  Sample Sentence: He is from a *heterodox* family and married a woman from an orthodox family.

  Related Words: ORTHODOX –a. conservative; religious

HETEROGENEOUS (het er uh JEEN yus): a. Dissimilar; foreign

  Trigger: HETEROGENEOUS -HOMOGENOUS

  Trigger Sentence: HETEROGENEOUS and HOMOGENOUS are antonyms.

  Sample Sentence: 22 pairs of human chromosomes are homogenous whereas the XY chromosome pair is *heterogeneous*.

  Related Words: HOMOGENOUS –a. similar

HEYDAY (HAY day): n. Prime, time of greatest success

  Trigger: HEY +DAY-"HAPPY DAY"

  Trigger Sentence: HEY DAYS are HAPPY DAYS and TOP DAYS.

  Sample Sentence: In his *heydays*, Uncle John was a great athlete.

HIATUS (hye AY tus): n. A pause or gap

  Trigger: HIATUS-HALTS

  Trigger Sentence: 1. HIATUS and HALTS carry the same meaning. 2. At bus shelter, the bus HALTS. This HALTING progress increases the HIATUS.

  Sample Sentence: My workaholic boss considers' holidays as a *hiatus* that hinder work!

HIDEBOUND (HIED bownd): a. Stubborn; narrow-minded

  Trigger: HIDE-BOUND (*BOUNDARY)

  Trigger Sentence: HIDEBOUND conservatives HIDE behind the BOUNDARIES of their orthodox beliefs; they are never out of BOUNDARIES.

  Sample Sentence: My *hidebound* uncle criticized my dad for marrying an older woman.

HIERARCHY (HYE eh rahr kee): n. Any system of persons ranked one above another

  Trigger: HIGHER-VERY HIGHER-VERY VERY HIGHER-ARCHY

  Trigger Sentence: Body of people in an organization is arranged from HIGHER to LOW RANK.

  Sample Sentence: Edwin was always conscious of his higher *hierarchy*; so kept his juniors at bay.

HIEROGLYPHIC (HY ur u GLIF ik): a. Picture writing; hard to decipher

  Trigger: HIEROGLYPHIC -HIGHER GRAPHICS

  Trigger Sentence: GRAPHIC means PICTURE WRITING; HIEROGLYPHICS is a PICTORIAL WRITING (like Mona-Lisa) and they are usually very DIFFICULT TO DECODE.

  Sample Sentence: Egyptian *hieroglyphics* have been deciphered by Egyptologists.

HINDRANCE (HIN drens): n. Obstruction; block
    Trigger: 1. HINDRANCE- NO ENTRANCE. 2. HINDER-HAMPER-HALTER
    Trigger Sentence: 1. HINDRANCE-NO ENTRANCE. 2. HINDER-HAMPER-HALTER are synonyms.
    Sample Sentence: There is no *hindrance* at the entrance of the temple.
    Related Words: HINDER - v. prevent

HIRSUTE (HUR soot): a. Hairy
    Trigger: 1.HIRS +sute. 2. HIRSUTE-HAIRS +SUIT
    Trigger Sentence: HIRS in the word HIRSUTE looks like HAIRS. His HAIRY SUIT is like a HIRSUTE animal.
    Sample Sentence: Jerry's English sheep dog is a *hirsute*; he is like a large sphere of fur.

HISTRIONIC (his tree AHN ik): a. Theatrical; overly emotional for effect
    Trigger: 1. HYSTERIA. 2. HISTRIONIC- HISTORIC
    Trigger Sentence: 1. People who exhibit HYSTERIA show EXCESSIVE EMOTIONS and their actions are usually HISTRIONIC. 2. Most of the dramas are based on HISTORIC events; HISTORY teachers tell and explain them in a HISTRIONIC manner.
    Sample Sentence: Women go through *histrionic* episodes due to hysteria.

HOARY (HOHR ee): a. White with age; old
    Trigger: HOARY-HAIRY-(WHITE HAIRY)
    Trigger Sentence: WHITE HAIRY or gray HAIRY people usually look HOARY (and old).
    Sample Sentence: The devotees paid homage to the *hoary* head of the Tibetan monastery.

HOAX (HOHKS): n. Deceptive trick; a practical joke
    Trigger: HOAX-JOKES (*PRACTICAL JOKES)
    Trigger Sentence: The PRACTICAL JOKES applied on her turn out be cruel HOAXES.
    Sample Sentence: We knew him for years before we learned that his identity was a *hoax*.

HOMAGE (AHM ij): n. Honor, respect
    Trigger: 1.HOMAGE-HOME AGED. 2. HOME PAGE
    Trigger Sentence: 1. When they went to OLD age HOME, they paid HOMAGE to the AGED members. 2. I pay HOMAGE to my HOME PAGE of my web-site.
    Sample Sentence: We paid *homage* to Dr.A.C.Rao for his achievements in Mechanical research.

HOMEOSTASIS (hoh me uh STEY sis): n. Maintenance of equilibrium or a stable bodily state
    Trigger: HOMEOSTASIS –"HOME-STAY-SITS"
    Trigger Sentence: The STAY at HOME for a month brought HOMEOSTASIS in my body.
    Sample Sentence: Upholding *homeostasis* is essential in our homes during the riots in the city.

HOMILY (HOM uh lee): n. A lecture on moral or religious topic
    Trigger: HOMILY-HOMELY LECTURE
    Trigger Sentence: At HOME my father gave us a long HOMILY about benefits of hard work.
    Sample Sentence: The priest gave us a long *homily* about forgiveness.
    Related Words: SERMON - a moralistic lecture

HOMOGENOUS (hoh MOJ uh nus): n. Similar; of the same kind
    Trigger: HOMO+GENES-SAME GENES
    Trigger Sentence: Because we share SAME GENES we are HOMOGENEOUS.

Sample Sentence: Humans are *homogenous* across the globe but differ geographically.

HONE (HON): v. Sharpen; whet

    Trigger: 1.HONE-CONE. 2. HONE-STONE

    Trigger Sentence: 1. When you HONE you get a CONE shaped edge which is sharp. 2. WHET STONE or STONE TOOLS are used to SHARPEN knifes.

    Sample Sentence: Sam *honed* his tennis game by playing four times a week.

HOSPITABLE (HOS pi tuhbul): a. Favorable to life and growth; sociable; receptive

    Trigger: 1.HOSPITABLE-HOSPITAL. 2. HOSPITABLE-HOST (** synonym variant)

    Trigger Sentence: For the sick, the HOSPITAL provides HOSPITABLE conditions.

    Sample Sentence: People in the village are extremely *hospitable.*

    Related Words: HOSPITALITY - n. kindness in welcoming guests

HOSTILITY (ho STIL i tee): n. Enmity, hatred

    Trigger: 1.HOST-HOSTILITY. 2. HOSPITALITY

    Trigger Sentence: 1. HOST exhibits HOSPITALITY- NOT HOSTILITY. 2. A HOST should not show HOSTILITY against his/her guests.

    Sample Sentence: The townspeople showed open *hostility* to outsiders.

    Related Words: HOSTILE - a. unfriendly

HUBRIS (HYOO bris): n. Excessive pride; arrogance

    Trigger: HUBRIS —"HUBBY+RICH"

    Trigger Sentence: 1. My RICH HUBBY is ARROGANT. 2. With RICH HUBBY she shows HUBRIS.

    Sample Sentence: Avoid being *hubristic* to get your paper work through bureaucratic bundles!

    Related Words: HUBRISTIC - a. excessive pride; Arrogant

HUMANE (hyoo MEYN): a. Compassionate, kind

    Trigger: HUMAN-HUMANITY

    Trigger Sentence: The conditions of the HUMAN beings are more HUMANE now.

    Sample Sentence: One should always treat other human beings or animals with *humanity* (n).

    Related Words: DEHUMANIZE –v. deprive of human character; make mechanical

HUMDRUM (HUHM drum): a. Dull or monotonous

    Trigger: HUMDRUM -DIM DRUM - (DRUM SOUND)

    Trigger Sentence: DIM DRUM gives DULL SOUND; DIM SOUND lacks VARIETY.

    Sample Sentence: Meena dreamt of galloping away on a horse back from the *humdrums* of city.

HUMILITY (hyoo MIL uh tee): n. Humbleness; lack of pride

    Trigger: HUMILITY-HUMBLE

    Trigger Sentence: 1. HUMILITY -HUMBLENESS are synonyms. 2. HUMILITY is in HUMBLENESS.

    Sample Sentence: With all my *humility*, I accept your gift and cherish it all my life.

    Related Words: HUMBLE - v. humiliate, shame

HUNCH (HUHNCH): n. A strong intuitive feeling

    Trigger: HUNCH- HUNK

Trigger Sentence: I had a sudden HUNCH that I was as mighty as a HUNK.

Sample Sentence: Yesterday Priya had a *hunch* that something was going to go wrong.

HYPERBOLE (hye PUR buh lee): n. Exaggeration or overstatement

Trigger: HYPERBOLE —HYPE

Trigger Sentence: While creating HYPE, the people resort to HYPERBOLEs.

Sample Sentence: The prices are a hype and *hyperbole* created by real estate mafia.

HYPOTHESIS (hi POTH uh sis): n. An assumption requiring a proof

Trigger: HYPOTHETICAL-THEORETICAL

Trigger Sentence: A THEORETICAL THESIS is a HYPOTHESIS; it requires practical proof.

Sample Sentence: The scientists conducted many experiments hoping to prove their *hypothesis*.

Related Words: HYPOTHETICAL - a. assumed; theoretical

ICONOCLAST (eye CON oh klast): n. One who destroys religious images or beliefs

Trigger: 1.ICON + BLAST. 2. ICON+CLASH

Trigger Sentence: 1. An ICONOCLAST BLASTS religious ICONS. 2. ICONOCLAST CLASH with the religious or orthodox ICONS.

Sample Sentence: 70's saw a generation of *iconoclastic* groups going against their own religion.

Related Words: ICONOCLASTIC - a. nonconformist; opposed to orthodox.

IDEOLOGIC (id ee LOJ ik): a. Concerned with ideas; theoretical

Trigger: IDEOLOGIC - IDEAS+ LOGIC

Trigger Sentence: This research is an IDEOLOGICAL application of theoretical IDEAS of Darwin.

Sample Sentence: We separated only because of *ideological* differences.

Related Words: IDEOLOGY - n. system of ideas of a group

IDIOCY (ID ee uh see): n. Extremely stupid behavior

Trigger: IDIOCY-IDIOT (*IDIOTIC BEHAVIOR)

Trigger Sentence: It is ironical that some IDIOTS complain about the IDIOCIES of other people.

Sample Sentence: She sensed the *idiocy* in their demands and dismissed them immediately.

IDIOSYNCRASY (ih dee oh SINK ruh see): n. Peculiarity, individual characteristic

    Trigger: IDIOSYNCRASY —"IDEAS+CRAZY"

    Trigger Sentence: He has IDIOSYNCRASY; His IDEAS are CRAZY and UNIQUE.

    Sample Sentence: People with *idiosyncrasy* tend to entertain crazy ideas.

IDOLATRY (eye DOLL ah tree): n. Hero Worship; admiration

    Trigger: IDOLATRY- IDOL

    Trigger Sentence: IDOLATRY means treating someone like an IDOL or a GOD.

    Sample Sentence: Your *idolatry* towards me is quite flattering but I am just another human.

IDYLLIC (eye DIL ik): a. Simple, Peaceful

    Trigger: IDYLLIC -IDEAL LIKE

    Trigger Sentence: IDEAL LIKE rural areas are IDYLLIC; simple and peaceful.

    Sample Sentence: Uncle Frank likes to paint *idyllic* and scenic seascapes.

IGNOBLE (ig NOH bul): a. Unworthy, not noble, low character

    Trigger: IGNOBLE –NOT + NOBLE

    Trigger Sentence: A person of IGNOBLE birth can never become NOBLE.

    Sample Sentence: "He is an *ignoble* person not worthy of this noble job"!

    Related Words: IGNOMINY –n. disgrace; humiliation

TIMOROUS tom went to photo shoot the tribes !

TIMOROUS : nervous, timid, frightened, scared

Memory Test-53 : Match each word and its memory trick to the corresponding definition.

S.N	WORD	MEMORY TRIGGER	S.N	DEFINITIONS	KEY
1	GRANDILOQUENT	Grand+ELOQUENT	A	absurdly odd, fantastic, ugly	
2	GRANDIOSE	Grand+pose	B	Calm, happy	
3	GRANDSTAND	Stand great	C	Credulous; easy to deceive	
4	GRATIFY	Satisfaction	D	Cunning; trickery	
5	GRATIS	GRANT is	E	Exaggerated; Magnificent	
6	GRATUITOUS	Gratuity	F	Fond of company	
7	GRAVITY	Grave (yard)	G	Free of charge	
8	GREGARIOUS	Congregation	H	Ghastly	
9	GRIEVOUS	GRIEF to US	I	Given freely; unjustified	
10	GRISLY	Grisly-GHOSTLY	J	Grief; very serious	
11	GROTESQUE	Grow+tusk	K	Laugh loudly	
12	GROVEL	Bow well	L	Looking exhausted; worn out	
13	GUFFAW	Hee-haw-haw	M	Outward appearance; mask	
14	GUILE	GUY + ill minded	N	Perform showily in order to impress	
15	GUISE	Disguise	O	Plead; crawl abjectly on ground	
16	GULLIBLE	Can be easily GULLED	P	Pompous, excessively eloquent	
17	HABITAT	Habit at - INHABIT	Q	Routine, overused, commonplace	
18	HACKNEYED	Lack new	R	Satisfy, please	
19	HAGGARD	haggard-beggar look	S	Seriousness or importance	
20	HALCYON	hall+DYAN	T	The natural home	

Memory Test-54 : Match each word and its memory trick to the corresponding definition.

S.N	WORD	MEMORY TRIGGER	S.N	DEFINITIONS	KEY
1	HALE	HALE-PALE (**antonyms)	A	A place of safety	
2	HALLMARK	Trade MARK	B	Aggressive or scolding speech	
3	HALLOWED	Holy--honored	C	Arrogantly superior	
4	HAMPER	halter (halt)	D	Chance; fate	
5	HAPHAZARD	Hap + hazard	E	Dangerous	
6	HAPLESS	Hapless -happy less	F	Destruction; disorder	
7	HAPPENSTANCE	Happen by chance	G	Encourage; comfort	
8	HARANGUE	Harass-tongue	H	Expedite, stepped up	
9	HARBINGER	Messenger-bringer-beginner	I	Extremely painful; distressing	
10	HARDHEADED	Practical headed	J	Fore runner; indication	
11	HARMONY	Harm no -harmony	K	Healthy, Robust	
12	HARROWING	Harrowing -harassing	L	Holy; sacred	
13	HASTEN	HASTEN –FAST run	M	Impede, delay	
14	HAUGHTY	Hottie gal nature !!	N	Listen; pay attention to	
15	HAVEN	HEAVEN is best place	O	Pleasure seeker	
16	HAVOC	VOLCANO created HAVOC	P	Practical; stubborn	
17	HAZARDOUS	HUNDRED DIES	Q	Random; Lacking order	
18	HEARKEN	Hear	R	Specific feature; emblem	
19	HEARTEN	Brave-heart	S	Unfortunate	
20	HEDONIST	He DON ist	T	Unity, symmetry	

Answers	EX.NO	1	2	3	4	5	6	7	8	9	10	11	12	13	14	15	16	17	18	19	20
	53	P	E	N	R	G	I	S	F	J	H	A	O	K	D	M	C	T	Q	L	B
	54	K	R	L	M	Q	S	D	B	J	P	T	I	H	C	A	F	E	N	G	O

Memory Test-55 : Match each word and its memory trick to the corresponding definition.

S.N	WORD	MEMORY TRIGGER	S.N	DEFINITIONS	KEY
1	HEED	Heedful-mindful	A	Authority over others	
2	HEGEMONY	He's MONEY	B	Deceptive trick; a practical joke	
3	HEINOUS	Hyena- villainous	C	Dissimilar; foreign	
4	HERALD	HEAR + ALL	D	Give notice of; announce	
5	HERESY	Heterodoxy	E	Group which governs as per rank	
6	HERETICAL	Theoretical-practical	F	Hairy	
7	HERMIT	Hermit -no permit	G	Hatefully bad; or shockingly evil	
8	HETERODOX	HETERO-ORTHO (antonyms)	H	Obstruction; block	
9	HETEROGENEOUS	NOT-homogenous	I	One who lives alone; recluse	
10	HEYDAY	Happy day	J	Opinion contrary to popular belief	
11	HIATUS	Hiatus-HALTS	K	Pause or gap	
12	HIDEBOUND	Never cross boundary	L	Pay attention to; take notice of	
13	HIERARCHY	higher- archy	M	Picture writing; hard to decipher	
14	HIEROGLYPHIC	Higher GRAPHICS	N	Respect, Honor	
15	HINDRANCE	No entrance	O	Stubborn; narrow-minded	
16	HIRSUTE	Hairs +suit	P	Theatrical; overly emotional foreffect	
17	HISTRIONIC	HYSTERIA acting	Q	Time of greatest success	
18	HOARY	HAIRY-white hairy	R	Unorthodox, radical	
19	HOAX	practical JOKES	S	Unorthodox; Unconventional	
20	HOMAGE	Home aged	T	White with age; old	

Memory Test-56 : Match each word and its memory trick to the corresponding definition.

S.N	WORD	MEMORY TRIGGER	S.N	DEFINITIONS	KEY
1	HOMEOSTASIS	Home-stay-sits	A	An assumption requiring a proof	
2	HOMILY	Homely lecture	B	Compassionate, kind	
3	HOMOGENOUS	Homo+genes-same genes	C	Concerned with ideas; theoretical	
4	HONE	Hone-cone. 2. Hone-stone	D	Dull or monotonous	
5	HOSPITABLE	Hospital- Hospitable-HOST	E	Enmity, hatred	
6	HOSTILITY	NO hospitality	F	Exaggeration or overstatement	
7	HUBRIS	HUBBY+RICH	G	Excessive pride; arrogance	
8	HUMANE	Human-HUMANITY	H	Extremely stupid behavior	
9	HUMDRUM	DIM drum	I	Hero Worship; admiration	
10	HUMILITY	Humble	J	Humbleness; lack of pride	
11	HUNCH	Hunk -guts	K	lecture on moral or religious topic	
12	HYPERBOLE	HYPE	L	Maintenance of a stable bodily state	
13	HYPOTHESIS	Hypothetical-theoretical	M	One who destroys religious images	
14	ICONOCLAST	Icon + blast	N	Peaceful, Simple	
15	IDEOLOGIC	Ideas+ logic	O	Peculiarity, individual characteristic	
16	IDIOCY	Idiot	P	Sharpen; whet	
17	IDIOSYNCRASY	Ideas+CRAZY	Q	Similar; of the same kind	
18	IDOLATRY	Treat like an IDOL	R	sociable; receptive	
19	IDYLLIC	IDEAL LIKE	S	strong intuitive feeling	
20	IGNOBLE	Not + NOBLE	T	Unworthy, low character	

Answers

EX.NO	1	2	3	4	5	6	7	8	9	10	11	12	13	14	15	16	17	18	19	20
55	L	A	G	D	J	R	I	S	C	Q	K	O	E	M	H	F	P	T	B	N
56	L	K	Q	P	R	E	G	B	D	J	S	F	A	M	C	H	O	I	N	T

WORD GROUPS DAY-14

★ **BEAUTIFUL LOOKING**

ADJECTIVES: aesthetic, graceful, elegant; comely, charming, winsome, personable

NOUNS: pulchritude

VERB: enhance, embellish, adorn

ANTONYMS: adj. ugly, homely, hideous, unprepossessing

★ **UGLY LOOKING**

ADJECTIVES: hideous, homely, unprepossessing

NOUNS: ugliness

VERB: mar, deface, disfigure

ANTONYMS: adj. beautiful, attractive

★ **DAPPER/TIDY APPEARANCE**

ADJECTIVES: dapper, spruce, prim, trim, debonair, elegant, chic, natty

NOUNS: dandy, fop

VERB: preen, primp

ANTONYMS: adj. dirty, disheveled, ruffled, rumpled.

★ **UNTIDY APPEARANCE**

ADJECTIVES: tousled, disheveled, unkempt, rumpled, bedraggled, ruffled; dowdy, slovenly, sloppy, slatternly

NOUNS: slovenliness, sloppiness

VERB: dishevel

ANTONYMS: adj. tidy

★ **COGNIZANT**

ADJECTIVES: aware, apprehensive, cognizant, conscious, sensible, sentient, witting

NOUNS: cognizance , perceptiveness

VERB: heed

ANTONYMS: adj. oblivious ,unwitting,, ignorant

★ **OBLIVIOUS/UNMINDFUL**

ADJECTIVES: heedless, inattentive, incognizant, preoccupied, undiscerning, unmindful, unobservant, unwitting; amnesia

NOUNS: oblivion

VERB: unrecognize

ANTONYMS: adj. concious

★ **VISIBLE - (Obvious to the eye)**

ADJECTIVES: perceptible, perceivable, noticeable, detectable, discernible; evident, apparent, manifest, transparent, clear, conspicuous, obvious, patent, prominent, salient, glaring; palpable, tangible

NOUNS: conspicuity

VERB: display

ANTONYMS: adj. concealed, obscure

★ **IMPERCEPTIBLE**

ADJECTIVES: unnoticeable, undetectable, indistinguishable, indiscernible, invisible, impalpable, unobtrusive; subtle, faint, fine; indistinct, obscure, vague

NOUNS: imperceptibility, subtlety

VERB: obscure

ANTONYMS: adj. noticeable

now that we have tied the holy knot...

we are together for life !

cats CONCATENATED !

Word List Day-15

IGNOMINY (IG nuh min ee): n. Shame; disgrace or dishonor

Trigger: 1. igNOMINY-NO MONEY-NO CREDIT. 2. IGNOBLE- NOT NOBLE

Trigger Sentence: 1. NO MONEY, you live in IGNOMINY.2. NO NOBLE family lives in IGNOMINY.

Sample Sentence: In the `Scarlet Letter', Hester Prynne's exploits are sinfully *ignominy*.

Related Words: IGNOBLE - a. not noble, low character.

ILLEGIBLE (ih LEJ uh bul): a. Impossible to read, unclear

Trigger: ILLEGIBLE-ILLITERATE

Trigger Sentence: An ILLITERATE writing is usually ILLEGIBLE; very difficult to read.

Sample Sentence: If the signatures are *illegible* the application will be rejected.

Related Words: LEGIBLE –a. readable

ILLIBERAL (ih LIB er ul): a. Narrow-minded; strictness

Trigger: ILLIBERAL-NOT LIBERAL

Trigger Sentence: The NOT so LIBERAL newspaper gave an ILLEBRAL view on nudity in movies.

Sample Sentence: We have become *illiberal* in our desire to curb what was once normal...

Related Words: 1.LIBERTY -n. freedom; license .2.LIBERAL –a. open-minded; generous

ILLICIT (ih LIS it): v. Illegal, unlawful

Trigger: 1. ILLICIT-ILL TO CITY. 2. ILLICIT-ILLEGAL

Trigger Sentence: 1. ILLS OF A CITY is ILLICIT drug trafficking. 2. All ILLICIT things are ILLEGAL.

Sample Sentence: The gang made most of its money from the sale of *illicit* drugs.

ILLUMINATE (ih LOO muh neyt): n. Clarify, light up

Trigger: ILLUMINATE-ILLUSTRATE

Trigger Sentence: 1. ILLUSTRATE is to MAKE CLEAR by examples. 2. The book is ILLUMINATED with lively ILLUSTRATIONS.

Sample Sentence: The art historian *illuminated* on the prehistoric cave paintings.

ILLUSORY (ih LOOS ree): n. Deceptive; not real

Trigger: ILLUSORY-IMAGINARY

Trigger Sentence: Mirages are ILLUSORY creating FALSE ILLUSION or FALSE IMAGINATION.

Sample Sentence: It is an *illusory* feeling that money brings happiness.

Related Words: ILLUSIVE -a. false; elusive

IMBECILITY (im buh SIL ih tee): n. Stupidity, silliness; mentally retarded

Trigger: IMBECILI+ITY- I'M BE SILLY+ITY

Trigger Sentence: "CILI" sounds like SILLY. IMBECILITY means INABILITY

Sample Sentence: Joey being *imbecility* naïve, he was often ill-treated by other boys.

IMBROGLIO (im BROHL yoh): n. An extremely confused or complicated situation

Trigger: IMBROglio-IN+ BRA +UGLY

Trigger Sentence: Imagine an UGLY ant IN BRA; it is creating IMBROGLIO (complicate situation).

Sample Sentence: USA is caught in the ugly *imbroglio* with Iraq.

Related Words: EMBROIL -v. involve in conflict, entangle

IMBUE (im BYOO): v. Fill with a feeling (or color); permeate

Trigger: IMBUE-I'M BLUE

Trigger Sentence: Sky and ocean are IMBUED or permeated with BLUE color.

Sample Sentence: Her poetry was *imbued* with love for nature.

IMMACULATE (ih MAK yuh lit): a. Perfectly clean

Trigger: IMMACULATE - MAC (MARK)- NO MARK

Trigger Sentence: The IMMACULATE dress is spotlessly free from any DIRT MARK.

Sample Sentence: The West Point cadets were *immaculate* as they lined up for inspection.

IMMANENT (IM uh nunt): a. Inherent; within the mind

Trigger: 1.IM (IN) + MAN. 2. IMMANENT-INHERENT. 3. PERMANENT

Trigger Sentence: 1. IN MAN there are IMMANENT (natural) qualities. 2. Individual traits are INHERENT by birth. They are IMMANENT than learnt. 3. IMMANENT qualities are PERMANENT.

Sample Sentence: She's got an *immanent* quality of compassion and love for animals.

IMMENSE (ih MENS): a. Enormous, massive

Trigger: 1.IMMENSE-IMMEASURABLE (** synonyms).2. IMMENSE-INTENSE

Trigger Sentence: 1. There is NO MENSURATION to measure the IMMENSE size of the boundless universe. 2. My INTENSE desire for you is IMMENSE.

Sample Sentence: Picasso was an artist of *immense* repute and talent.

Related Words: INTENSE –a. extreme; acute

IMMINENT (IM uh nunt): a. About to happen, impending

Trigger: 1. imMINENT -IMMEDIATE MOMENT. 2. IMMINENT-IMMEDIATE MINUTE

Trigger Sentence: 1. Danger is IMMINENT; it can happen at an IMMEDIATE MOMENT. 2. It is IMMINENT that the organization is going to fire you at any IMMEDIATE MINUTE.

Sample Sentence: When dark clouds encompass the sky, heavy shower is *imminent*.

IMMUNITY (im MYOO ni tee): n. Resistant to; exemption; freedom

Trigger: IMMUNITY-NO IMPURITY

Trigger Sentence: Vaccine gives IMMUNIZATION; so there are NO IMPURITIES in the body.

Sample Sentence: We were asked to eat healthy so as to strengthen our *immunity* system.

IMMURE (ih MYOOR): v. Confine, imprison

Trigger: 1. IMPURE-IMPURE. 2. IMPURE-"IN MURAL (WALL)"

Trigger Sentence: 1. IMPURE guy got IMMURED. 2. He was kept IN MURALS (MURALS-WALLS)

Sample Sentence: The murderer was *immured* for the rest of his life.

IMMUTABLE (i MYOO tuh bul): a. Unchangeable

Trigger: IMMUTABLE-IMMOVABLE

Trigger Sentence: 1. IMMUTABLE things are IMMOVABLE and IMMOBILE. 2. MUTABLE-

MOVABLE-CHANGEABLE.

Sample Sentence: The Rocky Mountains appear *immutable*; however, they shift in time.

Related Words: MUTABLE -a. liable to change.

IMPAIR (im PAIR): v. Injure, Hurt

Trigger: 1. IMPAIR-REPAIR. 2. IMPAIR-IMPALE

Trigger Sentence: 1. Doctors REPAIR an IMPAIRED person. 2. IMPAIR and IMPALE are synonyms.

Sample Sentence: The polo player's career got *impaired* due to a bad fall from his horse back.

Related Words: IMPAIRMENT -n. defect, flaw

IMPALE (im PALE): v. Pierce

Trigger: IMPALE -IN POLE

Trigger Sentence: 1. IMPALE enemy with sharp-edged POLE.2. IMPAIR an IMPALE are synonyms.

Sample Sentence: Stop *impaling* each other with those sarcastic and wordy stabs.

IMPASSE (IM pas): n. Deadlock, place from which there is no escape.

Trigger: 1. IMPASSE- NO PASS. 2. IMPASSE- IMPOSSIBLE.

Trigger Sentence: Without a PASSPORT you can NEVER PASS from this IMPASSE.

Sample Sentence: We have reached an *impasse* on the negotiations; neither side will budge.

IMPASSIONED (im PASH ind): a. Full of passion; emotional

Trigger: IMPASSIONED- I'm IN PASSION

Trigger Sentence: I'M IN PASSION with wildlife. My IMPASSIONED promise is unquestionable.

Sample Sentence: The lawyer made an *impassioned* argument in her defense.

IMPASSIVE (im PASS iv): a. Without feeling; not sensitive to emotion or pain

Trigger: 1. PASSIVE-NO ACTIVE. 2. IMPASSIVE-NO PASSION

Trigger Sentence: 1. PASSIVE - NO ACTIVE feelings. 2. IMPASSIVE person shows NO PASSION.

Sample Sentence: Nick kept his face *impassive* during the questioning, but his mind was racing.

Related Words: PASSIVE -n. disinterested; submissive; inert

IMPEACH (im PEECH): v. Accuse, charge with crime.

Trigger: IMPEACH-TEACH a lesson

Trigger Sentence: With an IMPEACHMENT the Congress can TEACH the US President a lesson.

Sample Sentence: The press members rescued a journalist who was wrongly *impeached*.

IMPECCABLE (im PEK uh bul): a. Faultless

Trigger: IMPECCA-"I'M PUKKA"

Trigger Sentence: I'M PUKKA means I'M PERFECT.

Sample Sentence: Jane chose *impeccable* marble stone for the interiors of her house.

IMPECUNIOUS (im pi KYOO nee us): a. Penniless; poor

Trigger: 1. IMPECUNIOUS-I'M PENURIOUS. 2. PENURIOUS-PENNY LESS (refer)

Trigger Sentence: 1. I'M PENURIOUS now. I was not IMPECUNIOUS by birth.
2. IMPECUNIOUS and PENURIOUS are synonyms.

Sample Sentence: I have seen him as an *impecunious* student living in bad conditions years ago.

Related Words: PECUNIARY –a. relating to money; financial

IMPEDE (im PEED): v. Obstruct; block

Trigger: 1. IMPEDANCE. 2. IMPEDE- NO SPEED

Trigger Sentence: 1. IMPEDANCE IMPEDES flow of current. 2. IMPEDE means to block SPEED.

Sample Sentence: A ghastly accident on the highway *impeded* our speedy of journey.

Related Words: IMPEDIMENT -n. obstacle, block

IMPEL (im PEL): v. Urge into action, drive or force onward

Trigger: 1. IMPEL-IMPULSE. 2. IMPEL-PROPEL

Trigger Sentence: 1. The profound religious IMPULSES IMPELLED her to a lifelong commitment to the MONASTERY. 2. IMPEL and PROPEL are synonyms.

Sample Sentence: She felt *impelled* to give a speech after the performance.

IMPENDING (im PEND ing): a. Nearing; approaching

Trigger: 1.IN +PENDING. 2. IMPENDING- SUSPENDING

Trigger Sentence: SUSPENDING work is STOPPED while IMPENDING things will happen IMMEDIATELY.

Sample Sentence: The *impending* danger cannot be suspended indefinitely.

IMPENETRABLE (im PEN uh truh bul): a. Impossible to enter; impossible to comprehend

Trigger: IMPENETRABLE -NO PENETRATION

Trigger Sentence: If something is IMPERMEABLE (no permit) it is going to be IMPENETRABLE.

Sample Sentence: The castle was built like a maze making it *impenetrable* to the enemy.

IMPENITENT (im PEN ih tent): a. Not feeling shame or regret.

Trigger: NOT+ PENITENT (REPENTANT)

Trigger Sentence: IMPENITENT criminals are NOT REPENTANT.

Sample Sentence: He stood unashamed as though *impenitent* of his sins.

IMPERATIVE (im PER uh tiv): a. Command, order, of vital importance

Trigger: IMPERIAL-IMPERIOUS-IMPERATIVE-AUTHORITATIVE

Trigger Sentence: IMPERIOUS EMPIRES give IMPERATIVE or AUTHORITATIVE orders.

Sample Sentence: It should be an *imperative* situation that sales of cigarettes be prevented.

IMPERCEPTIBLE (im pur SEP tah bul): a. Unnoticeable; undetectable

Trigger: 1. IM (NO) +PERCEPT (PERCEIVE). 2. NO CONCEPTS

Trigger Sentence: Quantum Physics is difficult to PERCEIVE; I've no CONCEPTS, so it is IMPERCEPTIBLE.

Sample Sentence: If there is no perception in your foot, it means it is numb. Things are *imperceptible* to numb organs.

IMPERIOUS (im PEER ee us): a. Arrogantly domineering

    Trigger: IMPERIOUS-EMPIRES

    Trigger Sentence: The emperor of an EMPIRE tends to be IMPERIOUS.

    Sample Sentence: His *imperiousness* indicates that he must have been a strict army commander!

IMPERTINENT (im PUR tn unt): a. Arrogant, insolent

    Trigger: IMPERTINENT-PERT (IMPERT-EXPERT)

    Trigger Sentence: An EXPERT tends to be IMPERTINENT (or PERT) about his dexterity in his/her field of specialization.

    Sample Sentence: I hold your remarks on my personal life as *impertinent* and I do resent them.

IMPERTURBABLE (im pur TURB uh bul): a. Calm, composed

    Trigger: 1.IM (NO) + DISTURB. 2. PERTURB-DISTURB

    Trigger Sentence: 1. IMPERTURBABLE people are NOT so easily DISTURBED; they are CALM. 2. PERTURB is to DISTURB.

    Sample Sentence: Vivekananda was not disturbed as he learnt how to remain *imperturbable*.

IMPERVIOUS (im PUR vee us): a. Impenetrable; incapable of being damaged

    Trigger: IM + PERVIOUS –NO PERMIT

    Trigger Sentence: If it is IMPERVIOUS, then there is NO PERMIT and nobody can enter.

    Sample Sentence: The Himalayas were *impervious* to Chengiz Khan to penetrate into India.

IMPETUOUS (im PECH oo wus): a. Violent, rash, hasty

    Trigger: 1.IMPETUOUS- IMPATIENCE. 2. IMPETUOUS-IMPACTS US

    Trigger Sentence: 1. MY PET dog is IMPETUOUS and IMPATIENT. 2. IMPETUOUS people act in a rash manner as if there is an IMPACT.

    Sample Sentence: *Impetuous* behavior has a negative impact on others.

IMPETUS (IM pi tus): n. Urge, stimulus

    Trigger: 1. IMPETUS -IMPULSE (synonyms). 2. IMPETUS-IMPACT US

    Trigger Sentence: His teachings had given us an IMPETUS and had an important IMPACT on us.

    Sample Sentence: There is an emerging research *impetus* in the area of aeronautical spaceships.

IMPINGE (im PINJ): v. Infringe, hit, collide with

    Trigger: 1.IM+PINGE-I'M PINCHED. 2. I'M PINGED-I'M PUNCHED

    Trigger Sentence: When I'M PINCHED and PUNCHED by my seniors to do illegal things at the college, they IMPINGED on my rights as an individual.

    Sample Sentence: Neighbors are demolishing their building and the *impinging* sound is horrible!

IMPLACABLE (im PLAK uh bul): a. Impossible to appease

    Trigger: 1. PLACABLE- PEACEABLE. 2. IMPLACABLE-IMPOSSIBLE TO PLEASE

    Trigger Sentence: 1. PLACABLE people are PLEASE+ ABLE. 2. It is IMPOSSIBLE TO PLEASE the IMPLACABLE people.

    Sample Sentence: It was impossible to negotiate with an *implacable* union leader.

IMPLAUSIBLE (im PLAWZ uh bul): a. Hard to believe, unlikely

Trigger: IMPLAUSIBLE-IMPOSSIBLE

Trigger Sentence: We believed that reaching moon was IMPLAUSIBLE until it became POSSIBLE.

Sample Sentence: It is *implausible* that at 66 years of age he completed a triple marathon!

Related Words: 1.PLAUSIBLE -n. reasonable, believable.2.IMPROBABLE –a. unlikely

IMPLICATE (IM pli keyt): v. Incriminate, show to be connected

Trigger: 1. IMPLICATE -IMPLY + CASE. 2. IMPLICATE-INCULPATE-INCRIMINATE

Trigger Sentence: 1. The criminal CASES IMPLY that "He is IMPLICATED in the scheme to defraud the government". 2. Implicate, inculpate and INCRIMINATE someone in a CRIME.

Sample Sentence: His business partner was *implicated* in the fraud case.

IMPLICIT (im PLIS it): a. Understood but not stated; tacit

Trigger: IMPLICIT

Trigger Sentence: In an IMPLICIT situation, things are IMPLIED.

Sample Sentence: I *implicitly* trust her, so I leave the work and the rest to her!

IMPLODE (im PLOHD): v. Burst inward

Trigger: IMPLODE-EXPLODE

Trigger Sentence: A vacuum chamber IMPLODES where as dynamite EXPLODES.

Sample Sentence: She might *implode* emotionally and damage herself further.

IMPOLITIC (im PAWL i tick): a. Unwise

Trigger: POLITIC-DIPLOMATIC

Trigger Sentence: POLITIC and IMPOLITIC are antonyms; POLITICIANS are POLITIC and DIPLOMATIC in nature.

Sample Sentence: *Impolitic* individuals are not diplomatic.

Related Words: POLITIC - a. wise; balanced

IMPONDERABLE (im PON der uh bul): a. Weightless

Trigger: IM (NO) + POND (POUND) +ABLE

Trigger Sentence: 1. Something which CANNOT be measured in POUNDS is IMPONDERABLE. 2. WEIGHTLESS things are "NOT CLEAR TO EYE" and hence "NOT MEASURABLE".

Sample Sentence: The vastness of space is *imponderable*.

Related Words: PONDEROUS –a. weighty; awkward

IMPORTUNE (im pawr TOON): v. Beg persistently

Trigger: 1. IMPORTUNE -IN POOR TUNE. 2. IMPOR+TUNE-I'M POOR.

Trigger Sentence: IN a POOR TUNE, the beggars IMPORTUNED for money.

Sample Sentence: Foreigners are *importuned* by beggars in all the touristy places of our country.

IMPOSTOR (im POS ter): n. One that assumes false identity for the purpose of deception

Trigger: 1.IMPOSTOR–IM+POSE-FALSE POSE. 2. IMPOSTOR-IMPERSONATOR (synonyms)

Trigger Sentence: The IMPOSTOR had a FALSE POSE in the photograph of passport to deceive.

Sample Sentence: The *impostor* carried a false passport, but was caught by the security.

Related Words: IMPOSTURE -n. Fraud; assuming a false identity

IMPOVERISH (im PAH vrish): v. Make poor; exhaust the strength

    Trigger: I'M in POVERTY

    Trigger Sentence: IMPOVERISH is to make someone or something POOR in quality, in quantity.

    Sample Sentence: USA was affected with poverty in 1930's and its citizens were *impoverished*.

IMPRECATION (im prih KAY shun): n. A curse

    Trigger: IMPRECATION- NO PRAY

    Trigger Sentence: He NEVER PRAYED to God; so he suffered IMPRECATIONS from him.

    Sample Sentence: It's an *imprecation* to live in a country where people are not hospitable.

IMPREGNABLE (im PREG nuh bul): a. Invulnerable

    Trigger: 1.IM (NO) + PREGNANT. 2. IMPREGNABLE-INVULNERABLE

    Trigger Sentence: 1. I'M NOT PREGNANT, so I'm IMPREGNABLE. 2. PREGNANT women are PREGNABLE or VULNERABLE to diseases.

    Sample Sentence: Her high-end ventures are *impregnably* astonishing!

IMPRESSIONABLE (im PRESH in uh bul): a. Easily influenced

    Trigger: IMPRESSED

    Trigger Sentence: IMPRESSIONABLE people get EASILY IMPRESSED with a smooth talk; they are usually INNOCENT by nature.

    Sample Sentence: A young child's mind Is highly *impressionable*. Childhood experiences leave strong impressions on their character.

IMPROBITY (im PROH bi tee): n. Wickedness; dishonesty

    Trigger: 1.IMPROBITY- IMPROPER. 2. IMPROBITY-IMPURITY

    Trigger Sentence: IMPROBITY involves IMPROPER DEALINGS and moral IMPURITIES.

    Sample Sentence: No one voted for Bhaskar, because he is known for *improbity* and immorality.

    Related Words: PROBITY -n. honesty

IMPROMPTU (im PRAHMP too): a. Without previous preparation; spontaneous,

    Trigger: 1.IMPROMPTU —"I'M PROMPT".2.IMPROMPTU-IMPROVISATION

    Trigger Sentence: PROMPT action or PROMPT lecture is known as IMPROMPTU; I'M PROMPT.

    Sample Sentence: *Impromptu* performance is a spontaneous improvisation of some action.

IMPROPRIETY (im pruh PRYE uh tee): n. Improperness; indecency

    Trigger: IMPROPRIETY- IMPROPER

    Trigger Sentence: IMPROPER behavior is known as IMPROPRIETY.

    Sample Sentence: It is improper for a professional to stand as an example for *impropriety*.

    Related Words: PROPRIETY – n. decency; politeness

IMPROVISE (IM pruh vyze): v. To compose extemporaneously

    Trigger: 1.IMPROVISE-IMPROMPTU. 2. I'M-PROVIDED

    Trigger Sentence: 1. IMPROMPTU and IMPROVISED are synonyms. 2. A.R. Rahman PROVIDED tunes SPONTANEOUSLY.

Sample Sentence: The guru encourages young actors to *improvise* so as to exercise creativity.

Related Words: IMPROMPTU –a. spontaneous; improvised

IMPUDENCE (IM pew duns): n. Arrogant, insolence

Trigger: 1. IMPUDENCE- (OVER) CONFIDENCE. 2. IMPUDE-I'M RUDE

Trigger Sentence: 1. OVER CONFIDENCE people exhibit IMPUDENCE. 2. IMPUDE sounds like I'M RUDE; As long as I remain RUDE, I'll be IMPUDENT.

Sample Sentence: My mother would not tolerate *impudence* behavior from anyone.

IMPUGN (im PYOON): v. Challenge; criticize

Trigger: 1.IMPUGN –IMP& UGLY. 2. I'M PUG

Trigger Sentence: 1. The boy IMPUGNED his rival kid by calling him IMP & UGLY. 2. I have a PUG dog that IMPUGNS any stranger entering our residence.

Sample Sentence: During elections the opposing candidates try to *impugn* others' integrity.

IMPUNITY (im PYOO nuh tee): n. Freedom from punishment

Trigger: 1. IMPUNITY - NO + PUNISH. 2. IMPUNITY -IMMUNITY

Trigger Sentence: 1. When there is NO PUNITIVE action it is known as IMPUNITY. 2. IMMUNITY is freedom from the attack of a disease.

Sample Sentence: The President of India has legal immunity. The constitution confers on him/her the right of *impunity*.

IMPUTE (im PYOOT): v. Attribute; charge

Trigger: 1.IMPUTE-IN PUT. 2. IMPUTE-IMPURE.

Trigger Sentence: 1. IMPUTE is to "PUT IN" the blame on someone. 2. People IMPUTE his bad habits to his IMPURE thoughts.

Sample Sentence: The manager *imputed* his own mismanagement as his subordinates' job.

INADVERTENT (in ad VUR tunt): v. Unintentional, inattentive

Trigger: INADVERTENTLY- INATTENTIVELY

Trigger Sentence: 1. As he was INATTENTIVE, he was INADVERTENTLY drawn into controversy. 2. ADVERTENTLY-ATTENTIVELY. 3. ADVERTISEMENTS are given to ATTRACT ATTENTION.

Sample Sentence: Oops! My important files *inadvertently* got deleted!

INALIENABLE (in EYL yuh nuh bul): a. Non-transferable; not to be taken away

Trigger: INALIENABLE- NO ALIEN-NOT ALIENABLE

Trigger Sentence: Life on the earth is our INALIENABLE right. NEVER allow ALIENS to share.

Sample Sentence: The basic rights of the citizen are *inalienable*.

Related Words: ALIENATE –v. separate; transfer; confiscate

INANE (i NAYN): a. Silly, senseless

Trigger: INANE-INSANE-NO SENSE

Trigger Sentence: Usually INSANE people become more INANE in human society.

Sample Sentence: How did you imagine making a film out of this *inane* script?!

Related Words: 1. INANITY -n. foolishness. 2. INSANE –a. senseless

INARTICULATE (in ar TIK yoo lit): v. Speechless; indistinct

Trigger: NO ARTICLE

Trigger Sentence: 1. He has NO ART of TALKING clearly. 2. The ARTICLE is NOT INARTICULATE.

Sample Sentence: If you remain *inarticulate*, you can never make it as a writer!

Related Words: ARTICULATE -a. fluent and clear in speech.

INCENDIARY (in SEN dee er ee): n. Arsonist; adj. Inflammatory

Trigger: INCENDIARY-INCENSE (STICK)

Trigger Sentence: With an INCENSE stick a fire is set by an INCENDIARY.

Sample Sentence: Since gas cans are *incendiary* they come with sealed lids.

INCENSE (in SENS): v. Make angry; enrage

Trigger: 1.INCENSE. 2. NONSENSE

Trigger Sentence: 1. INCENSE sticks BURNS; in the same way my boss BURNS with ANGER. 2. You INCENSED me by doing NONSENSE.

Sample Sentence: When we are overcome by *incense*, we tend to speak nonsense.

INCENTIVE (in SEN tiv): n. Stimulus; encouragement

Trigger: INCENTIVE-CENT

Trigger Sentence: The teacher offered CENTS as INCENTIVE to the students to do well in course.

Sample Sentence: Word Wizard book is at a discounted price as an *incentive* for the students.

INCEPTION (in SEP shun): n. Beginning, start

Trigger: INCEPTION-CONCEPTION-RECEPIION

Trigger Sentence: 1. In the INCEPTION we were given cordial RECEPTION.2. In the INCEPTION, CONCEPTION (pregnancy) starts with a single cell known as zygote.

Sample Sentence: She was involved with `project to protect the tiger' from its *inception*.

INCESSANT (in SES unt): a. Continuous, unceasing

Trigger: 1.INCESSANT- NO+ CEASE. 2. IN + CESSANT-IN +CONSTANT

Trigger Sentence: 1. There is NO CEASE to human greed. It is INCESSANT. 2. INCESSANT and CONSTANT are synonyms.

Sample Sentence: There was an *incessant* conflict between Communism and Capitalism. They were in constant friction during 1917 and 1991.

Related Words: 1.CEASE –v. stop. 2. CESSATION –n. stopping; ceasing

INCHOATE (in KOH it): a. Recently begun; elementary

Trigger: INCHOATIVE-IN CREATIVE

Trigger Sentence: INCHOATIVE means IN-CREATIVE stage; not developed into complete product.

Sample Sentence: Nano-technology is still *inchoate*, but this creative field has great potentiality.

INCIPIENT (in SIP ee unt): a. Initial, beginning

Trigger: 1. INCEPTIVE-CONTRACEPTIVE. 2. INCIPIENT-INCEPTION (refer)-INCEPTIVE

Trigger Sentence: CONTRACEPTIVE is useful to prevent INCEPTIVE pregnancy.

Sample Sentence: This musical group is inexperienced and still in its *incipient* point.

Related Words: INCEPTIVE -a. beginning

INCISIVE (in SYE siv): a. Sharp, cutting

Trigger: INCISOR-"IN SCISSOR"

Trigger Sentence: She is known for her INCISIVE comments just as tigers for their INCISOR tooth.

Sample Sentence: David is notorious for his *incisive* and utterly insensitive remarks.

INCITE (in SIGHT): v. Arouse to action; stir up; provoke

Trigger: INCITE –EXCITE (*synonyms)

Trigger Sentence: The crowd was EXCITED by the speaker's INCITING inflammatory speech.

Sample Sentence: "He *incited* feelings of love and compassion in me".

INCLEMENT (in KLEM unt): a. Stormy, cruel

Trigger: NO + CLEMENCY-NO MERCY

Trigger Sentence: 1. The INCLEMENT Dead Sea shows NO CLEMENCY. It kills you even if you make a small mistake. 2. Clement, inclement, clemency and inclemency belong to same family.

Sample Sentence: The game was postponed due to *inclement* weather.

Related Words: CLEMENCY -n. grace, mercy

INCOGNITO (in kog NEE toh): a. Anonymous, unknown

Trigger: INCOGNITO –NO RECOGNITION

Trigger Sentence: The king lived "INCOGNITO" as a butler; NO ONE would RECOGNIZE him.

Sample Sentence: The King lived *incognito* as a butler in the palace of the Nizam Empire.

INCOHERENT (in ko HER ent): a. Inconsistent, illogical; unintelligible

Trigger: 1. INCOHERENT-I CAN NOT HEAR IT. 2. INCOHERENT -INCONSISTENT

Trigger Sentence: 1. He is INCOHERENT in his speech. I CANNOT HEAR IT clearly. 2. His speech is INCOHERENT and INCONSISTENT.

Sample Sentence: Herb's description of the bank robbery was rather hysterical and *incoherent*.

Related Words: COHERENT -a. able to speak clearly and logically.

INCOMPATIBLE (in kuhm PAT uh bul): a. Inharmonious; unsuitable

Trigger: INCOMPATIBLE-NO COMPANY

Trigger Sentence: My wife is NOT a perfect COMPANY, in fact many couples are INCOMPATIBLE.

Sample Sentence: My pen drive is *incompatible* on your computer.

INCONGRUITY (in kuhn GROO i tee): n. The quality of disagreeing; inappropriate

Trigger: NOT CONGRUENT

Trigger Sentence: INCONGRUENT triangles are NOT IDENTICAL, so they DISAGREE in form.

Sample Sentence: US debt crisis is a result of non-congruent stance of Republican and Democratic parties. They are stuck with *incongruity*.

Related Words: INCONGRUOUS -a. inharmonious; unsuitable.

INCONSEQUENTIAL (in kon si KWEN shul): a. Unimportant; insignificant

Trigger: INCONSEQUENTIAL-NO SEQUENCE

Trigger Sentence: In a card game WITHOUT SEQUENCE -they seem INCONSEQUENTIAL.

Sample Sentence: Our government considers "planting trees" as an *inconsequential* matter.

Related Words: CONSEQUENTIAL -a. important; resultant

INCONSISTENCY (in kuhn SIS tuhn see): n. Incompatibility; lack of harmony

Trigger: NO CONSISTENCY

Trigger Sentence: Judge noticed that there is no CONSISTENCY in the lawyer's argument.

Sample Sentence: There is no seriousness in his commitments; his promises are *inconsistent.*

Related Words: CONSISTENT -a. same; coherent

INCONTROVERTIBLE (in kon trah VUR tih bul): a. Unquestionable; indisputable

Trigger: NO CONTROVERSY

Trigger Sentence: There was NO CONTROVERSY on Judge's verdict; since he had received an INCONTROVERTIBLE proof of the defendant's innocence.

Sample Sentence: The judge received an *incontrovertible* proof from the witness.

Memory Test-57 : Match each word and its memory trick to the corresponding definition.

S.N	WORD	MEMORY TRIGGER	S.N	DEFINITIONS	KEY
1	IGNOMINY	No money-NO CREDIT	A	About to happen, impending	
2	ILLEGIBLE	Illegible-ILLITERATE	B	Clarify, light up	
3	ILLIBERAL	Not liberal	C	Confine, imprison	
4	ILLICIT	Ill to city- ILLEGAL	D	Deadlock	
5	ILLUMINATE	Illuminate-ILLUSTRATE	E	Deceptive; not real	
6	ILLUSORY	Illusory-IMAGINARY	F	Enormous, massive	
7	IMBECILITY	I'm be SILLY	G	Extremely complicated situation	
8	IMBROGLIO	In+ bra +ugly	H	Fill with a feeling (or color); permeate	
9	IMBUE	BLUE color	I	Full of passion; emotional	
10	IMMACULATE	NO MARK	J	Illegal, unlawful	
11	IMMANENT	PERMANENT impression	K	Impossible to read, unclear	
12	IMMENSE	INTENSE size	L	Inherent; within the mind	
13	IMMINENT	Immediate MOMENT	M	Injure, Hurt	
14	IMMUNITY	No impurity	N	Narrow-minded; strictness	
15	IMMURE	IMPURE guy arrested	O	Perfectly clean	
16	IMMUTABLE	Immovable	P	Pierce	
17	IMPAIR	REPAIR an IMPAIRED	Q	Resistant to; exemption; freedom	
18	IMPALE	IN POLE	R	Shame; disgrace or dishonor	
19	IMPASSE	No pass- impossible	S	Silliness; mentally retarded	
20	IMPASSIONED	I'm in PASSION	T	Unchangeable	

Memory Test-58 : Match each word and its memory trick to the corresponding definition.

S.N	WORD	MEMORY TRIGGER	S.N	DEFINITIONS	KEY
1	IMPASSIVE	No passion	A	Arrogant, insolent	
2	IMPEACH	TEACH a lesson	B	Arrogantly domineering	
3	IMPECCABLE	I'm PUKKA-perfect	C	Calm, composed	
4	IMPECUNIOUS	I'm PENURIOUS-PENNY LESS	D	Charge with crime, accuse	
5	IMPEDE	NO SPEED	E	Command, order, of vital importance	
6	IMPEL	Impel-PROPEL	F	Faultless	
7	IMPENDING	In +PENDING	G	Impenetrable; impassable	
8	IMPENETRABLE	No penetration	H	Impossible to appease	
9	IMPENITENT	Not+ repentant	I	Impossible to enter	
10	IMPERATIVE	imperative-AUTHORITATIVE	J	Infringe, hit, collide with	
11	IMPERCEPTIBLE	(No) +percept (perceive).	K	Nearing; approaching	
12	IMPERIOUS	EMPIRES mentality	L	Not feeling shame or regret.	
13	IMPERTINENT	Pert –EXPERT mentality	M	Obstruct; block	
14	IMPERTURBABLE	(No) + DISTURB	N	Penniless; poor	
15	IMPERVIOUS	NO PERMIT	O	Stimulus, urge	
16	IMPETUOUS	IMPATIENCE	P	Unlikely, Hard to believe	
17	IMPETUS	IMPULSE	Q	Unnoticeable; undetectable	
18	IMPINGE	I'm PINCHED-punched	R	Urge into action, drive or force	
19	IMPLACABLE	Peaceable	S	Violent, rash, hasty	
20	IMPLAUSIBLE	Impossible-improbable	T	Without feeling; unemotional	

Answers

EX.NO	1	2	3	4	5	6	7	8	9	10	11	12	13	14	15	16	17	18	19	20
57	R	K	N	J	B	E	S	G	H	O	L	F	A	Q	C	T	M	P	D	I
58	T	D	F	N	M	R	K	I	L	E	Q	B	A	C	G	S	O	J	H	P

Memory Test-59 : Match each word and its memory trick to the corresponding definition.

S.N	WORD	MEMORY TRIGGER	S.N	DEFINITIONS	KEY
1	IMPLICATE	inculpate-incriminate	A	Arrogant, insolence	
2	IMPLICIT	Implied	B	Charge; Attribute	
3	IMPLODE	Implode-explode	C	Beg persistently	
4	IMPOLITIC	Not diplomatic	D	Burst inward	
5	IMPONDERABLE	no POUNDS	E	Challenge; criticize	
6	IMPORTUNE	In POOR TUNE	F	Compose extemporaneously	
7	IMPOSTOR	False pose	G	Curse	
8	IMPOVERISH	I'M in POVERTY	H	Easily influenced	
9	IMPRECATION	NO PRAY	I	Freedom from punishment	
10	IMPREGNABLE	INVULNERABLE	J	Improperness; indecency	
11	IMPRESSIONABLE	Easily IMPRESSED	K	Incriminate, show to be connected	
12	IMPROBITY	Moral IMPURITY	L	Invulnerable	
13	IMPROMPTU	I'm PROMPT	M	Make poor; exhaust the strength	
14	IMPROPRIETY	Improper	N	One that assumes false identity	
15	IMPROVISE	Impromptu- provided	O	Spontaneous	
16	IMPUDENCE	I'm RUDE	P	Understood but not stated	
17	IMPUGN	You are IMP& UGLY	Q	Unintentional, inattentive	
18	IMPUNITY	No + PUNISH	R	Unwise	
19	IMPUTE	IN PUT –IMPURE	S	Weightless	
20	INADVERTENT	INATTENTIVELY	T	Wickedness; dishonesty	

Memory Test-60 : Match each word and its memory trick to the corresponding definition.

S.N	WORD	MEMORY TRIGGER	S.N	DEFINITIONS	KEY
1	INALIENABLE	No alien-not alienable	A	Anonymous, unknown	
2	INANE	no sense	B	Arouse to action; provoke	
3	INARTICULATE	NO ART of TALKING	C	Arsonist; Inflammatory	
4	INCENDIARY	Incense (stick)	D	Beginning, start	
5	INCENSE	Don't do NONSENSE	E	Continuous, unceasing	
6	INCENTIVE	Give CENTS	F	Encouragement; Stimulus	
7	INCEPTION	RECEPTION is at !!	G	Incompatibility; lack of harmony	
8	INCESSANT	CONSTANT	H	Inconsistent, unintelligible	
9	INCHOATE	Inchoative-in creative	I	Inharmonious; unsuitable	
10	INCIPIENT	Incipient-inception	J	Initial, beginning	
11	INCISIVE	Incisor-"in scissor	K	Make angry; enrage	
12	INCITE	Incite –excite	L	Non-transferable	
13	INCLEMENT	MENCY-no MERCY	M	Recently begun; elementary	
14	INCOGNITO	No recognition	N	Sharp, cutting	
15	INCOHERENT	I CANNOT hear it	O	Silly, senseless	
16	INCOMPATIBLE	NO COMPANY	P	Speechless; indistinct	
17	INCONGRUITY	Not CONGRUENT	Q	Stormy, cruel	
18	INCONSEQUENTIAL	No sequence	R	The quality of disagreeing	
19	INCONSISTENCY	No consistency	S	Unimportant; insignificant	
20	INCONTROVERTIBLE	No controversy	T	Unquestionable; indisputable	

Answers

EX.NO	1	2	3	4	5	6	7	8	9	10	11	12	13	14	15	16	17	18	19	20
59	K	P	D	R	S	C	N	M	G	L	H	T	O	J	F	A	E	I	B	Q
60	L	O	P	C	K	F	D	E	M	J	N	B	Q	A	H	I	R	S	G	T

WORD GROUPS DAY-15

★ INTRODUCTION (Preface)

ADJECTIVES: prefatory, introductory, preliminary.

NOUNS: preface, prelude, introduction, prologue, preamble; overture, precursor

VERB: introduce, broach

ANTONYMS: adj. addendum, epilogue, postscript

★ CONCLUSION OF A SPEECH, EVENT OR BOOK

ADJECTIVES: closing ,summarizing

NOUNS: finale, epilogue, coda, ending; culmination, climax, conclusion; upshot; peroration;

VERB: end, climax

ANTONYMS: adj. beginning , origin

★ DENYING OF SELF

ADJECTIVES: ascetic , monastic, austere, abstemious, celibate, refraining ; Spartan; teetotal, temperate

NOUNS: recluse, hermit

VERB: abnegate , abstain, renounce

ANTONYMS: n. hedonist, sybarite

★ DISGUSTING/BAD SMELL

ADJECTIVES: fetid , malodorous, rancid, putrid, pungent, acrid, noisome, noxious

NOUNS: effluvium, miasma

VERB: reek, stink

ANTONYMS: adj. aromatic, fragrant, perfumed, redolent.

★ FRAGRANT/GOOD SMELL

ADJECTIVES: ambrosial, aromatic, balmy, delectable, delicious, odoriferous, odorous, perfumed, redolent, savory, spicy

NOUNS: fragrance , incense

VERB: savor, flavor

ANTONYMS: adj. noxious, putrid, stale, stinking

★ HARSH SOUNDING

NOUNS: cacophony, dissonance, din, clamor, clangor.

ADJECTIVES: strident, jarring, raucous, raspy, stentorian.

VERB: grate

ANTONYMS: adj.euphonious, mellifluous, melodious, dulcet, sonorous, harmonious.

★ Pleasant SOUNDING

NOUNS: mellifluence

ADJECTIVES: dulcet, euphonious, harmonic, mellifluous, mellifluent, resonant, silvery, sonorous, soothing, symphonious

VERB: mellow

ANTONYMS: adj. cacophonious, raspy

★ PREVENT-OBSTRUCT

ADJECTIVES: preventive, prophylactic;

NOUNS: deterrent, encumbrance, hindrance, impediment, restraint.

VERB: block, baulk, inhibit, impede, interrupt, fetter, forfend, frustrate, hinder, hamper, occlude, scotch, thwart; bridle , check, curb, delay, halt, retard, restrict; avert, foil, forestall, obviate, preclude, preempt; manacle, rein, restrain, repress, stifle, smother, suppress; disallow, prohibit, forbid, proscribe, exclude, debar, bar;

ANTONYMS: v.abet, aid, facilitate, foment, foster.

Word List Day-16

INCORPORATE (in KAWR per it): v. Make part of a whole; combine; united

    Trigger: IN+ CORPORATE

    Trigger Sentence: It is CORPORATE Company that INCORPORATES many different units.

    Sample Sentence: The music album *incorporated* many old songs to make a series.

INCORRIGIBLE (in KOR uh juh bul): a. Uncorrectable

    Trigger: NOT CORRIGIBLE (**CORRIGIBLE-CORRECTABLE-CURABLE)

    Trigger Sentence: INCORRIGIBLE drug addict is INCURABLE (**UNCORRECTABLE).

    Sample Sentence: Your son is not corrigible because he has an *incorrigible* bad attitude.

INCREDULITY (in kri DOO li tee): n. Tendency to disbelief

    Trigger: NO + CREDIT (BELIEF)

    Trigger Sentence: People with INCREDULITY give NO CREDIT to anyone- they NEVER BELIEVE.

    Sample Sentence: The visitors watched the chimpanzee paint on the canvas with *incredulity*!

    Related Words: INCREDULOUS - a. disbelieving, skeptical

INCUBATE (IN kyuh beyt): v. Hatch; develop

    Trigger: INCUBATOR

    Trigger Sentence: Researchers INCUBATED the eggs in the INCUBATOR.

    Sample Sentence: During the nestling season, birds *incubate* their young ones.

INCULCATE (in KUL keyt): v. Teach; implant

    Trigger: INCULCATE–CALCULATE

    Trigger Sentence: He INCULCATED in her students the value of mathematical CALCULATIONS.

    Sample Sentence: Parents must *inculcate* good manners to their children.

    Related Words: CALCULATED – a. planned; computed

INCUR (in KUR): v. Bring upon oneself; acquire

    Trigger: 1.INCUR-CURRENCY (*currency as debt). 2. INCUR –ACQUIRE (*Synonyms)

    Trigger Sentence: He foolishly INCURRED debts in CURRENCY beyond his ability to pay.

    Sample Sentence: It is a risky proposition and you might *incur* losses.

INDEBTED (in DET id): a. Obligated; beholden

    Trigger: DEBT

    Trigger Sentence: People who are IN DEBT are INDEBTED.

    Sample Sentence: We are in neck deep debt. We're *indebted* to many investors.

    Related Words: OBLIGATED –a. indebted; obliged

INDEFATIGABLE (in di FAT i guh bul): a. Tireless

    Trigger: NO FATIGUE

    Trigger Sentence: NO FATIGUE to an INDEFATIGABLE man.

    Sample Sentence: Japanese *indefatigably* toiled without fatigue to recover from the World War.

INDELIBLE (in DEL uh bul): a. Not able to be erased

Trigger: NOT+ DELETABLE

Trigger Sentence: INDELIBLE memories are NOT DELETABLE.

Sample Sentence: Princess Gayatri Devi was praised for her *indelible* beauty and grace.

INDEMNIFY (in DEM nuh fy): v. Pay for loss; compensate

Trigger: NO + DAMAGE

Trigger Sentence: 1. NOT to cause DAMAGE, we INDEMNIFY and provide COMPENSATION. 2.*(demn-damage; indemn-no damage); A DEMON causes DAMAGE.

Sample Sentence: The Birla Company generously *indemnifies* their workers if injured on job.

Related Words: CONDEMN - v. criticize; declare guilty

INDENTURE (in DEN cher): n. Bind as servant or apprentice to master; bond

Trigger: 1.INDENT- IN DEBT. 2. DEBENTURE

Trigger Sentence: 1. When I was IN DEBT, I worked as an INDENTURED servant. 2. As part of DEBENTURE, I served as an INDENTURED labor. 3. INDENTURED-INDEBTED are synonyms.

Sample Sentence: Times of *indentured* slavery are gone, now be aware of "dignity of labor"!

INDETERMINATE (in di TUR muh nit): a. Uncertain; indefinite

Trigger: UNDETERMINED

Trigger Sentence: If INDETERMINATE numbers of people exist their food needs are UNDETERMINED.

Sample Sentence: The influence of the universe on the earth is *indeterminate*.

Related Words: DETERMINATE —a. fixed; definite

INDIFFERENT (in DIF ur unt): a. Unmoved; unconcerned; mediocre

Trigger: INDIFFERENT —NOT DIFFERENT for good or bad

Trigger Sentence: If you remain INDIFFERENT, you are NOT DIFFERENT from reckless people.

Sample Sentence: My boyfriend is behaving *indifferent* towards me these days.

INDIGENOUS (in DIJ uh nus): a. Native; inborn

Trigger: INDIGENOUS- INDIAN + GENIUS

Trigger Sentence: 1. An INDIAN GENIUS INDIGENOUSLY created a submarine. 2. The indigenous Indians are genius. They know about many natural herbs.

Sample Sentence: Every nook and corner of India has an *indigenous* tribe with their individualistic ethnicities.

INDIGENT (IN di junt): a. Poor; needy

Trigger: 1.INDIAN GENT. 2. INDIGENCE (INDICA & ZENS). 3. OPULENCE (OPEL & LANCER)

Trigger Sentence: 1. INDIAN GENTS are INDIGENTS compare to Americans and Chinese. 2. (Indigence & opulence) INDICA & ZENS are owned by INDIGENT people and OPEL & LANCERS are owned by OPULENT people.

Sample Sentence: Ironically, *indigent* are the farmers who produce food grains for the country!

Related Words: OPULENT —a. wealthy; abundant

INDIGNATION (in dig NEY shun): n. Anger; anger at an injustice

Trigger: 1.INDIAN NATION-PAKISTAN NATION. 2. INDIGNATION –INDIGNITY

Trigger Sentence: 1. INDIAN NATION expressed INDIGNATION over PAKISTAN NATION for their collusion with terrorists. 2. The INDIGNITY inflicted on him aroused INDIGNATION.

Sample Sentence: The decision to shut the factory provoked *indignation* among the workers.

INDISCERNIBLE (in di ZUR nuh bul): a. Unclear; impossible to see

Trigger: 1. NOT DISCERNIBLE. 2. NOT DISCOVERING

Trigger Sentence: 1. Life remains INDISCERNIBLE until consciousness remains NOT DISCERNIBLE. 2. I am UNABLE to DISCOVER so it is INDISCERNIBLE to me.

Sample Sentence: Hidden under vines the crumbling old temple wall was almost *indiscernible*.

Related Words: DISCERNING - a. wise

INDISCRIMINATE (in di SKRIM uh nit): a. Choosing at random; aimless; confused

Trigger: INDISCRIMINATE-IN+THIS+CRIMINAL+ACT

Trigger Sentence: 1. IN THIS CRIMINAL ACT, the terrorists participated in an INDISCRIMINATE slaughter of innocent victims. 2. When we are involved in an INDISCRIMINATE act, we never know who is INNOCENT and who is CRIMINAL.

Sample Sentence: She uses an *indiscriminate* mixture of colors in designing her garments.

INDISPENSABLE (in di SPEN suh bul): a. Absolutely necessary, most essential; cannot be without

Trigger: INDISPENSABLE-NOT DISPENSABLE

Trigger Sentence: He is an INDISPENSABLE worker. He can't easily be DISPENSED.

Sample Sentence: These students are obviously *indolent* to miss their sports class.

Related Words: DISPENSABLE-a. unimportant; may be done with out

INDISSOLUBLE (in di SOL yuh bul): a. Cannot be destroyed; permanent

Trigger: INDESTRUCTIBLE

Trigger Sentence: INDISSOLUBLE contract is INDESTRUCTIBLE.

Sample Sentence: Some believe that marriages are *indissoluble* and are made in heaven!

INDOLENT (IN duh lunt): a. Lazy

Trigger: INDOLENT-"IDLE + GENT"

Trigger Sentence: 1. From INDOLE word remove "NO"-to get IDLE. 2. IDLE GENT is an INDOLENT.

Sample Sentence: These students are obviously *indolent* to miss their sports class.

INDUBITABLE (in DYOO bi tuh bul): a. Impossible to doubt; unquestionable

Trigger: 1. NOT DOUBTFUL. 2. INDUBITABLE -INDISPUTABLE

Trigger Sentence: Michael Jackson was an INDUBITABLE and INDISPUTABLE king of Pop music.

Sample Sentence: The Theory of Evolution is so *indubitable* that scientists do not doubt it.

INDULGENT (in DUL gent): a. Lenient; tolerant

Trigger: DULL GENT

Trigger Sentence: If student is a DULL GENT; the teachers are usually INDULGENT towards him.

Sample Sentence: Her grandparents were always *indulgent* and gave her freedom.

INDUSTRIOUS (in DUHS tree uhs): a. Hard-working, diligent

Trigger: INDUSTRIOUS -INDUSTRY

Trigger Sentence: In DUST INDUSTRY people are INDUSTRIOUS.

Sample Sentence: If you are *industrious*, this industry offers you a great scope to flourish.

INEFFABLE (in EF uh bul): a. Inexpressible; Unutterable

Trigger: INEFFABLE- NOT + F*** + ABLE

Trigger Sentence: 1. Don't talk F *** WORDS. 2. INEFFABLE and INEXPRESSIBLE are synonyms.

Sample Sentence: Her love for him is so *ineffable* that she is unable to express it.

INEPT (in EPT): a. Incompetent, silly

Trigger: 1. INEPT —"IN APT". 2. INEPT -ADEPT

Trigger Sentence: 1. INEPTITUDE means NO APTITUDE. 2. INEPT and ADEPT are antonyms.

Sample Sentence: I am *inept* in playing chess, but I am adept in playing tennis.

Related Words: INEPTITUDE - n. clumsiness

INERT (in URT): a. Inactive

Trigger: 1. INERT –INERTIA. 2. INERT -NOT ALERT

Trigger Sentence: 1. INERT materials are NOT ALERT. 2. INERT people live a life of INERTIA.

Sample Sentence: The intelligence department was so *inert* that it did not alert the Government about the possible terrorist attack.

INEVITABLE (in EV i tuh bul): a. Unavoidable

Trigger: 1.INEVITABLE-INESCAPABLE-INELUDIBLE. 2. VITAMINS

Trigger Sentence: 1. Death is INEVITABLE, INELUCTABLE, INESCAPABLE, INELUDIBLE and UNAVOIDABLE- no one can avoid. 2. VITAMINS are INEVITABLE for essential body functions.

Sample Sentence: Two things are *inevitable*; death and taxes!!!

INEXHAUSTIBLE (in ig ZAWS tuh bul): a. That cannot be entirely consumed or used up; unlimited

Trigger: INEXHAUSTIBLE-NOT EXHAUSTIBLE

Trigger Sentence: The INEXHAUSTIBLE supply of coal is NOT EXHAUSTIBLE.

Sample Sentence: He is an *inexhaustible* marathon runner.

Related Words: EXHAUSTIVE - a. very thorough; exhaustively complete

INEXORABLE (in EK sur uh bul): a. Inflexible; implacable; relentless

Trigger: INEXORABLE -INEXCUSABLE-INFLEXIBLE

Trigger Sentence: 1. INEXORABLE boss is INFLEXIBLE in nature. 2. INEXORABLE boss does not bend for INEXCUSABLE (never excuses) mistakes.

Sample Sentence: The army marched ahead with inflexible and *inexorable* determination.

INFALLIBLE (in FAL ah bul): a. Unfailing

Trigger: NO FALL-NO FAIL

Trigger Sentence: UNFAILING- INFALLIBLE people NEVER FAIL.

Sample Sentence: My team was *infallible* this year, apparently, we won the championship.

Related Words: FALLIBLE - n. liable to err

INFAMY (IN fuh mee): n. Bad reputation

Trigger: INFAMY-BAD FAME (synonyms)

Trigger Sentence: Being INFAMOUS (NOT FAMOUS for good things) is known as INFAMY.

Sample Sentence: Doing bad things will only earn you *infamy*.

Related Words: INFAMOUS –a. having a very bad reputation

INFIDELITY (in fi DEL i tee): n. Unfaithfulness, lack of belief

Trigger: 1. INFIDELITY-NO CONFIDENCE –PERFIDY. 2. PERFIDY-PERFECT NOT

Trigger Sentence: 1. I've NO CONFIDENCE on my girl friend; she is seeing another boy. 2. INFIDELITY to spouse is PERFIDY.

Sample Sentence: She was sure that her husband was guilty of *infidelity*.

Related Words: PERFIDY - N. unfaithfulness

INFINITESIMAL (in fin i TES uh mul): a. Minute; very tiny

Trigger: INFINITELY SMALL

Trigger Sentence: An INFINITELY SMALL object is known as INFINITESIMAL.

Sample Sentence: There are *infinitesimal* particles in the matter.

Related Words: 1. INFINITE –a. limitless. 2. DEFINITE –a. Clear; limited. 3. FINITE –a. having limits

INFIRMITY (in FUR mi tee): n. Sickness; weakness

Trigger: INFIRMITY-"NOT FIRM and strong"

Trigger Sentence: Due to illness, the sick can become INFIRM-LACK of FIRMNESS and strength.

Sample Sentence: My granny's has become weak and she is not able to bear her *infirmity*.

INFLATED (in FLEY tid): a. Swollen; exaggerate

Trigger: "IN+FLAT"-"IN FAT"

Trigger Sentence: INFLATE is to make something FAT, if it is FLAT

Sample Sentence: Wonder why the professional athletes get an *inflated* salary pack?!

Related Words: 1. BALLONED –a. inflated. 2. DEFLATED –a. collapsed, dispirited

INFLEXIBLE (in FLEK shubul): a. Rigid; stubborn; immovable

Trigger: INFLEXIBLE-NOT FLEXIBLE

Trigger Sentence: The NOT so FLEXIBLE army boss took an INFLEXIBLE stance on peace talks.

Sample Sentence: The military captain is an *inflexible* disciplinarian.

Related Words: RIGIDITY –n. stiffness; severity

INFLUX (IN fluks): n. Flowing into

Trigger: IN + FLUX —IN FLOW

Trigger Sentence: Any INFLOW is called INFLUX.

Sample Sentence: South Florida has an *influx* of northern tourists every winter.

Related Words: EXODUS –n. mass departure; exit

INFURIATE (in FYOOR ee yet): v. Make furious; anger

    Trigger: 1. INFURIATE-IRRITATE. 2. IN FURY (FURY-FURIOUS).

    Trigger Sentence: 1. I was INFURIATED by his IRRITATING comments. 2. IN fist of FURY (Hong Kong martial arts film), Bruce lee was INFURIATED.

    Sample Sentence: She was *infuriated* by his sarcastic comments.

INGENIOUS (in JEEN yus): a. Clever, resourceful

    Trigger: GENIUS

    Trigger Sentence: GENIUS (clever) people possess INGENIOUS qualities.

    Sample Sentence: The genius Einstein revealed his *ingeniousness* by relating space and time.

INGENUITY (in juh NYOO i tee): n. Inventive skill

    Trigger: INGEN-ENGINE (INVENT)

    Trigger Sentence: To create an ENGINE one should possess INGENUITY and INVENTIVE skill.

    Sample Sentence: James Watt's *ingenuity* came to surface when he invented steam engine.

INGENUOUS (in JEN yoo us): a. Innocent, Naive, trusting

    Trigger: GENUINE

    Trigger Sentence: GENUINE (frank & innocent) fellows have INGENUOUS qualities.

    Sample Sentence: She is *ingenuous*. Her story is genuine.

    Related Words: DISINGENUOUS –a. insincere

INGRAINED (in GREYND): a. Firmly fixed, deeply rooted

    Trigger: 1. "INGRAIN"-IN BRAIN". 2. INGRAINED-"IN TRAINED"

    Trigger Sentence: 1. His war-time experiences were INGRAINED IN his BRAIN. 2. When you get TRAINED the whole world list will be INGRAINED IN your BRAIN.

    Sample Sentence: The missionaries wanted to uproot the *ingrained* superstitions of the natives.

INGRATIATE (in GRAY shee ayt): v. Become popular with...

    Trigger: 1. "IN + GREAT". 2. IN GRACES

    Trigger Sentence: She has GREAT smile and it is INGRATIATING.

    Sample Sentence: Aishwarya Roy became *ingratiated* among Indian masses with her grace.

INHERENT (in HAYR unt): a. Belonging by nature or habit

    Trigger: 1.IN+ HER. 2. INHERENT-(IN-HEART)

    Trigger Sentence: INSIDE of HER HEART there are INHERENT qualities.

    Sample Sentence: The *inherent* property of the Earth is to rotate around the Sun.

INHIBIT (in HIB it): v. Hinder, or prevent

    Trigger: 1. INHIBIT-IN HIDE IT. 2. INHIBIT-PROHIBIT

    Trigger Sentence: When you HIDE IT INSIDE, it INHIBITS from expressing.

    Sample Sentence: Where freedom of speech is prohibited, there people *inhibit* their feelings.

    Related Words: PROHIBIT – v. forbid; ban

INIMICAL (i NIM i kul): a. Hostile, unfriendly

> **Trigger:** INIMI-ENEMY
>
> **Trigger Sentence:** "INIMI" in the word sounds like ENEMY.
>
> **Sample Sentence:** One tends to be *inimical* against one's enemy.

INIMITABLE (ih NIM i tuh bul): a. Impossible to imitate; matchless

> **Trigger:** INIMITABLE-impossible to IMITATE
>
> **Trigger Sentence:** Michael Jackson was an INIMITABLE performer; it was IMPOSSIBLE TO IMITATE his dancing and singing skills.
>
> **Sample Sentence:** Michael Jacksons' style of dancing is *inimitable*.
>
> Related Words: IMITATIVE –a. mimicking; copying

INIQUITY (ih NIK wi tee): n. Wickedness, injustice

> **Trigger:** INIQUITY-INEQUALITY
>
> **Trigger Sentence:** Showing INEQUALITY based on race, gender etc. can be termed as INIQUITY.
>
> **Sample Sentence:** The nation is still facing the *iniquities* of caste system.
>
> Related Words: INIQUITOUS –a. Wicked; unjust; immoral

INNATE (i NAYT): a. Native, inborn

> **Trigger:** 1. IN + NATE- NATIVE. 2. INNATE- IN NATURAL
>
> **Trigger Sentence:** 1. IN NATIVE places, people have INNATE qualities. 2. It is NATURAL for a human being to be INNATE dissatisfied whatever he may possess materially.
>
> **Sample Sentence:** With an *innate* sense of numbers Surya created his own math equations.
>
> Related Words: NATIVE –a. inborn; natural; local

INNOCUOUS (i NAHK yoo us): a. Harmless

> **Trigger:** INNOCUOUS-INNOCENT
>
> **Trigger Sentence:** 1. His INNOCENT face shows how INNOCUOUS he is. 2. NOXIOUS TOXINS are HARMFUL; whereas INNOCUOUS things are HARMLESS.
>
> **Sample Sentence:** Jennie's *innocuous* smile and innocent eyes made us to trust her instantly!

INNOVATIVE (IN uh vey tiv): a. New; inventive

> **Trigger:** INNOVATIVE-NOVEL
>
> **Trigger Sentence:** The INNOVATIVE teaching methods are completely NOVEL.
>
> **Sample Sentence:** The Apple Inc. is famous for stylistic *innovative* systems.
>
> Related Words: NOVELTY –n. something new

INNUENDO (in yoo EN doh): n. Hint, indirect suggestion (usually derogatory)

> **Trigger:** 1. INNUENDO -IN U A NOD. 2. innueNDO ("NDO" make it as "NOD")
>
> **Trigger Sentence:** 1. IN UR NOD there is an INDICATION and an INNUENDO. 2. NDO-NOD: nod is an indication.
>
> **Sample Sentence:** The bowler gave an *innuendo* to the wicket keeper in the form of a nod.

INORDINATE (in OR den it): a. Excessive, immoderate; disorderly

> **Trigger:** 1. NOT IN ORDER. 2. INORDINATE-EXTRAORDINARY
>
> **Trigger Sentence:** INORDINATE means NOT in ORDER; it is EXTRAORDINARY or out of ORDER.
>
> **Sample Sentence:** Cricket players' salaries are *inordinate* compared to the hockey players.

INQUISITOR (in KWIZ i ter): n. Investigator; questioner

Trigger: INQUISITOR-INQUIRER-ENQUIRER

Trigger Sentence: 1. IN a QUIZ (based on law) we got QUIZZED by an INQUISITOR. 2. INQUISITOR and INQUIRER are synonyms.

Sample Sentence: The witness had to answer the *inquisitors'* questions on the murder case.

Related Words: 1.INQUISITIVE –a. overly curious, questioning. 2. INQUEST - n. formal legal inquiry. 3. INQUIRY – n. a search for knowledge; question

INSATIABLE (in SAYSH uh bul): a. Unsatisfiable; extremely greedy

Trigger: INSATIABLE-UNSATISFIED

Trigger Sentence: People remain UNSATISFIED, if they desire INSATIABLE wealth.

Sample Sentence: Her desire for jewelry is *insatiable*.

INSCRUTABLE (in SKROO tuh bul): a. Not easily understood, mysterious

Trigger: IN- SCRIPT-TROUBLE

Trigger Sentence: I am IN TROUBLE to understand this INSCRUTABLE SCRIPT. This INSCRUTABLE SCRIPT is impossible to SCRUTINIZE or ANALYZE.

Sample Sentence: It is troublesome to script on Quantum Mechanics. It is an *inscrutable* subject.

INSENTIENT (in SEN shee unt): a. Insensible; lacking the ability to feel

Trigger: NOT + SENTIENT: (SENTIENT-SENSITIVE-SENSE)

Trigger Sentence: An INSENTIENT person is NOT SENSITIVE.

Sample Sentence: *Insentient* people are insensitive to others worries.

Related Words: 1. SENTIENT –a. sensitive in Perception. 2. INSENSIBLE –a. unconscious

INSIDIOUS (in SID ee us): a. Cunning; secretly harmful

Trigger: 1. INSIDIOUS-INSIDE US. 2. INSIDIOUS-"IN +HIDE+OUS"

Trigger Sentence: INSIDE US (SECRETLY) there are lots of INSIDIOUS plans to harm others.

Sample Sentence: It is *insidious* to live with hideous people.

INSIGHTFUL (IN sahyt ful): a. Perceptive; clear understanding

Trigger: INSIGHT-SIGHT

Trigger Sentence: His SIGHT of battlefield was INSIGHTFUL

Sample Sentence: Dr. Abdul Kalam gave some *insightful advice to the budding scientists.*

INSINUATE (in SIN yoo eyt): v. Hint; imply; creep in

Trigger: 1.IN SIGN U ATE. 2. INSINUATE-INTIMATE-INDICATE

Trigger Sentence: 1. SIGN means SIGNAL and SIGNAL is an INDICATION. 2. INSINUATE is to INTIMATE or INDICATE.

Sample Sentence: Put your foot in the business; you can soon *insinuate* into the field work later.

Related Words: INSINUATION - n. hint

INSIPID (in SIP id): a. Dull; tasteless

Trigger: INSIPID -NOT SIPPED

Trigger Sentence: The INSIPID sauce is NOT SIPPED because it is TASTELESS.

Sample Sentence: Your jokes are *insipid*... they are somewhat irksome to me.

INSOLENT (IN suh lunt): a. Rude and disrespectful

    Trigger: 1. INSULT. 2. INSOLENT -INSULT GENT

    Trigger Sentence: An INSULTING GENT is INSOLENT and IMPOLITE in attitude.

    Sample Sentence: That *insolent* lady insults gentlemen with her rude remarks.

    Related Words: INSOLENCE - n. arrogance

INSOLVENT (in SAWL vunt): a. Bankrupt; unable to pay one's debts

    Trigger: NOT SOLVED

    Trigger Sentence: 1. With an INSOLVENT, the money problem is NOT SOLVED.
2. Bankrupt means bank is ruptured and there is no money.

    Sample Sentence: ABC Company became *insolvent*, as all the three owners drew large salaries.

    Related Words: 1. SOLVENCY - n. ability to pay one's debts. 2. BANKRUPT –a. lacking; insolvent

INSOUCIANCE (in SOO see uhns): n. Lack of concern; lightheartedness

    Trigger: INSOUCIANCE-INSURANCE

    Trigger Sentence: This life INSURANCE plan allows the elderly to enjoy INSOUCIANCE life.

    Sample Sentence: Children play with *insouciance*, as if they do not have a care in the world!

    Related Words: INSOUCIANT –a. carefree; easygoing; nonchalant

INSTIGATE (IN stuh gayt): v. Urge, excite, provoke

    Trigger: 1.INSTIGATE-INITIATE. 2. INSTIGATOR-INITIATOR

    Trigger Sentence: An INSTIGATOR is an INITIATOR; she INSTIGATED and INITIATED the quarrel.

    Sample Sentence: He initiates a quarrel by making *instigating* comments on the other person.

INSUBORDINATE (in suh BAWR dn it): a. Disobedient; rebellious

    Trigger: NOT SUBORDINATE

    Trigger Sentence: The SUBORDINATE officer was dismissed for being INSUBORDINATE.

    Sample Sentence: The *insubordinate* soldiers were court-marshaled.

    Related Words: SUBORDINATE –a. under the authority of others

INSULAR (IN suh lur): a. Isolated; narrow-minded

    Trigger: INSULAR- ISOLATED

    Trigger Sentence: An INSULAR person is INSULATED and ISOLATED from other people.

    Sample Sentence: Coronado is an *insular* community located off the coast of San Diego.

INSURGENT (in SUR junt): a. Rebellious

    Trigger: INSURGENT -NOT SERVANT

    Trigger Sentence: My SERVANT becomes INSURGENT; says - I'm NOT a SERVANT; I am a Rebel.

    Sample Sentence: Rudra's *insurgent* ideas got toned down as he grew older and wiser!

    Related Words: INSURRECTION –n. Rebellion

INTELLIGIBLE (in TEL i juh bul): a. Understandable

    Trigger: INTELLIGIBLE-INTELLIGENT

Trigger Sentence: An INTELLIGENT teacher teaches a difficult topic with INTELLIGIBLE examples.

Sample Sentence: These young girls are *intelligible* enough to find their respective Mr. Right.

Related Words: UNINTELLIGIBLE –a. Impossible to understand

INTEMPERATE (in TEM per it): a. Excessive; immoderate; extreme

Trigger: INTEMPERATE- HOT TEMPER

Trigger Sentence: The HOT TEMPER guy exhibits INTEMPERATE anger.

Sample Sentence: *Intemperate* remarks of admin hawks (hostile persons) damaged a good deal.

Related Words: TEMPERATE –a. moderate; composed

INTERMINABLE (in TUR muh nuh bul): a. Endless; apparently endless

Trigger: INTERMINABLE -NO TERMINATION

Trigger Sentence: INTERMINABLE things appear to have NO TERMINAL point.

Sample Sentence: His speech was short, but seemed *interminable* to his uninterested audience.

INTERMITTENT (in ter MIT nt): a. Not continuous, on-off

Trigger: INTERMITTENT-INTERMISSION-INTERVAL

Trigger Sentence: They forecast INTERMITTENT rain throughout the day; in INTERMISSIONS.

Sample Sentence: It drizzled *intermittently* all day long.

INTERPLAY (IN ter pley): v. Interaction; reciprocal play or influence

Trigger: INTERPLAY-INTERACTION+PLAY

Trigger Sentence: The hunter enjoyed the INTERPLAY of animals in the forest.

Sample Sentence: It is important to understand the *interplay* between all living things.

INTERPOLATE (in TUR puh leyt): v. Insert between

Trigger: INTER+POLE- ENTER+POLE

Trigger Sentence: INTERPOLATE means INSERT A POLE between OTHER POLES and analyze the nature of the inserted pole with respect to other poles.

Sample Sentence: We welcome the *interpolation* of the Interpol in this case linking nations.

Related Words: EXTRAPOLATE – v. guess; infer

INTERPOSE (in ter POHZ): v. Be or come between; interfere

Trigger: 1.INTERPOSE- INSERT POSE. 2. INTERPOSE-INTERFERE (** synonyms)

Trigger Sentence: He INTERPOSED to stop by POSING himself in between the warring parties.

Sample Sentence: He *interposed* an opaque body between the light and eye.

INTERTWINE (in ter TWAHYN): a. Interlaced, interwoven

Trigger: INTERTWINED-INTERTWISTED

Trigger Sentence: INTERTWINED-INTERLACED-INTERLOCKED-INTERCONNECTED; are synonyms.

Sample Sentence: The strength of USA is inter-twisted and *intertwined* between Dollar and Military Power.

INTERVENE (in tur VEEN): v. Come between; interfere

> **Trigger:** 1. INTERVENE –INTERFERE. 2. INTERVAL

> **Trigger Sentence:** Intervene and interfere are synonyms. INTERVAL INTERVENES between first half and second half of a movie.

> **Sample Sentence:** USA interfered in Vietnam War; USSR also *intervened* in the controversy.

INTERWEAVE (in ter WEEV): v. To weave together

> **Trigger:** WEAVE TOGETHER; INTERTWINE-INTERWEAVE

> **Trigger Sentence:** INTERWOVEN-INTERTWINED-INTERTWISTED-INTERLACED-INTERLOCKED- INTERCONNECTED; are synonyms.

> **Sample Sentence:** PEARL programming and Statistics are *interwoven* and interlaced into Bioinformatics.

INTIMACY (IN tuh muh see): n. Closeness; warm friendship; privacy

> **Trigger:** INTIMACY-INTIMATE PRIVACY

> **Trigger Sentence:** After their INTIMATE union in PRIVACY, he felt he gained INTIMACY with her.

> **Sample Sentence:** He is just her friend; they are not in an *intimate* relationship.

> Related Words: INTIMATE – a. close; private

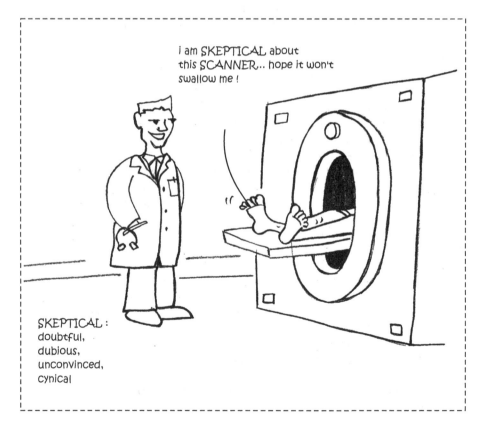

Memory Test-61 : Match each word and its memory trick to the corresponding definition.

S.N	WORD	MEMORY TRIGGER	S.N	DEFINITIONS	KEY
1	INCORPORATE	CORPORATE company	A	Absolutely necessary, most essential	
2	INCORRIGIBLE	incurable -uncorrectable	B	Anger; anger at an injustice	
3	INCREDULITY	No + credit (belief)	C	Bind as servant to master; bond	
4	INCUBATE	Incubator	D	Bring upon oneself; acquire	
5	INCULCATE	How to CALCULATE	E	Cannot be destroyed; permanent	
6	INCUR	Currency–acquire	F	Choosing at random; aimless-	
7	INDEBTED	Debt	G	Hatch; develop	
8	INDEFATIGABLE	No fatigue	H	Make part of a whole; combine	
9	INDELIBLE	Not+ DELETABLE	I	Native; inborn	
10	INDEMNIFY	No + damage	J	Not able to be erased	
11	INDENTURE	Indent- in debt- debenture	K	Obligated; beholden	
12	INDETERMINATE	Undetermined	L	Pay for loss; compensate	
13	INDIFFERENT	NOT DIFFERENT for good or bad	M	Poor; needy	
14	INDIGENOUS	Native Indian + genes	N	Teach; implant	
15	INDIGENT	Indian gents are	O	Tendency to disbelief	
16	INDIGNATION	Don't DIG at me	P	Tireless	
17	INDISCERNIBLE	Not discernible- Not discovering	Q	Uncertain; indefinite	
18	INDISCRIMINATE	In+this+criminal+act	R	Unclear; impossible to see	
19	INDISPENSABLE	Not dispensable	S	Unconcerned; unmoved; mediocre	
20	INDISSOLUBLE	INDESTRUCTIBLE.	T	Uncorrectable	

Memory Test-62 : Match each word and its memory trick to the corresponding definition.

S.N	WORD	MEMORY TRIGGER	S.N	DEFINITIONS	KEY
1	INDOLENT	Idle + gent	A	Bad reputation	
2	INDUBITABLE	Indubitable -indisputable	B	Clever, resourceful	
3	INDULGENT	On DULL GENT be indulgent	C	Flowing into	
4	INDUSTRIOUS	Dust industry	D	Hard-working, diligent	
5	INEFFABLE	Not + f*** + able	E	Impossible to doubt; unquestionable	
6	INEPT	Inept —"in apt"-no aptitude	F	Inactive	
7	INERT	Inertia- Inert -not alert	G	Incompetent, silly	
8	INEVITABLE	INESCAPABLE	H	Inexpressible; Unutterable	
9	INEXHAUSTIBLE	Not exhaustible	I	Inflexible; implacable; relentless	
10	INEXORABLE	Inexcusable-INFLEXIBLE	J	Lazy	
11	INFALLIBLE	NEVER FAIL	K	Lenient; tolerant	
12	INFAMY	NOT FAMOUS for good	L	Make furious; anger	
13	INFIDELITY	No confidence –perfidy	M	Minute; very tiny	
14	INFINITESIMAL	Infinitely small	N	Rigid; stubborn; immovable	
15	INFIRMITY	NOT FIRM and strong	O	Sickness; weakness	
16	INFLATED	In fat-make fat	P	Swollen; exaggerate	
17	INFLEXIBLE	Not flexible	Q	That cannot be entirely used up	
18	INFLUX	In flow	R	Unavoidable	
19	INFURIATE	Irritate-fury-furious	S	Unfailing	
20	INGENIOUS	GENIUS	T	Unfaithfulness, lack of belief	

Answers	EX.NO	1	2	3	4	5	6	7	8	9	10	11	12	13	14	15	16	17	18	19	20
	61	H	T	O	G	N	D	K	P	J	L	C	Q	S	I	M	B	R	F	A	E
	62	J	E	K	D	H	G	F	R	Q	I	S	A	T	M	O	P	N	C	L	B

Memory Test-63 : Match each word and its memory trick to the corresponding definition.

S.N	WORD	MEMORY TRIGGER	S.N	DEFINITIONS	KEY
1	INGENUITY	Create an ENGINE	A	Become popular with...	
2	INGENUOUS	Genuine	B	Belonging by nature or habit	
3	INGRAINED	It is IN BRAIN	C	Excessive, immoderate; disorderly	
4	INGRATIATE	In graces	D	Firmly fixed, deeply rooted	
5	INHERENT	In-heart	E	Harmless	
6	INHIBIT	In hide it-PROHIBIT	F	Hinder, or prevent	
7	INIMICAL	Enemy	G	Hint, indirect suggestion	
8	INIMITABLE	Impossible to IMITATE	H	Impossible to imitate; matchless	
9	INIQUITY	To show INEQUALITY	I	Innocent, Naive, trusting	
10	INNATE	Nate- NATIVE	J	Insensible; lacking the ability to feel	
11	INNOCUOUS	Innocent	K	Inventive skill	
12	INNOVATIVE	Novel	L	Investigator; questioner	
13	INNUENDO	In u a NOD	M	Native, inborn	
14	INORDINATE	Not in order; extra+ordinary	N	New; inventive	
15	INQUISITOR	Inquirer-ENQUIRER	O	Not easily understood, mysterious	
16	INSATIABLE	Unsatisfied	P	Perceptive; clear understanding	
17	INSCRUTABLE	In- script-trouble	Q	Secretly harmful; cunning	
18	INSENTIENT	Not + sentient-sensitive	R	Unfriendly, Hostile	
19	INSIDIOUS	Inside us-in +hide	S	Unsatisfiable; extremely greedy	
20	INSIGHTFUL	Clear Sight	T	Wickedness, injustice	

Memory Test-64 : Match each word and its memory trick to the corresponding definition.

S.N	WORD	MEMORY TRIGGER	S.N	DEFINITIONS	KEY
1	INSINUATE	In SIGN u ate	A	Bankrupt; unable to pay one's debts	
2	INSIPID	Not sipped	B	Be or come between; interfere	
3	INSOLENT	INSULT	C	Closeness; privacy	
4	INSOLVENT	Money problem NOT SOLVED	D	Come between; interfere	
5	INSOUCIANCE	Take Insurance	E	Disobedient; rebellious	
6	INSTIGATE	Instigate-INITIATE	F	Endless; apparently endless	
7	INSUBORDINATE	Not subordinate	G	Excessive; immoderate; extreme	
8	INSULAR	Insular- ISOLATED	H	Excite, provoke ; urge	
9	INSURGENT	Not servant	I	Hint; imply; creep in	
10	INTELLIGIBLE	Intelligent	J	Insert between	
11	INTEMPERATE	No temperate-no moderate	K	interaction; reciprocal play	
12	INTERMINABLE	No TERMINATION	L	Interlaced, interwoven	
13	INTERMITTENT	Intermission-interval	M	Isolated; narrow-minded	
14	INTERPLAY	Interaction+play	N	Lightheartedness; Lack of concern	
15	INTERPOLATE	Enter+a pole	O	Not continuous, on-off	
16	INTERPOSE	Insert pose	P	Rebellious	
17	INTERTWINE	Inter-twisted	Q	Rude and disrespectful	
18	INTERVENE	Interfere- Interval	R	Tasteless ; dull	
19	INTERWEAVE	Weave together	S	To weave together	
20	INTIMACY	Intimate privacy	T	Understandable	

Answers	EX.NO	1	2	3	4	5	6	7	8	9	10	11	12	13	14	15	16	17	18	19	20
	63	K	I	D	A	B	F	R	H	T	M	E	N	G	C	L	S	O	J	Q	P
	64	I	R	Q	A	N	H	E	M	P	T	G	F	O	K	J	B	L	D	S	C

WORD GROUPS DAY-16

★ **STIMULATE**

ADJECTIVES: hortatory, stimulating

NOUNS: incentive, impetus, fillip, stimulus

VERB: animate, arouse, elate, energize, enliven, exhilarate, exhort, foment, foster, galvanize, impel, incite, inflame, instigate, motivate, pique, prod, prompt, spur, urge, vivify, whet

ANTONYMS: v. calm, depress, discourage

★ **HELP-ASSIST**

ADJECTIVES: hortatory, supportive

NOUNS: advice, aid, avail, balm, nourishment, remedy, succor, support, sustenance, utility

VERB: abet, accommodate, advocate, bolster, boost, endorse, further, intercede, patronize, prop, root for, sanction, stimulate, sustain, uphold

ANTONYMS: v. block, check, counteract, hinder, injure, obstruct

★ **WITHDRAWAL-RETREAT**

VERB: retract , retreat, recant, recede, repudiate, renounce, renege, retrograde, reverse, revoke, rescind, abjure, disavow.

NOUNS: abeyance, respite, remission;

ADJECTIVES: retired, resigned.

ANTONYMS: v.advance; foster

★ **PACIFY:** soothe, calm;

ADJECTIVES: propitiatory, mollifying

NOUNS: appeasement, conciliation

VERB: assuage, alleviate, allay, appease, conciliate, ease, pacify, soothe, mitigate, palliate, abate, ameliorate, subdue, tranquillize, moderate; slake, sate, satiate

ANTONYMS: v. aggravate, exacerbate, deteriorate, intensify, worsen

★ **MAKE WORSE**

ADJECTIVES: exacerbating

NOUNS: intensification, worsening

VERB: aggravate, amplify, annoy, egg on, embitter, enrage, exacerbate, exasperate, excite, heighten, inflame, intensify, irritate, madden, provoke, vex, worsen

ANTONYMS: v. aid, calm, comfort, help, soothe

★ **IRRITATE –IRRITABLE**

ADJECTIVES: irritable, irascible, choleric, crabby, crotchety, cantankerous, dyspeptic, fractious, peevish, prickly, splenetic, testy, touchy

NOUNS: irritation, exasperation, indignation, impatience, chagrin, rage, fury, wrath; curmudgeon, gadfly

VERB: annoy, antagonize, anger, bother, badger, exasperate, irk, infuriate, gall, pester, pique, nag, nettle, madden, provoke, vex

ANTONYMS: v. please, gratify , mollify, pacify

★ **CALM NATURE-CALMNESS**

ADJECTIVES: placid, serene, tranquil, relaxed, unruffled, unperturbed; composed, equable, even-tempered; unexcitable, unflappable, phlegmatic

NOUNS: quietude, equanimity, equilibrium, imperturbability, sangfroid

VERB: soothe, pacify, placate, propitiate, mollify, appease, conciliate

ANTONYMS: adj. agitated , perturbed, turbulent

Word List Day-17

INTIMIDATE (in TIM i deyt): v. Frighten

> **Trigger:** INTIMIDATE–TIMID

> **Trigger Sentence:** The TIMID freshmen were INTIMIDATED by the seniors in the college.

> **Sample Sentence:** You are trying to corner and *intimidate* me for no fault of mine.

> Related Words: TIMID –a. shy

INTOLERANT (in TOL er unt): a. Bigoted; narrow-minded

> **Trigger:** INTOLERANT- NEVER TOLERATES

> **Trigger Sentence:** The INTOLERANT person is unwilling to TOLERATE difference of opinions.

> **Sample Sentence:** My boss is *intolerant* when it comes to granting sick leave.

> Related Words: INTOLERABLE – a. unbearable. 2. TOLERANT – a. open-minded; easy going

INTRACTABLE (in TRAK tuh bul): a. Hard to control; stubborn; unruly

> **Trigger:** INTRACTABLE-NOT TRACTABLE

> **Trigger Sentence:** INTRACTABLE people are NOT TRACTABLE; CANNOT keep them on a TRACK.

> **Sample Sentence:** The police could not control the *intractable* masses at the public meeting.

> Related Words: TRACTABLE –a. obedient

INTRANSIGENT (in TRAN suh junt): a. Uncompromising; stubborn

> **Trigger:** 1.NO TRANSFER. 2. INTRANSIGENT-INTRACTABLE (REF)

> **Trigger Sentence:** 1. An INTRANSIGENT gent is "CONTRA" to TRANSFER; he says NO CHANGE. 2. INTRACTABLE people are INTRANSIGENT.

> **Sample Sentence:** I do not accept this transfer for I can't work with *intransigent* people.

> Related Words: INTRANSIGENCE –n. unwillingness to compromise; stubbornness

INTREPID (in TREP id): a. Brave, fearless

> **Trigger:** 1. NOT TREPID (refer). 2. TREPID-means-TIMID

> **Trigger Sentence:** I am NOT TREPID or TIMID; I'm INTREPID; bold and brave.

> **Sample Sentence:** USA was *intrepid*, but USSR was equally not timid.

> Related Words: TREPID –a. fearful, timid

INTRICATE (IN truh kit): v. Complex, complicated

> **Trigger:** 1.IN THREE CASE. 2. INTRICATE-COMPLICATE

> **Trigger Sentence:** 1. IN 3 CASES of offence pending in 3 COURTS, he is in INTRICATE position. 2. INTRICATE design is COMPLICATED to understand.

> **Sample Sentence:** The novel's *intricate* plot will not be easy to essay out into a film.

> Related Words: EXTRICATE –v. free, release from intricate position.

INTRIGUE (IN treeg): v. To arouse the interest, plot

    Trigger: 1. INTRIGUE -IN + TRIGUE (TRICK). 2. INTRIGUING-INTERESTING

    Trigger Sentence: 1. IN TRICK there is an INTRIGUE or plot; the TRICKS are good at AROUSING-INTEREST. 2. INTRIGUING is nothing but INTERESTING.

    Sample Sentence: The subject of Epigenetics is so *intriguing* that it triggers my interest.

    Related Words: INTRIGUING (ad): v. Absorbing, fascinating.

INTRIGUING (in TREEG ing): a. Absorbing, fascinating

    Trigger: 1.INTRIGUING-"IN TRICK VIEWING". 2. INTRIGUING-INTERESTING

    Trigger Sentence: 1. In the magician's "IN TRICK VIEWING" show, children's had an INTRIGUING experience. 2. INTRIGUING and INTERESTING are synonyms.

    Sample Sentence: The story teller kept us captivated all night with his *intriguing* tales.

INTRINSIC (in TRIN sik): a. Essential; inherent; built-in

    Trigger: INTRINSIC-INTERNAL

    Trigger Sentence: INTRINSIC qualities are INTERNAL and ESSENTIAL; EXTRINSIC qualities are EXTERNAL and INESSENTIAL.

    Sample Sentence: Juliet has an *intrinsic* quality to help the needy just like her charitable father.

    Related Words: EXTRINSIC –a. external; unrelated

INTROSPECTIVE (in truh SPEC tiv): a. Self-examining, looking inwards

    Trigger: INTROSPECT-INSPECT INSIDE

    Trigger Sentence: INTROSPECTION is an INSPECTION of; INSIDE of ONESELF.

    Sample Sentence: Gandhiji often *introspected* himself In order to inspect his inside feelings.

INTUITION (in too ISH uhn): n. Immediate insight; Sixth sense

    Trigger: INTUITION -IN + TUITION

    Trigger Sentence: A student's INTUITION does not improve in TUITION; it improves only in natural environment.

    Sample Sentence: Meena has got an *intuitive* power; she foretells everything.

INUNDATE (IN un deyt): n. Flood, overflow; overwhelm

    Trigger: 1. INUNDANT-ABUNDANT. 2. IN UNDERWATER-INUNDATE

    Trigger Sentence: 1. INUNDANT means ABUNDANT of anything. 2. IN UNDER WATER, I'm INUNDATED (or flooded).

    Sample Sentence: China has *inundated* USA with abundant supply of cheap products.

INURED (in YOO rd): a. Accustomed to hardship; habituated

    Trigger: IN+URED —"IN USED"

    Trigger Sentence: I got USED to Hardships and pains.

    Sample Sentence: Soldiers become *inured* as they are used to face danger.

INVALIDATE (in VAL uh dayt): v. Weaken; destroy

    Trigger: NOT VALID

    Trigger Sentence: INVALIDATE is to make something NOT VALUABLE.

    Sample Sentence: Your entry is not valid. If you credit any expense it is *invalid* in accounting.

    Related Words: VALIDATE - n. make valid

INVALUABLE (in VAL yoo uh bul): a. Priceless, very valuable

Trigger: INVALUABLE-VERY VALUABLE

Trigger Sentence: He has provided INVALUABLE/VERY VALUABLE assistance.

Sample Sentence: My wife does my quality control which I find *invaluable.*

INVASIVE (in VEY siv): a. Tending to invade; aggressive

Trigger: INVASIVE-INVADE

Trigger Sentence: The INVASIVE cancer cells INVADED the whole body.

Sample Sentence: Dare work in an *invasive* ambiance where everyone is out to stab the other?

INVECTIVE (in VEK tiv): n. Abuse, criticism

Trigger: INVECTIVE -ENVY ACTIVE

Trigger Sentence: As his ENVY is still ACTIVE, he threw a bitter INVECTIVE at his ex-foe.

Sample Sentence: Will you stop being *invective* towards me for working long, it is just my duty.

Related Words: INVEIGH - v. attack with words

INVEIGH (in VAY): v. Attack with words; blame

Trigger: INVEIGH-ENVY

Trigger Sentence: With ENVY (jealousy) the people INVEIGH (blame) others.

Sample Sentence: Journalists' often *inveigh* against corruption in the daily news papers.

INVEIGLE (in VAY gul): v. Persuade (convince) by flattery

Trigger: INVEIGLE -INVITE+GAL

Trigger Sentence: He INVEIGLED A pretty youthful GIRL and INVITED her to dine him.

Sample Sentence: Rissa was *inveigled* by the street vendor to buy a fake Rolex watch.

INVERSE (in VURS): v. Opposite

Trigger: INVERSE-REVERSED

Trigger Sentence: In an INVERSE approach when the direct method failed he REVERSED.

Sample Sentence: Multiplication and division are *inverse* operations.

Related Words: INVERT - v. turn upside down; turn inside out

INVETERATE (in VET ur it): a. Deeply rooted, habitual

Trigger: INVETERATE-IN VETERANS

Trigger Sentence: IN VETERANS (old people) THE HABITS are INVETERATE (deeply rooted).

Sample Sentence: When it comes to playing cards, Jordan is an *inveterate* trickster.

INVIDIOUS (in VID ee us): a. Designed to create ill will or envy

Trigger: 1.INVIDIOUS-ENVY +odious. 2. INVIDIOUS-INSIDIOUS

Trigger Sentence: 1. Nobody likes INVIDIOUS people they are ODIOUSLY ENVIOUS. 2. INVIDIOUS and INSIDIOUS- both are harmful.

Sample Sentence: This *invidious* man makes money on the name of charity!

INVINCIBLE (in VIN suh bul): a. Impossible to conquer

    Trigger: NO WIN

    Trigger Sentence: NO WIN against INVINCIBLE man; one cannot win against an invincible man.

    Sample Sentence: Mohammad Ali wanted to win every fight and to remain *invincible*.

INVIOLABLE (in VYE uh luh bul): a. Incorruptible, impossible to violate

    Trigger: NOT TO VIOLATE

    Trigger Sentence: Venerable are INVIOLABLE; CANNOT VIOLATE the HOLINESS of such things.

    Sample Sentence: There are certain *inviolable* policies, you are supposed not to violate.

INVOKE (in VOHK): v. Call forth; request

    Trigger: INVOKE –"IN WAKE"-WAKE someone from inside

    Trigger Sentence: He INVOKED spirit by WAKING him with magical spell.

    Sample Sentence: Danseuse Gayatri *invoked* the spirit of the dancing Lord Siva in her dance.

    Related Words: INVOCATION - n. prayer asking for god's help

INVOLVED (in VOLVD): a. Complicated; convoluted

    Trigger: INVOLVED-CONVOLUTED (** synonyms)

    Trigger Sentence: The INVOLUTE problem is so INVOLVED/ CONVOLUTED that it REVOLVED in his mind.

    Sample Sentence: The "Inception" movie plot was too *involved* and concocted.

IOTA (eye OH tuh): n. Small quantity

    Trigger: IOTA- DOT

    Trigger Sentence: IOTa-a DOT; DOT means SMALL.

    Sample Sentence: Thank god he is gone; I don't have an *iota* of remorse for throwing him!

IRASCIBLE (i RAS uh bul): a. Hot-tempered; irritable

    Trigger: IRASCIBLE-IRRITABLE

    Trigger Sentence: IRASCIBLE person is usually IRRITABLE.

    Sample Sentence: Uncle Tim is a real grouch; he gets *irascible* to find kids playing on his lawn!

    Related Words: 1. IRE –n. anger. 2. IRATE –v. angry; enraged. 3. IRKSOME –a. irritating; annoying

IRKSOME (URK sum): a. Annoying; tedious

    Trigger: 1.IRKSOME-TIRESOME. 2. IRRITATING SOME

    Trigger Sentence: IRKSOME is TIRESOME and BORESOME.

    Sample Sentence: The *irksome* nature of our boss has become very tiresome to our employees.

IRONY (EYE ruh nee): n. Upshot of events contrary to what is expected; Sarcasm

    Trigger: IRONY-MONEY

    Trigger Sentence: FULL MONEY- no sleep; NO MONEY- full sleep; that is IRONY of the MONEY.

Sample Sentence: "Money honey"! My honey wants money, I don't have any, that is the *irony*!!!

Related Words: IRONIC - a. occurring in an unexpected and contrary manner.

IRRATIONAL (ih RASH uh nal): a. Illogical, lacking reason

Trigger: NOT RATIONAL

Trigger Sentence: He DOESN'T have RATIONAL analysis; he gets IRRATIONAL fears.

Sample Sentence: I find my husband's arguments as *irrational,* one-sided and chauvinistic!

IRRECONCILABLE (ih rek uhn SAHY luh bul): a. Incompatible; impossible to compromise

Trigger: NOT RECONCILABLE

Trigger Sentence: It is IMPOSSIBLE to COUNSEL the couple for RECONCILIATION, as they have IRRECONCILABLE differences.

Sample Sentence: The couple is heading for a divorce as they were totally *irreconcilable.*

Related Words: 1.RECONCILE –v. make compatible with.2.CONCILIATE –v. pacify; reconcile

IRREFUTABLE (ih ruh FYOOT uh bul): a. Undeniable; indisputable

Trigger: 1. NOT REFUSE. 2. IRREFUTABLE -INDISPUTABLE

Trigger Sentence: IRREFUTABLE theorem is INDISPUTABLE and CAN'T BE REFUSED with PROOF.

Sample Sentence: It is *irrefutable* and indisputable that primates evolved from mammals.

Related Words: REFUTE - v. prove false; rebut

IRREPROACHABLE (ir i PROH chuh bul): a. Faultless, blameless

Trigger: NOT REPROACHABLE –NOT IMPEACHABLE

Trigger Sentence: He has an IRREPROACHABLE character and UNIMPEACHABLE reputation.

Sample Sentence: His conduct as a judge is *irreproachable,* so trust him, and truth will triumph!

IRRESOLUTE (ih REZ uh loot): a. Indecisive; uncertain how to act

Trigger: lacking RESOLUTION

Trigger Sentence: I stood IRRESOLUTE to make some RESOLUTION to stop drinking in New Year.

Sample Sentence: The new president is hesitant and *irresolute,* so don't let him tackle matters.

IRREVERENCE (ih REV er uns): n. Lack of respect

Trigger: LACK OF REVERENCE (towards the sacred river Ganges)

Trigger Sentence: Certain young people show IRREVERENCE to the RIVER Ganges.

Sample Sentence: I cannot accept him as my student because he is *irreverent* towards elders.

ITINERARY (eye TIN uh rare ee): n. Plan of a trip

Trigger: ITINERANT DIARY- A MIGRANT DIARY

Trigger Sentence: AN ITINERANT or a MIGRANT DIARY is called ITINERARY.

Sample Sentence: I have noted down the *itinerary* of our Chief Guest in a diary.

Related Words: ITINERANT –n. wanderer

JABBER (JAB er): v. Talk rapidly or clumsily
   Trigger: JABBER-CHATTER-BLABBER-GIBBER
   Trigger Sentence: CHATTER, BLABBER, GIBBER and JABBER are synonyms.
   Sample Sentence: Some people just can't stop *jabbering*, don't their jaws pain?

JADED (JAY dud): a. Fatigued; tired
   Trigger: JADED-FADED-FATIGUED
   Trigger Sentence: FADED jeans pant and JADED face look the same.
   Sample Sentence: The jeans are so *jaded* that their color is completely faded.

JARGON (JAHR gun): n. Language used by a special group; technical terminology.
   Trigger: 1. JARGON -ARGON (CHEMISTRY). 2. JARGON- ORGAN (MEDICAL)
   Trigger Sentence: Just as ARGON is the JARGON of Chemistry- ORGAN is the JARGON of Biology.
   Sample Sentence: For a common man understanding the medical *jargon* is like Greek and Latin.

JEJUNE (ji JOON): a. Boring; immature
   Trigger: JEJUNE -JUNE
   Trigger Sentence: JUNE MONTH- holidays for students in India; life's going to be JEJUNE at home.
   Sample Sentence: Without vigor or color, without grace or ornament, her life is *jejunely* basic.

JEOPARDOUS (JEP er dus): a. Dangerous, hazardous
   Trigger: JEOPARDY-LEOPARD
   Trigger Sentence: It is JEOPARDOUS to underestimate the danger from a LEOPARD.
   Sample Sentence: Out of jealousy, she tried to *jeopardize* my chances of getting a job.
   Related Words: JEOPARDIZE - v. put at risk

JETTISON (JET uh sun): v. Throw or discard
   Trigger: 1. JETTISON-REJECT SOME. 2. JET (EJECT-REJECT)
   Trigger Sentence: 1. Let us JETTISON some of the REJECTED cartons into the ocean. Otherwise, our ship may sink. 2. JET JETTISONS the combustion gas and moves forward.
   Sample Sentence: The crew had to *jettison* the suspected cocaine cargo from the ship.

JINGOISM (JING goh iz um): n. Radical patriotism, aggressive chauvinism
   Trigger: JINGOISM -GENGHIS (KHAN)
   Trigger Sentence: GENGHIS KHAN, the Mongol Empire was famed for JINGOISM & PATRIOTISM.

Sample Sentence: When the war began many people were caught up in a wave of *jingoism*.

Related Words: JINGOIST - n. radical patriot; warmonger.

JOCOSE (joh KOHS): a. Playful or humorous

Trigger: JOCOSE–JOKES BOSS

Trigger Sentence: My JOCOSE Boss cuts lot of JOKES

Sample Sentence: Charlie is a *jocose* man who could make the most serious person smile.

Related Words: 1. JOCULAR - a. amusing; funny. 2. JOCUND –a. cheerful; jolly

JUBILATION (joo buh LEY shun): n. Joyfulness

Trigger: JUBILATION-JUBILEE+ CELEBRATION

Trigger Sentence: The JUBILATION/CELEBRATION of the crowd was seen at the silver JUBILEE.

Sample Sentence: This year's world cup victory is indeed an occasion for *jubilation*.

JUDICIOUS (joo DISH us): a. Sound in judgment; wise

Trigger: JUDGE

Trigger Sentence: A JUDGE should possess a JUDICIOUS mind.

Sample Sentence: Plan out your finances *judiciously* now, so as to avoid problems later.

Related Words: INJUDICIOUS - a. unwise

JUGGERNAUT (JUG ur not): n. Irresistible crushing force

Trigger: 1. JAGANNATH-PURI JAGANNATH. 2. JUGGERNAUT -BIGGER SHOT

Trigger Sentence: 1. Lord JAGANNATH chariot or sudarshan chakra was JUGGERNAUT for many rakshas. 2. The JUGGERNAUT is a BIGGER SHOT that destroyed the enemies.

Sample Sentence: The British coined the word *juggernaut* based on chariot of Puri Jagannath!

JUSTIFY (JUHS tuh fy): v. Defend; excuse; vindicate

Trigger: JUSTIFY-JUSTICE

Trigger Sentence: His JUSTICE was stern but absolutely JUSTIFIED.

Sample Sentence: Nice man you may be, but that doesn't *justify* your impulsive abusive behavior.

JUXTAPOSE (JUK stuh pohz): v. Place side by side

Trigger: JUXTAPOSE-OPPOSE (** near antonyms)

Trigger Sentence: JUXTAPOSE-posing side by side; OPPOSE-pose against each other.

Sample Sentence: The play is a tragedy *juxtaposed* in a backdrop of love and war.

KEEN (KEEN): n. sharp; perceptive; intense (of a feeling)

Trigger: KEEN-FINE (* synonyms)

Trigger Sentence: The KEEN pilots possess especially FINE eyesight.

Sample Sentence: He is a *keen* observer of politics, politicians and their policies.

KEN (KEN): n. Range of knowledge

Trigger: 1.KEN-KEEN. 2. KEN-LEARN

Trigger Sentence: 1. She is a KEEN learner. Her KEN is amazing. 2. LEARN according to one's KEN.

Sample Sentence: One develops *ken* over a period of time with experience and good schooling.

Related Words: 1.HEARKEN - v. hear, listen. 2. KEEN –a. sharp; eager

KERNEL (KUR nl): n. Central or vital part

Trigger: KERNEL-KEY + CENTRAL

Trigger Sentence: Make"KE" as"KEY"; KERNEL is KEY and CENTRAL point.

Sample Sentence: The *kernel* of the international monetary system is the US Central Bank.

KINDLE (KIN dl): v. Fire Up, inspire

Trigger: KINDLE-CANDLE

Trigger Sentence: 1. Let us KINDLE the CANDLES. 2. A CANDLE KINDLES hope in darkness.

Sample Sentence: Joe sent flowers and chocolates to *kindle* his chemistry with Pat.

Related Words: REKINDLE - v. revive; kindle again.

KNOTTY (NOT ee): a. Intricate; difficult; tangled

Trigger: KNOTTY

Trigger Sentence: 1. After TIE the KNOT (after marriage is done), the life is going to be KNOTTY-No more naughty. 2. When you KNIT, the problem gets KNOTTY.

Sample Sentence: Too many knots in the murder case make it *knotty* to solve the mystery.

KUDOS (KOO dohz): n. Praise; honor; glory

Trigger: KUDOS-JUDO

Trigger Sentence: The winning JUDO fighter received KUDOS from the Japanese people.

Sample Sentence: *Kudos* to this daredevil judo master and his dedicated pupils!

LABILE (LEY bul): a. Likely to change, unstable

Trigger: 1. LABILE-MOBILE .2. LABILE-"NO STABLE"

Trigger Sentence: LABILE is MOBILE and UNSTABLE. MOBILE phone technology is LABILE because it tends to keep on changing.

Sample Sentence: Let these *labile* times pass by; we shall soon be in a stable situation.

LABYRINTH (LAB uh rinth): n. Complicated network of passages; maze

Trigger: 1. LABYR - (LABOR). 2. LABYRINTHINE-"LAB WIRING LINE"

Trigger Sentence: 1. The String Theory of Universe is so LABYRINTHINE that it is LABORIOUS to understand. 2. In Electrical engineering LAB, WIRING LINE is a LABYRINTH of twists and turns.

Sample Sentence: The airplane's cockpit was a *labyrinth* of switches, wires and controls.

LACHRYMOSE (LAK ruh mohs): a. Tearful

Trigger: LACHRYMOSE —"la +CHRY + mose" -"CHRY-CRY"

Trigger Sentence: LACHRYMOSE things arouse CRY.

Sample Sentence: The second half of the film evolves into a *lachrymose* soap opera.

LACKADAISICAL (lak uh DEY zi kul): a. Listless, lacking energy

Trigger: LACKADAISICAL-"LACK OF ZEAL"

Trigger Sentence: LACK OF ZEAL is known as LACKADAISICAL.

Sample Sentence: They played the game *lackadaisically* due to lack of zeal among the team.

LACKLUSTER (LAK lus tur): a. Dull, mediocre

Trigger: LACK OF LUSTER

Trigger Sentence: The new building looks LACKLUSTER because the colors LACK LUSTER.

Sample Sentence: This theater group gave a *lackluster* portrayal of Shakespeare's play.

Related Words: LUSTROUS –a. shiny; splendid

LACONIC (luh KAHN ik): a. Using few words; brief and to the point

Trigger: LACONIC —"LACK + TONE +IC"

Trigger Sentence: If you LACK TONE and speak only a few words, you will remain LACONIC.

Sample Sentence: Being *laconic* and lucid is a skill where a big theory can be put in a nutshell.

LAITY (LEY i tee): n. People who are not members of the clergy; lay man

Trigger: LAITY-LAY

Trigger Sentence: The LAY people are called LAITY.

Sample Sentence: The *laity* has played an important role in the history of the church.

Related Words: 1.LAY - a. not having expertise; not clerical. 2. LAYMAN - n. someone who is not a clergyman or a professional person.

LAMBASTE (lam BAST): v. Attack verbally; beat

Trigger: LAMBASTE-BLAST

Trigger Sentence: In a VERBAL BLAST the coach LAMBASTED the players for poor performance.

Sample Sentence: The coach *lambasted* his football team for their poor performance.

LAMENT (la MINT): v. Express sorrow; mourn

Trigger: 1.LAMENT-CEMENT. 2. LAMENT-NO ENJOYMENT

Trigger Sentence: 1. When someone buried in CEMENT (cemetery), people express

LAMENT for them. 2. Many fresh employees have LAMENTED about LACK OF ENJOYMENT in the work.

Sample Sentence: The farmers *lamented* over their poor produce of rice crop this season.

LAMPOON (lam POON): v. Ridicule, mock

Trigger: LAMPOON – CARTOON

Trigger Sentence: News paper CARTOONS usually LAMPOON politicians.

Sample Sentence: The comedian *lampooned* the President in a light hearted manner.

LANGUID (LANG gwid): a. Slow; listless; lacking energy

Trigger: LANGUID-LAZY KID

Trigger Sentence: The LAZY KID proceeded in a LANGUID way.

Sample Sentence: The teacher's *languid* ways in teaching English Vocabulary did not help us.

LANGUISH (LANG gwish): v. Grow weak; lose animation

Trigger: LANGUISH-"LAND FISH"

Trigger Sentence: A FISH ON LAND immediately LANGUISHES.

Sample Sentence: We are *languishing* with no challenge or motivation in life, lets rediscover!

Related Words: 1.LANGUOR –n. weakness; apathy. 2. LANGUID –a. lacking energy

LARGESSE (lahr JES): n. Generous gift

Trigger: LARGESSE -LARGENESS

Trigger Sentence: The LARGENESS of his contribution reflects his LARGESSE.

Sample Sentence: The Johnsons' gave their entire *largess* to the animal rescue center.

LASCIVIOUS (luh SIVE ee us): a. Lustful

Trigger: LASCIVIOUS-LUSTY BOYS

Trigger Sentence: The LUSTY BOYS were arrested for their LASCIVIOUS behavior with the girls

Sample Sentence: Women complained against those *lascivious* men who were fired from jobs.

LASSITUDE (LAS uh tood): n. Laziness, Weariness

Trigger: LASSITUDE -LAZY + DUDE

Trigger Sentence: LAZY DUDES carry an attitude of LASSITUDE.

Sample Sentence: Due to hormonal imbalance, Niraja developed *lassitude* and gets tired easily.

LATENT (LAYT nt): a. Hidden; present but not visibly active; dormant

Trigger: LATENT-"LAY-TENT"

Trigger Sentence: 1. The activity of the group is LATENT from the sky because they LAID a TENT over them. 2. Some people TALENTS are LATENT.

Sample Sentence: As her cancer was in *latent* state, no one could make out that she was ill.

LATITUDE (LAT i tood): n. Freedom from narrow limitations

Trigger: LATITUDE —"LATE + ATTITUDE"

Trigger Sentence: If your ATTITUDE is good your boss gives freedom- i.e. LATITUDE. You can go LATE to the office and come LATE from the office.

Sample Sentence: Carla allowed her children a fair amount of *latitude*.

LAUD (LAWD): v. Praise

    Trigger: 1. LAUD-APPLAUD. 2. LAUD-LORD

    Trigger Sentence: 1. O, LORD! Let me LAUD and APPLAUD you for all your help. 2. LAUD, LAUDATORY, LAUDABLE, LAUDATION; belong to same family.

    Sample Sentence: The entire country *lauded* the Olympic champions.

    Related Words: LAUDABLE - n. worthy of praise

LAX (LAKS): a. Careless; loose

    Trigger: LACKS

    Trigger Sentence: He LACKS discipline. He is RELAXED and LAZY

    Sample Sentence: The coach was too *lax* on training, and his team lost shoddily.

    Related Words: LAXITY - n. negligence

LEGITIMIZE (li JIT uh mahyz): v. Make legal; authorize

    Trigger: LEGITIMIZE-LEGALIZE (** synonyms)

    Trigger Sentence: In Uruguay marijuana is LEGITIMIZED/ LEGALIZED.

    Sample Sentence: Marijuana should be *legitimized*.

    Related Words: LITIGANT - a. involved in a law suit.

LETHAL (LEE thul): a. Deadly

    Trigger: LETHAL-DEATH ALL

    Trigger Sentence: A LETHAL dose of drug was injected that caused his DEATH.

    Sample Sentence: The enemies sent a spy to mix a *lethal* medicine in the King's meal.

LETHARGY (LETH er gee): n. Laziness, lack of energy

    Trigger: 1. LETHARGY –LAZY. 2. LETHARGY -NO ENERGY

    Trigger Sentence: A person with LETHARGY is LAZY and possesses NO ENERGY to execute a job.

    Sample Sentence: I get *lethargic* during winters and feel like hibernating like the tortoises!

LEVITY (LEV i tee): n. Lack of seriousness, frivolity

    Trigger: LEVITY-GRAVITY

    Trigger Sentence: GRAVITY means SERIOUSNESS; at GRAVEYARD everyone is SERIOUS and maintains GRAVITY. LEVITY is opposite to GRAVITY.

    Sample Sentence: Our strict science teacher allowed no *levity* until the last day of the school.

    Related Words: GRAVITY – n. seriousness; severity; weight

LIAISON (lee ey ZAWN): n. 1. Secret love affair. 2. A channel for communication between groups

    Trigger: 1. LIAISON-LOVE SON. 2. LINE ON

    Trigger Sentence: 1. In this LOVE story, she acts a LIAISON between my SON and my enemy's daughter. 2. A communication LINE was ON; and it acts a LIAISON with neighboring country.

    Sample Sentence: There is a *liaison* between the two companies in their hand-in-glove dealings.

Memory Test-65 : Match each word and its memory trick to the corresponding definition.

S.N	WORD	MEMORY TRIGGER	S.N	DEFINITIONS	KEY
1	INTIMIDATE	TIMID were INTIMIDATED	A	Absorbing, fascinating	
2	INTOLERANT	Never tolerates	B	Abuse, criticism	
3	INTRACTABLE	Not tractable	C	Accustomed to hardship; habituated	
4	INTRANSIGENT	CONTRA to TRANSFER	D	Attack with words; blame	
5	INTREPID	Not trepid –NOT TIMID	E	Complex, complicated	
6	INTRICATE	Intricate-complicate	F	Brave, fearless	
7	INTRIGUE	In + "trigue" -trick	G	Flood, overflow; overwhelm	
8	INTRIGUING	In trick viewing-interesting	H	Frighten	
9	INTRINSIC	Internal	I	Hard to control; stubborn; unruly	
10	INTROSPECTIVE	Inspect inside	J	Immediate insight; Sixth sense	
11	INTUITION	In + tuition	K	Inherent; built-in; essential	
12	INUNDATE	In under water	L	narrow-minded; bigoted	
13	INURED	In used-GOT USED	M	Opposite	
14	INVALIDATE	Not valid	N	Persuade by flattery	
15	INVALUABLE	Very valuable	O	Plot, arouse the interest	
16	INVASIVE	Invade	P	Self-examining, looking inwards	
17	INVECTIVE	Envy active	Q	Tending to invade; aggressive	
18	INVEIGH	With envy	R	Uncompromising; stubborn	
19	INVEIGLE	Invite+gal	S	Very valuable, priceless	
20	INVERSE	Inverse-reversed	T	Weaken; destroy	

Memory Test-66 : Match each word and its memory trick to the corresponding definition.

S.N	WORD	MEMORY TRIGGER	S.N	DEFINITIONS	KEY
1	INVETERATE	In VETERANS	A	Annoying; tedious	
2	INVIDIOUS	ENVY +odious	B	Call forth; request	
3	INVINCIBLE	NO WIN	C	Complicated; convoluted	
4	INVIOLABLE	Not to violate	D	Contrary outcome of an event, Sarcasm	
5	INVOKE	IN WAKE	E	Deeply rooted, habitual	
6	INVOLVED	Involved-CONVOLUTED	F	Designed to create ill will or envy	
7	IOTA	Iota- DOT	G	Fatigued; tired	
8	IRASCIBLE	irascible-Irritable	H	Faultless, blameless	
9	IRKSOME	Tiresome-irritating some	I	Hot-tempered; irritable	
10	IRONY	No money-full sleep	J	Illogical, lacking reason	
11	IRRATIONAL	Not rational	K	Impossible to conquer	
12	IRRECONCILABLE	Not reconcilable	L	Impossible to violate, incorruptible,	
13	IRREFUTABLE	Irrefutable -INDISPUTABLE	M	Impossible to compromise	
14	IRREPROACHABLE	not IMPEACHABLE	N	Indecisive; uncertain how to act	
15	IRRESOLUTE	Lacking RESOLUTION	O	Lack of respect	
16	IRREVERENCE	Lack of REVERENCE	P	Language used by a special group	
17	ITINERARY	ITINERANT diary	Q	Plan of a trip	
18	JABBER	Chatter-blabber-gibber	R	Small quantity	
19	JADED	faded-fatigued	S	Talk rapidly or clumsily	
20	JARGON	ARGON - JARGON of Chemistry	T	Undeniable; indisputable	

Answers	EX.NO	1	2	3	4	5	6	7	8	9	10	11	12	13	14	15	16	17	18	19	20
	65	H	L	I	R	F	E	O	A	K	P	J	G	C	T	S	Q	B	D	N	M
	66	E	F	K	L	B	C	R	I	A	D	J	M	T	H	N	O	Q	S	G	P

Memory Test-67 : Match each word and its memory trick to the corresponding definition.

S.N	WORD	MEMORY TRIGGER	S.N	DEFINITIONS	KEY
1	JEJUNE	JUNE in India	A	Central or vital part	
2	JEOPARDOUS	LEOPARD is behind	B	Boring; immature	
3	JETTISON	REJECT SOME	C	Complicated network of passages	
4	JINGOISM	GENGHIS (KHAN) wars	D	Dangerous, hazardous	
5	JOCOSE	Jokes boss	E	Defend; excuse; vindicate	
6	JUBILATION	Jubilee+ celebration	F	Fire Up, inspire	
7	JUDICIOUS	JUDGE is	G	Intricate; difficult; tangled	
8	JUGGERNAUT	BIGGER SHOT	H	Irresistible crushing force	
9	JUSTIFY	JUSTICE is done	I	Joyfulness	
10	JUXTAPOSE	JUXTAPOSE-OPPOSE	J	Likely to change, unstable	
11	KEEN	FINE perception	K	Listless, lacking energy	
12	KEN	LEARN - KEN	L	Place side by side	
13	KERNEL	KEY + CENTRAL	M	Playful or humorous	
14	KINDLE	A CANDLE KINDLES	N	Praise; honor; glory	
15	KNOTTY	TIE the KNOT	O	Radical patriotism	
16	KUDOS	JUDO received KUDOS	P	Range of knowledge	
17	LABILE	NO STABLE	Q	Sharp; perceptive	
18	LABYRINTH	LAB WIRING LINE	R	Sound in judgment; wise	
19	LACHRYMOSE	la+CHRY+mose-cry	S	Tearful	
20	LACKADAISICAL	Lack of zeal	T	Throw or discard	

Memory Test-68 : Match each word and its memory trick to the corresponding definition.

S.N	WORD	MEMORY TRIGGER	S.N	DEFINITIONS	KEY
1	LACKLUSTER	Lack of luster	A	Attack verbally; beat	
2	LACONIC	Lack + tone	B	Careless; loose	
3	LAITY	LAY people are called LAITY	C	Deadly	
4	LAMBASTE	Blast verbally	D	Dull, mediocre	
5	LAMENT	Buried in CEMENT	E	Express sorrow; mourn	
6	LAMPOON	CARTOON	F	Freedom from narrow limitations	
7	LANGUID	Lazy kid	G	Generous gift	
8	LANGUISH	Land fish	H	Grow weak; lose animation	
9	LARGESSE	LARGENESS	I	Hidden; present but not visibly active	
10	LASCIVIOUS	lusty boys	J	Lack of seriousness, frivolity	
11	LASSITUDE	Lazy + dude	K	Lay man; everyone except clergy	
12	LATENT	Lay-tent	L	Laziness, lack of energy	
13	LATITUDE	Late + attitude	M	Laziness, Weariness	
14	LAUD	APPLAUD	N	Lustful	
15	LAX	RELAXED and LAZY	O	Make legal; authorize	
16	LEGITIMIZE	LEGALIZE	P	Praise	
17	LETHAL	DEATH ALL	Q	Ridicule, mock	
18	LETHARGY	Lazy--no energy	R	Secret love affair; channel for contact	
19	LEVITY	Opp. To GRAVITY	S	Slow; listless; lacking energy	
20	LIAISON	Love son- Line on	T	Using few words; brief	

Answers

EX.NO	1	2	3	4	5	6	7	8	9	10	11	12	13	14	15	16	17	18	19	20
67	B	D	T	O	M	I	R	H	E	L	Q	P	A	F	G	N	J	C	S	K
68	D	T	K	A	E	Q	S	H	G	N	M	I	F	P	B	O	C	L	J	R

WORD GROUPS DAY-17

★ ARCHAIC-OLD- OUTDATED

ADJECTIVES: ancient, antediluvian, bygone, fusty, obsolete, old-fashioned, outmoded, anachronistic, antiquated, primitive, superannuated, defunct, passé, dowdy

NOUNS: archaism

VERB: antiquate, outdate, obsolete.

ANTONYMS: adj. current, modern, new, present, young

★ MODERN

ADJECTIVES: avant-garde, coincident, concomitant, concurrent, contemporary, current, cutting-edge, latest, modernistic, modernized, modish, neoteric, newfangled, novel, prevailing, prevalent

NOUNS: vogue, trend, fad

VERB: regenerate, rejuvenate, renew, renovate, revamp, revive, update

ANTONYMS: adj. ancient, antiquated, obsolete, old-fashioned, outdated, passe

★ SECRET/SECRETIVE

ADJECTIVES: clandestine, covert, undercover, underground, surreptitious, stealthy, furtive, closet

NOUNS: privacy, secrecy ; confidentiality

VERB: cloak, conceal, veil, mask, shroud, envelop

ANTONYMS: adj. overt, public

★ OPEN-OBVIOUS

ADJECTIVES: apparent, definite, manifest, observable, open, patent, public, undisguised, visible; barefaced; blatant;

NOUNS: overtness

VERB: disclose, divulge, uncover

ANTONYMS: adj. concealed, hidden, private, secret

★ SUMMIT-PEAK

ADJECTIVES: vertical, sublime, supreme, topmost.

NOUNS: acme, apex, apogee, crest, crown, peak, pinnacle, summit, vertex, zenith.

VERB: climax, culminate, peak, surmount.

ANTONYMS: n.nadir, abyss, base.

★ AVOID-EVASIVE

ADJECTIVES: evasive, elusive

NOUNS: evasion, shunning

VERB: avert, elude, evade, dodge, hedge, shirk, skirt, escape; shun, abstain, refrain, eschew, desist

ANTONYMS: v.confront, seek, welcome.

★ CONFRONT/FACE/TOLERATE

ADJECTIVES: sustainable

NOUNS: confrontation

VERB: abide, accost, bear, brace, brave, brook, challenge, confront, contend, cope with, countenance, court, dare, deal with, defy, encounter, endure, meet, oppose, stomach, sustain, take, take it, tolerate, venture, withstand

ANTONYMS: v. avoid, retreat, run, withdraw

TANTALIZING muffin!

and they say ~ i eat like a GLUTTON... pig !

Word List Day-18

LIBERTINE (LIB ur teen): a. Debauchee; immoral person

    Trigger: 1. LIBERTINE –"LIBERTY + IN". 2. LIBIDINOUS.

    Trigger Sentence: 1. A LIBERTINE indulges LIBERTY-IN illicit relationships. 2. A LIBERTINE possesses LIBIDINOUS behavior.

    Sample Sentence: Don Juan could be considered a *libertine* as the story is told.

LICENTIOUS (lye SEN shus): a. Immoral; especially sexually unrestrained

    Trigger: 1. LICENTIOUS-LICENSE. 2. LIKE SENSUOUS.

    Trigger Sentence: LICENTIOUS person LIKES SENSUOUS pleasures; feels he has LICENSE for LUST.

    Sample Sentence: Because of his *licentious* behavior his wife seeks for a divorce.

    Related Words: LICENSE –n. freedom; permit

LIMN (LIM): v. Describe; outline

    Trigger: 1.LIMN-LINE. 2. LIMN-FILM

    Trigger Sentence: The FILM LIMNS a girl and OUTLINES her dark side of the life.

    Sample Sentence: The commentary *limns* the life of Mahatma Gandhi's freedom struggle.

LIMPID (LIM pid): a. Clear; Lucid

    Trigger: 1.LIMPID – LAMPED. 2. LIMPID -LIQUID

    Trigger Sentence: 1. We LAMPED the room it became LIMPID. 2. This pure LIQUID looks LIMPID.

    Sample Sentence: As editor, my work becomes easy with my journo submitting *limpid* reports.

LINGER (LING ger): v. Stay longer than usual; loiter; dawdle

    Trigger: 1.LINGER-LONGER. 2. LINGER-LOITER

    Trigger Sentence: 1. To LINGER is to take LONGER time. 2. LINGER and LOITER are synonyms.

    Sample Sentence: The longer you *linger*, more the time you will be wasting!

LIONIZE (LIE uh nize): v. Treat as a celebrity

    Trigger: LIONIZE

    Trigger Sentence: Treating a hero like A LION; In LION KING movie the LION was LIONIZED.

    Sample Sentence: The Lion's Club has *lionized* him as the savior of the nation.

LISTLESS (LIST lis): a. Lacking spirit or energy

    Trigger: LIST + LESS-"LIFELESS"-"SPIRITLESS"

    Trigger Sentence: If the leader himself becomes SPIRITLESS, the followers will become LISTLESS.

    Sample Sentence: The recession has left people *listless* and lifeless.

LITERAL (LIT erul): a. Factual; accurate; relating to or expressed in letters

    Trigger: LITERAL-LETTER

    Trigger Sentence: In a LITERAL translation of the article everything was explained with corresponding LETTER to LETTER with the original.

Sample Sentence: I was reading the *literal* translation of the book.

Related Words: 1.LITERATI - n. scholarly people, educated people. 2. LITERARY - a. relating to literature; scholarly, educated

LOATH (LOHTH): a. Reluctant; averse

Trigger: 1. LOATH-NO OATH. 2. LOATH-LOW

Trigger Sentence: 1. I DON'T take OATH, since I LOATH to take oath. 2. When you LOATH someone, you will show LOW opinion on them.

Sample Sentence: It was a *loathsome* experience to use those unclean public toilets!

Related Words: LOATHE - v. hate, detest

LOATHE (LOHTH): v. Dislike; abhor

Trigger: LOATHE-LOVETH

Trigger Sentence: LOATHE (hate) and LOVETH (love) are antonyms.

Sample Sentence: We *loathe* each other and can't stand eye to eye!

LONGEVITY (lon JEV i tee): v. Long life; length of life

Trigger: LONGEVITY-LONG LIFE

Trigger Sentence: The LONGEVITY of tires depends on how LONG and what LENGTH the car is driven.

Sample Sentence: With increasing *longevity*, we will lead retired life more than half of our lives!

LONGING (LAWNG ing): a. Having a strong desire for something

Trigger: LONGING-LOVING

Trigger Sentence: The LOVING boy friend LONGING for his girl friend.

Sample Sentence: People were *longing* for freedom in those long, long days of slavery.

LOQUACIOUS (lo KWAY shus): a. Extremely talkative

Trigger: 1.LOQ-LOCK. 2. LOQ-TALK

Trigger Sentence: LOCK your mouth. I can't bear your LOQUACITY.

Sample Sentence: The *loquacious* bride could not stop talking even during the wedding.

Related Words: LOQUACITY - n. talkativeness

LUCID (LOO sid): a. Clear, easily understood

Trigger: LUC+ID-"LOOK + ID"

Trigger Sentence: 1. If you LOOK at my ID, it will become LUCID that I am an employee of Microsoft. 2. LUCENT bulbs give brightness and so everything will be LUCID and clear.

Sample Sentence: Her poetry is *lucid* with lovely simple metaphors.

LUCRATIVE (LOO kruh tiv): a. Profitable

Trigger: 1. LUCRE-LOCKER. 2. LUCRATIVE-CREATIVE

Trigger Sentence: 1. This world belongs to LUCRE- (bank LOCKER where we keep MONEY). 2. CREATIVE jobs are LUCRATIVE and REMUNERATIVE.

Sample Sentence: His creative portrait will fetch him a *lucrative* price.

Related Words: LUCRE –n. money; profit

LUDICROUS (LOO di krus): a. Laughable; nonsensical

Trigger: LUDICROUS-RIDICULOUS (**synonyms)

Trigger Sentence: It is RIDICULOUS that the LUDICROUS actor has been named for an Oscar.

Sample Sentence: The charges against him were almost *ludicrous* and mind-boggling.

Related Words: ABSURD –a. ridiculous; nonsensical

LUGUBRIOUS (loo GOO bree us): a. Sad, sorrowful

Trigger: LUGUBRIOUS-LOOK +BURIALS

Trigger Sentence: I feel LUGUBRIOUS whenever I LOOK at the BURIAL ground.

Sample Sentence: His themes and style of writing is *lugubriously* long, worn-down and numbing.

LULL (LUHL): a. Temporary period of calm

Trigger: 1. LULL-DULL. 2. LULL-LULLABY. 2. The phrase: "Lull before the storm".

Trigger Sentence: 1. Sing a LULLABY to LULL baby to sleep. 2. In a LULL market, business is DULL.

Sample Sentence: It can bring us to tears or to our feet, drive us into battle or *lull* us to sleep...

LUMINOUS (LOO muh nus): a. Shining, issuing light

Trigger: LUMINOUS-ILLUMINATION

Trigger Sentence: The LUMINOUS electric lights have ILLUMINATED the arena.

Sample Sentence: My travel alarm clock is so *luminous* that it lights up my tent in the dark.

LURE (LOOR): v. Temp; entice; bait

Trigger: 1.LURE- LOVER. 2. LURE-LUST

Trigger Sentence: 1. She LURED me to fall in LOVE. 2. LUST for gold LURED her into smuggling.

Sample Sentence: You are trying to *lure* me with bribes; I will not budge an inch.

Related Words: ALLURE –v. tempt; attract

LURID (LOOR id): a. Shocking; sensational; graphic

Trigger: 1. LURID-HORRID-HORRIBLE. 2. LURID-LOOK RED-LOOK BLOOD RED

Trigger Sentence: 1. The LURID book of Dan Brown was received with a HORRID feeling in North America and Europe. 2. The portrait LOOKED LURID because it was painted with RED BLOOD.

Sample Sentence: She is loud and *lurid*. Well, she is an artist with an attitude!

LURK (LURK): v. Lie in wait; exist unobserved

Trigger: LURK- DARK (**LIE in DARK)

Trigger Sentence: She could tell there was someone out there LURKING in the DARK shadows.

Sample Sentence: She is well outwardly, yet her health issues seem to *lurk* under the surface.

LUSH (LUHSH): a. Rich, luxurious; full of plant growth

Trigger: LUSH-LAVISH (** synonyms)

Trigger Sentence: I always wanted live on a LUSH/LAVISH Kerala country side landscape.

Sample Sentence: The Amazon rain forest is *lush* with vegetation.

LUSTROUS (LUHS trus): a. Shiny, glossy

Trigger: LUSTROUS-LUMINOUS

Trigger Sentence: Silver is LUSTROUS and becomes LUMINOUS (illumines) under moonlight.

Sample Sentence: My black horse had *lustrous* long mane.

LUXURIANT (luhk SHOOR ee unt): a. Abundant; rich; fertile

    Trigger: LUXURIANT-LUXURIOUS.

    Trigger Sentence: The LUXURIOUS house is home to LUXURIANT gardens.

    Sample Sentence: South Africa is home to *luxuriant* forests and wild life.

MACABRE (muh KAH ber): a. Horrifying; Ghastly

    Trigger: MACABRE -MASSACRE

    Trigger Sentence: The MACABRE movie is full of MASSACRE.

    Sample Sentence: The novel is a *macabre* story of murder and madness.

MACERATE (MAS uh rayt): v. Soften or break up (food) by soaking in a liquid.

    Trigger: 1. MACERATE-MARINATE. 2. MACERATE-SATURATE (** synonyms)

    Trigger Sentence: 1. Leave the beef to MARINATE overnight. Then it will become MACERATED. 2. MACERATED food is SATURATED with water.

    Sample Sentence: Toilet paper is designed to *macerate* in water.

MACHIAVELLIAN (mak ee uh VEL ee un): n. a. Cunning, scheming

    Trigger: MACHIAVELLIAN - MAFIA + VILLAIN

    Trigger Sentence: MAFIA VILLAINS follow MACHIAVELLIAN methods for underground activities.

    Sample Sentence: History shows countless *Machiavellian* battles due to lust for power.

MACHINATION (mak uh NAY shun): n. Evil schemes, conspiracy

    Trigger: 1.MACHINE GUN. 2. MACHINATION-MACHIAVELLIAN

    Trigger Sentence: 1. The terrorists with MACHINE GUNS conceived a MACHINATION to destroy the NATIONS. 2. People with MACHIAVELLIAN minds keep working on MACHINATIONS.

    Sample Sentence: Can peace prevail if *machination* and meanness penetrates into the society?

MAELSTROM (MEYL strum): n. Whirlpool; commotion

    Trigger: MAELSTROM-STORM (**synonyms)

    Trigger Sentence: Due to STORM the ship was drawn into the MAELSTROM.

    Sample Sentence: I was caught in the *maelstrom* of the office hour traffic jam.

MAGISTERIAL (maj uh STEER ee ul): a. Authoritative; domineering

    Trigger: MAGISTERIAL -MAGISTRATE

Trigger Sentence: The MAGISTRATE has a MAGISTERIAL voice.

Sample Sentence: He spoke with a *magisterial* tone silencing almost everyone in the hall!

MAGNANIMOUS (mag NAN uh mus): a. Generous or forgiving

Trigger: MAGNANIMOUS —"MEGA + GENEROUS"

Trigger Sentence: The MAGNANIMOUS man helped people with MEGA GENEROUS donations.

Sample Sentence: `Caring Hands for Animals' is a group of activists who *magnanimously* spend their earnings for animal rescue.

Related Words: 1.MAGNANIMITY - n. generosity. 2.MAGNIFY –v. increase the size of; enlarge

MAGNILOQUENT (mag NIL uh kwunt): a. Boastful; pompous

Trigger: MAGNILOQUENT —"MEGA + ELOQUENT"

Trigger Sentence: Only MAGNILOQUENT leaders with MEGA ELOQUENCE can attract followers.

Sample Sentence: My aunt *magniloquently*, rather vulgarly displays her wealth.

MALADROIT (mal uh DROIT): a. Clumsy, bungling; tactless

Trigger: MAL (BAD) + ADROIT

Trigger Sentence: 1. A MALADROIT- CANNOT DRAW. 2. ADROIT- He can DRAW IT. He is an EXPERT.

Sample Sentence: What made you employ this *maladroit* of a man?! Messing is what he can do.

Related Words: ADROIT - a. clever or skillful.

MALEVOLENT (ma LEVO lunt): a. Evil; harmful

Trigger: MALEVOLENT-"MALE + VIOLENT"

Trigger Sentence: VIOLENT MALES tend to possess MALEVOLENT nature.

Sample Sentence: People who are *malevolent* in nature are generally incompetent!

Related Words: MALIGNANT - a. evil; malevolent

MALFEASANCE (mal FEE zunce): n. Wrongdoing

Trigger: 1.MALFEASANCE-MALPRACTICE. 2. MAL+FEASIBLE

Trigger Sentence: 1. The politician is blamed for MALFEASANCE for involving in MALPRACTICE. 2. FEASIBLE is DOABLE; but if it is WRONGDOING then it is called MALFEASANCE.

Sample Sentence: The mayor is at fault of *malfeasance* for giving contracts to his kin's company.

MALICE (MAL is): n. Ill-will, desire to harm another

Trigger: 1. MAL (bad) + LIES. 2. maLICE-LICE

Trigger Sentence: 1. Don't tell LIES with MALICE. 2. Don't live a MALICIOUS life like LICE.

Sample Sentence: I wonder why she developed *malice* against me, with no fault of mine.

Related Words: MALICIOUS - a. hateful; spiteful

MALIGN (muh LINE): adv. Speak evil of; bad mouth; defame

Trigger: MALIGN-"MAL+LIE+N"

Trigger Sentence: They told him all LIES and MALIGNED his mind.

Sample Sentence: Sheela was wrongfully *maligned* for indulging in a secret affair!

Related Words: MALIGNANT - a. evil; malevolent

MALINGER (muh LING ger): v. Fake illness to escape duty

Trigger: 1.MALINGER-BEGGER. 2. MAL+LINGER

Trigger Sentence: 1. A BEGGAR tends to be a MALINGERER because he finds excuses not to work. 2. A MALINGERER aimlessly LINGERS around to avoid doing serious work.

Sample Sentence: Judie often *malingers* to escape from her work.

Related Words: MALINGERER - n. one who pretends illness to escape duty

MALLEABLE (MAL ee uh bull): a. Flexible; adaptable

Trigger: 1.MALLEABLE-MOLDABLE. 2. MALLEABLE-FLEXIBLE

Trigger Sentence: 1. A MALLEABLE metal is easily MOLDABLE into a shape of your choice. 2. My boss is MALLEABLE. My work timings are quite FLEXIBLE.

Sample Sentence: The sculptor gave *malleable* metal and modeling clay to his students.

MANACLE (MAN uh kul): v. Restrain, Control

Trigger: MANACLE-MAN SHACKLE - MAN BUCKLE

Trigger Sentence: 1. The violent MAN was SHACKLED to a MANACLE. 2. BUCKLE this MAN'S wrists to MANACLE.

Sample Sentence: It is difficult to *manacle* my heavy powerful dog while I go walking with him.

MANDATE (MAN deyt): n. Order; charge

Trigger: MANDATE-MAND-COMMAND

Trigger Sentence: As a MANDATE the chancellor of the university COMMANDED regular tests.

Sample Sentence: It's *mandatory* that we must obey our boss.

Related Words: MANDATORY - a. obligatory

MANIFEST (MAN ih fest): a. Clear; obvious; visible

Trigger: 1.MANY FESTS. 2. MANIFESTO

Trigger Sentence: 1. MANY FESTS MANIFEST FESTIVE atmosphere. 2. The party's interests are MANIFESTED in an election MANIFESTO.

Sample Sentence: If you think positive, positivity will *manifest* in your life!

Related Words: MANIFESTO - a. declaration; statement of policy

MANIFOLD (MAN uh fowld): a. Many and various

Trigger: MANIFOLD - MANY FOLD

Trigger Sentence: There are MANIFOLD of opportunities in medical field.

Sample Sentence: Nanotechnology is *manifold*, multifaceted subject.

MARGINAL (MAR jih nul): a. Unimportant; borderline

Trigger: 1. MARGINAL-MARGIN. 2. MARGINAL-MINIMAL (**synonyms)

Trigger Sentence: Rough jots on the MARGIN of the page are of MARGINAL/MINIMAL value.

Sample Sentence: His diabetic condition is rather *marginal,* so not to worry.

MARRED (MAWRED): a. Damaged

Trigger: 1.MAR- SCAR. 2. MARRED-SCARRED

Trigger Sentence: The SCARS MARRED her beauty.

Sample Sentence: The pristine beauty of this lake is *marred* by people throwing plastic.

MARSH (MAHRSH): n. Soft wet land; morass

Trigger: 1. MARSH-MARINE. 2. MARSH-MARS

Trigger Sentence: 1. All MARINE lands are MARSH i.e. very wet and soft. 2. There is NO MARSH land on MARS because there is no water on its surface.

Sample Sentence: The *marshes* along the coast line support a plethora of plant life.

MARTINET (mart in ET): n. Strict disciplinarian

Trigger: MARTINET

Trigger Sentence: MARTIAL arts people and military MARSHALS are MARTINETS; STRICT.

Sample Sentence: The commanding officer is a *martinet* to the core.

MATERIALISM (muh TEER ee uh liz um): n. Desire for material riches with no spiritual concern

Trigger: 1. MATERIALISTIC. 2. "I am a Material Girl...." song by Madonna.

Trigger Sentence: MATERIALIST believes that physical comfort is the highest value

Sample Sentence: The modern society is preoccupied with *materialism;* it wants is money!

MATRIARCH (MEY tree ahrk): n. Female head of a family or tribe

Trigger: 1. MAA ARCH- JOAN OF ARC. 2. MATRI (MATA- MA); ARCH-RULE

Trigger Sentence: 1. JOAN OF ARC is the story of a MATRIARCH. 2. (MA) RULES; it is called MATRIARCHY. Patriarchy, matriarchy, oligarchy, anarchy, monarchy and hierarchy are related to ruling family.

Sample Sentence: She was the family's respected and elegant *matriarch*.

MAUDLIN (MAWD lin): a. Excessively sentimental

Trigger: 1.MAA. 2. MARY MAGDALENE

Trigger Sentence: 1. My MAA is usually MAUDLIN. 2. MAUDLIN sense derives from images of Mary MAGDALENE in weeping posture.

Sample Sentence: She became *maudlin* and started crying like a vulnerable baby.

MAVERICK (MAV rik): n. Rebel; nonconformist

Trigger: MAVERICK- RICKY MARTIN

Trigger Sentence: RICKY (MARTIN) was MAVERICK singer and dancer. He declared himself a gay.

Sample Sentence: Michael Jackson was known for his *maverick* sense of dressing!

MAWKISH (MAW kish): a. Overly sentimental

Trigger: MAWKISH —"MA + KISS"

Trigger Sentence: I am MAWKISH about receiving my MA's KISS before writing an exam.

Sample Sentence: My mom is so *mawkish* that whenever I go abroad, she cries!

MEAGER (MEE ger): a. Scanty; inadequate

Trigger: 1. MEAGER-NOT MAJOR-MINOR. 2. MEAGER- MISER

Trigger Sentence: 1. This MEAGER amount is enough to start this MINOR venture. 2. He is a MISER and lives with MEAGER means.

Sample Sentence: Padnil forgot all her *meager* beginning as a girl from a beggars' family.

Related Words: MISER –n. one who is stingy with money and is miserable

MEDIOCRE (mee dee OH kur): a. Ordinary; common place

   Trigger: 1. MEDIOCRE-MEDIUM LEVEL. 2. MEDIOCRITY-MEDIUM QUALITY

   Trigger Sentence: MEDIUM LEVEL in quality, performance, value or ability is called MEDIOCRE.

   Sample Sentence: In a *mediocre* society, uncreative people manage to make it big!

MEEK (MEEK): a. Timid; humble; submissive

   Trigger: MEEK-WEAK (**weak hearted)

   Trigger Sentence: She may seem WEAK and MEEK but it is all an act.

   Sample Sentence: She is rather a *meek* child dominated by her big brothers.

MELANCHOLY (MEL un kahl ee): n. Gloomy; morose

   Trigger: MELANCHOLIC-ALCOHOLIC

   Trigger Sentence: With an ALCOHOLIC husband, she always lives in MELANCHOLIC state.

   Sample Sentence: Many men try to forget their *melancholy* by consuming alcohol.

MELLIFLUOUS (meh LIF loo us): a. Sweetly flowing, melodious

   Trigger: MELLIFLUOUS-MELODIOUS FLOW

   Trigger Sentence: A MELLIFLUOUS song is MELODIOUS.

   Sample Sentence: The ringing of the church bells let off a *mellifluous* resonance in air.

MEMOIR (MEM wahr): n. Life story, autobiography, biography

   Trigger: MEMOIR-MEMORY

   Trigger Sentence: MEMOIR is a history created from personal experience and MEMORY.

   Sample Sentence: He has written a *memoir* of Bollywood in the 1950s.

MENACING (MEN is ing): a. Dangerous; threatening

   Trigger: 1.MENACE-MINUS. 2. MENACE sounds like MINUS

   Trigger Sentence: This underworld atmosphere is full of MENACE or MINUS SIGNS.

   Sample Sentence: Minus marks are *menacing* problems for many objective test takers.

   Related Words: MENACE - v. threaten, endanger

MENDACITY (men DAS i tee): n. Untruthfulness; dishonesty

   Trigger: MENDACITY-"MEN IN CITY"

   Trigger Sentence: 1. MEN IN CITY usually possess MENDACITY. 2. Cab MEN IN our CITY are notorious for their MENDACITY.

   Sample Sentence: It is only your *mendacity* that is not letting you join hands with us.

   Related Words: MENDACIOUS –a. deceptive; false

MENDICANT (MEN di kunt): n. Beggar

   Trigger: MENDICANT-"SPEND I CAN'T"

   Trigger Sentence: A MENDICANT says "SPEND I CAN'T"; I CAN'T SPEND anything, I am a beggar.

   Sample Sentence: The monks usually lead a *mendicant* life style.

MENIAL (MEE nee uhl): n. Servile; suitable for servants; mean

   Trigger: MENIAL-MANUAL labor

   Trigger Sentence: The MANUAL LABOR was employed to do MENIAL works.

   Sample Sentence: I was paid *menially* as a teacher in the government school.

MERCANTILE (MUR kun teel): a. Relating to trade or commerce

Trigger: MERCANTILE-MERCHANT

Trigger Sentence: MERCANTILE system is related to the MERCHANTS.

Sample Sentence: *Mercantile* needs were the main cause of migrations in the world!

Related Words: MERCENARY –n. Money oriented; marked by materialism

MERCURIAL (mur KYOOR ee ul): a. Capricious, changing; fickle

Trigger: MERCURIAL -MERCURY LEVEL

Trigger Sentence: MERCURY LEVEL in a thermometer is not stationary. It is MERCURIAL.

Sample Sentence: John's *mercurial* approach is not helping our project, so consider firing him.

MERETRICIOUS (mer uh TRISH us): a. Falsely attractive; tempting in a vulgar way

Trigger: MERETRICIOUS–MERIT TRICK US

Trigger Sentence: The MERETRICIOUS MERIT certificates given in schools TRICKS US to believe that we were great!

Sample Sentence: The carnival saw *meretriciously* cross dressed men in a procession.

METAMORPHOSIS (met uh MOR fuh sis): n. A complete change in form or nature

Trigger: MORPH

Trigger Sentence: Butterfly larva MORPHS itself several times before it makes a total METAMORPHOSIS into a butterfly.

Sample Sentence: Sohila was a tomboy, but soon she *metamorphosed* into a savvy young lady.

METAPHOR (MET uh fer): n. Figurative language; symbolic

Trigger: METAPHOR-"MEGASTAR-SUPERSTAR"

Trigger Sentence: The title 'MEGASTAR' is a METAPHOR. In METAPHORICAL language a human being is represented with other forms. It is also known as a FIGURATIVE LANGUAGE.

Sample Sentence: Her poems are complete with imaginative *metaphors*.

METAPHYSICS (met uh FIZ iks): n. The study of ultimate reality

Trigger: METAPHYSICS–MEDITATION PHYSICS

Trigger Sentence: The philosopher's MEDITATION on PHYSICS finally resulted in METAPHYSICS.

Sample Sentence: The mode of thought which dominates the modern capitalist philosophy and science is called the *metaphysics*.

METE (MEET): v. Divide and distribute, allot

Trigger: 1. METE-METER. 2. METE-MEAT

Trigger Sentence: With measuring METER the mother METED out MEAT to the kids.

Sample Sentence: The sergeant *meted* out arms and ammunition to the soldiers.

METEORIC (mee tee AWR ik): a. Fast and brilliant

Trigger: METEORIC-METEOR LIKE

Trigger Sentence: The METEORIC rise to fame was because of his METEOR LIKE brilliance.

Sample Sentence: We all wondered at his *meteoric* rise to fame.

METICULOUS (meh TIK yuh lus): a. Very careful and precise

   Trigger: 1.METICUL-METHODICAL. 2. METICULOUS- MORE ACCURATE

   Trigger Sentence: 1. METICULOUS is METHODICAL. 2. METICULOUS people insist ACCURACY.

   Sample Sentence: He is very *meticulous* about keeping his wardrobe clean and tidy.

METTLE (MET l): n. Courage; spirit

   Trigger: 1. METTLE-MEN BATTLE. 2. METTLE-MEDAL

   Trigger Sentence: 1. MEN showed METTLE in BATTLE. 2. MEDAL for his METTLE in BATTLE.

   Sample Sentence: The competition will test her *mettle* and persistence.

MIASMA (my AZ muh): n. Unhealthy poisonous vapor; unpleasant atmosphere

   Trigger: MIASMA-MY ASTHMA.

   Trigger Sentence: MY ASTHMA was due to MIASMA of cigar smoke.

   Sample Sentence: A *miasma* of tobacco smoke suffused the crowded bar.

MICROCOSM (MAHY kruh koz um): n. Small world; miniature of the universe

   Trigger: MICROCOSM-MICRO+COSMOS

   Trigger Sentence: MICRO means SMALL; COSMOS means UNIVERSE.

   Sample Sentence: The web has become a *microcosm* of our society.

MIDST (MIDST): n. Middle, core

   Trigger: MIDST-MIDDLE

   Trigger Sentence: We are in the MIDDLE of (MIDST of) remodeling our house.

   Sample Sentence: We were in the *midst* of the jungle when it started to rain.

MILIEU (mil YOO): n. Surroundings; means of expression

   Trigger: MILIEU – MY VIEW

   Trigger Sentence: In MY VIEW the big city offers intellectual MILIEU for innovative artists thrive.

   Sample Sentence: Family *milieu* has a significant impact on a child's development.

MINISCULE (MIN us kyool): a. Tiny, very small

   Trigger: MINUSCULE-"MINI-MOLECULE"

   Trigger Sentence: MINI MOLECULE is VERY SMALL.

   Sample Sentence: The subject of Nanotechnology deals with *miniscule* molecules.

MINATORY (MIN uh tohr ee): a. Threatening, menacing

   Trigger: MINATOR-MAN EATER

   Trigger Sentence: MAN EATER tiger is MINATORY.

   Sample Sentence: Jim Corbett shot a *minatory* man eater.

MINUTIAE (mi NOO shee uh): n. A small detail; petty matters

   Trigger: MINUTIAE —"MINUTE-MINI"

   Trigger Sentence: MINI DETAILS are known as MINUTIAE.

   Sample Sentence: If you make fuss on such *minutiae*, your stature in the eyes of your employees will become minute.

   Related Words: 1.MINIMAL - a. very small; least possible. 2. MINISCULE –a. very small. 3. MINUTE –a. tiny .4. MINION - n. slavish servant

Memory Test-69 : Match each word and its memory trick to the corresponding definition.

S.N	WORD	MEMORY TRIGGER	S.N	DEFINITIONS	KEY
1	LIBERTINE	Liberty in LUST	A	Clear, easily understood	
2	LICENTIOUS	Like sensuous plesures	B	Clear; Lucid	
3	LIMN	Line-film	C	Debauchee; immoral person	
4	LIMPID	LAMPED	D	Describe; outline	
5	LINGER	Longer -loiter	E	Dislike; abhor	
6	LIONIZE	You are LION king	F	Extremely talkative	
7	LISTLESS	Lifeless-spiritless	G	Factual; expressed in letters	
8	LITERAL	LETTER	H	Having a strong desire	
9	LOATH	NO to oath	I	Immoral; especially sexually	
10	LOATHE	LOATHE-LOVETH	J	Lacking spirit or energy	
11	LONGEVITY	long life	K	Laughable; nonsensical	
12	LONGING	LOVING to have	L	Long life; length of life	
13	LOQUACIOUS	LOCK-TALK	M	Profitable	
14	LUCID	LOOK + id .	N	Reluctant; averse	
15	LUCRATIVE	LUCRE in LOCKER	O	Sad, sorrowful	
16	LUDICROUS	RIDICULOUS	P	Shining, issuing light	
17	LUGUBRIOUS	look +burials	Q	Stay longer than usual; loiter	
18	LULL	Lull-dull; Lull-lullaby	R	Tempt; entice; bait	
19	LUMINOUS	ILLUMINATION	S	Temporary period of calm	
20	LURE	Lover lured me	T	Treat as a celebrity	

Memory Test-70 : Match each word and its memory trick to the corresponding definition.

S.N	WORD	MEMORY TRIGGER	S.N	DEFINITIONS	KEY
1	LURID	look red-look blood red	A	Authoritative; domineering	
2	LURK	LIE in DARK	B	Boastful; pompous	
3	LUSH	Lush-LAVISH	C	Clumsy, bungling; tactless	
4	LUSTROUS	LUMINOUS	D	Conspiracy , evil schemes	
5	LUXURIANT	LUXURIOUS	E	Cunning, scheming	
6	MACABRE	full of MASSACRE	F	Evil; harmful	
7	MACERATE	Marinate -saturate	G	Fake illness to escape duty	
8	MACHIAVELLIAN	Mafia + villain	H	Flexible; adaptable	
9	MACHINATION	Machine gun plot	I	Generous or forgiving	
10	MAELSTROM	STORM	J	Horrifying; Ghastly	
11	MAGISTERIAL	MAGISTRATE voice	K	Ill-will, desire to harm another	
12	MAGNANIMOUS	Mega + generous	L	Lie in wait; exist unobserved	
13	MAGNILOQUENT	Mega + ELOQUENT	M	Luxurious; full of plant growth	
14	MALADROIT	CANNOT DRAW it	N	Rich; abundant; fertile	
15	MALEVOLENT	Male + violent	O	Shiny, glossy	
16	MALFEASANCE	MALPRACTICE	P	Shocking; sensational; graphic	
17	MALICE	MAL (bad) + LIES	Q	Soften by soaking in a liquid	
18	MALIGN	Mal+LIE+n	R	Speak evil of; bad mouth; defame	
19	MALINGER	Beggar nature	S	Whirlpool; commotion	
20	MALLEABLE	Moldable -FLEXIBLE	T	Wrongdoing	

Answers	EX.NO	1	2	3	4	5	6	7	8	9	10	11	12	13	14	15	16	17	18	19	20
	69	C	I	D	B	Q	T	J	G	N	E	L	H	F	A	M	K	O	S	P	R
	70	P	L	M	O	N	J	Q	E	D	S	A	I	B	C	F	T	K	R	G	H

Memory Test-71 : Match each word and its memory trick to the corresponding definition.

S.N	WORD	MEMORY TRIGGER	S.N	DEFINITIONS	KEY
1	MANACLE	Man shackled	A	Clear; obvious; visible	
2	MANDATE	COMMAND	B	Damaged	
3	MANIFEST	Many fests-manifesto	C	Dangerous; threatening	
4	MANIFOLD	MANY fold	D	Desire for material possessions	
5	MARGINAL	MINIMAL –on margin	E	Excessively sentimental	
6	MARRED	SCARRED	F	Female head of a family or tribe	
7	MARSH	MARINE land	G	Gloomy; morose	
8	MARTINET	MARTIAL nature	H	Life story, autobiography	
9	MATERIALISM	MATERIALISTIC	I	Many and various	
10	MATRIARCH	JOAN OF ARC	J	Order; charge	
11	MAUDLIN	Maa- Mary Magdalene	K	Ordinary; common place	
12	MAVERICK	RICKY martin	L	Overly sentimental	
13	MAWKISH	MA + KISS	M	Rebel; nonconformist	
14	MEAGER	Not major-MINOR	N	Restrain, Control	
15	MEDIOCRE	MEDIUM level	O	Scanty; inadequate	
16	MEEK	WEAK hearted	P	Soft wet land; morass	
17	MELANCHOLY	Life with ALCOHOLIC	Q	Strict disciplinarian	
18	MELLIFLUOUS	MELODIOUS flow	R	Sweetly flowing, melodious	
19	MEMOIR	MEMORY	S	Timid; humble; submissive	
20	MENACING	MINUS signs	T	Unimportant; borderline	

Memory Test-72 : Match each word and its memory trick to the corresponding definition.

S.N	WORD	MEMORY TRIGGER	S.N	DEFINITIONS	KEY
1	MENDACITY	MEN in city	A	Beggar	
2	MENDICANT	Spend I CAN'T	B	Capricious, changing; fickle	
3	MENIAL	MANUAL labor	C	Complete change in form	
4	MERCANTILE	MERCHANT	D	Courage; spirit	
5	MERCURIAL	MERCURY LEVEL	E	Divide and distribute, allot	
6	MERETRICIOUS	Merit TRICK us	F	Falsely attractive	
7	METAMORPHOSIS	MORPH	G	Fast and brilliant	
8	METAPHOR	Megastar-superstar	H	Figurative language; symbolic	
9	METAPHYSICS	Meditation physics	I	Middle, core	
10	METE	Meter- Mete-meat	J	Relating to trade or commerce	
11	METEORIC	METEOR like	K	Small detail; petty matters	
12	METICULOUS	MORE ACCURATE	L	Small world	
13	METTLE	Men battle	M	Suitable for servants; Servile	
14	MIASMA	my asthma	N	Surroundings; means of expression	
15	MICROCOSM	Micro+cosmos	O	The study of ultimate reality	
16	MIDST	MIDDLE	P	Threatening, menacing	
17	MILIEU	MY VIEW	Q	Tiny, very small	
18	MINISCULE	mini-molecule	R	Unhealthy poisonous vapor	
19	MINATORY	MAN EATER	S	Untruthfulness; dishonesty	
20	MINUTIAE	MINI minutes	T	Very careful and precise	

Answers

EX.NO	1	2	3	4	5	6	7	8	9	10	11	12	13	14	15	16	17	18	19	20
71	N	J	A	I	T	B	P	Q	D	F	E	M	L	O	K	S	G	R	H	C
72	S	A	M	J	B	F	C	H	O	E	G	T	D	R	L	I	N	Q	P	K

WORD GROUPS DAY-18

★ PREDICT

ADJECTIVES: prescient, portentous , premonitory, foreseeable

NOUNS: auspice, harbinger, augury, omen, precursor

VERB: bode, forebode, forecast, foretell, foresee, prophesy, anticipate, envision, envisage; augur, herald, presage, portend, prognosticate

ANTONYMS: adj.unforeseeable, unanticipated.

★ UNCERTAIN

ADJECTIVES: ambiguous, ambivalent, conjectural, dubious, erratic, fitful, hazy, incalculable, indefinite, indeterminate, indistinct, irresolute, precarious, questionable, speculative, unclear, unforeseeable , unpredictable, unreliable, unresolved, unsettled, up vacillating, vague, variable, wavering

NOUNS: uncertainty, dubiety

VERB: unforesee

ANTONYMS: v. certain, clear, definite, determined, foreseeable, secure, sure, unchanging

★ CERTIFY

ADJECTIVES: certified, endorsed, authorized

NOUNS: certification

VERB: accredit, ascertain, assure, attest, authenticate, authorize, aver, avow, commission, confirm, corroborate, endorse, guarantee, license, profess, reassure, sanction, substantiate, swear, testify, validate, verify, vouch, warrant

ANTONYMS: v. contradict, counteract, deny, disavow, discredit, invalidate, reject, repudiate

★ CANCEL

ADJECTIVES: abolishable

NOUNS: abolition, annulment

VERB: abolish, abort, abrogate, annul, countermand, nullify, invalid, quash, repeal, rescind, revoke

ANTONYMS: v.allow, approve, establish, uphold

★ SEPARATE

ADJECTIVES: apart, apportioned, asunder, disparate, detached, discrete, disjointed, divergent, isolated

NOUNS: severance, estrangement, dichotomy

VERB: cleave, disband, disjoin, dissect, isolate, rupture, sever, sunder

ANTONYMS: adj. connected, joined, mixed, united

★ UNITE /UNITED/UNION

ADJECTIVES: cognate, concerted, congruent, conjugate, corporate, homogeneous, integrated, interwoven, unanimous

NOUNS: amalgam, conciliation, concord, concurrence, confluence, congregation, conjunction, consolidation, consensus, correlation, fusion, harmony, juncture, melding, symbiosis, synthesis, unanimity, unison

VERB: affiliate, ally, associate, coalesce, commingle, concatenate, conjoin, consolidate, converge, incorporate, intertwine, merge, unify

ANTONYMS: n. division, divorce, separation

Word List Day-19

MIRE (MYRE): v. To become stuck in difficult situation
    Trigger: MIRE-"MUDDY-TIRE"
    Trigger Sentence: 1. MY TIRE got MIRED in MUD. **2.** I ADMIRE you for removing me from MIRE.
    Sample Sentence: Life is a *mire*, learn to wire yourself out and help others too.
    Related Words: QUAGMIRE - n. a complex or difficult situation

MISANTHROPE (MIZ an thrope): n. One who hates human beings
    Trigger: MISANTHROPIST-PHILANTHROPIST (** antonyms)
    Trigger Sentence: A MISANTHROPIST hates HUMAN RACE; whereas a PHILANTHROPIST loves HUMAN RACE. He is a former MISANTHROPE who is now involved in PHILANTHROPIC activities.
    Sample Sentence: Gandhi was a philanthrope whereas Hitler was a *misanthrope*.
    Related Words: PHILANTHROPIST –n. charitable donor; benevolent person

MISAPPREHEND (mis ap ri HEND): v. Fail to understand
    Trigger: MISAPPREHEND-MISUNDERSTAND
    Trigger Sentence: MISUNDERSTANDING results in MISAPPREHENSION.
    Sample Sentence: She *misapprehended* my friendly remarks as being flirtatious.
    Related Words: COMPREHEND – v. understand

MISCREANT (MIS kree unt): n. Villain; criminal
    Trigger: MISCREANT-MISCREATE
    Trigger Sentence: The god's MISCREATION resulted in MISCREANTS.
    Sample Sentence: The use of video cameras at ATMs will identify the *miscreants*.

MISER (MI zer): n. One who is extremely stingy with money
    Trigger: MISER-MINOR
    Trigger Sentence: A MISER is MONEY spending wise a MINOR.
    Sample Sentence: This man with `rags to riches' story is still a *miser*!

MISNOMER (mis NOH mer): n. Wrong name
    Trigger: MISNOMER-MISTAKE in NAME
    Trigger Sentence: It is a MISTAKE in NAME him Casanova; as he never ever had a girl friend.
    Sample Sentence: Morning sickness is a *misnomer* – in fact nausea can strike any time.

MITIGATE (MIT uh gayt): v. To make less severe; alleviate
    Trigger: 1. MITIGATE-MITE. **2.** MITIGATE -MODERATE **3.** MITIGATE-NOT IRRITATE
    Trigger Sentence: 1. MITE is small; MITIGATE is to lessen esp. pain. **2.** MITIGATE is to MODERATE the intensity level. **3.** Do NOT get IRRITATED with mild pain. I will MITIGATE your joint pains.
    Sample Sentence: To *mitigate* the traffic problems, there is a proposal for a fly over.
    Related Words: UNMITIGATED –a. not lessened; complete

MNEMONIC (neh MAHN ik): n. A device used for memory

Trigger: MNEMONIC–MEMORY TRICK

Trigger Sentence: In this book MEMORY TRICKS are used as MNEMONICS to unravel the definitions of the difficult GRE words.

Sample Sentence: *Mnemonic* is used to help memorize the difficult GRE vocabulary.

MODEST (MOD ist): a. humble; moderate; simple, limited

Trigger: MODEST-MODERATE (**synonyms)

Trigger Sentence: He earns a MODERATE/MODEST salary

Sample Sentence: He is very *modest* about his achievements.

MODICUM (MOH di kum): n. Small quantity

Trigger: MODICUM-MODEST SUM

Trigger Sentence: MODEST SUM is known as MODICUM.

Sample Sentence: Your *modicum* of a skill is not enough to fix this machine.

MODISH (MOH dish): a. Stylish

Trigger: MOD-"MODERN" - MODEL

Trigger Sentence: The MODEL wore a MODISH gown to a fashion show.

Sample Sentence: The delegates wore *modish* suits and shiny shoes.

Related Words: 1.FADDISH –a. trendy. 2. OUTMODED –a. out of fashion

MOLLIFY (MAHL ih fye): v. Soothe

Trigger: MOLLIFY-LULL+ IFY

Trigger Sentence: By singing a LULLABY she managed to MOLLIFY the crying kid.

Sample Sentence: The mellifluous music has *mollified* her sadness to some extent.

Related Words: EMOLLIENT –n. soothing cream

MOLLYCODDLE (MOL ee kod ul): v. Spoil, pamper

Trigger: MOLLYCODDLE-MA+ CUDDLE

Trigger Sentence: My MA CUDDLES and MOLLYCODDLES me.

Sample Sentence: The way his parents *mollycoddle* Surya, he'll remain a spoiled brat for ever!

Related Words: CODDLE –v. pamper; treat gently

MOMENTARY (MOH mun ter ee): a. Brief; short lived

Trigger: MOMENTARY-brief MOMENT

Trigger Sentence: For a BRIEF MOMENT he experienced a MOMENTARY loss of consciousness.

Sample Sentence: It's a *momentary* pain; you can easily take this injection.

MOMENTOUS (moh MEN tuhs): a. Very important

Trigger: MOMENTOUS-great MOMENT

Trigger Sentence: The GREAT MOMENT in Indian Cricket was the MOMENTOUS world cup win.

Sample Sentence: The day we were tied in a wedlock will always be a *momentous* moment.

MONASTIC (muh NAS tik): a. Relating to the monks or monasteries; isolated

Trigger: 1.MONASTIC –MONK. 2. MONASTIC-MONK-MONO

Trigger Sentence: 1. A MONK lives a MONASTIC life. 2. Living in MONASTERIES is a MONO life.

Sample Sentence: He has a *monastic* focus and dedication to his music practice.

MONOLITHIC (mon uh LITH ik): n. Rigidly uniform

Trigger: MONOLITHIC-MONO+THICK

Trigger Sentence: The THICK MONUMENT with even material was made in MONOLITHIC stone.

Sample Sentence: This sculpture of Buddha was chiseled on a huge *monolithic* rock.

MONOTONY (muh NOT n ee): n. Tedious sameness

Trigger: MONOTONY-MONO+TONE

Trigger Sentence: She hated MONOTONY of the TONE of the soprano.

Sample Sentence: Mohan hated the *monotonous* city life and decided to travel to the hills.

MORATORIUM (mawr uh TAWR ee um): n. A suspension of an activity

Trigger: MORATORIUM-"MORE TIME"

Trigger Sentence: 1. Sir has given me MORE TIME to submit my assignment; I will submit it after SOME MORE TIME. 2. The two warring sides will extend their MORATORIUM for MORE TIME.

Sample Sentence: In 1986, the commission introduced a *moratorium* on all commercial hunting.

MORES (MOHR eez): n. The conventions; moral standards; ethics

Trigger: MORES-MORALS

Trigger Sentence: MORAL standards are known as MORES.

Sample Sentence: According to the *mores* of Chanakya, morals depend on the actions of enemies.

Related Words: IMMORALITY –n. lack of principles; wickedness

MORIBUND (MOR ih bund): a. Dying

Trigger: MORIBUND-MORTAL (DEAD)

Trigger Sentence: If you allow MORIBUND fears to overcome you, they become MORTAL soon.

Sample Sentence: With the evolution of computers, typewriters are *moribund* now.

Related Words: 1.MORTAL –a. deadly. 2. IMMORTAL –a. deathless .3.MORBID –a.sad; sickly

MOROSE (muh ROHS): a. Sad, sullen; ill-humoured

Trigger: MOROSE -MORE RUE

Trigger Sentence: If you continue to be MOROSE, the children will become MORE RUEFUL.

Sample Sentence: Danny's *morose* attitude is infectious, no one can be happy in his company.

MOSAIC (mo ZAY ik): n. Inlaid colorful stone decoration

Trigger: 1.MOSAIC. 2. MOSAIC-MUSIC

Trigger Sentence: 1. MOSAIC floor is done with MOSAIC tiles. 2. MUSIC is a MOSAIC of melodies.

Sample Sentence: I was awestruck by the intricate *mosaic* on the walls of the cathedral.

MUDDLE (MUHD l): v. Confuse; mess up

    Trigger: 1. MUDDLE- RIDDLE. 2. MUDDLE-MUDDY

    Trigger Sentence: 1. How I could MUDDLE over such a silly thing is still a big RIDDLE to me! 2. Don't MUDDLE my papers with your MUDDY hands.

    Sample Sentence: My editor *muddled* up all the paper work and blamed it on me!

MULTIFACETED (muhl tee FAS i tid): a. Having many facets; complex

    Trigger: MULTIFACETED -MULTI+FACES

    Trigger Sentence: He is MULTIFACETED. I saw his MULTIPLE FACES when I lived with him.

    Sample Sentence: A *multifaceted* approach to the education system is the need of the hour.

MULTIFARIOUS (muhl tuh FAIR ee us): a. Varied; greatly diversified

    Trigger: MULTIFARIOUS -MULTI+VARIOUS

    Trigger Sentence: The MULTIFARIOUS plants have been collected from VARIOUS countries.

    Sample Sentence: Having *multifarious* interests, Sheeba was known as the `jack of all arts'.

    Related Words: MULTITUDINOUS - a. many, very numerous.

MUNDANE (mun DAYN): a. Every day, worldly; not earthly

    Trigger: MONDAY-EVERYDAY

    Trigger Sentence: 1. I feel great on a Sunday, but MUNDANE on a MONDAY.2. This is a MUNDANE love story which we come across EVERYDAY.

    Sample Sentence: It is not a difficult thing... but a *mundane* task for me.

MUNIFICENT (myoo NEF uh sunt): a. Very Generous

    Trigger: MUNIFICENT -MONEY+CENT

    Trigger Sentence: My MUNIFICENT friend SENT MONEY throughout my unemployment period.

    Sample Sentence: Dr. Mote, in his will, left *munificent* wealth to the Mote marine Lab.

MURKY (MUR kee): a. Dark and gloomy

    Trigger: MURKY-MUDDY(** synonyms)

    Trigger Sentence: MUDDY water looks MURKY.

    Sample Sentence: It is a *murky* atmosphere, completely uninspiring to work.

MUSTER (MUS tur): v. Gather together, assemble for action.

    Trigger: 1. MUSTER-CLUSTER. 2. MUSTER-MASTER

    Trigger Sentence: 1. We have MUSTERED our strength by CLUSTERING all our resources. 2. He is a MASTER; he knows how to MUSTER the students.

    Sample Sentence: I *mustered* up some courage to question the politician in public.

MUTABLE (MYOO tuh bul): a. Changeable; unstable

    Trigger: 1. MUTABLE-MOVABLE. 2 .MUTABLE-NOT STABLE

    Trigger Sentence: Human epigenome is both MUTABLE and MOVABLE.

    Sample Sentence: Bob's business is in a *mutable* condition now.

    Related Words: MUTABILITY - n. ability to change; fickleness

MUTED (MYOO tid): a. Silent; hushed; made softer

    Trigger: 1.MUTED-QUIETED. 2. FLUTED-MUTED

Trigger Sentence: The MUTED/QUIET sound of a distant drum is almost silent.
2. The FLUTED song is MUTED.

Sample Sentence: Dictatorship was all about stifling the rebels and *muting* their voices.

MYOPIC (mye OP ik): a. Near-sighted; lack of foresight

Trigger: MYOPIC-MY OPAQUE (MY OPAQUE- "DARK")

Trigger Sentence: Near objects are OPAQUE to MYOPIC patients.

Sample Sentence: You are a *myopic* for focusing on the present and ignoring your future.

Related Words: MYOPIA -n. Lack of foresight; Narrow-mindedness

MYRIAD (MIR ee ud): n. Very large number

Trigger: "myriADS- moreADS"

Trigger Sentence: To face MYRIAD competitors, business firms give MORE ADS on products.

Sample Sentence: With *myriad* moods, the danseuse personified as the courtesan Chitrangada.

MYTH (MITH): n. A widely held but false belief; a traditional story accepted as history

Trigger: 1. MYTH-MYTHOLOGY. 2. MYTH-no TRUTH

Trigger Sentence: 1. Some people believe the MYTHS and legends of Indian MYTHOLOGY. 2. Most of the MYTHS are devoid of TRUTH.

Sample Sentence: The Indian *myth* on creation depicts the Gods creating a milky ocean, from which all living forms emerged.

NADIR (NAY der): n. The lowest point

Trigger: NADIR-UNDER

Trigger Sentence: NADIR and UNDER are synonyms.

Sample Sentence: Deep down in the *nadir* you will find the secret treasures of ocean life!

NAIVE (nah EEV): a. Innocent, lacking worldly wisdom

Trigger: 1. NAIVE-NATIVE. 2. NAIVE-BELIEVE

Trigger Sentence: 1. The NATIVE Aborigines of Australia are very NAIVE. 2. NAIVE persons BELIEVE everyone and everything.

Sample Sentence: My mom *naively* gave loan to our driver who took the money and absconded!

Related Words: NAIVETY - n. innocence; lacks experience

NARCISSISM (NAHR si siz em): n. Self-love; vanity

Trigger: 1. NARCISSIST-NAZI EGOIST. 2. NARCISSIST-NURSE

Trigger Sentence: 1. NAZI EGOISTS popularized NARCISSISM. 2. A NURSE gives up her NARCISSISM before she enters this noble profession.

Sample Sentence: Being a little *narcissistic* is not bad at all! Well, don't we all love ourselves?!

NASCENT (NAS unt): a. Incipient; just beginning

Trigger: NASCENT-RECENT

Trigger Sentence: Nanotechnology is still NASCENT. It is a RECENT scientific idea.

Sample Sentence: Modern art movement was still in its *nascent* state during the 19th century.

NATAL (NEYT l): a. Natural; biological

Trigger: 1.NATAL-NATURAL. 2. NATAL-NATIVE

Trigger Sentence: 1. NATURAL evolution is NATAL. 2. NATIVE Aborigines inhabit in NATAL land.

Sample Sentence: Mohan's diabetic condition is hereditary; it is ingrained in his *natal* system.

NEBULOUS (NEB yuh lus): a. Dark, cloudy, hazy

Trigger: NEBULOUS-NEBULA

Trigger Sentence: NEBULA is a CLOUD of cosmic dust; something NEBULOUS is DARK and HAZY.

Sample Sentence: She had only a *nebulous* memory of her grandmother's face.

NECROMANCY (NEK ruh man see): n. Black magic; dealing with the dead.

Trigger: 1. "NECRO+MAN + CY"-NEGRO MANS. 2. NECROMANCY-NECK+ROMES

Trigger Sentence: 1. NEGRO MAN (black) - African tribe believes in NECROMANCY (black magic). 2. In a NECROMANCY the NECK of the DEAD body roams from one place to another place.

Sample Sentence: She is a `black magic woman' who has the art of *necromancy* to evoke evil.

NEFARIOUS (ni FAIR ee us): a. Very Wicked

Trigger: NO FAIR NESS

Trigger Sentence: NEFARIOUS people possess NO FAIR qualities.

Sample Sentence: Not fair of Lance Armstrong to have achieved fame *nefariously*.

NEGATE (ni GEYT): v. Deny, nullify; cancel out

Trigger: NEGATE-NEGATIVE

Trigger Sentence: If you NEGATE this decision, it'll leave a NEGATIVE remark on your career.

Sample Sentence: Bob *negated* the idea of going into the mountains during monsoon.

Related Words: ABNEGATE - v. deny one-self

NEOLOGISM (nee OL uh jiz uhm): n. A newly invented word or phrase

Trigger: NEOLOGISM- NEW DIALOGUE

Trigger Sentence: This NEW DIALOGUE has NEW WORDS creating a NEOLOGISM for language.

Sample Sentence: The 2005 revision of words includes *neologisms* like podcast and spendy.

NEOPHYTE (NEE uh fyte): n. A beginner

Trigger: NEW TO THE FIGHT

Trigger Sentence: He is NEW TO FIGHT in the ring. He is a NEOPHYTE.

Sample Sentence: As a *neophyte* engineer you are bound to slip-up.

NEPOTISM (NEP uh tiz um): n. Favoritism shown to relatives

Trigger: NEPHEW+ ism

Trigger Sentence: He has shown NEPOTISM towards his NEPHEW.

Sample Sentence: The dictator was notorious for his rampant *nepotism*

NETTLE (NET l): v. Annoy; irritate

Trigger: 1. NETTLE-UNSETTLE. 2. NETTLE-NEEDLE. 3. NETTLE PLANT

Trigger Sentence: 1. This piece of music is NETTLESOME and UNSETTLING. 2. It is really NETTLESOME to insert thread through the eye of a NEEDLE.

Sample Sentence: It is *nettling* when all the lights are unnecessarily switched on in my house.

NEUTRALIZE (NOO truh lahyz): v. Make ineffective by counteract

Trigger: NEUTRALIZE-NEUTRAL +EQUALIZE

Trigger Sentence: If something is predominant, MINIMIZE and EQUALIZE by NEUTRALIZING.

Sample Sentence: Insulin *neutralizes* excess sugar content in blood; it's life saving for diabetics.

NEXUS (NEK sus): n. Connection

Trigger: NEXUS-CONNECTIONS

Trigger Sentence: The CONNECTIONS reveal that there is NEXUS between police and mafia.

Sample Sentence: There is a strong *nexus* between industries and political power. It is a money game they say!

NOCTURNAL (nok TUR nl): a. Active during the night

Trigger: NOCTURNAL-NOT +URINAL

Trigger Sentence: Going frequent to the URINALS is NOT a NOCTURNAL activity; it is a daytime/diurnal activity.

Sample Sentence: Bats are *nocturnal* creatures and are active during the dark.

Related Words: DIURNAL - a. active during the day; daily

NOISOME (NOY sum): a. Harmful; harmful smell

Trigger: 1. NOISOME-NOISE. 2. NOISOME-ANNOY SOME

Trigger Sentence: 1. Loud NOISE is NOISOME to ears. 2. The NOISE of fart gives NOISOME smell.

Sample Sentence: I could not take the *noisome* atmosphere around the slaughter houses.

NOMAD (NOH mad): a. Wandering, nomadic

Trigger: NOMAD- NO LAND

Trigger Sentence: A NOMAD has NO LAND of his own.

Sample Sentence: We lived a *nomadic* life, as my defense officer dad was often transferred from one corner of the county to the other.

NONCHALANCE (NON shuh lawns): n. Casually calm; apathy; indifference

Trigger: NONCHALANCE-NEGLIGENCE

Trigger Sentence: 1. NONCHALANCE and NEGLIGENCE are synonyms. 2. NONCHALANCE to tyrannical rulers tantamount to NEGLIGENCE of Democracy.

Sample Sentence: Some government officials are completely *nonchalant* towards their duties.

NONENTITY (non EN ti tee): n. A person of no importance; a nonexistent thing

Trigger: NONENTITY-NO ENTRY

Trigger Sentence: There is NO ENTRY for NONENTITIES in the President Dinner party.

Sample Sentence: The boss never allowed *nonentities* in his private meetings.

Related Words: NONDESCRIPT –a. mediocre person

NONPLUS (non PLUS): v. Perplex; confuse

Trigger: 1. NO PLUS. 2. NONPLUS-PERPLEX-COMPLEX

Trigger Sentence: 1. When COMPLEX problem is given...we get NONPLUSED and PERPLEXED. 2. I was NONPLUSED to notice that NO single judge had given me a PLUS score.

Sample Sentence: John's unusual rudeness *nonplused* his wife, who wondered "why"?!

Related Words: NONPLUSED - a. confused, embarrassed.

NORMATIVE (NAWR muh tiv): a. Standard, normal

Trigger: NORMATIVE-NORMAL

Trigger Sentence: NORMATIVE relates NORMAL or standard rules.

Sample Sentence: It is normal for Human Resource Department to follow *normative* guidelines.

NOSTALGIA (no STAL juh): n. Homesickness, Longing for the past

Trigger: NOSTALGIA- HOSTEL + GIA

Trigger Sentence: Went to HOSTEL, I felt NOSTALGIC; I remembered my mom in hostel.

Sample Sentence: Our reunion had *nostalgic* moments; we recalled those carefree old days.

NOSTRUM (NOS trum): n. False remedy; panacea

Trigger: 1. NOSTRUM -NOSE DRUM .2.NOSTRUM-NOSTRIL+DROP

Trigger Sentence: 1. The breathing yoga that involves NOSE DRUM claimed to cure all diseases was a NOSTRUM. 2. The NOSTRIL DROPS concoction prepared by the alternative medicine specialist claimed to cure the stubborn cold was indeed a NOSTRUM.

Sample Sentence: Your sweet words are just *nostrums;* not a cure for your incurable friend.

NOTABLE (NOH tuh bul): a. Remarkable; famous; honored

Trigger: NOTABLE-NOTEWORTHY (** synonyms)

Trigger Sentence: Anything WORTHY OF NOTICE is known as NOTABLE.

Sample Sentence: My book `Word Wizard' has steadily picked up and is now *notable* on shelves.

NOTORIOUS (noh TAWR ee us): a. Known for bad qualities

Trigger: NOTORIOUS-NOTED TERRORISTS

Trigger Sentence: This NOTORIOUS criminal has a nexus to many NOTED TERRORISTS.

Sample Sentence: Marley is *notorious* as a womanizer; women often complained against him.

Related Words: NOTORIETY: bad name; disrepute

NOURISH (NUR ish): v. Support; nurture

Trigger: 1. NOURISH-NURSE. 2. NOURISH-FLOURISH

Trigger Sentence: 1. A doctor may treat you, but it is a NURSE that NOURISHES you. 2. If we NOURISH children properly, they will FLOURISH.

Sample Sentence: She keeps *nourishing* her skin with herbs and fruit pulps to make it glow!

NOVELTY (NOV ul tee): n. Newness; unusual

Trigger: NOVELTY-INNOVATION

Trigger Sentence: This INNOVATION is a NOVELTY in fuel cell research.

Sample Sentence: To practice *novelty*, one should think innovatively.

Related Words: NOVEL - n. new, strange

NOVICE (NOV iss): n. Beginner

Trigger: 1. NOVICE-NOVEL. 2. NOVICE-NO WISE

Trigger Sentence: 1. Though he is NOVICE to this profession, he is contributing NOVEL ideas to the management. 2. It is NOT WISE to recruit a NOVICE for this responsible post.

Sample Sentence: The horse riding club caters to all, from nervous *novices* to expert riders.

Related Words: NOVITIATE - n. novice

NOXIOUS (NOK shuhs): a. Harmful, poisonous, or very unpleasant

Trigger: 1. NOXIOUS-TOXINS. 2. NOXIOUS- KNOCKS US

Trigger Sentence: 1. NOXIOUS air contains TOXINS. 2. NOXIOUS gas KNOCKS our consciousness.

Sample Sentence: We must trace the source of these *noxious* gases before they asphyxiate us.

Related Words: 1.OBNOXIOUS - a. Extremely unpleasant. 2. INNOCUOUS - a. harmless; innocent

NUANCE (NOO ahns): n. A shade of difference in meaning; a subtle distinction

Trigger: 1. NUANCE-"NEW SENSE". 2. "NUANCE-SUBSENSE"

Trigger Sentence: 1. This NEW SENSE of meaning of word developed a NUANCE. 2. Generally NUANCES has latent SUBSENSE.

Sample Sentence: The Taj Mahal's marble sparkles with the subtle *nuances* of changing light.

NUGATORY (NOO guh tawr ee): a. Worthless; useless

Trigger: NUGATORY-LAVATORY

Trigger Sentence: From LAVATORY NUGATORY (waste) things are routed out.

Sample Sentence: What a bunch of *nugatory* nuts they are, these boys have no purpose.

NULLIFY (NUL ih fy): v. To make useless

Trigger: NULL - (NIL)

Trigger Sentence: NULLIFY is to make something NULL (or NIL).

Sample Sentence: The judgment of the High Court becomes null if the Supreme Court *nullifies* it.

Related Words: ANNUL - v. cancel; put an end to

NURTURE (NUR cher): v. Foster; nourish, teach

Trigger: NURTURE-NURSE

Trigger Sentence: NURSE NURTURES the patients.

Sample Sentence: I recovered quickly from the illness as the *nurse* nurtured me with love!

OBDURATE (OB dyoo rit): a. Stubborn

Trigger: 1. OB + DURA (DURABILITY). 2. OBD-OLD

Trigger Sentence: 1. OLD people with DURATION usually become OBDURATE. 2. DURABILITY is related to TOUGHNESS & STUBBORN.

Sample Sentence: I got to be diplomatic in dealing with these *obdurate* people with rigid ideas.

OBEISANCE (oh BAY suns): n. Bow, bend with respect

Trigger: 1. OBEISANCE-OBEY. 2. OBEISANCE-OBEDIENCE

Trigger Sentence: One should show OBEDIENCE to parents and OBEISANCE to one's mentors.

Sample Sentence: Offering *obeisance* to her gurus, the young dancer stepped on to the stage.

OBFUSCATE (OB fuh skayt): v. Confuse; muddle; obscure

Trigger: 1.OBFUSCATED-OF CONFUSED. 2. OBFUSCATE-OBSCURE

Trigger Sentence: 1. The OBSCURE questions OBFUSCATED and CONFUSED the test takers. 2. Create FUSS to OBFUSCATE or CONFUSE the people.

Sample Sentence: Do not *obfuscate* the issue with your unrelated arguments.

OBJECTIVE (uhb JEK tiv): a. Impartial, not influenced by emotions; fair

Trigger: 1. OBJECT (goal oriented). 2. OBJECTIVE-SUBJECTIVE(** antonyms)

Trigger Sentence: 1. When one is goal (OBJECT) oriented and OBJECTIVE -one is not interested in personal matters. 2. OBJECTIVE and SUBJECTIVE (interested in subjects) are antonyms.

Sample Sentence: As an interviewer, please be *objective* (impartial) in your selection process.

Related Words: OBJECTIVITY - n. lack of emotional involvement

OBJURGATE (OB jer geyt): v. Criticize harshly; castigate

Trigger: OBJECT - OBJURGATE

Trigger Sentence: Teacher OBJECTED to my tantrums in the class room and OBJURGATED me.

Sample Sentence: Though racism is *objurgated* worldwide, it still prevails in the world!

Related Words: OBJURGATION - n. scolding, rebuking

OBLIQUE (oh BLEEK): a. Indirect; inclined; leaning

Trigger: OBLIQUE- line " / "

Trigger Sentence: OBLIQUE LINE (/is OBLIQUE; he gave OBLIQUE answers to direct questions.

Sample Sentence: Your *oblique* accusations are no less than back stabbing!

OBLITERATE (uh BLIT uh reyt): v. Erase; destroy

Trigger: 1. LITTER. 2. ALL BE LITERATE-ILLITERACY

Trigger Sentence: 1. Let us OBLITERATE the LITTER. 2. If you want, ALL BE LITERATES... let us OBLITERATE the ILLITERACY in India.

Sample Sentence: Alas, we could not *obliterate* illiteracy even after 66 years of independence.

OBLIVION (uh BLIV ee un): n. Forgotten or unknown

Trigger: 1. OFF+LIVING. 2. "OBLIVION"-O+BLIND+VISION

Trigger Sentence: 1. BLIND person LIVES a life OF OBLIVION. 2. If VISION is BLIND- live OBLIVION.

Sample Sentence: Once a sort after heroine, she passed into *oblivion* for reasons not known!

Related Words: OBLIVIOUS - a. unmindful; forgetful

OBLIVIOUS (uh BLIV ee us): a. Unmindful, inattentive; Unconscious

Trigger: 1. OBLIVIOUS- OFF+LIVING. 2. "OBLIVIOUS"-O+BLIND+VISIONS

Trigger Sentence: 1. With O + BLIND + VISIONS she was OBLIVIOUS to our warnings. 2. You have BLIND VISION if you remain OBLIVIOUS to the injustice in your surroundings.

Sample Sentence: Anand was completely *oblivious* of those conspiracies against him.

OBLOQUY (OB luh kwee): n. Abuse, defame, calumny

Trigger: OBLOQUY- O BLACKY

Trigger Sentence: By calling "O BLACKY"--" OH BLACKY" he passed OBLOQUY.

Sample Sentence: *Obloquy* and gossiping will not help you deal with people you dislike.

OBNOXIOUS (uhb NOK shus): a. Extremely unpleasant

Trigger: 1.OBNOXIOUS-OB+ KNOCKS US. 2. NOXIOUS- KNOCKS US

Trigger Sentence: OBNOXIOUS blow can KNOCK US down.

Sample Sentence: Alcohol is making you behave in an *obnoxious* manner.

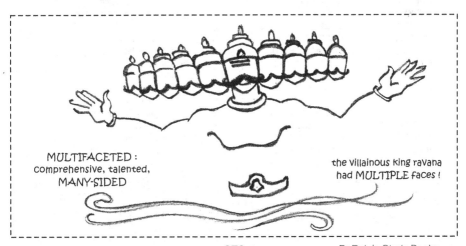

MULTIFACETED :
comprehensive, talented,
MANY-SIDED

the villainous king ravana
had MULTIPLE faces !

Memory Test-73 : Match each word and its memory trick to the corresponding definition.

S.N	WORD	MEMORY TRIGGER	S.N	DEFINITIONS	KEY
1	MIRE	MUDDY-tire	A	Become stuck in difficult situation	
2	MISANTHROPE	Mistaken anthropologist	B	Brief; short lived	
3	MISAPPREHEND	misunderstand	C	Device used for memory	
4	MISCREANT	He MISCREATES	D	Fail to understand	
5	MISER	Money s wise MINOR	E	Humble; moderate; limited	
6	MISNOMER	MISTAKE in NAME	F	Make less severe; alleviate	
7	MITIGATE	MITE is small	G	One who hates human beings	
8	MNEMONIC	MEMORY TRICK	H	One who is stingy with money	
9	MODEST	moderate	I	Relating to the monks; isolated	
10	MODICUM	Modest SUM	J	Rigidly uniform	
11	MODISH	Modern - MODEL	K	Small quantity	
12	MOLLIFY	LULL+ ify	L	Soothe	
13	MOLLYCODDLE	Ma+ CUDDLE	M	Spoil, pamper	
14	MOMENTARY	Brief MOMENT	N	Stylish	
15	MOMENTOUS	Great MOMENT	O	Suspension of an activity	
16	MONASTIC	monk-MONO	P	Tedious sameness	
17	MONOLITHIC	MONO+thick	Q	The conventions; moral standards	
18	MONOTONY	Mono+TONE	R	Very important	
19	MORATORIUM	Takes MORE TIME	S	Villain; criminal	
20	MORES	MORALS	T	Wrong name	

Memory Test-74 : Match each word and its memory trick to the corresponding definition.

S.N	WORD	MEMORY TRIGGER	S.N	DEFINITIONS	KEY
1	MORIBUND	MORTAL (dead)	A	Changeable; unstable	
2	MOROSE	More RUE	B	Confuse; mess up	
3	MOSAIC	Mosaic floor	C	Dark and gloomy	
4	MUDDLE	MUDDY in RIDDLE	D	Dying	
5	MULTIFACETED	Multi+faces	E	Every day, worldly; not earthly	
6	MULTIFARIOUS	Multi+various	F	Gather together	
7	MUNDANE	Monday-everyday	G	Having many facets; complex	
8	MUNIFICENT	MONEY+cent	H	Just beginning; Incipient	
9	MURKY	MUDDY	I	Inlaid colorful stone decoration	
10	MUSTER	Master-Muster-cluster	J	Innocent, lacking worldly wisdom	
11	MUTABLE	MOVABLE	K	Natural; biological	
12	MUTED	Muted-QUIETED	L	Near-sighted; lack of foresight	
13	MYOPIC	Myopic-my opaque	M	Sad, sullen	
14	MYRIAD	myriads- more+ads	N	Self-love; vanity	
15	MYTH	no TRUTH	O	Silent; hushed; made softer	
16	NADIR	Nadir-UNDER	P	The lowest point	
17	NAÏVE	Naïve-native; naive-believe	Q	Varied; greatly diversified	
18	NARCISSISM	NAZI EGOIST	R	Very Generous	
19	NASCENT	RECENT	S	Very large number	
20	NATAL	Natal-NATURAL	T	Widely held but false belief	

Answers	EX.NO	1	2	3	4	5	6	7	8	9	10	11	12	13	14	15	16	17	18	19	20
	73	A	G	D	S	H	T	F	C	E	K	N	L	M	B	R	I	J	P	O	Q
	74	D	M	I	B	G	Q	E	R	C	F	A	O	L	S	T	P	J	N	H	K

Memory Test-75 : Match each word and its memory trick to the corresponding definition.

S.N	WORD	MEMORY TRIGGER	S.N	DEFINITIONS	KEY
1	NEBULOUS	Nebula -CLOUD of gas	A	Active during the night	
2	NECROMANCY	Negro MAN performs	B	Annoy; irritate	
3	NEFARIOUS	No FAIRness	C	Beginner	
4	NEGATE	negative	D	Black magic; dealing with the dead	
5	NEOLOGISM	new dialogue	E	Casually calm; apathy; indifference	
6	NEOPHYTE	NEW to the fight	F	Connection	
7	NEPOTISM	NEPHEW+ ism	G	Dark, cloudy, hazy	
8	NETTLE	unsettle-needle	H	Deny, nullify; cancel out	
9	NEUTRALIZE	neutral +equalize	I	False remedy; panacea	
10	NEXUS	connections	J	Favoritism shown to relatives	
11	NOCTURNAL	NOT +URINAL	K	Harmful; harmful smell	
12	NOISOME	Noise polution	L	Homesickness, Longing for the past	
13	NOMAD	NO LAND to stay	M	Make ineffective by counteract	
14	NONCHALANCE	NEGLIGENCE of emotions	N	Newly invented word or phrase	
15	NONENTITY	NO ENTRY to this man	O	Perplex; confuse	
16	NONPLUS	NO PLUS; perplex-complex	P	Person of no importance	
17	NORMATIVE	NORMAL	Q	Remarkable; famous; honored	
18	NOSTALGIA	HOSTEL + gia	R	Standard, normal	
19	NOSTRUM	NOSTRIL+drop	S	Very Wicked	
20	NOTABLE	NOTEWORTHY	T	Wandering, nomadic	

Memory Test-76 : Match each word and its memory trick to the corresponding definition.

S.N	WORD	MEMORY TRIGGER	S.N	DEFINITIONS	KEY
1	NOTORIOUS	Noted terrorists	A	Abuse, defame, calumny	
2	NOURISH	Nurse- Nourish-flourish	B	Beginner	
3	NOVELTY	INNOVATION	C	Bend with respect, bow	
4	NOVICE	Novel-NO WISE	D	Confuse; muddle; obscure	
5	NOXIOUS	knocks us	E	Criticize harshly; castigate	
6	NUANCE	NOUNS-new sense	F	Erase; destroy	
7	NUGATORY	lavatory	G	Extremely unpleasant	
8	NULLIFY	Make nil	H	Forgotten or unknown	
9	NURTURE	NURSE-nourish	I	Foster; nourish, teach	
10	OBDURATE	Old with durability	J	Harmful, poisonous	
11	OBEISANCE	obey	K	Impartial, fair	
12	OBFUSCATE	of confused	L	Indirect; inclined; leaning	
13	OBJECTIVE	Not SUBJECTIVE	M	Known for bad qualities	
14	OBJURGATE	I -OBJECT (v)	N	Make useless	
15	OBLIQUE	OBLIQUE- line " / "	O	Newness; unusual	
16	OBLITERATE	Remove illiteracy	P	Shade of difference in meaning	
17	OBLIVION	Off+ LIVING	Q	Stubborn	
18	OBLIVIOUS	Mind is not LIVING	R	Support; nurture	
19	OBLOQUY	o blacky	S	Unmindful; Unconscious	
20	OBNOXIOUS	KNOCK US down	T	Worthless; useless	

Answers

EX.NO	1	2	3	4	5	6	7	8	9	10	11	12	13	14	15	16	17	18	19	20
75	G	D	S	H	N	C	J	B	M	F	A	K	T	E	P	O	R	L	I	Q
76	M	R	O	B	J	P	T	N	I	Q	C	D	K	E	L	F	H	S	A	G

WORD GROUPS DAY-19

★ **RENEGADE:** traitor, apostate

ADJECTIVES: apostate, disloyal, dissident, heterodox, mutinous, outlaw, radical, reactionary, rebel, recreant, traitorous, unfaithful.

NOUNS: defector, deserter, heretic, nonconformist, quisling, renegade, turncoat

VERB: apostatize

ANTONYMS: n. adherent, faithful, loyalist; obedient

★ **SUPPORT-SUPPORTER**

ADJECTIVES: advocate, apologist, champion, exponent, proponent, partisan, protagonist

NOUNS: advocacy; aegis, patronage; sustenance, subsistence, subsidy, succor

VERB: advocate, bolster, buttress, champion, espouse, endorse, foster, nurture, nourish, uphold; substantiate, corroborate, collaborate

ANTONYMS: n. detractor, critic

★ **WRONGDOING**

ADJECTIVES: diabolic, execrable, mercenary, venal

NOUNS: malpractice, vice, iniquity, villainy; felony, malfeasance, misdeed, misdemeanor, peccadillo, transgression

VERB: err, breach, flout; contravene, trespass, infringe, encroach

ANTONYMS: n. good deed

★ **CRUELTY**

ADJECTIVES: barbarous, brutal, bestial, coarse, despotic, diabolical, fiendish, savage, tyrannical, vicious

NOUNS: callousness, depravity, despotism, ferocity, malice, malignity, persecution, rancor, sadism, spite, truculence, venom

VERB: rampage

ANTONYMS: n. charity, compassion, mercy

★ **CORRUPT NATURE**

ADJECTIVES: depraved, degenerate, ignoble, immoral, iniquitous, miscreant, nefarious, reprobate, sordid, tainted, unscrupulous, venal, vile

NOUNS: fraudulence, depravity, turpitude, venality

VERB: adulterate, contaminate, debase, defile, suborn, tarnish

ANTONYMS: moral, ethical, irreproachable, scrupulous

★ **DEBAUCHERY**

ADJECTIVES: bacchanalian, debauched, dissipated, degenerate, immoral, lascivious, lecherous, lewd, lustful, libidinous, licentious, reprobate, promiscuous, salacious, wanton

NOUNS: degeneracy, depravity, iniquity, vice, perversion, impropriety, immorality; lechery, promiscuity, profligacy; decadence, turpitude

VERB: debauch

ANTONYMS: adj. chaste, virtuous

★ **VIRTUOUS**

ADJECTIVES: celibate, chaste, effectual, exemplary, incorruptible, inculpable, irreprehensible, moralistic, noble, praiseworthy, principled, righteous, saintly, unimpeachable, unsullied, untainted, untarnished, upright, wholesome, worthy

NOUNS: virtue, integrity, nobility, rectitude

VERB: benefit

ANTONYMS: adj. bad, sinful, unethical, vile, wicked

Word List Day-20

OBSCURE (ub SKYOOR): a. Vague, dark; unclear

    Trigger: OBSCURE-UNSURE

    Trigger Sentence: 1. I am UNSURE because it is still OBSCURE. 2. This person is OBSCURE; NOBODY is SURE about where he is living.

    Sample Sentence: *Obscure* dating by historians of this cave temple, further mystified it!

    Related Words: OBSCURITY - n. unclearness; anonymity

OBSEQUIOUS (ub SEE kwee us): a. Obedient or attentive; servile; sycophantic

    Trigger: 1. OB+SEQUI+OUS-OBEDIENT (synonyms). 2. SEQUENCE

    Trigger Sentence: In SEQUENCE (imagine playing cards) one thing FOLLOWS other; likewise if a servant- EXCESSIVELY FOLLOWS a boss he can be called an OBSEQUIOUS man.

    Sample Sentence: Nothing irritated her more than an excessively *obsequious* waiter.

OBSESSIVE (uhb SES i): v. / a. Compulsive; excessively preoccupied

    Trigger: OBSESSIVE-EXCESSIVE (thinking)

    Trigger Sentence: Dancers are OBSESSIVE about their weight; think EXCESSIVELY on losing it.

    Sample Sentence: He is an *obsessive* lover who never stops thinking about his girlfriend.

OBSOLETE (OB suh leet): a. Outdated; useless

    Trigger: OBSOLETE-OF SO LATE

    Trigger Sentence: OBSOLETE things are "OF SO LATE"; they are OUTDATED.

    Sample Sentence: Of late, Bell-bottom style is *obsolete*.

OBSTINATE (OB stuh nit): a. Stubbornly persistent; hard to control

    Trigger: OBSTINATE- OF+STONE + ate

    Trigger Sentence: 1. OBSTINATE person is made up OF STONE like a character. 2. How can you stay as OBSTINATE as a STONE?

    Sample Sentence: He *obstinately* snubbed us, when we persuaded him to give up smoking.

    Related Words: OBSTINACY - n. stubbornness; willfulness

OBSTREPEROUS (ob STREP er uh s): a. Noisy; undisciplined

    Trigger: 1.OBSTREPEROUS- BOISTEROUS (**synonyms) 2. STREPSILS

    Trigger Sentence: 1. BOISTEROUS (BOISTEROUS BOYS are NOISY) boys were OBSTREPEROUS. 2. My OBSTREPEROUS throat is under control after I used STREPSILS Tablets.

    Sample Sentence: It was difficult to control the *obstreperous* crowd at the public gathering.

OBTRUSIVE (ub TROO si): v. a. Undesirably noticeable; sticking out; protruding

    Trigger: OBTRUSIVE-PROTRUSIVE (**synonyms)

    Trigger Sentence: His PROTRUSIVE (protrusion-projection) bulge is OBTRUSIVE.

    Sample Sentence: Hyderabad has no more heritages; now there are *obtrusive* high-rises instead.

    Related Words: UNOBTRUSIVE - a. not conspicuous; not attracting attention

OBTUSE (ob TYOOS): a. Stupid; blunt

Trigger: 1. OBTUSE-NO + USE. 2. OBTUSE (dull)-ACUTE (sharp)

Trigger Sentence: "NO-USE"-"USELESS" brain is OBTUSE. It is OF NO USE arguing with an OBTUSE guy.

Sample Sentence: We laughed at his *obtuse* and meaningless doubts.

OBVIATE (OB vee eyt): v. Make unnecessary; get rid of

Trigger: OB (AGAINST) + VIA (WAY) - OBSTRUCT WAY

Trigger Sentence: 1. OBVIATE is to go against some one's way and OBSTRUCT that WAY. 2. OBVIATE anything that OBSTRUCTS your WAY.

Sample Sentence: Why don't we *obviate* this extravagant and unpractical proposal?!

OCCLUDE (uh KLOOD): v. Shut, close

Trigger: 1. CLUDE-CLUSE-CLOSE. 2. OCCLUDED-CLOSED

Trigger Sentence: The OCCLUDING Himalayas CLOSED the way for Ghengis khan to enter India.

Sample Sentence: Water pipe lines got *occluded* due to an unknown reason!

Related Words: OCCLUDED - a. obstructed

OCCULT (uh KULT): a. Not easily understood; secret; supernatural

Trigger: 1.OCCULT-DIFFICULT. 2. OCCULT-ADULT

Trigger Sentence: 1. OCCULT practices are DIFFICULT to understand. 2. Parents OCCULT (v) the ADULT rated movies from prying eyes of the teenage children.

Sample Sentence: The *occult* rituals of the secretive union were revealed only to its members.

Related Words: CULT —a. extreme religious sect

ODIOUS (OH dee us): a. Hateful; vile

Trigger: ODIOUS-TEDIOUS

Trigger Sentence: I am ODIOUS about TEDIOUS job of reading GRE/SAT word list.

Sample Sentence: The most *odious* of all things these days is driving on the city roads!

Related Words: 1.ODIUM - n. hatred .2.TEDIUM —n. boredom

OFFHAND (AWF hand): a. Casual; without preparation or thought

Trigger: "OFFHAND"-"HANDS-ON" (** near antonyms)

Trigger Sentence: The OFFHANDED piano recital showed his lack of HANDS ON EXPERIENCE.

Sample Sentence: The students made some *offhand* remarks about the new teacher.

OFFICIOUS (uh FISH us): a. Excessively pushy in offering one's service; bossy.

Trigger: 1.OFFICERS. 2. OFFICIALS

Trigger Sentence: 1. OFFICERS are OFFICIOUS towards girls in giving excessive. 2. The male workers felt unhappy with the OFFICIOUS behavior of the OFFICERS.

Sample Sentence: My *officious* officer tells everyone how to do their jobs.

OFFSET (awf SET): v. Compensate; balance

Trigger: OFFSET-SET OFF

Trigger Sentence: The SET gains OFFSET the losses.

Sample Sentence: His extraordinary skills *offset* his opponent's superior strengths.

Related Words: 1.UPSET - a. worried. 2. OUTSET - n. start; beginning. 3. ONSET - n. attack

OLFACTORY (ol FAK tuh ree): a. Related to sense of smell
  Trigger: OLFACTORY-OIL FACTORY
  Trigger Sentence: My OLFACTORY sense tells me that there is an OIL FACTORY nearby.
  Sample Sentence: *Olfactory* neuron - is a nerve cell involved in processing smell.
  Related Words: GUSTATORY - a. of or pertaining to taste.

OMINOUS (OM uh nu s): a. Threatening
  Trigger: OMINOUS-"O + MINUS (-Ve)"
  Trigger Sentence: A MINUS sign is considered to be OMINOUS in some societies.
  Sample Sentence: The weather was almost *ominous*, so we feared a thunder storm.

OMNIPOTENT (om NIP uh tunt): a. All powerful
  Trigger: OMNI (all) +POTENT
  Trigger Sentence: OMNIPOTENT people possess POTENTIAL energy.
  Sample Sentence: Superman is *omnipotent*. He has potential powers to accomplish impossible feats.
  Related Words: PLENIPOTENTIARY - a. has full authority.

OMNISCIENT (om NISH unt): a. Knowing everything
  Trigger: OMNI (ALL) +SCIENTIST
  Trigger Sentence: SCIENTISTS are curious to achieve OMNISCIENCE.
  Sample Sentence: I do not pretend to be omniscient, but as far as medicine is concerned, I am!
  Related Words: OMNIPOTENT – a. all-powerful. 2.OMNIPRESENT - a. present everywhere

ONEROUS (ON er us): a. Burdensome
  Trigger: ONEROUS-OWNERS
  Trigger Sentence: OWNER's life is usually ONEROUS.
  Sample Sentence: Owners of private buses have the *onerous* duty of ensuring safety.
  Related Words: ONUS - n. duty; burden

ONUS (OH nus): n. A burden, responsibility
  Trigger: 1. ONUS- ONEROUS-OWNERS. 2. ONUS-ON US
  Trigger Sentence: 1. The ONUS of proving our loyalty lies ON US. 2. The ONUS of proving their innocence lies in the OWNERS of the lodge.
  Sample Sentence: It is an *onus* on us to conserve our environment.

OPACITY (oh PAS i tee): n. Obscurity; unclear
  Trigger: OPACITY-OPAQUE
  Trigger Sentence: The condition of being OPAQUE is known as OPACITY.
  Sample Sentence: The OPACITY of the road is due to the OPAQUE weather.
  Related Words: OPAQUE - a. cloudy; unclear

OPINIONATED (uh PIN yuh ney tid): a. Stubborn; adherent to one's own opinion
  Trigger: OPINIONATED–rigid on OPINION
  Trigger Sentence: The OPINIONATED man is obstinate or rigid in OPINION.
  Sample Sentence: It is not easy to introduce new concepts to a bunch of *opinionated* old masters!

OPPORTUNE (OP er tyoon): a. Timely; proper

Trigger: OPPORTUNE-OPPORTUNITY

Trigger Sentence: At OPPORTUNE time you get good OPPORTUNITIES.

Sample Sentence: It is not an *opportune* time to invest in the stock market.

Related Words: INOPPORTUNE - a. untimely, inconvenient

OPPRESSIVE (uh PRES iv): a. Burdensome; tyrannical

Trigger: PRESSURE

Trigger Sentence: An OPPRESSOR (dictator) put solid PRESSURE (oppressive laws) on people.

Sample Sentence: Women in villages still lead an *oppressive* life dominated by chauvinistic men.

OPPROBRIUM (uh PROH bree um): n. Infamy, insult

Trigger: 1.OPP. –OPPOSITE. 2. OPPRO (APPROVE) + BRIUM

Trigger Sentence: 1. OPP. (OPPOSITE) people always talk OPPROBRIUM. 2. "OPP. TO APPROVE" is known as "OPPROBRIUM".

Sample Sentence: This star sportsman will face *opprobrium* for indulging in match fixing.

OPTIMUM (OP tuh mum): a. Most favorable; best

Trigger: OPTIMUM-MAXIMUM (** synonyms)

Trigger Sentence: Put MAXIMUM effort to get OPTIMUM result.

Sample Sentence: I would expect *optimum* results, since all my students who attended the GRE test had excellent training.

Related Words: OPTIMIST - n. one who looks on the positive side of things

OPULENT (OP yuh lunt): a. Wealthy, lavish; abundant

Trigger: 1.OPUL-OPEL. 2. OPULENT-AFFLUENT

Trigger Sentence: 1. OPULENT people buy OPEL car. 2. OPULENT and AFFLUENT are synonyms.

Sample Sentence: *Opulent* people do not have problems?! Their issues can be larger than life!

ORACULAR (oh RAK yuh ler): a. Prophetic; mysterious or ambiguous

Trigger: ORACLE-ORATION- ORATOR

Trigger Sentence: The prophet's ORACULAR ORATION about the future mystified many.

Sample Sentence: The ancient Greeks were prophetic with a great insight of *oracular* science.

Related Words: ORACLE –n. prophecy

ORDEAL (awr DEEL): n. Hardship; severe trail

Trigger: ORDEAL-HARD DEAL

Trigger Sentence: It is very difficult to DEAL with an ORDEAL.

Sample Sentence: It was indeed an *ordeal* for her to deal with an alcoholic husband.

ORGANIC (awr GAN ik): a. Natural; inherent; fundamental

Trigger: ORGANIC-ORGAN

Trigger Sentence: ORGANIC food is produced by ORGANIC farming.

Sample Sentence: The course is *organic*- with daily news and sporting updates.

Related Words: ORGANIZATION - n. systematic arrangement of elements

ORIGINATE (uh RIJ uh neyt): v. Begin; be created; develop
    Trigger: 1.ORIGINATE-ORIGIN .2.ORIGINATE-ORIGINAL
    Trigger Sentence: The flight ORIGINATES in Hyderabad ORIGIN.
    Sample Sentence: The custom of marriage *originated* during earlier times.

ORNATE (awr NEYT): a. Excessive in decorative detail
    Trigger: ORNATE-ORNAMENT
    Trigger Sentence: The king's palace is very ORNATE with gold ORNAMENTS.
    Sample Sentence: The ancient temple was *ornate* with sculptures of dancing seraphs.
    Related Words: 1.ADORN – v. decorate; 2.UNADORNED – a. simple; undecorated

OSSIFY (OS uh fi): v. Become hard or inflexible
    Trigger: OSSIFIED-"FOSSIL-FIED"
    Trigger Sentence: FOSSILS become OSSIFIED as time passes.
    Sample Sentence: The cartilage will *ossify*, to become bone.
    Related Words: FOSSILIZE – v. petrify; become unchanging

OSTENSIBLE (o STEN seh bul): a. Apparent, seem, pretended
    Trigger: "OSTEN + SIBLE"-VISIBLE (ostensible-visible)
    Trigger Sentence: The OSTENSIBLE life style of successful entrepreneurs is clearly VISIBLE.
    Sample Sentence: For all his *ostensible* wealth, he had no money to pay his employees.

OSTENTATIOUS (os ten TEY shus): a. Showy, pretentious; pompous
    Trigger: 1.OH + STUNT + STATUS. 2. OSTENTATIOUS-PRETENTIOUS
    Trigger Sentence: 1. Movie STUNTS are OSTENTATIOUS in nature; all are SHOWY.
    2. OSTENTATIOUS appearances tend to be PRETENTIOUS.
    Sample Sentence: People who are *ostentatious* tend to show off their status.
    Related Words: PRETENTIOUS –a. showy; feigning

OSTRACIZE (OS truh syze): v. Exclude from a group, banish
    Trigger: ostRACISM (-RACISM)
    Trigger Sentence: RACISM encourages people to OSTRACIZE the poor class from the society.
    Sample Sentence: Criminals are put in jails so as to *ostracize* them form the civil society.

OUTLANDISH (out LAN dish): a. Strange; unusual; bizarre
    Trigger: OUT OF THE LAND
    Trigger Sentence: The OUTLANDISH ornaments are brought into this country from foreign LAND.
    Sample Sentence: Touching snow for the first time in my life was an *outlandish* experience!

OUTMODED (out MOH did): a. Out-of-date; old-fashioned
    Trigger: 1. OUT+ MODERN. 2. OUTDATED
    Trigger Sentence: OUTDATED fashion is known as OUT OF DATE or OUTMODED.
    Sample Sentence: You cannot win a modern war with *outmoded* arms and ammunition.

OUTSTRIP (out STRIP): v. Excel; surpass

Trigger: OUTSTRIP-OUTSTANDING

Trigger Sentence: With OUTSTANDING show Bolt OUTSTRIPPED and OUTDISTANCED his rivals.

Sample Sentence: Our outstanding expenditure *outstrips* our outstanding income.

OVERLOOK (oh ver look): v. Ignore; excuse

Trigger: OVERLOOK - NO LOOK

Trigger Sentence: OVERLOOK is NOT to LOOK at the mistakes; IGNORE and EXCUSE.

Sample Sentence: Have a deeper look into the problem. Never *overlook* it.

OVERSHADOW (oh ver SHAD oh): v. Obscure; make less important

Trigger: OVERSHADOW -SHADOW

Trigger Sentence: The SHADOWS OVERSHADOW the sunlight and makes everything dark.

Sample Sentence: The shadow of inflation *overshadows* the prospects of a booming economy.

OVERHAUL (oh ver HAWL): v. Renovate; make overall repairs

Trigger: OVERHAUL- OVER-ALL

Trigger Sentence: When you OVERHAUL an engine go for an OVERALL REPAIR.

Sample Sentence: I need to *overhaul* my car before venturing on a long distance jaunt.

OVERT (oh VURT): a. Open to view

Trigger: OVERT-COVERT (refer)

Trigger Sentence: COVERT (COVERED) means SECRET; and OVERT means OPEN; COVERT and OVERT are antonyms.

Sample Sentence: in a Democracy, we should *overtly* discuss any sort of covert operations.

Related Words: COVERT - a. secret, hidden

OVERTURE (OH ver choor): n. Something introductory; prelude

Trigger: OVERTURE-OPENTUNE

Trigger Sentence: An OVERTURE is an OPEN-TUNE of a musical composition.

Sample Sentence: As an *overture* to Liberal Economy, China first opened up certain districts for free trade before tuning the entire country to a full-fledged Capitalist Economy.

OVERWEENING (OH ver WEE ning): a. Arrogant; immoderate

Trigger: OVERWEENING-"OVER + WINNING"

Trigger Sentence: The WINNING team appears OVERWEENING to the losing team.

Sample Sentence: Rahul is rich and famous, yet down to earth unlike his *overweening* cousins.

Related Words: OVERBEARING – a. bossy; arrogant

OVERWHELM (oh ver WELM): v. Overpower, flood, engulf

Trigger: 1. OVERWHELM-OVERFLOW. 2. OVERWHELM-OVERPOWER

Trigger Sentence: They were OVERWHELMED by an OVERFLOW of congratulatory letters.

Sample Sentence: 1. I was *overwhelmed* with happiness to see my nephew. 2. Spain *overwhelmed* Russia in the game of hockey.

OXYMORON (ok si MAWR on): n. A combination of contradictory words

   Trigger: OXY-MORON (sharp-dull)

   Trigger Sentence: OXY means "SHARP" like oxygen; MORON means "DULL".

   Sample Sentence: The phrase "thunderous silence" is an *oxymoron*.

PACIFY (PAS uh fie): v. Soothe, make calm

   Trigger: 1.PACIFIST-NO FIST. 2. PACIFY-PACIFIER

   Trigger Sentence: 1. PACIFIST never uses his FIST. 2. a PACIFIER PACIFIES the baby; comforts.

   Sample Sentence: When you are on a *pacifying* mission, you should not show your fist.

   Related Words: PACIFIST - n. lover of peace

PAEAN (PEE un): n. Song of praise; joy

   Trigger: 1. PAEAN-PIANO. 2. PAEAN- PAN (refer)

   Trigger Sentence: 1. With PIANO he sang a PAEAN (a song of praise) for his lover. 2. PAEAN is a song of PRAISE; whereas PAN is to CRITICIZE.

   Sample Sentence: The *paean* of piano music filled the auditorium.

PAINSTAKING (PAYN stay king): a. Careful; showing hard work

   Trigger: PAINS+TAKING

   Trigger Sentence: PAINSTAKING artist TAKES lot of PAINS by continuously carving a sculpture.

   Sample Sentence: Dr. Rao did a *painstaking* surgery for almost five hours to save the patient.

PALATABLE (PAL ih tah bul): a. Agreeable; tasty

   Trigger: PALATABLE-FULL EATABLE

   Trigger Sentence: All these EATABLE items are PALATABLE.

   Sample Sentence: Truth is not always palatable; don't they say truth is bitter?!

   Related Words: UNPALATABLE - a. not tasty.

PALLIATE (PAL ee eyt): v. Ease pain; make less severe

   Trigger: PALLIATE-PILL+ ATE

   Trigger Sentence: Once the patient ATE PILLS, it PALLIATED his suffering.

   Sample Sentence: If you cannot cure this disease, at least try to *palliate* the pain.

PALLID (PAL id): a. Pale; weak

> **Trigger:** PALLID-PALE + LID
>
> **Trigger Sentence:** The drooping EYELID and PALE face shows PALLID condition of an INVALID.
>
> **Sample Sentence:** Her complexion turned *pallid* due to prolonged illness and bad diet.

PALPABLE (PAL pah bul): a. Touchable; obvious, clear

> **Trigger:** 1.PALP-PALM. 2. PALPABLE-PERCEPTIBLE
>
> **Trigger Sentence:** 1. With PALM, body is PALPABLE. 2. PALPABLE & PERCEPTIBLE are synonyms.
>
> **Sample Sentence:** The Great Wall of China is not only perceptible from Mongolia but also *palpable* from the Moon.
>
> Related Words: IMPALPABLE - n. unable to be felt by touch; not easily understood.

PALTRY (PAWL tree): a. Worthless, petty, trivial, small

> **Trigger:** PALTRY-PETTY
>
> **Trigger Sentence:** PALTRY means PETTY; the company donated PALTRY $100 for flood relief.
>
> **Sample Sentence:** This is a *paltry* sum to pay for such a masterpiece.

PAN (PAN): v. Criticize harshly

> **Trigger:** FAN (ANTI)
>
> **Trigger Sentence:** A FAN never PANS his favorites. But an "ANTI-FAN" PANS the opposition.
>
> **Sample Sentence:** The script was unanimously *panned* by the critics for being redundant.

PANACEA (pan ih SEE uh): n. A cure-all

> **Trigger:** PANACEA -PAIN+ NAUSEA
>
> **Trigger Sentence:** PANACEA removes PAIN as well as NAUSEA
>
> **Sample Sentence:** Though this medicine is a real *panacea*, it causes nausea.

PANACHE (pa NASH): n. Style; flair, flamboyance

> **Trigger:** 1.PANACHE-MUSTACHE. 2. PANACHE- POSH
>
> **Trigger Sentence:** 1. To look POSH is his PANACHE. 2. The PANACHE of MOUSTACHE made him handsome.
>
> **Sample Sentence:** Many performers imitate Noel Coward, but few have his *panache* and style.

PANDEMIC (pan DEM ik): a. /n. Widespread; affecting the majority of the people

> **Trigger:** 1. PANDA-PANDEMIC. 2. PANDEMIC-EPIDEMIC
>
> **Trigger Sentence:** 1. PANDAS are PANDEMIC to China. 2. Widely EPIDEMIC like swine flu is known as PANDEMIC.
>
> **Sample Sentence:** Bird flu and dengue are considered *pandemic*.
>
> Related Words: 1.EPIDEMIC –a. widespread; outbreak. 2. ENDEMIC –a. local; limited to an area

PANDEMONIUM (pan duh MOH nee um): n. Wild disorder; Tumult, furor

> **Trigger:** 1. PANDEMONIUM-PANIC. 2. panDEMONium-DEMON
>
> **Trigger Sentence:** 1. PANDEMONIUM and PANIC are synonyms. 2. The teacher's DEMON-like appearance created a PANDEMONIUM in the classroom.

Sample Sentence: When the two ships collided at the harbor, *pandemonium* broke out.

PANDER (PAN der): v. Cater to the low desires of others

> **Trigger:** PANDER-UNDER (low)
>
> **Trigger Sentence:** Prostitutes WANDER to PANDER to boys for their UNDER (low) desires.
>
> **Sample Sentence:** Low graded films bow down and *pander* to the tastes of vulgar viewers.

PANEGYRIC (pan i JIR ik): n. Formal praise

> **Trigger:** "PANEGYRIC"-"FAN+LYRIC"
>
> **Trigger Sentence:** In a PANEGYRIC -- a FAN sings LYRIC about his heroine.
>
> **Sample Sentence:** A diehard fan of Sachin Tendulkar wrote a *panegyric* lyric.

PANORAMA (pan uh RAM ah): n. Wide view in all directions; comprehensive view

> **Trigger:** PANORAMA-DRAMA-RAMA
>
> **Trigger Sentence:** In a DRAMA, the PANORAMA of Lord RAMA'S image unfolds for the viewers.
>
> **Sample Sentence:** Via the external walkway, visitors get 360° of *panoramic* London skyline.

PARABLE (PAR ah bul): n. Moral story/tale, fable

> **Trigger:** PARABLE-FABLE
>
> **Trigger Sentence:** A MORAL FABLE is termed as PARABLE.
>
> **Sample Sentence:** Panchatantra is a timeless classic with hundreds of *parables* on morals.

PARADIGM (PAR ah dime): n. Model, example, pattern

> **Trigger:** 1. PARADIGM- PARADISE. 2. PARADIGM-PARAGON
>
> **Trigger Sentence:** 1. We dream of shaping our country as a PARADIGM of a PARADISE. 2. PARAGON and PARADIGM are synonyms.
>
> **Sample Sentence:** The new java language might turn existing computing *paradigm* upside down.

PARADOX (PAR uh doks): n. A statement that is seemingly contradictory to common sense and yet is perhaps true.

> **Trigger:** 1.DOX-DOGS; DOX-FOX. 2. ORTHODOX-HETERODOX
>
> **Trigger Sentence:** 1. DOGS appear like FOX; FOX appear like DOGS; it is a CONTRADICTION. 2. It is PARADOXICAL that some people are known for UNORTHODOX beliefs with ORTHODOX acts.
>
> **Sample Sentence:** The *paradox* is that fox is a foolish animal unlike its portrayal in stories.
>
> Related Words: PARADOXICAL - a. negate itself; contradictory.

PARAGON (PAR ah gon): n. Model of perfection

> **Trigger:** PARAGON-PARADISE
>
> **Trigger Sentence:** 1. A PARAGON-goes to a PARADISE; because he is a MODEL of perfection. 2. 'PARADISE LOST' is a PARAGON of John Milton's brilliant poetry.
>
> **Sample Sentence:** Perfect like a *paragon* he always inspired his students.

PARAMOUNT (PAR uh mount): a. More important than anything else; supreme

Trigger: parAMOUNT-AMOUNT

Trigger Sentence: AMOUNT (money) is the most important and PARAMOUNT thing in world.

Sample Sentence: Nutrition is of *paramount* concern to be addressed among the poor.

PARIAH (puh RY uh): n. Outcast; castaway

Trigger: PARIAH-MESSIAH

Trigger Sentence: PARIAH is almost near opposite to MESSIAH (Jesus, the Lord)

Sample Sentence: They looked down at me like I was some *pariah,* when I wore jeans.

PAROCHIAL (puh ROH kee ul): a. Narrow-minded; provincial

Trigger: PAROCHIAL -PARISH

Trigger Sentence: PARISH means a village or a PROVINCE; where LOCAL people are PAROCHIAL/NARROW –MINDED.... unlike city people who are COSMOPOLITAN.

Sample Sentence: The local leaders are creating *parochial* feelings among the citizens.

PARODY (PAR uh dee): n. Comical imitation of another work; spoof

Trigger: PARODY-PARROT-COMEDY

Trigger Sentence: The PARROT PARODIED (v) the man in a COMICAL fashion.

Sample Sentence: We laughed when the comedian *parodied* the Chief Minister's pronunciation.

PAROXYSM (PAR uk siz um): n. A sudden uncontrollable attack; fit

Trigger: 1.PAROXYSM- ORGASM. 2. PAROXYSM-PEROXIDE

Trigger Sentence: 1. The PAIR experienced PAROXYSM of ecstasy during an ORGASM. 2. When nitrogen PEROXIDE is inhaled people exhibit PAROXYSM.

Sample Sentence: He broke into a *paroxysm* of anger by finding his BMW wrecked by the driver.

PARRY (PAR ee): n. Ward off a blow, deflect

Trigger: 1. PARRY-HARRY (POTTER). 2. PARRY-QUERY

Trigger Sentence: 1. HARRY ducked under to PARRY the opponent's blow. 2. I know how to PARRY your QUERY.

Sample Sentence: Peter swiftly *parried* off from the psycho's blow and ran to safety.

PARSIMONY (PAHR suh moh nee): n. Miserliness; extreme stinginess

Trigger: PARSIMONY-PURSE+ MONEY

Trigger Sentence: PARSIMONIOUS NEVER PASS THE MONEY; never open PURSE to spend MONEY.

Sample Sentence: *Parsimonious* people don't spend money lavishly.

PARTIAL (PAHR shl): a. 1. Incomplete. 2. Showing favoritism

Trigger: 1. PART .2. PARTIALITY

Trigger Sentence: The first PART of this book gives PARTIAL description of the GRE wordlist.

Sample Sentence: A judge should not deliver a *partial* verdict; he got to be completely *impartial.*

Related Words: PARTIALITY - n. preference; bias

PARTISAN (PART ah zan): n. One sided; biased; committed to a party

Trigger: PARTISAN-"PARTY + FAN"

Trigger Sentence: 1. He is a PARTISAN PARTY FAN. 2. For a PARTISAN there is lot of PARTIALITY towards his PARTY.

Sample Sentence: Those *partisans* and puritans often behave like they are god sent to mankind!

PASSIVE (PAS iv): a. Submissive; apathetic; disinterested

Trigger: PASSIVE-ACTIVE (**antonyms)

Trigger Sentence: The SUBMISSIVE girl accepted her fate PASSIVELY.

Sample Sentence: The handcuffed prisoner stood *passively* before the judge.

PASTICHE (pa STEESH): n. Imitation of another's style in writing

Trigger: PASTICHE-"PASTE-EACH"

Trigger Sentence: It is an incidence of PASTICHE. The writer copied and PASTED EACH of the articles.

Sample Sentence: Her music compositions are a *pastiche*, in fact a blend of many choirs.

PATENT (PAT unt): a. Clear, obvious, innovative

Trigger: PATENT-LATENT (** near antonyms)

Trigger Sentence: Something LATENT is HIDDEN and something PATENT is CLEARLY VISIBLE.

Sample Sentence: The scientist has already taken more than a 100 *patents* in a latent manner.

Memory Test-77 : Match each word and its memory trick to the corresponding definition.

S.N	WORD	MEMORY TRIGGER	S.N	DEFINITIONS	KEY
1	OBSCURE	unsure	A	All powerful	
2	OBSEQUIOUS	OBEDIENT - SEQUENCE	B	Burdensome	
3	OBSESSIVE	EXCESSIVE	C	Casual; without preparation	
4	OBSOLETE	Of so LATE	D	Compensate; balance	
5	OBSTINATE	of+STONE + ate	E	Compulsive; excessively preoccupied	
6	OBSTREPEROUS	Strepsils	F	Excessively pushy; bossy.	
7	OBTRUSIVE	protrusion-projection	G	Hateful; vile	
8	OBTUSE	USELESS brain	H	Knowing everything	
9	OBVIATE	Obstruct way	I	Make unnecessary; get rid of	
10	OCCLUDE	Clude-cluse-CLOSE	J	Noisy; undisciplined	
11	OCCULT	Difficult	K	Not easily understood; secret	
12	ODIOUS	ODIOUS about TEDIOUS	L	Obedient or attentive; sycophantic	
13	OFFHAND	Without HANDS on experience	M	Outdated; useless	
14	OFFICIOUS	Officers- Officials	N	Related to sense of smell	
15	OFFSET	Offset-set off	O	Shut, close	
16	OLFACTORY	OIL FACTORY	P	Stubbornly persistent; hard to control	
17	OMINOUS	o + minus -omen	Q	Stupid; blunt	
18	OMNIPOTENT	OMNI (all) +POTENT	R	Threatening	
19	OMNISCIENT	Omni (all) +scientist	S	Undesirably noticeable; protruding	
20	ONEROUS	OWNERS life is ??	T	Vague, dark; unclear	

Memory Test-78 : Match each word and its memory trick to the corresponding definition.

S.N	WORD	MEMORY TRIGGER	S.N	DEFINITIONS	KEY
1	ONUS	Onus- onerous-owners	A	Apparent, seem, pretended	
2	OPACITY	My brain is OPAQUE	B	Become hard or inflexible	
3	OPINIONATED	rigid on OPINION	C	Begin; be created; develop	
4	OPPORTUNE	OPPORTUNITY	D	Burden, responsibility	
5	OPPRESSIVE	authoritative PRESSURE	E	Burdensome; tyrannical	
6	OPPROBRIUM	OPP. people talk	F	Excel; surpass	
7	OPTIMUM	MAXIMUM	G	Excessive in decorative detail	
8	OPULENT	own an OPEL car	H	Exclude from a group, banish	
9	ORACULAR	Oracle-oration- orator	I	Hardship; severe trail	
10	ORDEAL	HARD DEAL	J	Insult, Infamy	
11	ORGANIC	ORGANIC farming	K	Most favorable; best	
12	ORIGINATE	ORIGIN -ORIGINAL	L	Natural; inherent; fundamental	
13	ORNATE	gold ORNAMENTS	M	Obscurity; unclear	
14	OSSIFY	become OSSIFIED	N	Out-of-date; old-fashioned	
15	OSTENSIBLE	VISIBLE	O	Prophetic; mysterious or ambiguous	
16	OSTENTATIOUS	Movie STUNTS are ...	P	Showy, pretentious; pompous	
17	OSTRACIZE	Racism is cut	Q	Strange; unusual; bizarre	
18	OUTLANDISH	Out of the LAND	R	Stubborn on one's own opinion	
19	OUTMODED	OUTDATED	S	Timely; proper	
20	OUTSTRIP	OUTSTANDING	T	Wealthy, lavish; abundant	

Answers	EX.NO	1	2	3	4	5	6	7	8	9	10	11	12	13	14	15	16	17	18	19	20
	77	T	L	E	M	P	J	S	Q	I	O	K	G	C	F	D	N	R	A	H	B
	78	D	M	R	S	E	J	K	T	O	I	L	C	G	B	A	P	H	Q	N	F

Memory Test-79 : Match each word and its memory trick to the corresponding definition.

S.N	WORD	MEMORY TRIGGER	S.N	DEFINITIONS	KEY
1	OVERLOOK	no look	A	Tasty; agreeable	
2	OVERSHADOW	shadow	B	Arrogant; immoderate	
3	OVERHAUL	Over-all	C	Careful; showing hard work	
4	OVERT	OVERT-COVERT	D	combination of contradictory words	
5	OVERTURE	OPENTUNE	E	Criticize harshly	
6	OVERWEENING	Over + winning	F	Cure-all	
7	OVERWHELM	overflow	G	Ease pain; make less severe	
8	OXYMORON	OXYGEN-MORON	H	Ignore; excuse	
9	PACIFY	pacifier	I	Obscure; make less important	
10	PAEAN	PIANO - PAEAN	J	Open to view	
11	PAINSTAKING	Pains+taking	K	Overpower, flood, engulf	
12	PALATABLE	full eatable	L	Pale; weak	
13	PALLIATE	Pill+ ate	M	Renovate; make overall repairs	
14	PALLID	pale + lid	N	Something introductory; prelude	
15	PALPABLE	PALM is PALPABLE	O	Song of praise; joy	
16	PALTRY	PETTY	P	Soothe, make calm	
17	PAN	Anti-FAN pans	Q	Style; flair, flamboyance	
18	PANACEA	Pain+ nausea gone	R	Touchable; obvious, clear	
19	PANACHE	POSH-mustache	S	Widespread; affecting the majority	
20	PANDEMIC	Widely EPIDEMIC	T	Worthless, petty, trivial	

Memory Test-80 : Match each word and its memory trick to the corresponding definition.

S.N	WORD	MEMORY TRIGGER	S.N	DEFINITIONS	KEY
1	PANDEMONIUM	Panic -DEMON	A	1. Incomplete. 2. Showing favoritism	
2	PANDER	UNDER (low)	B	Cater to the low desires of others	
3	PANEGYRIC	FAN+LYRIC	C	Clear, obvious, innovative	
4	PANORAMA	Panorama-drama-rama	D	Comical imitation of another work	
5	PARABLE	FABLE	E	Formal praise	
6	PARADIGM	paradise -paragon	F	Imitation of another's style in writing	
7	PARADOX	Orthodox-heterodox	G	Miserliness; extreme stinginess	
8	PARAGON	Paragon-PARADISE	H	Model of perfection	
9	PARAMOUNT	AMOUNT is ultimate	I	Model, example, pattern	
10	PARIAH	Pariah-messiah	J	Moral story/tale, fable	
11	PAROCHIAL	Parochial -PARISH local	K	More important than anything else	
12	PARODY	Parrot-comedy	L	Narrow-minded; provincial	
13	PAROXYSM	Paroxysm-orgasm-peroxide	M	One sided; committed to a party	
14	PARRY	Avoid QUERY	N	Outcast; castaway	
15	PARSIMONY	Never pass the money	O	Statement that is seemingly contradictory	
16	PARTIAL	PART and Partiality	P	Submissive; apathetic; disinterested	
17	PARTISAN	Party + fan	Q	Sudden uncontrollable attack; fit	
18	PASSIVE	No ACTIVE	R	Ward off a blow, deflect	
19	PASTICHE	PASTE-each	S	Wide view in all directions	
20	PATENT	open LATENT	T	Wild disorder; Tumult, furor	

Answers	EX.NO	1	2	3	4	5	6	7	8	9	10	11	12	13	14	15	16	17	18	19	20
	79	H	I	M	J	N	B	K	D	P	O	C	A	G	L	R	T	E	F	Q	S
	80	T	B	E	S	J	I	O	H	K	N	L	D	Q	R	G	A	M	P	F	C

WORD GROUPS DAY-20

★ **PURITANICAL:** strict on moral and religious issues

ADJECTIVES: moralistic, strait-laced, prudish, prim, priggish; narrow-minded, censorious; austere, stern, severe, ascetic, abstemious

NOUNS: puritan, prude

VERB: xxxxxxxxxxx

ANTONYMS: permissive, liberal; freewheeling

★ **FEELING SORRY**

ADJECTIVES: apologetic, penitential, regretful

NOUNS: compunction, conscience, scruples, misgivings, demur, qualms, guilt, regret, contrition, self-reproach; penitence, penance, atonement, remorse

VERB: regret, repent

ANTONYMS: n. defiance, meanness

★ **MERCY**

ADJECTIVES: clement, compassionate, generous, gentle, humane, indulgent, lenient, liberal, pitiful, sympathetic, tender, tolerant

NOUNS: benevolence, boon, clemency, commiseration, forbearance, godsend, goodwill

VERB: condone,pardon

ANTONYMS: n. cruelty, intolerance, meanness, uncompassion

★ **FORGIVE/FORGIVENESS**

VERB: absolve, acquit, discharge, exonerate, exculpate, expiate, redeem, redress, vindicate

ADJECTIVES: exonerated, reprieved

NOUNS: acquittal, exculpation

ANTONYMS: v.blame, charge, condemn, convict, impeach, incriminate, obligate, punish, sentence

★ **CATHARSIS:** purification, emotional cleansing

ADJECTIVES: cathartic, expurgatory

NOUNS: ablution, cleansing, expurgation, purification, release

VERB: purge, bowdlerize

ANTONYMS: n. dirtying

★ **DRYNESS**

ADJECTIVES: arid, bare, barren, dehydrated, desiccated, droughty, impoverished, parched, sear, torrid

NOUNS: aridity

VERB: desiccate; wither, shrivel; drain, deplete

ANTONYMS: damp, wet, fertile

★ **WETNESS**

ADJECTIVES: damp, dank, saturated, teeming

NOUNS: dampness

VERB: deluge, drench, imbue, steep

ANTONYMS: dehydrate, dry

★ **MODICUM/SMALL AMOUNT**

ADJECTIVES: minute, infinitesimal

NOUNS: modicum, bit, crumb, fragment, iota, mite, morsel, speck, scrap, shred, smattering, scintilla, trifle, whit

VERB: minimize

ANTONYMS: n.large amount, lot

Word List Day-21

PATHETIC (puh THET ik): a. Touching; pitiful, causing compassion.

Trigger: 1. SYMPATHETIC. 2. Pathos (feelings)-sympathy (same feelings)-empathy (same feelings)-antipathy (anti-feelings)-apathy (no feelings).

Trigger Sentence: 1. PATHETIC state stirs SYMPATHY. 2. PATHETICAL - PITIFUL are synonyms.

Sample Sentence: It is a *pathetic* situation for the homeless across the world.

PATRON (PEY trun): n. A person who supports

Trigger: 1.PATER-FATHER.2.PATRON-PAT ON

Trigger Sentence: 1. FATHER or PATER supports. 2. The PATRON PATTED all his proteges ON the BACK for their good work.

Sample Sentence: I am looking for a *patron* who could help me set up my sculpture studio.

PATRONIZE (PEY truh nyze): v. Act superior towards, serve as a sponsor

Trigger: PATER-FATHER

Trigger Sentence: My PATER (or FATHER) is a SUPERIOR BOSS over all of us in the family.

Sample Sentence: During those good old days kings *patronized* music and arts in their courts.

PAUCITY (PAW si tee): a. Lack, scarcity

Trigger: 1.PAUCITY-POOR CITY. 2. PAUPER (beggar) + CITY

Trigger Sentence: In a PAUPER (BEGGAR) CITY everything is SCARCITY.

Sample Sentence: They closed down the old cake shop because of the *paucity* of customers.

PECCADILLO (pek ah DIL oh): n. A minor sin

Trigger: PECCADILLO- "PUKKA- NIL"

Trigger Sentence: NO ONE is PUKKA (English); everyone possesses some PECCADILLOES.

Sample Sentence: He got caught for mere *peccadilloes* while the major criminals escaped!

Related Words: IMPECCABLE -a. faultless; perfect

PECUNIARY (pi KYOO nee er ee): a. Related to money

Trigger: PECUNIARY-PENURY (**near antonym sense)

Trigger Sentence: He lived in PENURY as he never received any PECUNIARY benefits.

Sample Sentence: I am bad at *matters of pecuniary,* so I prefer an accountant to do my finances.

PEDAGOGUE (PED uh gog): n. Teacher; bookish teacher

    Trigger: PEDAGOGUE- PEDANT DIALOGUE

    Trigger Sentence: PEDANT pundit is my PEDAGOGUE; he taught me philosophical DIALOGUES.

    Sample Sentence: He was not a stuffy *pedagogue*; his classes were lively and amusing.

    Related Words: PEDAGOGY - n. education; art of teaching

PEDANTIC (puh DAN tik): a. Showing off learning; bookish

    Trigger: PEDANTIC-VEDANTIC; PEDANT-PUNDIT

    Trigger Sentence: This VEDANTI is PEDANTIC.

    Sample Sentence: Prof. Jones's lectures are *pedantic;* his students have tough time listening.

    Related Words: 1.PEDANT –a. bookish scholar 2. PEDAGOGUE -n. teacher

PEDESTRIAN (peh DES tree ahn): a. Ordinary; unimaginative

    Trigger: PEDESTRIAN PATH

    Trigger Sentence: PEDESTRIAN path is ROUTINE and BORING.

    Sample Sentence: How did you imagine that you will be awarded for your *pedestrian* prose?

PEEVISH (PEE vish): a. Angry, irritable

    Trigger: PEE +WISH

    Trigger Sentence: The frequent PEEING of the dog in the hall made him PEEVISH.

    Sample Sentence: The *peevish* babe did a pee on the expensive rug.

PEJORATIVE (pi JOR uh tiv): a. Having negative connotations; Belittle

    Trigger: 1. PIGGY RAT. 2. PEJORATIVE-NEGATIVE

    Trigger Sentence: 1. If you PEJORATIVELY call someone PIGGY RAT, it can lead to an altercation. 2. Talking NEGATIVE about someone!!

    Sample Sentence: What will you get by making *pejorative* remarks on my character?

PELL-MELL (PEL MEL): a. In confusion; disorderly

    Trigger: PELL-MELL –"HELTER-SKELTER"-"HURRY-SCURRY"

    Trigger Sentence: Helter-skelter; hurry-scurry, hodge-podge; PELL-MELL; topsy-turvy; all belong to same family.

    Sample Sentence: In the 'bull chasing' event in Spain, participants ran *pell-mell* and got trampled.

    Related Words: HELTER-SKELTER -a. hasty and disorderly

PELLUCID (puh LOO sid): a. Transparent; limpid; easy to understand

    Trigger: 1.PURE LIQUID. 2. PELLUCID-LUCID (refer)

    Trigger Sentence: 1. This PURE LIQUID is highly PELLUCID. 2. PELLUCID and LUCID are synonyms.

    Sample Sentence: I find his *pellucid* concepts in writing quite pleasant and pure.

PENANCE (PEN uhns): n. Self-imposed punishment

    Trigger: PENANCE-PENALTY

    Trigger Sentence: He is making PENANCE to pay PENALTY for his crime.

Sample Sentence: "Goddess Parvati did sever *penance* to beget the lord Siva as her husband...".

Related Words: 1.PENITENTIAL -a. relating to penance. 2. REPENT –v. regret one's past actions

PENCHANT (PEN chunt): n. A strong inclination; liking

Trigger: 1. PENCHANT-PENDANT (refer). 2. PENCHANT-ENCHANT-CHANT

Trigger Sentence: 1. Girls have PENCHANT for PENDANTS. 2. PENCHANT for ENCHANTING art.

Sample Sentence: Sohila has an inborn talent and *penchant* for singing and dancing.

Related Words: PENDANT –n. piece of jewelry designed to hang

PENSIVE (PEN siv): a. Dreamily thoughtful; expressing thoughtfulness with sadness

Trigger: PENSIVE-SUSPENSE

Trigger Sentence: The SUSPENSE drama kept the audience in a PENSIVE mood.

Sample Sentence: The author had an intellectual block; he was *pensive* and couldn't pen down his thoughts.

PENURIOUS (puh NYOOR ee us): a. Extremely poor, stingy

Trigger: 1. PENURY-no PENNY. 2. PENURIOUS-PENNY LESS

Trigger Sentence: 1. He is PENURIOUS as he is PENNILESS. 2. He NEVER SPENDS PENNY; stingy

Sample Sentence: He lived *penniless* and yet never complained of his penurious life.

Related Words: PENURY -n. poverty; stinginess

PERCEPTIVE (per SEP tiv): a. Sharp; wise; insightful

Trigger: PERCEPTIVE-CONCEPTIVE

Trigger Sentence: People with strong CONCEPTS are PERCEPTIVE in nature

Sample Sentence: The professor asked his research scholars to be *perceptive* and interpretative.

PEREGRINATION (per i gruh NEY shun): n. Journey, voyage

Trigger: 1. PEREGRINATION-MIGRATION. 2. PEREGRINATION- PILGRIMAGE

Trigger Sentence: PILGRIMAGE, PEREGRINATION and MIGRATION are synonyms.

Sample Sentence: The novel is about a woman *peregrinating* across the temple towns of India in search of spiritualism.

PEREMPTORY (puh REMP tuh ree): a. Authoritative; demanding and leaving no choice

Trigger: PEREMPTORY-PREEMPTORS -EMPERORS

Trigger Sentence: PREEMPTORS are known as EMPERORS; EMPERORS tend to be PEREMPTORY.

Sample Sentence: As a perfectionist, he *peremptorily* made his juniors work with promptness.

PERENNIAL (puh REN ee ul): a. Long lasting

Trigger: PERENNIAL-BIENNIAL-CENTENNIAL

Trigger Sentence: Annual-once a year; biennial-2 years; centennial-100 years; millennium-1000 years; PERENNIAL-INFINITE YEARS; means PERMANENT.

Sample Sentence: Floods are a *perennial* issue for people living by the river.

PERFIDY (PUR fi dee): n. Unfaithfulness; treachery

Trigger: 1. PERFIDY-"PERFECT NOT". 2. PERFIDY-INFIDELITY

Trigger Sentence: 1. A person with PERFIDY is NOT PERFECT. 2. INFIDELITY to one's spouse is perfidy.

Sample Sentence: *Perfidious* friends are back stabbers; more dangerous than your enemies.

Related Words: PERFIDIOUS -a. treacherous; disloyal

PERFUNCTORY (per FUNGK tuh ree): a. Superficial, not thorough; careless; that lacks enthusiasm

Trigger: PERFUNCTORY-NO FUNCTION

Trigger Sentence: It is useless if you FUNCTION PERFUNCTORILY with NO interest.

Sample Sentence: A *perfunctory* assessment will not help dig out the flaws of the factory.

PERIL (PER ul): n. Danger, risk

Trigger: PERIL-DEVIL-EVIL

Trigger Sentence: Because of the DEVIL my life is in a state of PERIL.

Sample Sentence: "He saw the rewards but not the *perils* of the crime".

Related Words: 1.PERILOUS -a. dangerous, risky. 2. IMPERIL -v. put at risk or in danger.

PERIPATETIC (per ih pah TIT ik): a. Moving; walking about

Trigger: PERIPATETIC-"PERI+PATH"

Trigger Sentence: PERI +PATH +TIC ; always implies on "PATH".

Sample Sentence: The *peripatetic* school of philosophy derives its name from the fact that Aristotle walked with his pupils while discussing philosophy with them.

PERIPHERAL (pur IF ur ul): a. Irrelevant, marginal; outer

Trigger: 1.PERIPHERAL-PERIPHERY. 2. PERIPHERAL-CENTRAL

Trigger Sentence: 1. PERIPHERAL issues touches only at the PERIPHERY. 2. In Communist country, the party plays the CENTRAL role whereas the Government plays the PERIPHERAL role.

Sample Sentence: I finished the major part of the project except those *peripheral* details.

Related Words: MARGINAL -a. peripheral; minimal

PERJURY (PUR juh ree): n. Act of lying under oath

Trigger: 1. PERJURY-JURY. 2. PERJURY-FORGERY

Trigger Sentence: 1. In front of JURY Bill Clinton showed PERJURY. 2. FORGERY is a form of PERJURY.

Sample Sentence: When witnesses challenged his statements, he got charged for *perjury*.

PERMEATE (PUR mee eyt): v. Enter, penetrate

Trigger: 1.PERMEATE-PERMIT. 2. PERMEATE-PENETRATE

Trigger Sentence: If you PERMIT light, it'll be PERMEATED and PENETRATED.

Sample Sentence: When the Moghals PERMITTED 'The East India Company' into India, it PERMEATED the entire country.

Related Words: IMPERMEABLE -n. impenetrable

PERNICIOUS (per NISH us): a. Highly destructive

Trigger: PERNICIOUS- POISONOUS-MALICIOUS

Trigger Sentence: 1. A POISONOUS chemical is PERNICIOUS. 2. MALICIOUS friends cause PERNICIOUS harm.

Sample Sentence: Racism gives rise to *pernicious* tensions.

PERPETRATE (PUR pi treyt): v. Commit a crime

Trigger: 1.PERPETRATE-PERFORM (BAD). 2. PERPETRATE-OPERATE

Trigger Sentence: 1. PERPETRATE is to PERFORM an illegal act .2. The terrorists OPERATE from Pakistan to PERPETRATE atrocities in India.

Sample Sentence: The bomb blast in school was the worst attack *perpetrated* by the terrorists.

PERPETUAL (per PECH oo ul): a. Everlasting; permanent

Trigger: PERPETUAL-PERENNIAL (** synonyms)

Trigger Sentence: PERENNIAL rivers are PERPETUAL.

Sample Sentence: He was a *perpetual* patron for the poor in the village.

Related Words: PERPETUATE -v. Make something last.

PERPLEX (per PLEKS): v. To make it complicated; confuse

Trigger: PERPLEX-COMPLEX

Trigger Sentence: The COMPLEXITY of human brain is PERPLEXING.

Sample Sentence: Why are you trying to *perplex* the matter instead of simplifying?

Related Words: PERPLEXED -a. baffled

PERQUISITE (PUR kwuh zit): n. Something in addition to regular pay; bonus

Trigger: 1.PERQ-PERK. 2. PERQUISITE-REQUISITE

Trigger Sentence: 1. Salary + PERKS; The short form of PERQUISITES is PERKS. 2. More than REQUISITE (required) is known as PERQUISITE.

Sample Sentence: Isn't a Benz car a great *perquisite* of my job?!

Related Words: REQUISITE -a. required; essential

PERSEVERANCE (pur suh VEER uns): n. Hard work, diligence

Trigger: 1.SEVERE work. 2. PERSEVERANCE –PERSISTENCE (** synonyms)

Trigger Sentence: In spite of SEVERE WORK load, he finished his task with sheer PERSEVERANCE.

Sample Sentence: With *perseverance* and patience Minoti, a single parent, brought up her kids.

PERSONIFICATION (per son uh fi KEY shun): n. A person who represents an abstract quality

Trigger: PERSON-IDENTIFICATION

Trigger Sentence: IDENTIFICATION with PERSONAL nature in an abstract quality is PERSONIFICATION.

Sample Sentence: Tall and graceful Gayatri convincingly *personified* the god Siva in the play.

Related Words: PERSONIFY -v. represent, embody

PERSONABLE (PUR suh nuh bul): a. Attractive

Trigger: PERSONABLE-PERSONALITY

Trigger Sentence: Public Relations Officers should have PERSONABLE PERSONALITY.

Sample Sentence: I need a *personable* receptionist for my office.

PERSPICACIOUS (pur spi KEY shus): a. Perceptive, having insight; astute

   Trigger: 1. PERS-PICACIOUS- PERSON PICASSO. 2. PER+SPICACIOUS- 'PER + SAGACIOUS"

   Trigger Sentence: 1. PICASSO was PERSPICACIOUS artist. 2. A PERSPICACIOUS person is PERCEPTIVE and SAGACIOUS.

   Sample Sentence: Tom being a *perspicacious* person will surely do well in his new career.

   Related Words: PERSPICACITY -n. keenness of perception.

PERSPICUOUS (per SPIK yoo us): a. Expressed clearly; transparent

   Trigger: PERS+PICUOUS-"PERS+ PICS"

   Trigger Sentence: The PERFECT PICS are so PERSPICUOUS that they obviously tell the story.

   Sample Sentence: 1. The author writes in a *perspicuous* style. 2. One of the outstanding features of this book is the *perspicuity* of its author.

   Related Words: PERSPICUITY -n. clarity of expression; transparency

PERT (PURT): a. Impertinent; bold

   Trigger: PERT-EXPERT

   Trigger Sentence: An EXPERT usually exhibits PERT attitude towards others.

   Sample Sentence: Angelina Jolie has a natural *pert* in her gait.

   Related Words: IMPERTINENT -a. Impudent; irrelevant

PERTINACIOUS (pur tn EY shus): a. Stubborn; persistent

   Trigger: 1.PERTINACIOUS-EXPERT IN ASIA'S. 2. PERTINACIOUS-TENACIOUS (** synonyms)

   Trigger Sentence: 1. He has become EXPERT IN ASIA'S games, because of his PERTINACIOUS nature. 2. PERTINACITY-TENACITY (or CAPACITY to hold).

   Sample Sentence: The *pertinacious* Mongols became expert horse riders in Asia before they invaded Europe.

   Related Words: TENACIOUS -a. stubborn; not easily loosened

PERTURB (per TURB): v. Disturb completely, agitate

   Trigger: PERTURB-DISTURB

   Trigger Sentence: PERTURB is to DISTURB completely.

   Sample Sentence: Mr. Simpson was *perturbed* due to family fights on property.

   Related Words: IMPERTURBABLE -a. calm, not easily disturbed.

PERUSE (puh ROOZ): v. Read with care

   Trigger: PERUSE-FOR USE

   Trigger Sentence: She is habituated to PERUSE all the instructions before USING the medicine.

   Sample Sentence: All of this information is available in the library for you to *peruse*.

PERVASIVE (per VEY siv): a. Spread throughout.

   Trigger: 1. VAST-VAST UNIVERSE. 2. PERVASIVE-"PARAM+SIVA"

   Trigger Sentence: 1. Our VAST UNIVERSE is PERVASIVE in all directions. 2. PARAM+SIVA, THE Lord is PERVASIVE in the VAST universe.

Sample Sentence: The spiritual master had a pervasive aura of peace and positivity.

Related Words: PERVADE – v. penetrate; spread out

PERVERSE (pur VERSE): a. Contrary; wicked; perverted

Trigger: 1.PERVERSE-REVERSE. 2. PERVERSE-PERVERTED (** synonyms)

Trigger Sentence: The PERVERTED man took PERVERSE satisfaction by REVERSING her work.

Sample Sentence: Those *perverse* headed boys often watch dirty, horror, violent films.

PESSIMISM (PES uh miz um): n. Belief that life is basically bad

Trigger: PESSIMISM-no POSITIVISM

Trigger Sentence: When someone possesses PESSIMISM there is NO POSITIVISM.

Sample Sentence: A sense of *pessimism* prevailed among the business community.

Related Words: OPTIMISM –n. state of hoping for the best

PESTILENTIAL (pes tl EN shul): a. Baneful, deadly; contagious

Trigger: PESTILENTIAL-PESTICIDE

Trigger Sentence: Wide range application of PESTICIDES is PESTILENTIAL to human societies.

Sample Sentence: What a pest of a person you are to spread a *pestilential* growth in my office.

PETRIFY (PE truh fye): v. Turn to stone, terrify

Trigger: 1.PETRI-PETROL. 2. PETRIFY-TERRIFY

Trigger Sentence: 1. PETROL is a rock oil; extracted from rock below the surface of earth. 2. She became PETRIFIED after watching the TERRIFYING murder.

Sample Sentence: The severe rules and regulations of this religion *petrified* us.

PETULANT (PET yoo lunt): a. Ill-tempered; irascible

Trigger: PETULANT-PET+VIOLENT

Trigger Sentence: My PET is VIOLENT and PETULANT.

Sample Sentence: Patricia has lived all her life with a *petulant* and pestering partner.

PHARISAIC (far uh SEY ik): a. Hypocritically religious; self-righteous

Trigger: PHARISAIC -P+HARI+SAI+C

Trigger Sentence: His devotion to HARI & SAI was PHARISAIC.

Sample Sentence: A true believer is natural, not *pharisaical* about his ethics and customs.

PHILANTHROPIST (fi LAN thruh pist): n. Lover of mankind; charitable donor

Trigger: PHIL (love) +ANTHROP (MANKIND)

Trigger Sentence: ANTHROPOLOGY (study of human race) & (Phil - love); a PHILANTHROPIST loves HUMAN RACE; whereas MISANTHROPE hates mankind.

Sample Sentence: My uncle was a *philanthropist* who headed many civic projects in our village.

Related Words: MISANTHROPE -a. hater of mankind.

PHILISTINE (FIL ih steen): a. Narrow- minded person; uncultured

Trigger: PHILISTINE-PALESTINE

Trigger Sentence: Israel believes that PALESTINE is a PHILISTINE nation.

Sample Sentence: The *philistines* opposed everything new and creative in art.

PHLEGMATIC (fleg MAT ik): a. Calm; not easily disturbed

Trigger: PHLEGM-FLAME LESS; NO FLAME- NO HOT

Trigger Sentence: 1. PHLEGMATIC appear cool and FLAME LESS. 2. NO-FLAME-NO PASSION or burning desire.

Sample Sentence: As a *phlegmatic* nurse, she maintains composure during emergencies.

PHONY (foh NEE): a. Fake; not authentic

Trigger: PHONY-PHONE

Trigger Sentence: Rural Indian consumers are lapping up Chinese-made PHONY Nokia PHONES.

Sample Sentence: The sales representative sold a *phony* watch with a designer logo.

PICARESQUE (pik uh RESK): a. Describing adventures of a person (usually a rogue)

Trigger: PICARESQUE-PICTURES of RISK

Trigger Sentence: In the PICARESQUE novels, writers PICTURE the RISKY adventures of heroes.

Sample Sentence: The History of Tom Jones, a Foundling (1749) is the best *picaresque* novel.

PICAYUNE (pik ee YOON): a. Worthless; petty; small-minded

Trigger: 1. PICAYUNE- PUNY (** synonyms) .2. PICAYUNE- PICK COIN in cents

Trigger Sentence: 1. The PICAYUNE people argued over even on the PUNY matters. 2. The beggar PICKED the five cent COINS; it was a PICAYUNE amount.

Sample Sentence: The peon gets a *picayune* amount as his salary.

PICTURESQUE (pik chuh RESK): a. Charming in appearance; visual

Trigger: PICTURESQUE – PICTURES

Trigger Sentence: Life of Pie is a PICTURESQUE book of boy's voyage with painted PICTURES.

Sample Sentence: The Taj hotel and its surrounding environments are exceptionally *picturesque*.

PIED (PYED): a. Multicolored; spotted

Trigger: 1. PIED-PIE CHART. 2. PIED-PAINTED

Trigger Sentence: 1. A PIE CHART is usually PIED. 2. A PIE CHART is PAINTED with colors.

Sample Sentence: The forest is home to many *pied* and *piebald* mules and wild horses.

Related Words: PIEBALD -a. spotted; of different colors

PIETY (PYE uh tee): n. Devotion; reverence for God

Trigger: PIETY-DEITY

Trigger Sentence: When a devotee stands in front of a DEITY, his/her PIETY becomes intensified.

Sample Sentence: Purity and *piety* were the subjects of discussion at the spiritual conclave.

Related Words: 1. PIOUS -a. devout; orthodox. 2. IMPIETY -n. lack of respect.

PILLAGE (PIL ij): v. Plunder; rob

   Trigger: PILLAGE-PIRATE+VILLAGE

   Trigger Sentence: A PIRATE of that ship PILLAGED this VILLAGE.

   Sample Sentence: After the earthquake, people *pillaged* the deserted stores for food.

PINNACLE (PIN uh kul): n. Summit, peak

   Trigger: 1. PINE + VERTICAL. 2. PINE+SCALE

   Trigger Sentence: 1. On PINE tree go VERTICAL to reach PINNACLE. 2. He scaled PINNACLES.

   Sample Sentence: The rising sun illuminated the *pinnacle* of the mountains.

PIONEER (pye uh NEER): n. An innovator, path-finder

   Trigger: 1.PIONEER-FOUNDER. 2. PIONEER-ENGINEER

   Trigger Sentence: This ENGINEER is a PIONEER and a FOUNDER of innovative technologies.

   Sample Sentence: She *pioneered* as the first lady pilot of the Indian Air Force.

   Related Words: PIONEERING -a. first, initial

PIOUS (PI us): a. Religious; devout

   Trigger: PIOUS-PRAYERS

   Trigger Sentence: Your PIOUS PRAYERS will be answered very soon.

   Sample Sentence: Sermons on `*piousness*, purity and cleansing thy minds' are his favorites!

   Related Words: IMPIOUS -a. ungodly; lacking respect.

PIQUANT (pi KONT): a. Spicy, having a sharp flavor; stimulating

   Trigger: 1.PIQUANT-PICKLE. 2. piQUANT-QUANT

   Trigger Sentence: 1. PUNGENT PICKLE is spicy and PIQUANT. 2. In "GRE" QUANT is PIQUANT and verbal is BORING.

   Sample Sentence: The pickle tasted so *piquant* that I gasped for water.

PIQUE (PEEK): v. Provoke; arouse, annoy

   Trigger: PIQUE- PRICK

   Trigger Sentence: Her PIQUING sarcasm still PRICKS me.

   Sample Sentence: Her rude remarks on my dressing sense *piqued* me.

PITFALL (PIT fawl): n. Hidden danger; a trap

   Trigger: PIT FALL

   Trigger Sentence: PITFALL is a PIT flimsily covered and used to capture animals.

   Sample Sentence: The poachers made *pitfalls* in the forest to trap animals.

PITH (PITH): n. Central or vital part; essence

   Trigger: 1. PITH-PI (π). 2. PITH- PATH- PART-central PART

   Trigger Sentence: 1. The PI (π) is PITH of Geometry. 2. The PITH of the movie lies in the CENTRAL PART of the movie.

   Sample Sentence: The *pith* of the whole narrative was that- everything is fair in love and war!

PITHY (PITH ee): a. Concise; brief and meaningful

   Trigger: PI +THY

Trigger Sentence: 1. PI-THY: the math symbol "PI" is CONCISE and has great meaning. 2. PYTHAGORAS theorem is PITHY (brief) in nature but it is ESSENTIAL for geometry.

Sample Sentence: I enjoy reading his essays because they are always compact and *pithy*.

Related Words: PITHINESS -n. brevity, conciseness.

PITTANCE (PIT unce): n. Small amount

Trigger: PITTANCE- PETTY ANTS

Trigger Sentence: PETTY ANTS need PITTANCE of food.

Sample Sentence: The graduate students had to work part-time for a mere *pittance.*

PIVOTAL (PIV uh tul): a. Central; critical

Trigger: 1. PIVOTAL-PI VITAL. 2. PIVOTAL-VITAL-CAPITAL

Trigger Sentence: 1. This PI (π) is VITAL for geometry. 2. CAPITAL is PIVOTAL for any country.

Sample Sentence: It is the *pivotal* part of the city where business bloomed in multifold.

PLACATE (PLAY keyt): v. To soothe; pacify

Trigger: 1. PLACATE- PLACE. 2. PLATE +CAKE

Trigger Sentence: 1. Ideal PLACE to PLACATE my wife. 2. A PLATE OF CAKE PLACATED his tummy.

Sample Sentence: My husband *placated* me after a fight.

Related Words: PLACABLE - a. easily calmed or placated.

PLACID (PLA sid): a. Calm and peaceful

Trigger: 1.PLACID-PLACE. 2. PLACID-PLACED

Trigger Sentence: 1. An IDEAL PLACE is PLACID. 2. I was PLACED so PLACIDLY in my life that I could not anticipate this cataclysm.

Sample Sentence: The Lake was *placid* until an alligator dramatically ripped up on the surface!

Related Words: PLACIDITY -n. serenity

PLAGIARISM (PLAY juh rism): n. Unauthorized copying

Trigger: PLAGIARISM-PLAY GUY + RISM

Trigger Sentence: Many Indian GUY PLAYS are PLAGIARIZED versions of English dramas.

Sample Sentence: *Plagiarism* in research departments is a serious offense.

PLAINTIVE (PLEYN tiv): a. Sad, mournful

Trigger: 1. PLAINTIVE- PAIN+GIVE. 2. COMPLAINT

Trigger Sentence: 1. The back PAIN GIVES PLAINTIVE experience. 2. With a medical COMPLAINT, the patient was in PLAINTIVE mood.

Sample Sentence: I heard a *plaintive* cry of a wounded animal in the woods.

PLASTICITY (pla STIS i tee): n. Flexibility, ability to be molded

Trigger: PLASTICITY-ELASTICITY (** synonyms)

Trigger Sentence: An object of PLASTICITY exhibits the characteristics of ELASTICITY.

Sample Sentence: *Plasticity* of young brains they say, that is why the children learn faster!

Related Words: PLASTIC -a. flexible

PLATITUDE (PLAT i tood): n. Trite remark; commonplace statement

Trigger: PLAT-FLAT

Trigger Sentence: Platitude is a FLAT, unexciting statement.

Sample Sentence: *Platitudes* in his speech were expected, for he cannot go beyond basics.

PLATONIC (pley TON ik): a. Free from romance or sex; spiritual

Trigger: PLATO LOVE-PLATONIC

Trigger Sentence: PLATO is a Greek philosopher; whose love is obviously PLATONIC in nature.

Sample Sentence: They are eternally in love- *platonic* love is what makes these spiritualists different from us.

PLAUDITS (PLAW dits): n. Praise; enthusiastic approval

Trigger: PLAUDITS-APPLAUDS

Trigger Sentence: LAUD; APPLAUD; LAUDATORY; LAUDATION; LAUDABLE; PLAUDITS; all belong to one family.

Sample Sentence: We received applauds and *plaudits* on our invention.

PLAUSIBLE (PLAW zuh bul): a. Believable, feasible

Trigger: PLAUSIBLE-POSSIBLE

Trigger Sentence: It is POSSIBLE, therefore may be believable and PLAUSIBLE.

Sample Sentence: My boss demanded all *plausible* opinions rather than far-fetching ideas.

Related Words: IMPLAUSIBLE -a. hard to believe

PLENITUDE (PLEN i tyood): n. Overabundance; completeness

Trigger: PLENITUDE-PLENTY DUDE

Trigger Sentence: He eats PLENTY when he sees PLENITUDE of food.

Sample Sentence: I gathered *plenitude* of research information on anthropological evolution.

PLETHORA (PLETH or ah): a. Excess; overabundance

Trigger: PLETHORA -PLENTY of FLORAS

Trigger Sentence: In my house there is a PLETHORA of FLORA.

Sample Sentence: She offered a *plethora* of excuses for her shortcomings.

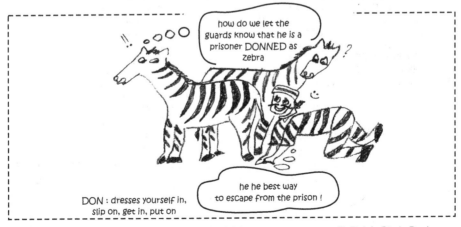

Memory Test-81 : Match each word and its memory trick to the corresponding definition.

S.N	WORD	MEMORY TRIGGER	S.N	DEFINITIONS	KEY
1	PATHETIC	Sympathetic- pity	A	Act superior towards	
2	PATRON	Pater-father-pat on	B	Authoritative	
3	PATRONIZE	Pater (father) is a BOSS	C	Expressing thoughtfulness with sadness	
4	PAUCITY	Poor + city	D	Extremely poor, stingy	
5	PECCADILLO	PUKKA- nil	E	Having negative connotations; Belittle	
6	PECUNIARY	Never in PENURY	F	In confusion; disorderly	
7	PEDAGOGUE	Pedant dialogue	G	Irritable, Angry	
8	PEDANTIC	pedant-pundit	H	Journey, voyage	
9	PEDESTRIAN	Pedestrian path	I	Lack, scarcity	
10	PEEVISH	Peeing causes	J	Minor sin	
11	PEJORATIVE	Piggy rat-imply negative	K	Ordinary; unimaginative	
12	PELL-MELL	Helter-skelter	L	Person who supports	
13	PELLUCID	Pure liquid -lucid	M	Related to money	
14	PENANCE	pay PENALTY	N	Self-imposed punishment	
15	PENCHANT	chant	O	Sharp; wise; insightful	
16	PENSIVE	SUSPENSE in sad	P	Showing off learning; bookish	
17	PENURIOUS	penny less	Q	Strong inclination; liking	
18	PERCEPTIVE	Strong concepts are perceptive	R	Teacher; bookish teacher	
19	PEREGRINATION	Migration-pilgrimage	S	Touching; pitiful, causing compassion	
20	PEREMPTORY	EMPERORS nature	T	Transparent; easy to understand	

Memory Test-82 : Match each word and its memory trick to the corresponding definition.

S.N	WORD	MEMORY TRIGGER	S.N	DEFINITIONS	KEY
1	PERENNIAL	Centennial-millennium	A	Act of lying under oath	
2	PERFIDY	PERFECT not	B	Attractive	
3	PERFUNCTORY	No FUNCTION	C	Bonus	
4	PERIL	Devil-evil presence	D	Commit a crime	
5	PERIPATETIC	Peri+PATH	E	Danger, risk	
6	PERIPHERAL	Periphery-not central	F	Enter, penetrate	
7	PERJURY	Jury -forgery	G	Everlasting; permanent	
8	PERMEATE	penetrate	H	Expressed clearly; transparent	
9	PERNICIOUS	Poisonous	I	Hard work, diligence	
10	PERPETRATE	PERFORM -bad	J	Highly destructive	
11	PERPETUAL	Perpetual-PERENNIAL	K	Impertinent; bold	
12	PERPLEX	COMPLEX	L	Irrelevant, marginal; outer	
13	PERQUISITE	SALARY + PERKS	M	Long lasting	
14	PERSEVERANCE	SEVERE work	N	Make it complicated; confuse	
15	PERSONIFICATION	Person-identification	O	Moving; walking about	
16	PERSONABLE	Nice PERSONALITY	P	Perceptive, having insight	
17	PERSPICACIOUS	Person PICASSO	Q	Person who represents	
18	PERSPICUOUS	Perfect PICS (pictures)	R	Stubborn; persistent	
19	PERT	Expert attitude	S	Superficial, not thorough; careless	
20	PERTINACIOUS	TENACIOUS	T	Unfaithfulness; treachery	

Answers	EX.NO	1	2	3	4	5	6	7	8	9	10	11	12	13	14	15	16	17	18	19	20
	81	S	L	A	I	J	M	R	P	K	G	E	F	T	N	Q	C	D	O	H	B
	82	M	T	S	E	O	L	A	F	J	D	G	N	C	I	Q	B	P	H	K	R

Memory Test-83 : Match each word and its memory trick to the corresponding definition.

S.N	WORD	MEMORY TRIGGER	S.N	DEFINITIONS	KEY
1	PERTURB	DISTURB	A	Baneful, deadly; contagious	
2	PERUSE	For use	B	Belief that life is basically bad	
3	PERVASIVE	VAST universe	C	Calm; not easily disturbed	
4	PERVERSE	perverted	D	Charming in appearance; visual	
5	PESSIMISM	No positivism	E	Contrary; wicked; perverted	
6	PESTILENTIAL	Pesticides	F	Describing adventures of a person	
7	PETRIFY	PETROL -ROCK oil	G	Devotion; reverence for God	
8	PETULANT	Pet+violent	H	Disturb completely, agitate	
9	PHARISAIC	P+HARI+SAI+c	I	Fake; not authentic	
10	PHILANTHROPIST	Phil (love) +anthrop	J	Hypocritically religious; self-righteous	
11	PHILISTINE	Palestine mentality ??	K	Ill-tempered; irascible	
12	PHLEGMATIC	NO FLAME- no hot	L	Lover of mankind; charitable donor	
13	PHONY	Chinese-made PHONE	M	Multicolored; spotted	
14	PICARESQUE	PICTURES of RISK	N	Narrow- minded person; uncultured	
15	PICAYUNE	PICK COIN in cents	O	Plunder; rob	
16	PICTURESQUE	Beautiful Pictures	P	Read with care	
17	PIED	painted	Q	Spread throughout	
18	PIETY	Piety-DEITY	R	Summit, peak	
19	PILLAGE	Pirate+village	S	Turn to stone, terrify	
20	PINNACLE	PINE+scale	T	Worthless; petty; small-minded	

Memory Test-84 : Match each word and its memory trick to the corresponding definition.

S.N	WORD	MEMORY TRIGGER	S.N	DEFINITIONS	KEY
1	PIONEER	FOUNDER	A	Believable, feasible	
2	PIOUS	prayers	B	Calm and peaceful	
3	PIQUANT	Piquant-PICKLE	C	Central or vital part; essence	
4	PIQUE	PRICKS me	D	Central; critical	
5	PITFALL	Pit FALL	E	Commonplace statement ; trite remark	
6	PITH	PATH- central PART	F	Concise; brief and meaningful	
7	PITHY	PI-thy	G	Excess; overabundance	
8	PITTANCE	PETTY ANTS	H	Flexibility, ability to be molded	
9	PIVOTAL	Pivotal-vital-capital	I	Free from romance or sex; spiritual	
10	PLACATE	PLACID life	J	Hidden danger; a trap	
11	PLACID	Ideal PLACE is placid	K	Innovator, path-finder	
12	PLAGIARISM	PLAY GUY + rism	L	Overabundance; completeness	
13	PLAINTIVE	PAIN+give	M	Praise; enthusiastic approval	
14	PLASTICITY	elasticity	N	Provoke; arouse, annoy	
15	PLATITUDE	Platitude is a FLAT	O	Religious; devout	
16	PLATONIC	Plato love	P	Sad, mournful	
17	PLAUDITS	Applauds	Q	Small amount	
18	PLAUSIBLE	possible	R	Soothe; pacify	
19	PLENITUDE	PLENTY dude	S	Spicy; stimulating	
20	PLETHORA	PLENTY of floras	T	Unauthorized copying	

Answers

EX.NO	1	2	3	4	5	6	7	8	9	10	11	12	13	14	15	16	17	18	19	20
83	H	P	Q	E	B	A	S	K	J	L	N	C	I	F	T	D	M	G	O	R
84	K	O	S	N	J	C	F	Q	D	R	B	T	P	H	E	I	M	A	L	G

WORD GROUPS DAY-21

★ **MANY - MANY**

ADJECTIVES: abounding, bountiful, copious, countless, crowded, innumerable, legion, manifold, multifarious, multifaceted, multitudinous, myriad, numerous, rife, sundry, teeming, umpteen, varied, various

NOUNS: horde, scads, swarm, slew, throng, multitude

VERB: multiply, proliferate.

ANTONYMS: adj. few, scarce

★ **COMPLICATED TASK**

ADJECTIVES: convoluted, involved, intricate, knotty, tangled, labyrinthine, Byzantine, tortuous; problematic, sophisticated, elaborate

NOUNS: intricacy, enigma

VERB: perplex, entangle, mystify

ANTONYMS: adj.easy, facile, simple, disentangle.

★ **EASY TASK**

ADJECTIVES: cursory, elementary, effortless, facile, obvious, oversimplified, sinecure, shallow, simplistic, superficial, uncomplicated, unexacting

NOUNS: facileness

VERB: facilitate

ANTONYMS: adj. arduous, complicated, confusing, difficult, hard, involved, laborious, profound

★ **ARDUOUS TASK**

ADJECTIVES: arduous, laborious, onerous, strenuous, taxing

NOUNS: hardship, drudgery

VERB: strain, exhaust

ANTONYMS: adj. easy, facile, sinecure

★ **HARD WORKING**

ADJECTIVES: assiduous, conscientious, diligent, industrious, painstaking, scrupulous, sedulous, studious, unflagging

NOUNS: assiduity, perseverance, persistence

VERB: persevere, persist, endure

ANTONYMS: adj. indolent, lazy, negligent, remiss

★ **ARROGANCE-ARROGANT ATTITUDE**

ADJECTIVES: conceited, haughty, hubristic, self-important, egotistic, superior, supercilious; overbearing, pert, pompous, presumptuous, bumptious, imperious, overweening; proud, immodest

NOUNS: hubris, smugness, pride, disdain, pomposity

VERB: arrogate, assume, usurp

ANTONYMS: adj. modest, humble, deferential, submissive.

★ **DOMINEERING ATTITUDE**

ADJECTIVES: arrogant, assertive, autocratic, bossy, despotic, dictatorial, egotistic, imperative, imperious, insolent, iron-fisted, overbearing, peremptory, tyrannical

NOUNS: peremptoriness , aggressiveness

VERB: browbeat, bully, coerce, intimidate

ANTONYMS: adj. submissive, surrendering, yielding

Word List Day-22

PLIABLE (PLYE ah bul): a. Flexible, adaptable; bendable

    Trigger: 1. PLIABLE-LIABLE-FLEXIBLE. 2. PLY-FLEXIBLE

    Trigger Sentence: PLYWOOD material is LIABLE to change; something PLIABLE is FLEXIBLE.

    Sample Sentence: If you make my work hours *pliable*, it helps me work at flexible hours.

    Related Words: PLIANT –a. flexible; easily influenced

PLUCK (PLUHK): n. Courage

    Trigger: LUCK-PLUCK-- (FORTUNE-BRAVE)

    Trigger Sentence: Like the Latin saying "fortune favors the brave", "LUCK favors the PLUCK".

    Sample Sentence: She showed *pluck* in plucking a lion's hair.

PLUMB (PLUM): a. Exactly vertical; checking perpendicularity

    Trigger: PLUMB-PLUMBER

    Trigger Sentence: Just like the cricket umpire checks whether the "LBW" is PLUMB, the PLUMBER checks the pipe to see whether it is PLUMB.

    Sample Sentence: The plumber made sure that the pipe was *plumb*.

PLIGHT (PLYTE): n. Bad or unfortunate condition or state

    Trigger: 1. PLIGHT-FLIGHT. 2. PLIGHT-FIGHT

    Trigger Sentence: 1. Bad PLIGHT in a FLIGHT journey... 2. FIGHT between nations brings PLIGHT.

    Sample Sentence: Please understand, she has been through a painful *plight*.

PLODDING (PLOD ding): a. Hard monotonous routine work

    Trigger: 1.PLODDING-PLOWING. 2. PLOD-SLOW

    Trigger Sentence: 1. He slowly PLODDED across while PLOWING the field; PLOWING a field is a hard monotonous work. 2. PLOD means SLOW WALK or WORK.

    Sample Sentence: Work in a government department *plods* along.

    Related Words: PLOD -v. walk heavily; work hard

PLUMMET (PLUHM it): v. Fall sharply

    Trigger: 1. PLUMMET-SUMMIT. 2. PLUMMET-COMET

    Trigger Sentence: 1. After reaching SUMMIT, share prices have PLUMMETED. 2. A COMET from Oort cloud is PLUMMETING towards the Earth.

    Sample Sentence: Stock prices *plummeted* again; it's like a game of snakes and ladders!

POIGNANT (POIN yunt): a. Intensely touching the emotions

    Trigger: POIGNANT-POINT (emotional)

    Trigger Sentence: EMOTIONAL POINTED scenes in movies are quite POIGNANT.

    Sample Sentence: Shakespeare's Romeo Juliet is a *poignant* play of love, war and separation.

POISE (POIZ): n. Composure; balance

Trigger: POISE-POSE-COMPOSURE

Trigger Sentence: POISED people maintain same POSE (CALM POSE).

Sample Sentence: She had a *poise* and grace while walking on the aisle to receive the award.

POLARIZE (POH luh ryze): v. Split into opposite factions

Trigger: POLE-(NORTH POLE-SOUTH POLE)

Trigger Sentence: You are in NORTH POLE; I am in SOUTH POLE; we are POLES APART.

Sample Sentence: The abortion issue *polarized* the country into pro and anti-abortion camps.

Related Words: POLARITY -n. presence of two opposing tendencies

POLEMIC (puh LEM ik): a. /n. Quarrelsome, disputatious

Trigger: POLEMIC-POLITIC

Trigger Sentence: Like election CONTESTS are CONTENTIOUS, POLITICS are POLEMIC in nature.

Sample Sentence: There is a political *polemic* between the two warring sides.

Related Words: POLEMICAL -a. quarrelsome; disputatious

POMPOUS (POM pus): a. Self-importance; overly proud

Trigger: POMPOUS-POMP (PUMP)

Trigger Sentence: 1. One who PUMPS iron and becomes muscular becomes POMPOUS. 2. John tends to become POMPOUS, when someone PUMPS him up with flattery.

Sample Sentence: She sounds like a *pompous* windbag...

Related Words: POMPOSITY -n. affectedly grand

PONDEROUS (PON der us): a. Weighty; unwieldy

Trigger: PONDEROUS-POUNDS

Trigger Sentence: As he gained another 10 POUNDS of weight, he appears PONDEROUS.

Sample Sentence: It's a *ponderous* assignment which cannot be done in a hasty manner.

Related Words: PONDER -v. think; consider

PONTIFICAL (pon TIF i kul): a. Pompous or pretentious; like pope

Trigger: 1. PONTIFICAL-PONTING. 2. PONTI-POINT

Trigger Sentence: 1. Ricky PONTING (Australian Batsman) was PONTIFICAL and pompous in nature. 2."Catch my point"-someone who TELLS POINTS are always PONTIFICAL in nature.

Sample Sentence: The *pontiff* attitude is characterized by grandiloquent and *pontifical* manners.

POROUS (POHR us): a. Full of pores; permeable

Trigger: POROUS-PORES

Trigger Sentence: With lot of PORES our country border has become POROUS.

Sample Sentence: Papers produced from the pulp are highly *porous*- it allows passage of water.

PORTEND (por TEND): v. Foretell, predict

    Trigger: PORTEND-"RE+PORT+END"

    Trigger Sentence: Mayan calendar PORTENDED on the END of the world with a future REPORT.

    Sample Sentence: We cannot *portend* how the end report will turn out to be.

    Related Words: PORTENTOUS -a. boding evil; impressive

PORTENTOUS (por TEN tus): a. Ominous; impressive

    Trigger: PORTENTOUS-POUR TENSION

    Trigger Sentence: The TENSION POURED in during the PORTENTOUS events.

    Sample Sentence: King Martin Luther spoke *portentous* words even on the night before he died.

POSEUR (poh ZUR): n. One who tries to impress others; pretender

    Trigger: POSEUR-POSER-POSE-POSES

    Trigger Sentence: 1. A POSEUR POSES in front of others. 2. Cinema POSES are ARTIFICIAL.

    Sample Sentence: Gullible girls fall prey to the pretentious *poseurs*.

POSIT (POZ it): v. Establish a view point; assume

    Trigger: POSIT-POSITION (present a POSITION)

    Trigger Sentence: He POSITED thirty basic POSITIONS in yoga.

    Sample Sentence: After going through your opinion letters, I *posit* that the majority wants to work from home!

    Related Words: POSTULATE -n. premise; basic principle

POSTHUMOUS (POS chuh mus): a. Occurring after death

    Trigger: POSTMORTEM -POST (after) + HUMAN

    Trigger Sentence: POST-MORTEM is done POSTHUMOUSLY.

    Sample Sentence: Sumedha received her late husband's bravery award *posthumously*.

POSTURE (POS cher): v. To assume an artificial pose; act artificially

    Trigger: POSTURE-POSE

    Trigger Sentence: A POSTURE is not natural. It is an artificial POSE.

    Sample Sentence: Her dance *postures* are very graceful like temple sculptures.

    Related Words: POSTURING -a. behaving unnaturally

POTENTATE (POHT n teyt): n. Powerful person; monarch

    Trigger: POTENTATE- POTENT STATE

    Trigger Sentence: The POTENTATE Empire was ruling the STATE with POTENT weapons.

    Sample Sentence: Kings prohibited their noblemen from making alliances with other *potentates*.

    Related Words: 1.POTENT -a. powerful; strong. 2. POTENTIAL –a. possible; latent. 3.PLENIPOTENTIARY -a. has full authority. 4.IMPOTENT –a. powerless; weak

POULTICE (POHL tis): n. Soothing application applied to inflamed portions of the body

    Trigger: POULTICE-ICE

    Trigger Sentence: He applied a pack of ICE as a POULTICE on the wounded area.

    Sample Sentence: The nurse applied herbal *poultice* over the inflamed parts of my hand.

PRAGMATIC (prag MAT ik): a. Practical, pertaining to practice

    Trigger: PRAGMATICAL-PRACTICAL (** synonyms)

    Trigger Sentence: PRAGMATIC people are PRACTICAL minded.

    Sample Sentence: His *pragmatic* view of education comes from years of work in the city schools.

PRATTLE (PRAT l): v. Chatter, babble

    Trigger: PRATTLE-CHATTER

    Trigger Sentence: CHATTERING with my girl friend I spent five hours on phone PRATTLING on about nothing in particular.

    Sample Sentence: My husband thinks I *prattle* a lot; how he wishes he married a calm lady.

PREAMBLE (PREE am bul): n. A preliminary statement

    Trigger: PREAMBLE- "PRE-READBLE" (** synonyms)

    Trigger Sentence: You can AMBLE through the Indian Constitution by reading the PREAMBLE.

    Sample Sentence: She gave a *preamble* of the whole subject before explaining it further.

PRECARIOUS (pri KAIR ee us): a. Risky; uncertain

    Trigger: 1. PRE+CARI (CARE). 2. PRECARIOUS-SERIOUS-DANGEROUS

    Trigger Sentence: 1. You got to be CAREFUL in PRECARIOUS situation. 2. PRECARIOUS, DANGEROUS & SERIOUS are synonyms.

    Sample Sentence: This cat *precariously* moved on the wall with dogs sleeping under!

PRECEDENCE (pri SEED ns): n. The condition of preceding others in importance

    Trigger: PRESIDENT PRECEDES

    Trigger Sentence: The PRECEDENCE is given to the PRESIDENT as he is will PRESIDE the meeting.

    Sample Sentence: We received his request first, so his issue takes *precedence* over yours.

PRECIPICE (PRES uh pis): n. Cliff; dangerous position

    Trigger: PRECIPICE-PRECARIOUS ICE

    Trigger Sentence: The slippery ICE at the PRECIPICE is PRECARIOUS

    Sample Sentence: On the snaky hilly roads, my car hit a tree and struck in a *precipice* spot.

PRECIPITATE (pri SIP i teyt): v. Rash; hasty; sudden; premature

    Trigger: PRECIPITATE-PARTICIPATE

    Trigger Sentence: When I PARTICIPATE in a contest, my dad PRECIPITATES and pushes me .

    Sample Sentence: How can you make a good pilot if your mind is often *precipitating*?

PRECIPITOUS (pri SIP i tus): a. Very steep, hasty

    Trigger: PRECI+PITOUS- PITS

    Trigger Sentence: From the PRECIPITOUS hill he has fallen into the PITS in a PRECIPITOUS way.

    Sample Sentence: The price of shares in the company dropped *precipitously*.

PRECIS (PREY see): n. Summary, shortened version of a work

    Trigger: PRÉCIS-PRECISE-CONCISE

    Trigger Sentence: He PREPARED a CONCISE report to make a PRÉCIS of the book.

Sample Sentence: He compiled six different scholars' research papers in a *précis* document.

Related Words: 1.PRECISE –a. exact. 2.IMPRECISE –a. inexact; inaccurate

PRECLUDE (pri KLOOD): v. Eliminate, prevent, make impossible

Trigger: 1.PRECLUDE-EXCLUDE. 2. PRECLUDE-PREVENT

Trigger Sentence: 1. DON'T INCLUDE this. 2. PREVENT and PRECLUDE him by EXCLUDE him from consideration.

Sample Sentence: This contract *precludes* me for over a year from working as a freelancer.

Related Words: OCCLUDE –v. close; shut

PRECOCIOUS (pri KOH shus): a. (Prematurely) genius; advanced in development

Trigger: PRECOCIOUS-PREMATURE +CONSCIOUS

Trigger Sentence: A PRECOCIOUS child has PREMATURELY developed CONSCIOUSNESS.

Sample Sentence: She is a *precocious* child always preoccupied in exploring newer subjects.

PRECURSOR (pri KUR ser): n. Forerunner

Trigger: PRE (before) + CURSOR

Trigger Sentence: 1. CURSOR is an INDICATOR; PRECURSOR is a PRE-INDICATOR. 2. A CURSOR works as a PRECURSOR for us to browse on the computer screen.

Sample Sentence: Bern is judged as *precursor* of the Romantic Movement, not a true Romantic.

Related Words: PREDECESSOR -n. one who came before

PREDATE (PREE deyt): v. Precede; occur prior to; antedate

Trigger: PREDATE-PREVIOUS DATE-PRECEDE

Trigger Sentence: On what PREVIOUS DATE did you come here? If you tell me a tentative date, I'll refer to the PREDATE register.

Sample Sentence: Stone tools *predate* bronze tools. Simple archeological fact!

Related Words: ANTEDATE -v. precede, predate

PREDICAMENT (pri DIK uh munt): n. A difficult or dangerous situation

Trigger: 1. PREDICAMENT-PREDICT + BAD. 2. PREY-PREDICAMENT-PREDATOR

Trigger Sentence: 1. I could not PREDICT the PREDICAMENT I was going to face. 2. Just imagine the PREDICAMENT the PREY would undergo while being chased by its PREDATOR!

Sample Sentence: This country with a *predicament* pool of people out to destroy humanity, is no good for normal life!

PREDILECTION (pred uh LEK shun): n. Preference; partiality

Trigger: PREDILECTION-PREFERENCE+SELECTION

Trigger Sentence: These employees are PRE-SELECTED ones. They constitute the bunch of candidates under the PREDILECTION of the Chairman.

Sample Sentence: My professor has a *predilection* for foreign students and ignores the locals.

PREDOMINANT (pri DOM uh nunt): a. Supreme; widespread

Trigger: PREDOMINANT-DOMINATE

Trigger Sentence: She is PREDOMINANT among new writers and completely DOMINATES them with her excellent rhetorical skills.

Sample Sentence: The social concern of child marriage *predominated* in the rural Rajasthan.

Related Words: PREVAILING -a. predominant; widespread

PREEMINENT (pre EM ih nunt): a. Most important, superior

Trigger: PREEMINENT- VERY EMINENT

Trigger Sentence: EMINEM is top rapper and he is PREEMINENT in the area of rap music.

Sample Sentence: She's the *preeminent* speaker of the council.

PREEMPT (pree EMPT): v. Acquiring something by acting first; supplant

Trigger: PREEMPTIVE-PREVENTIVE

Trigger Sentence: 1. PREVENTIVE, PREVENTATIVE and PREEMPTIVE belong to same family. 2. EMPTY the ENEMY before it acts is known as PREEMPTIVE action.

Sample Sentence: Israel *preempts* the targets of its enemy states. It is notorious for its preventive measures.

PREHENSILE (pri HEN sil): a. Capable of grasping or holding

Trigger: PREHENSILE-"FREE HANDS+ILE"

Trigger Sentence: My PREHENSILE FREE HANDS grabbed a pencil.

Sample Sentence: Monkeys have *prehensile* tails that can wrap up around a branch!

PREJUDICED (PREJ uh dis): a. Biased; preconception

Trigger: 1.PREJUD-PRE+JUDGE. 2. PREFERRED JUDGMENT

Trigger Sentence: 1. PREJUDGED (judged before hand) opinions are known as PREJUDICED. 2. The PREJUDICED give PREFERRED JUDGMENT not based of facts, but on the basis of their beliefs.

Sample Sentence: The orthodox Hindus were *prejudiced* on the issues of widow remarriage.

Related Words: UNPREJUDICED -n. impartial; unbiased

PRELUDE (PREY lood): n. Introduction; opening

Trigger: 1.PRELUDE-CONCLUDE. 2. PRELUDE-PRELIMINARY-PREFACE

Trigger Sentence: 1. PRELUDE is opposite to CONCLUDE. 2. A PRELUDE is a PRELIMINARY part.

Sample Sentence: Is training at Finishing Schools, a needed *prelude* before one takes up a job?

PREMEDITATED (pri MED ih tey tid): a. Preplanned, deliberate

Trigger: PRE + MEDITATE

Trigger Sentence: PREMEDITATED things associate with PRE-THINKING and PRE-PLANNING.

Sample Sentence: The assassins planned before committing the *premeditated* murder.

Related Words: UNPREMEDITATED -v. unplanned, unprepared

PREMISE (PREM is): n. Assumption; postulate

Trigger: PREMISE-PRESUME-ASSUME

Trigger Sentence: 1. PREMISE is to PRESUME and ASSUME. 2. On what PREMISE will you PRESUME her to be unreliable?

Sample Sentence: It is a simple *premise* that what goes up must come down!

Related Words: SURMISE –v. guess; presume

PREMONITION (pree muh NISH un): v. Forewarning; advance feeling

Trigger: 1. PREMONITION-PRENOTION. 2. PRE+MONK+NOTION

Trigger Sentence: 1. PREMONITION and PRENOTION are synonyms. 2. The MONK had a good PREMONITION that he would meet his guru soon.

Sample Sentence: I had a strange *premonition* that the plane would explode.

Related Words: ADMONISH -v. warn, scold

PREPOSTEROUS (pri POS trus): a. Absurd, ridiculous

Trigger: PREPOSTEROUS-MONKEY POSTERS

Trigger Sentence: 1. Monkey POSES look PREPOSTEROUS. 2. It is PREPOSTEROUS to fix Darwin's head on a MONKEY'S body in most of the image POSTERS on the internet.

Sample Sentence: The idea that extraterrestrials built the pyramids is *preposterous*.

PREROGATIVE (pri ROG uh tiv): n. An exclusive right; privilege

Trigger: PREROGATIVE-INTERROGATIVE

Trigger Sentence: Police officers are given INTERROGATIVE authority; it is their PREROGATIVE to INTERROGATE any person who proved guilty.

Sample Sentence: Voting right is the *prerogative* of the adult citizens only.

PRESAGE (PRES ij): v. Foretell, predict

Trigger: PRESAGE-"PRE +MESSAGE"

Trigger Sentence: These MESSAGES PRESAGED the bad news.

Sample Sentence: Most of the ill-fated events in the novel are *presaged* by ill-omens.

PRESCIENT (PREE shunt): a. Able to foresee future

Trigger: PRE (before) +SCIENCE (knowledge)- PRE SIGNS

Trigger Sentence: The SCIENTISTS possess PRESCIENT knowledge about the future. If you are PRESCIENT, you are in a position to guess the PRE SIGNS of a future event.

Sample Sentence: With *prescience* perfectness the numerologist calculated future.

PRESENTIMENT (pri ZEN tih munt): n. An intuitive feeling about the future

Trigger: PRESENTI-"PRE+SENSE"

Trigger Sentence: People endowed with PRESENTIMENT are able to PRE-SENSE future.

Sample Sentence: I had an uncomfortable *presentiment* before the interview.

PRESUME (pri ZOOM): v. Assume, take for granted

Trigger: PRESUME-ASSUME (ASSUME great)

Trigger Sentence: 1. PRESUME and ASSUME are synonyms. 2. He ASSUMES that he is great.

Sample Sentence: I wrongly *presumed* that he will never come back to his wife!

PRESUMPTUOUS (pri ZUMP choo us): a. Arrogant, taking liberties

Trigger: PRE + SUMPTUOUS - (SUMPTUOUS-SUM)

Trigger Sentence: 1. Just because your life is SUMPTUOUS (lot of sum), you should not become PRESUMPTUOUS. 2. When you request a SUM of money, you should not look PRESUMPTUOUS.

Sample Sentence: The *presumptuous* doctor didn't explain the cause of the disease.

PRETENTIOUS (pri TEN shus): n. Pretending; showy

    Trigger: PRETENTIOUS- PRETENSION- fake INTENTION

    Trigger Sentence: A PRETENTIOUS fraud is full of PRETENSION.

    Sample Sentence: The director made the film appear *pretentious,* rather than realistic.

    Related Words: UNPRETENTIOUS –a. plain; simple; understated

PRETERNATURAL (pree ter NACH rul): a. Supernatural; abnormal

    Trigger: PRETERNATURAL-SUPERNATURAL

    Trigger Sentence: The SUPERNATURAL skills of Superman match the PRETERNATURAL skills of Hanuman.

    Sample Sentence: She is not just sensuous but has a *preternatural* ability to enchant men!

PREVAIL (pri VEYL): n. Win; persuade

    Trigger: PREVAIL-PREVENT AIL

    Trigger Sentence: 1. The medicine PREVAILED by PREVENTING the illness of an AILING patient. 2. He PREVAILED in the battle by successfully PREVENTING the enemy.

    Sample Sentence: For centuries, music and dance *prevailed* in the temples of India.

PREVALENT (PREV uh lunt): a. Widespread, widely accepted.

    Trigger: 1.preVALENT-VALENTINE. 2. PREVALENT-PREDOMINANT

    Trigger Sentence: VALENTINE DAY is PREVALENT (everywhere) and PREDOMINANT in the world.

    Sample Sentence: Bell bottoms were *prevalent* in the 70's and were termed as "elephant legs"!

PREVARICATE (pri VAR i keyt): v. Lie, equivocate

    Trigger: 1.PREVARIcate-PRE+VARY. 2. PREVARICATE-EQUIVOCATE (refer)

    Trigger Sentence: 1. If you VARY from your PRIOR statement, your words tantamount to PREVARICATION. 2. People, who can cleverly EQUIVOCATE, can easily PREVARICATE as well. 3. Without VERIFICATION leads to PREVARICATION .

    Sample Sentence: During the hearings the witness was *prevaricating* to protect his friend.

    Related Words: PREVARICATION -n. lie

PRICKLY (PRIK lee): a. Very irritable

    Trigger: PRICKLY-PRICK

    Trigger Sentence: During summers, it is PRICKLY that the Sun PRICKS our backs.

    Sample Sentence: Nylon pants are *prickly*; I would prefer simple cottons for traveling.

PRIGGISH (prig): a. Exaggeratedly proper; arrogant

    Trigger: PRIGGISH (CLEAN)-PIGGISH (DIRTY)

    Trigger Sentence: PIGGISH means EXTREMELY DIRTY (pigs live dirtily); PRIGGISH means EXTREMELY PROPER.

    Sample Sentence: My *priggish* aunt Anna doesn't approve of my miniskirts.

PRIME (PRAHYM): a. The earliest stage, excellent, superior

    Trigger: 1. PRIME-PRIMITIVE. 2. PRIME-PRIME MINISTER

    Trigger Sentence: 1. For PRIMITIVE tribes, food and survival were of PRIME importance. 2. PRIME MINISTER plays PRIME role in India.

Sample Sentence: At 70 years of age, Jack has the vigor and enthusiasm of a man in his *prime*.

Related Words: 1.PRIMACY -n. superiority, state of being first. 2. SUPREMACY -n. superiority. 3. PRIMITIVE – a. old, ancient, uncultured. 4. PRIMORDIAL –a. early; original

PRIMORDIAL (prahy MAWR dee ul): a. Early; primary; existing at the beginning

Trigger: PRIMOR+DIAL-PRIMARY (** synonyms)

Trigger Sentence: PRIMORDIAL forests were PRIMARY resources for human survival.

Sample Sentence: Tom found some *primordial* Stone Age tools in the caves of Madhya Pradesh.

PRISTINE (PRIS teen): a. Ancient, primitive; unspoiled

Trigger: 1. PRISTINE-PRIEST. 2. PRISTINE-FRESH TEEN

Trigger Sentence: 1. People believe that PRIESTS are PRISTINE. 2. FRESH TEEN is PRISTINE.

Sample Sentence: 1. Snow should be *pristine* and sparkly. 2. My office is a mess as against her *pristine* work place.

PRIVATION (prye VEY shun): n. Hardship, want; poverty

Trigger: DEPRIVATION-PRIVATION-PRIVATE

Trigger Sentence: In PRIVATE companies the workers suffer PRIVATION; lack of money.

Sample Sentence: Due to long periods of economic *privation,* the factories are defunct now.

PRIVILEGE (PRIV lij): n. Special right not enjoyed by others

Trigger: 1.PRIVILEGE-"PRIME+VILLAGE". 2. PRIVATE + LEGAL

Trigger Sentence: 1. In my VILLAGE I've lot of PRIVILEGES, since I am a PRIME (no -1) member. 2. Special LEGAL rights are known as PRIVILEGES.

Sample Sentence: We had the *privilege* of being invited to the president's party.

PROBITY (PRO bi tee): n. Uprightness; honesty

Trigger: 1.PROBITY-PURITY. 2. PROBITY- never ROB

Trigger Sentence: 1. You stand as an example of PROBITY when you have PURITY of thought. 2. The person with PROBITY never ROB others.

Sample Sentence: If you possess proper behavior, then that will reflect your *probity*.

Related Words: IMPROBITY -n. wickedness

PROBLEMATIC (prob leh MAT ik): a. Troublesome; doubtful; debatable

Trigger: PROBLEMATIC-PROBLEM

Trigger Sentence: I faced the PROBLEMATIC PROBLEM of what to wear for the party.

Sample Sentence: The control over the usage of internet in office is quite *problematic*.

PROCLIVITY (PRO kliv i tee): n. A natural liking, inclination

Trigger: 1.PRO. 2. PRONE. 3. PROCLIVITY-PRO+CLIMB. 4.CLIENTS

Trigger Sentence: 1. I have a PROCLIVITY to become a PRO (Public Relations Officer). 2. He has PROCLIVITY for CLIMBING hills.

Sample Sentence: Arya had an artistic *proclivity* even as a young girl.

Related Words: 1.ACCLIVITY –n. upward slope. 2.DECLIVITY –n. downward slope. 3. INCLINATION -n. liking. 4. CLIENTELE –n. group of customers

PROCRASTINATE (pro KRAS tuh neyt): v. Delay or postpone

Trigger: 1. PROCRASTINATE-PROLONGATE. 2. PROCRASTINATE-PROGRESS LATE

Trigger Sentence: 1. PROCRASTINATE is to PROLONG an action. 2. When you PROCRASTINATE your PROGRESS is going to be LATE.

Sample Sentence: He *procrastinated* and missed the submission deadline.

PROD (PROD): v. Stir up; push, urge

Trigger: 1.PROD-"P (push) + ROD". 2. PROD-PRODUCE

Trigger Sentence: 1. PUSH with a ROD to PROD a bull. 2. To PRODUCE results, PROD the people.

Sample Sentence: Madav needs some *prodding* to finish his editorials on time.

PRODIGAL (PROD ih gul): a. Wasteful; reckless with money

Trigger: 1. PRODIGAL-PROUD GAL. 2. PRODIGAL-FRUGAL

Trigger Sentence: 1. I spent PRODIGAL amounts to impress the PROUD GAL. 2. We should stop our PRODIGAL expenditure and adopt FRUGAL methods.

Sample Sentence: I was deemed as the *prodigal* daughter for not listening to my parents.

PRODIGIOUS (pra DIJ us): a. Huge; enormous; marvelous

Trigger: PRODUCE+BIG+US

Trigger Sentence: 1. PRODIGIOUS things PRODUCE BIG. 2. Obama Care is a PRODIGIOUS task. To implement this scheme the Federal Government should PROCURE HUGE funds.

Sample Sentence: The Juggler performed *prodigiously* magical acts for rapt audiences.

PRODIGY (PROD i jee): n. Wonder; exceptional talented child (or person)

Trigger: 1.PRODIGY- PRO+DJ. 2. PRODIGY-PROUD GENIUS

Trigger Sentence: 1. This PRO (professional) DJ (disco- jockey) is a PRODIGY; he has enormous and unusual talent. 2. Parents are PROUD about their GENIUS/ PRODIGY.

Sample Sentence: Young Arjun is a *prodigy* with numbers; he can multiply, subtract or add any given big number instantly.

PROFANE (pro FAYN): v. To treat with abuse; violate; desecrate

Trigger: PROFANE-PORN + FAN

Trigger Sentence: A PORN FAN is PROFANE – a. he also violates religious things.

Sample Sentence: This talented young actor however *profaned* himself by becoming a porn star.

PROFICIENT (pruh FISH unt): a. Expert, competent

Trigger: PROFICIENT-EFFICIENT

Trigger Sentence: Become PROFICIENT in your subject, to become an EFFICIENT professor.

Sample Sentence: He has become very *proficient* at computer programming.

PROFLIGATE (PROF li git): a. Wasteful, wildly immoral

Trigger: 1.PROFLIGATE-PRODIGAL (replace "FL" with "D"). 2. PROFLIGATE- "PROFIT ATE"

Trigger Sentence: 1. PRODIGAL and PROFLIGATE are synonym variants; in place of "FL" keep "D"; profligate is a prodigal. 2. Politicians PROFLIGATE public money to EAT illegal PROFITS.

Sample Sentence: 1. She spent *profligately* on her cloths. 2. The *profligacy* of life in Caligula's Rome has shocked historians.

PROFOUND (pruh FOUND): a. Deep, not superficial; complete

    Trigger: PROFOUND-"SOUND+ PROF (PROFESSOR)"

    Trigger Sentence: A PROF (PROFESSOR) possesses SOUND and DEEP KNOWLEDGE.

    Sample Sentence: The professor has *profound* knowledge.

    Related Words: PROFUNDITY - n. deepness

PROFUSION (pruh FYOO zhun): n. Overabundance; wasteful spending

    Trigger: PROFUSIVE-PRO+EXCESSIVE

    Trigger Sentence: EXCESSIVE spending is known as PROFUSIVE; EXCESSIVE means PROFUSIVE.

    Sample Sentence: 1. Apples grow in *profusion* in this valley. 2. Food and drink was served in *profusion* at the princess's wedding party.

    Related Words: PROFUSIVE - a. Excessive spending; Lavish

PROGNOSIS (prog NOH sis): n. Prediction; probable outcome of a disease

    Trigger: PROGNOSIS-DIAGNOSIS

    Trigger Sentence: Analyzing the medical DIAGNOSIS the doctor says his PROGNOSIS is good.

    Sample Sentence: The coach had a hopeful *prognosis* on the team's performance in the finals.

PROHIBITIVE (pro HIB i tiv): a. Preventing, hindering

    Trigger: PROHIBITIVE-PROHIBIT

    Trigger Sentence: PROHIBITIVE means tending to PROHIBIT or forbid something.

    Sample Sentence: The tax was *prohibitive*.

    Related Words: 1.INHIBIT –v. check; hold back. 2. EXHIBIT -v. show; present

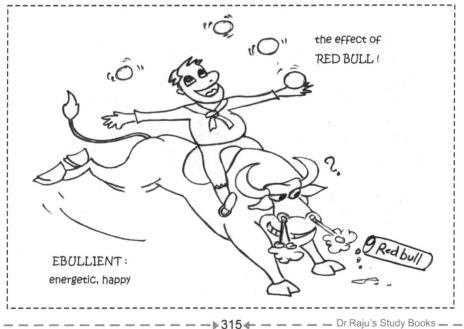

Memory Test-85 : Match each word and its memory trick to the corresponding definition.

S.N	WORD	MEMORY TRIGGER	S.N	DEFINITIONS	KEY
1	PLIABLE	Ply-flexible	A	Assume an artificial pose; act artificially	
2	PLUCK	Luck favors PLUCK	B	Bad or unfortunate state	
3	PLUMB	PLUMBER duty	C	Composure; balance	
4	PLIGHT	FIGHT brings plight	D	Courage	
5	PLODDING	PLOWING	E	Establish a view point; assume	
6	PLUMMET	From summit plummets	F	Exactly vertical; examine thoroughly	
7	POIGNANT	Point (emotional)	G	Fall sharply	
8	POISE	pose-composure	H	Flexible, adaptable	
9	POLARIZE	north pole-south pole	I	Foretell, predict	
10	POLEMIC	Politics are polemic	J	Full of pores; permeable	
11	POMPOUS	pomp (PUMP up)	K	Hard monotonous routine work	
12	PONDEROUS	POUNDS	L	Intensely touching the emotions	
13	PONTIFICAL	PONTING was pontifical	M	Occurring after death	
14	POROUS	PORES	N	Ominous; impressive	
15	PORTEND	REPORT+end	O	One who tries to impress others	
16	PORTENTOUS	Pour tension	P	Pompous or pretentious; like pope	
17	POSEUR	Poser-pose-poses	Q	Quarrelsome, disputatious	
18	POSIT	Posited - positions	R	Self-importance; overly proud	
19	POSTHUMOUS	Post (after) + human	S	Split into opposite factions	
20	POSTURE	Artificial POSE	T	Weighty; unwieldy	

Memory Test-86 : Match each word and its memory trick to the corresponding definition.

S.N	WORD	MEMORY TRIGGER	S.N	DEFINITIONS	KEY
1	POTENTATE	POTENT state	A	(Prematurely) genius; advanced	
2	POULTICE	Poultice-ICE	B	Acquiring something by acting first	
3	PRAGMATIC	Pragmatical-practical	C	Chatter, babble	
4	PRATTLE	chatter	D	Cliff; dangerous position	
5	PREAMBLE	Pre-READBLE	E	difficult or dangerous situation	
6	PRECARIOUS	Serious-DANGEROUS	F	Eliminate, prevent, make impossible	
7	PRECEDENCE	President precedes	G	Forerunner	
8	PRECIPICE	Precarious ICE	H	Most important, superior	
9	PRECIPITATE	Participate-RUN FAST	I	Powerful person; monarch	
10	PRECIPITOUS	Preci+pitous- PITS	J	Practical, pertaining to practice	
11	PRÉCIS	Precise-CONCISE	K	Precede; occur prior to; antedate	
12	PRECLUDE	Exclude--PREVENT	L	Preference; partiality	
13	PRECOCIOUS	Premature +conscious	M	preliminary statement	
14	PRECURSOR	Pre + CURSOR	N	Rash; hasty; sudden; premature	
15	PREDATE	Previous date	O	Risky; uncertain	
16	PREDICAMENT	PREDICT + BAD	P	Soothing application	
17	PREDILECTION	Preference+selection	Q	Summary, shortened version of a work	
18	PREDOMINANT	Dominate	R	Supreme; widespread	
19	PREEMINENT	Very eminent	S	The condition of preceding others	
20	PREEMPT	Preventive-empty before	T	Very steep, hasty	

Answers

EX.NO	1	2	3	4	5	6	7	8	9	10	11	12	13	14	15	16	17	18	19	20
85	H	D	F	B	K	G	L	C	S	Q	R	T	P	J	I	N	O	E	M	A
86	I	P	J	C	M	O	S	D	N	T	Q	F	A	G	K	E	L	R	H	B

Memory Test-87 : Match each word and its memory trick to the corresponding definition.

S.N	WORD	MEMORY TRIGGER	S.N	DEFINITIONS	KEY
1	PREHENSILE	Free HANDS+ile	A	Able to foresee future	
2	PREJUDICED	Preferred judgment	B	Absurd, ridiculous	
3	PRELUDE	PRELIMINARY-preface	C	An exclusive right; privilege	
4	PREMEDITATED	Pre + meditate	D	An intuitive feeling about the future	
5	PREMISE	Presume-assume	E	Arrogant, taking liberties	
6	PREMONITION	Pre+monk+notion	F	Assume, take for granted	
7	PREPOSTEROUS	Monkey POSTERS	G	Assumption; postulate	
8	PREROGATIVE	INTERROGATIVE authority	H	Biased; preconception	
9	PRESAGE	Pre +MESSAGE	I	Capable of grasping or holding	
10	PRESCIENT	pre SIGNS	J	Exaggeratedly proper; arrogant	
11	PRESENTIMENT	Pre+SENSE	K	Foretell, predict	
12	PRESUME	assume great	L	Forewarning; advance feeling	
13	PRESUMPTUOUS	Pre + sumptuous-sum	M	Introduction; opening	
14	PRETENTIOUS	Pretension- fake intention	N	Lie, equivocate	
15	PRETERNATURAL	Supernatural	O	Preplanned, deliberate	
16	PREVAIL	PREVENT all	P	Pretending; showy	
17	PREVALENT	Prevalent-predominant	Q	Supernatural; abnormal	
18	PREVARICATE	Pre+VARY-no verification	R	Very irritable	
19	PRICKLY	pricks	S	Widespread, widely accepted	
20	PRIGGISH	Not- PIGGISH (dirty)	T	Win; persuade	

Memory Test-88 : Match each word and its memory trick to the corresponding definition.

S.N	WORD	MEMORY TRIGGER	S.N	DEFINITIONS	KEY
1	PRIME	Primitive	A	Deep, not superficial; complete	
2	PRIMORDIAL	Primor+dial-primary	B	Delay or postpone	
3	PRISTINE	Pristine-fresh teen	C	Early; primary; existing at the beginning	
4	PRIVATION	Private industry job	D	Expert, competent	
5	PRIVILEGE	Private + LEGAL	E	Hardship, want; poverty	
6	PROBITY	Purity- Probity- never ROB	F	Huge; enormous; marvelous	
7	PROBLEMATIC	problem	G	natural liking, inclination	
8	PROCLIVITY	PRO+CLIMB	H	Overabundance; wasteful spending	
9	PROCRASTINATE	PROLONGATE time	I	Prediction	
10	PROD	P (push) + rod	J	Preventing, hindering	
11	PRODIGAL	Proud gal	K	Special right not enjoyed by others	
12	PRODIGIOUS	Produce+big+us	L	Stir up; push, urge	
13	PRODIGY	proud genius	M	The earliest stage, excellent	
14	PROFANE	Porn + fan	N	Treat with abuse; violate; desecrate	
15	PROFICIENT	Efficient	O	Troublesome; doubtful; debatable	
16	PROFLIGATE	PROFIT ATE-prodigal	P	Unspoiled; ancient, primitive	
17	PROFOUND	SOUND knowledge	Q	Uprightness; honesty	
18	PROFUSION	PROFUSIVE-pro+excessive	R	Wasteful, wildly immoral	
19	PROGNOSIS	diagnosis	S	Wasteful; reckless with money	
20	PROHIBITIVE	prohibit	T	Wonder; exceptional talented child	

Answers	EX.NO	1	2	3	4	5	6	7	8	9	10	11	12	13	14	15	16	17	18	19	20
	87	I	H	M	O	G	L	B	C	K	A	D	F	E	P	Q	T	S	N	R	J
	88	M	C	P	E	K	Q	O	G	B	L	S	F	T	N	D	R	A	H	I	J

WORD GROUPS DAY-22

★ **YIELDING ATTITUDE**

CEDE: give up (power or territory); grant

ADJECTIVES: yielding, compliant, submissive

NOUNS: cession, concession.

VERB: surrender, capitulate, cede, concede, relinquish, yield, waive, give up; abandon, forgo, sacrifice

ANTONYMS: v. possess, retain; resist

★ **OBEDIENT/ SUBMISSIVE NATURE-REPEATED**

ADJECTIVES: amenable, acquiescent, complaisant, compliant, docile, deferential, dutiful, malleable, obedient, obeisant, pliant, pliable, submissive, slavish, subservient, tame, tractable, unassertive, yielding

NOUN: compliance, passivity, resignation, servility

VERB: abide, comply, confirm, defer, heed, obey

ANTONYMS: adj. intransigent, intractable; v. repudiate.

★ **COMMODIOUS :** spacious, comfortable

ADJECTIVES: capacious, comfortable, convenient, expansive, extensive , voluminous

NOUNS: spaciousness

VERB: accommodate , harbor

ANTONYMS: adj. confined, cramped, inconvenient, small, squeezed, uncomfortable

★ **CRAMPED :** congested, overcrowded

ADJECTIVES: confined, crabbed, crowded, hemmed in, illegible, incommodious, indecipherable, minute, narrow, packed, pent, restricted, squeezed, taut, tight, tucked up, uncomfortable

NOUNS: congestion

VERB: circumscribe, clog, confine, constrain, encumber, impede, inhibit, restrict, shackle, stymie, thwart

ANTONYMS: adj. free, spacious,uncongested, uncrowded, uninhibited, unobstructed

★ **WITCHCRAFT:** magic, spell casting

ADJECTIVES: mystic, sorcerous

NOUNS: charisma, enchantment, incantation, jinx, necromancy, occult, spell, wizardry; demonism, diabolism, necromancy; clairvoyance, telepathy ; legerdemaln

VERB: conjure, bewitch

ANTONYMS:

★ **FOOD/DRINK**

ADJECTIVES: appetizing, comestible, culinary, delicious, edible, esculent, nutritious, palatable, piquant, savory, succulent, tasty, wholesome,

NOUNS: aliment, cuisine, fodder, larder, nourishment, provision, repast, subsistence, sustenance, viand, victual; potable, potion

VERB: gorge , nibble, guzzle, swallow,

ANTONYMS: adj. inedible, unpalatable

★ **TASTY**

ADJECTIVES: ambrosial, delectable, flavorsome, luscious, palatable, piquant, pungent, sapid, savory, spicy, tangy, toothsome

NOUNS: palatability

VERB: relish, savor

ANTONYMS: bland

Word List Day-23

PROLIFERATE (pruh LIF uh reyt): v. Grow quickly, multiply rapidly.

    Trigger: PRO+LIFE+RATE-(LIFE RATE)

    Trigger Sentence: LIFE RATE is PROLIFERATING.

    Sample Sentence: Rumors about the incident *proliferated* on the Internet.

PROLIFIC (pro LIF ik): a. Abundantly fruitful

    Trigger: PROLIFIC -PRO+LIFE; PRODUCTION OF LIFE

    Trigger Sentence: PROLIFIC - PRODUCES lot of LIFE; PROLIFIC apple tree PRODUCES lot of apples.

    Sample Sentence: He is a *prolific* writer who produced several works of fiction and nonfiction.

PROLIX (proh LIKS): a. Long and wordy

    Trigger: PROLIX-PROLONG

    Trigger Sentence: Epics were originally written in PROLIX and PROLONGED verses.

    Sample Sentence: His poetry is *prolix*, yet like slow poison it makes you concentrate into its pith.

    Related Words: PROLIXITY -n. tedious wordiness; verbosity

PROLOGUE (PROH log): n. Introduction, foreword

    Trigger: PROLOGUE-FIRST DIALOGUE

    Trigger Sentence: PROLOGUE is the FIRST DIALOGUE of the author.

    Sample Sentence: A *prologue* is mandatory to attract the attention of your audience.

    Related Words: EPILOGUE -n. concluding section

PROMINENT (PROM uh nunt): a. Renowned; important; noticeable

    Trigger: PROMINENT-EMINENT

    Trigger Sentence: The EMINENT rap singer Eminem is PROMINENT citizen of US.

    Sample Sentence: Rap singer Eminem in a flash became a *prominent* figure in the music world.

PROMISCUOUS (pruh MIS kyoo uhs): a. Immoral; wanton; indiscriminate; mixed

    Trigger: PROMISCUOUS- PRO+ MISSUS

    Trigger Sentence: You are referred as PROMISCUOUS, if you are PRO towards many MISSUS.

    Sample Sentence: Bill Clinton was criticized for his *promiscuous* lifestyle.

PROMULGATE (PROM ul geyt): v. Announce officially; promote

    Trigger: PROMULGATE-PROMOTE; "ULGA" is replaced by "O"

    Trigger Sentence: 1. PROMULGATE is to PROMOTE any theory or message or an idea; 2. The company PROMULGATED COLGATE tooth paste.

    Sample Sentence: Her ideas have been widely *promulgated* on the Internet.

PRONE (PROHN): a. Inclined to; prostrate

Trigger: 1.PRONE-PROSTRATE. 2. SUPINE (refer)-PRONE. 3. PRONE-PRO towards

Trigger Sentence: 1. PRONE and PROSTRATE (prostate gland is near stomach) positions are same. 2. SUPINE and PRONE positions are antonyms.

Sample Sentence: 1. Subdue the suspect and get him into a *prone* position. 2. He was *prone* to emotional outbursts under stress.

PRONOUNCE (pruh NOUNS): v. Utter, articulate

Trigger: PRONOUNCE-ANNOUNCE

Trigger Sentence: ANNOUNCE something clearly; PRONOUNCE things categorically.

Sample Sentence: He was *pronounced* dead upon arrival at the hospital.

PROPENSITY (pruh PEN si tee): n. Natural inclination

Trigger: PROCLIVITY-PROPENSITY-PRO

Trigger Sentence: 1. I have PROPENSITY for earning PROPERTY. 2. A Business PRO (professional) has PROPENSITY to quick thinking. 3. Men have PROPENSITY for quantity- women have PROCLIVITY for quality.

Sample Sentence: He has a *propensity* for crime, and he is incorrigible!

PROPHECY (PROF uh see): n. Prediction, forecast

Trigger: PROPHET-PROPHECY

Trigger Sentence: PROPHET tells about the FUTURE

Sample Sentence: A new *prophet* tends to terrorize people with his threatening prophecies.

Related Words: PROPHETIC -a. of prediction; forecasting

PROPINQUITY (proh PING kwi tee): n. Nearness; relationship

Trigger: 1. PROPINQUITY-PROXIMITY. 2. "P"+ RO + PIN + "Q" +UITY.

Trigger Sentence: 1. PROPINQUITY is PROXIMITY. 2. With P if you PIN Q it will be PROPINQUITY.

Sample Sentence: The world has become mechanical; there is hardly any *propinquity* among us.

PROPITIATE (pruh PISH ee eyt): v. Appease; calm

Trigger: 1. PROPITIATE-"PRO +PEACE+ ATE". 2. PROPITIATE -PROPHET + PITY

Trigger Sentence: 1. PRO towards PEACE. 2. Want a PROPHET PITY? You got to PROPITIATE him.

Sample Sentence: It is archaic to believe that sacrificing an animal will *propitiate* the angry gods!

Related Words: PROPITIATORY -a. appeasing; conciliating

PROPITIOUS (pruh PISH us): a. Favorable, fortunate, advantageous

Trigger: PROPITIOUS-PROFIT+US

Trigger Sentence: The trade between USA and China is mutually PROPITIOUS as it PROFITS both.

Sample Sentence: With all the resources in your kitty, it is a *propitious* time to start a business.

Related Words: UNPROPITIOUS -a. not propitious, not favorable.

PROPONENT (pruh POH nunt): n. Supporter, advocate

Trigger: PROPONENT-OPPONENT

Trigger Sentence: 1. PROPONENT and OPPONENT are antonyms. 2. Adam Smith was the PROPONENT of Capitalism whereas Karl Marx was the OPPONENT of it.

Sample Sentence: I don't need a *proponent* to support my good projects, they will be selected.

Related Words: EXPONENT –n. one who actively promotes

PROPOUND (pruh POUND): v. Propose an idea; present for discussion

Trigger: PROPOUND-PROPOSE (** synonyms)

Trigger Sentence: The professor expanded the theory PROPOUNDED/PROPOSED in his journal.

Sample Sentence: Einstein *propounded* many scientific theories which opened up a Pandora's Box of possibilities for generations to explore.

PROPRIETY (pruh PRYE uh tee): n. Fitness; correct conduct

Trigger: 1.PROPRIETY-PROPER. 2. PROPRIETY-APPROPRIATE

Trigger Sentence: 1. PROPER BEHAVIOR is known as PROPRIETY (or PROPERNESS). 2. Your conduct does not look APPROPRIATE to match your PROPRIETY.

Sample Sentence: *Propriety* and other mannerisms were part of the learning in military training.

Related Words: PROPRIETARY -a. of a proprietor, protected by a patent or trade mark

PROSAIC (proh ZEY ik): a. Dull, unimaginative, everyday

Trigger: 1.PROSAIC-PROSE LIKE. 2. PROSAIC-POETIC

Trigger Sentence: 1. PROSAIC (prose) approach is BORING; POETIC approach is IMAGINATIVE and INTERESTING. 2. POETRY is less PROSAIC than PROSE. A prosaic poet is unimpressive.

Sample Sentence: Though the ad writers had a creative campaign to publicize the company's newest product, the head office rejected it for a more *prosaic*, down-to-earth approach.

PROSCRIBE (proh SKRYBE): v. Prohibit, banish

Trigger: PROSCRIBE-PRESCRIBE (antonym Memory trick)

Trigger Sentence: Got stomach upset? Doctor PRESCRIBES curd rice and PROSCRIBES spicy food.

Sample Sentence: The Czar's prescribed *proscription* of Lenin to Siberia for his anti rule stance.

Related Words: CIRCUMSCRIBE -v. limit

PROTEAN (PRO tean): a. Versatile; taking of different forms

Trigger: PROTEAN-PROTEIN

Trigger Sentence: The PROTEIN is PROTEAN in nature; it is an organic compound of amino acids.

Sample Sentence: Kamal Hassan is a remarkable *protean* actor who could take on any role.

PROTRACT (proh TRAKT): v. Prolong; stretch

Trigger: PROTRACT-CONTRACT (** antonyms)

Trigger Sentence: PROTRACT is to PROLONG and CONTRACT is to SHRINK.

Sample Sentence: The highway project is being *protracted* by years of litigation.

Related Words: CONTRACT -v. to sink

PROVIDENT (PROV i dunt): a. Careful in spending; displaying foresight

Trigger: PROVIDENT -PROVIDENT FUND

Trigger Sentence: 1. people who PROVIDE MONEY for the future are PROVIDENT.
2. PROVIDENT people keep their money in PROVIDENT FUND for their future care.

Sample Sentence: My mom's *provident* measures keep us safe and alive in this foreign land.

Related Words: PROVIDENTIAL -a. peculiarly fortunate; lucky

PROVIDENTIAL (prov i DEN shul): a. Fortunate; lucky; opportune

Trigger: PROVIDENTIAL-PROVIDE accidental

Trigger Sentence: PROVIDENTIAL events PROVIDE ACCIDENTAL benefits.

Sample Sentence: *Providential* events like those heavenly signs bounded the birth of the Christ.

PROVINCIAL (pruh VIN shul): n. Rural; regional; narrow-minded

Trigger: PROVINCIAL-PROVINCE

Trigger Sentence: I am from small PROVINCE- in a well-read company I am uneasily PROVINCIAL.

Sample Sentence: His narrow *provincial* attitude often irritated her.

Related Words: PROVINCE -n. district, division; region

PROVISIONAL (pruh VIZH unl): a. Temporary; tentative

Trigger: PROVISIONAL-PROVISIONAL certificate

Trigger Sentence: The University has given a PROVISIONAL certificate for TEMPORARY use.

Sample Sentence: All bookings are considered *provisional* until full payment has been received.

PROVOKE (pruh VOHK): v. Irritate; stimulate

Trigger: 1.PROVOKE-PROMOTE. 2. PROVOKE-PRO+WAKE

Trigger Sentence: 1. PROVOKE is to PROMOTE bad sense like ANGER, IRRITATION. 2. It also PROMOTES good sense like EXCITEMENT. 3. His PROVOKING words WOKE us to awful situations.

Sample Sentence: His remarks *provoked* both tears and laughter.

Related Words: PROVOCATIVE -a. irritating; stimulating

PROWESS (PROW is): n. Extraordinary ability; bravery

Trigger: PROWESS-POWERS

Trigger Sentence: PROWESS is to have lot of POWERS.

Sample Sentence: Sachin is known for his *prowess* on the cricket field.

PROXIMITY (PROK sim i tee): n. Nearness

Trigger: PROXIMITY-APPROXIMATE

Trigger Sentence: The APPROXIMATE location is in close PROXIMITY to the old city.

Sample Sentence: Being a loner, he has not developed any kind of *proximity* with his employees.

PROXY (PROK see): n. A person authorized to act for another

Trigger: PROXY-APPROXIMATE

Trigger Sentence: The PROXY tries to APPROXIMATE his boss during the meeting.

Sample Sentence: The boss sent a *proxy* to cast the vote on behalf of him.

PRUDE (PROOD): n. Excessively proper or modest person

Trigger: PRUDE-CRUDE-RUDE

Trigger Sentence: 1. PRUDE is an antonym to CRUDE (or RUDE) person; PRUDE is a PROPER DUDE-(but bit excessive in exhibiting properness). 2. A PRUDE is a DUDE with PROPER etiquette.

Sample Sentence: He is too much of a *prude* to enjoy movies containing sex and violence.

Related Words: 1.PRUDERY -n. excessively modest behavior. 2. PRUDISH -a. excessively humble

PRUDENT (PROOD unt): a. Careful, wise

Trigger: PRUDENT- PRESIDENT

Trigger Sentence: 1. PRESIDENT is a PRUDENT/ WISE person. 2. A PROVIDENT man is PRUDENT.

Sample Sentence: Being *prudent* is the need of the hour when in crisis.

Related Words: IMPRUDENT –a. unwise; lacking caution

PRURIENT (PROOR ee unt): a. Lustful, obsessed with sex

Trigger: PRURIENT-PORN +ORIENT

Trigger Sentence: A PORN ORIENTED man is obsessed with PRURIENT thoughts.

Sample Sentence: She tried to avoid the *prurient* touch of her colleague.

PSEUDONYM (SOO duh nim): n. Pen name; false name

Trigger: PSEUDONYM -PSEUDO (false) + NAME

Trigger Sentence: A PSEUDONYM reflects the FALSE NAME of an author.

Sample Sentence: The notorious serial killer of females is known by the *pseudonym* of -Jack the Ripper.

Related Words: 1. ANONYMOUS -a. not named. 2. MISNOMER -n. use of a wrong name

PUERILE (PYOOR il): a. Childish; immature

Trigger: 1. PUERILE- PUBERTY. 2. PUER-PUTER + ILE

Trigger Sentence: 1. PUERILE ways fade at PUBERTY. 2. My PUTTER (son) nature is PUERILE.

Sample Sentence: The teenagers behaved in a *puerile* manner during the ceremony.

PUGNACIOUS (pug NEY shus): a. Inclined to quarrel; combative

Trigger: 1.PUG DOG. 2. PUGILIST (boxer). 2. PUGNACIOUS-PUSHY

Trigger Sentence: 1. A PUG dog or A PUGILIST tend to be PUGNACIOUS.
2. PUGNACIOUS people are PUSHY in nature.

Sample Sentence: There's one *pugnacious* member on the committee who won't agree to us.

Related Words: IMPUGN -v. challenge, criticize

PUISSANCE (PYOO uh suns): n. Power; strength

Trigger: PUISSANCE-POTENCE (** synonyms)

Trigger Sentence: The PUISSANCE of US economy is the POTENCY of its dollar.

Sample Sentence: He has proved himself as a *puissant* in the project.

Related Words: IMPUISSANCE -n. weakness

PULCHRITUDE (PUHL kri tood): n. Beauty; glory

Trigger: 1.PULCHRITUDE –PULSAR + DUDE. 2. PLUSH+RICH+ DUDE

Trigger Sentence: 1. On a PULSAR bike the DUDE is with a female PULCHRITUDE.
2. The PLUSH and RICH locality of the DUDE is full of PULCHRITUDE.

Sample Sentence: The flower show was like a plethora of *pulchritude*... enticing beauty.

PUNGENT (PUN gent): a. Biting; sharp in taste or smell; caustic

Trigger: PUNGENT-PUN GENT

Trigger Sentence: The GENT make PUNS of others; they are PUNGENT (bitter, biting, sarcastic).

Sample Sentence: I love the *pungent* taste of the tamarind pickle.

PUNITIVE (PYOO ni tiv): a. Punishing

Trigger: PUNITIVE-PUNISH

Trigger Sentence: PUNITIVE action is done to PUNISH the people.

Sample Sentence: If there are no strict *punitive* measures, criminals will escape their penalty.

Related Words: IMPUNITY -n. freedom from punishment

PURGE (PURJ): v. Purify; clean, remove dirt; free from guilt

Trigger: PURGE-PURE (pure by removing the dirt)

Trigger Sentence: PURGE is to make PURE by removing all the IMPURITIES

Sample Sentence: After all the sins, he tries to *purge* himself by confessing to the Church priest.

Related Words: 1.EXPURGATE -v. purify; censor. 2. PURGATORY –a. purifying; absolving

PURITANICAL (pyoor i TAN i kul): a. Strict on religious and moral issues, austere

Trigger: PURITANICAL -PURITY

Trigger Sentence: Excessive claim on MORAL PURITY can be identified as PURITANICAL behavior.

Sample Sentence: My *puritanical* aunt doesn't approve of my sexy outfits.

Related Words: PURIST -n. one who strictly adheres to purity of behavior (or speech, etc.)

PURPORT (pur PORT): n. Intention, meaning

Trigger: PURPORT-PURPOSE

Trigger Sentence: A pretty girl is dating a rich old man; the main PURPORT (or PURPOSE) of her affair with him can be easily understood.

Sample Sentence: The main *purport* of Europeans' visit to India is to learn yoga and meditation.

Related Words: PURPORTED -a. alleged; rumored; reputed

PUSILLANIMOUS (pyoo sih LAN ih muss): a. Cowardly, Fearful

Trigger: 1.PUSSY + ANIMAL. 2. PUSSY CAT

Trigger Sentence: 1. He is as PUSILLANIMOUS as a PUSSY CAT. 2. PUSILLANIMOUS ANIMAL runs away from aggressive animals.

Sample Sentence: Ashamed of his *pusillanimous* conduct during the war he resigned the Army!

QUAFF (KWOF): v. Drink with large gulps

    Trigger: QUAFF-"COUGH" (syrup)

    Trigger Sentence: The kid QUAFFED the tasty COUGH syrup.

    Sample Sentence: We spent the whole evening at a bar and *quaffed* few beers.

    Related Words: GUZZLE –v. drink greedily

QUACK (KWAK): n. Charlatan; impostor

    Trigger: 1.QUACK-FAKE. 2. QUACK-LACK truth

    Trigger Sentence: Don't encourage QUACKS. They are FAKE doctors.

    Sample Sentence: He is a *quack*; don't believe in his products, they are not exotic like he claims.

QUAINT (KWEYNT): a. Unusual, odd; old fashioned

    Trigger: 1.QUAINT-SAINT. 2. QUAINT-ACQUAINT

    Trigger Sentence: 1. Indian SAINTS look QUAINT to the foreigners. 2. We ACQUAINTED with QUAINT-looking people.

    Sample Sentence: He captured some pictures of those *quaint* and historic buildings.

QUALIFIED (KWOL uh fyde): a. 1.Limited; restricted (secondary sense). 2. Certified

    Trigger: QUALIFIED -QUALITY

    Trigger Sentence: Secondary meaning: LIMITED in QUALITY is known as QUALIFIED.

    Sample Sentence: He was now *qualified* to fly fighter air crafts.

    Related Words: 1.QUALIFY -v. make more specific, restrict. 2. UNQUALIFIED –a. unlimited

QUALM (KWAM): n. Misgiving, uneasy fear

    Trigger: QUALM- NO CALM

    Trigger Sentence: If you are in a QUALM, you CANNOT remain CALM.

    Sample Sentence: She has no *qualms* about buying pirated films.

QUANDARY (KWON dree): n. Dilemma; state of confusion

    Trigger: 1. QUANDARY-QUANTUM mechanics. 2. QUANDARY-QUERY

    Trigger Sentence: 1. One of the QUANDARIES of QUANTUM MECHANICS is the existence of GOD PARTICLE. 2. He was in QUANDARY with my perplexing QUERY.

    Sample Sentence: She was in such a *quandary* and didn't know whom to turn to for advice.

    Related Words: QUERY -n. inquiry; question

QUARANTINE (KWOR un teen): n. To isolate (esp. to prevent from contagious diseases)

    Trigger: 1. QUARANTINE –"QURAN-CONFINE". 2. QUARANTINE-CONFINE

Trigger Sentence: 1. The QURAN QUARANTINES people against bad habits. 2. If we QUARANTINE the carriers of this strange disease, we can CONFINE the spread of the disease.

Sample Sentence: We kept the dog under *quarantined* observation to determine his infection.

QUASH (KWOSH): v. Crush; subdue; suppress

    Trigger: 1. QUASH-CRUSH. 2. QUASH-SQUASH

    Trigger Sentence: 1. When we prepare a lemon SQUASH --we CRUSH the lemon.
    2. Let us QUASH some lemons and make SQUASH.

    Sample Sentence: If you try to *quash* my travel plans, I will never forgive you!

QUELL (KWEL): v. Suppress, crush; quiet

    Trigger: QUELL-KILL

    Trigger Sentence: The dictator KILLED rebellion by QUELLING signs of dispute during his regime.

    Sample Sentence: As a child my desire to become an actress was *quelled* by my parents.

QUERULOUS (KWER uh lus): a. Complaining; irritable

    Trigger: QUERULOUS-QUARRELSOME

    Trigger Sentence: QUARRELSOME persons exhibit QUERULOUS tendencies.

    Sample Sentence: Our Bus trip was spoiled by a couple of *querulous* passengers at the back.

QUIBBLE (KWIB ul): n. A slight objection or complaint

    Trigger: QUIBBLE-SQUABBLE-SMALL QUARREL

    Trigger Sentence: It is foolish to QUARREL over a QUIBBLE.

    Sample Sentence: My extremely protective mommy keeps *quibbling* on my hippy lifestyle.

QUIESCENT (kwye ES unt): a. Restful; temporarily inactive

    Trigger: QUIESCENT-"QUITE SENSE"

    Trigger Sentence: The volcano is QUIET; it has remained QUIESCENT for the last 400 years.

    Sample Sentence: These volcano fields have remained *quiescent* for years, but may not for long!

    Related Words: QUIESCENCE -n. calmness, quiet, absence of activity

QUINTESSENCE (kwin TES uns): n. Purest & highest embodiment; core

    Trigger: QUINTESSENCE–ESSENCE-ESSENTIAL

    Trigger Sentence: 1. She is the QUINTESSENCE (or ESSENCE) of punctuality. 2. Business acumen is an ESSENTIAL QUINTESSENCE for managers.

    Sample Sentence: Her *quintessential* beauty remains in her charitable deeds.

QUIP (KWIP): n. A clever or witty comment

    Trigger: QUIP-"QUICK+LIP"-QUICK TIP

    Trigger Sentence: Persons who QUIP well tend to have QUICK QUIPS on the TIPS of their LIPS.

    Sample Sentence: In a pat he could *quip* or give a sarcastic comment that could embarrass you!

QUIRK (KWURK): n. Sudden twist; caprice

    Trigger: QUIRK-JERK

    Trigger Sentence: QUIRK and JERK are synonyms. If he is QUIRKY means….he is a JERK in nature.

    Sample Sentence: To remain motionless for 24 hours without a single jerk is one of his *quirks*.

    Related Words: QUIRKINESS -v. oddness

QUISLING (KWIZ ling): n. Traitor; betrayer

    Trigger: QUISLING-DARLING (** near antonyms)

    Trigger Sentence: 1. MY DARLING has become a QUISLING. 2. SIBLINGS became QUISLINGS.

    Sample Sentence: The dictator declared- all *quislings* be hanged without any mercy.

QUIXOTIC (kwik SOT ik): a. Idealistic but impracticable

    Trigger: 1.QUIXOTICAL-HYPOTHETICAL-THEORETICAL. 2. QUIXOTIC –"QUICK +THICK"

    Trigger Sentence: 1. QUIXOTICAL means THEORETICAL and PRAGMATICAL means PRACTICAL. 2. QUIXOTIC - QUICK + THICK: a THICK fellow want to be QUICK; is it possible? It appears QUIXOTIC.

    Sample Sentence: Theoretical ideas remain *quixotic* without experimental evidence.

    Related Words: QUIXOTICAL -a. unrealistic

QUOTIDIAN (kwoh TID ee un): a. Daily, Commonplace, Customary

    Trigger: 1. QUOTIDIAN-QUOTE+DAILY. 2. QUOTODIAN-QUOTE-QUOTATION

    Trigger Sentence: 1. Display of QUOTATIONS in school premises is a QUOTIDIAN practice. 2. Explaining a DAILY QUOTE in the classroom is QUOTIDIAN routine to Mrs. Lloyd.

    Sample Sentence: Visiting the temple every Tuesday was Gita's *quotidian* practice.

RACONTEUR (ra kawn TYOOR): n. Story teller

    Trigger: 1. RECOUNT + TOUR. 2. BACK ON TOUR

    Trigger Sentence: The RACONTEUR, after BACK from the TOUR, RECOUNTED on the TOUR.

    Sample Sentence: He is such a good *raconteur* that the children listened to him all mesmerized!

    Related Words: RECKON -v. guess; estimate; understand

RAIL (REYL): v. Scold; complain bitterly

> **Trigger:** RAIL-HAIL (**antonyms)
>
> **Trigger Sentence:** 1. He RAILED at FAILURES .2. RAIL means scolding- HAIL means praising.
>
> **Sample Sentence:** The master *rails* at his servants for not coming on time.
>
> Related Words: HAIL –v. praise; salute

RAIMENT (REY munt): n. Clothing

> **Trigger:** RAIMENT-GARMENT (** synonyms)
>
> **Trigger Sentence:** The Raymond shop sells RAIMENT/GARMENTS.
>
> **Sample Sentence:** The model's first appearance in feminine *raiment* is quite arty and sensuous.

RAMBLE (RAM bul): v. To move or talk aimlessly

> **Trigger:** RAMBLE-"ROAM + BULL"
>
> **Trigger Sentence:** 1. RAMBLE like a ROAMING BULL! 2. ROAMING TALK means TALK aimlessly.
>
> **Sample Sentence:** Listening to my teacher *ramble*, I wondered if he'd ever get to the point.

RAMBUNCTIOUS (ram BUNK shuhs): a. Unruly, boisterous, uncontrollable

> **Trigger:** 1. RAMBUNCTIOUS-RAMBO+ANXIOUS. 2. RAM +BUNKS
>
> **Trigger Sentence:** 1. In the film, "Rambo and first blood" RAMBO was RAMBUNCTIOUS; his gun makes lot of NOISE; and he was UNCONTROLLABLE to the US military. 2. RAMBUNCTIOUS---RAM BUNKS the college and create RAUCOUS in the city.
>
> **Sample Sentence:** The *rambunctious* shouts of the crowd made boxer Rambo anxious.

RAMIFICATION (ram uh fi KEY shun): n. Branching out; subdivision; outgrowth

> **Trigger:** 1. RAMIFICATION-RAM BHAN. 2. RAMIFICATION-UNIFICATION
>
> **Trigger Sentence:** 1. There was RAMIFICATION of RAM BHAN (arrow); the OUTCOME was many rakshas were killed. 2. RAMIFICATION is branching out; almost opposite to UNIFICATION.
>
> **Sample Sentence:** The *ramifications* from the bifurcation of the country are unpredictable.
>
> Related Words: RAMIFY -v. branch out or cause to branch out

RAMPANT (RAM punt): a. Behaving violently; unrestrained; excessive

> **Trigger:** 1.RAMPANT-"RAM+PANT+ANT". 2. RAMPANT-REDUNDANT-ABUNDANT
>
> **Trigger Sentence:** 1. The ANTS in RAM PANTS had a RAMPANT time. 2. RAMPANT-REDUNDANT.
>
> **Sample Sentence:** Corruption is growing *rampantly* in India.

RAMSHACKLE (RAM shak ul): a. Falling to pieces, rickety

> **Trigger:** RAMSHACKLE-"RAM + SHACKY (SHAKY)"
>
> **Trigger Sentence:** 1. AN OLD RAM is SHACKY and SHAKY; he may COLLAPSE at any moment. 2. AN OLD SHACK (hut) is SHAKY; it may FALL DOWN into PIECES.
>
> **Sample Sentence:** A speeding vehicle left Ram's shaky cycle in a *ramshackle* state.

RANCOR (RAN kur): n. Bitterness; hatred

> **Trigger:** RANCOR-r+ ANCOR - ANGER

Trigger Sentence: Feeling of ANGER is RANCOR; Showing RANCOR and ANGER against rival.

Sample Sentence: Let us get out of this *rancor* rut and rest our animosity.

RAPACIOUS (ruh PAY shus): a. Greedy, Selfish; Predatory

Trigger: RAPACIOUS-RAPES

Trigger Sentence: This RAPACIOUS man RAPED her. Rapacious and ravenous are synonyms.

Sample Sentence: Hawks and other *rapacious* birds prey on variety of small animals.

RAPPORT (rah PORE): n. Close relationship; understanding

Trigger: RAPPORT-SUPPORT

Trigger Sentence: There is a RAPPORT between the members because of their mutual SUPPORT.

Sample Sentence: My teacher has a *rapport* with students and understanding our needs.

Related Words: RAPPROCHEMENT -n. the reestablishing of cordial relationships; reconciliation

RAREFY (RAIR uh fye): v. To make thin, or less dense

Trigger: RAREFY-RARE

Trigger Sentence: To make RARE (extremely thin or fine) in appearance is RAREFACTION.

Sample Sentence: People rarely live in mountain ranges as oxygen is *rarefied* here.

Related Words: RARIFIED –a. made less dense.

RATIFY (RAT uh fye): v. Approve formally; certify

Trigger: 1. RATIFY-CERTIFY. 2. RATIFICATION-CERTIFICATION

Trigger Sentence: RATIFY is to CERTIFY; your appointment is RATIFIED (or CERTIFIED).

Sample Sentence: Before the contract was put into effect, it had been *ratified* by the president.

Related Words: RATIFICATION -n. certification, sanction

RATIOCINATION (rash ee oh suh NAY shun): n. Process of reasoning, logical deduction

Trigger: RATIOCINATION-RATIO-RATIONALIZATION

Trigger Sentence: Aristotle, the father of RATIOCINATION introduced a logical process for RATIONALIZATION.

Sample Sentence: The forensic experts' *ratiocination* seemed to be the only scientific method.

RATIONAL (RASH nl): a. Logical, reasonable; intelligent, prudent

Trigger: 1. RATIO. 2. RATIONAL-REAL

Trigger Sentence: 1. RATIONALIZE, RATIONALITY, RATIONALIZATION, RATIONALE and RATIONAL; all belong to reasoning, knowledge and logic. 2. RATIONAL thinking needed for RATIO analysis.

Sample Sentence: Human beings are *rational* creatures.

Related Words: 1. RATIONALE -n. reasoning; grounds for an action. 2. IRRATIONAL -a. illogical, senseless. 3. RATIONALIZE -v. attempt to justify (an action) with logical reasoning

RAVAGE (RAV ij): v. Destroy; rob

    Trigger: RAVAGE-rain DAMAGE

    Trigger Sentence: Heavy torrential RAINS RAVAGED and DAMAGED the country side.

    Sample Sentence: The bull dozers sadly *ravaged* this beautiful 100 year old building.

RAVE (REYV): n. An extravagantly favorable review

    Trigger: RAVE-BRAVE

    Trigger Sentence: The critics RAVED about his BRAVE performance.

    Sample Sentence: People *raved* about the new film.

RAVENOUS (RAV uh nus): a. Desirous, extremely hungry

    Trigger: 1.RAVAN-RAVENOUS. 2. RAVENOUS-REVENUES

    Trigger Sentence: 1. Rakshas King RAVAN had 500 wives but still he was RAVENOUS about SITA. 2. Most of the Business people are RAVENOUS about REVENUES.

    Sample Sentence: The *ravenous* dog raided several garbage dumps in search of food.

RAZE (REYZ): v. Destroy; demolish

    Trigger: 1.RAZE-ERASE. 2. RAZE-RAYS

    Trigger Sentence: Ultraviolet RAYS ERASED and RAZED the planet.

    Sample Sentence: The bull dozer *razed* the heritage house, erasing all its traces of existence.

PLIGHT : dilemma, scrap, quandary

Memory Test-89 : Match each word and its memory trick to the corresponding definition.

S.N	WORD	MEMORY TRIGGER	S.N	DEFINITIONS	KEY
1	PROLIFERATE	LIFE rate is proliferating	A	Abundantly fruitful	
2	PROLIFIC	produces lot of LIFE	B	Announce officially; promote	
3	PROLIX	PROLONG	C	Appease; calm	
4	PROLOGUE	first DIALOGUE	D	Dull, unimaginative, everyday	
5	PROMINENT	EMINENT	E	Favorable, fortunate	
6	PROMISCUOUS	pro+ MISSUS	F	Fitness; correct conduct	
7	PROMULGATE	PROMOTE	G	Grow quickly, multiply rapidly	
8	PRONE	pro TOWARDS	H	Immoral; wanton; indiscriminate	
9	PRONOUNCE	ANNOUNCE	I	Inclined to; prostrate	
10	PROPENSITY	PRO for property	J	Introduction, foreword	
11	PROPHECY	PROPHET	K	Long and wordy	
12	PROPINQUITY	PROXIMITY	L	Natural inclination	
13	PROPITIATE	pro +PEACE+ ate	M	Nearness; relationship	
14	PROPITIOUS	PROFIT+us	N	Prediction, forecast	
15	PROPONENT	Not OPPONENT	O	Prohibit, banish	
16	PROPOUND	PROPOSE	P	Propose an idea	
17	PROPRIETY	Proper--appropriate	Q	Renowned; important; noticeable	
18	PROSAIC	PROSE like	R	Supporter, advocate	
19	PROSCRIBE	Not PRESCRIBED	S	Utter, articulate	
20	PROTEAN	PROTEINS	T	Versatile; taking of different forms	

Memory Test-90 : Match each word and its memory trick to the corresponding definition.

S.N	WORD	MEMORY TRIGGER	S.N	DEFINITIONS	KEY
1	PROTRACT	CONTRACT -shrink	A	Beauty; glory	
2	PROVIDENT	PROVIDENT fund	B	Biting; sharp in taste; caustic	
3	PROVIDENTIAL	provide ACCIDENTAL	C	Careful in spending; displaying foresight	
4	PROVINCIAL	PROVINCE	D	Careful, wise	
5	PROVISIONAL	PROVISIONAL certificate	E	Childish; immature	
6	PROVOKE	Promote- pro+WAKE	F	Excessively proper or modest person	
7	PROWESS	POWERS	G	Extraordinary ability; bravery	
8	PROXIMITY	APPROXIMATE	H	Fortunate; lucky; opportune	
9	PROXY	Proxy friend	I	Inclined to quarrel; combative	
10	PRUDE	prude-proper dude	J	Irritate; stimulate	
11	PRUDENT	prudent- PRESIDENT	K	Lustful, obsessed with sex	
12	PRURIENT	porn +orient	L	Nearness	
13	PSEUDONYM	pseudo (false) + name	M	Pen name; false name	
14	PUERILE	puberty	N	Person authorized to act for another	
15	PUGNACIOUS	pugilist -PUSHY	O	Power; strength	
16	PUISSANCE	POTENCE	P	Prolong; stretch	
17	PULCHRITUDE	PLUSH+rich+ dude	Q	Punishing	
18	PUNGENT	pun gent	R	Purify; remove dirt; free from guilt	
19	PUNITIVE	PUNISH	S	Rural; regional; narrow-minded	
20	PURGE	PURE	T	Temporary; tentative	

Answers	EX.NO	1	2	3	4	5	6	7	8	9	10	11	12	13	14	15	16	17	18	19	20
	89	G	A	K	J	Q	H	B	I	S	L	N	M	C	E	R	P	F	D	O	T
	90	P	C	H	S	T	J	G	L	N	F	D	K	M	E	I	O	A	B	Q	R

Memory Test-91 : Match each word and its memory trick to the corresponding definition.

S.N	WORD	MEMORY TRIGGER	S.N	DEFINITIONS	KEY
1	PURITANICAL	Moral PURITY	A	1.Limited. 2. certified	
2	PURPORT	PURPOSE ??	B	Charlatan; impostor	
3	PUSILLANIMOUS	PUSSY CAT nature ??	C	Clever or witty comment	
4	QUAFF	tasty COUGH syrup	D	Complaining; irritable	
5	QUACK	FAKE	E	Cowardly, Fearful	
6	QUAINT	Saint is QUAINT	F	Crush; subdue; suppress	
7	QUALIFIED	limited in QUALITY	G	Dilemma; state of confusion	
8	QUALM	NO CALM	H	Drink with large gulps	
9	QUANDARY	quantum -query	I	Idealistic but impracticable	
10	QUARANTINE	quran-CONFINE	J	Intention, meaning	
11	QUASH	crush	K	Isolate	
12	QUELL	KILL	L	Misgiving, uneasy fear	
13	QUERULOUS	QUARRELSOME	M	Purest embodiment; core	
14	QUIBBLE	squabble-small quarrel	N	Restful; temporarily inactive	
15	QUIESCENT	QUITE SENSE	O	Slight objection or complaint	
16	QUINTESSENCE	ESSENCE-essential	P	Strict on religious and moral issues	
17	QUIP	quick+lip-quick tip	Q	Sudden twist; caprice	
18	QUIRK	JERK	R	Suppress, crush; quiet	
19	QUISLING	No more DARLING	S	Traitor; betrayer	
20	QUIXOTIC	QUICK-THICK ??	T	Unusual, odd; old fashioned	

Memory Test-92 : Match each word and its memory trick to the corresponding definition.

S.N	WORD	MEMORY TRIGGER	S.N	DEFINITIONS	KEY
1	QUOTIDIAN	QUOTE+DAILY	A	Approve formally; certify	
2	RACONTEUR	RECOUNT + tour	B	Behaving violently; excessive	
3	RAIL	RAIL-HAIL	C	Bitterness; hatred	
4	RAIMENT	GARMENT	D	Branching out; subdivision; outgrowth	
5	RAMBLE	ROAM + BULL	E	Close relationship; understanding	
6	RAMBUNCTIOUS	ram +BUNKS	F	Clothing	
7	RAMIFICATION	Not UNIFICATION	G	Daily, Commonplace	
8	RAMPANT	ram+PANT+ant	H	Desirous, extremely hungry	
9	RAMSHACKLE	ram + SHAKY	I	Destroy; demolish	
10	RANCOR	r+ancor-ANGER	J	Destroy; rob	
11	RAPACIOUS	RAPES	K	Extravagantly favorable review	
12	RAPPORT	SUPPORT	L	Falling to pieces, rickety	
13	RAREFY	Make RARE	M	Greedy, Selfish; Predatory	
14	RATIFY	CERTIFY	N	Logical, reasonable; intelligent	
15	RATIOCINATION	ratio-rationalization	O	Make thin, or less dense	
16	RATIONAL	RATIONAL-real	P	Move or talk aimlessly	
17	RAVAGE	rain DAMAGE	Q	Process of reasoning, logical deduction	
18	RAVE	rave-BRAVE	R	Scold; complain bitterly	
19	RAVENOUS	I want REVENUES	S	Story teller	
20	RAZE	rays-ERASE	T	Unruly, boisterous, uncontrollable	

Answers	EX.NO	1	2	3	4	5	6	7	8	9	10	11	12	13	14	15	16	17	18	19	20
	91	P	J	E	H	B	T	A	L	G	K	F	R	D	O	N	M	C	Q	S	I
	92	G	S	R	F	P	T	D	B	L	C	M	E	O	A	Q	N	J	K	H	I

WORD GROUPS DAY-23

★ **CLOTHING**

ADJECTIVES: sartorial

NOUNS: raiment, habiliment

VERB: don

ANTONYMS: v. doff;denude, defrock,unfrock, divest

★ **LANDS**

ADJECTIVES: arable; fertile; bog, marsh , morass, mire, quagmire

NOUNS: fecundity

VERB: fructify

ANTONYMS: arid, barren, infertile ; fallow, unused;

★ **RURAL / WOODED AREAS**

ADJECTIVES: agrarian, bucolic, elysian, idyllic , pastoral, picturesque, rustic, sylvan

NOUNS: yokel, bumpkin

VERB: rusticate

ANTONYMS: adj. urban; sophisticated

★ **SMILE/LAUGH**

ADJECTIVES: smiling, grinning

NOUNS: laughter

VERB: smile, grin, smirk, simper, leer; laugh, chortle, chuckle, giggle, guffaw, snicker, snigger, titter

ANTONYMS: v.cry

★ **LAMENT:** mourn

ADJECTIVES: lachrymose, doleful, mournful.

NOUNS: elegy, requiem, dirge.

VERB: bewail, mourn, deplore.

ANTONYMS: v.celebrate, exult, praise.

★ **STORY**

ADJECTIVES: allegorical , metaphorical, figurative, emblematic

NOUNS: allegory, anecdote, chronicle, epic, fable, fiction, memoir, myth, narrative, parable, saga, tale; raconteur

VERB: narrate, chronicle, account, recount

ANTONYMS: n. fact

★ **PROVERB- SAYING**

NOUNS: adage, axiom, aphorism, apothegm, dictum, maxim, precept, truism; banality, cliché , platitude

ADJECTIVES: aphoristic, epigrammatic, proverbial, sententious

VERB: aphorize

ANTONYMS: n.absurdity; paradox

★ **THEATRICAL:** excessively dramatic, related to actors.

ADJECTIVES: dramatic, histrionic, thespian;

affected, exaggerated, mannered, melodramatic, operatic, ostentatious, staged, stilted

NOUNS: theatricality, vaudeville

VERB: dramatize , hyperbolize, sensationalize

ANTONYMS: adj. undramatic, real.

★ **BLIGHT:** disease, plague

ADJECTIVES: dammed, infernal

NOUNS: affliction, bane, blight, canker, contamination, curse, decay, pestilence, scourge, withering, woe

VERB: afflict, infect, mar, devastate, demolish

ANTONYMS: blessing

Word List Day-24

REBUKE (ri BYOOK): v. Criticize severely; scold harshly

    Trigger: 1. REBUKE-PUKE. 2. REBUKE- NUKE (nuclear weapons)

    Trigger Sentence: 1. You cowardly little PUKES!! The boss REBUKED at the subordinates. 2. NUKE is to ATTACK with nuclear weapons, where as REBUKE is to ATTACK with WORDS.

    Sample Sentence: North Korea got *rebuked* from the world to decide to go ahead with its nuke.

REBUT (ri BUT): v. Contradict, refuse with proof

    Trigger: 1.RE + BUT .2. BUTT

    Trigger Sentence: 1."BUT" word itself is CONTRADICTION. 2. The scientist claimed that he had created a human infant, BUT the claim was REBUTTED to be only a hoax.

    Sample Sentence: Godman showed his butt when his miracles were *rebutted* by a rationalist

    Related Words: 1. REBUTTAL -n. contradiction, opposition. 2. REBUFF – v. reject; snub

RECALCITRANT (ri KAL si trunt): a. Stubborn, rebellious, unruly

    Trigger: RECALCITRANT-RELUCTANT-RESISTANT

    Trigger Sentence: RECALCITRANT people tend to be RELUCTANT and RESISTANT to CHANGE; recalcitrance, reluctance and resistance are synonyms.

    Sample Sentence: Don't be reluctant to oppose any *recalcitrant* person.

RECANT (ri KANT): v. Give up; disavow, retract a previous statement.

    Trigger: 1. RECANT-RECALL (refer). 2. RECANT- CAN'T

    Trigger Sentence: 1. RECANT means RECALL (call back or withdraw) the previous ACTION. 2. When you RECANT, "IT CAN'T BE DONE".

    Sample Sentence: Witnesses *recanted* their testimony as the court let out their names in news.

RECAPITULATE (ree kuh PICH uh leyt): v. Summarize

    Trigger: RECAPITULATE-RECAP-RECAPTURE

    Trigger Sentence: RECAPITULATE what you have learnt- you will RECAPTURE your knowledge.

    Sample Sentence: Our professor advised us to *recapitulate* our thesis for any changes.

    Related Words: 1.RECAP -v. summarize. 2. CAPITULATE –v. surrender

RECIDIVISM (ri SID uh viz um): n. Habitual return to crime

    Trigger: RECIDIVISM-ROWDYISM

    Trigger Sentence: People who have innate tendency for ROWDYISM tend to be RECIDIVISTIC.

    Sample Sentence: *Recidivism* is a fact as 90% of convicted sex offenders will relapse.

RECIPROCAL (ri SIP ruh kul): a. Mutual; interchangeable

Trigger: RECIPROCAL- RECIPROCATE

Trigger Sentence: In a RECIPROCAL action we RECIPROCATED the favor by helping our neighbor.

Sample Sentence: My husband does not *reciprocate* my love.

Related Words: RECIPROCATE -v. return; repay

RECLUSE (REK loos): n. Loner, hermit

Trigger: reCLUSE-CLUSE-CLOSE

Trigger Sentence: Living a secret, lonely life; a RECLUSE CLOSES himself from society.

Sample Sentence: I am not able to put up with my husband's *reclusive* behavior.

Related Words: SECLUDE –v. isolate; place in solitude

RECONCILE (REK un syl): v. Reunite, make friendly; make consistent

Trigger: RE + CONCILE (COUNCIL)

Trigger Sentence: If people engage in fighting...COUNSEL them for RECONCILIATION.

Sample Sentence: All the factions of the council have decided to *reconcile* their differences.

Related Words: 1. CONCILIATE -v. pacify, reconcile. 2. IRRECONCILABLE -a. unwilling to compromise

RECONDITE (REK un dyte): a. Profound, secret, difficult to understand

Trigger: RECONDITE-RECONDUCT

Trigger Sentence: Imagine a professor of physics having profound knowledge RE-CONDUCTED the quantum physics class; since quantum physics is so RECONDITE to understand.

Sample Sentence: He is a spiritualist who delves in reasoning those *recondite* concepts.

RECONNAISSANCE (ri KON uh suns): n. Survey of enemy by soldiers; gather info in enemy terrain

Trigger: RECONNAISSANCE-RECOGNIZANCE (** synonyms)

Trigger Sentence: RECOGNIZANCE of an enemy by SURVEY is known as RECONNAISSANCE

Sample Sentence: The police made a preliminary *reconnaissance* in mufti before the mass meet.

Related Words: RECONNOITERING -n. exploring in order to gain information

RECOURSE (ri KOHRS): n. A source of help in a difficult situation

Trigger: 1.RECOURSE-SOURCE .2.RECOURSE-COURSE

Trigger Sentence: 1. Go to a SOURCE for help. 2. Short term GRE COURSE is a nice RECOURSE or a good RESOURCE to increase the score.

Sample Sentence: Whenever business people need source of 'Capital', they tend to take *recourse* to commercial banks for loan.

Related Words: RESOURCEFUL –a. having inner resources; imaginative

RECRUDESCENT (ree kroo DES uns): a. Reappearing; erupting again

Trigger: RECRUdescent-RECRU-RECUR

Trigger Sentence: Something that RECURS (RE+ OCCUR) AGAIN is known as RECRUDESCENT.

Sample Sentence: Terrorism has become *recrudescent* as terror activities recur consistently.

RECTITUDE (REK ti tyood): n. Morality; correctness of judgment

    Trigger: RECTITUDE -CORRECT + DUDE

    Trigger Sentence: A CORRECT DUDE always sticks to the path of RECTITUDE.

    Sample Sentence: He was renowned for his *rectitude* and integrity.

RECUPERATE (ri KYOO puh reyt): v. Recover

    Trigger: RECUPER-RECOVER

    Trigger Sentence: After doctors OPERATED, the patient got RECUPERATED/RECOVERED.

    Sample Sentence: To *recuperate* from its losses, the company is trying to recover its debts.

REDEMPTIVE (ri DEMP tiv): a. Delivering from sin or evil; making amends

    Trigger: REDEMPTIVE-EMPTY (EMPTY evil or sin)

    Trigger Sentence: REDEMPTIVE suffering of the Christ EMPTIED the universe from sin.

    Sample Sentence: *Redemptive* work of Jesus was able to repair the world from sin.

    Related Words: REDEEM -v. save from sins; free from debt; convert into cash.

REDOUBTABLE (rih DOUT uh buhl): a. Arousing fear; formidable

    Trigger: 1.DOUBT. 2. REDOUBTABLE-RESPECTABLE

    Trigger Sentence: 1. REDOUBTABLE people cause or create DOUBT or FEAR in others. 2. Napoleon always remained RESPECTABLE to his REDOUBTABLE enemies.

    Sample Sentence: The young climbers got lost in the *redoubtable* deep hills.

REDRESS (ree DRES): v. Dress gain; correct a wrong; remedy

    Trigger: RE+ DRESS

    Trigger Sentence: If a DRESS is defective, the store REDRESSES the customer with compensation.

    Sample Sentence: The king realized his mistake and *redressed* his earlier injustice judgments.

REDUNDANT (rih DUN dunt): a. Superfluous; repetitious

    Trigger: 1. REDUNDANT –ABUNDANT. 2. REDUNDANT-RE+DONE+ DONE+++

    Trigger Sentence: 1. When there is ABUNDANT quantity of food grains in our storehouses, it is REDUNDANT to import more. 2. Why have you REDONE the work? It's absolutely REDUNDANT to waste one's talent on such duplication.

    Sample Sentence: Avoid *redundant* expressions in your writing.

REFRACTORY (ri FRAK tuh ree): a. Stubborn or unmanageable

    Trigger: REFRACT –REACT against

    Trigger Sentence: REFRACTORY people tend to REACT AGAINST. Why REACT AGAINST me?

    Sample Sentence: Coach declared that all the *refractory* players will be ejected from the team.

REFRAIN (ri FREYN): v. Abstain; restrain oneself

    Trigger: 1. REFRAIN-RESTRAIN-RESTRICT. 2. REFRAIN- REFUSE + RAIN

    Trigger Sentence: 1. REFUSE to go in the RAIN; children REFRAINED to go to school. 2. REFRAIN means to RESTRAIN/RESTRICT oneself. 3. Refrain, constrain, restrain and abstain are synonyms.

    Sample Sentence: I kept myself *refrained* from alcohol for over a decade now.

REFUTE (ri FYOOT): v. Prove false

    Trigger: REFUTE-REFUSE with proof

    Trigger Sentence: To REFUTE is to REFUSE with proof

    Sample Sentence: There were several futile attempts to *refute* Einstein's theory.

    Related Words: IRREFUTABLE –a. incontrovertible; positive

REGAL (REE gul): a. Royal

    Trigger: 1. REGAL-ROYAL. 2. REGAL-LEGAL

    Trigger Sentence: 1. All LEGAL things are given by REGAL or ROYAL people. 2. ROYAL families have some REGAL entitlements.

    Sample Sentence: The actress's *regal* looks makes her a perfect choice to play Cleopatra.

REGENERATE (ri JEN er it): a. Reformed spiritually or morally

    Trigger: RE +GENERATE- GENERATE AGAIN

    Trigger Sentence: Many spiritual persons turn REGENERATE by redemption from error.

    Sample Sentence: Not easy to *regenerate* criminal minded people and put them into positivity.

    Related Words: UNREGENERATE -a. sinful; not reformed

REGIMEN (REJ uh mun): n. Prescribed diet and habits

    Trigger: REGIMEN-"REG (regulation) +MEN"

    Trigger Sentence: 1. REGIMEN implies Rules and REGULATIONS for MANKIND to follow for orderliness. 2. In a Doctor's REGIME one has to follow health REGIMEN.

    Sample Sentence: The soldiers had to follow a strict *regimen* despite the adverse weather.

    Related Words: REGIME -n. mode of rule

REHABILITATE (ree uh BIL i teyt): a. Restore to good conditions

    Trigger: REHAB-"RE + HABITS"

    Trigger Sentence: The REHAB clinic REHABILITATED the upset person by restoring his HABITS.

    Sample Sentence: The drug addict was successfully *rehabilitated*.

REIGN (RAYN): n. Rule, sovereignty

    Trigger: REIGN-REGION

    Trigger Sentence: Hyderabad REGION was once in the REIGN of *Nawabs*.

    Sample Sentence: Rani Arundhati took over the *reigns* during the 16th century.

    Related Words: SOVEREIGN -a. self-governing; supreme

REIN (REYN): v. To check or stop

    Trigger: 1. REIN-RESTRAIN. 2. REIN-no RUN

    Trigger Sentence: 1. Firmly hold the REINS to RESTRAIN the horse. 2. Once the sledge-rider let loose the REINS, then the dogs started to RUN fast.

    Sample Sentence: If Luther couple doesn't *rein* their children, they will never learn to behave.

REINFORCE (ree in FAWRS): v. Strengthen or support

    Trigger: RE+IN+FORCE; FORCE-FORTE

    Trigger Sentence: Let us REINFORCE our demands with FORCEFUL voice.

    Sample Sentence: Thank you for *reinforcing* me to get back to writing after my sabbatical.

RELEGATE (REL i geyt): v. Demote, assign to an inferior position

    Trigger: 1. RELEGATE-DELEGATE. 2. RELEGATE-RELOCATE-"RE+LOW+CATE"

    Trigger Sentence: A higher ranker RELOCATED to a LOWER RANK; as A DELEGATE is RELEGATED.

    Sample Sentence: If a person does not accomplish his delegated work his position is *relegated*.

RELENT (ri LENT): v. Give in; become less severe.

    Trigger: RELENT-RELAX

    Trigger Sentence: 1. RELENT is to RELAX rigidity. 2. RELENTING implies RELAXING SEVERE rules.

    Sample Sentence: My application was initially declined, but the Municipality *relented* in the end.

    Related Words: UNRELENTING -a. relentless, not yielding.

RELENTLESS (ri LENT lis): a. Oppressively constant; harsh or inflexible

    Trigger: 1. RELENTLESS+"RELAX +LESS". 2. RELENTLESS-"REST +LESS"

    Trigger Sentence: 1. WITHOUT being RELAXED or WITHOUT taking REST, he is involved in RELENTLESS pursuit. 2. UNRELENTING involves UN-RELAXING (UNYIELDING) the rules.

    Sample Sentence: The hunter *relentlessly* explored the jungle for a kill.

RELEVANT (REL uh vunt): a. Pertinent; related to the current subject

    Trigger: 1.RELEVANT- REAL EVENT. 2. RELEVANT-RELATED (** synonyms)

    Trigger Sentence: The REAL EVENTS and the RELATED analysis in the book are RELEVANT today.

    Sample Sentence: Your good research is however not *relevant* to our department.

    Related Words: IRRELEVANT -a. unconnected; impertinent

RELINQUISH (ri LING kwish): v. Give up; renounce; yield

    Trigger: 1.RELINQUISH-RELEASE WISH. 2. RELINQUISH-RELISH (refer)

    Trigger Sentence: 1. RELINQUISH is to RELEASE (give up) your WISH. 2. I used to RELISH FISH; now I RELINQUISHED.

    Sample Sentence: The court ordered him to *relinquish* the custody of his child.

RELUCTANCE (ri LUK tuns): n. Unwillingness, hesitance

    Trigger: RELUCTANCE-RESISTANCE

    Trigger Sentence: RELUCTANCE is to offer RESISTANCE

    Sample Sentence: I *reluctantly* took this project, but now I have begun to enjoy it!

REMARKABLE (ri MAHR kuh bul): a. Extraordinary; unusual

    Trigger: REMARKABLE- MARK TWAIN

    Trigger Sentence: 1. MARK Twain is a REMARKABLE author of UNUSUAL talent. 2. Getting 100 % MARKS in a subject is something REMARKABLE.

    Sample Sentence: Mark Twain's subtle humour is *remarkable*.

    Related Words: UNREMARKABLE -a. common

REMEDIAL (ri MEE dee ul): a. Curing; corrective

    Trigger: REMEDIAL-REMEDY

    Trigger Sentence: REMEDIAL powers of herbal REMEDIES are documented in Ayurvedic journals.

Sample Sentence: No point taking *remedial* measures now after the damage is already done!

Related Words: 1. IRREMEDIABLE -a. Incurable; cannot be corrected. 2. IRREPARABLE - a. impossible to repair

REMINISCENCE (rem uh NIS uns): n. Recollection of past events

Trigger: 1. REMINI-REMIND. 2. REMINISCENCE-REMEMBERENCE

Trigger Sentence: This place REMINDS me of my childhood REMINISCENCES.

Sample Sentence: An emotional *reminiscence* intensifies our remembrance capability strong.

Related Words: REMINISCE -v. remember the past.

REMISS (rih MISS): a. Negligent

Trigger: REMISS -RE (again) + MISS

Trigger Sentence: If you REPEATEDLY MISS, you are REMISS (negligent) in your duties.

Sample Sentence: If you *remiss* this opportunity, you will miss a golden chance to prosper.

REMNANT (REM nunt): n. Remainder; leftover

Trigger: REMNANT-REMAINS

Trigger Sentence: REMNANT means a tiny part that REMAINS once its main part no more exists.

Sample Sentence: These relics are *remnant*s of the bygone era.

REMONSTRATE (ri MON streyt): v. Protest; object

Trigger: REMONSTRATE-"RE-DEMONSTRATE"

Trigger Sentence: In a REMONSTRATION, thousands DEMONSTRATED against corruption.

Sample Sentence: Millions of people *remonstrate* against the growing corruption in India.

RENAISSANCE (REY nuh sonce): n. Rebirth of art and literature

Trigger: RENAI-RENEW

Trigger Sentence: RENEWAL of art and literature period is known as RENAISSANCE period.

Sample Sentence: During *renaissance*, Europeans discovered a renewed sense of achievement.

RENDER (REN der): v. Give; provide; deliver; represent

Trigger: 1.RENDER-TENDER. 2. RENDER-SURRENDER

Trigger Sentence: 1. They RENDERED aid to the needy by TENDERING two million dollars. 2. After the SURRENDER, they had to RENDER the estate.

Sample Sentence: Beethoven *rendered* some of the finest musical compositions.

RENEGE (ri NEG): v. Deny

Trigger: RENEG-"RE+NEG"-"REPLY NEGATIVE"

Trigger Sentence: NEGATIVE reply implies "DENIAL".

Sample Sentence: If your reply is negative, people *renege* on their promise of voting you.

Related Words: RENEGADE –n. traitor; rebel

RENOUNCE (ri NOWNCE): v. Abandon; disown; repudiate

Trigger: reNOUNCE-NOUNCE-NUNS

Trigger Sentence: The RENOWNED NUNS RENOUNCED social life and lead a life in seclusion.

Sample Sentence: Nuns *renounce* family life in favor of spiritual life.

REPARATION (rep uh RAY shun): n. Compensation; amends

Trigger: REPARATION-"REPAIR + ACTION"

Trigger Sentence: As a REPAIR ACTION, Germany was forced to pay REPARATIONS to its rival countries after the First World War.

Sample Sentence: He had to pay *reparations* for all the damage done in the gaming bar.

REPEAL (ri PEEL): v. Revoke, annul

Trigger: REPEAL-APPEAL

Trigger Sentence: 1. After the APPEAL the third umpire REPEALED (REVERSED) the decision. 2. After defendant had APPEALED to the Supreme Court, it REPEALED the case by reversing the High Court judgment.

Sample Sentence: Time to *repeal* those defunct acts from the law books.

REPERTOIRE (REP er twar): n. List of works/skills that a person is ready to perform

Trigger: REPERTOIRE-RESERVOIR (** synonyms)-(an artist RESERVOIR)

Trigger Sentence: The new mall has endless REPERTOIRE/RESERVOIR of summer cloths.

Sample Sentence: Tendulkar's batting *repertoire* includes both defensive and offensive strokes.

REPINE (ri PAHYN): v. Complain, fret

Trigger: REPINE-RE+PAIN

Trigger Sentence: 1. Whenever there is PAIN we COMPLAIN. 2. We REPAIN on RAPES in India.

Sample Sentence: If you keep *repining* over the bad event, you can't recover from mental pain.

REPLETE (ri PLEET): a. Filled to satisfaction; complete; sated

Trigger: REPLETE-COMPLETE

Trigger Sentence: REPLETE is to have COMPLETE stomach.

Sample Sentence: It is a complete book of yoga. It is *replete* with various yogic postures.

REPLICA (REP li kuh): n. Copy

Trigger: REPLICA-REPLICATE-DUPLICATE (** synonyms)

Trigger Sentence: I bought a miniature REPLICA/DUPLICATE of the Taj Mahal.

Sample Sentence: *Replicas* of various extinct species are displayed in the Washington Museum.

Related Words: REPLICATE -v. duplicate; reproduce

REPREHEND (rep ri HEND): v. Reprimand, rebuke

Trigger: 1. RAPE HAND. 2. REPREHEND-REPRIMAND-REPROACH-REPROBATE-REPROOF-REPROVE

Trigger Sentence: 1. He has HAND in that RAPE case, so people have REPREHENDED him. 2. Reprehend, reprimand, reproach, reprobate, reprove all are synonym variants. 3. When we APPROVE we PRAISE, when we REPROVE we CRITICIZE or BLAME.

Sample Sentence: The book reviewers *reprehended* the fiction's redundant plot.

Related Words: REPREHENSIBLE -a. deserving blame

REPREHENSIBLE (rep ri HEN suh bul): a. Deserving blame

Trigger: REPREHENSIBLE-RE+ PRETENSION+ ABLE

Trigger Sentence: His REPEATED PRETENSION about his adultery was REPREHENSIBLE.

Sample Sentence: The book reviewers criticized the *reprehensible* acts of violence in the plot.

REPRESS (ri PRES): a. Restrain, crush; suppress

Trigger: REPRESS-SUPPRESS-PRESS

Trigger Sentence: China REPRESSES or SUPPRESSES her dissidents very efficiently.

Sample Sentence: *Repressed* by a domineering society, the tribes were almost nonexistent.

REPRIEVE (ri PREEV): n. Temporary relief; respite

Trigger: REPRIEVE-RELIEVE-RELIEF (** synonyms)

Trigger Sentence: The rescue team in the last minute REPRIEVED/RELIEVED the mountaineers.

Sample Sentence: With hectic itinerary, our sojourn at the coconut lagoons was a good *reprieve*.

REPRIMAND (REP ruh mand): v. Scold severely; rebuke

Trigger: REPRIMAND-"RAPE+REMAND"

Trigger Sentence: 1. If a criminal involves in "RAPE" he will be REPRIMANDED and sent to jail. 2. Reprehend, reprimand, reproach, reprobate, reprove all are synonym variants.

Sample Sentence: My parents *reprimand* me for my nightly jaunts.

REPROACH (ri PROHCH): v. Blame, accuse; express disapproval

Trigger: 1.REPROACH-IMPEACH. 2. REPROACH-REPROVE

Trigger Sentence: 1. The court IMPEACHED him when he brought REPROACH with his irresponsible behavior; reprehend, reprimand, reproach, reprobate, reprove all are synonym variants. 2. When we APPROVE we praise, when we REPROVE we criticize or blame.

Sample Sentence: The religious body *reproached* Bob for being the black sheep against the cult.

Related Words: BEYOND/ABOVE REPROACH: blameless, above suspicion

REPROBATE (REP ruh bayt): n. A person hardened in sin.

Trigger: REPROBATE-"RAPE + ROB + ATE"

Trigger Sentence: 1. n. One who does RAPES & ROBS is a REPROBATE. 2. v. Reprehend, reprimand, reproach, reprobate, reprove-all are synonym variants. 3. Approbation (approve); Reprobation (reprove); disapprobation (disapprove).

Sample Sentence: Against our will, the council put this *reprobate* rowdy in the campaign.

Related Words: REPROBATE -v. censure

REPROVE (ri PROOV): v. Criticize; rebuke

Trigger: REPROVE-APPROVE (** antonyms)

Trigger Sentence: 1. Boss APPROVES girls, but if it is a boy he REPROVES. 2. Reprove and disapprove are synonyms; reprehend, reprimand, reproach, reprobate, reprove-all are synonyms. 3. When we APPROVE we praise, when we REPROVE we criticize or blame.

Sample Sentence: I was disheartened to know that all my endeavors were *reproved*.

REPUDIATE (ri PYOO dee eyt): v. Disown; disavow

Trigger: REPUDIATE-"REFUSE DATE"

Trigger Sentence: 1. He REFUSED his DATE to save his repute. 2. REPUDIATION and REJECTION are synonyms.

Sample Sentence: This rich man *repudiated* all the donations that he promised to grant.

REPUGNANCE (ri PUG nuns): n. Aversion, loathing

Trigger: REPUGNANCE-REPELLENCE-REPULSION

Trigger Sentence: 1. REPELLENCE and REPUGNANCE are synonyms. 2. A REPELLENT like mosquito REPELLENT REPELS (hates or drives away) mosquitoes.

Sample Sentence: They expressed their *repugnance* at the idea of cutting trees.

Related Words: REPUGNANT -a. disgusting; opposed

REQUISITE (REK wuh zit): n. Necessary requirement

Trigger: REQUISITE-REQUIRED

Trigger Sentence: Food is REQUISITES and REQUIREMENTS of life; perquisites are luxuries.

Sample Sentence: Food, shelter and clothing are basic *requisites* of life.

REQUITE (ri KWAHYT): v. Repay; revenge

Trigger: RE +QUITE-make someone QUITE-REVENGE

Trigger Sentence: 1. Make them QUITE by REQUITE. 2. I'll be QUITE only after I take REQUITE (revenge). 3. QUITE-peaceful; REQUITE-revenge.

Sample Sentence: Our guru advised us not to *requite* even our enemies.

Related Words: UNREQUITED - a. not reciprocated.

RESCIND (ri SIND): v. Cancel

Trigger: 1.RECESSION-RESCIND. 2. RESCIND-RESIGNED

Trigger Sentence: 1. During the RECESSION all appointment orders were CANCELLED. 2. After his appointment has been RESCINDED, he has RESIGNED.

Sample Sentence: The work order of waterlines was *rescinded* due to bureaucratic problems.

RESENTMENT (ri ZENT munt): n. Anger; bitterness; displeasure

Trigger: RESENTMENT-BAD SENTIMENT

Trigger Sentence: 1. BAD SENTIMENT (feeling) is called RESENTMENT. 2. When people SENTIMENTS are hurt there is RESENTMENT.

Sample Sentence: She did not display her feelings of *resentment* against her ex-husband.

RESIDUAL (ri ZIJ oo ul): a. Remainder

Trigger: RESIDUAL-RESIDUE

Trigger Sentence: If there is no RESIDUE there is no RESIDUAL quantity.

Sample Sentence: Though *residual,* the money left by his father is enough to lead a comfy life.

RESILIENT (ree ZILL yunt): a. Elastic, quickly recovering from failure

Trigger: 1. "RESILIENT-RE+EASILY+BENT". 2. "RESILIENT-NOT SILENT"

Trigger Sentence: 1. RESILIENT springs or materials are not resistant; they are EASILY BENT. 2. RESILIENT person is NOT SILENT after the defeat; he easily recovers from sadness or defeat.

Sample Sentence: 1. Bring some *resilience* into your system dude, for failures are bound to happen, also success is inevitable! 2. The Indian economy is remarkably *resilient.*

RESOLUTION (rez uh LOO shun): n. Determination

Trigger: RESOLUTION-SOLUTION

Trigger Sentence: Till I find the SOLUTION I've RESOLUTION and DETERMINATION; imagine New Year RESOLUTIONS.

Sample Sentence: With a strong *resolution* she managed to complete the monumental task.

Related Words: 1. RESOLUTE -a. determined. 2. IRRESOLUTE -v. indecisive. 3. RESOLVE - n. firm decision, resoluteness.

RESPITE (RES pit): n. Time for rest; interval of relief

Trigger: RESPITE-"REST+BIT"

Trigger Sentence: REST A BIT is known as RESPITE.

Sample Sentence: Our teacher gave a two day *respite* before the exams.

RESPLENDENT (ri SPLEN dunt): a. Shining brilliantly; splendid

Trigger: RESPLENDENT-SPLENDID (** synonyms)

Trigger Sentence: The fields were RESPLENDENT with SPLENDID flowers.

Sample Sentence: She shimmered like a *resplendent* full moon.

Related Words: REFULGENT -a. shining; brilliant

RESTITUTION (res ti TOO shun): n. Restoration to a previous condition; reparation, compensation, reimbursement

Trigger: RESTITUTION-RESTORATION (** synonyms)

Trigger Sentence: RESTITUTION is nothing but RESTORATION of the previous condition.

Sample Sentence: The judge ordered *restitution* of property taken by the accused.

RESTIVE (RES tiv): a. Restless; uncontrollable

Trigger: 1.RESTIVE-RESTLESS. 2. RESTIVE-RESISTIVE

Trigger Sentence: 1. A RESTIVE person is RESTLESS and RESISTANT. 2.He is RESISTIVE too.

Sample Sentence: 1.Baba spent a *restive* night worrying about the next day's exam.

2. The *restive* bull threw its head and dragged its hoofs.

RESTRAINED (ri STREYND): a. Repressed, understated

Trigger: RESTRAINED-RESTRICTED

Trigger Sentence: RESTRICTED in emotions; RESTRAINED person is RESTRICTED in great ecstasy.

Sample Sentence: She has unassuming beauty, understated elegance and *restrained* behavior.

Related Words: UNRESTRAINED -a. uncontrolled

RESTRICTIVE (ri STRIK tiv): a. Imposing limits

Trigger: RESTRICTIVE-RESTRICT-STRICT

Trigger Sentence: The STRICT parents create RESTRICTIVE home environment for the kids.

Sample Sentence: The teenagers are eager to escape from *restrictive* home environments.

RESUMPTION (ri ZUHMP shun): n. Beginning again

Trigger: RESUMPTION-RESUME

Trigger Sentence: The act of RESUMING is known as RESUMPTION.

Sample Sentence: There was *resumption* of the game, after the rains faded away.

RESURGENT (ri SUR junt): a. Rising again; reviving

Trigger: RE+SURGE-"SURGERY"

Trigger Sentence: After SURGERY the patient is RESURGENT.

Sample Sentence: After hitting rock bottom in his career, Vishnu *resurged* like a phoenix.

RESUSCITATE (ri SUHS i teyt): v. Revive; restore to life

Trigger: 1.RESUSC-RESCUE. 2. RESUSCITATE-REACTIVATE

Trigger Sentence: 1. Doctors RESUSCITATED the comatose man to RESCUE from death. 2. Resuscitate, resurrect, reactivate, reanimate, rehabilitate, revitalize and revive are synonyms.

Sample Sentence: The patient stopped breathing but doctors were able to *resuscitate* him.

Related Words: RESURRECTION –n. revival

RETAIN (ri TEYN): v. Keep; employ

Trigger: 1.RETAIN-REMAIN. 2. RETAIN-MAINTAIN

Trigger Sentence: 1. If you RETAIN, it will REMAIN with you. 2. In order to RETAIN employees, you got to MAINTAIN good relationships.

Sample Sentence: My grandparents insisted on *retaining* and following old customs.

Related Words: 1.DETAIN -v. arrest; stop. 2. RETENTIVE -a. having a good memory

RETALIATION (ri TAL ee ey shun): n. Revenge

Trigger: RETALIATION-"RE+ACTION"

Trigger Sentence: RETALIATION is a REACTION and REVENGE.

Sample Sentence: The union threatened to *retaliate* if their demands were not met.

Related Words: RETALIATE -v. take revenge.

RETICENT (RET ih sunt): a. Remaining silent; reserved

Trigger: 1.RETICENT-REST & SILENT. 2. RETICENCE-SILENCE

Trigger Sentence: 1. A RETICENT person is SILENT and RESERVED. 2. RETICENCE implies SILENCE.

Sample Sentence: Ray being a *reticent* man, people mistook him to be snobby.

Memory Test-93 : Match each word and its memory trick to the corresponding definition.

S.N	WORD	MEMORY TRIGGER	S.N	DEFINITIONS	KEY
1	REBUKE	Rebuke-puke	A	Arousing fear; formidable	
2	REBUT	but - show BUTT	B	Contradict, refuse with proof	
3	RECALCITRANT	RELUCTANT-resistant	C	Criticize severely; scold harshly	
4	RECANT	RECALL	D	Delivering from sin or evil	
5	RECAPITULATE	RECAP the main point	E	Difficult to understand; secret	
6	RECIDIVISM	ROWDYISM	F	Dress gain; correct a wrong	
7	RECIPROCAL	reciprocate	G	Habitual return to crime	
8	RECLUSE	CLUSE-CLOSE	H	Loner, hermit	
9	RECONCILE	Council -Re + concile	I	Morality; correctness of judgment	
10	RECONDITE	RE-CONDUCT	J	Mutual; interchangeable	
11	RECONNAISSANCE	RECOGNIZANCE	K	Reappearing; erupting again	
12	RECOURSE	SOURCE	L	Recover	
13	RECRUDESCENT	Recru-RECUR	M	Repetitious; Superfluous	
14	RECTITUDE	CORRECT + dude	N	Retract a previous statement; give up	
15	RECUPERATE	Recuper-RECOVER	O	Reunite, make friendly	
16	REDEMPTIVE	EMPTY evil or sin	P	Source of help in a difficult situation	
17	REDOUBTABLE	Create DOUBT in enemy	Q	Stubborn or unmanageable	
18	REDRESS	Re+ dress	R	Stubborn, rebellious, unruly	
19	REDUNDANT	re+done+ done+	S	Summarize	
20	REFRACTORY	REACT against	T	Survey of enemy; gathering information	

Memory Test-94 : Match each word and its memory trick to the corresponding definition.

S.N	WORD	MEMORY TRIGGER	S.N	DEFINITIONS	KEY
1	REFRAIN	RESTRAIN-RESTRICT	A	Become less severe; Give in	
2	REFUTE	REFUSE with proof	B	Abstain; restrain oneself	
3	REGAL	Regal-ROYAL	C	Check or stop	
4	REGENERATE	generate again	D	Curing; corrective	
5	REGIMEN	REG (regulation) +MEN	E	Demote, assign to an inferior position	
6	REHABILITATE	Rehab	F	Extraordinary; unusual	
7	REIGN	REGION	G	Give up; renounce; yield	
8	REIN	no RUN	H	Negligent	
9	REINFORCE	Re+in+force-FORTE	I	Oppressively constant; harsh	
10	RELEGATE	Relocate-re+LOW+cate	J	Pertinent; related to	
11	RELENT	relax	K	Prescribed diet and habits	
12	RELENTLESS	RELAX +less	L	Prove false	
13	RELEVANT	RELATED	M	Recollection of past events	
14	RELINQUISH	Release wish	N	Reformed spiritually or morally	
15	RELUCTANCE	RESISTANCE	O	Remainder; leftover	
16	REMARKABLE	MARK Twain - REMARKABLE	P	Restore to good conditions	
17	REMEDIAL	remedy	Q	Royal	
18	REMINISCENCE	REMEMBRANCE	R	Rule, sovereignty	
19	REMISS	RE (again) + MISS	S	Strengthen or support	
20	REMNANT	REMAINS	T	Unwillingness, hesitance	

Answers	EX.NO	1	2	3	4	5	6	7	8	9	10	11	12	13	14	15	16	17	18	19	20
	93	C	B	R	N	S	G	J	H	O	E	T	P	K	I	L	D	A	F	M	Q
	94	B	L	Q	N	K	P	R	C	S	E	A	I	J	G	T	F	D	M	H	O

Memory Test-95 : Match each word and its memory trick to the corresponding definition.

S.N	WORD	MEMORY TRIGGER	S.N	DEFINITIONS	KEY
1	REMONSTRATE	re-demonstrate	A	Abandon; disown; repudiate	
2	RENAISSANCE	RENAI-RENEW	B	Blame, express disapproval	
3	RENDER	Surrender-give TENDER	C	Compensation; amends	
4	RENEGE	reply negative	D	Complain, fret	
5	RENOUNCE	NUNS renounced	E	Copy	
6	REPARATION	Repair + action	F	Criticize; rebuke	
7	REPEAL	After appeal ban is repealed	G	Deny	
8	REPERTOIRE	an artist RESERVOIR	H	Deserving blame	
9	REPINE	COMPLAIN	I	Disown; disavow	
10	REPLETE	complete	J	Filled to satisfaction; complete	
11	REPLICA	replicate-DUPLICATE	K	Give; provide; deliver; represent	
12	REPREHEND	Rape hand	L	List of works by an artist	
13	REPREHENSIBLE	Re+ PRETENSION+ able	M	person hardened in sin.	
14	REPRESS	Suppress-press	N	Protest; object	
15	REPRIEVE	relieve-relief	O	Rebirth of art and literature	
16	REPRIMAND	RAPE+remand	P	Reprimand, rebuke	
17	REPROACH	REPROVE	Q	Restrain, crush; suppress	
18	REPROBATE	Rape + ROB + ate	R	Revoke, annul	
19	REPROVE	No APPROVE	S	Scold severely; Rebuke	
20	REPUDIATE	refuse date	T	Temporary relief; respite	

Memory Test-96 : Match each word and its memory trick to the corresponding definition.

S.N	WORD	MEMORY TRIGGER	S.N	DEFINITIONS	KEY
1	REPUGNANCE	Repellence-repulsion	A	Anger; displeasure	
2	REQUISITE	required	B	Aversion, loathing	
3	REQUITE	make someone QUITE	C	Beginning again	
4	RESCIND	RESIGNED	D	Cancel	
5	RESENTMENT	Bad SENTIMENT	E	Determination	
6	RESIDUAL	RESIDUE	F	Elastic, recovering from failure	
7	RESILIENT	Re+EASILY+BENT	G	Imposing limits	
8	RESOLUTION	New year RESOLUTION	H	Keep; employ	
9	RESPITE	rest+bit	I	Necessary requirement	
10	RESPLENDENT	SPLENDID	J	Remainder	
11	RESTITUTION	RESTORATION	K	Remaining silent; reserved	
12	RESTIVE	RESTLESS-resistive	L	Repressed, understated	
13	RESTRAINED	RESTRICTED	M	Restless; uncontrollable	
14	RESTRICTIVE	restrict-STRICT	N	Restoration to a previous condition	
15	RESUMPTION	RESUME	O	Revenge	
16	RESURGENT	After SURGERY	P	Revenge, Repay	
17	RESUSCITATE	Resusc-RESCUE	Q	Revive; restore to life	
18	RETAIN	Retain-remain--maintain	R	Rising again; reviving	
19	RETALIATION	RE+ACTION"	S	Shining brilliantly; splendid	
20	RETICENT	rest & silent	T	Time for rest; interval of relief	

Answers

EX.NO	1	2	3	4	5	6	7	8	9	10	11	12	13	14	15	16	17	18	19	20
95	N	O	K	G	A	C	R	L	D	J	E	P	H	Q	T	S	B	M	F	I
96	B	I	P	D	A	J	F	E	T	S	N	M	L	G	C	R	Q	H	O	K

WORD GROUPS DAY-24

★ HEALTHY-HEALTH GIVING

ADJECTIVES: beneficial, salubrious, salutary, wholesome; hale, robust , hardy, sturdy, vigorous

NOUNS: salubrity

VERB: heal, ameliorate, remedy

ANTONYMS: adj.insalubrious, unwholesome

★ CALAMITY: disaster, tragedy

ADJECTIVES: calamitous, catastrophic, dire

NOUNS: adversity, affliction, calamity, cataclysm, catastrophe, distress, misadventure, misfortune, mishap, plight scourge, trial, tribulation

VERB: indemnify, repay

ANTONYMS: n. boon, fortune, good luck, joy, profit

★ LUCK

ADJECTIVES: fortuitous, adventitious, providential, opportune; auspicious, propitious

NOUNS: kismet, serendipity; happenstance

VERB: happen upon, chance upon

ANTONYMS: adj. deterministic; predictable; unlucky

★ QUIXOTIC: idealistic, impractical

ADJECTIVES: chimerical, chivalrous, idealistic, impracticable, unrealistic, utopian, visionary

NOUNS: idealist

VERB: dream

ANTONYMS: adj. believable, realistic, sensible, practical

★ COMPENSATION

ADJECTIVES: compensatory

NOUNS: amends, atonement, defrayal, indemnity, redress, reimbursement, requital, reparation, restitution

VERB: indemnify, repay

ANTONYMS: n. damage, fine, forfeiture, penalty

★ TERSE

ADJECTIVES: brief, concise, synoptical, succinct, pithy, laconic, elliptical; brusque, abrupt, curt, incisive, blunt, terse, trenchant

NOUNS: abridgement, brevity, compendium, précis, synopsis

VERB: abridge, abbreviate, curtail, retrench, truncate

ANTONYMS: adj.lengthy, long-winded, prolix, wordy

★ SUPERFLUOUS: extra, unnecessary

ADJECTIVES: excessive, exorbitant, extraneous, gratuitous, inessential, inordinate, overflowing, redundant, spare, supererogatory, supernumerary, unwarranted

NOUNS: superfluity ,surplus, glut, plethora, profusion

VERB: overflow

ANTONYMS: adj. necessary ,integral

if i stay here for 5 more minutes, i will get knocked out due to this NOXIOUS smell

NOXIOUS : harmful, toxic, deadly smell

Word List Day-25

RETIRING (ri TYR ing): v. Shy; modest

    Trigger: RETIRING-RETIRED from public life

    Trigger Sentence: The model RETIRED from public appearances since her character is RETIRING

    Sample Sentence: The *retiring* beautiful lady left the party preferring privacy.

RETRACT (ri TRAKT): v. Withdraw, take back

    Trigger: RETRACT-"RE TAKE"-"TAKE BACK"

    Trigger Sentence: RETRACT is to TAKE BACK the decision or word given to someone.

    Sample Sentence: The pilot *retracted* the landing gear soon after takeoff.

RETREAT (ree TREET): v. /n. Withdraw, depart

    Trigger: 1.RETREAT-RETRACT (refer).2. Summer RETREAT-DEFEAT

    Trigger Sentence: 1. RETRACT and RETREAT are synonyms. 2. Instead of fighting, the army has gone back and relaxed in summer RETREAT. RETREAT also means DEFEAT.

    Sample Sentence: She *retreated* from public life after her defeat in the elections.

RETRENCH (ri TRENCH): v. Cut down or reduce (Expenses Etc.)

    Trigger: RETRENCH-RETURN TO BENCH

    Trigger Sentence: Back ON BENCH after RETRENCHMENT in job market.

    Sample Sentence: Wal-Mart is expanding, while its competitors are *retrenching* in recession.

RETRIEVE (re TREEV): v. Recover; bring back

    Trigger: RETRIEVE-REVIVE (** synonyms)

    Trigger Sentence: The author's writing RETRIEVES/REVIVES the past.

    Sample Sentence: The file data was *retrieved* from the old computer.

RETROGRESS (re truh GRES): v. Move backward; revert to a previous condition

    Trigger: RETROGRESS-REGRESS-PROGRESS

    Trigger Sentence: If there is NO PROGRESS, life RETROGRESSES to worse conditions.

    Sample Sentence: The quality of research has begun to *retrogress* as an upshot of budget cut.

    Related Words: REGRESSION -n. act of moving backward

RETROSPECTIVE (re truh SPEK tiv): a. Looking back on the past

    Trigger: RETROSPECT-RE +INSPECT (** back inspection)

    Trigger Sentence: In a RETROSPECTIVE show, the critics' RE-INSPECTED artist's early work.

    Sample Sentence: This exhibition is a comprehensive *retrospective* of the artist's early work.

REVAMP (ree VAMP): v. Renovate, revise

    Trigger: REVAMP- REVISE

    Trigger Sentence: REVAMP is to REVISE for improvement.

    Sample Sentence: I can *revamp* that old sofa and make it look brand new.

REVELATION (rev uh LEY shun): n. Act of showing; disclosure

    Trigger: REVELATION-REVEAL

    Trigger Sentence: The book REVEALED many shocking REVELATIONS about the president's life.

    Sample Sentence: The shocking *revelation* is likely to break hearts of many of his female fans.

REVERBERATE (ri VUR buh reyt): v. Echo; resound

    Trigger: REVERBERATE-"RE+VIBRATE"

    Trigger Sentence: SOUND VIBRATIONS REVERBERATE-recur again and again.

    Sample Sentence: Our voices *reverberated* in the caves.

REVERE (ri VEER): v. Venerate, respect deeply

    Trigger: 1. REVERE – Paul REVERE. 2. REVERE-RIVER

    Trigger Sentence: 1. Paul REVERE is REVERED by Americans. 2. In India Ganga RIVER is greatly REVERED.

    Sample Sentence: With all *revere* and regards I thank you from the bottom of my heart.

    Related Words: 1. REVERENCE -n. sense of deep respect. 2. IRREVERENCE –n. lack of respect

REVERIE (REV uh ree): n. Daydream, preoccupation

    Trigger: REVERIE-"RIVER+EYE"

    Trigger Sentence: He spent the day in REVERIE before the RIVER with dreamy EYES.

    Sample Sentence: The nun had a romantic *reverie* before waking to realities of her celibate life!

REVILE (ri VYLE): v. Insult, criticize abusively

    Trigger: 1. rEVILe-EVIL. 2. RE+VILE

    Trigger Sentence: 1. When we REVILE a person we TALK EVIL. 2. VILIFY and REVILE - synonyms.

    Sample Sentence: Why am I being *reviled* without my mistake?!

    Related Words: VILIFY –v. slander; defame

REVIVE (ri VYV): v. Return to life: become active.

    Trigger: RE+VIVE- RE +LIVE

    Trigger Sentence: TO REVIVE means to LIVE AGAIN.

    Sample Sentence: The performance was a *revival* of sorts of the bygone classical drama.

REVOKE (ri VOHK): v. Cancel, retract

    Trigger: REVOKE-REVERSE

    Trigger Sentence: 1. To REVOKE is to REVERSE decision; license is given but cancelled (revoked-reversed). 2. Revocable decisions are reversible; If it is IRREVOCABLE, it is IRREVERSIBLE.

    Sample Sentence: Their privileges were *revoked* after their misconduct in the office.

    Related Words: IRREVOCABLE - a. unchangeable

RHETORICAL (ri TOR i kul): a. Pertaining to art of speaking and writing effectively

    Trigger: RHETORICAL-"RIGHT +ORAL"

Trigger Sentence: The ORATOR uses RIGHT ORAL skills in RHETORICAL way to impress listeners.

Sample Sentence: Sri Arobindo's writings are intense and *rhetorical*; they draw me into an internalized world of mind.

Related Words: RHETORIC -n. art of effective communication

RIBALD (RIB uld): a. Obscene; vulgar

Trigger: 1. RIBALD-BALD-BAD. 2. RIBALD-VERY BAD

Trigger Sentence: A BALD BAD guy was watching a RIBALD BLUE film.

Sample Sentence: She was embarrassed by the *ribald* language of her boss.

RIFE (RYFE): a. Abundant; current

Trigger: RIFE-LIFE

Trigger Sentence: The Ocean is RIFE with LIFE.

Sample Sentence: The production of grains is unexpectedly *rife*; however, the issue is storage space lest the grains go down the drains during rains!

RIFT (RIFT): n. Split; cleave

Trigger: RIFT-CLEFT-SLIT-SPLIT (** synonyms)

Trigger Sentence: The couple hoped to avoid RIFT/SPLIT in their relationship.

Sample Sentence: Those hills were *rifted* by the earthquake.

RIG (RIG): v. Fix; manipulate

Trigger: RIG- RIGID- FIXED- (so RIG means FIX)- RIGID things are FIXED.

Trigger Sentence: Match FIXED is match RIGGED; likewise ELECTION FIXED- election RIGGED.

Sample Sentence: The politician *rigged* the election.

Related Words: RIGID –a. stiff; inflexible; strict; adamant

RIGOROUS (RIG er us): v. Harsh, severe; demanding, strictly accurate

Trigger: RIGOROUS-RIGID + ONEROUS (** synonyms)

Trigger Sentence: RIGOROUS work is RIGIDLY accurate and ONEROUSLY perfect.

Sample Sentence: He developed six-pack abs with a *rigorous* exercise routine.

Related Words: RIGOR -n. severity; harshness

RISIBLE (RIZ uh bul): a. Laughable

Trigger: 1.RISIBLE-RIDICULOUS. 2. RISIBLE-ROUSE

Trigger Sentence: 1. RIDICULOUS acts are RISIBLE. 2. RISIBLE acts AROUSE laughter

Sample Sentence: Jacob's *risible* stories pep up the otherwise somber atmosphere.

RISQUE (ri SKEY): a. Indecent; racy

Trigger: RISQUÉ-RISKY

Trigger Sentence: It is RISKY to speak RISQUÉ language in the class room.

Sample Sentence: He sang a song with *risqué* lyrics.

RIVETING (RIV it ing): a. Fascinating; engrossing

Trigger: RIVET

Trigger Sentence: 1. We use RIVET for holding and gripping; If the movie is RIVETING you get RIVETED to chair. 2. For some people READING is RIVETING.

Sample Sentence: This British historian found the prehistoric cave paintings of India *riveting*.

ROBUST (roh BUST): a. Strong, healthy, vigorous

Trigger: ROBUST -ROBOT

Trigger Sentence: ROBOT is always represented as ROBUST. It is very strong and sturdy.

Sample Sentence: *Robust* like a horse, he is a star performer in the circus.

ROCOCO (roh KOH koh): a. Excessively ornate; intricate

Trigger: 1.ROCOCO- ROCK & CO. 2. ROCOCO- ROW COCO

Trigger Sentence: 1. ROCK & CO musicians usually wear ROCOCO style of ornaments . 2. The COCOnuts were arranged in a ROW in ROCOCO style in Kerala coconut gardens.

Sample Sentence: *Rococo* style is an 18th-century style of art and architecture characterized by the use of elaborate ornamentation.

ROTUND (roh TUND): n. Round in Shape; Fat

Trigger: ROTUND-ROUND

Trigger Sentence: Drop "t" from "ROTUND" to get ROUND; ROTUND person is ROUND SHAPED.

Sample Sentence: My cat is *rotund* like a pumpkin.

Related Words: 1. ROTUNDITY - n. roundedness; quality of having a full or deep voice. 2. ROTUNDA -n. a round building, esp. with a dome

ROW (ROH): n. Argue, fight

Trigger: ROW -ARROW

Trigger Sentence: Imagine in a ROW they fight with ARROWS.

Sample Sentence: They had a *row* over a silly issue.

RUDIMENTARY (roo duh MEN tuh ree): a. Elementary; not fully developed; crude

Trigger: RUDE+ELEMENTARY

Trigger Sentence: 1. CRUDE oil is in RUDIMENTARY form. 2. ELEMENTARY class people are RUDIMENTARY by nature.

Sample Sentence: The education system in this backward country still remains *rudimentary*.

RUEFUL (ROO ful): a. Sorrowful; sad; regretful

Trigger: RUEFUL-SORROWFUL (** synonyms)

Trigger Sentence: She looked at me with RUEFUL/SORROWFUL smile and apologized

Sample Sentence: She was *rueful* for her own wrong doings.

Related Words: RUE -v. regret, mourn

RUMINATE (ROO muh neyt): v. Think deeply about something; ponder

Trigger: 1.RUMINATE-MEDITATE. 2. RUMINATE-"RUM + ROOMMATE".

Trigger Sentence: My ROOMMATE after taking RUM always RUMINATES about his love affairs.

Sample Sentence: He *ruminated* over the proposition of an overseas job.

RUNIC (ROO nik): a. Of the ancient class; having some secret meaning

Trigger: 1.RUNIC-RUBIK'S CUBE. 2. RUNIC- PURANIC

Trigger Sentence: 1. He created a RUBIK'S cube with RUNIC alphabets. 2. PURANIC language Sanskrit had RUNIC script.

Sample Sentence: Sumerian *runic* inscriptions have got mysterious symbols.

RUSE (ROOZ): n. Trick, ploy

   Trigger: 1.RUSE-ROSE. 2. RUSE-USE TRICK

   Trigger Sentence: 1. Guys offer ROSE to RUSE the girls. 2. A RUSE was USED to escape prison.

   Sample Sentence: His act was just a cunning *ruse* to get me to go out with him.

RUTHLESS (ROOTH lus): a. Merciless; cruel

   Trigger: RUTHLESS-RECKLESS

   Trigger Sentence: The RECKLESS man had a RUTHLESS disregard for others' feelings.

   Sample Sentence: Though he was *ruthless* in chasing criminals, he was rather mild on punishing.

SABOTAGE (SAB uh tahzh): v. Intentionally damage

   Trigger: SABOTAGE-SUBVERT+DAMAGE (** synonyms)

   Trigger Sentence: 1. SABOTAGE is to DAMAGE. 2. In a SUBVERSIVE plan the SABOTEUR DAMAGED the project.

   Sample Sentence: Angry workers were responsible for the *sabotage* of the machines.

   Related Words: SABOTEUR -n. one who maliciously causes damage

SACCHARINE (SAK er in): a. Coyly sweet; excessive sentimental

   Trigger: SACCHARINE-SUGAR IN

   Trigger Sentence: 1. Excessively SUGARY sentiments were IN the SACCHARINE love story. 2. The artificial sweetener is SACCHARIN; the adjective 'excessively sweet' is known as saccharine.

   Sample Sentence: The film had a lot of blood shed, but ended *saccharinely* of happy ever after.

   Related Words: CLOYING –a. sicken with an excess (of richness, sweetness or emotion)

SACRILEGIOUS (sak ruh LIJ uhs): a. Profane; desecrating

   Trigger: SACRILEGIOUS-IRRELIGIOUS

   Trigger Sentence: All IRRELIGIOUS acts are known as SACRILEGIOUS.

   Sample Sentence: They accused him of committing a *sacrilege* against their religion.

SACROSANCT (SAK roh sangt): a. Most sacred; inviolable

   Trigger: SACROSANCT-"SACRED + SAINT"

   Trigger Sentence: SACROSANCT things must be kept SCARED and NOT VIOLATED at any cost; SAINT (extremely holy person) is the MOST SACRED person.

Sample Sentence: The burial grounds were considered *sacrosanct* by Aztec's tribe.

SAGACIOUS (suh GEY shus): a. Wise, shrewd

    Trigger: 1.SAGACIOUS-SAGE. 2. SAGACIOUS —"SUGGEST US"

    Trigger Sentence: 1. SAGES are SAGACIOUS. 2. SAGACIOUS people SUGGEST US.

    Sample Sentence: Caron hopes that the court will reach a *sagacious* decision in her case.

    Related Words: 1. SAGE –a. wise, learned. 2. SAGACITY -n. wisdom, judiciousness

SAGE (SEYJ): n. / a. Wise, learned

    Trigger: 1.SAGE-PAGE. 2. SAGE-WISE

    Trigger Sentence: SAGES are sage and wise; they know everything on each and every PAGE.

    Sample Sentence: In Chinese culture, the grandparents are regarded as the *sages* of the family.

SALIENT (SAY lee unt**): a.** Prominent; important

    Trigger: 1.SALIENT-SAIL POINT. 2. SALIENT-ALIEN

    Trigger Sentence: 1. The SAILING POINT for the sailing ship is SALIENT from the lighthouse. 2. The planet hunter's most SALIENT achievement was finding an ALIEN.

    Sample Sentence: He has written all the *salient* features of Hinduism in over four volumes.

SALUBRIOUS (suh LOOB ree uss): a. Healthful

    Trigger: 1. SALUBRIOUS -SALLU- (Salman Khan). 2. SALUBRIOUS- "SOLVE + BRUISE"

    Trigger Sentence: 1. SALLU Bhai in SALUBRIOUS lifestyle. 2. SALUBRIOUS climate SOLVE BRUISES.

    Sample Sentence: A regimen of daily exercise is *salubrious* to a person's well-being.

SALUTARY (SAL yuh ter ee): a. Beneficial; wholesome

    Trigger: 1. SALUTARY-SANITARY. 2. SALUTARY-SALUTE

    Trigger Sentence: 1. SANITARY regulations lead to a SALUTARY life. 2. It is very SALUTARY to SALUTE the colonel in order to show respect.

    Sample Sentence: The low interest rates should have a *salutary* effect on business.

SALVAGE (SAL vij): a. Rescue from loss

    Trigger: 1. SALVAGE-"SAVE +DAMAGE". 2. SALVAGE-SAVAGE-DAMAGE

    Trigger Sentence: 1. SAVE from SAVAGE (damage) is SALVAGE. 2. Devil SAVAGES-god SALVAGES.

    Sample Sentence: They *salvaged* the ship from sinking.

    Related Words: SAVAGE a. /v. - cruel; ruthless; attack brutally

SANCTIFY (SANK tih fye): v. Make holy; purify

    Trigger: SANCTIFY-SAINT+IFY

    Trigger Sentence: The new SAINT left the monastery SANCTIFIED.

    Sample Sentence: The saint *sanctified* their marriage.

    Related Words: SANCTUARY -n. Sacred place; shelter, refuge

SANCTIMONIOUS (sank tih MOH nee us): v. Pretending to be religious; self-righteous

    Trigger: SANCTIMONIOUS-"SAINT & MONK"

Trigger Sentence: Some of the SAINTS and MONKS are identified with SANCTIMONIOUS deeds.

Sample Sentence: He passes *sanctimonious* comments on morality while he himself is shady.

SANGUINARY (SANG gwuh ner ee): a. Bloody; murderous

Trigger: 1.SANGUINARY-SANK IN GORY .2. SANGUINARY – not SANCTUARY

Trigger Sentence: In a SANGUINARY/GORY war the Japanese SANK American ships IN Pearl Harbor.

Sample Sentence: Some men get sadistic pleasure by seeing *sanguinary* and brutality on screen.

SANGUINE (SANG gwin): a. Cheerful; hopeful

Trigger: SANGUINE-"SANG+WIN"

Trigger Sentence: She SANG well and we will WIN; we are quite SANGUINE about our WIN

Sample Sentence: He is *sanguine* about the company's future.

SARDONIC (sahr DON ik): a. Sarcastic, cynical

Trigger: 1.SARDONIC-SARCASTIC. 2. SARD-SARDAR

Trigger Sentence: Jokes made on SARDARS are usually SARDONIC and SARCASTIC.

Sample Sentence: The movie is all about a *sardonic* look at modern life.

SARTORIAL (sahr TOHR ee uhl): a. Pertaining to tailors

Trigger: 1. SARTORIAL-TAILORS. 2. SARTORIAL-SARI+TAILOR

Trigger Sentence: 1. In "SARTORIAL", find all the letters of the word "TAILORS". 2. When SARI-TORE, to fix you require a TAILOR.

Sample Sentence: The fashion design students had a lecture on the *sartorial* finesse in works.

SATIATE (SEY shee eyt): v. Satisfy fully

Trigger: SATIATE-SATISFY

Trigger Sentence: 1. SATE, SATED, SATISFY, SATURATE, SATIATE; all belong to same family. 2. The people are always UNSATISFIED, if they possess INSATIABLE desire of wealth.

Sample Sentence: 1.Krish is all *satiated* by feeding himself on those computer games!! 2. Her desire for jewelry is *insatiable*.

Related Words: 1.INSATIABLE -a. unsatisfiable; extremely greedy. 2. SATE-v. satisfy

SATURNINE (SAT er nahyn): a. Gloomy, sad

Trigger: SATURN

Trigger Sentence: He is SATURNINE (sad) because he is affected by SATURN planet.

Sample Sentence: Do not be misled by his *saturnine* face; he is not as gloomy as he looks.

SAVAGE (SAV ij): a. Violent, uncivilized; v. attack brutally

Trigger: SAVAGE-DAMAGE

Trigger Sentence: SAVAGE is to attack and DAMAGE brutally.

Sample Sentence: He wrote *savage* satires about people he didn't like.

SAVANT (SAV unt): n. Scholar

    Trigger: SAVANT-VEDANT

    Trigger Sentence: A SAVANT (SCHOLAR) can talk VEDANTA

    Sample Sentence: David has an incredible memory, but he is not a *savant*.

SAVORY (SEY vuh ree): a. Tasty, pleasing

    Trigger: SAVORY-"SPICY FLAVORY"

    Trigger Sentence: The SAVORY chicken curry is SPICY and emanates FLAVOR.

    Sample Sentence: You are on a bland diet; please don't demand for a special *savory* palette.

    Related Words: 1.UNSAVORY -a. morally offensive; disgusting. 2. SAVOR -v. enjoy

SCANT (SKANT): a. Little, meager

    Trigger: 1.SCANT-SCARCE-SCARCITY. 2. SCANTY-PLENTY (** antonyms)

    Trigger Sentence: 1. When there is SCARCITY the amount is SCANT and SCARCE. 2. SCANTY is opposite to PLENTY.

    Sample Sentence: She paid *scant* attention to the facts.

    Related Words: SCARCE -a. rare, insufficient

SCARCE (SKAIRS): a. Rare, not abundant, in short supply

    Trigger: SCARCE-SCARCITY (** synonym variants)

    Trigger Sentence: Fresh vegetables were scarce during the drought

    Sample Sentence: Food was *scarcely* provided to the slaves in Africa.

    Related Words: SPARSE -n. not dense; few

SCATHING (SKEY thing): a. Bitterly severe; injurious

    Trigger: 1. SCATHING-SCOLDING. 2. SCATHING-SCARY THING

    Trigger Sentence: 1. A SCOLDING boss makes SCATHING remarks. 2. SCARY THING had a SCATHING effect on the kids.

    Sample Sentence: He wrote a *scathing* review of the book.

SCHISM (SIZ uhm): n. Division, slit

    Trigger: SCHISM-ISM

    Trigger Sentence: 1. Hinduism and Islamism- there is SCHISM. 2. Because of RACISM there is SCHISM among races.

    Sample Sentence: *Schism* between the offensive and the defensive teams needs to be resolved.

SCOFF (SKOF): v. Mock, deride

    Trigger: SCOFF-LAUGH (** synonyms)

    Trigger Sentence: SCOFF is to LAUGH AT the people in a mocking way.

    Sample Sentence: The boss *scoffed* at his subordinates' impractical ideas.

SCORN (SKOHRN): v. Mock; reject with contempt

    Trigger: 1. SCORN-SCOLD. 2. SCORN-PORN

    Trigger Sentence: 1. The boss SCOLDING expression is full of SCORN. 2. The PORN heroine was SCORNED by the public.

    Sample Sentence: Since Bobby is a spoilsport, his friends often *scorned* him.

SCOURGE (SKURJ): n. Whip; lash; sever punishments

    Trigger: 1.SCOURGES-SCARS. 2. SCOURGES-CURSES (** synonyms)

Trigger Sentence: 1. The SCARS are due to SCOURGES. 2. Disease and famine are SCOURGES/CURSES of the humanity.

Sample Sentence: It's a struggle to get out of this *scourge* situation in of the war zone area.

SCRUPLE (SKROO puhl): v. Hesitate on ethical grounds

Trigger: SCRUPLES-COUPLES

Trigger Sentence: 1. The married COUPLES have SCRUPLES. They hesitate to do wrong things because of moral conscience. 2. UNSCRUPULOUS means NO ETHICS.

Sample Sentence: He lied outright and did not even *scruple* about it.

Related Words: UNSCRUPULOUS -a. unprincipled, immoral

SCRUPULOUS (SKROO pyu les): a. Extremely thorough; conscientious

Trigger: SCRUPULOUS-SCULPTURES

Trigger Sentence: When you make SCULPTURES, SCRUPULOUS effort is needed.

Sample Sentence: This editorial requires *scrupulous* attention.

SCRUTINIZE (SKROOT uh nyze): v. Examine closely and critically

Trigger: 1.SCRUTINIZE-ANALYZE. 2. SCRUTINIZE-"SCREW+TINI+EYES"

Trigger Sentence: When you SCREW TINY things you SCRUTINIZE and ANALYZE it carefully.

Sample Sentence: Her performance was carefully *scrutinized* by her employer.

SCURRILOUS (SKUR uh luhs): a. Obscene, indecent

Trigger: 1. SCURRILOUS-SKIRT LESS. 2. SCURRILOUS-SCANDALOUS

Trigger Sentence: 1. The ruffians use SCURRILOUS language on SKIRT LESS girls walking on the ramp.2. SCURRILOUS and SCANDALOUS are synonyms.

Sample Sentence: I cannot take his *scurrilous* behavior towards me anymore!

SCURVY (SKUR vee): a. Vulgar; despicable

Trigger: SCURVY-CURVY

Trigger Sentence: 1. Watching CURVY girls is SCURVY. 2. When one gets SCURVY disease one would look nasty and VULGAR.

Sample Sentence: We never expected her to turn out so *scurvy* and shabbily dressed.

SCUTTLE (SKUHT l): v. 1. Move quickly; 2. Sink

Trigger: 1. SCUTTLE-SHUTTLE. 2. SCUTTLE-"SHIP+CUT+LE"

Trigger Sentence: 1. The SHUTTLE SCUTTLED across the badminton court. 2. They SCUTTLED a ship after CUTTING holes through the bottom.

Sample Sentence: Many species of reptiles *scuttle* around the brushwood.

SECESSION (si SESH un): n. Withdrawal; separation

Trigger: SECESSION-no PROCESSION

Trigger Sentence: Instead of going with the PROCESSION, a section of the troops were in SECESSION.

Sample Sentence: Seema's boss demanded for a *secession* of her complaint against him so as to keep her job intact!

Related Words: RECESSION –n. withdrawal; slow economy

SECLUDE (si KLOOD): v. Keep away from other people

Trigger: 1. SECLUDE-EXCLUDE. 2. SECLUDED- SEPARATELY CLOSED

Trigger Sentence: Women were SECLUDED and EXCLUDED from getting in to scientific societies.

Sample Sentence: I wish to run away from this maddening crowd and live in *seclusion* in jungles.

SECTARIAN (sek TAIR ee un): a. Narrow-minded; limited; related to a religious sect

Trigger: SECTARIAN-SECT (**sections-not whole)

Trigger Sentence: Most SECTARIANS are intolerant of the views of other religious SECTS.

Sample Sentence: Some religions are harshly *sectarian*.

SECULAR (SEK yuh lur): a. Non-religious in nature; worldly; temporal

Trigger: 1. SECULAR-SACRED (**near antonyms). 2. SECULAR-NOT SPIRITUAL

Trigger Sentence: SECULAR things are not related to SACRED or religious things.

Sample Sentence: India is a *secular* republic with a democratic government.

SEDATE (si DEYT): a. Calm; composed; grave

Trigger: SEDATE-STEADY

Trigger Sentence: A SEDATE person possesses STEADY attitude.

Sample Sentence: Everyone at the funeral was sedate silent.

SEDENTARY (SED en ter ee): a. Requiring sitting

Trigger: SEDENTARY-"SIT+ENTRY"

Trigger Sentence: All DATA ENTRY jobs are SEDENTARY jobs.

Sample Sentence: *Sedentary* jobs are those that require little activity.

SEDULOUS (SED yuh luss): a. Hardworking, diligent

Trigger: 1.SEDULOUS-STUDIOUS. 2. SEDULOUS-SCHEDULES

Trigger Sentence: 1. SEDULOUS guys are STUDIOUS. 2. SEDULOUS guys work in all three SCHEDULES of a day.

Sample Sentence: The football team's *sedulous* practice sessions produced a winning team.

Related Words: SEDULITY -n. diligence

SEEMLY (SEEM lee): a. Proper; appropriate

Trigger: SEEMLY-"SEE FAMILY & HOMELY"

Trigger Sentence: SEE FAMILY and HOMELY (of course comely) girls, they LOOK SEEMLY (see-look; LOOK PROPERLY).

Sample Sentence: He is a young man of *seemly* appearance and robust health.

Related Words: UNSEEMLY -a. improper, indecorous. 2. SEAMY –a. morally degraded

SEETHE (SEETH): v. Be disturbed; anger; boil

Trigger: 1.SEETHE-SOOTHE (** near antonyms). 2. SEETHE-TEETH

Trigger Sentence: 1. When a person is SEETHING with anger, SOOTHING words are going to calm his soul. 2. When Boxer Tyson SEETHE he usually bites the opponents with his TEETH.

Sample Sentence: The rural masses *seethed* with discontent; thus revolted against government.

SEGREGATE (SEG ri geyt): v. Separate

Trigger: 1. SEGREGATE-SEPARATE . 2. SEGREGATE-AGREGATE-CONGREGATE

Trigger Sentence: 1. SEGREGATE and SEPARATE are synonyms. 2. SEGREGATE and AGGREGATE are antonyms.

Sample Sentence: The fishermen *segregated* the marketable fish from the junk fish which they returned to the sea.

SEMANTIC (si MAN tik): a. Of the study of the meaning and use of words and phrases

Trigger: SEMANTIC-SEE MEANING

Trigger Sentence: SEMANTIC interpretations usually SEE MEANING of the words in a sentence.

Sample Sentence: Teachers use *semantic* maps to teach vocabulary.

SEMINAL (SEM uh nl): a. Original, influencing future developments

Trigger: 1.SEMINAL-SEMINAR. 2. SEMINAL-ORIGINAL

Trigger Sentence: In a SEMINAR professors present SEMINAL (original) ideas and later they encourage other people to work on them.

Sample Sentence: Freud is regarded as a *seminal* thinker who shaped the course of psychology.

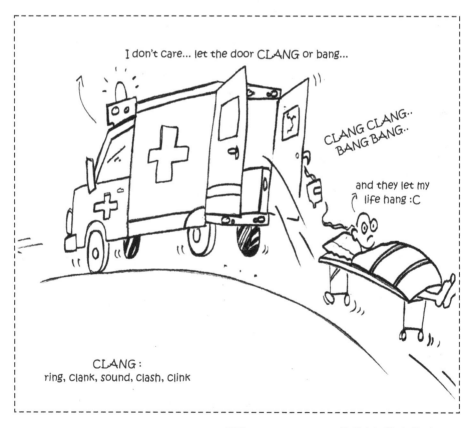

Memory Test-97 : Match each word and its memory trick to the corresponding definition.

S.N	WORD	MEMORY TRIGGER	S.N	DEFINITIONS	KEY
1	RETIRING	RETIRED from life	A	Abundant; current	
2	RETRACT	"RE TAKE"-"take back"	B	Act of showing; disclosure	
3	RETREAT	Summer RETREAT-DEFEAT	C	Cancel, retract	
4	RETRENCH	RETURN to bench	D	Cut down or reduce (Expenses Etc.,)	
5	RETRIEVE	Retrieve-REVIVE	E	Daydream, preoccupation	
6	RETROGRESS	no PROGRESS	F	Depart , Withdraw	
7	RETROSPECTIVE	Re +INSPECT	G	Echo; resound	
8	REVAMP	REVISE	H	Fix; manipulate	
9	REVELATION	REVEAL	I	Insult, criticize abusively	
10	REVERBERATE	RE+VIBRATE	J	Looking back on the past	
11	REVERE	Paul REVERE- Ganges RIVER	K	Move backward; get worse	
12	REVERIE	River+EYE	L	Obscene; vulgar	
13	REVILE	Talk-EVIL	M	Pertaining to art of speaking effectively	
14	REVIVE	re +LIVE	N	Recover; bring back	
15	REVOKE	REVERSE decision	O	Renovate, revise	
16	RHETORICAL	right +ORAL	P	Return to life: become active	
17	RIBALD	very BAD SCENE	Q	Shy; modest	
18	RIFE	Ocean is RIFE with LIFE.	R	Split; cleave	
19	RIFT	cleft-slit-split	S	Venerate, respect deeply	
20	RIG	Rig- RIGID- fixed	T	Withdraw, take back	

Memory Test-98 : Match each word and its memory trick to the corresponding definition.

S.N	WORD	MEMORY TRIGGER	S.N	DEFINITIONS	KEY
1	RIGOROUS	Rigid + ONEROUS	A	Argue, fight	
2	RISIBLE	RIDICULOUS-ROUSE	B	Cloyingly sweet; excessive sentimental	
3	RISQUÉ	RISKY language	C	Elementary; not fully developed	
4	RIVETING	Rivet for GRIP	D	Excessively ornate; intricate	
5	ROBUST	Robot is strong	E	Fascinating; engrossing	
6	ROCOCO	ROCK & co style	F	Harsh, severe; demanding	
7	ROTUND	Round	G	Having some secret meaning	
8	ROW	Row -ARROW	H	Indecent; racy	
9	RUDIMENTARY	Rude+ELEMENTARY	I	Intentionally damage	
10	RUEFUL	SORROWFUL	J	Laughable	
11	RUMINATE	Roommate-MEDITATE.	K	Merciless; cruel	
12	RUNIC	Rubik's cube	L	Most sacred; inviolable	
13	RUSE	USE trick	M	Profane; desecrating	
14	RUTHLESS	Ruthless-RECKLESS	N	Round in Shape; Fat	
15	SABOTAGE	Subvert+damage	O	Sorrowful; sad; regretful	
16	SACCHARINE	SUGAR IN	P	Strong, healthy, vigorous	
17	SACRILEGIOUS	IRRELIGIOUS	Q	Think deeply about something	
18	SACROSANCT	Sacred + saint	R	Trick, ploy	
19	SAGACIOUS	Sage- suggest us	S	Wise, shrewd	
20	SAGE	Know PAGE	T	Wise, learned	

Answers

EX.NO	1	2	3	4	5	6	7	8	9	10	11	12	13	14	15	16	17	18	19	20
97	Q	T	F	D	N	K	J	O	B	G	S	E	I	P	C	M	L	A	R	H
98	F	J	H	E	P	D	N	A	C	O	Q	G	R	K	I	B	M	L	T	S

Memory Test-99 : Match each word and its memory trick to the corresponding definition.

S.N	WORD	MEMORY TRIGGER	S.N	DEFINITIONS	KEY
1	SALIENT	Sail point	A	Beneficial; wholesome	
2	SALUBRIOUS	SOLVE + BRUISE	B	Bitterly severe; injurious	
3	SALUTARY	SANITARY or SALUTE	C	Bloody; murderous	
4	SALVAGE	Save +damage	D	Cheerful; hopeful	
5	SANCTIFY	SAINT+ify	E	Division, slit	
6	SANCTIMONIOUS	Fake SAINT & MONK	F	Gloomy, sad	
7	SANGUINARY	SANK in GORY	G	Healthful	
8	SANGUINE	Sang+WIN	H	Little, meager	
9	SARDONIC	SARCASTIC	I	Make holy; purify	
10	SARTORIAL	sari+TAILOR	J	Mock, deride	
11	SATIATE	SATISFY	K	Pertaining to tailors	
12	SATURNINE	SATURN effect	L	Pretending to be religious	
13	SAVAGE	He DAMAGEs	M	Prominent; important	
14	SAVANT	VEDANTA	N	Rare, not abundant	
15	SAVORY	Spicy flavor	O	Rescue from loss	
16	SCANT	Scanty-no plenty	P	Sarcastic, cynical	
17	SCARCE	Scarce-scarcity	Q	Satisfy fully	
18	SCATHING	SCOLDING	R	Scholar	
19	SCHISM	RACISM - SCHISM	S	Tasty, pleasing	
20	SCOFF	LAUGH	T	Violent, uncivilized	

Memory Test-100 : Match each word and its memory trick to the corresponding definition.

S.N	WORD	MEMORY TRIGGER	S.N	DEFINITIONS	KEY
1	SCORN	Scold--porn	A	Be disturbed; anger; boil	
2	SCOURGE	Scourges-SCARS	B	Calm; composed; grave	
3	SCRUPLE	COUPLE ethics	C	Examine closely and critically	
4	SCRUPULOUS	SCULPTURES work	D	Extremely thorough; conscientious	
5	SCRUTINIZE	Analyze-screw+tini+eyes	E	Hardworking, diligent	
6	SCURRILOUS	SKIRT LESS	F	Hesitate on ethical grounds	
7	SCURVY	CURVY - SCURVY	G	Keep away from other people	
8	SCUTTLE	Shuttle- ship+cut+le"	H	Mock; reject with contempt	
9	SECESSION	No PROCESSION	I	Move quickly; Sink	
10	SECLUDE	SEPARATELY closed	J	Narrow-minded; limited	
11	SECTARIAN	SECT feelings	K	Non-religious in nature; worldly	
12	SECULAR	Secular-not SACRED	L	Obscene, indecent	
13	SEDATE	STEADY	M	Of the study of the meaning and use of words	
14	SEDENTARY	SIT+ENTRY	N	Original, influencing future developments	
15	SEDULOUS	Studious-schedules	O	Proper; appropriate	
16	SEEMLY	See FAMILY girl	P	Requiring sitting	
17	SEETHE	Opp. SOOTHE	Q	Separate	
18	SEGREGATE	SEPARATE	R	Vulgar; despicable	
19	SEMANTIC	See MEANING	S	Whip; lash; sever punishments	
20	SEMINAL	Seminar- ORIGINAL	T	Withdrawal; separation	

Answers

EX.NO	1	2	3	4	5	6	7	8	9	10	11	12	13	14	15	16	17	18	19	20
99	M	G	A	O	I	L	C	D	P	K	Q	F	T	R	S	H	N	B	E	J
100	H	S	F	D	C	L	R	I	T	G	J	K	B	P	E	O	A	Q	M	N

WORD GROUPS DAY-25

★ **ANCILLARY:** secondary, extra, assistant
ADJECTIVES: accessory, adjuvant, auxiliary, collateral, concomitant, incident, secondary, subordinate, subservient, subsidiary
NOUNS: auxiliary, ancillary, appurtenance
VERB: supplement
ANTONYMS: adj. necessary, needed

★ **ESSENTIAL, NECESSARY**
ADJECTIVES: capital, cardinal, chief, crucial, foremost, fundamental, imperative, indispensable, main, necessary, needful, prerequisite, principal, requisite ; compelling, decisive, exigent, expedient, fundamental, incumbent on, indispensable, mandatory, momentous, obligatory, paramount, prime, quintessential, significant, specified, unavoidable, vital
NOUNS: principle, quintessence, requisite
VERB: necessitate, entail, warrant
ANTONYMS: adj. accessory, auxiliary, inessential, minor, secondary, subsidiary, unimportant

★ **INNATE:** inborn, natural
ADJECTIVES: congenital, connate, hereditary, inborn, inbred, indigenous, ingrained, inherent, inherited, instinctive, intrinsic, intuitive, natural
NOUNS: innateness
VERB: naturalize
ANTONYMS: adj. acquired, extrinsic, learned

★ **SPONTANEOUS:** impromptu, natural

ADJECTIVES: ad-lib, automatic, extempore, impromptu, improvised, instinctive, involuntary, natural, offhand, unplanned, unstudied; impetuous, impulsive, voluntary
NOUNS: spontaneity
VERB: improvise , extemporize
ANTONYMS: deliberate, intended, planned, premeditated, studied

★ **JARGON :** specialized or technical language, dialect
ADJECTIVES: jargon-laden
NOUNS: argot, cant, colloquialism, dialect, gibberish, idiom, lexicon, lingo, neologism, parlance, patois, slang, vernacular
VERB: jargonize
ANTONYMS: n. standard

★ **PRIVILEGE:** special individual right not enjoyed by others
ADJECTIVES: privileged ,exclusive
NOUNS: allowance, appurtenance, authority, benefit, boon, concession, entitlement, exemption, favor, franchise, grant, immunity, liberty, license, perquisite, prerogative, sanction
VERB: privilege
ANTONYMS: detriment, disadvantage

★ **ERASE:** remove, rub out
ADJECTIVES: eradicable
NOUNS: eradication
VERB: abolish, annul, annihilate, delete, efface, excise, expunge, extirpate, negate, nullify, obliterate
ANTONYMS: imprint, insert; reinstate

Word List Day-26

SENILITY (si NIL i tee): n. Old age; feeblemindedness of old age

Trigger: SENILITY-SENIORITY

Trigger Sentence: SENIOR CITIZENS are OLD CITIZENS.

Sample Sentence: I thought you are sensible, but you have gone *senile* like an old man!

Related Words: SENESCENT –a. growing older

SENTENTIOUS (sen TEN shus): a. Terse, concise; aphoristic

Trigger: SENTENTIOUS-SENTENCES

Trigger Sentence: MORALISTIC SENTENCE statements are SENTENTIOUS; Most of the proverbs consists moralistic sentences.

Sample Sentence: President Clinton gave a *sententious* talk on the value of honesty in politics.

SENTIENT (SEN shunt): a. Capable of sensation; aware; sensitive

Trigger: 1.SENTIENT-SENTIMENT. 2. "SENSE+ENT"

Trigger Sentence: 1. If you have SENTIMENT you can feel SENSE and being SENTIENT towards others. 2. Imagine ENT (ear, nose, tongue) SENSES.

Sample Sentence: Humans and animals are *sentient*, while rocks are not.

Related Words: INSENTIENT -n. inanimate, lacking consciousness, inability to feel

SEQUENTIAL (si KWEN shul): a. Successive, following, subsequent, consecutive

Trigger: SEQUENTIAL-SEQUENCE

Trigger Sentence: SEQUENTIAL things are characterized by regular SEQUENCE.

Sample Sentence: He arranged the cards in a *sequential* order.

Related Words: SUBSEQUENT -a. following; happening after

SERE (SEER): a. Dry, parched

Trigger: SERE-SEAR-SOAR

Trigger Sentence: When temperatures SOAR with SEARING heat the lands become SERE.

Sample Sentence: The Sahara belt in summers has a *sere* landscape and eerie breezy sounds.

SERENDIPITY (ser un DIP i tee): n. An instance of fortunate discovery; luck

Trigger: SERENDIPITY-"SUDDEN DIP +ITY"

Trigger Sentence: After SUDDEN DIP in water, in a SERENDIPITOUS moment Archimedes found a LUCKY DISCOVERY; and said eureka...

Sample Sentence: The lovers found each other by pure *serendipity*.

SERENE (se REEN): a. Calm; tranquil

Trigger: SERENE-SCENE

Trigger Sentence: GREEN areas are full of SERENE SCENES.

Sample Sentence: Dia was an image of *serenity* as she walked on the aisle in her wedding gown.

SERMON (SUR mun): n. Any serious speech, discourse esp. on a moral issue; preaching

    Trigger: SERMON–"SERIOUS + MONK"

    Trigger Sentence: SERIOUS TALK given by a MONK about moral living is known as a SERMON.

    Sample Sentence: Thousands of people flocked towards the Buddhist Kalachakra initiation to hear the His holiness Dalai Lama's *sermon* at Amaravati.

    Related Words: SERMONIZE -v. preach, lecture on religious issues

SERVILE (SUR vil**): a.** Slavish; subservient

    Trigger: SERVILE–SERVE

    Trigger Sentence: The SERVANTS at his home bear SERVILE attitude.

    Sample Sentence: The stewards at the star hotel are *servile* towards the rich and famous!

    Related Words: SERVITUDE -n. slavery; bondage

SEVER (SEV ur): v. Cut, separate

    Trigger: SEVER–SHAVER

    Trigger Sentence: A SHAVER SEVERS; cuts or SEPARATES.

    Sample Sentence: The guillotine was an execution device invented to *sever* the head.

SHACKLE (SHAK ul): v. Chain; fetter, manacle

    Trigger: 1.SHACKLE–BUCKLE. 2. SHACKLE–OBSTACLE

    Trigger Sentence: 1. With a BUCKLE he SHACKLED a man and tied his ankles.

    2. SHACKLES and OBSTACLES are synonyms.

    Sample Sentence: They *shackled* the legs of the prisoners with heavy iron chains.

SHAM (SHAM): v. Pretend, deceive, n. fraud, fake

    Trigger: 1.SHAM–SCAM. 2. SHAM–SCHEME

    Trigger Sentence: 1. A SHAM is a SCAM. 2. SHYAM (Krishna) plays SHAM on others.

    Sample Sentence: Their marriage was all a *sham*.

SHARD (SHAHRD): n. Fragment, generally of pottery

    Trigger: 1.SHARD-S (small) + HARD. 2. SHARD–SHRED

    Trigger Sentence: 1. SHARD can be SMALL portion of any HARD material like pottery, ceramic material. 2. SHARD and SHRED are fragments.

    Sample Sentence: *Shards* of terracotta were found during the excavations at the Indus Valley.

SHIRK (SHURK): v. Avoid (responsibility, work, etc.), malinger

    Trigger: SHIRK–WORK

    Trigger Sentence: SHIRK is to avoid WORK.

    Sample Sentence: O'Brian never *shirked* from doing his duty.

SHODDY (SHOD ee**): a.** Cheap, inferior; fake

    Trigger: 1.SHODDY–SHOWY. 2. SHODDY-goes to SHED

    Trigger Sentence: 1. Cheap and SHOWY dress is SHODDY. 2. SHODDY car goes to repair SHED.

    Sample Sentence: *Shoddy* construction lead to the collapse of the building.

SHREWD (SHROOD**): a.** Clever; sharp

    Trigger: SHREWD- SHARP DUDE

Trigger Sentence: The SHARP DUDE is SHREWD about his business investments.

Sample Sentence: He is a *shrewd* businessman.

SHUN (SHUN): v. Keep away from

Trigger: 1. SHUN-SUN. 2. SHUN-SHIRK (** synonyms)

Trigger Sentence: SHUN the SUN; AVOID direct SUN; it might cause skin cancer due to UV RAYS.

Sample Sentence: The laborers who belonged to the union *shunned* the non-union workers.

SIMILE (SIM uh lee): n. Comparison of one thing with another

Trigger: SIMILE-SIMILAR

Trigger Sentence: "She is SIMILAR to rose" is a SIMILE.

Sample Sentence: She's "as fierce as a tiger" is a *simile*, but "She's a tiger when she's angry" is a metaphor.

SIMPLISTIC (sim PLIS tik): a. Oversimplified; unrealistically simple

Trigger: SIMPLISTIC- SIMPLIFIED- SIMPLE

Trigger Sentence: The SIMPLISTIC style to a complex problem seems UNREALISTICALLY SIMPLE.

Sample Sentence: The orator's interpretation of the Hindu Vedas was somewhat *simplistic*.

Related Words: OVERSIMPLIFY –v. simplify excessively

SIMULATE (SIM yuh lit): v. Imitate, pretend

Trigger: 1.SIMULATE-IMITATE. 2. SIMULA-SIMILAR

Trigger Sentence: 1. SIMULATE is to IMITATE (not original; it is fake). 2. "SIMULATE" is to pretend "SIMILAR" like someone or something else.

Sample Sentence: The model will be used to *simulate* the effects of an earthquake.

SINECURE (SY ni kyoor): n. High paid job that needs little effort

Trigger: 1.SINECURE-SECURE. 2. SINECURE-SOFTWARE

Trigger Sentence: 1. Govt. SECURE jobs are usually SINECURE. 2. These days SOFTWARE jobs have become SINECURE.

Sample Sentence: My job is no *sinecure*; I work long hours and have much responsibility.

SINGULAR (SING gyu ler): a. Unique; odd; extraordinary

Trigger: SINGULAR-SINGLE

Trigger Sentence: SINGULAR girl say, "I am SINGLE but not ready to mingle".

Sample Sentence: There is some *singularity* about Thailand that draws thousands everyday.

Related Words: PECULIAR –a. strange; unique

SINISTER (SIN ih ster): n. Evil

Trigger: 1. SINister-SIN. 2. SINISTER-MONSTER

Trigger Sentence: 1. SIN is an EVIL. 2. SINISTER and MONSTERS are evils.

Sample Sentence: There was something *sinister* about him that his colleagues feared about!

SINUOUS (SIN yoo uss): a. Winding, twisting

Trigger: SINUOUS-SINE (WAVES)

Trigger Sentence: SINE WAVE is SINUOUS in nature.

Sample Sentence: The River Yamuna flowed in a *sinuous* trail through the lush green valleys.

SKEPTIC (SKEP tic): a. Skeptical, doubtful

Trigger: SKEPTIC-SKEPT-SUSPECT

Trigger Sentence: SKEPTIC always SUSPECTS.

Sample Sentence: The scientists have *skeptical* approach to the beliefs on miracles.

Related Words: SKEPTICAL -a. doubtful

SKETCHY (SKECH ee): a. Not thorough; superficial; incomplete

Trigger: SKETCHY- SKETCH

Trigger Sentence: The SKETCH of our plan of action is a little SKETCHY; we got to be more clear.

Sample Sentence: Details of how the online publishing service would benefit us are still *sketchy*.

SKIRT (SKURT): v. Avoid

Trigger: SKIRT-SKIP (** synonyms)

Trigger Sentence: We SKIRTED/SKIPPED the class to avoid the boring lecture.

Sample Sentence: We took a road that *skirted* the city to avoid traffic.

SKITTISH (SKIT ish): a. Nervous; restive

Trigger: 1.SKITTISH-KITTEN. 2. SKITTISH-BRITISH

Trigger Sentence: 1. KITTEN is always NERVOUS; and moves in a SKITTISH fashion. 2. During BRITISH rule India was in SKITTISH state.

Sample Sentence: The kitten would become *skittish* and hide under the sofa by seeing the dog.

SKULLDUGGERY (SKUL dug uh ree): n. Deception, trickery

Trigger: 1.SKULDUGGERY- SKULL+ DIGGING. 2. SKULL-SKILL (CUNNING)

Trigger Sentence: 1. His SKULL is full of SKULLDUGGERY; he digs SKULLS and sells them illegally to hospitals. 2."SKUL" in the word sounds like "SKILL"; interpret it as CUNNING SKILL.

Sample Sentence: The Company resorted to deceit and *skullduggery* to avoid taxes.

SLACKEN (SLAK un): v. Slow down; loosen

Trigger: SLACK-LACK (** LACK of speed or LACK of tightness)

Trigger Sentence: 1. He SLACKENED his pace as he LACKED energy. 2. Due to LACK OF TENSION, his grip on the rope SLACKENED.

Sample Sentence: He accused the government of *slack* supervision on uncontrolled corruption.

SLAKE (SLAYK): v. Quench; satisfy

Trigger: 1. SLAKE-LAKE. 2. SLAKE-FLAKE

Trigger Sentence: 1. LAKE SLAKES (reduces) my thirst. 2. Corn FLAKES SLAKE (relieve) my hunger.

Sample Sentence: Jeannie *slaked* her nicotine craving by going outdoors for smoking.

SLANDER (SLAN dur): n. Defamation, false statements about someone

Trigger: SLANDER-"SLANG"+"SCANDAL"

Trigger Sentence: SLANG LANGUAGE is used in a SLANDER, to spread a SCANDAL.

Sample Sentence: The movie star sued the magazine for *slandering* her.

SLATTERNLY (SLAT ern lee): a. Untidy; slovenly

Trigger: SLATTERNLY-SLIT & TORN

Trigger Sentence: A filthy SLATTERNLY slut was wearing a SLIT and a TORN dress.

Sample Sentence: The prostitute appeared *slatternly* with sleazy cloths.

SLEIGHT (SLYT): n. Skill in using hands; dexterity

Trigger: SLEIGHT-SMART & BRIGHT (** near synonyms)

Trigger Sentence: As an eight year old, he was SLEIGHT (SMART & BRIGHT) at writing on SLATE.

Sample Sentence: Our old carpenter has a gift of *sleight;* watch his hands move like a machine!

SLIGHT (SLYT): v. Neglect; snub

Trigger: SLIGHT-LIGHT

Trigger Sentence: She SLIGHTED her boy friend by taking him LIGHTLY in front of others.

Sample Sentence: He had been *slighted* in front of all the members of the jury.

SLOTH (SLAWTH): n. Laziness

Trigger: SLOTH-"SLOW+TH"

Trigger Sentence: A SLOTH is SLOW and LAZY.

Sample Sentence: Why do you *sloth* like a couch potato?!

SLOVENLY (SLUV un lee): a. Untidy; careless

Trigger: 1. SLOVENLY-CLEANLY (** antonyms). 2. SLOVENY-"LOVELY"-"HEAVENLY"

Trigger Sentence: 1. SLOVENLY and CLEANLY are antonyms. 2. SLOVENLY person does not look LOVELY and HEAVENLY.

Sample Sentence: He dressed in a *slovenly* manner to the party.

SLUGGARD (SLUHG erd): n. Lazy person

Trigger: SLUG-SLOW; "SLUGGISH-SLOWISH"

Trigger Sentence: SLUGGISH and SLOWISH are synonyms.

Sample Sentence: "You are a *sluggard*, a drone, a leech," the father yelled at his lazy son.

Related Words: SLUGGISH -a. slow, lethargic

SMUG (SMUHG): n. Self-satisfied, self-righteous

Trigger: SMUGNESS-SMUGGLERS

Trigger Sentence: 1. SMUGGLERS are ARROGANT & COMPLACENT in nature. 2. Whatever they do, they feel that they are RIGHT in their own way.

Sample Sentence: It's OK to celebrate your victory, but try not to be too *smug* about it.

Related Words: SMUGNESS -n. quality of being self-satisfied, complacency

SNARE (SNAIR): v. Catch in a trap

Trigger: 1.SNARE-SNAKE. 2. ENSNARE, SNARE, SNATCH (catch the unaware)

Trigger Sentence: 1. The snake catchers SNARED a SNAKE. 2. SNARE, SNATCH (CATCH) and ENSNARE are synonyms

Sample Sentence: The gangster *snared* her into drug addiction.

Related Words: ENSNARE -v. catch in a trap

SOBER (SOH ber): a. Not drunk; calm; clear headed; serious; drab

Trigger: SOBER- NO BEER

Trigger Sentence: I took NO BEER and totally SOBER for several weeks.

Sample Sentence: Rao's *sobriety* frightened some; he was always silent and serious.

SODDEN (SOD n): a. Soaked; dull, esp. from drink

Trigger: SODDEN-SOAK IN

Trigger Sentence: He stood at the door SODDEN (or SOAKED) by the rain.

Sample Sentence: He hung his *sodden* raincoat near the radiator to dry up.

SOLEMN (SOL uhm): a. Serious, formal, sincere

Trigger: SOLEMN-"SOLO +MAN"

Trigger Sentence: 1. SOLO-MAN (a single living man) is always SERIOUS. 2. King SOLOMON was SOLEMN; and maintained SOLEMNITY.

Sample Sentence: He spoke in a *solemn* and thoughtful manner.

Related Words: SOLEMNITY -n. seriousness; gravity

SOLICIT (sa LIS it): v. Seek; request earnestly

Trigger: 1.SOLICITING-SEEKING. 2 SOLICIT- SOUL SAID

Trigger Sentence: 1. SOLICITING is nothing but SEEKING. 2. my SOUL SAID in a SOLICITING manner – god please help me!

Sample Sentence: Despite *soliciting* the missionary, reverend Mathew was not posted to the church in his home town Kerala.

Related Words: UNSOLICITED -a. unrequested, uninvited

SOLICITOUS (suh LIS uh tis): a. Concerned; worried

Trigger: 1. SOLICITOUS-"SOUL+ SIT ON US". 2. SOLICITOUS-CONSOLE- DISCONSOLATE

Trigger Sentence: SOLICITOUS parents are very concerned; they CONSOLE and SOLACE when I feel DISCONSOLATE.

Sample Sentence: I appreciated his *solicitous* inquiry about my health.

SOLITARY (SOL i ter ee): a. Alone; single

Trigger: SOLITARY-SOLO

Trigger Sentence: A SOLO DUDE leads a SOLITARY life.

Sample Sentence: He is a man of a *solitary* nature and didn't welcome people into his privacy.

Related Words: SOLITUDE –n. loneliness

SOLITUDE (SOL i tyood): n. Being alone; seclusion

Trigger: SOLITUDE-SOLO DUDE

Trigger Sentence: A SOLO DUDE is in SOLITUDE; he wants to stay "SOLO".

Sample Sentence: I enjoy the peace and *solitude* of the woods.

SOLVENT (SAHL vunt): a. Able to pay all debts

Trigger: SOLVENT-"SOLVE+RENT"

Trigger Sentence: As the money problem is SOLVED; I can pay the room RENT and be SOLVENT.

Sample Sentence: After years of hard work to earn and pay back, Frank finally became *solvent*.

Related Words: INSOLVENT -a. bankrupt; unable to pay one's debts

SOMATIC (suh MAT ik): a. of the body; physical

Trigger: SOMATIC-ROMANTIC

Trigger Sentence: ROMANTIC feelings stimulate SOMATIC senses.

Sample Sentence: Spiritualism is all about soul, and materialism is all *somatic*.

SOMBER (SOM bur): a. Gloomy, depressing

Trigger: 1. SOMBER-BOMBER. 2. SOMBER-SOME BEER

Trigger Sentence: 1. BOMBER ATTACK made everyone SOMBER. 2. If you are in SOMBER mood have SOME BEER you will be silly and CHEERFUL.

Sample Sentence: The village was shrouded in a *somber* silence with a farmer's suicide issue.

SOMNOLENT (SOM nuh lunt): a. Sleepy; half-asleep

Trigger: 1. SOMNOLENT-STIMULANT. 2. INSOMNIA (lack of sleep)-SOMNOLENT (sleepy)

Trigger Sentence: 1. Coffee is STIMULANT and wine is SOMNOLENT. 2. If you are affected with INSOMNIA you will never feel SOMNOLENT.

Sample Sentence: He is still *somnolent* and jetlagged after traveling down from the other part of the globe.

Related Words: INSOMNIA -n. sleeplessness

SONOROUS (SON uh russ): a. Resonant

Trigger: SONOROUS-SNORERS

Trigger Sentence: SNORERS are producing SONOROUS sound.

Sample Sentence: Suddenly the silence of the valley was broken by the *sonorous* humming of the church bells as though a message from the skies was scattering across the cold hills!

SOOTHE (SOOTH): v. Ease; calm

Trigger: SOOTHE-SMOOTH

Trigger Sentence: The SMOOTH tone of her voice and SMOOTH taste of the wine give a SOOTHING effect.

Sample Sentence: The doctor prescribed medication to *soothe* Cheryl's back pain.

Related Words: SOOTHING -a. calming

SOPHISTICATED (suh FIS ti key tid): n. Worldly-wise; cultured; complex

Trigger: SOPHISTICATED-PHILOSOPHER

Trigger Sentence: PHILOSOPHERS like Aristotle are SOPHISTICATED people.

Sample Sentence: She was a *sophisticated* and well-traveled woman.

SOPORIFIC (sap uh RIF ik): a. Sleepy; sleep-causing

Trigger: 1. SOPOR-SUPPER+OVER. 2. SOPOR-SLEEPOVER

Trigger Sentence: "SOPOR" sounds "SUPPER"; after SUPPER/dinner is OVER, we get SOPORIFIC.

Sample Sentence: The doctor gave some kind of *soporific* medicine to Sonia for resting

SORDID (SAWR did): a. Dirty, filthy; base; ignoble

Trigger: SORDID-SOILED (** synonyms)

Trigger Sentence: The SORDID bar on the edge of the town was full of SOILED visitors.

Sample Sentence: The social worker was upset by the *sordid* shelters provided to the homeless.

SPARE (SPAIR): v. /a. Use frugally, just sufficient; thin

    Trigger: 1.SPARE-RARE. 2. SPARE-BARE

    Trigger Sentence: 1. Indian Sadhu led a BARE life; 2. SPARINGLY he indulged in luxury; RARELY did he spend money.

    Sample Sentence: 1.In his childhood he lived on a *spare* diet. 2. The library had a *spare* but efficient look. 3. They are a *sparing* couple who are trying to save up enough for a house.

    Related Words: SPARING -a. economical; meager, limited

SPARSE (SPAHRS): a. Thinly scattered; scanty; not dense

    Trigger: SPARSE-SCARCE (** scarcity)

    Trigger Sentence: Trees are SPARSE in the desert because the rain is SCARCE.

    Sample Sentence: My father has got *sparse* hair on his head, he is rather balding! Hehe!

SPARTAN (SPAHR tn): a. Lacking luxury and comfort; strictly disciplined

    Trigger: SPARTAN-SPARTA-SPARE-BARE

    Trigger Sentence: 1. People from SPARTA lead a SPARTAN life with SPARE food. 2. STALIN was a SPARTAN disciplinarian.

    Sample Sentence: People from Sparta had a *Spartan* upbringing.

SPECIFIC (spi SIF ik): a. Unique; precise; limited

    Trigger: SPECIFIC-SPECIAL (** synonyms)

    Trigger Sentence: There is a SPECIFIC word for this SPECIAL kind of feeling…

    Sample Sentence: Give a *specific* and a clear list of your requirements for the trip.

    Related Words: 1. SPECIFIED -a. clearly described; marked; stated. 2. GENERAL -a. of all things

SPECIOUS (SPEE shus): a. Misleading, deceptive; fallacious

    Trigger: 1.SPECIOUS-SUSPECIOUS. 2. SPECIOUS-SPECTACLES

    Trigger Sentence: 1. Political SPEECHES are always SPECIOUS; have a SUSPICIOUS look on them. 2. SPECTACLES are for LOOKS; but LOOKS are usually DECEPTIVE.

    Sample Sentence: Medical doctors always viewed acupuncture as *specious*.

SPECTRUM (SPEK trum): n. Range of colors; broad range of connected ideas or events

    Trigger: SPECTRUM -COLOR SPECTRUM

    Trigger Sentence: A color SPECTRUM consists of broad range of colors.

    Sample Sentence: A rainbow reveals a wide *spectrum* of colors.

SPECULATE (SPEK yuh leyt): v. Theorize, Guess

    Trigger: SPECULATE-PROSPECTS

    Trigger Sentence: Investors SPECULATE about the future PROSPECTS of the share market.

    Sample Sentence: I never *speculated* that one day I will have to leave this city.

SPLENETIC (spli NET ik): a. Irritable; spiteful

    Trigger: SPLENETIC-SPLEEN DISORDER

Trigger Sentence: He became SPLENETIC because of the SPLEEN disorder and pain.

Sample Sentence: The *splenetic* outburst from the public is often a cause of unrest.

SPONTANEOUS (spon TEY nee us): a. Unplanned; instinctive; natural

Trigger: SPONTANEOUS-SPOT- on the SPOT

Trigger Sentence: SPONTANEOUSLY we hired her ON THE SPOT.

Sample Sentence: Though emotions are *spontaneous*, they can be controlled to some extent.

SPORADIC (spuh RAD ik): a. Irregular, fitful, occasional, infrequent

Trigger: SPORADIC-PERIODIC

Trigger Sentence: SPORADIC things occur IRREGULARLY and PERIODIC things occur REGULARLY.

Sample Sentence: John's stomach pain was *sporadic*, so the doctor put him through some tests.

Related Words: SPASMODIC –a. irregular; intermittent

SPURIOUS (SPYOOR ee us): a. False; forged; illogical

Trigger: SPURIOUS-IMPURE

Trigger Sentence: SPURIOUS things are NOT PURE, they are BOGUS.

Sample Sentence: It was a *spurious* Picasso painting that wouldn't have fooled an art expert.

SPURN (SPURN): v. Reject, scorn

Trigger: 1.SPURN-PORN. 2. SPURN- SPIT+TURN

Trigger Sentence: 1. PORN heroine was SPURNED by the public. 2. SPURN is to TURN DOWN or TURN AWAY from someone.

Sample Sentence: The heroine *spurned* the villain's advances.

SQUABBLE (SKWOB uhl): n. A minor quarrel; tiff

Trigger: SQUABBLE-"S + QUARREL"

Trigger Sentence: "SMALL QUARREL" is known as "A SQUABBLE".

Sample Sentence: The fishermen *squabbled* among each other for who should dispatch their catch in the first cargo.

SQUALID (SKWOL id): a. Dirty; unpleasant; morally dirty

Trigger: 1.SQUALID-SORDID-SOILED (** synonyms). 2. SQUALID-SCANDAL

Trigger Sentence: 1. The SOILED youngsters were hanging around SQUALID casinos. 2. The SCANDAL is rather a SQUALID affair.

Sample Sentence: The actress had to initially live in a *squalid* one-bedroom apartment.

SQUALOR (SKWOL er): n. Dirtiness; degradation; filth

Trigger: 1.SQUALOR-SMALL LABOR. 2. SQUALID-SOILED (** synonyms)

Trigger Sentence: 1. LABOR people are identified with lot of SQUALOR. 2. SOILED characters hang around SQUALID casinos.

Sample Sentence: Kolkata was a byword for urban *squalor* and labor unrest.

SQUANDER (SKWON der): v. Waste

Trigger: SQUANDERER-SPENDER

Trigger Sentence: SQUANDERER is a SPENDER who SPENDS excessive money.

Sample Sentence: He *squandered* his entire wife's money by gambling in casinos.

SQUASH (SKWOSH): v. Crush; quell

    Trigger: 1.SQUASH-SQUEEZE. 2. SQUASH-QUASH-CRUSH

    Trigger Sentence: When you prepare lemon SQUASH we CRUSH and SQUEEZE lemon.

    Sample Sentence: The boss *squashed* my idea immediately.

STAID (STAYED): a. Sober, sedate

    Trigger: STAID-STAYED

    Trigger Sentence: The STAID personality STAYED cool and calm.

    Sample Sentence: Jia seeks divorce from her husband only because he was *staid* and boring.

STANCH (STANCH): v. Stop the flow of liquid (**also staunch)

    Trigger: STANCH-STAND

    Trigger Sentence: STANCH is to cause to STAND the blood flow.

    Sample Sentence: The doctor *stanched* the blood flow by stitching up the injury on my head.

    Related Words: STAUNCH -a. steadfast; unwavering

STARK (STAHRK): a. 1. Extreme; 2. Bare, plain, austere; 3. Harsh

    Trigger: STARK-"STAR+DARK"

    Trigger Sentence: STARRY night is in STARK contrast to the DARK night.

    Sample Sentence: The old facade of the building is in *stark* contrast to the modernist interiors.

STARTLE (STAHR tl): v. Surprise suddenly; alarm

    Trigger: STARTLE-START sudden

    Trigger Sentence: SUDDEN START might keep you STARTLED; since SUDDEN START is SHOCKING.

    Sample Sentence: The results will *startle* those who think that children benefit from having a stay-at-home mum.

    Related Words: STARTLING -a. shocking; surprising

STASIS (STEY sis): n. Stoppage

    Trigger: STASIS-STATIC

    Trigger Sentence: STATIC condition is MOTIONLESS; STASIS is also a condition of MOTIONLESS.

    Sample Sentence: The country is in economic *stasis*.

    Related Words: HOMEOSTASIS -n. metabolic equilibrium

STATIC (STAT ik): a. Motionless; unchanging

    Trigger: STATIC-STAY & STICK

    Trigger Sentence: In a STATIC condition the things STAY and STICK/FIX to a particular condition.

    Sample Sentence: The gold prices are likely to remain *static* for some time now.

STATUS QUO (status KWOH): n. Existing state or condition

    Trigger: STATUS QUO- existing STATUS

    Trigger Sentence: The existing STATE of affairs is known as STATUS QUO.

    Sample Sentence: I am content with the *status quo* and do not like change...like known devil better than unknown angel!

Memory Test-101 : Match each word and its memory trick to the corresponding definition.

S.N	WORD	MEMORY TRIGGER	S.N	DEFINITIONS	KEY
1	SENILITY	Senior citizens	A	An instance of fortunate discovery; luck	
2	SENTENTIOUS	Moralistic sentence	B	Avoid (responsibility, work, etc.)	
3	SENTIENT	Sense+ENT	C	Aaware; sensitive	
4	SEQUENTIAL	SEQUENCE	D	Calm; tranquil	
5	SERE	sear-SOARing heat	E	Chain; fetter, manacle	
6	SERENDIPITY	Sudden DIP +ity	F	Cheap, inferior; fake	
7	SERENE	GREEN-scenes	G	Clever; sharp	
8	SERMON	Serious + monk	H	Comparison of one thing with another	
9	SERVILE	SERVE	I	Concise; terse, aphoristic	
10	SEVER	SHAVER severs	J	Cut, separate	
11	SHACKLE	Buckle -obstacle	K	Dry, parched	
12	SHAM	Sham-SCAM- scheme	L	Fragment, generally of pottery	
13	SHARD	SHRED	M	Fraud, fake	
14	SHIRK	Avoid WORK	N	Imitate, pretend	
15	SHODDY	Showy-goes to SHED	O	Keep away from	
16	SHREWD	SHARP dude	P	Old age; feeblemindedness of old age	
17	SHUN	Avoid SUN -shirk	Q	Oversimplified; unrealistically simple	
18	SIMILE	SIMILAR to rose	R	Serious speech, esp. on a moral issue	
19	SIMPLISTIC	Simplified	S	Slavish; subservient	
20	SIMULATE	Imitate-similar	T	Successive, following, consecutive	

Memory Test-102 : Match each word and its memory trick to the corresponding definition.

S.N	WORD	MEMORY TRIGGER	S.N	DEFINITIONS	KEY
1	SINECURE	SECURE job	A	Avoid	
2	SINGULAR	SINGLE never mingle	B	Catch in a trap	
3	SINISTER	Sin-MONSTER	C	Deception, trickery	
4	SINUOUS	SINE (waves)	D	Defamation, false statements	
5	SKEPTIC	SUSPECT	E	Evil	
6	SKETCHY	SKETCH	F	High paid job that needs little effort	
7	SKIRT	SKIP	G	Laziness	
8	SKITTISH	KITTEN nature	H	Lazy person	
9	SKULLDUGGERY	SKULL+ digging	I	Loosen; Slow down	
10	SLANDER	Slang+scandal	J	Neglect; snub	
11	SLATTERNLY	SLIT & TORN dress	K	Nervous; restive	
12	SLACKEN	LACK of tightness	L	Not thorough; incomplete	
13	SLAKE	LAKE -flake	M	Quench; satisfy	
14	SLEIGHT	SMART & BRIGHT	N	Self-satisfied, self-righteous	
15	SLIGHT	Take him LIGHT	O	Skeptical, doubtful	
16	SLOTH	SLOW+th	P	Skill in using hands	
17	SLOVENLY	not LOVELY	Q	Unique; odd; extraordinary	
18	SLUGGARD	Sluggish-SLOWISH	R	Untidy; careless	
19	SMUG	SMUGGLERS nature	S	Untidy; slovenly	
20	SNARE	SNAKE catch	T	Winding, twisting	

Answers	EX.NO	1	2	3	4	5	6	7	8	9	10	11	12	13	14	15	16	17	18	19	20
	101	P	I	C	T	K	A	D	R	S	J	E	M	L	B	F	G	O	H	Q	N
	102	F	Q	E	T	O	L	A	K	C	D	S	I	M	P	J	G	R	H	N	B

Memory Test-103 : Match each word and its memory trick to the corresponding definition.

S.N	WORD	MEMORY TRIGGER	S.N	DEFINITIONS	KEY
1	SOBER	No BEER	A	Able to pay all debts	
2	SODDEN	SOAK+EN	B	Alone; single	
3	SOLEMN	SOLO +MAN	C	Being alone; seclusion	
4	SOLICIT	SOLICITING-SEEKING	D	Concerned; worried	
5	SOLICITOUS	SOUL+ SIT ON US	E	Dirty, filthy; base; ignoble	
6	SOLITARY	SOLO life.	F	Ease; calm	
7	SOLITUDE	SOLO+DUDE	G	Gloomy, depressing	
8	SOLVENT	Money problem is SOLVED	H	Lacking luxury; strictly disciplined	
9	SOMATIC	ROMANTIC feelings	I	Not drunk; calm; serious; drab	
10	SOMBER	After BOMBER attack	J	Physical; of the body	
11	SOMNOLENT	INSOMNIA	K	Resonance	
12	SONOROUS	SNORERS produce	L	Seek; request earnestly	
13	SOOTHE	SMOOTH effect	M	Serious, formal, sincere	
14	SOPHISTICATED	PHILOSOPHERS	N	Sleepy; half-asleep	
15	SOPORIFIC	SLEEPOVER	O	Sleepy; sleep-causing	
16	SORDID	SOILED	P	Soaked; dull, esp. from drink	
17	SPARE	RARE -BARE	Q	Thinly scattered; scanty; not dense	
18	SPARSE	SCARCE	R	Unique; precise; limited	
19	SPARTAN	SPARTA-SPARE-BARE	S	Use frugally, just sufficient	
20	SPECIFIC	SPECIAL	T	Worldly-wise; cultured; complex	

Memory Test-104 : Match each word and its memory trick to the corresponding definition.

S.N	WORD	MEMORY TRIGGER	S.N	DEFINITIONS	KEY
1	SPECIOUS	Be SUSPICIOUS	A	broad range of connected ideas	
2	SPECTRUM	Color spectrum	B	Crush; quell	
3	SPECULATE	PROSPECTS of future	C	Dirtiness; degradation; filth	
4	SPLENETIC	SPLEEN disorder	D	Dirty; unpleasant; morally dirty	
5	SPONTANEOUS	on the SPOT	E	existing state or condition	
6	SPORADIC	Not PERIODIC	F	Extreme; austere; Harsh	
7	SPURIOUS	Not PURE	G	False; forged; illogical	
8	SPURN	SPIT+TURN	H	Irregular, fitful, occasional	
9	SQUABBLE	Small + QUARREL	I	Irritable; spiteful	
10	SQUALID	SOILED	J	minor quarrel; tiff	
11	SQUALOR	Small labor -SOILED	K	Misleading, deceptive; fallacious	
12	SQUANDER	SPENDER	L	Motionless; unchanging	
13	SQUASH	quash-CRUSH	M	Reject, scorn	
14	STAID	STAYED	N	Stop the flow of liquid	
15	STANCH	Stanch-STAND	O	Sedate, Sober	
16	STARK	STAR opp. to DARK	P	Stoppage	
17	STARTLE	START sudden	Q	Surprise suddenly; alarm	
18	STASIS	STATIC	R	Guess, Theorize,	
19	STATIC	STAY & STICK	S	Unplanned; instinctive; natural	
20	STATUS QUO	Existing STATUS	T	Waste	

Answers

EX.NO	1	2	3	4	5	6	7	8	9	10	11	12	13	14	15	16	17	18	19	20
103	I	P	M	L	D	B	C	A	J	G	N	K	F	T	O	E	S	Q	H	R
104	K	A	R	I	S	H	G	M	J	D	C	T	B	O	N	F	Q	P	L	E

WORD GROUPS DAY-26

★ **PARAGON:** model of perfection; ideal
ADJECTIVES: exemplary
NOUNS: apotheosis, archetype, cynosure, epitome, exemplar, paradigm, personification, prototype, quintessence, sublimation
VERB: epitomize , symbolize, personify
ANTONYMS: n. worst

★ **HABITAT:** home, residence
ADJECTIVES: domestic, indoor.
NOUNS: abode, domicile, dwelling, environment, habitation, haunt, haven, purlieu, terrain, territory.
VERB: home
ANTONYMS: n. unnatural surroundings

★ **INVINCIBLE:** undefeatable, unbeatable
ADJECTIVES: impassable, impregnable, indomitable, insuperable, inviolable, invulnerable, unassailable, unconquerable, insurmountable
NOUNS: invincibility
VERB: immunize ,inoculate
ANTONYMS: adj. conquerable, destructible

★ **VULNERABLE :** unprotected; susceptible.
ADJECTIVES: assailable, endangered, exposed, liable, prone to, pregnable, sensitive, susceptible, tender, unprotected
NOUNS: susceptibility, impressionability
VERB: expose; make vulnerable
ANTONYMS: adj. guarded, protected, safe, secure

★ **SUBJUGATE :** (defeat, bring under control)
ADJECTIVES: repressive
NOUNS: subjugation, repression
VERB: conquer, vanquish, defeat, crush, quash, enslave, subdue, subordinate, suppress
ANTONYMS: v. free, liberate

★ **RELINQUISH:** give up, let go
ADJECTIVES: resigned
NOUNS: renunciation
VERB: abandon, abdicate, abnegate, cede, renounce, sacrifice, waive, resign, surrender, yield
ANTONYMS: retain, hold, keep, continue

★ **ABJURE:** renounce upon oath
ADJECTIVES: repudiatory
NOUNS: abjuration
VERB: renounce, relinquish, retract, forgo, disavow, abandon, deny, repudiate, give up, eschew, abstain from, refrain from; forsake, forswear, abnegate
ANTONYMS: affirm, espouse, embrace

★ **WANDER**
ADJECTIVES: ambulatory, peripatetic, rambling, discursive, vagrant, migratory, nomadic
NOUNS: migrant, itinerant, nomad; vagabond, vagrant
VERB: amble, circumambulate, divagate, diverge, loiter, maunder, meander, peregrinate, ramble, saunter, straggle, stray, traipse, tramp, vagabond
ANTONYMS: stay

Word List Day-27

STEADFAST (STED fast): a. Loyal; unchanging

 Trigger: STEADFAST-"STEADY + FAST"

 Trigger Sentence: STEADFAST people are STEADY and maintain STABLE relationships with single lover, single party etc.

 Sample Sentence: We worked *steadfastly* in this factory for over two decades.

STEALTH (STELTH): n. Secret, sneakiness; slyness

 Trigger: STEALTH-"STEAL WEALTH"

 Trigger Sentence: STEAL WEALTH in a STEALTHY and SECRET manner.

 Sample Sentence: I thought those *stealthy* vamps were there only in the stories and TV serials, now Shahi makes a real life one!

STEEP (STEEP): v. Soak; immerse; saturate

 Trigger: STEEP-WEEP

 Trigger Sentence: He STEEPED himself into a WEEPING letter for his lost lover.

 Sample Sentence: He *steeped* himself into those timeless romantic classics.

STELLAR (STEL er): a. Relating to the stars; brilliant

 Trigger: 1. STELLAR-SOLAR (** synonyms). 2. STELLAR-CONSTELLATION

 Trigger Sentence: CONSTELLATION is a configuration of STELLAR bodies.

 Sample Sentence: The film star has given a *stellar* performance.

STENTORIAN (sten TOR ee un): a. Very loud

 Trigger: 1. STENTORIAN-STUNT + ORIAN. 2. STEN GUN. 3. STENTORIAN-TEN TONES

 Trigger Sentence: 1. STEN GUNS made STENTORIAN sounds in STUNT SCENES of a Hollywood movie. 2. TEN TONES simultaneously produced STENTORIAN sound.

 Sample Sentence: Our teacher has a *stentorian* voice, and so he doesn't need a loudspeaker!

STERN (STURN): a. Strict, severe; harsh

 Trigger: STERN-STALIN

 Trigger Sentence: Russian dictator STALIN was a STERN disciplinarian.

 Sample Sentence: 1. The commander gave me a *stern* look. 2. My boss is *stern* authoritarian.

STICKLER (STIK lar): n. Strict disciplinarian; perfectionist

 Trigger: 1. STICKLER-STICK. 2. STICK-STRICT

 Trigger Sentence: 1. STICKLER is one who STICKS to a set of rules, a perfectionist. 2. My boss is a STICKLER and he is very STRICT and STICKS to the rules and regulations.

 Sample Sentence: The track coach was a *stickler* for fitness and preparation.

STIFLE (STAHY ful): v. Suppress; quell; inhibit

 Trigger: 1. STIFLE-STIFF-STILL. 2. STIFLE-RIFLE

 Trigger Sentence: With a RIFLE he STIFLED her voice and made her completely STILL.

 Sample Sentence: She tried hard to *stifle* her yawns during the boring lecture meeting.

STIGMA (STIG muh): n. A symbol of disgrace; brand

Trigger: STIG+MA-"STICK+MARK"

Trigger Sentence: Make faults, I beat you with a STICK; the STICK MARK on your body is STIGMA.

Sample Sentence: The *stigma* of slavery remained long after it had been abolished.

Related Words: STIGMATIZE -v. brand as disgraceful.

STILTED (STIL tid): a. Pompous; artificial; stiff

Trigger: 1. STILTED-STILL style. 2. STILTED-TITLED

Trigger Sentence: 1. The model's STYLE in the STILL for magazine ad was STILTED (artificial). 2. The TITLED (Like- Sir. Dr. Sr.) people conversation usually bears a STILTED tone.

Sample Sentence: The speaker made *stilted* remarks which were anything but meaningful!

STINT (STINT): v. Set limits, be frugal

Trigger: 1. STINT-STRICT. 2. STINT-STRICT-RESTRICT

Trigger Sentence: 1. Father is STRICT and RESTRICTS. 2. STRICT parents LIMIT or RESTRICT kids.

Sample Sentence: When I was young, I gave a restrained *stint* as a model and soon gave up!

STIPULATE (STIP yuh leyt): v. Specify; make express conditions

Trigger: 1. STIPULATE-SPECIFICATE-SPECIFY. 2. STIPULATION-SPECIFICATION

Trigger Sentence: STIPULATE and SPECIFICATE (to specify conditions) are synonyms.

Sample Sentence: The rules *stipulate* that players must wear uniforms.

STOIC (STOH ik): a. Impassive; unmoved by joy or passion

Trigger: STOIC-"STONE LIKE"

Trigger Sentence: "STONE-LIKE"--> Just like a STONE; no pain, no emotions; nonchalant.

Sample Sentence: Ann appeared *stoic* in defeat, but she cried like a baby in her privacy.

STOLID (STAHL id): a. Unemotional, impassive; dull

Trigger: STOLID-SOLID; ROCK SOLID

Trigger Sentence: NO FLUID from his eyes; he is SOLID and STOLID; no emotions.

Sample Sentence: With almost *stolid* expression, the laid-back police officer listened to her sad encounter with her assailants.

STRATAGEM (STRAT uh juhm): n. Clever trick; deceptive scheme

Trigger: STRATAGEM-STRATEGY

Trigger Sentence: 1. STRATEGY and STRATAGEM are synonyms. 2. In chess, STRATEGIES are applied to DECEIVE the opponent.

Sample Sentence: The bank tried varied stratagems to get out of the financial mismanagement.

Related Words: STRATEGIC -a. tactical, politic

STRATIFY (STRAT uh fye): v. Arrange into layer; divide into classes

Trigger: 1. STRAT-STAT. 2. STRATIFY- CLASSIFY. 3. STRAT- STRAIGHT (LAYER)

Trigger Sentence: 1. A STATISTICIAN STRATIFIES or CLASSIFIES the list of names according to the "CASTES". 2. STRAIGHT LAYERS; layer by layer CLASSIFY; geologist can do that.

Sample Sentence: 1. Income distribution often *stratifies* a society. 2. The geological rock formation showed *stratified* areas.

STRICTURE (STRIK cher): n. Restriction; severe criticism

    Trigger: 1. STRICTURE-STRICT SIR. 2. STRICTURE-"STRICT LECTURE"

    Trigger Sentence: 1. My STRICT SIR applied many STRICTURES/RESTRICTIONS in the class room. 2. In a STRICT LECTURE he voiced STRICTURES on morals and mores of society.

    Sample Sentence: The cinema critic made a few *strictures* on the young directors' debut film.

STRIDENT (STRYD nt): a. Loud and harsh; insistent

    Trigger: STRIDENT-STRIKE + DENT

    Trigger Sentence: If you STRIKE a car to make a DENT, it is going to produce a STRIDENT sound.

    Sample Sentence: The new band needs more practice to sound less *strident*.

STRIFE (STRYFE): n. Conflict, discord

    Trigger: STRIFE-STRIKE

    Trigger Sentence: Students are on STRIKE, since there is STRIFE (fight) with the college principal.

    Sample Sentence: It is their personal family *strife* that we should not get into.

STRINGENT (STRIN junt): a. Binding; rigid

    Trigger: STRINGENT-"STRICT+GENT"

    Trigger Sentence: A STRICT GENT nature is STRINGENT; Very STRICT in maintaining regulations.

    Sample Sentence: Military colleges have *stringent* rules of conduct.

STRIVE (STRIVE): v. Try hard; compete

    Trigger: 1.STRIVE-STRONG DRIVE. 2. STRIVE-TRY hard (** synonyms)

    Trigger Sentence: With a STRONG DRIVE she always STRIVED for perfection.

    Sample Sentence: This Company will *strive* for excellence in service delivery.

STUDIED (STUD eed): a. Deliberate; not spontaneous; carefully practiced

    Trigger: STUDIED –steady STUDY

    Trigger Sentence: After carefully STUDYING the repercussions, he has given a STUDIED reply.

    Sample Sentence: The boss gave a *studied* approval to my proposal.

    Related Words: UNSTUDIED –a. natural; not spontaneous; not learned

STULTIFY (STUHL tuh fie): v. Make useless; cause to appear stupid; frustrate

    Trigger: STULT-STUPID-STUN

    Trigger Sentence: STULTIFY is to make someone STUPID (stupefy-refer) and USELESS; STULTIFY is to make someone STUN.

    Sample Sentence: 1.The government has been *stultified* by political dramas. 2. Their behavior *stultified* the boss's hard work.

STUPEFY (STOO puh fie): v. Stun, make senseless

    Trigger: 1. STUP-STUN. 2. STUP-STUPID

    Trigger Sentence: To STUN is to make STUPEFIED; to make STUPID is to make STUPEFIED.

Sample Sentence: The magician's trick *stupefied* the audience.

Related Words: STUPOR –n. unconscious state; apathy

STYGIAN (STIJ ee un): n. Dark; hellish

Trigger: STYGIAN-SATAN

Trigger Sentence: A SATAN made my life STYGIAN.

Sample Sentence: I got lost in the *stygian* chilling cave with stinking bats and striking lizards!

STYMIE (STY mee): v. Hold back; hinder

Trigger: STYMIE-"TIE ME"

Trigger Sentence: He STYMIED me; with a rope around my legs he TIED ME.

Sample Sentence: The central government *stymied* the use of internet in prisons.

SUAVE (SWAHV): v. Sophisticated; smooth

Trigger: SUAVE- NAÏVE (** near antonyms)

Trigger Sentence: A NAÏVE man does not know how to behave in SUAVE fashion.

Sample Sentence: She is blue-blooded, *suave* and sophisticated.

SUBDUE (sub DOO): v. Overcome, defeat; gain control over

Trigger: SUBDUE-SUB-"SUBORDINATE"

Trigger Sentence: SUBORDINATE can easily be SUBDUED

Sample Sentence: 1. "Goddess Durga *subdued* the demons to prevail peace…". 2. Alexis' soothing words *subdued* the child's fear.

Related Words: SUBDUED -a. defeated; submissive; reduced in intensity.

SUBJECTIVE (sub JEK tiv): a. Influenced by personal feelings or opinions; biased, prejudiced

Trigger: SUBJECTIVE-SUBJECT (thing or person)

Trigger Sentence: If you are NONOBJECTIVE/ SUBJECTIVE you are interested in PERSONAL matters; you will say I'm INTERESTED in this SUBJECT or INTERESTED in another SUBJECT.

Sample Sentence: In reviewing applicants, we consider both objective and *subjective* criteria.

Related Words: SUBJECTIVELY -v. based on individual thoughts and feelings

SUBJUGATE (SUB ju geyt): v. Conquer, bring into submission

Trigger: SUBJUGATE-SUBDUE-SUB-SUBORDINATE (** synonyms)

Trigger Sentence: The government SUBDUED/SUBJUGATED/SUBORDINATED the rebellion.

Sample Sentence: Alexander *subjugated* many empires.

SUBLIME (suh BLYME): n. Noble; awesome

Trigger: 1.SUBLIME-PRIME. 2. SUBLIME-SUPREME

Trigger Sentence: 1. PRIME minister is in SUBLIME stage. 2. SUBLIME things are SUPREME.

Sample Sentence: The priest's *sublime* voice and sermon made him the object of reverence.

Related Words: 1.SUBLIMINAL –a. Below the threshold; imperceptible .2. SUBLIMATE –v. Purify; direct energy into useful activities

SUBMISSIVE (sub MIS iv): a. Yielding; meek

    Trigger: SUBMISSIVE-SUB (** subordinate)

    Trigger Sentence: My SUB is always SUBMISSIVE.

    Sample Sentence: The manager replaced fractious workers with *submissive* employees.

SUBORDINATE (sub BOR duh nit): v. Make subservient; dominate

    Trigger: make SUBORDINATE

    Trigger Sentence: The superior man SUBORDINATED the weaker people

    Sample Sentence: My *subordinates* are hard working since I take good care of them.

SUBPOENA (sub PEE nuh): n. A writ order summoning a witness to appear

    Trigger: SUBPOENA-"SUB +PENAL"

    Trigger Sentence: SUBORDINATE receives SUBPOENA from court in a PENAL offense.

    Sample Sentence: The judiciary sent a *subpoena* to the witness to attend the court.

SUBSERVIENT (SUB sur vee unt): a. Subordinate; behaving like a slave; obsequious

    Trigger: SUBSERVIENT-SUB + SERVANT

    Trigger Sentence: He is a SUBSERVIENT SERVANT to the party bosses.

    Sample Sentence: My mother was always like a *subservient* to my bossy father.

SUBSIDE (sub SYDE): v. Become less intense; decline

    Trigger: SUBSIDE-SUBTRACT ONE SIDE

    Trigger Sentence: When we SUBTRACT one SIDE- it SUBSIDES.

    Sample Sentence: The doctor assured us that the pain would eventually *subside*.

SUBSIDIARY (sub SID ee er ee): a. Secondary, lesser in importance

    Trigger: SUBSIDIARY-SUB+SECONDARY

    Trigger Sentence: All SECONDARY things are called SUBSIDIARIES.

    Sample Sentence: Hockey remains a *subsidiary* sport as against cricket in our country.

SUBSIDY (SUB si dee): n. Financial assistance; support

    Trigger: SUBSIDY-SUBSISTENCE-SUBSTANCE

    Trigger Sentence: Government gives SUBSISTENCE - SUBSIDY to the poor.

    Sample Sentence: Government offers *subsidies* for farmers in case of crop failure.

    Related Words: SUBSIDIZE -v. provide financial assistance.

SUBSTANTIAL (sub STAN shul): a. Important; considerable; ample

    Trigger: 1. SUBSTANTIAL-SUBSTANCE. 2. SUBSTANTIAL-ESSENTIAL

    Trigger Sentence: Keep on adding SUBSTANCE, to make it SUBSTANTIAL and ESSENTIAL.

    Sample Sentence: A *substantial* number of people commute to work through metros.

    Related Words: SUBSTANTIATE -v. prove, strengthen

SUBSUME (sub SOOM): v. Include; encompass

    Trigger: SUBSUME- SUB+SUM

    Trigger Sentence: All SUB colors like red, yellow, green and blue are SUMMED up and SUBSUMED under the term "color".

    Sample Sentence: The new Word Wizard book *subsumes* the content from the earlier version.

SUBTERFUGE (SUB ter fyooj): n. Deception; ruse

    Trigger: 1.REFUGEE .2. SUBTERFUGE- it is a RUSE (** synonyms)

    Trigger Sentence: The REFUGEES escaped from the country by a SUBTERFUGE/RUSE.

    Sample Sentence: The drug dealer managed to *subterfuge* the police to escape.

SUBTLE (SUT ul): a. Difficult to perceive: obscure; fine; clever

    Trigger: 1. SUBTLE-SUBTITLE. 2. SUBTLE- SUB TELL

    Trigger Sentence: 1. Without SUBTITLES the English movie is SUBTLE for the commoner to understand. 2. "SUB+TELL"UNDERHANDED way of TELLING or EXPRESSING is also known as SUBTLE sense.

    Sample Sentence: 1.*Subtle* yet expressive, the classical dancer had her own individualistic style of performance. 2. Jenny's way of flirting with her eyes was *subtle*.

    Related Words: SUBTLETY -n. ingenuity; delicacy; perceptiveness

SUBVERT (sub VURT): v. Overthrow; undermine the power of authority

    Trigger: 1.SUBVERT-INVERT-REVERT. 2. SUBMARINE

    Trigger Sentence: 1. SUBVERT is to INVERT or REVERT an established government. 2. SUBMARINES are usually employed by Nations to SUBVERT the other countries.

    Sample Sentence: Do not *subvert* your enemy's power, just be cautious.

    Related Words: SUBVERSIVE -a. disruptive

SUCCINCT (sek SINGKT): a. Brief; terse; compact

    Trigger: SUCCINCT-SHORT CUT

    Trigger Sentence: SUCCINCT is to express in a SHORT CUT fashion.

    Sample Sentence: The attorneys had a *succinct* discussion before the hearing.

SUCCOR (SUCK ur): n. /v. Aid, assist; support

    Trigger: 1. SUCCOR-SUPPOR-SUPPORT. 2. SUCCOR-SECURE

    Trigger Sentence: 1. Replace "cc" with "pp" to get meaning. 2. SUCCOR is to give a SECURE life.

    Sample Sentence: The volunteers *succored* the wounded victims of the hurricane.

SUCCUMB (suh KUM): v. Yield; die

    Trigger: SUCCUMB- SUCK UNDER- SURRENDER (** synonyms)

    Trigger Sentence: They finally SUCCUMBED when a strong rip tide SUCKED their boat UNDER.

    Sample Sentence: Thousands of cows have *succumbed* to the disease.

SUFFRAGE (SUF rij): n. The right to vote

    Trigger: SUFFRAGE-"SUPER-AGE"

    Trigger Sentence: After we reach SUPER-AGE (after teenage) we get SUFFRAGE/voting right.

    Sample Sentence: Kathryn learned about the women's *suffrage* movement, which gave women the right to vote.

SULLEN (SUH lun): a. Gloomy, Silently Angry

    Trigger: SULLEN-SWOLLEN (EYES)

    Trigger Sentence: With SWOLLEN eyes the guy looks quite SULLEN and SAD.

    Sample Sentence: Bill's roommate became quite *sullen* when Rick reminded him he hadn't paid his share of the rent.

SULLY (SUHL ee): v. Dirty; tarnish

    Trigger: SULLY-SOILY (** synonyms)

    Trigger Sentence: My dissolute son SOILED/SULLIED our family reputation.

    Sample Sentence: Indian cricket team league's name has been *sullied* by match fixings.

SUNDRY (SUN dree): a. Various, miscellaneous

    Trigger: SUNDRY-"SUNDAY-LAUNDRY"

    Trigger Sentence: On a SUNDAY my LAUNDRY is full of SUNDRY garments ready for cleansing.

    Sample Sentence: The provisional store is full of *sundry* stuff.

SUMPTUOUS (SUMP choo us): a. Rich, lavish

    Trigger: SUMPTUOUS- SUM

    Trigger Sentence: If you have lot of SUM; you can buy SUMPTUOUS cloths for yourself.

    Sample Sentence: My friend Neil treated me with a *sumptuous* Italian lunch at the restaurant.

SUPERCILIOUS (soo per SIL ee us): a. Arrogant, condescending, patronizing

    Trigger: 1. SUPERCILIOUS-SUPER SENIORS. 2. SUPERCILIOUS-SUPERIORITY

    Trigger Sentence: 1. Our SUPER SENIORS are SUPERCILIOUS. 2. Your SUPERCILIOUS behavior reflects your SUPERIORITY feelings.

    Sample Sentence: Albert's *supercilious* behavior made him unpopular among the players.

SUPERFICIAL (soo pur FISH ul): a. Not thorough; shallow, trivial

    Trigger: SUPERFICIAL-SURFICIAL (SURFACE)

    Trigger Sentence: If you only look at the SURFACE, you will understand things SUPERFICIALLY.

    Sample Sentence: Fortunately, Nancy's injuries were *superficial*, minor scrapes and bruises.

SUPERFLUOUS (soo PUR floo us): a. Excessive; overabundant, unnecessary

    Trigger: SUPERFLUOUS-"SUPER+FLOWS"

    Trigger Sentence: Rain water is SUPERFLUOUS to ocean. It already OVERFLOWS with water.

    Sample Sentence: His language is *superfluous* and dramatic not good for journalism.

SUPERLATIVE (suh PUR lu tiv): a. Superb; best

    Trigger: SUPERLATIVE-SUPER LAD

    Trigger Sentence: The SUPER LAD did a SUPERLATIVE/SUPERB performance in the dancing show.

    Sample Sentence: Michal Jackson's *superlative* shows can't be superseded by others.

SUPERSEDE (soo pur SEED): v. Take the place of; supplant

    Trigger: SUPERSEDE-SUPERCEDE-SUPER+SEED

    Trigger Sentence: 1. The SUPER SEED has only to SUPERSEDE one more player to win the championship. 2. A TOP SEEDED player never CONCEDES defeat; he always SUCCEEDS.

    Sample Sentence: Former stars were being *superseded* by younger actors.

SUPINE (soo PYNE): a. Lying on the back; passive

    Trigger: SUPINE-SPINE

Trigger Sentence: Though SPINE is located SUPINE, it plays a role in maintaining body posture.

Sample Sentence: He stayed *supine* for months after hurting his back in a horse riding accident.

SUPPLANT (suh PLANT): v. Replace; usurp

Trigger: SUPPLANT-UP PLANT

Trigger Sentence: When season changes, we SUPPLANT old PLANTS with new PLANTS.

Sample Sentence: Bolsheviks uprooted the Czar and *supplanted* feudalism from Russia.

SUPPLICATE (SUP li keyt): v. Ask or beg humbly

Trigger: SUPPLICATE-SUPPLY CAKE

Trigger Sentence: The philanthropist regularly SUPPLIES CAKE to SUPPLICANTS.

Sample Sentence: The bishop *supplicated* his town people to help the victims of the earthquake.

Related Words: SUPPLIANT –a. entreating; beseeching

SUPPOSITION (sup uh ZISH un): n. Hypothesis; assumption

Trigger: 1. SUPPOSITION-SUPPOSE. 2. SUPPOSITION-ASSUMPTION

Trigger Sentence: 1. 'SUPPOSE' is the 'verb' form whereas its 'noun' form is 'SUPPOSITION'. 2. Every business starts with an ASSUMPTION. Every invention starts with a SUPPOSITION.

Sample Sentence: The earlier *supposition* that the earth was flat was proven false.

SUPPRESS (suh PRES): v. Stifle; subdue; inhibit

Trigger: SUPPRESS-SUB + PRESS

Trigger Sentence: The national PRESS is SUPPRESSING the news.

Sample Sentence: Sarada *suppressed* her emotions and pain and refuses to share.

SURFEIT (SUR fit): n. /v. Overindulge; oversupply; satiate

Trigger: 1.SURFEIT-SIR+FAT. 2. SURFEIT-SURPLUS

Trigger Sentence: 1. My SIR SURFEITS his FAT body. 2. My FAT SIR eats SURPLUS food.

Sample Sentence: What will you do with all this *surfeit* of raw substance in your factory?

SURLY (SUR lee): a. Rude; irritable

Trigger: SURLY-"SUR-SIR" LI

Trigger Sentence: 1. Many of our SIRS are SURLY in nature. 2. JET LI acted as a SURLY villain in Lethal Weapon movie.

Sample Sentence: Earlier I found him to be somewhat *surly*, but now he is boorishly loud.

SURMISE (sur MIZE): v. Guess

Trigger: SURMISE-SIR WISE

Trigger Sentence: My WISE SIR SURMISED that I was not interested in studies.

Sample Sentence: In medieval period people *surmised* many theories about the sunrise.

SURMOUNT (ser MOUNT): v. Overcome (a difficulty)

Trigger: SURMOUNT-MOUNT

Trigger Sentence: Human spirit could even SURMOUNTED the MOUNT Everest.

Sample Sentence: The workshop let the students identify their skills and *surmount* their fears.

Related Words: INSURMOUNTABLE -a. can't be overcome, can't be defeated.

SURPASS (ser PAS): a. Exceed

> **Trigger:** PASS BEYOND; SURPASS-OVERPASS
>
> **Trigger Sentence:** 1. Ussian Bolt PASSED beyond and SURPASSED everyone.2. If we increase the pace of our sledge, we will SURPASS others behind and reach the PASSAGE first.
>
> **Sample Sentence:** Her performance in the college *surpassed* beyond expectations.

SURREAL (suh REE ul): a. Strange, unreal

> **Trigger:** SURREAL-UNREAL-NOT REAL
>
> **Trigger Sentence:** Modern art is SURREAL in nature. It does NOT reflect REAL ideas.
>
> **Sample Sentence:** There is a *surreal* quality to Jane's paintings; her flowers look real and unreal!

SURREPTITIOUS (sur ep TISH us): a. Secret, hidden, furtive

> **Trigger:** 1. SURREPTITIOUS-SUSPICIOUS. 2. SURREPTITIOUS- SOME REPTILES
>
> **Trigger Sentence:** 1. SOME REPTILES like rattle snakes live SURREPTITIOUS life.
> 2. His SURREPTITIOUS nature has made everyone SUSPICIOUS of his moves.
>
> **Sample Sentence:** Helen *surreptitiously* crept around the car so that to get the cat out from under it.

SURROGATE (SUR uh git): n. Substitute

> **Trigger:** SURROGATE-SUBROGATE-SUBSTITUTE
>
> **Trigger Sentence:** SURROGATE mothers are SUBSTITUTE mothers.
>
> **Sample Sentence:** A *surrogate* mother is a woman who agrees to bear a child for someone else.

SUSCEPTIBLE (suh SEP tuh bul): a. Easily influenced; having little resistance; vulnerable

> **Trigger:** 1.SUSCEPTIBLE-ACCEPTING .2.SUSCEPTIBLE-SEPTIC
>
> **Trigger Sentence:** 1. A SUSCEPTIBLE person tends to ACCEPT everybody's suggestions without SUSPECTING. 2. He is SUSCEPTIBLE to SEPTIC infection.
>
> **Sample Sentence:** The virus can infect *susceptible* individuals.

SUSTAIN (suh STEYN): v. Nourish, support; Experience

> **Trigger:** SUSTAIN -MAINTAIN
>
> **Trigger Sentence:** MAINTAIN and SUSTAIN are synonym variants. If you want to SUSTAIN in politics, you need to MAINTAIN wide range contacts.
>
> **Sample Sentence:** Only faith and hope *sustained* us during those difficult times.

SWAY (SWEY): v. Influence, affect; swing

> **Trigger:** SWAY-swing WAY
>
> **Trigger Sentence:** Whenever you SWING curvy body, he follows whichever WAY you go. You hold such a SWAY over him.
>
> **Sample Sentence:** Elders *swing* towards spiritualism while the young *sway* towards materialism.

SWERVE (SWURV): v. Turn abruptly, deviate

> **Trigger:** SWERVE-CURVE
>
> **Trigger Sentence:** When there is a CURVE you will have to SWERVE.
>
> **Sample Sentence:** He lost control of the car and swerved toward a tree.
>
> Related Words: UNSWERVING-a. steady; not fickle; straight

SWINDLE (SWIN dl): v. Cheat

Trigger: SWINDLE-SMUGGLE; SWINDLER-SMUGGLER

Trigger Sentence: 1. She SMUGGLED cigarettes across boarder by SWINDLING.
2. BUNDLE of money DWINDLED because someone has SWINDLED.

Sample Sentence: She was gullible and trusting, an easy victim for the *swindler* who came along.

SYBARITE (SIB er ite): n. Lover of luxury

Trigger: 1. SYBAR-BAR.2. SYBARITE-CIGAR+LIGHT

Trigger Sentence: 1. He is a SYBARITE and he spends most of his time in a BAR.
2. He is a SYBARITE. He studded his CIGAR LIGHT with a diamond.

Sample Sentence: The prince was remembered as a self-indulgent *sybarite*, not as a warrior.

SYCOPHANT (SIK uh funt): a. Servile flatterer; toady

Trigger: SYCOPHANT –SICK OF FANS

Trigger Sentence: Madonna was SICK of SYCOPHANT FANS; who wanted her to striptease.

Sample Sentence: Sam is *sycophant,* a self-seeker trying to win favor by flattering the influential.

SYLVAN (SIL vun): a. Relating to wooded regions; forest like

Trigger: SYLVAN-SILICON

Trigger Sentence: In SILICON VALLEY there are NO SYLVAN areas; SYLVAN VALLEY is WOODED JUNGLE where as SILICON VALLEY is a CONCRETE JUNGLE.

Sample Sentence: My great grand parents settled in those thick *sylvan* hinterlands of Andaman Islands in the early 19th century.

SYMBIOSIS (sim bee OH sis): n. Two different species living together and both benefit from this

Trigger: SYMBIOSIS –SAME+ BIOLOGICAL SIS

Trigger Sentence: The SYMBIOSIS with my BIOLOGICAL SIS helped both of us grow spiritually.

Sample Sentence: This book explores the literary *symbiosis* of languages from across continents.

SYMBOLIC (sim BOL ik): a. Representative, figurative; related to a symbol

Trigger: SYMBOLIC-SYMBOL

Trigger Sentence: SYMBOLIC representation is characterized by the use of SYMBOLS.

Sample Sentence: The poet *symbolically* used changing seasons as a backdrop for his mood swinging love lyrics.

SYMPATHY (SIM puh thee): n. Sharing of same feelings

Trigger: 1. SYMPATHY-ANTIPATHY (*antonyms).2.SYMPATHY-SAME PITY

Trigger Sentence: Don't show SYMPATHY, its fine; but don't develop ANTIPATHY against me.

Sample Sentence: 1. His *sympathies* were always with the underdog. 2. *Sympathetic* understanding of ones ethnicities and beliefs is necessary for anthropological studies.

Related Words: 1.SYMPATHETIC -a. compassionate, likable .2.EMPATHY –n. sympathy

Memory Test-105 : Match each word and its memory trick to the corresponding definition.

S.N	WORD	MEMORY TRIGGER	S.N	DEFINITIONS	KEY
1	STEADFAST	STEADY + fast	A	Arrange into layer; divide into classes	
2	STEALTH	STEAL wealth	B	Binding; rigid	
3	STEEP	STEEP into WEEP	C	Clever trick; deceptive scheme	
4	STELLAR	CONSTELLATION	D	Conflict, discord	
5	STENTORIAN	STEN gun- ten tones	E	Impassive; unmoved by joy or passion	
6	STERN	STALIN nature	F	Loud and harsh; insistent	
7	STICKLER	Stick-STRICT	G	Unchanging; loyal	
8	STIFLE	STIFF-rifle	H	Pompous; artificial; stiff	
9	STIGMA	Stick+MARK	I	Relating to the stars; brilliant	
10	STILTED	STILL style	J	Restriction; severe criticism	
11	STINT	strict-RESTRICT	K	Secret, sneakiness; slyness	
12	STIPULATE	Specificate-specify	L	Set limits, be frugal	
13	STOIC	STONE like	M	Soak; immerse; saturate	
14	STOLID	rock SOLID	N	Specify; make express conditions	
15	STRATAGEM	STRATEGY	O	Strict disciplinarian; perfectionist	
16	STRATIFY	Stat -CLASSIFY	P	Strict, severe; harsh	
17	STRICTURE	STRICT sir	Q	Suppress; quell; inhibit	
18	STRIDENT	Strike + DENT	R	Symbol of disgrace; brand	
19	STRIFE	On STRIKE	S	Unemotional, impassive; dull	
20	STRINGENT	STRICT+GENT	T	Very loud	

Memory Test-106 : Match each word and its memory trick to the corresponding definition.

S.N	WORD	MEMORY TRIGGER	S.N	DEFINITIONS	KEY
1	STRIVE	STRONG DRIVE	A	Based on personal feelings; biased	
2	STUDIED	steady STUDY	B	Become less intense; decline	
3	STULTIFY	STUPID-STUN	C	Conquer, bring into submission	
4	STUPEFY	STUN-STUPID	D	Deliberate; not spontaneous	
5	STYGIAN	SATAN	E	Financial assistance; support	
6	STYMIE	TIE ME	F	Hellish ;Dark	
7	SUAVE	Not NAÏVE	G	Hold back; hinder	
8	SUBDUE	Make him SUB	H	Important; considerable; ample	
9	SUBJECTIVE	SUBJECT (thing or person)	I	Include; encompass	
10	SUBJUGATE	Make him SUB	J	Make subservient; dominate	
11	SUBLIME	PRIME -SUPREME	K	Make useless; cause to appear stupid	
12	SUBMISSIVE	SUB (subordinate)	L	Noble; awesome	
13	SUBORDINATE	make SUBORDINATE	M	Overcome, defeat; gain control over	
14	SUBPOENA	SUB +PENAL	N	Secondary, lesser in importance	
15	SUBSERVIENT	SUB + SERVANT	O	Sophisticated; smooth	
16	SUBSIDE	SUBTRACT ONE SIDE	P	Stun, make senseless	
17	SUBSIDIARY	SUB+SECONDARY	Q	Subordinate; behaving like a slave	
18	SUBSIDY	Give SUBSTANCE	R	Try hard; compete	
19	SUBSTANTIAL	ESSENTIAL	S	Writ order summoning a witness to appear	
20	SUBSUME	SUB+SUM-consume	T	Yielding; meek	

Answers	EX.NO	1	2	3	4	5	6	7	8	9	10	11	12	13	14	15	16	17	18	19	20
	105	G	K	M	I	T	P	O	Q	R	H	L	N	E	S	C	A	J	F	D	B
	106	R	D	K	P	F	G	O	M	A	C	L	T	J	S	Q	B	N	E	H	I

Memory Test-107 : Match each word and its memory trick to the corresponding definition.

S.N	WORD	MEMORY TRIGGER	S.N	DEFINITIONS	KEY
1	SUBTERFUGE	REFUGEE escapes	A	Aid, assist; support	
2	SUBTLE	Subtitle- SUB TELL	B	Arrogant, condescending	
3	SUBVERT	Invert-REVERT- Submarine	C	Ask or beg humbly	
4	SUCCINCT	Short CUT	D	Brief; terse; compact	
5	SUCCOR	Support-SECURE	E	Deception; ruse	
6	SUCCUMB	SUCK UNDER	F	Dirty; tarnish	
7	SUFFRAGE	Super-age	G	Excessive; unnecessary	
8	SULLEN	SWOLLEN (eyes)	H	Gloomy, Silently Angry	
9	SULLY	SOILY	I	Hypothesis; assumption	
10	SUMPTUOUS	Sumptuous- sum	J	Lying on the back; passive	
11	SUNDRY	Sunday-LAUNDRY	K	Not thorough; shallow, trivial	
12	SUPERCILIOUS	SUPERIORITY	L	Obscure; fine; clever	
13	SUPERFICIAL	SURFICIAL –SURFACE	M	Overthrow; undermine the power	
14	SUPERFLUOUS	Super+FLOWS	N	Replace; usurp	
15	SUPERLATIVE	SUPER LAD	O	Rich, lavish	
16	SUPERSEDE	super+seed-succeed	P	Superb; best	
17	SUPINE	Lie on SPINE	Q	Take the place of; supplant	
18	SUPPLANT	UP PLANT	R	The right to vote	
19	SUPPLICATE	Please SUPPLY CAKE	S	Various, miscellaneous	
20	SUPPOSITION	assumption	T	Yield; die	

Memory Test-108 : Match each word and its memory trick to the corresponding definition.

S.N	WORD	MEMORY TRIGGER	S.N	DEFINITIONS	KEY
1	SUPPRESS	Sub + PRESS	A	A cooperative relationship	
2	SURFEIT	Sir+fat -SURPLUS	B	Cheat	
3	SURLY	SIR LI	C	Easily influenced; vulnerable	
4	SURMISE	Sir WISE	D	Exceed	
5	SURMOUNT	MOUNT the problem	E	figurative; related to a symbol	
6	SURPASS	Pass beyond	F	Guess	
7	SURREAL	unreal-not real	G	Influence, affect; swing	
8	SURREPTITIOUS	some REPTILES	H	Lover of luxury	
9	SURROGATE	substitute	I	Nourish, support; Experience	
10	SUSCEPTIBLE	Accepting -SEPTIC	J	Overcome (a difficulty)	
11	SUSTAIN	MAINTAIN	K	Overindulge; oversupply; satiate	
12	SWAY	swing WAY	L	Relating to wooded regions; forest like	
13	SWERVE	CURVE	M	Rude; irritable	
14	SWINDLE	SMUGGLE	N	Secret, hidden, furtive	
15	SYBARITE	BAR loving	O	Servile flatterer; toady	
16	SYCOPHANT	Sick of fans	P	Sharing of same feelings	
17	SYLVAN	No SILICON valley	Q	Stifle; subdue; inhibit	
18	SYMBIOSIS	Same+ biological sis	R	Strange, unreal	
19	SYMBOLIC	Symbol	S	Substitute	
20	SYMPATHY	SAME PITY	T	Turn abruptly, deviate	

Answers EX.NO	1	2	3	4	5	6	7	8	9	10	11	12	13	14	15	16	17	18	19	20
107	E	L	M	D	A	T	R	H	F	O	S	B	K	G	P	Q	J	N	C	I
108	Q	K	M	F	J	D	R	N	S	C	I	G	T	B	H	O	L	A	E	P

WORD GROUPS DAY-27

★ **EMANCIPATE:** free from slavery

ADJECTIVES: liberatory

NOUNS: manumission

VERB: discharge, enfranchise, liberate, manumit, unfetter

ANTONYMS: hold, imprison, incarcerate

★ **LATITUDE:** freedom of thought or action, liberty

ADJECTIVES: independent, unrestrained

NOUNS: leeway, flexibility, liberty, license

VERB:

ANTONYMS: restriction

★ **IMPRISON** (put in jail, constrain)

ADJECTIVES:

NOUNS: incarceration, detention

VERB: apprehend, circumscribe, closet, constrain, detain, fetter, immure, impound, incarcerate, occlude, remand, restrain, shackle, trammel

ANTONYMS: v. free, let go, release

★ **IMMINENT** (about to happen)

ADJECTIVES: impending, proximate, near, forthcoming, expected, anticipated, looming; unavoidable

NOUNS: imminence

VERB: impend

ANTONYMS: adj. distant, doubtful, far, later

★ **SILENT –SILENCE**

ADJECTIVES: hushed, inaudible; quiet, mute, reticent, taciturn, secretive, tight-lipped; tacit, implicit

NOUNS:

VERB: quietude, tranquility; taciturnity; reticence

ANTONYMS: adj. audible, noisy

★ **BOISTEROUS** (Noisy, Wild)

ADJECTIVES: clamorous, impetuous, obstreperous, rambunctious, raucous, riotous, tumultuous, unrestrained, unruly, uproarious, vociferous

NOUNS: turbulence

VERB: clamor

ANTONYMS: adj. calm, quiet, restrained, silent

★ **DORMANT** (Inactive, Sleeping)

ADJECTIVES: abeyant, comatose, fallow, inert, latent, lethargic, lurking, passive, potential, quiescent, sluggish, slumbering, torpid

NOUNS: quiescence, hibernation, repose

VERB: vegetate, languish, laze

ANTONYMS: adj. active, lively

★ **SPEED-ALERT**

ADJECTIVES: agile, brisk, nimble, swift

NOUNS: alacrity, celerity, immediacy, speed

VERB: bolt, dart, gallop, hurtle, scurry, scuttle, scamper, hasten

ANTONYMS: v. dawdle, slow, leisurely; decelerate, procrastinate, postpone

Word List Day-28

SYNCHRONOUS (SING kruh nus): a. Similarly timed; simultaneous with

    Trigger: SYNC

    Trigger Sentence: As their minds SYNC perfectly, Watson and Crick presented a new SYNCHRONOUS theory on the structure of DNA.

    Sample The drug produces an increased *synchrony* of the brain waves.

SYNERGY (SIN er jee): n. Combined action

    Trigger: SYNERGY-SYNC+ENERGY

    Trigger Sentence: There is more ENERGY when the two groups SYNC; that is called SYNERGY.

    Sample Sentence: We see considerable *synergy* in the merger of the two business houses.

SYNOPTIC (si NOP tik): a. Providing a general overview, summary

    Trigger: SYNOPTIC-SYNOPSIS

    Trigger Sentence: Since I got no time to read, give me a SYNOPTIC report of the events.

    Sample Sentence: We were asked to submit a *synoptic* summation of a voluminous text.

SYNTHESIS (SIN thuh sis): n. Combination of parts to make whole

    Trigger: SYNTHESIS-SYNDICATE

    Trigger Sentence: For a perfect SYNTHESIS of ideas a large bank SYNDICATE has been formed.

    Sample Sentence: Water can be *synthesized* from oxygen and hydrogen gas.

TABOO (ta BOO): n. Prohibition; ban

    Trigger: TABOO-TOBACCO

    Trigger Sentence: In our society smoking TOBACCO is considered a TABOO.

    Sample Sentence: In our traditional societies, drinking alcohol is considered a *taboo*.

TACIT (TASS it): a. Understood without being stated

    Trigger: TACIT-"TALK + SHUT"

    Trigger Sentence: When people make TACIT deals, they don't TALK- keep their mouths SHUT.

    Sample Sentence: My maid with a *tacit* expression nodded and went out of the room.

TACITURN (TAS ih turn): a. Silent, talking little

    Trigger: 1. TACITURN-"TALK + TURN". 2. TAC (Sounds like TALK)

    Trigger Sentence: TACITURN never TALKS. He TURNS AWAY from TALKING.

Sample Sentence: Joseph was so *taciturn* we couldn't tell if he had enjoyed the party or not.

TACTICAL (TAK tikul): a. Related to tactics; wise; expedient

Trigger: TACTICAL- TACTFUL (** synonyms)

Trigger Sentence: The TACTFUL politician used TACTICAL methods to defeat his rival.

Sample Sentence: The government is being *tactical* in imposing taxes on imported goods.

Related Words: TACTLESS - a. marked by a lack of tact; impolite

TACTILE (TAK til): a. Perceptible by touch; tangible

Trigger: TACTILE-"TACT"-"CONTACT"

Trigger Sentence: Your CONTACT (touch) is TACTILE.

Sample Sentence: His callused hands have lost their *tactile* sensitivity.

TAINT (TAYNT): v. Pollute; corrupt; bring shame

Trigger: 1.TAINT-STAIN (** synonyms). 2. TAINT-PAINT

Trigger Sentence: 1. His repute got TAINTED/ STAINED by scandals. 2. Shirt is TAINTED in PAINT.

Sample Sentence: Despite his good deeds, the *taint* of the scandal followed him for years.

TANGENTIAL (tan JEN shul): a. Peripheral, only slightly connected, divergent

Trigger: TANGENTIAL-TANGENT LIKE

Trigger Sentence: Word TANGENT is taken from math. TANGENT TOUCHES circle only at a single point (on PERIPHERY); it does NOT touch at CENTRAL.

Sample Sentence: 1.These arguments are *tangential* to the main point. 2. The romance part is only *tangential* in the novel.

TANGIBLE (TAN juh bul): a. Touchable; real; palpable

Trigger: TANGIBLE-"TOUNGUE+BLE"

Trigger Sentence: With TONGUE one can feel the TANGIBLE taste of the juice.

Sample Sentence: The *tangible* evidence that Billy was back home was that of the raided fridge!

Related Words: INTANGIBLE -a. cannot be seen or touched, insubstantial

TANTALIZE (TAN tl ize): v. Tease; torture with disappointment

Trigger: TANTALIZE- TEMPT + EYES

Trigger Sentence: 1. TANTALIZING means TEASING. 2. Girls with their TEMPTING EYES TANTALIZE boys. 3. Any TANTALIZING thing TEMPTS the EYES of an infant.

Sample Sentence: Jessica *tantalized* many with her sensual dance and beauty on stage.

Related Words: TANTALIZING -a. attractive but cannot be attained.

TANTAMOUNT (TAN tuh mount): a. Equivalent in effect or value

Trigger: TA & TA - EQUAL AMOUNTS

Trigger Sentence: EQUAL AMOUNT is called TANTAMOUNT.

Sample Sentence: Being invited to a charity ball is *tantamount* to being asked for a donation.

TARNISH (TAHR nish): v. Blacken, and stain

Trigger: 1.TARNISH-TAR. 2. TARNISH-VARNISH

Trigger Sentence: 1. Apply ROAD TAR (which is black color) to TARNISH; TAR TARNISHES walls. 2. VARNISH protects wood from getting TARNISHED.

Sample Sentence: They believed that inter-caste nuptials would *tarnish* their community.

Related Words: TAR -v. tarnish, spoil

TAUNT (TAWNT): v. Tease, mock; harass

Trigger: TAUNT-HAUNT

Trigger Sentence: The ghost HAUNTED her and TAUNTED her

Sample Sentence: Indian cricket fans *taunted* the visiting English team.

TAUT (TAWT): a. Tight; ready

Trigger: 1.TAUT-TIGHT. 2. TAUTEN- TIGHTEN. 3. TAUTNESS-TIGHTNESS

Trigger Sentence: Slim fit TIGHT jeans are TAUT.

Sample Sentence: 1.The rope was drawn *taut*. 2. The book is a *taut* thriller.

Related Words: TAUTEN -v. become taut

TAUTOLOGY (taw TOL uh jee): a. Needless repetition

Trigger: TAUTOLOGY-TWO+ TOLD+ LOGY

Trigger Sentence: To TELL TWO times something like "adequate enough" is a TAUTOLOGY.

Sample Sentence: To say that something is `return back' is a *tautology*.

TAWDRY (TAW dree): a. Cheap and gaudy

Trigger: 1. TAWDRY-TODDY. 2. GAUDY BODY

Trigger Sentence: 1. The tribes dress TAWDRY and drink TODDY; get intoxicated during the forest festival. 2. Prostitute wears GAUDY (showy) cloths to attract TAWDRY customers.

Sample Sentence: The wedding venue was *tawdrily* decorated with bright plastic flowers.

TAXONOMY (tak SON uh mee): n. The branch of science concerned with classification.

Trigger: 1. TAXONOMY-"TAXI+NAME". 2. TAX

Trigger Sentence: 1. TAXI NAME is CLASSIFIED from low end (Maruthi 800); Verna (middle), Skoda (high end), Benz (very high end) etc. 2. To collect the TAXES from the public, government generally CLASSIFIES various income groups.

Sample Sentence: Chandrahasa finds *taxonomy* interesting; she did well in scientific cataloging.

TEDIOUS (TEE dee us): a. Tiresome, boring

Trigger: TEDIOUS-"TIRES US"

Trigger Sentence: 1. Any TEDIOUS work TIRES US. 2. It is TIRESOME to watch TEDIOUS movie.

Sample Sentence: He gave a *tedious* speech, while all we wanted was to have dinner and go!

TEEM (TEEM): v. Be full of; swarm with

Trigger: TEEM-TEAM

Trigger Sentence: My TEAM is TEEMED with lot of girls.

Sample Sentence: People *teemed* on the streets to see the wining world cup cricket team.

TEMERITY (tuh MER i tee): n. Reckless boldness; rashness

Trigger: TEMERITY-TIMIDITY

Trigger Sentence: TEMERITY is opposite to "TIMIDITY".

Sample Sentence: She had the *temerity* to ask my boyfriend if she could go out with him!

TEMPERATE (TEM prit): a. Moderate, self-controlled, restrained

    Trigger: 1. TEMPERATE-"EVEN TEMPER". 2. TEMPERATE-MODERATE

    Trigger Sentence: 1. TEMPERATE people are EVEN-TEMPERED. 2. TEMPERATE and MODERATE (in terms of drinking) are synonyms.

    Sample Sentence: 1. Being a *temperate* man, he did not jump into the argument. 2. He was *temperate* in his consumption of alcoholic beverages.

    Related Words: 1.TEMPERANCE -n. moderation; abstinence from alcoholic Beverages. 2. INTEMPERATE -a. overindulgent; lacking self-control

TEMPESTUOUS (tem PES choo us): a. Stormy, violent, turbulent

    Trigger: TEMPESTUOUS-hot TEMPER

    Trigger Sentence: HOT-TEMPER person is usually TEMPESTUOUS. That man has a TEMPESTUOUS TEMPER.

    Sample Sentence: The defendant's *tempestuous* outburst almost shook the court room!

    Related Words: TEMPERAMENTAL -a. variable, changeable, irritable

TEMPORAL (TEM per ul): a. Limited by time; not lasting forever; mundane

    Trigger: TEMPORAL-TEMPORARY

    Trigger Sentence: TEMPORAL things are TEMPORARY; anything related to TIME is TEMPORAL.

    Sample Sentence: 1.Music is a *temporal* act. 2. Our existence in this world is *temporal*.

TENABLE (TEN uh bul): a. Reasonable; capable of maintained

    Trigger: 1. TENABLE-DEFENDABLE. 2. TEN+ ABLE-"TEN out of TEN"

    Trigger Sentence: 1. When TENDU (Tendulakr) was there, the score was DEFENDABLE & TENABLE. 2. If your theory is TENABLE, you'd receive TEN out of TEN.

    Sample Sentence: 1. I find your theory *untenable* and I reject it. 2. The *tenable* theory is that a giant meteor strike set off a chain of events resulting in the demise of the dinosaurs.

    Related Words: UNTENABLE -n. undefendable

TENACIOUS (teh NEY shus): a. Holding fast; tough

    Trigger: 1. TENACIOUS-TENDU (TENDULKAR). 2. TENACIOUS-TEENAGERS

    Trigger Sentence: 1. TENDULKAR was TENACIOUS; he played persistently for 24 years without giving up. 2. TEENAGERS are TENACIOUS; very stubborn.

    Sample Sentence: A *tenacious* trainer, she adheres to her grueling swimming schedule.

    Related Words: TENACITY -n. grasping; stubbornness

TENDENTIOUS (ten DEN shuhs): a. Biased; having an aim

    Trigger: TENDENTIOUS -TENDENCY

    Trigger Sentence: TENDENTIOUS people have TENDENCY to be one sided; my sir has a TENDENCY towards girls.

    Sample Sentence: 1. He made extremely *tendentious* remarks. 2. The department's *tendentious* methods are open to challenge.

TENDER (TEN der): v. Offer, propose; a. soft, delicate

> **Trigger:** 1.TENDER-ATTENDER-RENDER. 2. TENDER-UNDER (AGE)
>
> **Trigger Sentence:** 1. ATTENDER TENDERED his services. 2. UNDER AGE kids are TENDER /SOFT.
>
> **Sample Sentence:** In a *tender* the art dealer *tendered* $1 million for a Hussain painting.

TENUOUS (TEN yoo us): a. Thin, rare; slim

> **Trigger:** 1.TENUOUS-THINNISH. 2. TENUOUS-TENNIS (PLAYERS)
>
> **Trigger Sentence:** 1 .Hydrogen is very TENUOUS. It is THINNER than any other element in the Universe. 2. TENNIS players play a lot; they look TENUOUS, slender and slim.
>
> **Sample Sentence:** 1. He showed *tenuous* claim to ownership. 2. He has *tenuous* grasp on reality.
>
> Related Words: 1. ATTENUATE -v. make thin. 2. EXTENUATE-v. make smaller; lessen seriousness

TEPID (TEP id): a. Lukewarm; half-hearted

> **Trigger:** TEMP-MID
>
> **Trigger Sentence:** 1. MID-TEMP (neither too hot nor too cold) is called TEPID. 2. MIDDLE range TEMPERATURES are very TEPID.
>
> **Sample Sentence:** She gave a *tepid* dance performance.
>
> Related Words: TORRID –a. hot; passionate

TERSE (TURS): a. Concise, pithy, curt

> **Trigger:** TERSE-"TINY+VERSE"
>
> **Trigger Sentence:** The TERSENESS of the poet is reflected in the TINY VERSES.
>
> **Sample Sentence:** Hemingway is best known for his *terse* style of writing.

TETHER (TETH er): v. Tie with a rope

> **Trigger:** TETHER-"TIE HER"
>
> **Trigger Sentence:** He TIED HER and TETHERED her with a leather rope.
>
> **Sample Sentence:** We *tethered* the boat to the dock.

THESPIAN (THES pee uhn): a. Related to drama

> **Trigger:** 1.THEATER MAN-THESPIAN. 2. THESPIAN-THE ESPN
>
> **Trigger Sentence:** 1. Shakespeare was a complete THEATRE MAN. He spent his life on THESPIAN activities. 2. The ESPN (is NOT a THESPIAN) interviews sports persons, not THESPIAN people.
>
> **Sample Sentence:** It's a drama contest in which the best *thespian* wins.

THORNY (THAWR nee): a. Causing difficulty; problematic

> **Trigger:** THORNY-THORN
>
> **Trigger Sentence:** The THORNY critic's views on my art poked me like THORNS.
>
> **Sample Sentence:** The doctor avoided giving his views on the *thorny* issues of abortion.

THRESHOLD (THRESH ohld): n. Edge; lower limit; beginning; door step

> **Trigger:** THRESHOLD-HOLD
>
> **Trigger Sentence:** HOLD the door…. till I reach the THRESHOLD.
>
> **Sample Sentence:** He is on the *threshold* of manhood.

THRIFT (THRIFT): n. Saving, economizing

   Trigger: THRIFT-SPENDTHRIFT (** antonyms)

   Trigger Sentence: A SPENDTHRIFT is NOT THRIFTY.

   Sample Sentence: China's capacity for *thrift* has long perplexed economists.

   Related Words: THRIFTY -a. economical

THRIVE (THRYV): v. Prosper, flourish

   Trigger: THRIVE-SURVIVE-LIVE

   Trigger Sentence: Once Homo sapiens SURVIVED the initial difficulties, they started to THRIVE.

   Sample Sentence: *"Thriving* on the good will and faith of your customers is important".

   Related Words: THRIVING -a. succeeding, prospering

THWART (THWAWRT): v. Oppose; frustrate, baffle

   Trigger: 1. THWART-THREAT. 2. THWART-THE WAR

   Trigger Sentence: 1. With a THREAT, I can THWART his attempts. 2. THE WAR THWARTED economic progress.

   Sample Sentence: The threat of a nuclear disaster *thwarted* the USA and the USSR from warring.

TIMID (TIM id): a. Shy, lacking in courage or confidence

   Trigger: TIMID-"TIM HIDE"

   Trigger Sentence: As TIM was very TIMID, he HID in a barn to escape from his enemies.

   Sample Sentence: She's very *timid* and shy to meet strangers.

   Related Words: TIMOROUS -a. shy; timid

TIMOROUS (TIM ur us): a. Afraid; fearful

   Trigger: TIMOROUS- TIMID OF US

   Trigger Sentence: TIMID and TIMOROUS are synonyms. The TIMOROUS fellow is TIMID OF US.

   Sample Sentence: It was heartbreaking to see a *timorous* little lost girl in the caravan!

   Related Words: TIMID -a. shy, fearful

TIRADE (TYE rayd): n. Extended scolding; harangue; denunciation

   Trigger: TIRADE-(RADE)-DEGRADE

   Trigger Sentence: In a lengthy TIRADE he DEGRADED everyone.

   Sample Sentence: My mom never gets tired of her *tirades*! She just nags and nags...

TORPID (TOR pid): a. Slow, listless; inert

   Trigger: 1.TORPID-not RAPID. 2. TORPID-STUPID

   Trigger Sentence: 1. A TORPID batsman does NOT make runs RAPIDLY. 2. A TORPID thinker becomes a STUPID businessman.

   Sample Sentence: A *torpid* sloth bear refused to budge off its tree branch.

   Related Words: TORPOR -n. Lazy; sluggish

TORPOR (TOR per): n. Lazy; sluggish; dormancy

   Trigger: TORPOR-not TOPPER

Trigger Sentence: 1. Want to be a TOPPER? Then don't be a TORPOR. 2. TORPID is not RAPID.

Sample Sentence: Nothing seemed to arouse him from his *torpor* tendencies.

TORRID (TOR id): a. Hot; scorching; passionate

Trigger: 1.TORRID-TEPID. 2. TORRID-TOO RED

Trigger Sentence: 1. TOO RED hot sun makes a TORRID day. 2. TORRID-TEPID-antonym variants.

Sample Sentence: Mills and Boons, the classic romantic novels delved upon *torrid* love affairs.

TORTUOUS (TOR choo wus): a. Full of twists and turns; complicated

Trigger: TORT-TORQUE-TORSION

Trigger Sentence: Stand at the centre of TORTUOUS tornado, to get a live example of TORQUE.

Sample Sentence: His shortcut through the forest turned out to be *tortuous* and tiresome.

TOTALITARIAN (tohtal i TAIR ee un): a. Authoritarian; despotic; intolerant of opposition

Trigger: TOTALITARIAN-TOTAL AUTHORITARIAN

Trigger Sentence: A TOTALITARIAN is an AUTHORITARIAN who exercises TOTAL control over life.

Sample Sentence: There was *totalitarian* dictatorship in Nazi Germany

TOTALITY (toh TAL I tee): n. Whole; the quality of being complete

Trigger: TOTALITY-TOTAL

Trigger Sentence: The state of being TOTAL is known as TOTALITY.

Sample Sentence: In *totality* all of us did manage to fill the auditorium to its capacity.

TOUT (TOUT): v. Praise or publicize highly

Trigger: 1.TOUT-TELL OUT. 2. TOUT-SHOUT

Trigger Sentence: 1. TOUT is to TELL OUTSIDE that a particular product is a great one. 2. TOUT is SHOUTING in a positive way.

Sample Sentence: You can see him on TV ads *touting* his hair products.

TRACTABLE (TRAK tuh bul): a. Docile, easily managed

Trigger: TRACTABLE-TRACK

Trigger Sentence: Follow this particular TRACK to make this mysterious case TRACTABLE.

Sample Sentence: Boris's dog was easy to train because he was friendly and *tractable*.

Related Words: INTRACTABLE -a. inflexible, stubborn

TRADUCE (truh DOOS): v. Defame, slander

Trigger: TRADUCE-REDUCE image

Trigger Sentence: She TRADUCES her husband everywhere by REDUCING his image.

Sample Sentence: She was *traduced* and humiliated in the party.

TRAITOR (TREY ter): n. Betrayer

Trigger: 1. TRAITOR-TWO TIMER. 2. TRAITOR-BETRAYER (** synonyms)

Trigger Sentence: As a TRAITOR he BETRAYED his team by playing badly for personal gains.

Sample Sentence: *Traitor* betrays his country by delivering military secrets to the enemy.

TRANQUIL (TRANG kwil): v. Calm, quiet

    Trigger: TRANQUIL-TURN COOL

    Trigger Sentence: These TRANQUIL surroundings TURN even TRUCULENT individuals COOL.

    Sample Sentence: The house was *tranquil* at last as the kids moved outside to play.

TRANSCENDENT (tran SEN dunt): a. Surpassing; exceeding ordinary limits.

    Trigger: TRANSCEND- ASCEND beyond

    Trigger Sentence: Descend is to go down; ascend is to go up; crescendo is to gradually going up; TRANSCEND is to ASCEND beyond NORMAL LIMITS.

    Sample Sentence: The star players' *transcendental* performance made a winning team.

TRANSCRIBE (tran SCRYB): v. Copy; make a written copy

    Trigger: TRANSCRIBE- DESCRIBE the speech on paper

    Trigger Sentence: In a TRANSCRIPTION, the scribe DESCRIBED the President's speech.

    Sample Sentence: The pundit *transcribed* the oral history of Vedas.

TRANSGRESSION (trans GRESH uhn): n. Violation of law, sin

    Trigger: TRANSGRESSION-"TRAIN+AGRESSION"

    Trigger Sentence: To TRAIN AGGRESSION in militants can be called TRANSGRESSION; TRANSGRESSIVE (being aggressive) act is an OFFENSIVE behavior.

    Sample Sentence: He was expelled from his services for of drunken driving and *transgression*.

TRANSIENT (TRAN zee unt): a. Temporary, momentary; staying a short time

    Trigger: 1. TRANS (CHANGES). 2. TRANSIENT-TRANSITORY (** synonyms)

    Trigger Sentence: 1. Anything that TRANSFERS is not permanent. It is TRANSIENT. 2. Everything in this Universe is TRANSITORY. Some insects are so TRANSIENT that they live only few hours.

    Sample Sentence: Little astronaut in the making, Arya, can identify the *transient* stars in the sky!

TRANSITORY (TRAN si tohr ee): a. Not permanent; fleeting

    Trigger: TRANSITORY-TRANCE-TEMPORARY

    Trigger Sentence: 1. TRANSITORY and TRANSIENT are synonyms. 2. TRANCE is a TEMPORARY phenomenon.

    Sample Sentence: Recession is only a temporary phase between two financial *transitory* booms.

TRANSMUTE (tranz MYOOT): v. Change; convert to something different

    Trigger: TRANSMUTE-TRANSLATE

    Trigger Sentence: 1. MUTABLE-changeable; IMMUTABLE-immovable-unchangeable; TRANSMUTE-change. 2. DNA is TRANSMUTED into RNA which is then TRANSLATED into protein.

    Sample Sentence: The former criminal *transmuted* into a hero by saving a drowning kid.

TRANSPARENT (trans PAR unt): a. Easily detected or seen through; obvious

    Trigger: TRANSPARENT-APPARENT

    Trigger Sentence: 1. That which appears is APPARENT! 2. TRANSPARENT and APPARENT are synonyms.

    Sample Sentence: As a truthful officer, Vikas Raj, always believed in *transparency* at work.

TRAVAIL (tre VAYL): n. Painfully difficult or burdensome

    Trigger: TRAVAIL-TRAVEL

    Trigger Sentence: TRAVEL has become TRAVAIL, because of TRAFFIC jams, rush and pollution.

    Sample Sentence: Modern medicine has helped lessen the *travails* of childbirth.

TRAVERSE (TRAV ers): v. Travel across

    Trigger: TRAVERSE-TRAVEL ACROSS (** synonyms)

    Trigger Sentence: A bridge TRAVERSES/TRAVELS ACROSS the river.

    Sample Sentence: *Traversing* through the oceans and continents, millions of birds migrate.

TREACHERY (TRECH uh ree): n. Betrayal of trust; the quality of being deceptive

    Trigger: 1.TREACHERY-TRICKERY. 2. TREASON-TROJAN (HORSE)

    Trigger Sentence: 1. TRICKERY is a form of TREACHERY. 2. TROJAN horse was used as TREASON during Troy seize.

    Sample Sentence: Mata Hari was a famous German spy who was *treacherous* to her own native France during World War I.

    Related Words: 1.TREACHEROUS -a. unfaithful; dangerous. 2. TREASON -n. Betrayal; disloyalty

TREMULOUS (TREM yuh lus): a. Shaking; wavering

    Trigger: TREMULOUS-TREMORS -TREMBLES

    Trigger Sentence: A TREMULOUS voice consists of TREMORS or TREMBLES.

    Sample Sentence: The servants *tremulously* faced the wrath of their master.

TRENCHANT (TREN chunt): a. Cutting; keen; Clear-cut

    Trigger: 1.TRENCH ANT-"FRENCH CUT". 2. TRENCHANT-ANT

    Trigger Sentence: 1. TRENCH sounds like FRENCH CUT; An ANT TRENCHANTLY cuts a portion of a leaf before it carries it to the mound.2. If you talk CLEAR-CUT it is called as a TRENCHANT TALK.

    Sample Sentence: Julia used her *trenchant* tongue while discussing her ex-husband.

TREPID (TREP id): a. Timid; Fearful

    Trigger: 1.TREPID-TIMID. 2. TREPID-TRAPPED

    Trigger Sentence: 1. When you get TRAPPED by criminals you'd feel TREPID. 2. If you are TREPID, accept that you are TIMID and try to overcome your fear.

    Sample Sentence: As animal lovers, you are brave and not *trepid* to shrink away from snakes!

    Related Words: TREPIDATION -n. fear

TRIBULATION (trib yuh LEY shun): n. Suffering; trial

    Trigger: TRIBUL+ATION-TROUBLE (** synonyms)

    Trigger Sentence: You're going to have a lot of TROUBLE in this world, you'll have TRIBULATION.

    Sample Sentence: Life is not all about troubles and *tribulations,* but also of pleasures and revels.

TRIFLING (TRAHY fling): a. Trivial, unimportant

    Trigger: 1.TRIFLE-TRIVIAL. 2. TRIFLE-LITTLE

    Trigger Sentence: 1. TRIVIAL and TRIFLE are synonyms. 2. TRIFLE minded people pay attention to the LITTLE things of no importance.

Sample Sentence: Deciding what you want to do for a living is not a *trifling* matter.

Related Words: TRIFLE -n. a thing of little value or importance, small amount.

TRITE (TRYT): a. Hackneyed; commonplace; tired

> **Trigger:** TRY IT....TRY IT...TRY IT...TRY IT...
>
> **Trigger Sentence:** TRY IT...TRY IT....TRY IT... Everything will be ROUTINE and you get TIRED.
>
> **Sample Sentence:** Doris's speech was energetic but *trite*; she said the same old things.
>
> Related Words: TIRED -a. boring, dull

TRIVIAL (TRIV ee ul): a. Unimportant, insignificant

> **Trigger:** TRI (THREE) + VIA (WAY)--TRIVIAL
>
> **Trigger Sentence:** THREE WAYS meet to form a junction; at junction people talk TRIVIAL matters.
>
> **Sample Sentence**: Those youngsters meet at the tri-way junction and discuss *trivial* things.

TRUCE (TROOS): n. Cease-fire; respite

> **Trigger:** TRUCE-TRUE PEACE
>
> **Trigger Sentence:** To cause PEACE there must be a TRUCE between two countries.
>
> **Sample Sentence:** Both the sides on the war front agreed to a 24-hour *truce* on Christmas Eve.

TRUCULENT (TRUK yu lunt): a. Cruel; harsh; destructive

> **Trigger:** TRUCULENT-"TRUCK +VIOLENT"
>
> **Trigger Sentence:** A TRUCULENT TRUCK driver got drunk and VIOLENTLY crushed car.
>
> **Sample Sentence:** Die-hard fans became *truculent* and violent after their favorite team lost.
>
> Related Words: TRUCULENCE -n. ferocity

TRUNCATE (TRUNG keyt): v. Shorten, cut the top of

> **Trigger:** TRUNCATE-"TRUNK+CUT"
>
> **Trigger Sentence:** Image a TRUNCATED cone problem in math where its TRUNK portion is CUT.
>
> **Sample Sentence:** Due to lack of time, Praveena had to *truncate* her speech.

TRYST (TRIST): n. Meeting; date

> **Trigger:** TRYST-TIE+WRIST
>
> **Trigger Sentence:** My date caught my WRIST and came closer in a secret TRYST.
>
> **Sample Sentence:** My *tryst* with the beach babies at Florida was quite amusing!

TUMID (TYOO mid): a. 1. Swollen. 2. Pompous, bombastic

> **Trigger:** TUMOR-TUMID-TUMMY
>
> **Trigger Sentence:** He had a TUMID TUMMY since he has TUMOR in his stomach.
>
> **Sample Sentence:** He'd just been in a fight, and was nursing his *tumid* lip.
>
> Related Words: TURGID –a. Swollen; pompous, bombastic

TUMULT (TYOO mult): v. Commotion; disorder; noise

> **Trigger:** TUMULTUOUS- TUMBLED US

Trigger Sentence: TUMULTUOUS crowd at kumbh-mela TUMBLED US. The First World War TUMBLED the world into a TUMULT.

Sample Sentence: As a contrast the garden is set against the *tumult* of downtown Manhattan.

Related Words: TUMULTUOUS -a. characterized by unrest or disorder

TURBID (TUR bid): a. Muddy, clouded with disturbed sediment

Trigger: TURBID-DISTURBED

Trigger Sentence: Having its sediment DISTURBED, the water was TURBID.

Sample Sentence: Step carefully; the water is *turbid* near the pond.

TURBULENT (TUR byuh lunt): a. Disturbed; causing violence

Trigger: 1.TURBULENT-DISTURBED (** synonyms). 2. TURBULENT-VIOLENT (** synonyms)

Trigger Sentence: The country is DISTURBED with TURBULENT rebels.

Sample Sentence: I had *turbulent* childhood with my alcoholic father throwing tantrums.

TURGID (TUR jid): a. 1. Swollen; 2.pompous, bombastic

Trigger: 1. TURGID-TUMID-TUMOR. 2. TURGID-SURGED. 3. TURGID-TURTLE

Trigger Sentence: 1. TURGID and TUMID are synonyms. 2. The tent became TURGID as the wind SURGED into it. 3. The TURTLE top shell appears TURGID.

Sample Sentence: They have led a *turgid* life with all the comforts in the world at their feet.

Related Words: TUMID -a. Swollen; pompous, bombastic

RAZE : destroy, demolish!

Memory Test-109 : Match each word and its memory trick to the corresponding definition.

S.N	WORD	MEMORY TRIGGER	S.N	DEFINITIONS	KEY
1	SYNCHRONOUS	SYNC perfectly	A	Blacken, and stain	
2	SYNERGY	SYNC+ENERGY	B	Cheap and gaudy	
3	SYNOPTIC	Synopsis	C	Combination of parts to make whole	
4	SYNTHESIS	SYNDICATE	D	Combined action	
5	TABOO	Ban TOBACCO	E	Equivalent in effect or value	
6	TACIT	Talk + shut	F	Needless repetition	
7	TACITURN	TURN away from TALK	G	Overview, summary	
8	TACTICAL	TACTFUL	H	Perceptible by touch; tangible	
9	TACTILE	Tact-CONTACT	I	Peripheral, only slightly connected	
10	TAINT	STAIN reputation	J	Pollute; corrupt; bring shame	
11	TANGENTIAL	Tangent like	K	Prohibition; ban	
12	TANGIBLE	TOUNGUE+ble	L	Related to tactics; wise; expedient	
13	TANTALIZE	TEMPT + eyes	M	Silent, talking little	
14	TANTAMOUNT	Equal AMOUNT	N	Similarly timed; simultaneous with	
15	TARNISH	Apply ROAD TAR	O	Tease, mock; harass	
16	TAUNT	HAUNTED her	P	Tease; torture with disappointment	
17	TAUT	TIGHT	Q	The branch of science for classification	
18	TAUTOLOGY	Two+ told+ logy	R	Tight; ready	
19	TAWDRY	Toddy- Gaudy body	S	Touchable; real; palpable	
20	TAXONOMY	Taxi+name	T	Understood without being stated	

Memory Test-110 : Match each word and its memory trick to the corresponding definition.

S.N	WORD	MEMORY TRIGGER	S.N	DEFINITIONS	KEY
1	TEDIOUS	Tires us	A	Be full of; swarm with	
2	TEEM	TEEMED with girls	B	Biased; having an aim	
3	TEMERITY	no TIMIDITY	C	Causing difficulty; problematic	
4	TEMPERATE	Even temper	D	Concise, pithy, curt	
5	TEMPESTUOUS	Hot TEMPER	E	Edge; lower limit; beginning; door step	
6	TEMPORAL	Temporary	F	Flourish , Prosper	
7	TENABLE	Defendable -TEN out of TEN	G	Holding fast; tough	
8	TENACIOUS	TEENAGERS nature	H	Limited by time; mundane	
9	TENDENTIOUS	TENDENCY towards	I	Lukewarm; half-hearted	
10	TENDER	UNDER (age); ATTENDER	J	Oppose; frustrate, baffle	
11	TENUOUS	THINNISH	K	Reasonable; capable of maintained	
12	TEPID	TEMP-MID	L	Reckless boldness; rashness	
13	TERSE	TINY+VERSE	M	Related to drama	
14	TETHER	TIE HER	N	Saving, economizing	
15	THESPIAN	THEATER man	O	Self-controlled, Moderate, restrained	
16	THORNY	THORN in my flesh	P	Soft, delicate; Offer, propose	
17	THRESHOLD	HOLD the door	Q	Thin, rare; slim	
18	THRIFT	Not SPENDTHRIFT	R	Tie with a rope	
19	THRIVE	SURVIVE-LIVE	S	Tiresome, boring	
20	THWART	THREAT	T	Violent, Stormy, turbulent	

Answers

EX.NO	1	2	3	4	5	6	7	8	9	10	11	12	13	14	15	16	17	18	19	20
109	N	D	G	C	K	T	M	L	H	J	I	S	P	E	A	O	R	F	B	Q
110	S	A	L	O	T	H	K	G	B	P	Q	I	D	R	M	C	E	N	F	J

Memory Test-111 : Match each word and its memory trick to the corresponding definition.

S.N	WORD	MEMORY TRIGGER	S.N	DEFINITIONS	KEY
1	TIMID	Tim HIDE	A	Afraid; fearful	
2	TIMOROUS	TIMID of us	B	Authoritarian; despotic	
3	TIRADE	(Rade)-DEGRADE	C	Betrayer	
4	TORPID	Not RAPID -STUPID	D	Calm, quiet	
5	TORPOR	Not TOPPER	E	Change; transform	
6	TORRID	too RED SUN	F	Copy; make a written copy	
7	TORTUOUS	Tort-torque-torsion	G	Defame, slander	
8	TOTALITARIAN	Total authoritarian	H	Easily managed , Docile	
9	TOTALITY	TOTAL	I	Extended scolding; harangue	
10	TOUT	TELL OUT	J	Full of twists; complicated	
11	TRACTABLE	On TRACK	K	Hot; scorching; passionate	
12	TRADUCE	REDUCE image	L	Lazy; sluggish; dormancy	
13	TRAITOR	TWO TIMER -betrayer	M	Not permanent; fleeting	
14	TRANQUIL	TURN COOL	N	Praise or publicize highly	
15	TRANSCENDENT	ASCEND beyond	O	Shy, lacking confidence	
16	TRANSCRIBE	DESCRIBE on paper	P	Slow, listless; inert	
17	TRANSGRESSION	Train+AGRESSION	Q	Surpassing; exceeding ordinary limits	
18	TRANSIENT	TRANSITORY	R	Temporary, momentary	
19	TRANSITORY	Trance-TEMPORARY	S	Violation of law, sin	
20	TRANSMUTE	TRANSLATE	T	Whole; complete	

Memory Test-112 : Match each word and its memory trick to the corresponding definition.

S.N	WORD	MEMORY TRIGGER	S.N	DEFINITIONS	KEY
1	TRANSPARENT	APPARENT	A	Cease-fire; respite	
2	TRAVAIL	TRAVEL has become	B	Commotion; disorder; noise	
3	TRAVERSE	TRAVEL across	C	Cruel; harsh; destructive	
4	TREACHERY	Trickery	D	Cutting; keen; Clear-cut	
5	TREMULOUS	TREMORS -trembles	E	Disturbed; causing violence	
6	TRENCHANT	French cut –ANT bite	F	Easily detected; obvious	
7	TREPID	Timid -TRAPPED	G	Hackneyed; commonplace; tired	
8	TRIBULATION	TRIBUL-TROUBLE	H	Meeting; date	
9	TRIFLING	TRIVIAL- little	I	Muddy, cloudy; murky	
10	TRITE	Try it….try it…TIRED	J	Painfully difficult or burdensome	
11	TRIVIAL	TRI WAY matters	K	Shaking; wavering	
12	TRUCE	TRUE PEACE	L	Shorten, cut the top of	
13	TRUCULENT	Truck +VIOLENT	M	Suffering; trial	
14	TRUNCATE	Trunk+CUT	N	Swollen ;Pompous	
15	TRYST	Tie+WRIST	O	Swollen ;Pompous	
16	TUMID	TUMMY	P	The quality of being deceptive	
17	TUMULT	TUMBLED US	Q	Timid; Fearful	
18	TURBID	DISTURBED	R	Travel across	
19	TURBULENT	DISTURBANCE	S	Trivial, unimportant	
20	TURGID	TUMID-TUMMY	T	Unimportant, insignificant	

Answers EX.NO	1	2	3	4	5	6	7	8	9	10	11	12	13	14	15	16	17	18	19	20
111	O	A	I	P	L	K	J	B	T	N	H	G	C	D	Q	F	S	R	M	E
112	F	J	R	P	K	D	Q	M	S	G	T	A	C	L	H	N	B	I	E	O

WORD GROUPS DAY-28

★ **SPEED UP**

ADJECTIVES: exigent

NOUNS: hurry, haste, urgency

VERB: accelerate, dispatch, expedite, precipitate, hasten ; facilitate

ANTONYMS: v. retard, hinder, delay

★ **RASH/RASHNESS**

ADJECTIVES: reckless, impulsive, impetuous, headlong, hasty, foolhardy, precipitate; careless, heedless, imprudent, foolish; injudicious, hare-brained.

NOUNS: impetuosity

VERB: precipitate, trigger, expedite.

ANTONYMS: adj. prudent, cautious

★ **COGITATION/THINKING**

ADJECTIVES: contemplative, reflective, pensive; wistful

NOUNS: cerebration, contemplation, deliberation, meditation, reflection, rumination, speculation

VERB: cogitate, muse, ponder, ruminate

ANTONYMS: n. ignorance; v. disregard, ignore

★ **CHAOS-DISORDER**

ADJECTIVES: chaotic , topsy-turvy, jumbled. Helter-skelter

NOUNS: disarray, entropy, mayhem, bedlam, pandemonium, havoc, turmoil, tumult, commotion, upheaval, uproar; anarchy, lawlessness;

VERB: disrupt , addle, muddle.

ANTONYMS: n. harmony, order, quiet; system

★ **CONFUSE/CONFUSION**

ADJECTIVES: mysterious, disconcerting; garbled

NOUNS: perplexity, daze

VERB: bewilder, baffle, muddle, mystify, bemuse, puzzle, confound, nonplus, obfuscate

ANTONYMS: v. enlighten, elucidate

★ **PREVIOUS**

ADJECTIVES: antecedent, anterior, antediluvian, antebellum, earlier, erstwhile, ex, one-time, past, precedent

NOUNS: precedence

VERB: precede, antecede, predate, antedate

ANTONYMS: adj. current, future, later, present

★ **GAPS-OPENINGS**

NOUNS: aperture, crevice, fissure, orifice; arroyo, canyon, ravine; lull, hiatus, interstice, interregnum, respite; rift, rent; schism, chasm

VERB: breach

ADJECTIVES: hiatal

ANTONYMS: n. closure

★ **REVIVAL:** renewal, restoration; reactivation

NOUNS: recrudescence, regeneration, rejuvenation, renaissance, renewal, resurgence, resurrection, resuscitation, revitalization

ADJECTIVES: revived, rehabilitated

VERB: recuperate, rekindle, renovate, resurrect, resuscitate, revitalize, revamp ; animate, overhaul, invigorate

ANTONYMS: n. destruction, suppression, disappearance.

Word List Day-29

TURMOIL (TUR moyl): n. Great commotion and confusion

Trigger: 1. TURN+OIL. 2. TURMOIL-TURN BOIL

Trigger Sentence: 1. When we TURN OIL, OIL will be in great TURMOIL and disorder. 2. When we BOIL, water molecules will be in TURMOIL.

Sample Sentence: She grew up in the *turmoil* of 1960s, amid race riots and war protests.

TURPITUDE (TUR puh tood): n. Wickedness; depravity

Trigger: 1. TURPITUDE- CORRUPT+DUDE. 2. TURPITUDE-RECTITUDE (**antonyms)

Trigger Sentence: 1. A CORRUPT DUDE's attitude is TURPITUDE. 2. TURPITUDE is not RECTITUDE.

Sample Sentence: Pete's *turpitude* ways were evident in the way he spoke to his colleagues.

TUTELARY (TOOT l er ee): a. Providing protective supervision

Trigger: TUTE-TUITION

Trigger Sentence: The TUTELARY angel acted as a TUTOR to me.

Sample Sentence: My guru has *tutelary* powers, I feel comforted in his presence.

Related Words: TUTELAGE —n. tutorship; guardianship

TYRANNY (TEER uh nee): n. Oppression; cruel government

Trigger: 1. TYRANNY-TIE+REIGN. 2. TYRANNY-VILLANY

Trigger Sentence: 1. in a TYRANNY REIGN... the ruler TIEs the people and press them under car TIRES. 2. The VILLAINY of TYRANNICAL leaders is well-documented in history.

Sample Sentence: The Russians revolted against the *tyranny* of the the Czar.

TYRO (TY row): n. Beginner, novice

Trigger: TYRO-PRO (professional)

Trigger Sentence: 1. Takes time for a TYRO to turn into a PRO. 2. MAESTRO is opposite to TYRO.

Sample Sentence: I could tell that Roger was a *tyro* chess player.

UBIQUITOUS (yoo BIK who tus): a. Present, or found everywhere

Trigger: 1. UBIQUITOUS-UBIQ-U BIG. 2. UBIQUITOUS-MOSQUITOES

Trigger Sentence: 1. When U are BIG, you are UBIQUITOUS. 2. MOSQUITOES and BISCUITS are UBIQUITOUS.

Sample Sentence: McDonald's restaurants are *ubiquitous* around the world.

ULTERIOR (ul TEER ee ur): a. Secret, unstated and often questionable

Trigger: ULTERIOR-INTERIOR-EXTERIOR

Trigger Sentence: The ULTERIOR motives are not apparent; they are INTERIOR feelings; "not on exterior-outside".

Sample Sentence: Sue's *ulterior* motive as a helper nurse was only to meet an eligible doctor.

UMBRAGE (UM brij): v. Anger; resentment

Trigger: umbRAGE-RAGE

Trigger Sentence: When ANGREZ people ruled India, Indian people took UMBRAGE at them.

Sample Sentence: America took *umbrage* when Japan bombed Pearl Harbor.

Related Words: RAGE –n. anger, fury; passion

UNASSUMING (un uh SOOM ing): a. Humble, modest

Trigger: UN+AS+SUM

Trigger Sentence: He has no SUM (money); so UNASSUMING guy is HUMBLE and MODEST.

Sample Sentence: Hundreds of people lived in those *unassuming* small houses on the riverside.

Related Words: ASSUMING -a. supposing, taking for granted; arrogant.

UNCANNY (UN kan ee): a. Strange, mysterious

Trigger: 1.UNCANNY-UN+CAN'T. 2. UNCANNY-FUNNY-UNUSUAL

Trigger Sentence: 1. It is UNUSUAL for anyone to have such UNCANNY ability to read the minds of others. 2. UNCANNY man does the things that other people CAN'T.

Sample Sentence: John's wife has an *uncanny* ability to anticipate his words.

Related Words: CANNY –a. cautious, cunning, shrewd

UNCONSCIONABLE (un KONSH un uh bul): a. Immoral; excessive

Trigger: UNCONSCIONABLE-NO (moral) CONSCIENCE

Trigger Sentence: CONSCIENCELESS terrorists were involved in UNCONSCIONABLE killings.

Sample Sentence: Your *unconscionable* delay in delivering your work is unpardonable!

Related Words: CONSCIONABLE -a. conscientious; careful

UNCOUTH (un KOOTH): a. Clumsy, crude, strange

Trigger: 1. UNCOUTH-UNCIVIL-UNCOMBED. 2. UN+YOUTH

Trigger Sentence: 1. UNCOUTH-UNCIVIL-UNCOMBED are synonyms. 2. These days YOUTH appear UNCOUTH.

Sample Sentence: *Uncouth* behavior is especially inappropriate in churches.

Related Words: COUTH -a. highly sophisticated, of good manners.

UNCTUOUS (UNK choo us): a. Oily; insincerely suave or smooth

Trigger: 1.UNCT-OINT. 2. UNCTUOUS-FUNCTIONS

Trigger Sentence: 1. `UNCT-OINT' unction, unctuous, unguent, ointment- all same family. 2. The new employee made an UNCTUOUS effort to appear sincere in carrying out his FUNCTIONS.

Sample Sentence: The politician made an *unctuous* effort to appear religious to the voters.

UNDAUNTED (un DAWN tid): a. fearless, Courageous

Trigger: 1.DAUNT (refer). 2. UNDAUNTED-DAUNTLESS

Trigger Sentence: You can't DAUNT those UNDAUNTED warriors.

Sample Sentence: The firefighters were *undaunted* with the dangerous conditions they faced.

Related Words: DAUNTLESS -a. bold

UNDERMINE (UN dur myne): v. Weaken; sap

Trigger: UNDERMINE-"UNDER+MINE (MINUS SIGN)"

Trigger Sentence: UNDER the building there is a bomb MINE. So the building strength is UNDERMINED.

Sample Sentence: A minus sign *undermines* the value of a natural number.

UNDERRATE (un der REYT): v. Underestimate, undervalue, belittle

Trigger: UNDERRATE-UNDERESTIMATE

Trigger Sentence: EXAGGERATE is to OVERESTIMATE where as UNDERRATE is to UNDERESTIMATE.

Sample Sentence: Don't underestimate her just because she received *underrated* results.

Related Words: UNDERSTATED -a. represent as less important; downplay

UNDERSCORE (un dur SKAWR): v. Emphasize, Underline

Trigger: UNDERSCORE-GRE SCORE

Trigger Sentence: Get a good GRE SCORE; the importance of GRE SCORE should be UNDERSCORED for an admission into a graduate program.

Sample Sentence: The teacher arrived early to *underscore* and explain the rules of examination.

Related Words: 1. UNDERLINE -v. emphasize. 2.UNDERCUT -v. weaken, undermine 3.UNDERPIN -v. support. 4. UNDERMINE -v. weaken. 5. UNDERGIRD; support

UNDERSTATED (un der STEY tid): a. Expressed in a subtle and effective way; state less strongly

Trigger: UNDERSTATED-STATE LOW

Trigger Sentence: UNDERSTATED statement is STATED restrainedly.

Sample Sentence: The facts of the story were *understated* to meet the censor's requirements.

UNDULATE (UN ju leyt): v. Move with wave like motion

Trigger: 1.UNDULATE-UNDER WATER. 2. UNDULATE-MODULATE (** synonyms)

Trigger Sentence: 1. In UNDER WATER the waves move in an UNDULATED fashion. 2. The singer's voice is UNDULATED/ MODULATED

Sample Sentence: As she stood on the rock facing the sea, her skirt *undulated* with the breeze.

UNEQUIVOCAL (uhn ee KWIV uh kul): a. Clear, obvious; plain

Trigger: 1.UNEQUIVOCAL-UNIVOCAL. 2. EQUIVOCAL-DOUBLE-VOCAL (DOUBLE TONGUE)

Trigger Sentence: 1. UNIVOCAL (single voice) people are UNEQUIVOCAL. 2. EQUIVOCAL-DOUBLE VOCAL people are MISLEADING.

Sample Sentence: They univocally elected her the president. Such *unequivocal* election is rare.

Related Words: EQUIVOCAL -a. ambiguous, doubtful

UNEXCEPTIONABLE (un ik SEP shuh nuh bul): a. Not open to criticism; completely acceptable

Trigger: 1.UNEXCEPTIONABLE –UNOBJECTIONABLE.2. EXCEPTIONABLE-EXCEPT

Trigger Sentence: 1. The judgmental acumen of judges should be UNEXCEPTIONABLE that they should be UNOBJECTIONABLE. 2. The nastily EXCEPTIONABLE writing was EXCEPTED from print.

Sample Sentence: A judge's ethics should be *unexceptionable*.

Related Words: EXCEPTIONABLE –a. objectionable, may be protested.

UNEXCEPTIONAL (un ik SEP shuh nl): a. Usual; ordinary

Trigger: 1.EXCEPTIONAL-EXCELLENT.2. UNEXCEPTIONAL-NO EXCELLENT

Trigger Sentence: 1. EXCEPTIONAL ability is EXCELLENT ability. INCEPTION movie by Christopher Nolan is EXCEPTIONAL. 2. The UNEXCEPTIONAL qualities of the chairman are NOT EXCELLENT.

Sample Sentence: As an actor he was *unexceptional*, but as a singer he was exceptional!

Related Words: EXCEPTIONAL –a. Extraordinary; superior

UNFETTER (uhn FET er): v. Free or Release from chains

Trigger: 1.UNFETTER-RUN BETTER. 2. UN + FETTER

Trigger Sentence: When you are UNFETTERED, you can RUN BETTER.

Sample Sentence: Forest authorities *unfettered* those wild boars into the jungles after chipping and coding them for number study.

Related Words: 1.UNFETTERED -a. liberated.2.FETTER – v. chain; hinder

UNFLAPPABLE (un FLAP uh bul): a. Calm; not easily upset

Trigger: UNFLAPPABLE-UN+ FLOP

Trigger Sentence: Great people never get upset with FLOPS; they keep UNFLAPPABLE attitude.

Sample Sentence: James bond carried his *unflappable facade as a style statement!*

UNGAINLY (uhn GAYN lee): a. Awkward; clumsy; unwieldy

Trigger: 1. NO GAIN. 2. UNGAINLY-UNGRACEFUL

Trigger Sentence: 1. UNGRACEFUL and UNGAINLY are synonyms. 2. UNGAINLY - WON'T GAIN.

Sample Sentence: I was *ungainly* as an adolescent, as graceful as a cow on ice!

UNINITIATED (un ih NISH ee itd): a. Inexperienced; not initiated

Trigger: UN+ INITIATE

Trigger Sentence: If you are NOT yet INITIATED, It is unfamiliar to the UNINITIATED.

Sample Sentence: Hindu nuptials seemed like weird rituals to the *uninitiated* western minds.

Related Words: INITIATE –v. cause (a process or action) to begin

UNIQUE (yoo NEEK): a. Singular; rare; matchless

Trigger: UNIQUE-UNI-ONE

Trigger Sentence: Royal Bengal tiger is a UNIQUE animal.

Sample Sentence: Dr. Rajendra has a *unique* sense of humor and comic timing.

UNIVERSAL (yoo nuh VUR sul): a. Allover; ubiquitous

Trigger: UNIVERSAL-present in entire UNIVERSE

Trigger Sentence: Everyone should possess UNIVERSAL aspiration for a better UNIVERSE

Sample Sentence: Since global warming is a *universal* aspect, the entire earth gets effected.

UNIVOCAL (yoo NIV uh kul): a. Having one meaning; unambiguous

Trigger: ONE VOCAL

Trigger Sentence: ONE VOCAL- ONE MEANING only

Sample Sentence: The *univocal* law of all religions across the globe is simple, do good be good!

Related Words: UNEQUIVOCAL -a. clear; unambiguous.

UNKEMPT (un KEMPT): a. Disheveled; uncared for appearance

Trigger: UNKEMPT-"UN + KEPT"

Trigger Sentence: 1. KEMPT means KEPT everything TIDILY. 2. UNKEMPT is opposite to KEMPT.

Sample Sentence: The County admin is inspecting and giving notices *unkempt* lawns.

UNOBTRUSIVE (uhn ub TROOS ihv): a. Not visible; not attracting attention; not blatant

Trigger: UNOBTRUSIVE-no PROTRUSION

Trigger Sentence: If there is no PROTRUSION (projection) it will be UNOBTRUSIVE.

Sample Sentence: A good waiter is efficient and *unobtrusive*.

Related Words: OBTRUSIVE -a. undesirably noticeable

UNPALATABLE (un PAL uh tuh bul): a. Not tasty

Trigger: UNPALATABLE-UNEATABLE (** synonyms)

Trigger Sentence: Spicy Indian Biryani and honey is an UNPALATABLE/UNEATABLE combination.

Sample Sentence: Truth is usually bitter... and *unpalatable*.

UNPRECEDENTED (un PRESS i den tid): a. Never done or known before

Trigger: 1.UNPRECEDENTED -FIRST PRESIDENT. 2. NO PRECEDING EVENT

Trigger Sentence: The FIRST PRESIDENT inaugural oath ceremony is obviously UNPRECEDENTED.

Sample sentence The foot ball team has seen *unprecedented* success this year.

UNPREPOSSESSING (un pree puh ZES ing): a. Unattractive

Trigger: UNPREPOSSESING- UNPRESENTABLE

Trigger Sentence: 1. It does NOT POSSESS good looks. 2. UNPRESENTABLE and UNPREPOSSESSING are synonyms.

Sample Sentence: The actress's first appearance was however *unprepossessing*.

Related Words: PREPOSSESSING –a. impressive; attractive

UNRAVEL (un RAV ul) v.Untwist; solve

Trigger: UNRAVEL-REVEAL

Trigger Sentence: By REVEALING its secret, he UNRAVELED the mystery.

Sample Sentence: Astronauts have *unraveled* some of the mysteries of the Milky Way.

UNREMITTING (un ri MIT ing): a. Non-stop, continuous; never relaxing

   Trigger: UNREMITTING- UN+QUITTING- UN+RETIRING

   Trigger Sentence: The UNREMITTING rain has been UN+QUITTING for the last 20 days.

   Sample Sentence: My perfectionist boss is known for his *unremitting* attention to detail.

UNRULY (un ROO lee): a. Unmanageable; disobedient

   Trigger: UNRULY-UN+RULE

   Trigger Sentence: The UNRULY teenagers in the school are NOT following the RULES.

   Sample Sentence: *Unruly* trainees were thrown out of the army school.

UNSCATHED (uhn SKEYTHD): a. Unharmed, not Hurt

   Trigger: UNSCATHED-"UN (NO) +SCARRED"

   Trigger Sentence: 1. The president escaped the assassination attempt UNSCATHED and UNSCARRED. 2. Unscarred, unscratched and unscathed are synonyms.

   Sample Sentence: His lost dog however managed to come back home *unscathed*.

UNSEEMLY (un SEEM lee): a. Improper; indecent

   Trigger: 1.UNSEEMLY-NOT SEEMLY. 2. UNSEEMLY- UN+SHAME (shameless)

   Trigger Sentence: It is UNSEEMLY / NOT SEEMLY to use profane language in movies.

   Sample Sentence: Everyone was shocked by her *unseemly* conduct at the party.

UNSIGHTLY (uhn SAHYT lee): a. Ugly

   Trigger: 1.UN (NOT) + SIGHT (see). 2. BEAUTIFUL SIGHT

   Trigger Sentence: What a BEAUTIFUL SIGHT ? (It's opposite- UNSIGHTLY- UNBEAUTIFUL).

   Sample Sentence: Mining created an *unsightly* grayish gash on these otherwise green ranges.

UNSOUND (un SOUND): a. Unhealthy; weak; faulty

   Trigger: UNSOUND –NOT SOUND

   Trigger Sentence: UNSOUND banking practices are NOT SOUND financially.

   Sample Sentence: The building is structurally *unsound*.

UNSPARING (un SPAIR ing): a. 1. Cruel; not merciful. 2. Generous, not stingy (second sense)

   Trigger: UNSPARING-NOT SPARING

   Trigger Sentence: My boss is UNSPARINGLY severe; he NEVER SPARES anyone in his criticism.

   Sample Sentence: The actor *unsparingly* donated to the animal welfare organization.

UNSUNG (uhn SUHNG): a. Not honored, not celebrated or praised

   Trigger: UNSUNG-NOT SUNG

   Trigger Sentence: UNSUNG heroes' achievements are NOT praised in SONGS.

   Sample sentience: He was an *unsung* hero of India's world cup cricket history.

UNTENABLE (uhn TEN uh bul): a. Undefendable; not able to be maintained

   Trigger: UNTENABLE-UNDEFENDABLE

   Trigger Sentence: 1. UNTENABLE fort is UNDEFENDABLE. 2. TENABLE and UNTENABLE are antonyms.3. Your reasons are so UNTENABLE that they are UNDEFENDABLE in the court-of-law.

Sample Sentence: The house was neglected for so long that it is now *untenable*.

Related Words: TENABLE -n. capable of being defended against attack.

UNTOWARD (un TOH ward): a. Unfavorable; causing trouble

Trigger: UN+TOWARD

Trigger Sentence: If something good is NOT TOWARDS you, it will be UNTOWARD for you.

Sample Sentence: *Untoward* incidents like this fistfight in the office should never recur!

UNTRAMMELED (un TRAM uh ld): a. Not limited; not curbed

Trigger: 1.UNTRAMMELED – UN+TRAM. 2. UNTRAVELED (almost opposite)

Trigger Sentence: TRAM runs only on track. UNTRAMMELED things are not restricted by track.

Sample Sentence: She has the gift of a fresh explorative eye and an *untrammeled* curiosity.

UNTUTORED (un TOO terd): a. Untrained; uneducated

Trigger: UNTUTORED-NOT TUTORED

Trigger Sentence: WITHOUT being TUTORED - UNTUTORED people will be lacking in skills.

Sample Sentence: Despite being *untutored* Varma showed great flair in business administration.

UNWARRANTED (un WORE un tid): a. Unjustified; unreasonable; ground less

Trigger: UNWARRANTED (without warranty) -UNWANTED

Trigger Sentence: 1. UNWANTED gossips is UNWARRANTED. 2. Without arrest WARRANT, imprisonment is UNWARRANTED.

Sample Sentence: The allegations proved to be *unwarranted*.

UNWIELDY (un WEELD ee): a. Awkward, unmanageable, burdensome

Trigger: 1.UNWIELDY-UNYIELDING. 2. NOT HANDY

Trigger Sentence: 1. North Korea is UNWIELDY to the demands of USA and remains defiantly UNYIELDING for decades. 2. My son has become UNWIELDY and he is NOT at all HANDY to me.

Sample Sentence: A sledge hammer is *unwieldy* and dangerous.

Related Words: WIELD -v. exercise (influence); handle with skill (e.g. a weapon).

UNWITTING (un WIT ing): a. Unintentional; unaware

Trigger: UNWITTING-UN+ WILLING (not willing to do)

Trigger Sentence: An UNWITTING/UNWILLING mistake may be ignored.

Sample Sentence: His often passes *unwitting* remarks, which however cannot be ignored.

UNWONTED (uhn WOHN tid): a. Unaccustomed, unusual

Trigger: I WON"T

Trigger Sentence: 1. I WON'T do it, it is UNWONTED. 2. UNWANTED desires are UNWONTED; not habituated.

Sample Sentence: He was surprised by her *unwonted* cheerfulness.

Related Words: WON'T -n. habit

UPBRAID (up BREYD): v. Severely criticize or scold

Trigger: 1.BRIDE-UP-"BRIDE GROOM". 2. UPBRAID- DEGRADE

Trigger Sentence: 1. The BRIDE UPBRAIDED the BRIDEGROOM for coming late to the wedding. 2. The teacher UPBRAIDED the student by DEGRADING him harshly for his irresponsible behavior.

Sample Sentence: Pat never expected that his presentation will be *upbraided* in the conference.

UPHEAVAL (up HEE vul): n. A violent disruption; a major change

Trigger: UPHEAVAL-UP EVIL

Trigger Sentence: The EVIL is UP and it made an UPHEAVAL.

Sample Sentence: The civil rights movement marked a period of social *upheaval* in the U.S.

UPROOT (up ROOT): v. Pull out of the ground, eradicate

Trigger: UPROOT-ROOT OUT

Trigger Sentence: UPROOT is to PULL it from ROOTS and rip it out of place.

Sample Sentence: Can we ever be able to *uproot* racial discrimination?

URBANE (ur BANE): a. Polite, elegant; refined

Trigger: URBANE-URBAN

Trigger Sentence: 1. URBAN people have REFINED and POLITE manners; whereas RUSTIC people have RUDE manners. 2. URBAN people tend to learn superficial URBANE etiquette.

Sample Sentence: Mallika married an uneducated thug and not the *urbane* gentleman.

Related Words: URBANITY -n. polished courtesy

USURP (yoo ZURP): v. Seize another's power; supplant

Trigger: USURP- "USE UR POWER"

Trigger Sentence: USE UR POWER to USURP the enemy. If YOU want to SURPASS, USURP them.

Sample Sentence: City council was accused of *usurping* the mayors' powers into their hold.

USURY (YOO zhur ee): n. Lending money at high interest rates

Trigger: 1. USURY-TREASURY. 2. USURY-(>USUAL %)

Trigger Sentence: TREASURY lends money at USURY-more than USUAL INTEREST.

Sample Sentence: Credit card interest rates are usually *usury*!

UTOPIAN (yoo TOHP ee un): a. Perfect or idealistic but impracticable

Trigger: 1.UTOPIAN-U+TOP+IAN. 2. UTOPIAN-ETHIOPIAN

Trigger Sentence: 1. AN UTOPIAN believes in the TOP QUALITY. 2. An ETHIOPIAN cannot be a UTOPIAN; whereas EUROPEANS feel they are UTOPIAN.

Sample Sentence: Imagine living in a *utopian* world, where there is perfection and peace!

VACILLATE (VAS uh layt): v. Fluctuate; Waver

 Trigger: VACILLATE-OSCILLATE

 Trigger Sentence: My mind is VACILLATING just like a pendulum OSCILLATES.

 Sample Sentence: She *vacillated* on the issue of adopting a baby girl.

VACUOUS (VAK yoo wus): a. Empty; lacking in ideas

 Trigger: VACUOUS-VACANT- VACUUM

 Trigger Sentence: 1. My brain is VACANT and NO MATTER in it. 2. VACUUM is void. Universe has emerged from this VACUOUS state.

 Sample Sentence: It is a dull and *vacuous* film... no substance in it!

 Related Words: VACUITY -n. emptiness; absence of matter or meaning

VAGARY (vuh GAR ee): n. Caprice, whim

 Trigger: VAGARY-VARY

 Trigger Sentence: VAGARY-VARY; a VARYING thing is usually UNPREDICTABLE

 Sample Sentence: Wilson is bothered with his girlfriend's *vagaries*, whims and fancies.

 Related Words: VAGARIOUS -a. capricious, whimsical

VAGRANT (VEY grunt): n. Wanderer

 Trigger: VAGRANT-MIGRANT

 Trigger Sentence: The MIGRANT population had a VAGRANT life.

 Sample Sentence: Ria's dog got lost and became a *vagrant;* he came back home though.

 Related Words: 1. VAGARY –n. caprice. 2. VAGABOND –n. wanderer

VAIN (VEYN): a. 1. Proud; egotistical. 2. Useless

 Trigger: 1. VAIN-I'M MAIN. 2. VAIN-NO GAIN (second sense)

 Trigger Sentence: 1. The VAIN man says "I'm MAIN". 2. NO GAIN, in VAIN attempt.

 Sample Sentence: 1. *Vain* and vanity is what she carried over her shoulders. 2. All her hard work went down the drain while she cried in *vain!*

 Related Words: 1.VANITY -n. excessive pride; conceit. 2. VAINGLORIOUS –a. boastful

VALEDICTORY (val i DIK tu ree): a. Relating to a farewell

 Trigger: VALEDICTORY- FAREWELL DICTATION

 Trigger Sentence: In a VALEDICTORY function, the orator DICTATED a FAREWELL speech.

 Sample Sentence: Our principal gave a touching farewell speech during our *valedictory* function.

VALIANT (VAL yunt): a. Brave; daring

 Trigger: 1. VALIANT-vaLIANt-LION (** synonyms). 2. VALIANT-GALLANT (** synonyms)

Trigger Sentence: In a VALIANT attempt he fought like a LION.

Sample Sentence: The Vijayanagara King *valiantly* won the battle.

Related Words: VALOROUS -n. brave; courageous

VALIDATE (VAL i deyt): a. Confirm; legalize

Trigger: 1.VALID-SOLID. 2. VALID-VALUE-VALUABLE

Trigger Sentence: 1. SOLID reasoning is VALID. 2. VALID argument is VALUABLE and is VALIDATED. 3. INVALID statements have NO VALUE and they are INVALIDATED.

Sample Sentence: The couple decided to marry and *validate* their relationship.

Related Words: INVALIDATE - v. annul; disprove

VALOR (VAL er): a. Bravery

Trigger: 1. VALIANT-GALLANT-MILITANT. 2. VALOR-SAILOR-JAILOR

Trigger Sentence: 1. All MILITANTS are VALIANT. 2. A SAILOR and a JAILOR show VALOR. 3. Val- (strong) valuable, validate, valiant, valorous belong to same family.

Sample Sentence: The border security forces with all their *valor* and grit guard the county.

Related Words: VALOROUS -a. brave, valiant

VANGUARD (VAN gahrd): n. Forerunners; advanced forces

Trigger: VANGUARD-ADVANCE GUARD (** synonyms)

Trigger Sentence: The VANGUARD/ADVANCE GUARD troops marched ahead in the battle.

Sample Sentence: Michael Jackson was the *vanguard* of pop music.

Related Words: AVANT-GARDE -a. radically new or original

VANITY (VAN i tee): n. 1. Feelings of excessive pride. 2. Worthless

Trigger: VANITY-VAIN (** synonyms)

Trigger Sentence: The beautiful actress described her accomplishments with VANITY/VAINNESS.

Sample Sentence: Those rich women carried *vanity* and pride as their baggage!

VANQUISH (VANG kwish): v. Crush by using force; quell

Trigger: VANQUISH-"VAN CRUSH"

Trigger Sentence: The perpetrators VANQUISHED their enemy in a VAN CRUSH.

Sample Sentence: Henrietta *vanquished* her drug addiction to return to normal life.

Related Words: VANQUISHED -a. decisively defeated in combat.

VAPID (VA pid): a. Dull, unimaginative; insipid; tasteless

Trigger: 1. VAPID-STUPID. 2. VAPID-"NOT RAPID"

Trigger Sentence: 1. I am VAPID as my brain is STUPID. 2. VAPID brain is NOT RAPID in grasping.

Sample Sentence: They have all the money in the world but have a *vapid* weak lifestyle.

VARIANCE (VAIR ee uns): n. Difference; variation

Trigger: VARIANCE-VARIATION (** synonyms)

Trigger Sentence: There was some VARIANCE /VARIATION in the opinion.

Sample Sentence: He had *variance* thought processes with his own peculiar principles.

Related Words: VARIED -a. different, diverse

VARIEGATED (VAYR ee uh gay tid): a. Many-colored

Trigger: VARIEGATED-VARIETY

Trigger Sentence: VARIEGATED is marked by VARIETY of colors.

Sample Sentence: Rudolph painted the room in *variegated* rainbow colors.

VAUNTED (VAWN tid): a. Boasted; highly publicized

Trigger: VAUNTED-most WANTED

Trigger Sentence: I'm most WANTED man in this world; every girl WANTS me; he BOASTS.

Sample Sentence: The film crashed at the box office despite the *vaunted* publicity.

VEGETATE (VEJ i teyt): v. Lead a dull and inactive life

Trigger: VEGETATE-VEGETABLE

Trigger Sentence: VEGETARIANS generally lead a DULL AND INACTIVE life; where as NON-VEGETARIANS are FEROCIOUS.

Sample Sentence: I spent the weekend vegetating at home like a couch potato.

VEHEMENT (VEE uh munt): a. Forceful, intensely emotional; marked with vigor

Trigger: 1.VEHEMENT-HE MEANT IT. 2. VEHEMENT-VIOLENT

Trigger Sentence: With VIOLENT emotions he has given a VEHEMENT warning; HE MEANT IT!

Sample Sentence: I *vehemently* oppose the inhuman animal slaughter houses.

VEIL (VEYL): v. Cover; hide

Trigger: VEIL-SEAL-CONCEAL

Trigger Sentence: VEIL and SEAL are synonyms. The dark VEIL CONCEALS a secret behind it.

Sample Sentence: Under the *veil* of descending darkness the cats prowled on the streets.

Related Words: UNVEIL -v. uncover, reveal

VENAL (VEE nul): a. Capable of being bribed; corruptible

Trigger: VENAL-PENAL

Trigger Sentence: 1. A VENAL officer, will be sent to a PENAL court; unless VENAL deeds are PENALIZED, it is difficult to bring social transparency. 2. VENDOR sells; VENAL officer is for sale!

Sample Sentence: The town's *venal* administration was quickly voted out by the headquarters.

Related Words: VENALITY -n. corruption

VENERATE (VEN uh reyt): v. Respect, revere

Trigger: VENUS RATED

Trigger Sentence: Greeks VENERATE VENUS, the Goddess of Beauty. VENUS god is VENERABLE.

Sample Sentence: 1. She is *venerated* for noble services. 2. With all my *veneration* I bow to you.

Related Words: 1. VENERATION -n. reverence, respect. 2. VENERABLE -a. deserving respect.

VENGEANCE (VEN juns): n. Revenge

Trigger: VENGE-AVENGE-REVENGE

Trigger Sentence: 1.AVENGE, REVENGE-VENGEANCE belong to same family with minor variations. 2. The boy did not forget his VENGEANCE until he took REVENGE after 35 years.

Sample Sentence: Prince Bhima as a *vengeance* killed the villainous Dhuryodhana for abusing the Pandava queen Draupadi.

Related Words: REVANCHE –n. revenge

Memory Test-113 : Match each word and its memory trick to the corresponding definition.

S.N	WORD	MEMORY TRIGGER	S.N	DEFINITIONS	KEY
1	TURMOIL	TURN+OIL -turn boil	A	Anger; resentment	
2	TURPITUDE	CORRUPT dude	B	Beginner, novice	
3	TUTELARY	Provide TUITION	C	Clear, obvious; plain	
4	TYRANNY	TIE+REIGN- VILLAINY	D	Clumsy, crude, strange	
5	TYRO	Not yet PRO	E	Emphasize, Underline	
6	UBIQUITOUS	UBIQ-U BIG	F	Expressed in a subtle way	
7	ULTERIOR	INTERIOR-inside	G	fearless, Courageous	
8	UMBRAGE	RAGE	H	Great commotion and confusion	
9	UNASSUMING	Un+as+sum-no SUM	I	Humble, modest	
10	UNCANNY	FUNNY-unusual	J	Immoral; excessive	
11	UNCONSCIONABLE	NO CONSCIENCE	K	Move with wave like motion	
12	UNCOUTH	UNCIVIL-uncombed	L	Oily; insincerely suave or smooth	
13	UNCTUOUS	Unct-OINT	M	Oppression; cruel government	
14	UNDAUNTED	DAUNTLESS	N	Present, or found everywhere	
15	UNDERMINE	Under+MINE	O	Providing protective supervision	
16	UNDERRATE	UNDERESTIMATE	P	Secret, unstated	
17	UNDERSCORE	UNDERLINE	Q	Strange, mysterious	
18	UNDERSTATED	STATE low	R	Underestimate, undervalue, belittle	
19	UNDULATE	Under water -modulate	S	Weaken; sap	
20	UNEQUIVOCAL	UNIVOCAL meaning	T	Wickedness; depravity	

Memory Test-114 : Match each word and its memory trick to the corresponding definition.

S.N	WORD	MEMORY TRIGGER	S.N	DEFINITIONS	KEY
1	UNEXCEPTIONABLE	UNOBJECTIONABLE	A	Allover; ubiquitous	
2	UNEXCEPTIONAL	NO EXCELLENT	B	Awkward; clumsy; unwieldy	
3	UNFETTER	RUN BETTER	C	Disheveled; uncared for appearance	
4	UNFLAPPABLE	Un+ FLOP	D	Free or Release from chains	
5	UNGAINLY	UNGRACEFUL	E	Having one meaning; unambiguous	
6	UNINITIATED	NOT yet INITIATED	F	Improper; indecent	
7	UNIQUE	Uni-ONE	G	Inexperienced; not initiated	
8	UNIVERSAL	Present in entire UNIVERSE	H	Never done or known before	
9	UNIVOCAL	ONE VOCAL only	I	Non-stop, never relaxing	
10	UNKEMPT	Un + kept	J	Not easily upset; Calm	
11	UNOBTRUSIVE	No PROTRUSION	K	Not open to criticism or objection	
12	UNPALATABLE	UNEATABLE	L	Not tasty	
13	UNPRECEDENTED	No PRECEDING event	M	Not visible; not attracting attention	
14	UNPREPOSSESSING	UNPRESENTABLE	N	Singular; rare; matchless	
15	UNRAVEL	Unravel-REVEAL	O	Ugly	
16	UNREMITTING	un+QUITTING- un+retiring	P	Unattractive	
17	UNRULY	UN+RULE	Q	Unharmed, Not Hurt	
18	UNSCATHED	no+SCARRED	R	Unmanageable; disobedient	
19	UNSEEMLY	un+shame (shameless)	S	Untwist; solve	
20	UNSIGHTLY	NOT+ SIGHT	T	Usual; ordinary	

Answers	EX.NO	1	2	3	4	5	6	7	8	9	10	11	12	13	14	15	16	17	18	19	20
	113	H	T	O	M	B	N	P	A	I	Q	J	D	L	G	S	R	E	F	K	C
	114	K	T	D	J	B	G	N	A	E	C	M	L	H	P	S	I	R	Q	F	O

Memory Test-115 : Match each word and its memory trick to the corresponding definition.

S.N	WORD	MEMORY TRIGGER	S.N	DEFINITIONS	KEY
1	UNSOUND	NOT SOUND	A	A violent disruption; a major change	
2	UNSPARING	NOT SPARING	B	Awkward, unmanageable	
3	UNSUNG	NOT SUNG	C	Cruel; not merciful; Generous	
4	UNTENABLE	UNDEFENDABLE	D	Empty; lacking in ideas	
5	UNTOWARD	NOT TOWARDS you	E	Fluctuate; Waver	
6	UNTRAMMELED	UN+TRAM – no TRAM	F	Lending money at high interest rates	
7	UNTUTORED	not TUTORED	G	Not honored, not praised	
8	UNWARRANTED	without WARRANTY	H	Not limited; not curbed	
9	UNWIELDY	Not HANDY	I	Perfect or idealistic but impracticable	
10	UNWITTING	UN+ WILLING	J	Polite, elegant; refined	
11	UNWONTED	I WON'T	K	Pull out of the ground, eradicate	
12	UPBRAID	DEGRADE	L	Seize another's power; supplant	
13	UPHEAVAL	up EVIL	M	Severely criticize or scold	
14	UPROOT	ROOT OUT	N	Unaccustomed	
15	URBANE	URBAN	O	Undefendable; unjustifiable	
16	USURP	USE UR POWER	P	Unfavorable; causing trouble	
17	USURY	TREASURY -(>usual %)	Q	Unhealthy; weak; faulty	
18	UTOPIAN	u+TOP+ian	R	Unintentional; unaware	
19	VACILLATE	OSCILLATE	S	Unjustified; unreasonable	
20	VACUOUS	vacant- VACUUM	T	Untrained; uneducated	

Memory Test-116 : Match each word and its memory trick to the corresponding definition.

S.N	WORD	MEMORY TRIGGER	S.N	DEFINITIONS	KEY
1	VAGARY	VARY nature	A	Boasted; highly publicized	
2	VAGRANT	MIGRANT	B	Brave; daring	
3	VAIN	I'm MAIN; NO GAIN	C	Bravery	
4	VALEDICTORY	Farewell DICTATION	D	Capable of being bribed; corruptible	
5	VALIANT	Valiant-LION	E	Caprice, whim	
6	VALIDATE	Make Valid-solid	F	Confirm; legalize	
7	VALOR	Valiant-gallant-militant	G	Cover; hide	
8	VANGUARD	advance GUARD	H	Crush by using force; quell	
9	VANITY	VAIN –I am MAIN	I	Difference; variation	
10	VANQUISH	VAN CRUSH	J	Dull, unimaginative; insipid	
11	VAPID	stupid-NOT RAPID	K	Feelings of excessive pride	
12	VARIANCE	VARIATION	L	Forceful, intensely emotional	
13	VARIEGATED	VARIETY of colors	M	Forerunners; advanced forces	
14	VAUNTED	most WANTED	N	Lead a dull and inactive life	
15	VEGETATE	VEGETABLE life	O	Many-colored	
16	VEHEMENT	he meant it -VIOLENT	P	Proud; egotistical; Useless	
17	VEIL	Veil-seal-CONCEAL	Q	Relating to a farewell	
18	VENAL	PENAL crime	R	Respect, revere	
19	VENERATE	VENUS rated	S	Revenge	
20	VENGEANCE	AVENGE-revenge	T	Wanderer	

Answers	EX.NO	1	2	3	4	5	6	7	8	9	10	11	12	13	14	15	16	17	18	19	20
	115	Q	C	G	O	P	H	T	S	B	R	N	M	A	K	J	L	F	I	E	D
	116	E	T	P	Q	B	F	C	M	K	H	J	I	O	A	N	L	G	D	R	S

WORD GROUPS DAY-29

★ **GRANDIOSE:** pompous, impressive

ADJECTIVES: bombastic, flamboyant, fustian, impressive, imposing, magnificent, ostentatious, pompous, majestic, splendid, resplendent, elaborate; august, palatial, stately, luxurious, opulent

NOUNS: grandiosity, grandeur, pomposity

VERB: enrich

ANTONYMS: adj. humble, modest; unpretentious

★ **ORNAMENTAL**

ADJECTIVES: baroque, elaborate, embellished, extravagant, flamboyant, florid, grotesque, ornamented, ornate, rococo

NOUNS: arabesque, embroidery, adornment, trinket

VERB: adorn, bedeck, emblazon, festoon

ANTONYMS: adj. plain, unadorned, undecorated

★ **BOMBASTIC**

NOUNS: rhetoric , hyperbole, pomposity, verbosity, prolixity

ADJECTIVES: bombastic, blustering, declamatory, tumid, turgid, pompous, verbose, ornate, orotund, high-sounding, ostentatious, grandiloquent, magniloquent, sonorous

VERB: declaim

ANTONYMS: adj. plain, simple; understated

★ **SHOWY -FLAMBOYANT**

ADJECTIVES: pretentious, flamboyant, extravagant, ornate, ostentatious; baroque, rococo.

NOUNS: chic, panache, flair, élan.

VERB: exhibit

ANTONYMS: adj. simple, restrained, modest.

★ **BOASTFUL/PROUD ABOUT ONESELF**

ADJECTIVES: boastful, bragging, swaggering, bumptious, conceited, egotistical, vainglorious

NOUNS: braggadocio, gasconade; braggart, blowhard; narcissism, vanity

VERB: brag, boast, swagger

ANTONYMS: adj. deprecating, modest

★ **TAWDRY (LOOK CHEAP)**

ADJECTIVES: garish, gaudy, glaring, meretricious, raffish, shoddy, tawdry, vulgar

NOUNS: gaudiness.

VERB:

ANTONYMS: adj. nice, sophisticated, tasteful

★ **BRANDISH:** exhibit aggressively, wave

ADJECTIVES: flaunting

NOUNS: flourish

VERB: wave, wield; display, expose, flaunt

ANTONYMS: adj. not show, subtle

★ **OLD AGE**

ADJECTIVES: hoary, senile, superannuated

NOUNS: dotage, senescence, senility; veteran

VERB: superannuate

ANTONYMS: adj. adolescence, infancy, youth

Word List Day-30

VENTURESOME (VEN cher sum): a. Bold

Trigger: VENTURESOME-ADVENTURESOME

Trigger Sentence: ADVENTURESOME guys are VENTURESOME.

Sample Sentence: The *venturesome* man ran into a burning house to pull out people to safety.

VERACITY (vuh RAS uh tee): n. Truthfulness

Trigger: 1. VERACITY-VERITY-VERIFY. 2. VERACITY-MENDACITY (refer)

Trigger Sentence: 1. Judge VERIFIED the VERACITY of the witness statements. 2. MENDACITY and VERACITY are antonyms. 3. Veracity, verity and verify (verify truth) belong to same family.

Sample Sentence: The police doubted the *veracity* of the informer from the militant base.

Related Words: 1.VERACIOUS -a. truthful. 2. VERITY –n. truth

VERBOSE (ver BOHS): a. Wordy

Trigger: VERB+BOSS-OVERDOSE

Trigger Sentence: VERBOSE-"OVERDOSE +VERBS"; VERBOSE - GRE VERBAL Reasoning is VERBOSE because it consists of an OVERDOSE of words.

Sample Sentence: 1. She writes *verbosely*. 2. He is a *verbose* orator; not economical with words.

Related Words: 1. VERBOSITY -n. excess of words. 2. VERBIAGE –n. wordiness

VERDANT (VUR dunt): a. Lush with vegetation; green; inexperienced

Trigger: 1.VEG+PLANT. 2. VERDANT-VERANDA

Trigger Sentence: 1. "VER" in the word is made as "VEG"; DANT-sounds like PLANT - VEG PLANT is GREEN. 2. My VERANDA is VERDANT. Most PLANT VEGETARIAN is a VERDANT.

Sample Sentence: The hills are *verdant* with a variety of medicinal plants.

Related Words: VERDURE - v. greenness of vegetation; fresh condition

VERISIMILAR (ver uh SIM uh ler): a. Appearing to be true or real; probable

Trigger: 1.VERISIMILAR-"VERY+SIMILAR". 2. FACSIMILE

Trigger Sentence: 1. VERISIMILAR is SIMILAR to the truth. 2. There are many VERISIMILAR FACSIMILES of Leonardo Da Vin Ci's Mona Lisa.

Sample Sentence: The wax models of the celebrities were *verisimilar* and illusionistic.

Related Words: VERISIMILITUDE -n. the appearance of being true or real

VERITABLE (VER i tuh bul): n. Real, actual

Trigger: 1. VERITABLE-VERIFIABLE. 2. VERACITY-VERITY-VERIFY

Trigger Sentence: 1. VERITABLE things are VERIFIABLE. 2. Veracity, verity, veritable, verifiable and verify (verify for truth) belong to same family.

Sample Sentence: The *veritable* law of attraction is that opposites' attract!

VERNACULAR (ver NAK yuh ler): a. Local or living language; mass style

Trigger: VERNACULAR-VULGAR-VULGATE

Trigger Sentence: Written in VULGAR way to draw readers of VERNACULAR language.

Sample Sentence: He writes essays in a very easy-to-read, *vernacular* style.

VERSATILE (VUR suh tl): a. Having many skills; having great diversity

Trigger: 1.VERSATILE-VARIETY. 2. VERSATILE-VARIABLE

Trigger Sentence: He is a VERSATILE actor who acted in VARIETY of roles.

Sample Sentence: He is an exceptionally *versatile* artist with an amazing quality of multitasking.

VERTIGO (VUR tuh go): n. Feeling of dizziness

Trigger: VERTIGO –"VERTICAL GO"

Trigger Sentence: Some get VERTIGO, when they view from the top of the VERTICAL place.

Sample Sentence: I suffered *vertigo* for few seconds while riding on the merry-go-round.

VESTIGE (VES tij): n. A trace or remnant

Trigger: 1. VESTIGE-WASTAGE. 2. VESTIGE-INVESTIGATE

Trigger Sentence: 1. WASTAGE is a REMAINDER. 2. INVESTIGATE to find all VESTIGIAL organs in body.3. Any VESTIGE organ like human appendix is an organ of WASTAGE. NOT DEVELOPED.

Sample Sentence: 1. Sudha's diamond ring was the last of *vestiges* left from her ancestors. 2. These heritage structures are only a *vestige*, but they do reflect the grandiose bygone.

Related Words: VESTIGIAL –a. not fully developed in mature animals; of a remnant

VEX (VEX): v. Annoy; distress

Trigger: VEX-EX (LOVER)

Trigger Sentence: 1. VEXED with EX-LOVER. 2. Think of EX-WIFE, EX-BOYFRIEND, you get VEXED.

Sample Sentence: Jimmy was *vexed* after being stuck in a stalled elevator.

VIABLE (VIE uh bul): a. Workable, practicable; capable of living

Trigger: 1. VIABLE-DOABLE. 2. VIABLE-LIVABLE

Trigger Sentence: 1. Make LIVEABLE and VIABLE decisions. 2. VIABLE options are DOABLE.

Sample Sentence: The desert is not a *viable* location for planting fruit trees.

VICARIOUS (vy CARRY us): a. Substitute, experienced through another

Trigger: VICARIOUS-"VICEROYS" ("VICE-CHAIRMAN"-"VICE-PRESIDENT")

Trigger Sentence: The ROY experienced VICARIOUS feelings through VICEROYS. VICEROY, VICE-PRESIDENT and VICE-CHAIRMAN- these people are substitutes.

Sample Sentence: With a *vicarious* pleasure I saw this film on deep diving underwater discovery.

VICE (VAHYS): n. Moral weakness; depravity

Trigger: 1.VILE-VICE. 2. VICE-not NICE

Trigger Sentence: 1. The VILE (evil) man acts VICE. 2. VICE upsets the NICE nature of the society.

Sample Sentence: The society characterizes prostitution as a *vice*.

VICIOUS (VISH us): a. Cruel or violent

Trigger: 1. VICIOUS-MALICIOUS. 2. VICIOUS-VICES (3.VICE-NICE)

Trigger Sentence: 1. It is VICIOUS to be in the company of MALICIOUS men. 2. VICIOUS things consist of VICES. 3. VICE and NICE are antonyms.

Sample Sentence: There's no need to be *vicious* for small issues in life.

Related Words: VICE -n. a bad habit

VICISSITUDE (vih SISS ih tude): n. Changes of fortune

Trigger: 1. VICISSITUDES-VACILLATIONS-OSCILLATIONS. 2. VICISSITUDE-VISITED

Trigger Sentence: 1. VACILLATIONS (oscillations) and VICISSITUDES are synonyms. 2. The superstitious couple VISITED many Hindu temples to overcome VICISSITUDES in their life.

Sample Sentence: *Vicissitudes* in life brings in variety like the ups and downs of merry-go-round!

VIGILANT (VIJ uh lunt): a. Watchful; attentive

Trigger: 1. VIGILANT-INVIGILATOR. 2. VIGILANT-NEGLIGENT (** antonyms)

Trigger Sentence: The INVIGILATORS are VIGILANT in the examination hall.

Sample Sentence: Customs officers are *vigilant* to check on for smuggled goods in the baggage.

VIGOR (VIG er): n. Physical Strength; energy

Trigger: VIGOR-SUGAR

Trigger Sentence: The SUGAR has given him additional VIGOR.

Sample Sentence: My horse is getting old but he still has lot of *vigor* to go.

Related Words: VIGOROUS –a. strong; robust

VILIFY (VIL ih fie): v. Slander; to speak ill of

Trigger: VILIFY-VILLAIN

Trigger Sentence: Hero VILIFIES the VILLAIN; EVIL minded people are VILIFIED by the public.

Sample Sentence: Both the generals *vilified* each other as unpatriotic turncoats.

Related Words: 1.VILIFICATION -n. slander, defamation. 2.REVILE –v. abuse

VINDICATE (VIN di keyt): v. Clear from blame; justify, support

Trigger: VINDICATE-"WIN THE CASE"

Trigger Sentence: If we WIN THE CASE, it will VINDICATE us from all the blame.

Sample Sentence: The evidences will completely *vindicate* her.

VINDICTIVE (vin DIK tiv): a. Revengeful; spiteful

Trigger: VINDICTIVE-REACTIVE

Trigger Sentence: REACTIVE (revengeful) people like VIN DIESEL are VINDICTIVE in nature.

Sample Sentence: After being fired, the *vindictive* clerk spread vile rumors against the firm.

VINTAGE (VIN tij): a. Antiquated; high quality; classic

Trigger: 1.VINATGE- WINE-AGE. 2. VINTAGE-OLD AGE

Trigger Sentence: A VINTAGE wine is an AGED WINE.

Sample Sentence: The Charlie Chaplin movie is a *vintage* comedy of the silent movie era.

VIRTUAL (VUR choo ul): a. Practical; being in essence

Trigger: VIRTUAL-not ACTUAL-but almost close to ACTUAL

Trigger Sentence: The web-site provides the VIRTUAL tour of the university if not the ACTUAL.

Sample Sentence: Some universities are using *virtual* class rooms to impart on-line training.

VIRTUOSO (vur choo OH soh): n. Highly skilled artist

Trigger: VIRTUOSO-PICASSO-MAESTRO

Trigger Sentence: PICASSO is an artistic VIRTUOSO.

Sample Sentence: Paul Cezanne was a *virtuoso*; his paintings are housed in world museums.

VIRTUOUS (VUR choo us): a. Good; morally excellent

Trigger: VIRTUE-WERE TRUE

Trigger Sentence: The virgins WERE TRUE; they are women of VIRTUE.

Sample Sentence: Virtuosity and *virtuousness* is something rare in today's generation.

VIRULENT (VIR uh lunt): a. Extremely poisonous; hostile; bitter

Trigger: VIRULENT- VIRAL-VIRUS

Trigger Sentence: VIRAL fever is VIRULENT. VIRUS is more VIRULENT than a natural calamity.

Sample Sentence: A *virulent* rumor ruined Priyanka's chances of getting married.

Related Words: VIRULENCE -n. toxicity; hatred, antagonism

VISAGE (VIZ ij): n. Face; appearance

Trigger: VISAGE-IMAGE

Trigger Sentence: Her face is the mirror IMAGE of her mother's VISAGE.

Sample Sentence: John Abraham is a well-built wrestler with a vigorous *visage*.

VISCOUS (VIS kus**): a.** Sticky and thick

Trigger: 1.VISCOUS-VICKS. 2. VISCOUS-STICKS

Trigger Sentence: 1. The VICKS vaporub cold balm is VISCOUS. 2. The VISCOUS glue STICKS.

Sample Sentence: Honey has turned *viscous* and waxy in this cold weather.

Related Words: 1. VISCID -a. adhesive; viscous. 2. INVISCID -a. having zero viscosity

VITAL (VAHYT l): n. Crucial; critical; living; lively

Trigger: VITAL-VITAMINS

Trigger Sentence: VITAMINS are VITAL nutrients required for normal metabolism in the body.

Sample Sentence: A good leader is *vital* for a great social order.

VITIATE (VISH ee eyt): v. Spoil; make inoperative

Trigger: VITIATE-VIOLATE

Trigger Sentence: The VIOLENT storm VITIATED all the crops in the region.

Sample Sentence: Do not *vitiate* their minds with your silly wily doubts.

VITRIOLIC (vi tree AHL ik): a. Bitterly scathing; caustic

    Trigger: VITRIOLIC-ALCOHOLIC

    Trigger Sentence: An ALCOHOLIC husband is VITRIOLIC by nature.

    Sample Sentence: *Vitriolic* and egocentric women do exist among us, out to damage our peace.

VITUPERATE (vy TOO puh reyt): v. Abuse, scold

    Trigger: VITUPERATE-RATE- BERATE-DENIGRATE

    Trigger Sentence: Critics usually RATE a movie; they RATE, BERATE and VITUPERATE bad movies.

    Sample Sentence: Those prisoners are callous, so *vituperation* will not help mend their ways.

    Related Words: VITUPERATIVE -a. abusive

VIVACIOUS (vi VAY shus): a. Lively; animated; sprightly

    Trigger: VIVACIOUS - VIVA

    Trigger Sentence: Drink VIVA and become VIVACIOUS and lively.

    Sample Sentence: Joan's *vivacious* personality was infectious; she always made us laugh.

    Related Words: VIVACITY -n. gaiety, cheer, enthusiasm

VIVID (VIV id): a. Lively; intensely bright, distinct

    Trigger: 1.VIVID-VIVA-VIVACIOUS. 2. VIVID-VIDEO

    Trigger Sentence: 1. Vibrant COLOR dress is VIVID and VIVACIOUS. 2. The VIDEO is VIVID.

    Sample Sentence: The book includes many *vivid* illustrations.

VOCIFEROUS (voh SIF er us): a. Noisy, clamorous

    Trigger: VOCIFEROUS-VOICES +FEROCIOUS

    Trigger Sentence: Too many FEROCIOUS VOICES create VOCIFEROUS atmosphere.

    Sample Sentence: I am getting a headache to continuously listen to this *vociferous* woman!

VOGUE (VOHG): n. Popular fashion

    Trigger: VOGUE-PROVOGUE

    Trigger Sentence: The models wear PROVOGUE apparels because it is in VOGUE.

    Sample Sentence: Retro music and dressing is in *vogue* now.

VOLATILE (VOL uh tul): a. Changeable; explosive; evaporating easily

    Trigger: VOLATILE- VOLCANO

    Trigger Sentence: An active VOLCANO is VOLATILE; it can erupt at any minute.

    Sample Sentence: The share market in India is quite *volatile*.

VOLITION (voh LISH un): n. Act of making a choice or decision

    Trigger: 1.VOLITION-"V+OPTION". 2. VOLUNTEER

    Trigger Sentence: 1. An OPTION of own VOLITION. 2. He VOLUNTEERED to act on his VOLITION.

    Sample Sentence: She selected this weird dress on her own *volition*.

VOLUBLE (VOL yuh bul): a. Fluent; talkative, glib
    Trigger: VOLUBLE-VOLUME
    Trigger Sentence: She was a VOLUBLE speaker, talking VOLUMES.
    Sample Sentence: Such a *voluble* woman she is that she did not let us say a word!
    Related Words: VOLUBILITY -n. fluency, talkativeness

VOLUMINOUS (vuh LOO muh nus): a. Capacious, bulky; large
    Trigger: VOLUMINOUS-large VOLUME
    Trigger Sentence: There is VOLUMINOUS (many VOLUMES) literature in robotics research.
    Sample Sentence: With layers of warm clothing in winters, we tend to look *voluminous*.

VOLUPTUOUS (vuh LUP choo wus): a. Sensuous; luxurious; having an attractive full figure
    Trigger: VOLUPTUOUS-"VOLUME + PLUS"
    Trigger Sentence: Woman with good a VOLUME OF FIGURE at right parts looks VOLUPTUOUS.
    Sample Sentence: She is a *voluptuous* young woman with a great sense of sensuous dressing!

VORACIOUS (vaw REY shus): a. Excessively greedy; devouring
    Trigger: VORACIOUS-CARNIVOROUS
    Trigger Sentence: The CARNIVOROUS wolves are VORACIOUS.
    Sample Sentence: Vamsi is a *voracious* reader who whips off over three books every week.

VORTEX (VAWR teks): n. Whirlpool; engulfing situation
    Trigger: 1.VORTEX-VERTEX. 2. Imagine yourself twisting in a "V"
    Trigger Sentence: From the VERTEX of the wave the boat sucked down into the VORTEX.
    Sample Sentence: Some nations are still struggling in the *vortex* of a war and unrest.

VOUCHSAFE (vouch SAFE): v. Grant; concede
    Trigger: VOUCHSAFE—gift VOUCHER
    Trigger Sentence: A gift VOUCHER is VOUCHSAFED to the customer.
    Sample Sentence: He *vouchsafed* an explanation for all the questions thrown at him.

VULNERABLE (VUL ner uh bul): a. Unprotected; susceptible
    Trigger: VULNERABLE-UNABLE
    Trigger Sentence: The UNABLE person is very VULNERABLE to the disease
    Sample Sentence: Veena is *vulnerable* young innocent girl from a village.

WAGGISH (WAG ish): a. Joking, witty

   Trigger: 1.WAG-RAG. 2. WAGGING-RAGGING

   Trigger Sentence: The WAGGISH seniors RAGGED the juniors.

   Sample Sentence: As a prankster he overlooked the damage caused with his *waggish* tricks.

WAIL (WEYL): v. Cry out loudly; lament

   Trigger: 1.WAIL-AIL (ILL). 2. WAILING-WEEPING

   Trigger Sentence: 1. AILING people started WAILING. 2. WAILING is called WEEPING; wail, bewail, wailing are alternate forms of the same meaning.

   Sample Sentence: She *wailed* over the death of her dog.

   Related Words: BEWAIL -v. cry, wail; grieve

WANE (WAYN): v. Decrease in size or strength

   Trigger: WAXING-WANING (** antonyms)

   Trigger Sentence: 1. There is BUILD UP of WAX in ear…Ear WAX. 2. WAXING-increasing; WANING —decreasing; the moon WAXES and then WANES.

   Sample Sentence: By the late 70s, the band's popularity had begun to *wane*.

WANTON (WON tn): a. Sexually immodest; unrestrained

   Trigger: 1. WANTON-WANT ON & ON. 2. WANTON-WOMAN

   Trigger Sentence: 1. A WANTON ---WANTS ON & ON. 2. WANTON wants WOMAN.

   Sample Sentence: They slandered her for being a *wanton* woman with many male friends!

WARRANTED (WAR un tid): a. Authorized; justified

   Trigger: WARRANTED-WANTED

   Trigger Sentence: On a WANTED man an arrest WARRANT is WARRANTED; justified and wanted.

   Sample Sentence: The way military men get punished for small mistakes is *unwarranted*.

   Related Words: 1.WARRANT -v. justify; permit. 2. WARRANTY -n. guarantee

WARY (WAR ee): a. Very cautious

   Trigger: WARY-BEWARE

   Trigger Sentence: BEWARE of the dogs…Be WARY and cautious.

   Sample Sentence: Saif was *wary* of entering into the room filled with strangers.

   Related Words: WARINESS -n. cautious (about possible dangers or problems)

WASTREL (WEY strul): n. Person who wastes

Trigger: WASTREL-WASTED

Trigger Sentence: The WASTREL WASTED lot of his inherited money in foolish pursuits.

Sample Sentence: He is a young upper-class *wastrel*, courtesy his rich background!

WATERSHED (WATER shed): n. Crucial turning point

Trigger: WATERSHED-WATERGATE scandal

Trigger Sentence: The WATERGATE scandal was a WATERSHED in the politics of the US in 1970s.

Sample Sentence: Winning a lottery was a *watershed* moment in her life.

WAVER (WAY ver): v. Hesitate; be unsure

Trigger: 1.WAVER-WAY? 2. WAVER-VARY (** synonyms)

Trigger Sentence: This WAY!! Or that WAY!!! He WAVERS to choose a WAY!!

Sample Sentence: Finally Patricia decided to say "I do", after *wavering* on her wedding choice.

WAX (WAKS): v. Increase, grow

Trigger: WAXING-WANING

Trigger Sentence: 1. WAXING and WANING are antonyms. 2. Imagine there is build up of ear WAX that you are going to WANE it.

Sample Sentence: Sales instantly *waxed* after prices got cut down.

WEAN (WEEN): v. Give up a habit

Trigger: WEAN-LEAN

Trigger Sentence: To become LEAN the TEEN decided to WEAN herself away from fatty foods.

Sample Sentence: The puppies were weaned off their mother's milk before they were adopted.

WELTER (WEL ter): n. Confusion, disorder

Trigger: WELTER-(HELTER-SKELTER)

Trigger Sentence: 1. The room is in a total WELTER because kids threw things HELTER-SKELTER. 2. If you throw a stone in WATER it moves in TURBULENT fashion.

Sample Sentence: It is difficult to hear in the *welter* of noises during the city carnivals.

Related Words: HELTER-SKELTER —a. confused; disorderly

WHEEDLE (WEED l): v. Coax; entice; deceive by flattery

Trigger: 1.WHEEDLE-PLEADED. 2. WHEEDLE-NEEDLE (**near antonyms)

Trigger Sentence: 1. He PLEADED and WHEEDLED into going along. 2. Instead of WHEEDLING, he NEEDLED her with his sarcastic remarks.

Sample Sentence: He is just trying to *wheedle* you; don't you know your actual worth?!

WHET (WET): v. Sharpen; stimulate

Trigger: 1. WHET-CUT. 2. WHET-WET

Trigger Sentence: 1. WHETSTONE is used for CUTTING and SHARPENING. 2. You need to WHET your knife before you CUT vegetables. You better WET the edge of the knife before you WHET it.

Sample Sentence: 1. Prehistoric stone tools were *whetted* on a stone itself. 2. The aromas from this road side eatery always *whets* up my appetite.

WHIMSY (WIM zee): a. An odd or fanciful idea; impulsiveness

Trigger: 1.WHIMSY-FANCY. 2. WHIM-HIM

Trigger Sentence: 1. WHIMSY woman FANCIES being young. 2. Rely on HIM? He acts on WHIM!

Sample Sentence: The new designers created a windy *whimsical* fancy works.

Related Words: 1.WHIM -n. a sudden change of mind. 2. WHIMSICAL -a. capricious; amusing

WILLFUL (WIL ful): a. Intentional; headstrong

Trigger: 1.WILLFUL-"SELF-WILLED". 2. WILLED

Trigger Sentence: 1. She is a SELF-WILLED, WILLFUL girl. 2. The action was WILLED and WILLFUL.

Sample Sentence: He has shown a *willful* neglect for his wife's feelings.

WILY (WILE ee): a. Cunning, artful

Trigger: 1. WILY - (wi+LIE). 2. WILY -SLY-(S+LIE)

Trigger Sentence: 1. The people who LIE are WILY in nature. 2. WILY and SLY are synonyms.

Sample Sentence: The *wily* young boy was able to sneak into the stadium without a ticket.

Related Words: SLY -a. cunning; secretive

WINCE (WINS): v. Shrink back (with fear or pain); recoil

Trigger: 1.WINCE-PINS. 2. WINCE-RINSE

Trigger Sentence: She WINCED when an acupuncturist inserted PINS in her body.

Sample Sentence: She *winced* like a touch-me-not-plant as the doctor pulled out the syringe.

WINNOW (WIN oh): v. Separate the good from the bad; sift

Trigger: WINNOW- WIN NOW

Trigger Sentence: NOW a WIN in the game WINNOWS/separate good performers from the bad.

Sample Sentence: My granny *winnowed* the grains using a sieve.

WINSOME (WIN some): a. Attractive; agreeable; charming

Trigger: WIN +SOME-HANDSOME

Trigger Sentence: You will look WINSOME/ HANDSOME, when you WIN SOME games.

Sample Sentence: Praneeth is a *winsome* young man who becomes the centre of attraction.

Related Words: WHOLESOME -a. beneficial; good for health

WISTFUL (WIST ful): a. Sadly thoughtful; full of longing

Trigger: 1.WISTFUL-WOEFUL (** near synonyms). 2. WISTFUL –WISHFUL (** near synonyms)

Trigger Sentence: 1. A WISTFUL memoir made me WOEFUL. 2. WISHFUL eyes appear WISTFUL.

Sample Sentence: He became nostalgically *wistful by* listening to those old romantic classics.

WITHER (WITH er): v. Dry up or shrivel; decay

    Trigger: 1. WITHER- NO WATER. 2. WITHER -WEATHER

    Trigger Sentence: 1. If there is NO WATER, the plants will quickly WITHER away. 2. Dry WEATHER, flowers have WITHERED.

    Sample Sentence: My lush green lawn *withered*, as my lazy gardener did not water the plants.

    Related Words: WITHERING -a. weakening

WITTICISM (WIT ih siz um): n. Witty remark; wise saying

    Trigger: WITTICISM-WITTY (witty criticism)

    Trigger Sentence: The WITTY CRITIC is famous for WITTICISM

    Sample Sentence: Irish poet, Oscar Wilde is famous for his sharp *witticisms*.

    Related Words: 1. WITLESS -a. foolish; silly (**unwise). 2. UNWITTING –a. unknowing; unaware

WIZENED (WIZ und): a. Wrinkled with age; withered

    Trigger: WIZENED-old WIZARD

    Trigger Sentence: The WIZARD Dumbledore in "Harry-Potter" movies was a WIZENED old man.

    Sample Sentence: Yoda in the Star Wars movies is a *wizened* old man.

WOEFUL (WOH ful): a. Unhappy; sorrowful

    Trigger: WOEFUL-RUEFUL-SORROWFUL

    Trigger Sentence: WOEFUL, RUEFUL and SORROWFUL are synonyms. The team members were RUEFUL over their own WOEFUL performance.

    Sample Sentence: She has a *woeful* expression out of self pity!

    Related Words: 1. WOE -n. pain; sadness; misfortune. 2. WOEBEGONE sad, depressed

WORLDLY (WURLD lee): a. Earthly, temporal, material; sophisticated

    Trigger: WORLDLY-WORLD

    Trigger Sentence: 1. Life in this WORLD is WORLDLY; the WORLDLY possessions only give you the material comforts of the WORLD. They don't help you realized the spiritual purpose of life.

    Sample Sentence: She is *worldlier* than her elder sister.

    Related Words: UNWORLDLY -a. unaccustomed or unusual.

WRANGLE (RANG gul): v. Quarrel

    Trigger: WRANGLE-WRESTLE

    Trigger Sentence: WRANGLE and WRESTLE are synonyms. The members of the two political parties WRESTLED over the vexing WRANGLE.

    Sample Sentence: This couple kept *wrangling* throughout in the train journey.

WRATH (RATH): n. Anger; fury

    Trigger: 1.WRATH-RAGE. 2. WRATH-SOOTHE (** near antonyms)

    Trigger Sentence: 1. WRATH and RAGE are synonyms. 2. SOOTHE the WRATH to calm them.

    Sample Sentence: The puritans feared the *wrath* of God for their sins.

    Related Words: WRATHFUL -a. angry

XENOPHOBIA (zen uh FOH-bee uh): n. Fear of foreigners or hatred for foreigners

Trigger: XENOPHOBIA-"SEE+ NEW+ PHOBIA"

Trigger Sentence: People with XENOPHOBIA suffer with PHOBIA, whenever they SEE NEW people from foreign origin.

Sample Sentence: Stalin used anti-Semitism to fuel Great Russian *xenophobia* after 1947.

YEARN (YURN): v. Desire, long, crave

Trigger: 1.YEARN-EARN. 2. YEARN-YEAR

Trigger Sentence: 1. Most of the people YEARN to EARN more money, fame, love, etc. 2. After YEARS of my life in a foreign country, I am YEARNING to see my motherland.

Sample Sentence: In long distance marriages, couples eternally *yearn* for their spouses!

YIELD (YEELD): v. Surrender; give in

Trigger: YIELD in a FIELD

Trigger Sentence: The new methods have YIELDED a nice mango YIELD (n) in the FIELD.

Sample Sentence: He finally *yielded* to the wild party temptations in Thailand.

Related Words: YIELD -n. output; income

ZEALOT (ZEL ut): n. A fanatical follower of a religion or policy

Trigger: 1. ZEALOT-"ZEAL+ LOT". 2. ZEALOT-BIGOT. 3. JEALOUS

Trigger Sentence: 1. He has LOT OF ZEAL. 2. ZEALOT person is a BIGOT. 3. A ZEALOT (or a BIGOT) is a JEALOUS person; he NEVER TOLERATES others.

Sample Sentence: Those *zealots* think of themselves as guardians of their religion.

ZEALOUS (ZEL us): a. Having or showing zeal

Trigger: ZEAL LOVES

Trigger Sentence: A ZEALOUS person is full of ZEAL and ZEST.

Sample Sentence: Being a *zealous* mountaineer, Neil had climbed Mount Everest over six times!

ZENITH (ZEE nith): n. Point in sky directly overhead; summit

Trigger: 1. ZENITH-ZEN DYAN. 2. ZENITH-BENEATH

Trigger Sentence: 1. ZEN meditation leads to ZENITH of life. 2. BENEATH –below-ZENITH - (top).

Sample Sentence: 1. Lost in the jungles, we know it was noon, as the Sun had reached its *zenith*. 2. Mohan was at the *zenith* of his career when he decided to renounce the world!

ZEPHYR (ZEF er): n. Gentle breeze

Trigger: ZEPHYR-BREEZY FUR

Trigger Sentence: The BREEZE from the ZEPHYR gently stirred her coat's FUR.

Sample Sentence: As he waited near the river, his ladylove walked into his arms like a *zephyr*.

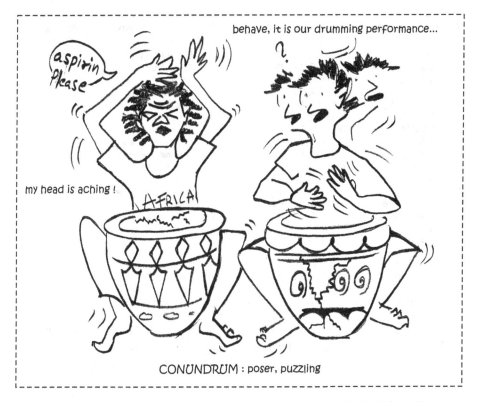

CONUNDRUM : poser, puzzling

Memory Test-117 : Match each word and its memory trick to the corresponding definition.

S.N	WORD	MEMORY TRIGGER	S.N	DEFINITIONS	KEY
1	VENTURESOME	ADVENTURESOME guys	A	Annoy; distress	
2	VERACITY	VERITY-VERIFY	B	Appearing to be true or real	
3	VERBOSE	Verb+BOSS-OVERDOSE	C	Bold	
4	VERDANT	VEG+PLANT -veranda	D	Changes of fortune	
5	VERISIMILAR	VERY+SIMILAR- FACSIMILE	E	Clear from blame; justify	
6	VERITABLE	VERIFIABLE	F	Cruel or violent	
7	VERNACULAR	VULGAR-VULGATE	G	Feeling of dizziness	
8	VERSATILE	VARIETY of talents	H	Having many skills	
9	VERTIGO	VERTICAL GO	I	Indirect, through another	
10	VESTIGE	WASTAGE-investigate	J	Local or living language; natural style	
11	VEX	Imagine EX (lover)	K	Lush with vegetation; inexperienced	
12	VIABLE	DOABLE	L	Moral weakness; depravity	
13	VICARIOUS	VICE ROY- VICARIOUS feelings	M	Physical Strength; energy	
14	VICE	Vile- -NOT NICE	N	practicable; capable of living	
15	VICIOUS	MALICIOUS	O	Real, actual	
16	VICISSITUDE	vacillations-OSCILLATIONS	P	Slander; to speak ill of	
17	VIGILANT	INVIGILATOR	Q	trace or remnant	
18	VIGOR	SUGAR gave VIGOR	R	Truthfulness	
19	VILIFY	VILIFY the VILLAIN	S	Watchful; attentive	
20	VINDICATE	WIN THE CASE	T	Wordy	

Memory Test-118 : Match each word and its memory trick to the corresponding definition.

S.N	WORD	MEMORY TRIGGER	S.N	DEFINITIONS	KEY
1	VINDICTIVE	REACTIVE - VIN DIESEL	A	Abuse, scold	
2	VINTAGE	WINE-AGE-OLD AGE	B	Act of making a choice or decision	
3	VIRTUAL	Close to ACTUAL	C	antiquated; high quality; classic	
4	VIRTUOSO	PICASSO-MAESTRO	D	Bitterly scathing; caustic	
5	VIRTUOUS	WERE TRUE	E	Capacious, bulky; large	
6	VIRULENT	VIRAL-VIRUS	F	Changeable; explosive	
7	VISAGE	Real IMAGE	G	Crucial; critical; living	
8	VISCOUS	VICKS-STICKS	H	Extremely poisonous; hostile	
9	VITAL	VITAMINS	I	Face; appearance	
10	VITIATE	VITIATE-VIOLATE	J	Fluent; talkative, glib	
11	VITRIOLIC	ALCOHOLIC nature	K	Good; morally excellent	
12	VITUPERATE	Critics RATE a movie	L	Highly skilled artist	
13	VIVACIOUS	Drink VIVA	M	Lively; intensely bright, distinct	
14	VIVID	VIVA-VIVACIOUS -VIDEO	N	Lively; animated; sprightly	
15	VOCIFEROUS	VOICES +FEROCIOUS	O	Noisy, clamorous	
16	VOGUE	wear PROVOGUE	P	Popular fashion	
17	VOLATILE	active VOLCANO is VOLATILE	Q	Practical; being in essence	
18	VOLITION	V+OPTION- VOLUNTEER	R	Revengeful; spiteful	
19	VOLUBLE	Sound VOLUME	S	Spoil; make inoperative	
20	VOLUMINOUS	large VOLUME	T	Sticky and thick	

Answers

EX.NO	1	2	3	4	5	6	7	8	9	10	11	12	13	14	15	16	17	18	19	20
117	C	R	T	K	B	O	J	H	G	Q	A	N	I	L	F	D	S	M	P	E
118	R	C	Q	L	K	H	I	T	G	S	D	A	N	M	O	P	F	B	J	E

Memory Test-119 : Match each word and its memory trick to the corresponding definition.

S.N	WORD	MEMORY TRIGGER	S.N	DEFINITIONS	KEY
1	VOLUPTUOUS	VOLUME + PLUS girl	A	An odd or fanciful idea	
2	VORACIOUS	CARNIVOROUS wolves	B	Authorized; justified	
3	VORTEX	VERTEX twisting in a "V"	C	Coax; entice; deceive by flattery	
4	VOUCHSAFE	gift VOUCHER	D	Confusion, disorder	
5	VULNERABLE	UNABLE	E	Crucial turning point	
6	WAGGISH	WAGGISH seniors RAGGED	F	Cry out loudly; lament	
7	WAIL	WAILING-WEEPING	G	Decrease in size or strength	
8	WANE	WASTE away	H	Excessively greedy; devouring	
9	WANTON	WANTS ON & ON- WOMAN	I	Give up a habit	
10	WARRANTED	Arrest WARRANT	J	Grant; concede	
11	WARY	BEWARE	K	Hesitate; be unsure	
12	WASTREL	WASTED	L	Increase, grow	
13	WATERSHED	WATERGATE scandal	M	Joking, witty	
14	WAVER	Which WAY?? -VARY	N	Person who wastes	
15	WAX	Build up of WAX	O	Sensuous; luxurious	
16	WEAN	to become LEAN- WEAN	P	Sexually immodest; unrestrained	
17	WELTER	HELTER-SKELTER	Q	Sharpen; stimulate	
18	WHEEDLE	NEED - PLEADE	R	Unprotected; susceptible	
19	WHET	WHET-CUT	S	Very cautious	
20	WHIMSY	FANCY	T	Whirlpool; engulfing situation	

Memory Test-120 : Match each word and its memory trick to the corresponding definition.

S.N	WORD	MEMORY TRIGGER	S.N	DEFINITIONS	KEY
1	WILLFUL	SELF-WILLED	A	Anger; fury	
2	WILY	wi+LIE	B	Attractive; charming	
3	WINCE	WINCE-PINS -RINSE	C	Cunning, artful	
4	WINNOW	WIN NOW	D	Desire, long, crave	
5	WINSOME	HANDSOME	E	Dry up or shrivel; decay	
6	WISTFUL	WOEFUL	F	Earthly, temporal; sophisticated	
7	WITHER	NO WATER	G	fanatical follower	
8	WITTICISM	WITTY	H	Fear/hatred of foreigners	
9	WIZENED	old WIZARD	I	Gentle breeze	
10	WOEFUL	RUEFUL-SORROWFUL	J	Having or showing zeal	
11	WORLDLY	Life in this WORLD	K	Intentional; headstrong	
12	WRANGLE	WRESTLE	L	Point in sky directly overhead	
13	WRATH	RAGE –no SOOTHE	M	Quarrel	
14	XENOPHOBIA	SEE+ NEW+ PHOBIA	N	Sadly thoughtful; full of longing	
15	YEARN	EARN-YEAR	O	Separate the good from the bad	
16	YIELD	YIELD in a FIELD	P	Shrink back ; recoil	
17	ZEALOT	ZEAL+ LOT-JEALOUS	Q	Surrender; give in	
18	ZEALOUS	ZEAL LOVES	R	Unhappy; sorrowful	
19	ZENITH	ZENITH-ZEN DYAN	S	Witty remark; wise saying	
20	ZEPHYR	BREEZY FUR	T	Wrinkled with age; withered	

Answers	EX.NO	1	2	3	4	5	6	7	8	9	10	11	12	13	14	15	16	17	18	19	20
	119	O	H	T	J	R	M	F	G	P	B	S	N	E	K	L	I	D	C	Q	A
	120	K	C	P	O	B	N	E	S	T	R	F	M	A	H	D	Q	G	J	L	I

WORD GROUPS DAY-30

★ **FLAGRANT:** conspicuously offensive; very noticeable

ADJECTIVES: blatant, glaring, obvious, patent, overt, conspicuous, barefaced, shameless, brazen; egregious, notorious, outrageous, scandalous, disgraceful, dreadful, gross.

NOUNS: flagrance, enormity

VERB: obtrude

ANTONYMS: adj. concealed, mild, moral, restrained, subtle

★ **NUANCE:** slight difference, shading

ADJECTIVES: suggestive

NOUNS: degree, fine distinction, gradation, nicety, refinement, shade, subtlety, tinge, variation

VERB: nuance

ANTONYMS: n. patent difference, lack of subtlety, sharp distinction

★ **ALLUSION:** indirect reference; hint

ADJECTIVES: allusive, indirect

NOUNS: casual remark, citation, connotation, denotation, indication, inference, innuendo, insinuation, intimation, mention, suggestion

VERB: allude, advert, refer, imply, hint at, suggest

ANTONYMS: n. reality,

★ **EUPHEMISM:** nice way of saying something

ADJECTIVES: euphemistic, mild, diplomatic, polite, inoffensive

NOUNS: circumlocution, delicacy, polite term, indirect term, substitute, alternative, understatement, genteelism, pretense

VERB: euphemise

ANTONYMS: n. patent difference, lack of subtlety, sharp distinction

★ **EMPHASIZE:** stress, make more clearly defined

ADJECTIVES: assertive, categorical, emphatic, explicit, unqualified

NOUNS: emphasis, prominence, significance

VERB: affirm, articulate, assert, enunciate, underline, highlight, spotlight, foreground; belabor; accent, accentuate, underline, underscore

ANTONYMS: v. depreciate, ignore, play down, understate

★ **SARCASTIC COMMENTS**

ADJECTIVES: acerbic, caustic, cynical, cutting, derisive, ironical, mordant, mordacious, sardonic, scathing, scornful, sharp, trenchant

NOUNS: contempt

VERB: disdain

ANTONYMS: adj.respectful, complimentary, flattering

★ **DEFAME:** damage the good reputation of

ADJECTIVES: abusive, calumnious, opprobrious, scurrilous, vituperative.

NOUNS: aspersion, calumny, libel, vilification.

VERB: defame, slander, malign, smear, traduce, vilify, besmirch, stigmatize, disparage, denigrate, discredit, decry

ANTONYMS: v. approve, commend, compliment, exalt, praise

Quick Review

A

ABANDON (v): Give up (an action or practice) completely

ABASE (v): Humiliate, degrade

ABASH (v): Embarrass

ABATE (v): Reduce; become less

ABDICATE (v): Give up; renounce

ABERRANT (adj): Deviant; abnormal

ABET (v): Help or encourage, usually in some wrongdoing

ABEYANCE (n): Suspended action; temporary inactivity

ABHOR (v): Hate, dislike

ABIDING (adj): Continuous; permanent

ABJECT (adj): Utterly hopeless; shameful

ABJURE (v): Renounce upon oath; deny

ABOLISH (v): Cancel, put an end to

ABOMINATE (v): Hate; to dislike

ABORTIVE (adj): Unsuccessful, fruitless

ABOUND (v): be plentiful; overflow with

ABRASIVE (adj): Harsh in manner; a substance that abrades

ABREAST (adj): Up-to-date; side by side; well-informed

ABRIDGE (v): Shorten

ABROGATE (v): Abolish; cancel officially

ABRUPT (adj): Unexpectedly sudden; curt; rude

ABSCISSION (n): The act of cutting off

ABSCOND (v): Depart secretly and hide

ABSOLUTE (adj): Complete, totally unlimited, certain

ABSOLVE (v): Pardon; forgive an offense

ABSTAIN (v): Avoid, refrain from

ABSTEMIOUS (adj): Self- control, especially in the consumption of food and drink

ABSTRACT (adj):Theoretical; difficult to understand; (n) Summary

ABSTRUSE (adj): Ambiguous, difficult to understand; obscure

ABUT (v): To border upon; adjoin

ABYSMAL (adj): Immeasurably deep or wretched; bottomless

ACCEDE (v): Agree, assent

ACCENTUATE (v): Stress or emphasize; intensify

ACCESSORY (n): Additional object; useful but not essential thing

ACCLAIM (v): Praise publicly

ACCOLADE (n): An expression of praise; award

ACCOMPLICE (n): Partner in crime

ACCORD (n): Agreement (v) to grant, give

ACCOUNT (v): Give a view; (n) Explanation, report

ACCRETION (n): An increase in amount; addition

ACCUSE (v): v. place blame, charge with a crime

ACERBIC (adj): Bitter; sharp-tempered

ACKNOWLEDGE (v): Recognize; admit

ACME (n): Top, peak; highest point

ACOLYTE (n): An assistant or follower

ACQUIESCENCE (n): Passive acceptance; yielding

ACQUISITIVE (adj): Strongly desirous of acquiring and possessing

ACQUIT (v): Discharge, set free; exonerate

ACRID (adj): Sharp; bitterly pungent

ACRIMONY (n): Bitterness or ill feeling

ACTUATE (v): Activate, motivate

ACUMEN (n): Shrewdness, keenness and depth of perception

ACUTE (adj): Shrewd, mentally sharp, critical

ADAMANT (adj): Hard; stubborn, rigid

ADDLE (v): Confuse; mix up

ADDRESS (v): Speak to, deal with; discuss

ADDUCE (v): To cite as evidence; offer as an example

ADEPT (adj): Skilled, expert

ADHERE (v): Stick fast to; be devoted to.

ADJUNCT (n): Something added on or attached; supplement

ADMONISH (v): Warn, scold

ADORE (v): Admire, venerate

ADORN (v): Decorate, enhance

ADROIT (adj): Clever, skillful

ADULATION (n): Excessive admiration, flattery

ADULTERATE (v): Make impure, spoil

ADUMBRATE (v): To suggest or disclose partially

ADVERSARY (n): Enemy; rival
ADVERSE (adj): Bad; miserable
ADVOCACY (n): Support
AESTHETIC (adj): Concerned with beauty; artistic
AFFABLE (adj): Good-natured and sociable; friendly
AFFECT (n): Influence, attack (of a disease)
AFFECTED (adj): Artificial; faked to impress
AFFINITY (n): Attraction; closeness
AFFIRM (n): State to be true; confirm
AFFLICTION (n): Suffering, pain; torment
AFFLUENT (adj): Wealthy, plentiful
AFFRONT (v): Insult, offend
AGGRANDIZE (v): Enhance, Exaggerate
AGGREGATE (v/n): Gather; accumulate
AGGRIEVE (v): Cause sorrow; offend
ALACRITY (n): Promptness; cheerful readiness
ALARMING (a): Worrisome, a warning of danger
ALBEIT (conj): Although, even though
ALCHEMY (n): A medieval chemistry
ALIENATE (v): To make unfriendly, separate
ALLAY (v): Calm; pacify
ALLEGE (v): State without proof
ALLEGORY (n): Symbolic story, metaphor
ALLEVIATE (v): Relieve; lessen the severity of...
ALLOY (v): Mix metals; corrupt by adding other substances
ALLUDE (v): To refer indirectly; hint
ALLURE (v): Tempt, attract
ALOOF (adj): Reserved or reticent; Indifferent; detached
ALTERCATION (n): Noisy quarrel
ALTRUISM (n): Unselfish; philanthropy
AMALGAM (n): A mixture or blend
AMATEUR (adj): Not professional, novice
AMBIGUOUS (adj): Doubtful or uncertain in meaning
AMBIVALENCE (n): A state of having both positive and negative feelings towards a subject
AMELIORATE (v): Improve; get better
AMENABLE (adj): Easily managed; willing
AMEND (v): Change; correct
AMITY (n): Friendship, friendly ties
AMOROUS (n): Full of love; loving
AMORPHOUS (adj): Formless; lacking shape or definition
AMPLE (adj): Plenty, full

AMPLIFY (v): Intensify; make stronger; clarify by expanding
ANACHRONISM (n): Something or someone misplaced in time.
ANALOGOUS (adj): Similar, comparable
ANARCHY (n): Lawlessness, absence of government
ANATHEMA (n): Curse; solemn curse
ANECDOTE (n): A short entertaining story describing an amusing incident
ANIMADVERSION (n): Criticism; aspersion
ANIMATED (adj): Lively, energetic
ANIMOSITY (n): Strong hostility or enmity
ANNEX (v): Extension, add
ANNIHILATE (v): To destroy completely
ANNOTATE (v): Make explanatory notes; comment
ANNUL (v): Cancel; make invalid
ANODYNE (adj): Reducing pain; soothing
ANOINT (v): Consecrate; rub oil on a person's head.
ANOMALY (n): Irregularity, Abnormality
ANONYMOUS (adj): Not named, unknown
ANTAGONIST (n): Adversary; opponent
ANTECEDENT (n): Something going before...
ANTEDATE (v): To be of older date than; precede in time
ANTEDILUVIAN (adj): Ancient; antiquated
ANTICIPATE (v): Look forward to; expect
ANTIDOTE (n): A remedy to counteract a poison or disease
ANTINOMIAN (n): One who rejects a socially established morality
ANTIPATHY (n): Aversion, hatred
ANTIQUATED (adj): Out-of-date, obsolete
ANTITHETIC (adj): Opposing; negating
APATHY (n): No feeling, indifferent
APEX (n): The highest or culminating point; climax
APHORISM (n): Concise saying; pithy
APLOMB (n): Self-confidence
APOCRYPHAL (adj): Not genuine; untrue
APOLITICAL (adj): Not political; not interested in politics
APOLOGIST (n): One who speaks in defense of something; advocate
APOSTATE (n): Traitor; one who abandons his religious or political beliefs
APPALLING (adj): Shocking, horrifying
APPARENT (adj): Readily perceived or

understood; obvious

APPARITION (n): A ghost; phantom

APPEASE (v): Soothe, relieve

APPELLATION (n): Name, title

APPOSITE (adj): Appropriate

APPRAISE (v): Estimate value

APPRECIATE (v): 1. Be thankful for. 2. Rise in value or price. 3. Be fully aware of

APPREHEND (v): Arrest (someone) for a crime

APPREHENSION (adj): Anxious or fearful especially of future evil: foreboding

APPRISE (v): Inform

APPROBATION (n): Approval; praise

APPROPRIATE (v/adj): (v) Take without permission, (adj) suitable

APROPOS (adj): Appropriate; relevant, suitable

APT (adj) : Appropriate; intelligent

ARABLE (adj): Fit for growing crops

ARBITRARY (adj): 1. Based on random choice; capricious 2. Autocratic

ARCANE (adj): Secret, mysterious; understood by few

ARCHAIC (adj): Ancient; no longer used

ARCHETYPE (n): Original model, prototype

ARDOR (n): Enthusiasm; fervor

ARDUOUS (adj): Hard, laborious

ARID (adj): Dry, barren

ARISTOCRATIC (adj): Of the noble class; refined

ARRAIGN (v): Accuse; indict

ARTICULATE (v): Clearly express; effective

ARTIFICE (n): Trickery; deception

ARTLESS (adj): Without guile; open and honest

ASCENT (n): Climbing; rising up; upward slope

ASCERTAIN (v): Find out for certain; clarify

ASCETIC (adj): A person who practices self-denial; austere

ASCRIBE (v): Attribute to, charge to

ASPERITY (n): Sharpness, bad temper

ASPERSION (n): Slander; false rumor

ASPIRE (v): Seek to attain a goal, dream for...

ASSAIL (v): Assault, attack

ASSENT (v/n): (v) Agree, accept

ASSERT (v): State strongly

ASSIDUOUS (adj): Hardworking, diligent

ASSIMILATE (v): Fully understand; absorb

ASSUAGE (v): Sooth, make less severe

ASTONISHING (adj): Surprising, shocking

ASTOUNDING (adj): Amazing, Shocking

ASTRAY (v): Away from the correct direction

ASTUTE (adj): Clever; keen, shrewd

ASUNDER (adv): Into separate parts

ASYLUM (n): Shelter, refuge

ATAVISTIC (adj): Characteristic of a former era

ATONE (v): Make amends for; pay for

ATROCITY (n): Cruel act of violence

ATROPHY (n): Wasting away

ATTAIN (v): To accomplish, gain

ATTENUATE (v): Make thin; weaken

ATTEST (v): Testify; bear witness

ATTRITION (n): Gradual decrease in numbers; wearing down by friction

ATTUNED (adj) : in harmony; in sympathetic relation

ATYPICAL (adj): Unusual, not normal

AUDACIOUS (adj): Bold; daring

AUGMENT (v): Increase; add to

AUGURY (n): Omen; prediction

AUSPICIOUS (adj): Favorable, beneficent

AUSTERE (adj): Severely simple; unadorned; strict

AUTHENTICATE (v): Prove genuine

AUTHORITARIAN (adj): Demanding absolute obedience to authority; dictatorial

AUTHORITATIVE (adj): Commanding; reliable

AUTONOMY (n): Independence; self-government

AVANT-GARDE (adj): Radically new or original; unusually new

AVARICE (n): Greed; lust for power or wealth

AVER (v): To declare true; affirm

AVERSE (adj): Strongly disliking or opposed

AVERT (v): Prevent, turn away

AVID (adj): Keen interest; greedy

AVOCATION (n): Hobby or minor occupation

AVOW (v): Declare; confess

AVUNCULAR (adj): Like an uncle

AWE (n): Solemn wonder

AWRY (adj): Distorted; crooked

AXIOMATIC (adj): Self-evident truth requiring no proof, certain

B

BADINAGE (n): Witty conversation

BAFFLE (v): Confuse; frustrate

BALEFUL (adj): Harmful, threatening, malevolent

BALK (v): Refuse to proceed
BALM (n): Something that relieves pain
BANAL (adj): Lacking originality; ordinary
BANEFUL (adj): Destructive, harmful
BANISH (v): Expel; dismiss
BARD (n): A poet
BAROQUE (adj): Highly ornate
BARREN (adj): Infertile, unproductive
BARRICADE (n): Blockade, barrier; obstruction
BASK (v): Luxuriate; derive pleasure in warmth
BAWDY (adj): Vulgar, obscene
BEACON (n/v): Warning light; lighthouse; guide
BEDIZEN (v): To dress in a vulgar manner
BEDLAM (n): A scene of uproar and confusion
BEFUDDLE (v): Confuse
BEGUILE (v): Mislead, deceive; charm
BEHEMOTH (adj): A huge creature
BEHOLDEN (adj): Obligated; indebted; in debt
BELEAGUER (v): Harass; besiege; attack
BELIE (v): Show to be false; contradict; fake
BELITTLE (v): Disparage; decry
BELLICOSE (adj) :Warlike; combative
BELLIGERENT (adj): Quarrelsome; aggressive
BEMUSE (v): Confuse
BENEDICTION (n): Blessing
BENEFACTOR (n): Sponsor, donor
BENEFICENT (adj): Kind; good
BENEFICIARY (n): One who benefits from something; heir
BENEVOLENT (n): Generous, kind
BENIGN (adj): Favorable and not harmful; not malignant
BENISON (n): Blessing, benediction
BENT (n): A strong inclination or interest; natural talent
BEQUEATH (v): Leave property to someone in a will; hand down.
BERATE (v): Scold strongly
BEREFT (adj): Deprived of; lacking
BESEECH (v): Beg; to request earnestly
BESIEGE (v): Surround a place, esp. with an army, harass
BETRAY (v): Be disloyal, reveal a secret
BEWILDERING (adj): Extremely confusing
BIASED (adj): favoring one person or side over another
BIFURCATE (v): split into two, divide into two
BIGOT (n): A person who is one-sided and prejudiced in his views; intolerant to others opinions

BILIOUS (adj): Irritable; cranky
BILK (v): Cheat; defraud
BIZARRE (adj): Very strange or unusual; odd
BLAND (adj): Tasteless; mild; boring
BLANDISH (v): Coax with flattery; persuade
BLASE (adj): Bored with pleasure or dissipation
BLASPHEMOUS (adj): Irreverent; sacrilegious; profane
BLATANT (adj): Loudly offensive; extremely obvious
BLEAK (adj): Depressing, unhappy, sad
BLEMISH (n): (n) Flaw, fault, defect
BLIGHT (n): Disease, decay
BLITHE (adj): Happy; carefree
BLUDGEON (v): To hit forcefully; n. club
BLUNT (adj): 1. Characterized by truthfulness in speech, curt. 2. Not sharp
BOGUS (adj): Not genuine; artificial, sham
BOHEMIAN (adj): Unconventional (in an artistic way)
BOISTEROUS (adj): Noisy; violent, rough
BOLSTER (v): Support, reinforce
BOMBAST (n): Pompous; using inflated language
BONHOMIE (n): Good-natured friendliness
BOON (n): Benefit; blessing
BOOR (n): A rude or insensitive person
BOWDLERIZE (v): Expurgate; purify
BRAGGART (n): Boaster, show off
BRANDISH (v): Wave around; exhibit aggressively
BRAZEN (adj): Shameless or arrogant
BREACH (n): Violation; crack, gap
BREVITY (n): Briefness, shortness
BRIDLE (v): Bring under control
BRISTLING (adj): Showing irritation; raising like bristles
BRITTLE (adj): Likely to break; fragile; frail
BROACH (v): Introduce; open up
BROOK (v): Tolerate; bear
BRUSQUE (adj): Curt, abrupt; rude
BRUTALITY (n): Cruelty, ruthless
BUCOLIC (adj): Rural, pastoral
BUNGLE (v): Mismanage, blunder
BUOYANT (n): Able to float; cheerful; optimistic
BUREAUCRACY (n): Any large administrative system with numerous rules and regulations
BURGEON (v): To grow rapidly; blossom

BURLESQUE (n): Comic imitation
BURNISH (v): Make shiny by rubbing, polish
BUTTRESS (v): Support, reinforce
BYZANTINE (adj): Excessively complicated

C

CABAL (n): A Small group of secret plotters, group of conspirators
CACOPHONY (n): Discord, harshness in sound
CADGE (v) : beg for money
CAJOLE (v): Tempt, persuade with flattery
CALAMITY (n): Disaster; catastrophe
CALLOUS (adj): Hard; heartless; unsympathetic
CALLOW (adj): Inexperienced; very young
CALUMNY (n): A false statement to injure the reputation; slander
CAMOUFLAGE (n/v): Disguise; conceal; hide
CANDID (adj): Honest, open
CANDOR (n): Openness, sincerity
CANONICAL (adj): Conforming to orthodox rules
CANT (n): 1. Hypocrisy, false religiousness. 2. Jargon
CANTANKEROUS (adj): Bad-tempered, irritable
CANYON (n): A deep narrow valley with steep sides
CAPACIOUS (adj): Spacious, comfortable
CAPITULATE (v): Surrender
CAPRICIOUS (adj): Fickle, changeable; impulsive
CAPTIOUS (adj): Fault-finding, picky
CARDINAL (n): Main, chief
CARICATURE (n): Comical distortion
CARNAGE (n): Destruction of life
CARNAL (adj): Fleshly; Sensual
CARP (v): Find fault
CASTIGATE (v): Criticize; scold; punish
CATACLYSM (n): A violent upheaval or disaster; earthquake, flood
CATALYST (n): cause of change
CATASTROPHE (n): Disaster, calamity, cataclysm
CATEGORICAL (adj): Absolute, certain; without reservations
CATER TO (v): Supply something desired; pamper
CATHARSIS (n): Emotional cleansing through drama; purging
CATHOLIC (adj): Universal; embracing everything; liberal
CAUSAL (adj): Related cause and effect
CAUSTIC (adj): Corrosive, sarcastic; biting comments
CAVIL (v): Make petty or unnecessary objections
CEASE (v) : end, stop
CEDE (v): Yield; surrender
CELERITY (n): Alacrity, rapidity, speed
CELIBATE (n): Away from sensual (sexual) desires; unmarried
CENSORIOUS (adj): Fault finding; critical
CENSURE (v): Blame; criticize
CEREBRAL (adj): 1. n. An Intellectual Person, 2.adj. Relating To the Brain
CEREMONIOUS (adj): Formal; polite
CERTITUDE (n): Certainty, sureness
CESSATION (n): Stopping, ceasing
CHAGRIN (n): Displeasure, strong feelings of embarrassment
CHAMPION (v): Defend, support
CHANT (n): Sing, recite
CHAOS (n): Complete disorder and confusion
CHARISMA (n): A personal attractiveness
CHARLATAN (n): Fraud, one who claims more skill or knowledge than he actually has
CHARY (adj): Careful, cautious, wary
CHASTE (n): Pure, virginal, modest
CHASTEN (v): To punish; discipline
CHASTISE (v): Punish; criticize harshly
CHAUVINIST (n): Person who is extremely patriotic
CHECK (v): To block; stop motion
CHECKERED (adj): Marked by various changes in fortune
CHERISH (v): Relish; love
CHIC (adj): Elegantly and stylishly fashionable
CHICANERY (n): Trickery; deception
CHIDE (v): Scold, yell at
CHIMERICAL (adj): Illusory; imaginary
CHIVALROUS (adj): Courteous, Courageous
CHOLERIC (adj): Quick to Anger
CHRONIC (adj): Lasting (as of an illness); constant
CHRONOLOGY (adj): An order of events from the earliest to the latest
CHURLISH (adj): Boorish; rude
CIPHER (v/n): Code, a secret method of writing

CIRCUITOUS (adj): Roundabout, not direct

CIRCUMLOCUTION (n): Indirect or roundabout expression; verbosity

CIRCUMSCRIBE (adj): Limit; confine

CIRCUMSPECT (v): Cautious; prudent

CIRCUMVENT (v): Outwit; baffle; surround

CITE (v): Quote, commend

CIVILITY (n): Politeness, courtesy

CLAIRVOYANCE (n): Extrasensory perception, sixth sense

CLAMOR (n): Loud Noise

CLANDESTINE (adj): Done secretly

CLANGOR (n): Loud resounding noise

CLAUSTROPHOBIA (n): fear of enclosed spaces

CLEMENCY (n): Grace, mercy, leniency

CLERGY (n): People who work in religious ministry

CLICHE (n): Overused (expression or phrase); trite remark

CLOAK (v): Cover, conceal

CLOISTER (v): Shut away; seclude

CLOYING (adj): Distaste because of excessively sweet or sentimental

COAGULATE (v): Thicken; become clotted

COALESCE (v): Combine, fuse

COARSE (adj): Rough texture

COAX (v): Persuade (someone) by flattery; tempt

CODA (n): Concluding section; finale

CODICIL (v): A supplement to a will

COERCE (v): Force, compel to do something

COEVAL (adj): Living at the same time as; contemporary

COGENT (adj): Convincing

COGITATE (v): Contemplate, think over

COGNIZANT (adj): Having knowledge; aware

COHERENT (adj): Logically connected; understandable; consistent

COHESIVE (adj): Union; well integrated

COLLABORATE (v): Work together, cooperate

COLLUSION (n): Conspiracy

COLORED (adj): Influence; biased; deceptive

COLOSSUS (n): Very big statue; something that is huge

COMBATIVE (adj): Eager to fight

COMELY (adj): Attractive, pretty

COMMENDABLE (adj): Deserving praise

COMMENSURATE (adj): Equal in extent; having a common measure

COMMISERATE (v): Sympathize, pity

COMMODIOUS (adj): Spacious, comfortable

COMMONPLACE (adj): Ordinary, everyday; uninteresting

COMMOTION (n): Confusion, turmoil

COMPATIBLE (adj): Harmonious; agreeable

COMPELLING (adj): Powerful; convincing

COMPENDIUM (n): A brief summary of a larger work

COMPLACENT (adj): Self-satisfied, overly pleased with oneself

COMPLAISANT (adj): Willing to please others; obliging

COMPLEMENT (v): Complete; be the perfect counterpart

COMPLIANT (adj): Yielding, ready to comply

COMPLICITY (n): Partnership (in wrongdoing)

COMPORT (v): Behave; bear oneself

COMPOSED (adj): Self-controlled, calm

COMPOSURE (n): Calmness

COMPREHEND (v): Understand; apprehend

COMPREHENSIVE (adj): Thorough; inclusive, complete

COMPROMISE (n): 1. To come to agreement by mutual concession (positive sense) 2. Bring into disrepute or danger by reckless behavior (negative sense)

CONCATENATE (v): Link together, connect one to another

CONCAVE (adj): Curving inward; hollow

CONCEDE (v): Admit; yield

CONCEIT (n): Self love; arrogance; a fanciful notion

CONCEPTION (n): Creation; beginning of an idea

CONCILIATE (v): Reunite, make friendly; calm; pacify

CONCISE (adj): Brief; succinct; terse

CONCOCT (v): Invent

CONCOMITANT (adj): Occurring together; accompanying

CONCORD (n): Harmony, agreement

CONCUR (v): Agree, work together

CONDENSED (adj): Made shorter; reduced to dense form

CONDESCEND (v): 1. humiliate 2. Act in a proud manner

CONDIGN (adj): Well-deserved; merited

CONDONE (v): Forgive, pardon

CONDUCIVE (v): Encouraging, helpful

CONFER (v): Give, grant, or bestow

CONFINE (v): Limit, restrict

CONFORMIST (n): One who conforms to the established norms

CONFOUND (v): Confuse; puzzle

CONFRONT (v): Stand face to face; challenge

CONGENIAL (adj): Pleasant; friendly

CONGRUITY (n): The quality of agreeing; being suitable

CONGRUOUS (adj): In agreement or harmony

CONNIVE (v): Plot, scheme, conspire

CONNOISSEUR (n): Expert, aesthete; judge of art

CONNOTATION (n): Suggested or implied meaning of an expression

CONSANGUINITY (n): Kinship, connection

CONSCIENTIOUS (adj): Thorough and assiduous; careful

CONSENSUS (n): General agreement

CONSENT (v): Agree; approve

CONSEQUENTIAL (adj): Resultant, subsequent, important

CONSERVATISM (n): Desire to preserve traditions, resistance to change

CONSIDERABLE (adj): Substantial, notably large

CONSIDERATE (adj): Thoughtful; respectful; kind

CONSOLE (v): lessen the suffering of; encourage

CONSOLIDATE (v): Make stronger or more solid, merge

CONSPICUOUS (adj): Noticeable, easy to see

CONSPIRACY (n): Plot; secret plan

CONSTERNATION (n): Fear or dismay

CONSTRAINT (n): Compulsion; repression of feelings

CONSTRICT (v): Squeeze; restrict the freedom of

CONSTRUE (v): Interpret; explain

CONSUMMATE (v): Perfect, fulfill, complete

CONTEMPLATE (v): To consider carefully; look at thoughtfully

CONTEMPT (v): Disdain; disrespect

CONTEND (v): Compete; struggle

CONTENTION (n): Contest; Conflict

CONTENTIOUS (adj): Quarrelsome

CONTEST (n): Dispute, competition, match

CONTIGUOUS (adj): Touching; Adjacent

CONTINGENT (adj): Dependent upon,

happening by chance; n. representative group

CONTRADICTION (n): Statement opposite to what was already said

CONTRAVENE (adj): Oppose; contradict

CONTRITE (adj): Penitent; sorry

CONTRIVED (adj): Forced; artificial; not spontaneous

CONTROVERT (v): Refute; oppose, challenge

CONTUMACIOUS (adj): Rebellious; head strong

CONTUMELY (adv): Rudeness; contemptuous behavior

CONUNDRUM (n): Difficult problem; dilemma

CONVALESCE (v): Recover, get well after sickness

CONVENTIONAL (adj): Ordinary; routine; formal

CONVERGE (v): Meet, come together

CONVERSE (n): Opposite

CONVICTION (n): A determined belief, declaration of guilt (*second sense)

CONVIVIAL (adj): Friendly; cheerful, jolly

CONVOKE (v): Call to meeting, summon

CONVOLUTED (adj): Twisted; involved, intricate

COPIOUS (adj): Bountiful; abundant, plentiful

CORDIAL (adj): Friendly; warm; heartfelt

CORNUCOPIA (n): Abundance; a symbol of plenty

COROLLARY (adj): Something that naturally follows; result

CORPOREAL (adj): Bodily; material

CORPULENT (adj): Fat, obese

CORROBORATE (v): Confirm; support with evidence

COSMOPOLITAN (adj): Sophisticated; related to the whole world

COUNTENANCE (n/v): (n) Appearance; face, (v) Tolerate; support

COUNTERFEIT (adj): Forged, fake, false

COUNTERMAND (v): Cancel an order

COUNTERPOINT (n): contrasting item; opposite

COUP (n): A victorious accomplishment; sudden attack

COURT (v): Seek to gain; seek love

COVERT (adj): Secret

COVETOUS (adj): Having a great desire; greedy, envious

COWER (v): Shrink with fear

COZEN (v): Cheat; deceive
CRAFTY (adj): Cunning, deceptive
CRASS (adj): Rude, ill-mannered
CRAVEN (adj): Fearful, cowardly; dastard
CREDENCE (n): Belief, credit
CREDIBLE (n): Reliable; dependable
CREDULITY (n): Tendency to believe too readily; gullibility
CREED (n): Any system of religious beliefs
CRESCENDO (n): Gradual increase in loudness of the music, climax
CRESTFALLEN (adj): Sad and disappointed
CRINGE (v): Shrink back, flinch; recoil (in surprise or fear)
CRONYISM (n): Favoritism shown to friends
CROTCHETY (adj): 1. Bad-tempered. 2. Having unusual ideas
CRUDE (adj): Unrefined; natural; rudimentary
CRUX (n): Essential or main point
CRYPTIC (adj): Secret; mysterious
CULMINATE (v): Climax; conclude
CULPABLE (n): Deserving blame
CUMBERSOME (adj): Burdensome, heavy
CUPIDITY (n): Greed
CURMUDGEON (n): Ill-tempered, stingy person
CURSORY (adj): Casual, hastily done
CURT (adj): Rudely brief; abrupt
CURTAIL (v): Reduce, cut short
CYNIC (n): A person who disbelieves
CYNOSURE (n): Center of attraction

D

DABBLE (v): To work superficially
DAMPEN (n): Make moist; discourage
DAUNT (v): To scare; intimidate
DAWDLE (v): Delay, waste time
DAZZLE (v): Amaze, fascinate; blind with bright light
DEARTH (n): A scarcity; lack of something
DEBACLE (n): Downfall; defeat; disaster
DEBASE (v): Lower the value or character of; degrade
DEBAUCHERY (n): Excessive indulgence in sex, alcohol, or drugs
DEBILITATE (v): Make very weak; incapacitate
DEBRIS (n): Scattered rubbish or remains; fragments
DEBUNK (v): Ridicule, expose as false; disprove
DECADENCE (n): Decline, decay

DECEITFUL (adj): Deceptive, dishonest
DECIDUOUS (adj): Falling off as leaves; short-lived
DECIMATE (v): Kill a large part of...
DECIPHER (v): Decode; interpret
DECLAIM (v): To speak loudly and pompously
DECLIVITY (n): Descent, decline
DECOROUS (adj): Polite; socially correct
DECORUM (n): Good manners; politeness
DECREPIT (adj): Weak, frail; worn out by age
DECRY (v): Condemn; criticize
DEDUCE (v): Derive by reasoning
DEEM (v): Regard in a specified way; suppose
DEFACE (v): Destroy; disfigure
DEFAME (v): Damage the good reputation of; malign
DEFAULT (n): Failure to act; Failure to pay loan on time
DEFER (v): Postpone, delay, respect (second sense)
DEFERENCE (n): Respect, reverence
DEFIANT (adj): Resisting, opposing
DEFICIT (n): Lack; shortage
DEFILE (v/n): To make dirty or filthy; to pollute
DEFINITIVE (adj): Decisive; most reliable
DEFLECT (v): Divert; deviate
DEFT (adj): Adept, skillful
DEFUNCT (v): Dead; no longer in use
DEGENERATE (v): Deteriorate; become worse
DEGRADE (v): To reduce in status, rank etc., demote
DEIFY (v): Turn into god; Idolize
DEJECTED (v): Depressed, sad
DELECTABLE (adj): Delicious; delightful
DELETERIOUS (adj): Harmful
DELIBERATE (adj): To think carefully, intentional, methodical
DELINEATE (v): Describe or portray
DELUDE (v): Deceive, to mislead
DEMAGOGUE (n): False leader of people
DEMARCATE (v): Set apart; Mark off the boundaries
DEMEAN (v): Humiliate, degrade
DEMEANOR (n): Behavior, conduct; bearing
DEMISE (n): Death
DEMOTIC (adj): Of the common people, popular
DEMUR (v): Object; hesitate
DEMURE (adj): Calm and polite; modest; coy

DEMYSTIFY (adj): Clarify; free from mystery or obscurity

DENIGRATE (v): Criticize; blacken

DENOTATIVE (n): Indicating; representing, naming

DENOUEMENT (n): Outcome; conclusion (in a novel, play, film etc.)

DENOUNCE (v): Condemn; criticize

DEPICT (v): Portray; describe

DEPLETE (v): Empty, reduce

DEPLORE (v): Disapprove of; regret

DEPOSE (v): Dismiss; remove from the office

DEPRAVITY (n): Corruption; moral perversion

DEPRECATE (v): Disapprove; belittle

DEPRIVE (v): Prevent from having; deny

DERELICTION (n): Neglecting of one's duty, negligence

DERIDE (v): Mock, ridicule

DERIVATIVE (adj): Copied or adopted; lacking originality

DEROGATIVE (adj): Belittling, disparaging

DESCRY (v): See from far away

DESECRATE (v): Damage the sacred places; insult

DESICCATE (v): To dry out completely

DESIST (v): Stop; cease

DESOLATE (adj): Abandoned, neglected

DESPAIR (n): To lose all hope

DESPICABLE (adj): Deserving hatred and contempt

DESPISE (v): To regard with hate; scorn

DESTITUTE (adj): Poor, penniless

DESUETUDE (n): A state of nonuse

DESULTORY (adj): Aimless, random; digressing

DETACHED (adj): Not attached; aloof; impartial

DETAIN (v): Delay; arrest

DETER (v): Discourage, prevent

DETERIORATE (v): Get worse; weaken

DETERMINISTIC (adj): Pertaining to determinism (doctrine which states that there is a reason for everything and all is predestined)

DETRACTOR (n): Critic; one who belittles

DETRIMENTAL (adj): Injurious, harmful

DEVASTATE (v): Destroy; ruin

DEVIATE (v/n): Turn away from a norm; depart, diverge

DEVIOUS (adj): Not straightforward; dishonest

DEVISE (v): Plan, invent; think up

DEVOID (adj): Lacking; empty

DEXTEROUS (adj): Skillful

DIABOLIC (adj): Devilish, wicked

DIAPHANOUS (adj): Filmy, transparent; sheer

DIATRIBE (n): An angry speech; criticism

DICEY (adj): Dangerous, risky; uncertain

DICHOTOMY (n): Split, branching into two parts (especially contradictory ones)

DIDACTIC (adj): Instructive, teaching

DIFFER (v): Be dissimilar, distinct

DIFFERENTIATE (v): Distinguish, make different

DIFFIDENCE (n): Shyness

DIFFUSE (v/ adj): (v) Scatter; (adj) Wordy, rambling

DIGRESSION (n): Deviation from the main point

DILAPIDATED (v): Spoiled because of neglect

DILATE (v): Expand, enlarge

DILATORY (adj): Delaying

DILETTANTE (adj): Superficial, amateur; dabbler

DILIGENT (adj): Industrious, hard-working

DIMINUTION (n): Reduction, decrease

DIN (n): A loud continued noise

DIRE (adj): Terrible, disastrous

DISABUSE (v): Correct a false impression; undeceive

DISAFFECTED (adj): 1. Not satisfied. 2. Disloyal

DISAPPROBATION (n): Disapproval, condemnation

DISARRAY (n): Lack of order, mess

DISAVOWAL (n): Denial, rejection

DISCERN (adj): To see things clearly; recognize

DISCLOSE (v): Reveal

DISCOMFIT (v): Make uneasy, discomfort

DISCONCERT (v): Upset; disorder; confuse

DISCORD (n): Disagreement, disharmony

DISCOUNT (v): Disregard, ignore

DISCREDIT (n): Defame; disbelieve

DISCREET (v): Careful; diplomatic; subtle

DISCREPANCY (n): Lack of consistency; difference

DISCRETE (adj): Separate and distinct

DISCRETION (n): Caution, careful judgment

DISCRIMINATE (v): Recognize a difference, treat differently (*negative sense)

DISDAIN (v): To view with disrespect

DISENCHANT (v): Let down; disappoint

DISENFRANCHISE (v): Deprive of civil rights

DISENTANGLE (v): Free from complex position, extricate

DISGRUNTLED (adj): Angry or dissatisfied

DISHEARTEN (adj): Discourage; dispirit

DISHEVELED (adj): Untidy, disordered

DISINCLINATION (v): Dislike; unwillingness

DISINGENUOUS (adj): Insincere, not naïve, hypocritical

DISINTERESTED (adj): Free from selfish motive; unbiased

DISJOINTED (adj): Disconnected, disordered

DISJUNCTION (N): State of being disconnected

DISMAY (n/v): Dishearten

DISPARAGE (v): Belittle; discourage

DISPARATE (v): Dissimilar, different

DISPARITY (n): Inequality; difference

DISPASSIONATE (adj): Impartial; calm

DISPEL (v): Scatter, expel, drive away

DISPIRIT (v): Dishearten, discourage

DISPOSITION (n): Your usual mood; character

DISPUTATIOUS (adj): Fond of having arguments

DISQUIET (n): Anxiety, uneasiness

DISSEMBLE (v): Disguise, pretend

DISSEMINATE (v): To scatter or spread widely

DISSENT (v): Disagree

DISSIDENT (adj): Opposing, dissenting

DISSIPATE (v): Waste (money, energy etc.,); squander

DISSOLUTE (adj): Loose in moral

DISSOLUTION (n): Separation, death of morals

DISSONANCE (n): Discord; difference

DISSUADE (v): Discourage; persuade not to do

DISTEND (v): Swell, expand

DISTILL (adj): Purify; refine; extract an essence

DISTINCT (adj): Clearly different

DISTINGUISH (v): See as different; recognize

DISTORT (v): Deform; falsify; twist

DISTRAUGHT (adj): Upset; distracted by anxiety

DIURNAL (adj): Daily; active during the day

DIVERGE (v): Vary and go in a different direction

DIVERSITY (n): Variety; difference

DIVEST (v): Strip; deprive

DIVISIVE (adj): Creating disunity

DIVULGE (v): Reveal, disclose

DOCILE (adj): Manageable, obedient

DOCTRINAIRE (n/adj): A person who tries to apply some theory; inflexible; dogmatic

DOCTRINE (n): Set of guide lines to a particular subject, opinion; dogma

DOGGED (adj): Determined, stubborn

DOGMA (n): System of religious laws or beliefs

DOGMATIC (adj): Opinionated, rigid, authoritative

DOLDRUMS (n): A dull, depressed mood; Lack of energy

DOLEFUL (adj): Sad, sorrowful

DOLOROUS (adj): Sorrowful

DOLT (n): Stupid person

DOMINANT (adj): Most prominent, powerful

DON (v): To put on

DORMANT (adj): Inactive, Sleeping, Lazy

DOSSIER (n): A file of documents or records; detailed report

DOUR (adj): Gloomy; unfriendly; stubborn

DOWNRIGHT (adj): Straightforward; utter, complete

DRAB (adj): Dull, cheerless, lacking color

DRACONIAN (adj): Excessively harsh; cruel

DREAD (n): Fear; terror

DROLL (adj): Humorous, odd, funny

DROUGHT (n): Lack of rain, abnormally dry weather

DRUDGERY (n): Tiring work; menial labor

DUBIOUS (adj): Doubtful; questionable

DUCTILE (adj): Malleable, flexible

DULCET (adj): Sweet sounding, melodious

DUPE (v): v.Deceive, trick; n. fool

DUPLICITY (n): Double dealing; hypocrisy

DURESS (n): Coercion, forcible restraint

DWINDLE (v): Reduce; shrink

E

EARNEST (n): Seriousness, industriousness

EBULLIENT (adj): Full of energy; excitement

ECCENTRIC (adj): Irregular, odd; bizarre

ECCLESIASTIC (adj): Pertaining to the church or religion

ECHELON: n. level; rank

ECLECTIC (adj): Selecting from various sources

ECLIPSE (v): Darken, surpass

ECSTASY (n): Joy; rapture

EDIFICATION (n): Education, instruction

EFFACE (v): Erase, rub-out

EFFECTUAL (adj): Effective; able to produce the desired effect

EFFERVESCENT (adj): Full of energy; producing

bubbles of gas

EFFETE (a): worn-out, exhausted; decadent

EFFICACY (adj): Effective; effectiveness

EFFRONTERY (n): Shameless Boldness; impudence

EFFULGENT (adj): Radiant, shining brightly

EFFUSIVE (adj): Gushing; Overflowing

EGALITARIAN (n): Advocate of equal rights

EGREGIOUS (adj): Outrageously bad, clearly wrong

ELATED (adj): Happy; overjoyed

ELEGY (n): Sorrowful poem; lament

ELICIT (v): Extract from; draw out by discussion

ELITE (n): A group of people considered to be superior in a society or organization.

ELIXIR (n): Cure-all; panacea

ELOQUENCE (n): Fluent or persuasive speaking

ELUCIDATE (v): Make clear, explain

ELUDE (v): Evade, avoid

ELUSIVE (adj): Difficult to catch; evasive

EMACIATE (v): Make lean, make thin

EMANCIPATE (v): Set free; liberate

EMBARGO (n): A legal prohibition on commerce; ban

EMBELLISH (v): Adorn, ornament, and decorate

EMBEZZLE (v): Steal

EMBLEMATIC (v): Symbolic

EMBROIL (v): In a difficult situation; entangle

EMEND (v): Correct errors; improve

EMINENT (adj): Famous, prominent

EMPATHY (n): Understanding, sympathy

EMPHATIC (adj): Forceful, definite, clear

EMPIRICAL (adj): Based on experience

EMULATE (v): Imitate; rival

ENAMOUR (adj): Be filled with love.

ENCHANT (v): Delight; charm

ENCOMIUM (n): Praise, eulogy

ENCOMPASS (v): Include comprehensively; enclose

ENCROACH (v): Trespass, occupy beyond set limits

ENCUMBER (v): Burden

ENDEAVOR (v): Try hard; make an effort to achieve a goal

ENDEMIC (adj): Native, local, limited to an area.

ENDORSE (v): Approve; support

ENDOW (v): Grant; give especially a large gift;

give ability

ENDURING (v): Lasting; surviving

ENERVATE (v): Weaken, tiring

ENFRANCHISE (v): Give the right to vote to

ENGAGE (v): Attract; employ; commit; confront

ENGENDER (v): Produce, cause

ENHANCE (v): Improve; Increase

ENIGMA (n): A mysterious thing

ENLIGHTENED (adj): Knowledgeable, broad-minded

ENMITY (n): Hatred; animosity

ENNUI (n): Boredom

ENORMITY (n): Hugeness (in a bad sense); immensity

ENRAGE (v): Infuriate, anger

ENRICH (v): Improve the quality or value of, make better

ENSCONCE (v): Settle comfortably; hide

ENSHROUD (v): To shroud; conceal, to cover

ENTAIL (v): Necessitate; require; involve

ENTANGLE (v): To complicate; to twist together

ENTHRALL (v): Captivate, enslave

ENTICE (v): Tempt, attract; lure

ENTITLE (v): Give the right to; give a title to

ENTRENCH (v): Settle comfortably; encroach

ENUMERATE (v): Mention one by one, list

ENUNCIATE (v): Speak clearly

ENVISION (v): To picture or visualize; imagine

EPHEMERAL (adj): Short-lived, fleeting

EPIDEMIC (n/adj): Plague, something which spreads quickly (i.e. a disease)

EPIGRAM (n): Short and witty saying

EPILOGUE (n): Short speech at conclusion

EPISODIC (adj): Occurring at irregular intervals

EPISTLE (n): Long formal letter, missive

EPITOME (n): Perfect example; embodiment

EQUABLE (adj): Uniform, steady; calm

EQUANIMITY (n): Calmness; emotional stability

EQUILIBRIUM (n): Balance

EQUIPOISE (n): Balance, equilibrium

EQUITABLE (adj): Fair and impartial

EQUIVOCAL (adj): Ambiguous; intentionally misleading

EQUIVOCATE (v): Lie; mislead; use words with double meanings

ERADICATE (v): Destroy

ERODE (n): Wear away; eat away

ERRATIC (adj): Odd; unpredictable

ERRONEOUS (adj): False; wrong

ERSATZ (adj): An artificial or inferior substitute

ERSTWHILE (adv): Formerly, previously

ERUDITE (adj): Learned, educated

ESCHEW (v): Avoid

ESOTERIC (adj): Hard to understand; known only to the chosen few

ESPOUSE (v): Adopt; support

ESTIMABLE (adj): Admirable; worthy

ESTRANGE (v): Separate from, make unfriendly

ETERNAL (adj): Lasting; without end

ETHOS (n): Beliefs or character of a group

ETIQUETTE (n): Social behavior; protocol

EULOGY (n): Praise, commendation

EUPHEMISM (n): A good word substituted for an offensive word

EUPHONY (n): Sweet sound

EUPHORIA (n): A feeling of intense happiness and elation

EVADE (v): Avoid, shirk

EVANESCENT (adj): Vanishing; temporary

EVENHANDED (n): Fair; impartial

EVERLASTING (adj): Continuing forever; eternal

EVINCE (v): Show clearly

EVOKE (v): Wake, recall to the conscious mind

EXACERBATE (v): Worsen, aggravate

EXACTING (adj): Extremely demanding; precise

EXALT (v): Raise in rank; praise

EXASPERATE (v): Vex

EXCERPT (n): Selected portion

EXCISE (v): To remove by cutting

EXCLUSIVE (adj): Limited to a select few; expensive

EXCORIATE (v): Criticize strongly

EXCULPATE (v): Clear from blame

EXECRABLE (adj): Extremely bad or unpleasant

EXECRATE (v): Extreme hate; to dislike strongly; curse

EXEMPLARY (adj): Serving as a model or example, outstanding

EXHORT (v): Urge; encourage strongly

EXIGENCY (n): Urgent situation

EXODUS (n): Mass departure

EXONERATE (v): Free from burden; acquit

EXORBITANT (adj): Excessive

EXORCISE (v): Expel an evil spirit

EXOTIC (adj): Strange; foreign; not native

EXPATIATE (v): Talk at length, amplify, elaborate

EXPATRIATE (n): One who lives in a foreign country; exile

EXPEDIENT (adj): Convenient and practical; wise

EXPEDITE (v): Hasten, to speed up

EXPEND (v): Spend; use up

EXPIATE (v): Make amends for a sin

EXPLICIT (adj): Clearly expressed; definite; outspoken

EXPONENTIAL (adj): Characterized by extremely rapid increase

EXPOSTULATE (v): Protest

EXPUNGE (v): Remove, cancel

EXQUISITE (adj): Very beautiful and delicate, intense

EXTANT (adj): Still existing; current

EXTEMPORE (adj): Spontaneous, impromptu, without prior preparation

EXTENUATE (v): Lessen; weaken

EXTINCT (adj): No longer living

EXTIRPATE (v): Destroy, uproot

EXTOL (v): Exalt, praise

EXTRANEOUS (adj): Not essential, superfluous

EXTRAPOLATE (v): Guess; infer

EXTRAVAGANT (adj): Wasteful, lavish, costly

EXTRICATE (v): Free, disentangle

EXTRINSIC (adj): External, not essential, extraneous

EXTROVERT (n): An outgoing person

EXUBERANT (n): Cheerful; abundant, plentiful

EXULT (v): Be happy, rejoice

F

FABRICATED (adj): Fake, forged; made up

FACADE (n): Front face (of a building); artificial or deceptive front face

FACETIOUS (adj): Humorous, inappropriate joking

FACILE (adj): Easily done, oversimplified (*negative sense)

FACILITATE (v): To make easier; promote

FACTIOUS (adj): Quarrelsome, dissentious

FACTITIOUS (adj): False, artificial

FALLACIOUS (adj): False; misleading

FALLIBLE (adj): Liable to fail

FALLOW (adj): Uncultivated; plowed but not sowed

FALTER (v): Hesitate to act; waver

FANATIC (adj): Extreme, radical, zealous

FANCY (n): Idea; illusion; whim

FASTIDIOUS (adj): Over particular, difficult to please

FATHOM (v): Comprehend; investigate

FATUOUS (adj): Stupid; silly

FAWN (v): To seek favor by flattering

FAZE (n): Frighten; disturb

FEALTY (n): Loyalty, faithfulness

FEASIBLE (adj): Possible, likely

FECKLESS (adj): Careless and irresponsible

FECUNDITY (n): Fertility; fruitfulness

FEEBLE (adj): Weak

FEIGN (v): Pretend

FEINT (v): To trick by cunning

FELICITOUS (adj): Well chosen or apt, pleasing

FELICITY (n): Happiness; ability

FEND (v): Ward off; resist

FERAL (adj): Wild, untamed

FERVENT (adj): Ardent; hot

FERVOR (n): Intense and passionate feeling

FESTER (v): To cause irritation; rankle

FETID (adj): Unpleasant smell

FETTER (v): Chain; hamper

FIASCO (n): A complete failure

FICKLE (adj): Changeable, faithless

FICTITIOUS (adj): Not real; imaginary

FIDELITY (n): Loyalty

FIGURATIVE (adj): Using a figure of speech; metaphorical; not literal

FILIAL (adj): Relating to a son or daughter

FILIBUSTER (v): Block legislation by making long speeches

FINESSE (n): Delicate Skill; subtlety

FINICKY (adj): Excessively particular, fussy

FITFUL (adj): Intermittent; sporadic

FLABBY (v): Weak; drooping; loose

FLACCID (adj): Flabby; not firm; soft

FLAG (v): Grow weak, Droop

FLAGRANT (adj): Visibly bad; outrageous; blatant

FLAMBOYANT (adj): Showy, ornate

FLAW (n): Fault or weakness

FLEDGLING (n): Inexperienced

FLEETING (adj): Temporary; transient

FLIMSY (adj): Delicate; thin; poorly made; weak

FLINCH (v): Shrink, hesitate

FLIPPANCY (n): Careless attitude, disrespectfulness

FLORID (adj): Flowery; overly decorated; reddish

FLOUNDER (v): Struggle; move awkwardly

FLOURISH (v): Prosper; grow well

FLOUT (v): Reject; mock

FLUCTUATE (v): Waver; change

FOIBLE (n): Weak point; a minor flaw

FOIL (v): Defeat, frustrate

FOLLY (n): Foolishness

FOMENT (v): Stir up, stimulate

FOOLHARDY (ADJ): Rash, fearless

FORAGE (v): Search for food; raid

FORBEARANCE (n): Tolerance; patience

FORBID (v): Ban; prohibit

FOREBODE (v): To predict or foretell

FOREGROUND (v): Move into the foreground to make more prominent

FORENSIC (adj): Legal; relating to the public debate

FORESEE (v): Be aware of beforehand; predict

FORESIGHT (v): Ability to foresee

FORESTALL (v): Prevent by taking advance action

FORFEIT (v): Lose; surrender

FORGO (v): Go without; to give up.

FORMIDABLE (adj): Fearsome; redoubtable

FORSAKE (v): Desert; abandon; renounce

FORTE (n): Strong point, special talent

FORTHRIGHT (adj): Frank; direct

FORTITUDE (n): Courage; bravery

FORTUITOUS (adj): By chance; accidental

FOSTER (v): Encourage, nurture

FOUNDER (v): Sink; fail completely

FRACAS (n): Noisy quarrel; brawl

FRACTIOUS (adj): Rebellious, unruly

FRAIL (adj): Weak; fragile

FRAUDULENT (adj): Deceitful; dishonest

FRENETIC (adj): Wildly excited; frenzied

FRENZY (n): Uncontrollable excitement

FRESCO (n): Fresh painting on a plaster

FRITTER (v): Waste

FRIVOLOUS (adj): Lacking in seriousness, carefree

FROWARD (adj): Contrary, rebellious

FRUCTIFY (v): To make fruitful

FRUGAL (adj): Economical, care in spending

FULMINATE (v): Explode; strongly attack

FULSOME (adj): Disgustingly excessive

FURTIVE (adj): Stealthy; secret

FUSION (n): Combination; union

FUTILE (n): Useless; worthless

G

GADFLY (n): An irritating person

GAFFE (n): An embarrassing blunder; mistake

GAINSAY (v): Deny; contradict

GALLANT (adj): Brave; courageous

GALVANIZE (v): Stimulate; shock or excite.

GAMBIT (n): An opening action that is calculated to gain an advantage; tactic

GAMBOL (v): To jump about playfully; skip

GARBLED (v): Confused; jumbled

GARGANTUAN (adj): Enormous, huge

GARNER (v): Gather; store up

GARRULOUS (adj): Unnecessarily talkative; wordy

GAUCHE (adj): Awkward; clumsy

GAUDY (adj): Vulgarly showy; flashy

GAUNT (adj): Lean; haggard

GAWKY (adj): Awkward, clumsy

GENERIC (adj): Referring to a class or group; not specific

GENRE (n): Particular type, category (esp of art, literature)

GERMANE (adj): Relevant, appropriate

GERMINAL (adj): Creative; original

GIGANTIC (adj) : Huge; tremendous

GINGERLY (adj): Cautiously, carefully

GIST (n): Essence; main idea

GLIB (adj): Fluent but insincere; slick

GLOAT (v): Boast greatly; express evil self-satisfaction

GLUM (adj): Dejected; gloomy; ill-natured

GLUT (n): Excessive supply, overabundance

GLUTTON (n): Overeater

GOAD (v): Urge on

GORGE (v): Stuff oneself with food; (n) Deep ravine

GOSSAMER (adj): Very light, delicate

GOUGE (v): Over charge; swindle

GRADATION (n): Gradual change; transition in stages

GRANDILOQUENT (adj): Pompous, loud, excessively eloquent

GRANDIOSE (adj): Magnificent; exaggerated

GRANDSTAND (v): Perform showily in order to impress the audience

GRATIFY (v): Satisfy, please

GRATIS (adj): Free of charge.

GRATUITOUS (adj): Given freely; unjustified

GRAVITY (adj): Seriousness or importance

GREGARIOUS (adj): Fond of company

GRIEVOUS (adj): (Of something bad) very serious

GRISLY (adj): Ghastly

GROTESQUE (adj): Fantastic, absurdly odd, ugly

GROVEL (v): Plead; crawl abjectly on ground

GUFFAW (v): To laugh loudly

GUILE (n): Cunning; trickery

GUISE (n): Outward appearance; mask

GULLIBLE (adj): Credulous; easy to deceive

H

HABITAT (n): The natural home

HACKNEYED (adj): Routine, overused, commonplace

HAGGARD (adj): Looking exhausted; worn out

HALCYON (adj): Calm, happy

HALE (adj): Robust, healthy

HALLMARK (n): Specific feature; emblem

HALLOWED (adj): Holy; sacred

HAMPER (v): (v) Impede, delay

HAPHAZARD (adj): Lacking order; random

HAPLESS (adj): Unfortunate

HAPPENSTANCE (n): Chance; fate

HARANGUE (n/v): Aggressive or scolding speech

HARBINGER (n): Fore runner; indication

HARDHEADED (adj): Practical; stubborn

HARMONY (n): Unity, symmetry

HARROWING (adj): Extremely painful; distressing

HASTEN (v): Expedite, stepped up

HAUGHTY (adj): Arrogantly superior

HAVEN (n): A place of safety

HAVOC (n): Destruction; disorder

HAZARDOUS (adj): Dangerous

HEARKEN (v): listen; pay attention to

HEARTEN (v): Encourage; comfort

HEDONIST (n): Pleasure seeker

HEED (v): Pay attention to; take notice of

HEGEMONY (n): Authority over others

HEINOUS (adj): Hatefully bad; or shockingly evil

HERALD (v): To give notice of; announce

HERESY (n): Opinion contrary to popular belief, unorthodox religious belief

HERETICAL (adj): Unorthodox, radical

HERMIT (n): One who lives alone; recluse
HETERODOX (adj): Unorthodox; unconventional
HETEROGENEOUS (adj): Dissimilar; foreign
HEYDAY (n): Prime, time of greatest success
HIATUS (n): A pause or gap
HIDEBOUND (adj): Stubborn; narrow-minded
HIERARCHY (n): Any system of persons ranked one above another
HIEROGLYPHIC (adj): Picture writing; hard to decipher
HINDRANCE (n): Obstruction; block
HIRSUTE (adj): Hairy
HISTRIONIC (adj): Theatrical; overly emotional for effect
HOARY (adj): White with age; old
HOAX (n): Deceptive trick; a practical joke
HOMAGE (n): Honor, respect
HOMEOSTASIS (n): Maintenance of equilibrium or a stable bodily state
HOMILY (n): A lecture on moral or religious topic
HOMOGENOUS (n): Similar; of the same kind
HONE (v): Sharpen; whet
HOSPITABLE (adj): Favorable to life and growth; sociable
HOSTILITY (n): Enmity, hatred
HUBRIS (n): Excessive pride; arrogance
HUMANE (adj): Compassionate, kind
HUMDRUM (adj): Dull or monotonous
HUMILITY (n): Humbleness; lack of pride
HUNCH (n): A strong intuitive feeling
HYPERBOLE (n): Exaggeration or overstatement
HYPOTHESIS (n): An assumption requiring a proof

I

ICONOCLAST (n): One who destroys religious images or beliefs
IDEOLOGIC (adj): Concerned with ideas; theoretical
IDIOCY (n): Extremely stupid behavior
IDIOSYNCRASY (n): Peculiarity, individual characteristic
IDOLATRY (n): Hero Worship; admiration
IDYLLIC (adj): Simple, Peaceful
IGNOBLE (adj): Unworthy, not noble, low character

IGNOMINY (n): Shame; disgrace or dishonor
ILLEGIBLE (adj): Impossible to read, unclear
ILLIBERAL (adj): Narrow minded; bigot; strictness
ILLICIT (v): Illegal, unlawful
ILLUMINATE (n): Clarify, light up
ILLUSORY (n): Deceptive; not real
IMBECILITY (n): Stupidity, silliness; mentally retarded
IMBROGLIO (n): An extremely confused or complicated situation
IMBUE (v): Fill with a feeling (or color); permeate
IMMACULATE (adj): Perfectly clean
IMMANENT (adj): Inherent; within the mind
IMMENSE (adj): Enormous, massive
IMMINENT (adj): About to happen, impending
IMMUNITY (n): Resistant to; exemption; freedom
IMMURE (v): Confine, imprison
IMMUTABLE (adj): Unchangeable
IMPAIR (v): Injure, hurt
IMPALE (v): Pierce
IMPASSE (n): Deadlock, place from which there is no escape.
IMPASSIONED (adj): Full of passion; emotional
IMPASSIVE (adj): Without feeling; not sensitive to emotion or pain
IMPEACH (v): Accuse, charge with crime.
IMPECCABLE (adj): Faultless
IMPECUNIOUS (adj): Penniless; poor
IMPEDE (v): Obstruct; block
IMPEL (v): Urge into action, drive or force onward
IMPENDING (adj): Nearing; approaching
IMPENETRABLE (adj): Impossible to enter; impossible to comprehend
IMPENITENT (adj): Not feeling shame or regret
IMPERATIVE (adj): Command, order, of vital importance
IMPERCEPTIBLE (adj): Unnoticeable; undetectable
IMPERIOUS (adj): Arrogantly domineering
IMPERTINENT (adj): Arrogant, insolent
IMPERTURBABLE (adj): Calm, composed
IMPERVIOUS (adj): Impenetrable; incapable of being damaged
IMPETUOUS (adj): Violent, rash, hasty

IMPETUS (n): Urge, stimulus

IMPINGE (v): Infringe, hit, collide with

IMPLACABLE (adj): Impossible to appease

IMPLAUSIBLE (adj): Hard to believe, unlikely

IMPLICATE (v): Incriminate, show to be connected

IMPLICIT (adj): Understood but not stated; tacit

IMPLODE (v): Burst inward

IMPOLITIC (adj): Unwise

IMPONDERABLE (adj): Weightless

IMPORTUNE (v): Beg persistently

IMPOSTOR (n): One that assumes false identity for the purpose of deception

IMPOVERISH (v): Make poor; exhaust the strength

IMPRECATION (n): A curse

IMPREGNABLE (adj): Invulnerable

IMPRESSIONABLE (adj): Easily influenced

IMPROBITY (n): Wickedness; dishonesty

IMPROMPTU (adj): Without previous preparation; spontaneous

IMPROPRIETY (n): Improperness; indecency

IMPROVISE (v): To compose extemporaneously

IMPUDENCE (n): Arrogant, insolence

IMPUGN (v): Challenge; criticize

IMPUNITY (n): Freedom from punishment

IMPUTE (v): Attribute; charge

INADVERTENT (v): Unintentional, inattentive

INALIENABLE (adj): Non-transferable; not to be taken away

INANE (adj): Silly, senseless

INARTICULATE (v): Speechless; indistinct

INCENDIARY (n): (n). Arsonist; (adj). Inflammatory

INCENSE (v): Make angry; enrage

INCENTIVE (n): Stimulus; encouragement

INCEPTION (n): Beginning, start

INCESSANT (adj): Continuous, unceasing

INCHOATE (adj): Recently begun; elementary

INCIPIENT (adj): Initial, beginning

INCISIVE (adj): Sharp, cutting

INCITE (v): Arouse to action; stir up; provoke

INCLEMENT (adj): Stormy, cruel

INCOGNITO (adj): Anonymous, unknown

INCOHERENT (adj): Inconsistent, illogical; unintelligible

INCOMPATIBLE (adj): Inharmonious; unsuitable

INCONGRUITY (n): The quality of disagreeing; inappropriate

INCONSEQUENTIAL (adj): Unimportant; insignificant

INCONSISTENCY (n): Incompatibility; lack of harmony

INCONTROVERTIBLE (adj): Unquestionable; indisputable

INCORPORATE (v): Make part of a whole; combine; united

INCORRIGIBLE (adj): Uncorrectable

INCREDULITY (n): Tendency to disbelief

INCUBATE (v): Hatch; develop

INCULCATE (v): Teach; implant

INCUR (v): Bring upon oneself; acquire

INDEBTED (adj): Obligated; beholden

INDEFATIGABLE (adj): Tireless

INDELIBLE (adj): Not able to be erased

INDEMNIFY (v): Pay for loss; compensate

INDENTURE (n): Bind as servant to master; bond

INDETERMINATE (adj): Uncertain; indefinite

INDIFFERENT (adj): Unmoved; unconcerned; mediocre

INDIGENOUS (adj): Native; inborn

INDIGENT (adj): Poor; needy

INDIGNATION (n): Anger; anger at an injustice

INDISCERNIBLE (adj): Unclear; impossible to see

INDISCRIMINATE (adj): Choosing at random; aimless; confused

INDISPENSIBLE (adj) : Absolutely necessary; cannot be without

INDISSOLUBLE (adj): Cannot be destroyed; permanent

INDOLENT (adj): Lazy

INDUBITABLE (adj): Impossible to doubt; unquestionable

INDULGENT (adj): Lenient; tolerant

INDUSTRIOUS (adj): Hard-working, diligent

INEFFABLE (adj): Inexpressible; unutterable

INEPT (adj): Incompetent, silly

INERT (adj): Inactive

INEVITABLE (adj): Unavoidable

INEXHAUSTIBLE (adj): That cannot be entirely consumed; unlimited

INEXORABLE (adj): Inflexible; implacable; relentless

INFALLIBLE (adj): Unfailing

INFAMY (n): Bad reputation

INFIDELITY (n): Unfaithfulness, lack of belief

INFINITESIMAL (adj): Minute; very tiny

INFIRMITY (n): Sickness; weakness

INFLATED (adj): Swollen; exaggerate

INFLEXIBLE (adj): Rigid; stubborn; immovable

INFLUX (n): Flowing into

INFURIATE (v): Make furious; anger

INGENIOUS (adj): Clever, resourceful

INGENUITY (n): Inventive skill

INGENUOUS (adj): Innocent, naive, trusting

INGRAINED (adj): Firmly fixed, deeply rooted

INGRATIATE (v): Become popular with...

INHERENT (adj): Belonging by nature or habit

INHIBIT (v): Hinder, or prevent

INIMICAL (adj): Hostile, unfriendly

INIMITABLE (adj): Impossible to imitate; matchless

INIQUITY (n): Wickedness, injustice

INNATE (adj): Native, inborn

INNOCUOUS (adj): Harmless

INNOVATIVE (adj): New; inventive

INNUENDO (n): Hint, indirect suggestion (usually derogatory)

INORDINATE (adj): Excessive, immoderate; disorderly

INQUISITOR (n): Investigator; questioner

INSATIABLE (adj): Unsatisfiable; extremely greedy

INSCRUTABLE (adj): Not easily understood, mysterious

INSENTIENT (adj): Insensible; lacking the ability to feel

INSIDIOUS (adj): Cunning; secretly harmful

INSIGHTFUL (adj): Perceptive; clear understanding

INSINUATE (v): Hint; imply; creep in

INSIPID (adj): Dull; tasteless

INSOLENT (adj): Rude and disrespectful

INSOLVENT (adj): Bankrupt; unable to pay one's debts

INSOUCIANCE (n): Lack of concern; lightheartedness

INSTIGATE (v): Urge, excite, provoke

INSUBORDINATE (adj): Disobedient; rebellious

INSULAR (adj): Isolated; narrow-minded

INSURGENT (adj): Rebellious

INTELLIGIBLE (adj): Understandable

INTEMPERATE (adj): Excessive; immoderate; extreme

INTERMINABLE (adj): Endless; apparently endless

INTERMITTENT (adj): Not continuous, on-off

INTERPLAY (v) : Interaction; reciprocal play or influence

INTERPOLATE (v): Insert between

INTERPOSE (v): Be or come between; interfere

INTERTWINE (adj): Interlaced, interwoven

INTERVENE (v): Come between; interfere

INTERWEAVE (v): To weave together

INTIMACY (n): Closeness; warm friendship; privacy

INTIMIDATE (v): Frighten

INTOLERANT (adj): Bigoted; narrow-minded

INTRACTABLE (adj): Hard to control; stubborn; unruly

INTRANSIGENT (adj): Uncompromising; stubborn

INTREPID (adj): Brave, fearless

INTRICATE (v): Complex, complicated

INTRIGUE (v): To arouse the interest, plot

INTRIGUING (adj): Absorbing, fascinating

INTRINSIC (adj): Essential; inherent; built-in

INTROSPECTIVE (adj): Self-examining, looking inwards

INTUITION (n): Immediate insight; Sixth sense

INUNDATE (n): Flood, overflow; overwhelm

INURED (adj): Accustomed to hardship; habituated

INVALIDATE (v): Weaken; destroy

INVALUABLE (adj): Priceless, very valuable

INVASIVE (adj): Tending to invade; aggressive

INVECTIVE (n): Abuse, criticism

INVEIGH (v): Attack with words; blame

INVEIGLE (v): Persuade (convince) by flattery

INVERSE (v): Opposite

INVETERATE (adj): Deeply rooted, habitual

INVIDIOUS (adj): Designed to create ill will or envy

INVINCIBLE (adj): Impossible to conquer

INVIOLABLE (adj): Incorruptible, impossible to violate

INVOKE (v): Call forth; request

INVOLVED (adj): Complicated; convoluted

IOTA (n): Small quantity

IRASCIBLE (adj): Hot-tempered; irritable

IRKSOME (adj): Annoying; tedious

IRONY (n): An outcome of events contrary to what might have been expected; Sarcasm

IRRATIONAL (adj): Illogical, lacking reason

IRRECONCILABLE (adj): Incompatible;

impossible to compromise
IRREFUTABLE (adj): Undeniable; indisputable
IRREPROACHABLE *(adj):* Faultless, blameless
IRRESOLUTE (adj): Indecisive; uncertain how to act
IRREVERENCE (n): Lack of respect
ITINERARY (n): Plan of a trip

J

JABBER (v): Talk rapidly or clumsily
JADED (adj): Fatigued; tired
JARGON (n): Language used by a special group; technical terminology
JEJUNE (adj): Boring; immature
JEOPARDOUS (adj): Dangerous, hazardous
JETTISON (v): Throw or discard
JINGOISM (n): Radical patriotism, aggressive chauvinism
JOCOSE (adj): Playful or humorous
JUBILATION (n): Joyfulness
JUDICIOUS (adj): Sound in judgment; wise
JUGGERNAUT (n): Irresistible crushing force
JUSTIFY (v): Defend; excuse; vindicate
JUXTAPOSE (v): Place side by side

K

KEEN (adj): sharp; perceptive; intense (of a feeling)
KEN (n): Range of knowledge
KERNEL (n): Central or vital part
KINDLE (v): Fire Up, inspire
KNOTTY (adj): Intricate; difficult; tangled
KUDOS (n): Praise; honor; glory

L

LABILE (adj): Likely to change, unstable
LABYRINTH (n): Complicated network of passages; maze
LACHRYMOSE (adj): Tearful
LACKADAISICAL (adj): Listless, lacking energy
LACKLUSTER (adj): Dull, mediocre
LACONIC (adj): Using few words; brief and to the point
LAITY (n): People who are not members of the clergy; lay man
LAMBASTE (v): Attack verbally; beat
LAMENT (v): Express sorrow; mourn
LAMPOON (v): Ridicule, mock

LANGUID (adj): Slow; listless; lacking energy
LANGUISH (v): Grow weak; lose animation
LARGESSE (n): Generous gift
LASCIVIOUS (adj): Lustful
LASSITUDE (n): Laziness, Weariness
LATENT (adj): Hidden; present but not visibly active; dormant
LATITUDE (n): Freedom from narrow limitations
LAUD (v): Praise
LAX (adj): Careless; loose
LEGITIMIZE (v): Make legal; authorize
LETHAL (adj): Deadly
LETHARGY (n): Laziness, lack of energy
LEVITY (n): Lack of seriousness, frivolity
LIAISON (n): 1. Secret love affair. 2. A channel for communication between groups
LIBERTINE (adj): Debauchee; immoral person
LICENTIOUS (adj): Immoral; especially sexually unrestrained
LIMN (v): Describe; outline
LIMPID (adj): Clear; Lucid
LINGER (v): Stay longer than usual; loiter; dawdle
LIONIZE (v): Treat as a celebrity
LISTLESS (adj): Lacking spirit or energy
LITERAL (adj): Factual; accurate; relating to or expressed in letters
LOATH (adj): Reluctant; averse
LOATHE (v): Dislike; abhor
LONGEVITY (v): Long life; length of life
LONGING (adj): Having a strong desire for something
LOQUACIOUS (adj): Extremely talkative
LUCID (adj): Clear, easily understood
LUCRATIVE (adj): Profitable
LUDICROUS (adj): Laughable; nonsensical
LUGUBRIOUS (adj): Sad, sorrowful
LULL (adj): Temporary period of calm
LUMINOUS (adj): Shining, issuing light
LURE (v): Temp; entice; bait
LURID (adj): Shocking; sensational; graphic
LURK (v): Lie in wait; exist unobserved
LUSH (adj): Rich, luxurious; full of plant growth
LUSTROUS (adj): Shiny, glossy
LUXURIANT (adj): Abundant; rich; fertile

M

MACABRE (adj): Horrifying; ghastly

MACERATE (v): Soften or break up (food) by soaking in a liquid
MACHIAVELLIAN (adj): Cunning, scheming
MACHINATION (n): Evil schemes, conspiracy
MAELSTROM (n): Whirlpool; commotion
MAGISTERIAL (adj): Authoritative; domineering
MAGNANIMOUS (adj): Generous or forgiving
MAGNILOQUENT (adj): Boastful; pompous
MALADROIT (adj): Clumsy, bungling; tactless
MALEVOLENT (adj): Evil; harmful
MALFEASANCE (n): Wrongdoing
MALICE (n): Ill-will, desire to harm another
MALIGN (adj/v): Speak evil of; bad mouth; defame
MALINGER (v): Fake illness to escape duty
MALLEABLE (adj): Flexible; adaptable
MANACLE (v): Restrain, Control
MANDATE (n): Order; charge
MANIFEST (adj): Clear; obvious; visible
MANIFOLD (adj): Many and various
MARGINAL (adj): Unimportant; borderline
MARRED (adj): Damaged
MARSH (n): Soft wet land; morass
MARTINET (n): Strict disciplinarian
MATERIALISM (n): A desire for wealth and material possessions with little interest in spiritual matters
MATRIARCH (n): Female head of a family or tribe
MAUDLIN (adj): Excessively sentimental
MAVERICK (n): Rebel; nonconformist
MAWKISH (adj): Overly sentimental
MEAGER (adj): Scanty; inadequate
MEDIOCRE (adj): Ordinary; common place
MEEK (adj): Timid; humble; submissive
MELANCHOLY (n): Gloomy; morose
MELLIFLUOUS (adj): Sweetly flowing, melodious
MEMOIR (n): Life story, autobiography
MENACING (adj): Dangerous; threatening
MENDACITY (n): Untruthfulness; dishonesty
MENDICANT (n): Beggar
MENIAL (n): Servile; suitable for servants; mean
MERCANTILE (adj): Relating to trade or commerce
MERCURIAL (adj): Capricious, changing; fickle
MERETRICIOUS (adj): Falsely attractive; tempting in a vulgar way

METAMORPHOSIS (n): A complete change in form or nature
METAPHOR (n): Figurative language; symbolic
METAPHYSICS (n): The study of ultimate reality
METE (v): Divide and distribute, allot
METEORIC (adj): Fast and brilliant
METICULOUS (adj): Very careful and precise
METTLE (n): Courage; spirit
MIASMA (n): Unhealthy poisonous vapor; unpleasant atmosphere
MICROCOSM (n): Small world; miniature of the universe
MIDST (n): Middle, core
MILIEU (n): Surroundings; means of expression
MINATORY (adj): Threatening, menacing
MINISCULE (adj): Tiny, very small
MINUTIAE (n): A small detail; petty matters
MIRE (v): To become stuck in difficult situation
MISANTHROPE (n): One who hates human beings
MISAPPREHEND (v): Fail to understand
MISCREANT (n): Villain; criminal
MISER (n): One who is extremely stingy with money
MISNOMER (n): Wrong name
MITIGATE (v): To make less severe; alleviate
MNEMONIC (n): A device used for memory
MODEST (adj): humble; moderate; simple, limited
MODICUM (n): Small quantity
MODISH (adj): Stylish
MOLLIFY (v): Soothe
MOLLYCODDLE (v): Spoil, pamper
MOMENTARY (adj): Brief; short lived
MOMENTOUS (adj): Very important
MONASTIC (adj): Relating to the monks or monasteries; isolated
MONOLITHIC (n): Rigidly uniform
MONOTONY (n): Tedious sameness
MORATORIUM (n): A suspension of an activity
MORES (n): The conventions; moral standards; ethics
MORIBUND (adj): Dying
MOROSE (adj): Sad, sullen; ill-humoured
MOSAIC (n): Inlaid colorful stone decoration
MUDDLE (v): Confuse; mess up
MULTIFACETED (adj): Having many facets; complex

MULTIFARIOUS (adj): Varied; greatly diversified
MUNDANE (adj): Every day, worldly; not earthly
MUNIFICENT (adj): Very Generous
MURKY (adj): Dark and gloomy
MUSTER (v): Gather together, assemble for action
MUTABLE (adj): Changeable; unstable
MUTED (adj): Silent; hushed; made softer
MYOPIC (adj): Near-sighted; lack of foresight
MYRIAD (n): Very large number
MYTH (n): A widely held but false belief; a traditional story accepted as history

N

NADIR (n): The lowest point
NAIVE (adj): Innocent, lacking worldly wisdom
NARCISSISM (n): Self-love; vanity
NASCENT (adj): Incipient; just beginning
NATAL (adj): Natural; biological
NEBULOUS (adj): Dark, cloudy, hazy
NECROMANCY (n): Black magic; dealing with the dead
NEFARIOUS (adj): Very Wicked
NEGATE (v): Deny, nullify; cancel out
NEOLOGISM (n): A newly invented word or phrase
NEOPHYTE (n): A beginner
NEPOTISM (n): Favoritism shown to relatives
NETTLE (v): Annoy; irritate
NEUTRALIZE (v): Make ineffective by counteract
NEXUS (n): Connection
NOCTURNAL (adj): Active during the night
NOISOME (adj): Harmful; harmful smell
NOMAD (adj): Wandering, nomadic
NONCHALANCE (n): Casually calm; apathy; indifference
NONENTITY (n): A person of no importance; a nonexistent thing
NONPLUS (v): Perplex; confuse
NORMATIVE (adj): Standard, normal
NOSTALGIA (n): Homesickness, longing for the past
NOSTRUM (n): False remedy; panacea
NOTABLE (adj): Remarkable; famous; honored
NOTORIOUS (adj): Known for bad qualities
NOURISH (v): Support; nurture
NOVELTY (n): Newness; unusual

NOVICE (n): Beginner
NOXIOUS (adj): Harmful, poisonous, or very unpleasant
NUANCE (n): A shade of difference in meaning; a subtle distinction
NUGATORY (adj): Worthless; useless
NULLIFY (v): To make useless
NURTURE (v): Foster; nourish, teach

O

OBDURATE (adj): Stubborn
OBEISANCE (n): Bow, bend with respect
OBFUSCATE (v): Confuse; muddle; obscure
OBJECTIVE (adj): Impartial, not influenced by emotions; fair
OBJURGATE (v): Criticize harshly; castigate
OBLIQUE (adj): Indirect; inclined; leaning
OBLITERATE (v): Erase; destroy
OBLIVION (n): Forgotten or unknown
OBLIVIOUS (adj): Unmindful, inattentive
OBLOQUY (n): Abuse, defame
OBNOXIOUS (adj): Extremely unpleasant
OBSCURE (adj): Vague, dark; unclear
OBSEQUIOUS (adj): Obedient or attentive; sycophantic
OBSESSIVE (adj): Compulsive; excessively preoccupied
OBSOLETE (adj): Outdated; useless
OBSTINATE (adj): Stubbornly persistent; hard to control
OBSTREPEROUS (adj): Noisy; undisciplined
OBTRUSIVE (adj): Undesirably noticeable; protruding
OBTUSE (adj): Stupid; blunt
OBVIATE (v): Make unnecessary; get rid of
OCCLUDE (v): Shut, close
OCCULT (adj): Not easily understood; secret; supernatural
ODIOUS (adj): Hateful; vile
OFFHAND (adj): Casual; without preparation or thought
OFFICIOUS (adj): Excessively pushy in offering one's service; bossy
OFFSET (v): Compensate; balance
OLFACTORY (adj): Related to sense of smell
OMINOUS (adj): Threatening
OMNIPOTENT (adj): All powerful
OMNISCIENT (adj): Knowing everything
ONEROUS (adj): Burdensome

ONUS (n): A burden, responsibility

OPACITY (n): Obscurity; unclear

OPINIONATED (adj): Stubborn; adherent to one's own opinion

OPPORTUNE (adj): Timely, proper

OPPRESSIVE (adj): Burdensome; tyrannical

OPPROBRIUM (n): Infamy, insult

OPTIMUM (adj): Most favorable; best

OPULENT (adj): Wealthy, lavish; abundant

ORACULAR (adj): Prophetic; mysterious or ambiguous

ORDEAL (n): Hardship; severe trail

ORGANIC (adj): Natural; inherent; fundamental

ORIGINATE (v): Begin; be created; develop

ORNATE (adj): Excessive in decorative detail

OSSIFY (v): Become hard or inflexible

OSTENSIBLE (adj): Apparent, seem, pretended

OSTENTATIOUS (adj): Showy, pretentious; pompous

OSTRACIZE (v): Exclude from a group, banish

OUTLANDISH (adj): Strange; unusual; bizarre

OUTMODED (adj): Out-of-date; old-fashioned

OUTSTRIP (v): Excel; surpass

OVERHAUL (v): Renovate; make overall repairs

OVERLOOK (v): Ignore; excuse

OVERSHADOW (v): Obscure; make less important

OVERT (adj): Open to view

OVERTURE (n): Something introductory; prelude

OVERWEENING (adj): Arrogant; immoderate

OVERWHELM (v): Overpower, flood, engulf

OXYMORON (n): A combination of contradictory words

PACIFY (v): Soothe, make calm

PAEAN (n): Song of praise; joy

PAINSTAKING (adj): Careful; showing hard work

PALATABLE (adj): Agreeable; tasty

PALLIATE (v): Ease pain; make less severe

PALLID (adj): Pale; weak

PALPABLE (adj): Touchable; obvious, clear

PALTRY (adj): Worthless, petty, trivial

PAN (v): Criticize harshly

PANACEA (n): A cure-all

PANACHE (n): Style; flair, flamboyance

PANDEMIC (adj/n): Widespread; affecting the majority of the people

PANDEMONIUM (n): Wild disorder; Tumult, furor

PANDER (v): Cater to the low desires of others

PANEGYRIC (n): formal praise

PANORAMA (n): Wide view in all directions; comprehensive view

PARABLE (n): Moral story/tale, fable

PARADIGM (n): Model, example, pattern

PARADOX (n): A statement that is seemingly contradictory to common sense and yet is perhaps true

PARAGON (n): Model of perfection

PARAMOUNT (adj): More important than anything else; supreme

PARIAH (n): Outcast; castaway

PAROCHIAL (adj): Narrow-minded; provincial

PARODY (n): Comical imitation of another work; spoof

PAROXYSM (n): A sudden uncontrollable attack; fit

PARRY (n): Ward off a blow, deflect

PARSIMONY (n): Miserliness; extreme stinginess

PARTIAL (adj): 1. Incomplete. 2. Showing favoritism

PARTISAN (n): One sided; biased; committed to a party

PASSIVE (adj): Submissive; apathetic; disinterested

PASTICHE (n): Imitation of another's style in writing

PATENT (adj): Clear, obvious, innovative

PATHETIC (adj): Touching; pitiful, causing compassion.

PATRON (n): A person who supports

PATRONIZE (v): Act superior towards, serve as a sponsor

PAUCITY (adj): Lack, scarcity

PECCADILLO (n): A minor sin

PECUNIARY (adj): Related to money

PEDAGOGUE (n): teacher

PEDANTIC (adj): Showing off learning; bookish

PEDESTRIAN (adj): Ordinary; unimaginative

PEEVISH (adj): Angry, irritable

PEJORATIVE (adj): Having negative connotations; Belittle

PELL-MELL (adj): In confusion; disorderly

PELLUCID (adj): Transparent; limpid; easy to understand

PENANCE (n): Self-imposed punishment

PENCHANT (n): A strong inclination; liking

PENSIVE (adj): Dreamily thoughtful; expressing thoughtfulness with sadness

PENURIOUS (adj): Extremely poor, stingy

PERCEPTIVE (adj): Sharp; wise; insightful

PEREGRINATION (n): Journey, voyage

PEREMPTORY (adj): Authoritative; demanding and leaving no choice

PERENNIAL (adj): Long lasting

PERFIDY (n): Unfaithfulness; treachery

PERFUNCTORY (adj): Superficial; careless; that lacks enthusiasm

PERIL (n): Danger, risk

PERIPATETIC (adj): Moving; walking about

PERIPHERAL (adj): Irrelevant, marginal; outer

PERJURY (n) : act of lying under oath

PERMEATE (v): Enter, penetrate

PERNICIOUS (adj): Highly destructive

PERPETRATE (v): Commit a crime

PERPETUAL (adj): Everlasting; permanent

PERPLEX (v): To make it complicated; confuse

PERQUISITE (n): Something in addition to regular pay; bonus

PERSEVERANCE (n): Hard work, diligence

PERSONABLE (adj): Attractive

PERSONIFICATION (n): A person who represents an abstract quality

PERSPICACIOUS (adj): Perceptive, having insight; astute

PERSPICUOUS (adj): Expressed clearly; transparent

PERT (adj): Impertinent; bold

PERTINACIOUS (adj): Stubborn; persistent

PERTURB (v): Disturb completely, agitate

PERUSE (v): read carefully; examine in detail

PERVASIVE (adj): Spread throughout.

PERVERSE (adj): Contrary; wicked; perverted

PESSIMISM (n): Belief that life is basically bad

PESTILENTIAL (adj): Baneful, deadly; contagious

PETRIFY (v): Turn to stone, terrify

PETULANT (adj): Ill-tempered; irascible

PHARISAIC (adj): Hypocritically religious; self-righteous

PHILANTHROPIST (n): Lover of mankind; charitable donor

PHILISTINE (adj): Narrow- minded person; uncultured

PHLEGMATIC (adj): Calm; not easily disturbed

PHONY (adj) : fake; not authentic

PICARESQUE (adj): Describing adventures of a person (usually a rogue)

PICAYUNE (adj): Worthless; petty; small-minded

PICTURESQUE (adj): Charming in appearance; visual

PIED (adj): Multicolored; spotted

PIETY (n): Devotion; reverence for God

PILLAGE (v): Plunder; rob

PINNACLE (n): Summit, peak

PIONEER (n): An innovator, path-finder

PIOUS (adj): Religious; devout

PIQUANT (adj): Spicy, having a sharp flavor; stimulating

PIQUE (v): Provoke; arouse, annoy

PITFALL (n): Hidden danger; a trap

PITH (n): Central or vital part; essence

PITHY (adj): Concise; brief and meaningful

PITTANCE (n): Small amount

PIVOTAL (adj): Central; critical

PLACATE (v): To soothe; pacify

PLACID (adj): Calm and peaceful

PLAGIARISM (n): Unauthorized copying

PLAINTIVE (adj): Sad, mournful

PLASTICITY (n): Flexibility, ability to be molded

PLATITUDE (n): Trite remark; commonplace statement

PLATONIC (adj): Free from romance or sex; spiritual

PLAUDITS (n): Praise; enthusiastic approval

PLAUSIBLE (adj): Believable, feasible

PLENITUDE (n): Overabundance; completeness

PLETHORA (adj): Excess; overabundance

PLIABLE (adj): Flexible, adaptable; bendable

PLIGHT (n): Bad or unfortunate condition or state

PLODDING (adj): Hard monotonous routine work

PLUCK (n): Courage

PLUMB (adj): Exactly vertical; checking perpendicularity

PLUMMET (v): Fall sharply

POIGNANT (adj): Intensely touching the emotions

POISE (n): Composure; balance

POLARIZE (v): Split into opposite factions

POLEMIC (adj/n): Quarrelsome, disputatious

POMPOUS (adj): Self-importance; overly proud

PONDEROUS (adj): Weighty; unwieldy

PONTIFICAL (adj): Pompous or pretentious; like pope

POROUS (adj): Full of pores; permeable

PORTEND (v): Foretell, predict

PORTENTOUS (adj): Ominous; impressive

POSEUR (n): One who tries to impress others; pretender

POSIT (v): Establish a view point; assume

POSTHUMOUS (adj): Occurring after death

POSTURE (v): To assume an artificial pose; act artificially

POTENTATE (n): Powerful person; monarch

POULTICE (n): Soothing application applied to inflamed portions of the body

PRAGMATIC (adj): Practical, pertaining to practice

PRATTLE (v): Chatter, babble

PREAMBLE (n): A preliminary statement

PRECARIOUS (adj): Risky; uncertain

PRECEDENCE (n): The condition of preceding others in importance

PRECIPICE (n): Cliff; dangerous position

PRECIPITATE (v): Rash; hasty; sudden; premature

PRECIPITOUS (adj): Very steep, hasty

PRECIS (n): Summary, shortened version of a work

PRECLUDE (v): Eliminate, prevent, make impossible

PRECOCIOUS (adj): (Prematurely) genius; advanced in development

PRECURSOR (n): Forerunner

PREDATE (v): Precede; occur prior to; antedate

PREDICAMENT (n): A difficult or dangerous situation

PREDILECTION (n): Preference; partiality

PREDOMINANT (adj): Supreme; widespread

PREEMINENT (adj): Most important, superior

PREEMPT (v): Acquiring something by acting first; supplant

PREHENSILE (adj): Capable of grasping or holding

PREJUDICED (adj): Biased; preconception

PRELUDE (n): Introduction; opening

PREMEDITATED (adj): Preplanned, deliberate

PREMISE (n): Assumption; postulate

PREMONITION (v): Forewarning; advance feeling

PREPOSTEROUS (adj): Absurd, ridiculous

PREROGATIVE (n): An exclusive right; privilege

PRESAGE (v): Foretell, predict

PRESCIENT (adj): Able to foresee future

PRESENTIMENT (n): An intuitive feeling about the future

PRESUME (v): Assume, take for granted

PRESUMPTUOUS (adj): Arrogant, taking liberties

PRETENTIOUS (n): Pretending; showy

PRETERNATURAL (adj): Supernatural; abnormal

PREVAIL (n): Win; persuade

PREVALENT (adj): Widespread, widely accepted

PREVARICATE (v): Lie, equivocate

PRICKLY (adj): Very irritable

PRIGGISH (adj): Exaggeratedly proper; arrogant

PRIME (adj): The earliest stage, excellent, superior

PRIMORDIAL (adj): Early; primary; existing at the beginning

PRISTINE (adj): Ancient, primitive; unspoiled

PRIVATION (n): Hardship, want; poverty

PRIVILEGE (n): Special right not enjoyed by others

PROBITY (n): Uprightness; honesty

PROBLEMATIC (adj): Troublesome; doubtful; debatable

PROCLIVITY (n): A natural liking, inclination

PROCRASTINATE (v): Delay or postpone

PROD (v): Stir up; push, urge

PRODIGAL (adj): Wasteful; reckless with money

PRODIGIOUS (adj): Huge; enormous; marvelous

PRODIGY (n): Wonder; exceptional talented child (or person)

PROFANE (v): To treat with abuse; violate; desecrate

PROFICIENT (adj): Expert, competent

PROFLIGATE (adj): Wasteful, wildly immoral

PROFOUND (adj): Deep, not superficial; complete

PROFUSION (n): Overabundance; wasteful spending

PROGNOSIS (n): Prediction; probable outcome of a disease

PROHIBITIVE (adj): Preventing, hindering

PROLIFERATE (v): Grow quickly, multiply rapidly.

PROLIFIC (adj): Abundantly fruitful

PROLIX (adj): Long and wordy

PROLOGUE (n): Introduction, foreword

PROMINENT (adj): Renowned; important; noticeable

PROMISCUOUS (adj): Immoral; wanton; indiscriminate

PROMULGATE (v): Announce officially; promote

PRONE (adj): Inclined to; prostrate

PRONOUNCE (v): Utter, articulate

PROPENSITY (n): Natural inclination

PROPHECY (n): Prediction, forecast

PROPINQUITY (n): Nearness; relationship

PROPITIATE (v): Appease; calm

PROPITIOUS (adj): Favorable, fortunate

PROPONENT (n): Supporter, advocate

PROPOUND (v): Propose an idea; present for discussion

PROPRIETY (n): Fitness; correct conduct

PROSAIC (adj): Dull, unimaginative, everyday

PROSCRIBE (v). Prohibit, banish

PROTEAN (adj): Versatile; taking of different forms

PROTRACT (v): Prolong; stretch

PROVIDENT (adj): Careful in spending; displaying foresight

PROVIDENTIAL (adj): Fortunate; lucky; opportune

PROVINCIAL (n): Rural; regional; narrow-minded

PROVISIONAL (adj): Temporary; tentative

PROVOKE (v): Irritate; stimulate

PROWESS (n): Extraordinary ability; bravery

PROXIMITY (n): Nearness

PROXY (n): A person authorized to act for another

PRUDE (n): Excessively proper or modest person

PRUDENT (adj): Careful, wise

PRURIENT (adj): Lustful, obsessed with sex

PSEUDONYM (n): Pen name; false name

PUERILE (adj): Childish; immature

PUGNACIOUS (adj): Inclined to quarrel; combative

PUISSANCE (n): Power; strength

PULCHRITUDE (n): Beauty; glory

PUNGENT (adj): Biting; sharp in taste or smell;

caustic

PUNITIVE (adj): Punishing

PURGE (v): Purify; clean, remove dirt; free from guilt

PURITANICAL (adj): Strict on religious and moral issues, austere

PURPORT (n): Intention, meaning

PUSILLANIMOUS (adj): Cowardly, Fearful

QUACK (n): Charlatan; impostor

QUAFF (v): Drink with large gulps

QUAINT (adj): Unusual, odd; old fashioned

QUALIFIED (adj): 1.Limited (secondary sense). 2. Certified

QUALM (n): Misgiving, uneasy fear

QUANDARY (n): Dilemma; state of confusion

QUARANTINE (n): To isolate (esp. to prevent from contagious diseases)

QUASH (v): Crush; suppress

QUELL (v): Suppress, crush; quiet

QUERULOUS (adj): Complaining; irritable

QUIBBLE (n): A slight objection or complaint

QUIESCENT (adj): Restful; temporarily inactive

QUINTESSENCE (n): Purest & highest embodiment; core

QUIP (n): A clever or witty comment

QUIRK (n): Sudden twist; caprice

QUISLING (n): Traitor; betrayer

QUIXOTIC (adj): Idealistic but impracticable

QUOTIDIAN (adj): Daily, commonplace, customary

RACONTEUR (n): Story teller

RAIL (v): Scold; complain bitterly

RAIMENT (n): Clothing

RAMBLE (v): To move or talk aimlessly

RAMBUNCTIOUS (adj): Unruly, boisterous

RAMIFICATION (n): Branching out; subdivision; outgrowth

RAMPANT (adj): Behaving violently; unrestrained; excessive

RAMSHACKLE (adj): Falling to pieces, rickety

RANCOR (n): Bitterness; hatred

RAPACIOUS (adj): Greedy, selfish; predatory

RAPPORT (n): Close relationship; understanding

RAREFY (v): To make thin, or less dense

RATIFY (v): Approve formally; certify

RATIOCINATION (n): Process of reasoning, logical deduction

RATIONAL (adj): Logical, reasonable; intelligent

RAVAGE (v): Destroy; rob

RAVE (n): An extravagantly favorable review

RAVENOUS (adj): Desirous, extremely hungry

RAZE (v): Destroy; demolish

REBUKE (v): Criticize severely; scold harshly

REBUT (v): Contradict, refuse with proof

RECALCITRANT (adj): Stubborn, rebellious, unruly

RECANT (v): Give up; retract a previous statement

RECAPITULATE (v): Summarize

RECIDIVISM (n): Habitual return to crime

RECIPROCAL (adj): Mutual; interchangeable

RECLUSE (n): Loner, hermit

RECONCILE (v): Reunite, make friendly; make consistent

RECONDITE (adj): Profound, secret, difficult to understand

RECONNAISSANCE (n): Survey of enemy by soldiers for gathering information

RECOURSE (n): A source of help in a difficult situation

RECRUDESCENT (adj): Reappearing; erupting again

RECTITUDE (n): Morality; correctness of judgment

RECUPERATE (v): Recover

REDEMPTIVE (adj): Delivering from sin or evil; making amends

REDOUBTABLE (adj): Arousing fear; formidable

REDRESS (v): Dress gain; correct a wrong; remedy

REDUNDANT (adj): Superfluous; repetitious

REFRACTORY (adj): Stubborn or unmanageable

REFRAIN (v): Abstain; restrain oneself

REFUTE (v): Prove false

REGAL (adj): Royal

REGENERATE (adj): Reformed spiritually or morally

REGIMEN (n): Prescribed diet and habits

REHABILITATE (adj): Restore to good conditions

REIGN (n): Rule, sovereignty

REIN (v): To check or stop

REINFORCE (v): Strengthen or support

RELEGATE (v): Demote, assign to an inferior position

RELENT (v): Give in; become less severe

RELENTLESS (adj): Oppressively constant; harsh or inflexible

RELEVANT (adj): Pertinent; related to the current subject

RELINQUISH (v): Give up; renounce; yield

RELUCTANCE (n): Unwillingness, hesitance

REMARKABLE (adj): Extraordinary; unusual

REMEDIAL (adj): Curing; corrective

REMINISCENCE (n): Recollection of past events

REMISS (adj): Negligent

REMNANT (n): Remainder; leftover

REMONSTRATE (v): Protest; object

RENAISSANCE (n): Rebirth of art and literature

RENDER (v): Give; provide; deliver; represent

RENEGE (v): Deny

RENOUNCE (v): Abandon; disown; repudiate

REPARATION (n): Compensation; amends

REPEAL (v): Revoke, annul

REPERTOIRE (n): List of works/skills that a person is ready to perform

REPINE (v): Complain, fret

REPLETE (adj): Filled to satisfaction; complete; sated

REPLICA (n): Copy

REPREHEND (v): Reprimand, rebuke

REPREHENSIBLE (adj): Deserving blame

REPRESS (adj): Restrain, crush; suppress

REPRIEVE (n): Temporary relief; respite

REPRIMAND (v): Scold severely; Rebuke

REPROACH (v): Blame, accuse; express disapproval

REPROBATE (n): A person hardened in sin

REPROVE (v): Criticize; rebuke

REPUDIATE (v): Disown; disavow to grant

REPUGNANCE (n): Aversion, loathing

REQUISITE (n): Necessary requirement

REQUITE (v): Repay; revenge

RESCIND (v): Cancel

RESENTMENT (n): Anger; bitterness; displeasure

RESIDUAL (adj): Remainder

RESILIENT (adj): Elastic, quickly recovering from failure

RESOLUTION (n): Determination

RESPITE (n): Time for rest; interval of relief

RESPLENDENT (adj): Shining brilliantly; splendid

RESTITUTION (n): Restoration to a previous condition; compensation

RESTIVE (adj): Restless; uncontrollable

RESTRAINED (adj): Repressed, understated

RESTRICTIVE (adj): Imposing limits

RESUMPTION (n): Beginning again

RESURGENT (adj): Rising again; reviving

RESUSCITATE (v): Revive; restore to life

RETAIN (v): Keep; employ

RETALIATION (n): Revenge

RETICENT (adj): Remaining silent; reserved

RETIRING (v): Shy; modest

RETRACT (v): Withdraw, take back

RETREAT (v/n): Withdraw, depart

RETRENCH (v): Cut down or reduce (expenses etc.)

RETRIEVE (v): Recover; bring back

RETROGRESS (v): Move backward; revert to a previous condition

RETROSPECTIVE (adj): Looking back on the past

REVAMP (v): Renovate, revise

REVELATION (n): Act of showing; disclosure

REVERBERATE (v): Echo; resound

REVERE (v): Venerate, respect deeply

REVERIE (n): Daydream, preoccupation

REVILE (v): Insult, criticize abusively

REVIVE (v): Return to life: become active

REVOKE (v): Cancel, retract

RHETORICAL (adj): Pertaining to art of speaking and writing effectively

RIBALD (adj): Obscene; vulgar

RIFE (adj): Abundant; current

RIFT (n) : split; cleave

RIG (v): Fix; manipulate

RIGOROUS (v): Harsh, severe; strictly accurate

RISIBLE (adj): laughable

RISQUE (adj) : indecent; racy

RIVETING (adj): Fascinating; engrossing

ROBUST (adj): Strong, healthy, vigorous

ROCOCO (adj): Excessively ornate; intricate

ROTUND (n): Round in Shape; Fat

ROW (n): Argue, fight

RUDIMENTARY (adj): Elementary; not fully developed; crude

RUEFUL (adj): Sorrowful; sad; regretful

RUMINATE (v): Think deeply about something; ponder

RUNIC (adj): Of the ancient class; having some secret meaning

RUSE (n): Trick, ploy

RUTHLESS (adj): Merciless; cruel

S

SABOTAGE (v): Intentionally damage

SACCHARINE (adj): Cloyingly sweet; excessive sentimental

SACRILEGIOUS (adj): Profane; desecrating

SACROSANCT (adj): Most sacred; inviolable

SAGACIOUS (adj): Wise, shrewd

SAGE (n/adj): Wise, learned

SALIENT (adj): Prominent; important

SALUBRIOUS (adj): Healthful

SALUTARY (adj): Beneficial; wholesome

SALVAGE (adj): Rescue from loss

SANCTIFY (v): Make holy; purify

SANCTIMONIOUS (v): Pretending to be religious; self-righteous

SANGUINARY (adj): Bloody; murderous

SANGUINE (adj): Cheerful; hopeful

SARDONIC (adj): Sarcastic, cynical

SARTORIAL (adj): Pertaining to tailors

SATIATE (v): Satisfy fully

SATURNINE (adj): Gloomy, sad

SAVAGE (adj): Violent, uncivilized

SAVANT (n): Scholar

SAVORY (adj): Tasty, pleasing

SCANT (adj): Little, meager

SCARCE (adj): Rare, not abundant, in short supply

SCATHING (adj): Bitterly severe; injurious

SCHISM (n): Division, split

SCOFF (v): Mock, deride

SCORN (v): Mock; reject with contempt

SCOURGE (n): Whip; lash; sever punishments

SCRUPLE (v): Hesitate on ethical grounds

SCRUPULOUS (adj): Extremely thorough; conscientious

SCRUTINIZE (v): Examine closely and critically

SCURRILOUS (adj): Obscene, indecent

SCURVY (adj): Vulgar; despicable

SCUTTLE (v): 1. Move quickly; 2. Sink

SECESSION (n): Withdrawal; separation

SECLUDE (v): Keep away from other people

SECTARIAN (adj): Narrow-minded; limited

SECULAR (adj): Non-religious in nature;

worldly; temporal

SEDATE (adj): Calm; composed; grave

SEDENTARY (adj): Requiring sitting

SEDULOUS (adj): Hardworking, diligent

SEEMLY (adj): Proper; appropriate

SEETHE (v): Be disturbed; anger; boil

SEGREGATE (v): Separate

SEMANTIC (adj): Of the study of the meaning and use of words and phrases

SEMINAL (adj): Original, influencing future developments

SENILITY (n): Old age; feeblemindedness of old age

SENTENTIOUS (adj): Terse, concise; aphoristic

SENTIENT (adj): Capable of sensation; aware; sensitive

SEQUENTIAL (adj): Successive, following, subsequent

SERE (adj): Dry, parched

SERENDIPITY (n): An instance of fortunate discovery; luck

SERENE (adj): Calm; tranquil

SERMON (n): Any serious speech esp. on a moral issue; preaching

SERVILE (adj): Slavish; subservient

SEVER (v): Cut, separate

SHACKLE (v): Chain; fetter, manacle

SHAM (v/n): Pretend, deceive

SHARD (n): Fragment, generally of pottery

SHIRK (v): Avoid (responsibility, work, etc.)

SHODDY (adj): Cheap, inferior; fake

SHREWD (adj): Clever; sharp

SHUN (v): Keep away from

SIMILE (n): Comparison of one thing with another

SIMPLISTIC (adj): Oversimplified; unrealistically simple

SIMULATE (v): Imitate, pretend

SINECURE (n): High paid job that needs little effort

SINGULAR (adj): Unique; odd; extraordinary

SINISTER (n): Evil

SINUOUS (adj): Winding, twisting

SKEPTIC (adj): Skeptical, doubtful

SKETCHY (adj): Not thorough; superficial; incomplete

SKIRT (v): Avoid

SKITTISH (adj): Nervous; restive

SKULLDUGGERY (n): Deception, trickery

SLACKEN (v): Slow down; loosen

SLAKE (v): Quench; satisfy

SLANDER (n): Defamation, false statements about someone

SLATTERNLY (adj): Untidy; slovenly

SLEIGHT (n): Skill in using hands; dexterity

SLIGHT (v): Neglect; snub

SLOTH (n): Laziness

SLOVENLY (adj): Untidy; careless

SLUGGARD (n): Lazy person

SMUG (n): Self-satisfied, self-righteous

SNARE (v): Catch in a trap

SOBER (adj): Not drunk; calm; serious; drab

SODDEN (adj): Soaked; dull, esp. from drink

SOLEMN (adj): Serious, formal, sincere

SOLICIT (v): Seek; request earnestly

SOLICITOUS (adj): Concerned; worried

SOLITARY (adj): Alone; single

SOLITUDE (n): Being alone; seclusion

SOLVENT (adj): Able to pay all debts

SOMATIC (adj): Of the body; physical

SOMBER (adj): Gloomy, depressing

SOMNOLENT (adj): Sleepy; half-asleep

SONOROUS (adj): Resonant

SOOTHE (v): Ease; calm

SOPHISTICATED (n): Worldly-wise; cultured; complex

SOPORIFIC (adj): Sleepy; sleep-causing

SORDID (adj): Dirty, filthy; base; ignoble

SPARE (v/adj): (v) Use frugally, (adj) just sufficient; thin

SPARSE (adj): Thinly scattered; scanty; not dense

SPARTAN (adj): Lacking luxury and comfort; strictly disciplined

SPECIFIC (adj): Unique; precise; limited

SPECIOUS (adj): Misleading, deceptive; fallacious

SPECTRUM (n): Range of colors; broad range of connected ideas or events

SPECULATE (v): Theorize, Guess

SPLENETIC (adj): Irritable; spiteful

SPONTANEOUS (adj): Unplanned; instinctive; natural

SPORADIC (adj): Irregular, occasional

SPURIOUS (adj): False; illogical

SPURN (v): Reject, scorn

SQUABBLE (n): A minor quarrel; tiff

SQUALID (adj): Dirty; unpleasant; morally dirty

SQUALOR (n): Dirtiness; degradation; filth
SQUANDER (v): Waste
SQUASH (v): Crush; quell
STAID (adj): Sober, sedate
STANCH (v): Stop the flow of liquid
STARK (adj): 1. Extreme; 2. Plain, austere; 3. Harsh
STARTLE (v): Surprise suddenly; alarm
STASIS (n): Stoppage
STATIC (adj): Motionless; unchanging
STATUS QUO (n): existing state or condition ☺ (adj): Loyal; unchanging
STEALTH (n): Secret, sneakiness; slyness
STEEP (v): Soak; immerse; saturate
STELLAR (adj): Relating to the stars; brilliant
STENTORIAN (adj): Very loud
STERN (adj): Strict, severe; harsh
STICKLER (n): Strict disciplinarian; perfectionist
STIFLE (v): Suppress; quell; inhibit
STIGMA (n): A symbol of disgrace; brand
STILTED (adj): Pompous; artificial; stiff
STINT (v): Set limits, be frugal
STIPULATE (v): Specify; make express conditions
STOIC (adj): Impassive; unmoved by joy or passion
STOLID (adj): Unemotional, impassive; dull
STRATAGEM (n): Clever trick; deceptive scheme
STRATIFY (v): Arrange into layer; divide into classes
STRICTURE (n): Restriction; severe criticism
STRIDENT (adj): Loud and harsh; insistent
STRIFE (n): Conflict, discord
STRINGENT (adj): Binding; rigid
STRIVE (v): Try hard; compete
STUDIED (adj): Deliberate; not spontaneous; carefully practiced
STULTIFY (v): Make useless; cause to appear stupid
STUPEFY (v): Stun, make senseless
STYGIAN (n): Dark; hellish
STYMIE (v): Hold back; hinder
SUAVE (v): Sophisticated; smooth
SUBDUE (v): Overcome, defeat; gain control over
SUBJECTIVE (adj): Based on or influenced by personal feelings, or opinions; biased
SUBJUGATE (v): Conquer, bring into submission
SUBLIME (n): Noble; awesome
SUBMISSIVE (adj): Yielding; meek
SUBORDINATE (v): Make subservient; dominate
SUBPOENA (n): A writ order summoning a witness to appear
SUBSERVIENT (adj): Subordinate; behaving like a slave; obsequious
SUBSIDE (v): Become less intense; decline
SUBSIDIARY (adj): Secondary, lesser in importance
SUBSIDY (n): Financial assistance; support
SUBSTANTIAL (adj): Important; considerable; ample
SUBSUME (v): Include; encompass
SUBTERFUGE (n): Deception; ruse and escaped with his goods
SUBTLE (adj): Difficult to perceive; obscure; fine; clever
SUBVERT (v): Overthrow; undermine the power of authority
SUCCINCT (adj): Brief; terse; compact
SUCCOR (n/v): Aid, assist; support
SUCCUMB (v): Yield; die
SUFFRAGE (n): The right to vote
SULLEN (adj): Gloomy, Silently Angry
SULLY (v): Dirty; tarnish
SUMPTUOUS (adj): Rich, lavish
SUNDRY (adj): Various, miscellaneous
SUPERCILIOUS (adj): Arrogant, condescending
SUPERFICIAL (adj): Not thorough; shallow, trivial
SUPERFLUOUS (adj): Excessive; overabundant, unnecessary
SUPERLATIVE (adj): Superb; best
SUPERSEDE (v): Take the place of; supplant
SUPINE (adj): Lying on the back; passive
SUPPLANT (v): Replace; usurp
SUPPLICATE (v): Ask or beg humbly
SUPPOSITION (n): Hypothesis; assumption
SUPPRESS (v): Stifle; subdue; inhibit
SURFEIT (n/v): Overindulge; oversupply; satiate
SURLY (adj): Rude; irritable
SURMISE (v): Guess
SURMOUNT (v): Overcome (a difficulty)
SURPASS (adj): Exceed
SURREAL (adj): Strange, unreal
SURREPTITIOUS (adj): Secret, hidden

SURROGATE (n): Substitute

SUSCEPTIBLE (adj): Easily influenced; having little resistance; vulnerable

SUSTAIN (v): Nourish, support; experience

SWAY (v): Influence, affect; swing

SWERVE (v): Turn abruptly, deviate

SWINDLE (v): Cheat

SYBARITE (n): Lover of luxury

SYCOPHANT (adj): Servile flatterer; toady

SYLVAN (adj): Relating to wooded regions; forest like

SYMBIOSIS (n): Two different species living together and both benefit from this

SYMBOLIC (adj): Representative, figurative; related to a symbol

SYMPATHY (n): Sharing of same feelings

SYNCHRONOUS (adj): Similarly timed; simultaneous with

SYNERGY (n): Combined action

SYNOPTIC (adj): Providing a general overview, summary

SYNTHESIS (n): Combination of parts to make whole

T

TABOO (n): Prohibition; ban

TACIT (adj): Understood without being stated

TACITURN (adj): Silent, talking little

TACTICAL (adj): Related to tactics; wise; expedient

TACTILE (adj): Perceptible by touch; tangible

TAINT (v): Pollute; corrupt; bring shame

TANGENTIAL (adj): Peripheral, only slightly connected, divergent

TANGIBLE (adj): Touchable; real; palpable

TANTALIZE (v): Tease; torture with disappointment

TANTAMOUNT (adj): Equivalent in effect or value

TARNISH (v): Blacken, and stain

TAUNT (v): Tease, mock; harass

TAUT (adj): Tight; ready

TAUTOLOGY (adj): Needless repetition

TAWDRY (adj): Cheap and gaudy

TAXONOMY (n): The branch of science concerned with classification

TEDIOUS (adj): Tiresome, boring

TEEM (v): Be full of; swarm with

TEMERITY (n): Reckless boldness; rashness

TEMPERATE (adj): Moderate, self-controlled, restrained

TEMPESTUOUS (adj): Stormy, violent, turbulent

TEMPORAL (adj): Limited by time; not lasting forever; mundane

TENABLE (adj): Reasonable; capable of maintained

TENACIOUS (adj): Holding fast; tough

TENDENTIOUS (adj): Biased; having an aim

TENDER (v): Offer, propose; adj. soft, delicate

TENUOUS (adj): Thin, rare; slim

TEPID (adj): Lukewarm; half-hearted

TERSE (adj): Concise, pithy, curt

TETHER (v): Tie with a rope

THESPIAN (adj): Related to drama

THORNY (adj): Causing difficulty; problematic

THRESHOLD (n): Edge; lower limit; beginning; door step

THRIFT (n): Saving, economizing

THRIVE (v): Prosper, flourish

THWART (v): Oppose; frustrate

TIMID (adj): Shy, lacking in courage or confidence

TIMOROUS (adj): Afraid; fearful

TIRADE (n): Extended scolding; harangue

TORPID (adj): Slow, listless; inert

TORPOR (n): Lazy; sluggish

TORRID (adj): Hot; scorching; passionate

TORTUOUS (adj): Full of twists and turns; complicated

TOTALITARIAN (adj): Authoritarian; despotic; intolerant of opposition

TOTALITY (n): Whole; the quality of being complete

TOUT (v): Praise or publicize highly

TRACTABLE (adj): Docile, easily managed

TRADUCE (v): Defame, slander

TRAITOR (n): Betrayer

TRANQUIL (v): Calm, quiet

TRANSCENDENT (adj): Surpassing; exceeding ordinary limits

TRANSCRIBE (v): Copy; make a written copy

TRANSGRESSION (n): Violation of law, sin

TRANSIENT (adj): Temporary, momentary; staying a short time

TRANSITORY (adj): Not permanent; fleeting

TRANSMUTE (v): Change; convert to something different

TRANSPARENT (adj): Easily detected or seen through; obvious

TRAVAIL (n): Painfully difficult or burdensome

TRAVERSE (v): Travel across

TREACHERY (n): Betrayal of trust; the quality of being deceptive

TREMULOUS (adj): Shaking; wavering

TRENCHANT (adj): Cutting; keen; clear-cut

TREPID (adj): Timid; fearful

TRIBULATION (n): Suffering; trial

TRIFLING (adj): Trivial, unimportant

TRITE (adj): Hackneyed; commonplace; tired

TRIVIAL (adj): Unimportant, insignificant

TRUCE (n): Cease-fire; respite

TRUCULENT (adj): Cruel; harsh; destructive

TRUNCATE (v): Shorten, cut the top of

TRYST (n): Meeting; date

TUMID (adj): 1.Swollen. 2. Pompous, bombastic

TUMULT (v): Commotion; disorder; noise

TURBID (adj): Muddy, clouded with disturbed sediment

TURBULENT (adj): Disturbed; causing violence

TURGID (adj): 1.Swollen; 2.pompous, bombastic

TURMOIL (n): Great commotion and confusion

TURPITUDE (n): Wickedness; depravity

TUTELARY (adj): Providing protective supervision

TYRANNY (n): Oppression; cruel government

TYRO (n): Beginner, novice

U

UBIQUITOUS (adj): Present, or found everywhere

ULTERIOR (adj): Secret, unstated and often questionable

UMBRAGE (v): Anger; resentment

UNASSUMING (adj): Humble, modest

UNCANNY (adj): Strange, mysterious

UNCONSCIONABLE (adj): Immoral; excessive

UNCOUTH (adj): Clumsy, crude, strange

UNCTUOUS (adj): Oily; insincerely suave or smooth

UNDAUNTED (adj): fearless, courageous

UNDERMINE (v): Weaken; sap

UNDERRATE (v): Underestimate, undervalue, belittle

UNDERSCORE (v): Emphasize, underline

UNDERSTATED (adj): Expressed in a subtle way; state less strongly

UNDULATE (v): Move with wave like motion

UNEQUIVOCAL (adj): Clear, obvious; plain

UNEXCEPTIONABLE (adj): Not open to criticism or objection; completely acceptable

UNEXCEPTIONAL (adj): Usual; ordinary

UNFETTER (v): Free or release from chains

UNFLAPPABLE (adj): Calm; not easily upset

UNGAINLY (adj): Awkward; clumsy; unwieldy

UNINITIATED (adj): Inexperienced; not initiated

UNIQUE (adj): Singular; rare; matchless

UNIVERSAL (adj): Allover; ubiquitous

UNIVOCAL (adj): Having one meaning; unambiguous

UNKEMPT (adj): Disheveled; uncared for appearance

UNOBTRUSIVE (adj): Not visible; not attracting attention

UNPALATABLE (adj): Not tasty

UNPRECEDENTED (adj): Never done or known before

UNPREPOSSESSING (adj): Unattractive

UNRAVEL (v): Untwist; solve

UNREMITTING (adj): Non-stop, continuous; never relaxing

UNRULY (adj) Unmanageable; disobedient

UNSCATHED (adj): Unharmed, not hurt

UNSEEMLY (adj): Improper; indecent

UNSIGHTLY (adj): Ugly

UNSOUND (adj) : Unhealthy, weak; faulty

UNSPARING (adj): 1. Cruel; not merciful; 2. Generous, not stingy (second sense)

UNSUNG (adj): Not honored, not celebrated or praised

UNTENABLE (adj): Undefendable; not able to be maintained

UNTOWARD (adj): Unfavorable; causing trouble

UNTRAMMELED (adj): Not limited; not curbed

UNTUTORED (adj): Untrained; uneducated

UNWARRANTED (adj): Unjustified; unreasonable; ground less

UNWIELDY (adj): Awkward, unmanageable, burdensome

UNWITTING (adj): Unintentional; unaware

UNWONTED (adj): Unaccustomed

UPBRAID (v): Severely criticize or scold

UPHEAVAL (n): A violent disruption; a major change

UPROOT (v): Pull out of the ground, eradicate

URBANE (adj): Polite, elegant; refined

USURP (v): Seize another's power; supplant

USURY (n): Lending money at high interest rates

UTOPIAN (adj): Perfect or idealistic but impracticable

V

VACILLATE (v): Fluctuate; Waver

VACUOUS (adj): Empty; lacking in ideas

VAGARY (n): Caprice, whim

VAGRANT (n): Wanderer

VAIN (adj): 1. Proud; egotistical.2. Useless

VALEDICTORY (adj): Relating to a farewell

VALIANT (adj): Brave; daring

VALIDATE (adj): Confirm; legalize

VALOR (adj): Bravery

VANGUARD (n): Forerunners; advanced forces

VANITY (n): 1. Feelings of excessive pride; 2. Worthless

VANQUISH (v): Crush by using force; quell

VAPID (adj): Dull, unimaginative; insipid; tasteless

VARIANCE (n): Difference; variation

VARIEGATED (adj): Many-colored

VAUNTED (adj): Boasted; highly publicized

VEGETATE (v): Lead a dull and inactive life

VEHEMENT (adj): Forceful, intensely emotional; marked with vigor

VEIL (v): Cover; hide

VENAL (adj): Capable of being bribed; corruptible

VENERATE (v): Respect, revere

VENGEANCE (n): Revenge

VENTURESOME (adj): Bold

VERACITY (n): Truthfulness

VERBOSE (adj): Wordy

VERDANT (adj): Lush with vegetation; green; inexperienced

VERISIMILAR (adj): Appearing to be true or real; probable

VERITABLE (n): Real, actual

VERNACULAR (adj): Local or living language; natural style

VERSATILE (adj): Having many skills; having great diversity

VERTIGO (n): Feeling of dizziness

VESTIGE (n): A trace or remnant

VEX (v): Annoy; distress

VIABLE (adj): Workable, practicable; capable of living

VICARIOUS (adj): Substitute, experienced through another

VICE (n): Moral weakness; depravity

VICIOUS (adj): Cruel or violent

VICISSITUDE (n): Changes of fortune

VIGILANT (adj): Watchful; attentive

VIGOR (n): Physical Strength; energy

VILIFY (v): slander; defame

VINDICATE (v): Clear from blame; justify, support

VINDICTIVE (adj): Revengeful; spiteful

VINTAGE (adj) : Antiquated; high quality; classic

VIRTUAL (adj): Practical; being in essence

VIRTUOSO (n): Highly skilled artist

VIRTUOUS (adj): Good; morally excellent

VIRULENT (adj): Extremely poisonous; hostile; bitter

VISAGE (n): Face; appearance

VISCOUS (adj): Sticky and thick

VITAL (n): Crucial; critical; living; lively

VITIATE (v): Spoil; make inoperative

VITRIOLIC (adj): Bitterly scathing; caustic

VITUPERATE (v): Abuse, scold

VIVACIOUS (adj): Lively; animated; sprightly

VIVID (adj): Lively; intensely bright, distinct

VOCIFEROUS (adj): Noisy, clamorous

VOGUE (n): Popular fashion

VOLATILE (adj): Changeable; explosive; evaporating easily

VOLITION (n): Act of making a choice or decision

VOLUBLE (adj): Fluent; talkative, glib

VOLUMINOUS (adj): Capacious, bulky; large

VOLUPTUOUS (adj): Sensuous; having an attractive full figure

VORACIOUS (adj): Excessively greedy; devouring

VORTEX (n): Whirlpool; engulfing situation

VOUCHSAFE (v): Grant; concede

VULNERABLE (adj): Unprotected; susceptible

W

WAGGISH (adj): Joking, witty
WAIL (v): Cry out loudly; lament
WANE (v): Decrease in size or strength
WANTON (adj): Sexually immodest;
unrestrained
WARRANTED (adj): Authorized; justified
WARY (adj): Very cautious
WASTREL (n): Person who wastes
WATERSHED (n): Crucial turning point
WAVER (v): Hesitate; be unsure
WAX (v): Increase, grow
WEAN (v): Give up a habit
WELTER (n): Confusion, disorder
WHEEDLE (v): Entice; deceive by flattery
WHET (v): Sharpen; stimulate
WHIMSY (adj): An odd or fanciful idea;
impulsiveness
WILLFUL (adj): Intentional; headstrong
WILY (adj): Cunning, artful
WINCE (v): Shrink back (with fear or pain);
recoil
WINNOW (v): Separate the good from the
bad; sift
WINSOME (adj): Attractive; agreeable

WISTFUL (adj): Sadly thoughtful; full of longing
WITHER (v): Dry up or shrivel; decay
WITTICISM (n): Witty remark; wise saying
WIZENED (adj) : Wrinkled with age; withered
WOEFUL (adj): Unhappy; sorrowful
WORLDLY (adj): Earthly, temporal, material;
sophisticated
WRANGLE (n): quarrel
WRATH (n): Anger; fury

X

XENOPHOBIA (n): Fear of foreigners or hatred
for foreigners

Y

YEARN (v): Desire, long, crave
YIELD (v): Surrender; give in

Z

ZEALOT (n): A fanatical follower of a religion
or policy
ZEALOUS (adj): Having or showing zeal
ZENITH (n): Point in sky directly overhead;
summit
ZEPHYR (n): Gentle breeze

CONFOUNDED : confused, mystified, baffled

Acknowlegements

This advanced version reflects the collaborative efforts of an outstanding team of students, educators and designers. Their insights and talents have been incorporated into this latest version of word wizard.

Creating this book based on memory trick has resulted from the direct interaction with the student community esp. in the class room. Though some of the memory trick content has been inadvertently duplicated in other publications, web pages published by open resources and community forums over a period of time, I received some incredibly helpful feedback from few students who are also good friends. Many thanks to every student at Dr Raju's educational academy.

I am grateful to English language educator Mr. Prasad Ravi, who researched, refined and updated many of the sample sentences used in this advanced version.

Pratima Sagar was responsible for creating the book design. I thank her not only for her creative talent, but also her flexibility through multiple revisions. Her extensive experience as an editor enhanced the literary content of this revised version.

Kavitha Gayatri, Wife! Whose love and encouragement allowed me to finish this journey. She already has my heart so I will just give her a heartfelt "thanks." Jaya Surya, my son, a vivacious handsome hulk and Chandra Hasa, my beautiful daughter, I owe my loving thanks to them. They have lost lots of quality time with me for my obsession with this work.

I have to thank my parents PSN Raju (late father) and Jayaprada for their love throughout my life. I also want to thank to my in-laws (DGK & Saradha) for their unconditional support. My special thanks to my large family ---from my side –sisters, brother-in-laws, nephews, nieces; ----from my wife side—sisters, brothers, nephews and nieces.

Colleagues of the Institute also deserve my sincerest thanks, their friendship and assistance has meant more to me than I could ever express. I could not complete my work without their invaluable friendly assistance. Special thanks go to the teachers Rama Krishna Reddy (The man of Maths), Krishna (IELTS teacher), and Neena (language teacher). A big thanks go to the consultancy and counseling team Ganapathi Raju (VISA expert), Ravali (Qaunt), Subba Lakshmi, Neelima, Bobby, Varma, Lakshmi, and Alekhya. Thanks and many varied reasons to Pavan, Krishna, Gopal and Padma.

Finally, I am forever indebted to my Late Guru Professor A.C.Rao who inspired in my life to think creatively.

Dr. Raju

Professor Dr Prasad Raju V.V.N.R Pathapati (aka Dr Raju) received his B.E, M.E, MS, PhD degrees in Mechanical Engineering from Gulbarga, BITS (Pilani), University Of Connecticut (Storrs, US) and Pt. Ravishankar Shukla University (GEC,Raipur-presently NI I, raipur) respectively.

Dr. Raju is a well admired Professor & Scientist in the field of theoretical and dynamic modeling of Kinematics, Robotics and Fuel Cells. He published and reviewed several papers in International journals such as ASME (American Society Of Mechanical Engineers, US), SAE (Society for Automotive Engineers, Michigan US). Elsevier Science (Renewable Energy) etc.Dr Raju has also worked as a Director, Principal, Professor, Head of the Department and Visiting Research Scholar in Reputed Engineering Colleges and Universities in India and Abroad.

Dr Raju founded Dr Raju's Educational Academy in 2006. Out of passion Dr.Raju has developed unique memory trick based vocabulary teaching with aid of visuals and first one to use more than 3000 cartoons in the world in GRE® Coaching !!!! and first one to implement visual GRE® in the world !!!!, equally appreciated both by student and academic communities. He has been relentlessly imparting this knowledge to many students for the last 10 years, who were later guided by him to world renowned institutes like MIT, John Hopkins, U PENN, UCLA, UT Austin, Purdue, PENN State, Cornell etc., He has immense knowledge regarding the wide ranging courses and programs in MS, PhD and MBA offered by different institutions in the US.

Dr Raju's web sites (www.drrajus.com,www.msatus.com,www.drrajus.in) has been accessed by more than 3000 people every day for his guidance in Graduate programs in all branches of engineering, science and business.